Bilinguality and Bilingualism

Second edition

This updated and revised edition of Hamers and Blanc's successful textbook presents state-of-the-art knowledge about languages in contact from individual bilinguality to societal bilingualism.

The book is both multidisciplinary and interdisciplinary in approach, and analyses bilingualism at individual, interpersonal and societal levels. Linguistic, cognitive and sociocultural aspects of bilingual development are explored, as are problems such as bilingual memory and polyglot aphasia. Hamers and Blanc analyse the relationship between culture, identity and language behaviour in multicultural settings, as well as the communication strategies in interpersonal and intergroup relations. They also propose theoretical models of language processing and development, which are then applied to bilingual behaviour. Other topics reviewed include language shift, pidgins and creoles, language planning and bilingual education.

This new edition reflects the changes in the theoretical approaches to bilingualism since the late 1980s and includes sections on language attrition, languages in contact and neuropsychological aspects of bilinguality. The book will be invaluable to students, teachers and scholars interested in bilingualism in a range of disciplines including psycholinguistics, linguistics, the social sciences, education and language planning.

Josiane F. Hamers is a Professor of Psycholinguistics and Bilingualism in the Département de Langues et Linguistique at the Université Laval, Québec. She has published widely in journals – including the *International Journal of Sociology of Language*, *Journal of Language and Social Psychology* and *Langue et Société* – and has written chapters and books in both English and French. **Michel H. A. Blanc** is Emeritus Reader in Applied Linguistics and Bilingualism at Birkbeck College, University of London. He has published numerous books and articles on bilingualism, French language and linguistics, and applied linguistics.

Bilinguality and Bilingualism

Second edition

Josiane F. Hamers and Michel H. A. Blanc

Université Laval, Québec and *Birkbeck College, University of London*

CAMBRIDGE
UNIVERSITY PRESS

CAMBRIDGE UNIVERSITY PRESS
Cambridge, New York, Melbourne, Madrid, Cape Town, Singapore, São Paulo

Cambridge University Press
The Edinburgh Building, Cambridge CB2 2RU, UK

Published in the United States of America by Cambridge University Press, New York

www.cambridge.org
Information on this title: www.cambridge.org/9780521640497

Originally published in French as *Bilingualité et bilinguisme*
by Pierre Mardaga, Editeur 1983
and © Pierre Mardaga, Editeur, Liège, Bruxelles

First published in English by Cambridge University Press 1989 as
Bilinguality and Bilingualism
English translation © Cambridge University Press 1989

Second edition published in English by Cambridge University Press 2000
© Cambridge University Press 2000
Reprinted 2003

A catalogue record for this publication is available from the British Library

ISBN-13 978-0-521-64049-7 hardback
ISBN-10 0-521-64049-0 hardback

ISBN-13 978-0-521-64843-1 paperback
ISBN-10 0-521-64843-2 paperback

Transferred to digital printing 2005

Contents

Figures

Tables

Foreword to the second edition

Since writing the foreword for this remarkable work, I realise how quickly time flies by and how research accumulates. It is difficult, except for the dedicated, to keep up to date and to realise that research has branched out into new and unpredictable domains. One can't help but get a broader education from a book like this one because it brings the reader up to date on bilingualism with a realisation of the depth of the subject, from old to new research. However, what may surprise the reader most is that bilingualism has become something more than multidisciplinary: it reviews in detail how psychologists, sociologists, ethnographers, linguists and informationists each present their views of the phenomena of bilingualism.

What is new is that the field has become interdisciplinary, that is, even though all sorts of specialists are focusing on the bilingual and the processes of bilingualism, only a few keep up with and know about more than one or possibly two neighbouring disciplines. Few think about bilingualism in an integrated, interdisciplinary manner. With that aim in mind, this book is completely rewritten and even better than the 1989 edition. In one of their conclusions, Josiane and Michel place us ahead of time by sketching out what an adequate, more complete description of bilingualism is likely to be. We glean what their view of the superstructure is likely to look like, and that's where this work gets really exciting.

The superstructure itself has been constructed and described from the first chapter on. There is no rush in their basic descriptions; the authors patiently and comfortably (from the reader's view) take each research effort apart fully, pointing out its potentials and its limitations. Sometimes it seems that the limitations overwhelm the positive aspects of a study, and this might be discouraging to young researchers or researchers-to-be. The authors are, however, essentially kind about research: with its apparent faults, the research attempt is often all that is available for superstructure building, and it is used, tentatively, in the construction. The authors realise, of course, that they are describing a particular feature, one part only, and that their own theories will be open to higher-level critiques. Research on bilingualism need not, therefore, be watertight to be useful, even though the authors show their appreciation when a more complete, more basic study has to be relied on.

How has the superstructure they have in mind come about? It seems that it is based on an attractive assembly of elements within a single discipline; these become the ultimate fundamentals. Each research attempt in the past or in the present derives from a presumed fundamental, and each fundamental has to pass the test of being tried and tested. This means that it has to be rigorously conducted, made public and made repeatable. In scientific terms this means that research of value has to be methodologically tight and show reliability. Thus, researchers-to-be will find much they can do within their own discipline (or possibly two or three disciplines) that they have invested time and energy in. What this book shows them is how the more integrative, interdisciplinary theories yet to come will be able to construct more and better fundamentals from within each discipline. This will aid them in their attempts to understand the fascinating world of bilingual behaviour. Incidentally, no one within a single discipline theory is likely to cover all the explanations that are needed. The psychologist, linguist or biologist is likely to realise that bilingualism – or language itself – must be more than some type of complex 'instinct'; nor will concepts like social-class differences, ethnolinguistic backgrounds or even sociolinguistic experiences by themselves be adequate explanations. This book therefore gives us believable notions of what bilingualism actually entails. It educates the reader beautifully.

I still believe (as I did in 1989) that no one else could have written such a book. Nor could any pair of others have done the job so well. It takes the fortunate and exceptional backgrounds of these particular scholars to do it. Josiane Hamers, a cognitive psychologist interested in the psycholinguistic aspects of bilingualism, spent her formative years in Belgium, a society where the social battle raged between Flemish and Walloon people. She then came to Montreal for graduate work, researching and teaching in a new society where an English–French social battle entertains her now. The fortunate part is the similarly rich background of Michel Blanc, and this is what makes this writing pair unique. Michel's formative years were spent in France, and his professional experiences in applied linguistics and sociolinguistics were in London. He has very likely been endlessly entertained by the social stereotypes of French and British people that fly back and forth across the Channel. He has now settled in the hills of Umbria in central Italy where his triculturality starts to develop. What a pair they make!

We have to congratulate them and thank them for the splendid education they offer us in this new edition.

Wallace E. Lambert
Annecy-le-Vieux

Preface

This second edition is an updated, revised and restructured version of the first edition originally published in 1989. All chapters have been altered. We have deleted two chapters: the one on second language acquisition has now been omitted because the explosion in the amount of research necessitates a book on its own; however, we have retained some important aspects, integrating these into other chapters; for example, the social psychological processes at work in second language acquisition are discussed in Section 8.5 and communication strategies in second language learning in Section 9.2.2.3. The other deleted chapter is that on interpretation. We believe that the field is more relevant to cognitive psychology but has little to do with bilingual processing.

Owing to the rapid changes in the theoretical approaches and the increase in experiments and studies in the field, a number of chapters have been split up. Former Chapter 1 has been split into two chapters: Chapters 1 and 2. In addition to the definitions of bilingualism, the new Chapter 1 presents theoretical guiding principles which we follow throughout the book. The new Chapter 2 deals with the dimensions and measurement of bilinguality and bilingualism. Chapters 3, 4 and 5 are concerned with bilingual development and its consequences and in Chapter 5 we propose a social cognitive interactional model of bilingual development. Chapters 6 and 7 review the state of the art in the neuropsychology of bilinguality and the bilingual's information processing. Social psychological and interpersonal aspects are treated in Chapters 8 and 9, while Chapter 10 looks at societal bilingualism. Finally, Chapter 11 is concerned with language planning in education and with bilingual education.

In our revision work we have also taken into account the public and personal comments and criticisms addressed to the first edition, although on the whole we have been greatly encouraged by these comments and criticisms. Lastly, we have learned from our own research findings.

Our special thanks go to Wallace E. Lambert who read the first draft of the manuscript and whose useful comments and sound advice helped us improve the quality of this book. We also gratefully acknowledge the comments and encouragement of our colleagues, in particular Richard Clément, Zita De Koninck and Itesh Sachdev. We are thankful to our research assistants, Isabelle Barrière, Ouafaâ Zouali and M'hammed Abdou, for their work on the bibliography and the figures.

We especially thank Georgette Hamers, Donna Lamping and Aurora Restaino for their continuing interest, support, encouragement and patience. Our special thanks go to the Département de Langues et Linguistique at the Université Laval for its support and to the Department of Applied Linguistics at Birkbeck College, University of London for its hospitality, to Jim Tyson and Giordano Castagnoli for their technical assistance. At Cambridge University Press, thanks are due to Andrew Winnard (commissioning editor), Martin Mellor (copy editor), Ann Mason (proofreader) and Karl Howe (senior production controller). Last but not least, we are extremely grateful to Qirul, Libellule and Bidule for their unconditional feline support which inspired us so much throughout the writing of this book.

We alone accept full responsibility for the shortcomings of the book.

Josiane F. Hamers and Michel H. A. Blanc
Quebec City, *London* and *Monte Santa Maria Tiberina*

Introduction

Languages in contact, that is bilingualism at the societal level and bilinguality, its counterpart at the individual level, are an integral part of human behaviour. With globalisation and increasing population movements due to immigration and greater geographical and social mobility, and with the spread of education, contacts between cultures and individuals are constantly growing. While bilingual individuals already outnumber monolinguals, it can be expected that this trend will continue in the twenty-first century.

In this book we attempt to present the state of the art on the principal issues of bilingualism and languages in contact. Our approach is multidisciplinary insofar as we study the various phenomena at different levels of analysis: we analyse languages in contact first in the language behaviour of the individual, next in interpersonal relations, and finally at the societal level where we consider the role of language in intergroup relations. A better understanding of languages in contact calls not only for a multidisciplinary approach but for an interdisciplinary integration of these diverse disciplines (Blanc & Hamers, 1987). One of the major problems of an interdisciplinary approach is the integration of the macro- and the micro-levels of analysis. Because of the great methodological and theoretical difficulties, very few scholars have attempted it, and even fewer succeeded. If at times our discussions lack an interdisciplinary scope, it is because the state of the art does not allow it yet.

Each level of analysis requires specific disciplinary approaches: psychological at the individual level, social psychological at the interpersonal level, and sociological at the intergroup level. These disciplines are brought together when the different levels of analysis meet. We discuss only those theoretical constructs which either have been empirically confirmed or for which empirical verification is possible. We have rejected unsound and unverifiable models or, if we mention them, it is to stress their theoretical and methodological flaws. We have treated in a critical way data not based on theoretical assumptions, as well as theories based solely on anecdotal evidence; furthermore, we have not relied either on models constructed on the grounds of evidence stemming from isolated case studies. However, we do not ignore this evidence, provided that it can confirm experimental data, or if it is the only available evidence. If we have ignored psychoanalytical approaches to bilingual behaviour, this is because we do not feel competent to evaluate them. We refer the interested reader to Amati Mehler, Argentieri & Canestri (1990). Typologies of bilingualism are mentioned only when they are based on some theoretical grounds and have therefore a predictive character; we consider a typology useful only in as far as a new classification of phenomena permits a better understanding of the psychological, sociological and linguistic processes and their interplay when languages are in contact.

It must be borne in mind that in English there is an ambiguity in the term *language*, which sometimes refers to a general communication process, rule-governed and shared by all humans (in French *langage*) and sometimes to the code of a specific speech community with its own rules (in French *langue*) (see also Le Page & Tabouret-Keller, 1985). As the reader continues, he or she will probably become aware that language does not necessarily have the same meaning in the different chapters. In the early chapters on the individual's language behaviour we use a more 'focused' definition of language, that is, it is defined as an abstract entity distinct from others, whereas in the later chapters we sometimes refer to a 'diffuse' definition, i.e. distributed on a continuum (see Le Page, 1978). In yet other chapters we take 'language' to mean a linguistic code used by a group of speakers who stand in a similar relationship to it and perceive it to be different from other linguistic codes.

Another problematic concept is that of *mother tongue*. UNESCO (1953: 46) defines it as 'the language which a person acquires in early years and which normally becomes its natural instrument of thought and communication'. At the psychological level the mother tongue can be defined as the first linguistic experience during the formative years of language development, regardless of the number of codes present and their use (Hamers, 1979). This means that the child's linguistic experience may vary from a differential use of several codes to the use of a single code. This definition has far-reaching implications when it comes to choosing a language of instruction for the child.

Our main concern is the identification of universals of behaviour when two or more languages are in contact. The phenomenon of language behaviour cannot be studied in isolation, as it is in constant interaction with other phenomena, namely with culture. Although language is part of culture there is no simple cause-and-effect relation between the two; rather, they are in constant interplay. When a chapter focuses on the one or other aspect, it must be kept in mind that one aspect of language behaviour, for example interpersonal features, cannot be explained if other dimensions, e.g. intergroup relations, are ignored. This focusing, therefore, is a momentary simplification which enables us to analyse the phenomenon more closely. Similarly, when we use a dichotomisation, for example compound vs. coordinate bilinguality, it must be understood as two extreme poles on a continuum rather than as two distinct entities.

In trying to understand behavioural processes there is a danger of reifying such conceptual constructs as language, culture, society, cognition, frames, scripts, and so on. Because we view these concepts only as theoretical constructs which enable us to understand better human behaviour and are convinced that they do not exist in the absence of human behaviour, we have tried to avoid their reification. It is in this frame of mind that all constructs used throughout the book must be understood. We have proposed a set of theoretical guiding principles which we follow throughout the book and attempt to apply at all levels of analysis.

In Chapter 1, after reviewing a number of definitions of bilingualism which we reject as one sided, we put forward a general interactional model of human behaviour which we apply to language behaviour and development. In Chapter 2 we define a number of dimensions which enable us to analyse the different facets of bilinguality and of bilingualism. We then describe and discuss the different measures that have been developed to assess bilingualism at the individual and the societal level.

In Chapters 3 and 4 we address the issue of bilingual development. The empirical research data on the bilinguistic ontogenesis is discussed in Chapter 3: we analyse the simultaneous and early consecutive development of bilinguality. We also review the specific case of bilinguality when one of the languages is gestural and the other articulated. We finally discuss individual language attrition and loss. In Chapter 4 we study the cognitive and sociocultural dimensions of the ontogenesis of bilinguality

Chapter 5 deals more specifically with the social and psychological foundations of bilingual development: after analysing the nature of language behaviour and development we stress the role of social networks and socialisation. We propose a social cognitive interactional model of language and bilingual development. At the end of the chapter we examine different types of bilinguality through a number of hypothetical case studies.

Chapters 6 and 7 deal with the neuropsychological foundations of bilinguality and with information processing in the bilingual. In Chapter 6 we look at the empirical evidence from polyglot aphasics and brain-intact bilinguals. We compare the neuropsychological functioning of bilinguals with that of monolinguals and look at differences in hemispheric preference. Chapter 7 examines the psychological mechanisms relevant to bilingual information processing, that is, representational mechanisms and in particular memory, and the access to these. Several models of representation and access are discussed and we stress the necessity of a hierarchical model. We further give a brief review of the bilingual's non-verbal behaviour.

The next two chapters deal with the social psychological dimensions of binguality. In Chapter 8 we examine the relationship between culture, identity and language behaviour in a multicultural environment. After a discussion of the relationship between language and culture, we analyse the bilingual's cultural identity and the social psychological processes which determine interethnic interpersonal relations. We end this chapter with a discussion of the social psychological processes which are relevant to second language acquisition. Chapter 9 addresses the issue of the interaction between interpersonal relations and linguistic behaviour: in the first part speech-accommodation theory and its consequences for bilinguistic behaviour and bilingual speech mode are discussed, while in the second part we describe communication strategies specific to intercultural interactions, such as code selection, speech modification, code-switching, code-mixing and borrowing

In Chapter 10 we turn to the analysis of societal bilingualism. The relationship between multiculturalism and intergroup relations are discussed from a sociolinguistic and social psychological standpoint. The role of language in intergroup behaviour is approached from different perspectives: language as a symbol and instrument of group identity, the concept of ethnolinguistic vitality and the interface between language and ethnicity in a multicultural setting. In the second part of this chapter we review the different types of sociolinguistic variations that arise from languages in contact: bilingual speech repertoires, diglossia, language shift, pidginisation, creolisation and decreolisation. We analyse their implications for language behaviour and linguistic theory. Finally we discuss language-planning policies and their consequences for groups and individuals with special reference to literacy.

Chapter 11 deals with language planning in education and with bilingual education. We first discuss the issue of literacy when languages are in contact, with special reference to developing countries and ethnolinguistic minorities. We then review bilingual education for majority/socially-advantaged children, in particular the immersion programs. We further examine the issue of educational programs for ethnolinguistic minority children. Finally, we briefly look at the potentials of community bilingual education.

This book is meant for all those who are interested in language behaviour or those who work with bilinguals: psychologists, psycholinguists, sociologists and sociolinguists, linguists, educators, language teachers, speech therapists and administrators who have to plan bilingual education. Even though it has been necessary sometimes to give complex technical details, we have tried to define the bilingual's behaviour in a way accessible to all readers, regardless of their disciplinary background. Explanations are given in the text or in notes. Some of the most important terms and concepts we use are defined in a Glossary at the end of the book. This, we hope, will further help the reader unfamiliar with certain terms and concepts. Throughout this book we use the masculine form as a generic term, unless otherwise specified; 'he', 'him' and 'his' refer therefore to a person, regardless of gender.

Given the magnitude of the problem, some analyses may have escaped us. We apologise to the authors we have unwittingly left out and to those we have misinterpreted, either because we had to summarise their view in a few sentences or because we had to synthesise approaches and disciplines with which we are not very familiar. We will be rewarded if this book informs the reader on the state of the art of languages in contact. We hope that she or he will have a better grasp of these issues after reading this book. Our goal will have been attained if this reading provokes many challenging questions. However, we do not necessarily provide all the answers. So much is yet to come from research not yet thought of.

1   Definitions and guiding principles

The aim of this book is to review critically the state of the art in the field of languages in contact. By 'languages in contact' we mean 'the use of two or more codes in interpersonal and intergroup relations as well as the psychological state of an individual who uses more than one language'. We distinguish between bilingualism and bilinguality. The concept of bilingualism refers to the state of a linguistic community in which two languages are in contact with the result that two codes can be used in the same interaction and that a number of individuals are bilingual (societal bilingualism); but it also includes the concept of bilinguality (or individual bilingualism). Bilinguality is the psychological state of an individual who has access to more than one linguistic code as a means of social communication; the degree of access will vary along a number of dimensions which are psychological, cognitive, psycholinguistic, social psychological, social, sociological, sociolinguistic, sociocultural and linguistic (Hamers, 1981).

1.1   DEFINITIONS

The concept of bilingualism seems at first sight to be non-problematical. According to Webster's dictionary (1961) bilingual is defined as 'having or using two languages especially as spoken with the fluency characteristic of a native speaker; a person using two languages especially habitually and with control like that of a native speaker' and bilingualism as 'the constant oral use of two languages'. In the popular view, being bilingual equals being able to speak two languages perfectly; this is also the approach of Bloomfield (1935: 56), who defines bilingualism as 'the native-like control of two languages'. In contradistinction to this definition which includes only 'perfect bilinguals' Macnamara (1967a) proposes that a bilingual is anyone who possesses a minimal competence in only one of the four language skills, listening comprehension, speaking, reading and writing, in a language other than his mother tongue. Between these two extremes one encounters a whole array of definitions as, for example, the one proposed by Titone (1972), for whom bilingualism is the individual's capacity to

6

speak a second language while following the concepts and structures of that language rather than paraphrasing his or her mother tongue.

All these definitions, which range from a native-like competence in two languages to a minimal proficiency in a second language, raise a number of theoretical and methodological difficulties. On the one hand, they lack precision and operationalism: they do not specify what is meant by native-like competence, which varies considerably within a unilingual population, nor by minimal proficiency in a second language, nor by obeying the concepts and structures of that second language. Can we exclude from the definitions of bilingual someone who possesses a very high competence in a second language without necessarily being perceived as a native speaker on account of a foreign accent? Can a person who has followed one or two courses in a foreign language without being able to use it in communication situations, or again someone who has studied Latin for six years, legitimately be called bilingual? Unless we are dealing with two structurally different languages, how do we know whether or not a speaker is paraphrasing the structures of his mother tongue when speaking the other language?

On the other hand, these definitions refer to a single dimension of bilinguality, namely the level of proficiency in both languages, thus ignoring non-linguistic dimensions. For example, Paradis (1986: xi), while suggesting that bilinguality should be defined on a multidimensional continuum, reduces the latter to linguistic structure and language skill. When definitions taking into account dimensions other than the linguistic ones have been proposed, they too have been more often than not limited to a single dimension. For example, Mohanty (1994a: 13) limits the definition of bilingualism to its social-communicative dimension, when he says that 'bilingual persons or communities are those with an ability to meet the communicative demands of the self and the society in their normal functioning in two or more languages in their interaction with the other speakers of any or all of these languages'.

More recent definitions insist on the specific characteristics of the bilingual. For example, Grosjean (1985a) defines a bilingual speaker as more than the sum of two monolinguals in the sense that the bilingual has also developed some unique language behaviour. Equally for Lüdi (1986) bilinguality is more than an addition of two monolingual competences, but an extreme form of polylectality.[1]

Baetens Beardsmore (1982) has listed some definitions and typologies of bilingualism, very few of which are multidimensional. These dimensions are further discussed in Section 2.2. But we have no intention of reviewing all the definitions or typologies that have been put forward for bilingualism. In this book, we will mention only those which are operational and can be applied in empirical research or those which are based on a theoretical construct. While discussing most of the important theoretical approaches to the study of bilingualism, we will also propose our own approach, which follows from the theoretical guiding principles underpinning the study of language behaviour outlined in the next section. It should be clearly understood that any adequate model of bilingual behaviour must be consistent with a more general model of language behaviour.

1.2   GENERAL GUIDELINES TO LANGUAGE BEHAVIOUR

In our view, language behaviour does not and cannot exist outside the functions it serves. By this we mean that language is in the first place a tool developed and used to serve a number of functions, both social and psychological, which can be classified in two main categories: communicative and cognitive (for more details, see, for example, Halliday, 1973; Bruner, 1990). Language does not exist in itself but has a use for the overall behaviour which is meaningful in a given culture. Functions of language are universal but the linguistic forms vary across languages and cultures. To some extent language is one of the variables which define culture. Moreover, language cannot be isolated from other aspects of behaviour. When language is processed by an individual it is always intermingled with cognitive and affective processes.

1.2.1   A functional approach to language behaviour

According to Bates & MacWhinney (1982) there are at least two levels of language processing: the functional level, where all the meanings and intentions to be expressed are represented; and, the formal level, at which all the surface forms used in the language are represented. Function plays a strong causal role in the way particular forms have evolved over time and in the way those forms are used by adults and acquired by children. Language is not just a device for generating structures but is seen as a potential for making meaning (Halliday, 1975). The linguistic system is only one form of the realisation of the more general semiotic system which constitutes the culture. In our approach we make a distinction between social functions, cognitive functions and semiotic-linguistic functions. Among the many cognitive functions that language fulfils, the semiotic-linguistic function (actor, action, goal) plays an active role in constructing meaning and therefore in developing formal language. Functions precede forms in the development and use of language, in the sense that forms are mapped onto the functions they serve.

Although the study of language can be conducted at several levels of analysis, in our view the nature of language behaviour, like that of other complex human behaviours, remains the same regardless of the level of analysis:[2]

(1) There is a constant interaction between the dynamics of language behaviour at the societal level and language behaviour at the individual level. In other words, whereas at the individual level we view language behaviour, at least in part, as the outcome of societal factors, we consider also that language behaviour at the societal level is the outcome of individual language behaviour.

(2) At all levels and between levels there is a constant and complex mapping process between the form of language behaviour and the function it is meant to fulfil. We consider that the approach of the competition model used at the individual level (see Bates & Mac-Whinney, 1987) applies equally at the societal level.

(3) Language behaviour is the product of culture and as such it follows the rules of enculturated behaviour. It is not a mere product of a biological endowment, but it is a product of culture, transmitted from one generation to the next in the socialisation process and appropriated by each individual; but, in turn, language behaviour moulds culture, that is, cultural representations are shaped by language behaviour.

(4) Self-regulation is a characteristic of all higher-order behaviours and therefore of language behaviour. By this we mean that a behaviour is not a mere response to stimuli but that it takes into account past experience; furthermore, it does not follow a pattern of trial and error but is an evaluative response calling upon the individual's cognitive and emotional functioning, adapted to a given situation.

(5) Finally, one concept central to this dynamic interaction between the societal and the individual level is valorisation. By valorisation we mean the attribution of certain positive values to language as a functional tool, that is, as an instrument which will facilitate the fulfilment of communicative and cognitive functioning at all societal and individual levels (Hamers & Blanc, 1982). The concept of valorisation is of the utmost importance in language-contact situations.

In addition, when two languages are in contact there can be a state of equilibrium between the two languages at each level and for each form–function mapping, in which case the use of both languages is constant and predictable. This equilibrium is not unlike the one existing in ecological systems. Any change of the relation between the two languages, due to a change in form–function mapping or to a change in valorisation at any level, will provoke a change in language behaviour.

Interactions between the dynamics of individual behaviour and the dynamics of the environment are current in biology and in evolutionary sciences. For example, the Neolithic revolution started with a change in individual behaviour, as a few humans started cultivating edible grasses rather than gathering them; when the behaviour spread and was adopted by a growing number of individuals, it started shaping the environment as woodlands gave way to cultivated fields; as cultivated fields spread, they in turn influenced the structure of the society which became organised around agriculture; this in turn changed the structures and called for a more collective behaviour in production and distribution, thereby changing the power relations in the society. Thus, a new form of behaviour (cultivating) served an existing function (need for food); when this mapping of form and function – that is when the new form of behaviour – became linked to the existing function, spread to a large enough number of individuals, this in turn changed the form of the landscape (from woods to fields) which came to serve the function of food growing. This twofold interplay between individual and society and between form and function is characteristic of processing in complex human behaviour.

Another example involving language behaviour is that of the origin of writing in Mesopotamia (see Schmandt-Besserat, 1992). Before a new language behaviour, i.e. writing, could come into existence, it started as a single mapping between form and function. Tokens with a specific shape (form) were designed and used as symbols for specific objects (e.g. a jar of oil) in order to record agricultural products (function); these symbols were first used in a one-to-one relationship with the objects (for example, five ovoid tokens stood for five jars). Next, a primitive system of counting appeared, e.g. one token was marked with five incisions. An important cognitive step was taken when an ovoid token (form) no longer represented a specific jar but the concept of jar and when the incisions represented an abstract concept of number (new functions). By introducing a system of counting (form), a large number of functions could be served; abstracting the concept of number enabled people to count any object. However, this did not happen before the use of the tokens had spread to a large enough area of the Ancient Near East and they were used by a critical but not necessarily large number of individuals. This critical mass[3] consisted of a few individuals who had power and status in the society (bureaucrats, administrators and scribes).

Each individual who had to use the system had also to develop the new concepts at the individual level. For example, at the cognitive level, a distinction had to be made between 'how much' and 'how many'. Each new form invented had to serve a specific function. In turn, creating a new form–function mapping and a new system would first be reflected in the individual's use of language and, in a next stage, in the language used in society. By creating a new system, new forms had to be invented not only to designate the new concepts (e.g. forms to denote 50, 250, 2500, but also to express the relations between 5, 50 and 500). These signs expressing abstract numbers indicated a new threshold in counting. When abstract counting was appropriated by the society, it gave rise to a new system of data storage and communication with the development of numerals and cuneiform pictography, that is, a writing system, which, in turn, would facilitate the development of a type of literacy.[4]

Introducing an individual to the language used in literacy, mainly through the means of learning to read and write, will induce changes in his or her language behaviour. For example, processing a written text calls to a greater extent on the use of decontextualised language. When few people were literate, the behaviour of individuals was changed with little effect on the social structures. As more and more people become literate, linguistic forms are mapped onto new cognitive functions; when a critical mass is reached, a need for new social institutions, such as schools (form), is created. In turn, these institutions serve the function of literacy; as the need to fulfil this function continues to grow, new norms, which evolve into a recognised fundamental right for education (form), are created. This, in turn, shapes individual behaviour: when schooling becomes compulsory, all individuals in a given society are expected to master reading and writing, thus shaping their own individual behaviour.

In their competition model Bates & MacWhinney (1982) suggest that, in language development, mapping occurs between two levels, the functional and the formal. This model is congruent with more general theories in psychology, in particular with connectionism, such as Hebb's neurophysiological theory of cell-assembly[5] (Hebb, 1949; 1968). It is also in line with the studies of language development which discuss the importance of the functional aspects of language (see, for example, Halliday, 1973; 1975). The two-level mapping between function and linguistic form is based on the assumption that linguistic forms are developed to express meanings and communicative intentions. As language develops, form–function mapping is not necessarily a one-to-one correlation: a single form can be mapped onto different functions, e.g. *it's cold in here* might have a referential function, meaning *the temperature is low*, or an instrumental-regulatory function meaning *turn on the radiator*. Conversely a single function may be served by several linguistic forms: an order can be expressed by an imperative, an interrogative, etc. Furthermore, three types of mapping are involved: form–function, function–function and form–form. These three types of mapping do not work independently in the language system but occur simultaneously; for example, for the utterance *I play*, a form–function mapping *I(agent)–I(linguistic form)* occurs simultaneously with another form–function mapping *I(agent)–play(linguistic form)*, a function–function mapping *I(agent)–play(act)* and a form–form mapping *I(linguistic form)–play(linguistic form)*.

Similar phenomena can be observed at the societal level. A typical example is provided by the pidginisation process (see Section 10.3.5). Pidgins are auxiliary languages (form) developed for the purpose of minimal communication between individuals/groups speaking mutually unintelligible vernaculars (function). In the pidginisation process, limited and simplified linguistic forms are developed. As the need for communication increases in the society (function), so new forms are created by the speakers. Gradually these new forms serve extended functions. Eventually the pidgin evolves into a creole (form), becomes the mother tongue of the next generation, and thereby serves new functions.

The forms of language are not static but undergo constant changes due to social changes; for example:

- a change of accent as a sign of distinctiveness, or a change of language use or language form as a result of language planning, e.g. a language compulsory in education;
- new technologies such as the introduction of computer technology using English;
- and contact with other languages as for example the conquest of England by the Normans.

New forms apply to old functions, as when a new expression is used by teenagers; in the same way old forms apply to new functions, as for example the English word *save* in using a computer; or new forms can be developed for new functions (e.g. new terminology). Forms can be created, e.g. *television*, or borrowed from other languages, as the French word *garage* in English. Forms can cease to be used if they no longer serve functions, as is the case in L_1-attrition in immigrants.

At the individual level higher-order behaviour is self regulated. While the behaviour is performed, the individual takes into account feedback mechanisms and readjusts constantly his behaviour. An example of this type of behaviour is speech accommodation in interpersonal communication interaction (as when a speaker switches languages to be understood by a non-native speaker; see further Section 9.1). We argue that similar mechanisms occur also at a collective level. For example, in the process of pidginisation a group of speakers from different cultural and linguistic backgrounds adjust to their new situation by developing a new code in order to communicate both with one another and with their masters (see Section 10.3.5).

All societies value language as a tool of communication and of cognition;

however, they tend to valorise certain functions more than others, e.g. the cognitive function in school. If different varieties of language, e.g. accents, are present in the society, one variety may be valued to the detriment of others. A similar situation obtains in the case of multilingual societies. One or more languages will be highly valued, while others will be devalorised. At the individual level a similar mechanism operates. To the extent that the adults around the child value the use of language for certain functions, he will also value the use of language for these functions and thus develop these aspects. The extreme importance of valorisation is evidenced at all societal and individual levels. For example, at the societal level, if a minority language is not valorised and used as a tool for education, language attrition and language shift are likely to occur. At the individual level, the positive valorisation of all or some of the values linked to the formal and functional aspects of language will help to elaborate and trigger off a motivational process for learning and using those aspects of language.

To sum up, in analysing language behaviour we will focus on different societal and individual levels: societal (institutions, groups and social class), social networks and interpersonal relations, individual (developmental, socio-affective, cognitive and neuropsychological processes as well as language behaviour). At each of these levels, we view language behaviour as dynamic: there are constant interactions amongst the determining factors within and between the different levels; for example, we cannot draw a complete picture of lexical development unless we also take into consideration relevant aspects of syntactic development, cognitive growth, interpersonal relations and social class. Language behaviour is the outcome not only of the multiple interactions between different factors, but also of social and psychological mediating processors. For instance, a social determinant like social class does not influence language production directly, but is mediated by the social networks; the acquisition of a second language is not only a function of the teaching method, but is also mediated by, for example, attitudes in the community and by individual motivation.

1.2.2 A general model of language behaviour

The following model is based on the functional approach to language behaviour described in the preceding section. In this functional approach we view language processing as a sequence of levels of processing embedded in one another; that is, the micro-levels are embedded in more macro-levels. If, for example, we analyse language processing at the level of social networks, it is embedded in language processing at the societal level; if we consider language processing at the interpersonal level it is embedded in social networks; language processing at the personal level is in turn embedded in interpersonal relations. Society is also a multilevel construction: language as shared behaviour is processed in terms of rules, norms and roles; this behaviour can be analysed in terms of institutions, classes or groups. In a similar way, at the individual level language behaviour is processed in terms of development, cognitive functioning, social psychological mechanisms, neuropsychological functioning or linguistic output. It is understood that these different levels of processing are not independent from one another.

The interface between the societal and the individual levels is situated in the interpersonal interactions actualised through the social network (Hamers, 1987). Our approach is schematised in Figure 1.1. It must be pointed out that language behaviour is present at all levels $<A>$, $<B>$, $<C>$ and $<D>$. Furthermore, each level can be represented at different times: X_0, X_1, X_2, etc. Given that a particular language behaviour occurs at a time X_1, this behaviour produced by an individual will result on the one hand from an interplay between embedded structures, i.e. the social structure, the social networks, the interpersonal interaction occurring at a time X_1; and, on the other hand, from a similar interplay at an earlier time, X_0. This earlier interplay is a determining antecedent (past experience) from the onset of language development onwards which will fulfil an important role in the self-regulation of the present behaviour. In addition, present language behaviour is likely to play a role in shaping future collective language behaviour, provided that a critical mass of individuals have adopted this behaviour. A critical mass presupposes a number of speakers but the size of the mass may vary as a function of the power and status of the speakers.

At each level we consider that similar mechanisms operate: an intake (i/t) from the previous level will integrate with elements from the present level including past experience and present evaluation (x) and will through self-regulation, feedback mechanisms and form–function mapping produce an output (o/p) that will serve as input (i/p) for the next embedded level.

At a time X_1 level $<A>$ provides an input *(a)* for an embedded level $<B>$; at level $<B>$ all or part of this input is restructured as *(b)* (i/t), which is integrated with some specific characteristics of $<B>$ (xb) to produce [*(b)*;xb]. Let us take as an example a bilingual situation, e.g. the case of French and Arabic in France. The societal level $<A>$ provides an output *(a)* of two languages with a status difference: a high status official language, French, and a low status immigrant language, Arabic; French is dominant over Arabic. Both languages are unequally valorised in the society. At the social network level $<B>$ there will be an intake *(b)* from this status difference which will be integrated with the status of Arabic as the mother tongue, which is more valorised and the language of communication in the network (xb) to produce [*(b)*;xb]. These two elements integ-

LEVELS A   B   C   D

TIME

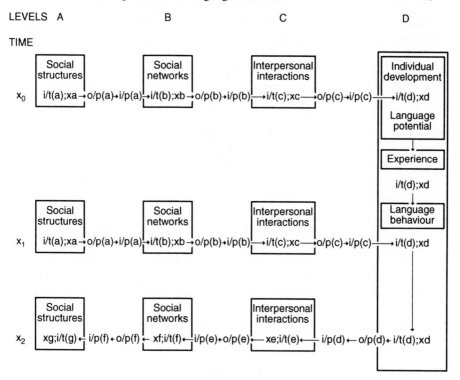

Figure 1.1   A general model of language behaviour

rated together $[(b);xb]$ will redefine the relative status of French and Arabic in the network: French might still be perceived as dominant, but Arabic will be more valorised, used to a greater extent and serve more functions (e.g. communicative and affective functions); mapping of the choice of language onto a given situation will occur in a different way from the preceding level. The use of both languages in the network will differ from the use of both languages in the larger society.

The use and status of both languages in the social network $[(b);xb]$ will in turn serve as input for interpersonal interactions (level $<C>$); with an (i/t) (c) from this i/p, individuals will integrate their own contribution (xc) (for example the degree of mastery in both languages) to produce $[(c);xc]$. At the interpersonal level $<C>$, which is the interface between the societal and the individual levels, Arabic (along with French or not) will be transmitted as the mother tongue to the infant with a status perceived in the interpersonal relations. At the individual level $<D>$ the child will first develop Arabic as his mother tongue with the presence of some French around him; as the child's social networks extend to include the school and the peer group, the relative status and valorisation of both languages will change and the intake from the interpersonal level will vary: the input of French will increase drastically. The child's i/t $((d)$ at level $<D>$) from the interpersonal relations in the networks (in terms of status and mastery) will be integrated with its own specific characteristics (xd) to produce $[(d);xd]$ which will determine linguistic output. It must be borne in mind that the child's characteristics include the intake received at a time X_0, that is, all former experience, including the developmental aspects. It must be noted that this personal input in the infant is limited to a communicative and language potential whereas in the already socialised adult it includes a number of social/emotional and cognitive dimensions. The interplay between the intake during childhood and the developing characteristics of the child (e.g. cognitive development) $[(d);xd]$ will in turn produce the final individual language behaviour of the adult speaker at level $<A>$. This is however not a linear relation, since level $<D>$ will in turn provide an input for level $<D>$ which will receive an intake (e), which will, in turn, integrate it (xe) to produce $[(e);xe]$, and so on until it produces an input (f) for level $<A>$ at a time X_2. However, in order for the individual input to have an effect on level $<A>$ a critical mass must be reached. For example, if enough individuals use and want to maintain Arabic and if they have enough power and status, they can impose new institutions such as schooling in Arabic. This will change the social structures, which will affect the language behaviour of the next generation.

1.2.3   Developmental aspects of language behaviour

Modelling of language behaviour has been developed to a greater extent at the individual level than at the societal level. Generally these models are rooted in a larger framework of psychological theorising. For example, Bruner (1990) views language development as part of a general model of cognitive development rooted in social interactions; Piaget's (1970) constructivist approach to language is embedded in a more general approach to human behaviour, calling on a model of equilibrium between adaptation and accommodation; Bates & MacWhinney's (1982) competition model is a general psycholinguistic model of language processing based on a connectionist approach of the study of behaviour. According to Pinker (1996) a comprehensive theory of language acquisition must consider the following aspects: the state of the child at the onset of acquisition; the linguistic input and its context; the mental algorithms that turn this input into knowledge about the language; the end state of the process, i.e. a grammatically competent speaker, and the evolution of the process, i.e. what children understand and produce during the acquisition process.

Linguistic and psychological approaches to language acquisition differ in the emphasis they put onto and the relative importance they attribute to each of these aspects. Pinker (1996), for example, while recognising the role played by parental input in child language acquisition, emphasises the role played by mental algorithms, considered to be innate. Bates & MacWhinney (1982) rather emphasise the role of input characteristics (form, functions, cues) which interact with the child's cognitive processing (mapping, evaluation) to produce competing potential outputs amongst which the most likely will be chosen. Bruner (1990) insists on the internalisation of communicative functions and the development of intentions at the prelinguistic stage.

Our aim here is not to enter into this type of debate but rather to explain our own positions on the development of language behaviour in order to analyse the development of bilinguality in the light of general theorising which is congruent with the guidelines mentioned in Section 1.2.1. In Chapter 5 we propose a theoretical approach to the development of bilinguality based on broader general assumptions of child language development.

In our functional approach we consider that language development is rooted in the social interactions with the significant others; furthermore it has an important social psychological component and an equally important cognitive component (Hamers & Blanc, 1982). Functions that language will later serve are developed before the child acquires the linguistic forms. According to Bruner (1975a), before developing language the child learns some communicative functions through cooperative actions, which are arrived at through joint attention with the adults who are interacting with the child. The child is initially equipped with 'a set of predispositions to construe the social world and to act upon our construals' (Bruner, 1990: 73). Through interactions with others he will develop a prelinguistic readiness for meaning, i.e. a context sensitivity which will enable him to make the linguistic forms present in the environment his own.

Considering our general approach described above, language development which occurs at level <D> receives an input (c) from level <C> through the joint actions and the interpersonal interactions with the significant others. In turn these interactions occur in the social networks of the significant others, essentially the family network <B>, from which they receive an input (b); the social network level <B> receives an input (a) from the societal level <A>.

According to the competition model (Bates & MacWhinney, 1989) language acquisition is guided by form–function correlations; these correlations give meaning to language. These correlations exist in the input amongst other cues which the children are able to pick up. Although children are able to pick up other cues, i.e. recurring patterns in the sound stream, this process is facilitated when meaning is available. However, language acquisition has also a perceptual/motor prerequisite: the child must be able to perceive forms before any form–function mapping can occur. Once forms have been identified in the input, they can be mapped onto existing communicative functions. According to connectionism form–function, form–form and function–function correlations will occur in order to form complex higher-order organisations (such as nodules or cell-assemblies) which are responsible for the complexities of language processing.

We make a further distinction between communicative, cognitive and linguistic functions. By communicative function we mean the social-communicative functions language is serving in the interactions, such as the instrumental (*I want*), regulatory (*do as I tell you*) and interactional (*me and you*) function. The cognitive functions include heuristic (use of the language to organise and analyse knowledge) and mathetic (use of language for the purpose of discovery and learning) functions. The linguistic functions refer to the specific functions served by semantic elements, such as actor, action and goal, in an utterance. It should be stressed that there is not a one-to-one relationship between form and function: one form can be mapped onto several functions and one function can be mapped onto several forms.

Two important aspects of language development must be taken into consideration. First, form–function mapping will not occur outside a valorisation process. Second, as soon as elements of language are acquired they will be used as a cognitive tool and important interactions between language and cognitive functioning will develop.

The valorisation process deals with the affective dimension of language development. For the child to develop language he must first valorise language, i.e. attribute a certain positive value to the functions language is meant to serve (Hamers & Blanc, 1982). To the extent that the adults around him (level <B>) value the use of language for certain functions, the child will also value the use of language for these functions and thus develop these aspects. As a child's environment (levels <C> and <B>) attaches certain values to language, the child, taking his environment as a model, internalises those values important for the significant others <B>, for his social networks <C> and for his community <A>. Those valorised aspects of language are those that enable the child to build up the social psychological mechanisms relevant to his language development; it is those very aspects that determine the evaluative dimension of language, the child's own affective relation to his language. The child (level <D>) will thus construct a certain notion of prestige conferred on language and language functions by society (level <A>), which, after they have been moulded at levels <B> and <C>, he will internalise. This affective dimension of language behaviour will play the role of an important mediator in the process of language development, i.e. in construing the motivational mechanisms, more particularly when different languages are present in the child's environment (see further Chapter 8). In some cases it will also be relevant to the construction of the social/cultural/ethnic identity.

As soon as language develops it becomes an important tool of cognitive functioning. This function is what Bruner (1975b) calls 'analytic competence', the conceptual-linguistic abilities involving 'the prolonged operation of thought processes exclusively on linguistic representations and propositional structures'. Linguistic representations are not stored in their original input form but undergo a processing and are stored in propositional forms. The conceptual-linguistic abilities are crucial in the comprehension of abstract concepts, the analysis of linguistic statements, the understanding of subtle semantic distinctions, etc. They will in turn play an important role in the further growth of language behaviour, and particularly in the development of metalinguistic awareness and metalinguistic ability, which are both crucial to the development of literacy. According to Bialystok & Ryan (1985a) the literacy-oriented use of language rests on two independent cognitive operations: (1) the analysis of knowledge which calls upon the manipulation of representations and (2) the cognitive control which is responsible for selecting and coordinating the required information within a given time and space. Metalinguistic activities require high levels of information processing in terms of both analysis and control.

Bialystok & Ryan's information-processing model is different from most connectionist approaches in the sense that they assume that language processing occurs at two different levels and that language development undergoes a progressive analysis and restructuring of the mental representations of language: at a first level, the language form–function mapping consists of a set of semantic relations that organise our knowledge of the world; at a deeper level, the metalinguistic level, the underlying mental representations must be organised around forms and structures and must indicate how forms relate to meaning. At the metalinguistic level, the analysed representations of linguistic knowledge are formal symbolic rather than semantic or empirical, and the structures of these categories are explicit (Bialystok, 1991). However, the notion of mapping as developed by Bates & MacWhinney (1982) seems equally important to their approach.

Finally, as we argued earlier (Hamers & Blanc, 1982), an important concept in analysing language development is that of feedback mechanisms, operating within and between the different levels. By feedback mechanism we mean that the more the child is successful in using language to fulfil a particular function, the more value he will attach to it, hence the more motivated he will be to use it for that particular function. On the other hand, the less successful the child is in using language for a particular function, the less value he will attribute to it and as a result the less motivated he will be to use language for that particular function. Thus every cognitive and social psychological processing will be intensified by the effect of its own feedback mechanism, which will operate as an amplifier.

When two or more languages are in contact they may be in a state of equilibrium or in a changing relation, at all levels (individual, interpersonal and societal). Any change in the form–function mapping or in the valorisation of either language leads to concomitant changes in language behaviour, and vice versa.

To sum up, in our view, the original input for language development comes from the child's social environment, via the social networks and the significant interactions with others. Perceptual processes must enable the child to pick up the meaningful cues. Internalisation processes of meaning, of language forms and of language values will serve as building blocks for his own language representations and processing mechanisms at the linguistic, at the cognitive and at the social psychological level. Cognitive processing, including mapping procedures, analysis of linguistic knowledge and control of linguistic processing, will shape the development of linguistic behaviour.

1.2.4   Collective aspects of language behaviour

Although no similar model at the societal level exists, we believe that this functional approach is equally valid at this level in the case of a monolingual society and is congruent with many social theories of language. Furthermore, it can be applied mutatis mutandis to language contact situations.

1.2.4.1   Monolingual situation

In addition to its communicative (message) and cognitive (intelligence) functions, language has a social function. By this we mean that any utterance carries a social meaning in that it reflects the position of its speaker in the power relations in the society which confers a particular social value to this utterance. It can be said that the whole social structure is present in every language interaction and that every interaction is mapped onto the social structure. Language is not homogeneous any more than society is; variation is inherent in language because language behaviour varies along social dimensions (e.g. social class). Languages and varieties of language (accents, dialects, sociolects, codes) have a recognised value on the linguistic market (Bourdieu, 1982) and can be placed on a hierarchical scale according to their distance from the official, legitimate norm. Power relations between language varieties vary as a function of their speakers' access to the legitimate norm, and any discourse takes its social meaning from its relation to the linguistic market. Variations in discourse (i.e. in language behaviour) are a result of the interplay between the objective dynamic forces of the market and the way in which the individual perceives, evaluates and responds to these forces.

Language behaviour is linked to the market not only by its conditions of application (language use) but also by its conditions of acquisition (language acquisition/learning). The different language varieties and their values are learned in particular markets, first in the family, then at school, and so on, that is in the individual's social networks, where different functions and forms of language are transmitted and valorised. The interpersonal relations in the social networks are, therefore, the locus where the societal level and the individual level meet. The structures of social networks influence the individual's language behaviour: a dense, close-knit, multiplex network is a factor of ingroup solidarity, maintenance of local, non-standard norms, and resistance to linguistic change; whereas a diffuse, loose and simplex network implies social mobility and is therefore open to code change and the influence of outside norms (Milroy, 1980).

In summary, language behaviour at the interpersonal interactional level is the result of the dynamic interplay between the objective power relations at the societal level which confer unequal values to language and varieties of language and the individual's perception and evaluation of these, together with his own language experience acquired and used in the social networks. (For an attempt to synthesise these various aspects see Prujiner, Deshaies, Hamers, Blanc, Clément & Landry, 1984.)

1.2.4.2   Bilingual situation

When one language is present in the society and the social networks it is used for all functions, though differentially, as a reflection of the social structure. When two or more languages are in contact, their relative functional use is of the utmost importance; functional use, in addition, shapes relative valorisation of the languages, and vice versa.

When two languages are in contact in the society, they may be used to a different extent, in different domains and for different functions in a state of functional equilibrium. In the case of diglossia, the uses of each language are determined at the societal level. In that case we have a predictable form–function mapping (e.g. German-speaking Switzerland, where the respective uses of High German for certain functions and Schwyzer-tüütsch for others are in complementary distribution in the society).

This state of equilibrium can be observed at all levels. However, if the equilibrium is disrupted at one level, it will disrupt the equilibrium at all other levels. For example, a change in the relative use of the two languages in the social networks, e.g. when the individual has a new network because of a job change, will inevitably provoke a change in the language behaviour of the individual. A change in the use of two languages at the societal level, like, for example, introducing a compulsory language of schooling (e.g. French in Quebec for the children of immigrants), will bring about a change in the use of language in the social network, hence in the interpersonal interactions and the language behaviour of the individual. When enough individuals start changing their language behaviour (e.g. using French instead of English), this will in turn modify language use in the interpersonal contacts (children will use French with their friends), in the social network (the peer group will use French) and hence at the societal level.

We will apply the functional model to the phenomenon of language shift and language attrition. Language shift is defined as the change from the use of one language to the use of another language across generations; language attrition is a shift occurring within one individual (for further details see Sections 3.5 and 10.4). In both cases it refers to the loss of functions, forms and language skills. The shift is complete when parents of one generation cease to transmit their language to their children and when the latter are no longer motivated to acquire an active competence in that language. Thus, language shift begins at the interpersonal level. What is the dynamic interaction between social, psychological and linguistic factors which determines language shift or language maintenance in a group? We will base our analysis on Gal's (1979) ethnographic study of a language shift in a German-Hungarian community in Austria. (The reader is referred to Section 10.3.3 for a more detailed analysis.)

At a time X_1 the societal level $<A>$ provides an input (a) of two language groups with a power difference (the German-speaking group is demographically and socially dominant) and two languages with a status difference (German is the high-status official language associated with urban values, while Hungarian is the low-status language/dialect associated with rural values). At the societal level, therefore, the two languages are unequally valorised; this is reflected in the asymmetry in the linguistic competence of the two groups, Hungarians being bilingual in Hungarian and German, Austrians monolingual in German. At the social network level $<B>$ this status difference is integrated with the more valorised Hungarian language/dialect as mother tongue and language of communication and emotion: in their dense and multiplex networks Hungarians still use their first language among themselves. But the presence of one Austrian in a dominant Hungarian network is sufficient to trigger a switch to German in interpersonal interactions with him/her. The status and use of the two languages in the social network are reflected at the interpersonal and personal levels. At the interpersonal level <C>, Hungarian is transmitted as mother tongue to the infant with a higher status perceived in the interpersonal interactions. At the personal level <D> the Hungarian child first develops Hungarian as his/her mother tongue; he/she is also aware of the use of German around him/her. As the child's social networks extend to include the school and the peer group, the relative status and thus the relative valorisation of the two languages changes again: the input from German at school and in the new network increases dramatically; modern urban values, associated with German language and culture, influence the child who starts speaking German in asymmetrical interpersonal interactions with Hungarians of the older generation in their own rural social network, while the latter is still using Hungarian only. As they grow up, many young Hungarians enter a German-speaking labour market and marry into a German-speaking family (new domains), thus extending even more widely their German-speaking networks. For example, a Hungarian woman marrying into an Austrian family, even if she decides to speak Hungarian to her children, soon code-switches between Hungarian and German with them; her Hungarian and that of her children inevitably is influenced by German. The shift and the attrition are already under way. Eventually, at time level X_2 a Hungarian mother in a German-dominated network may not even transmit her mother tongue to her children. When enough individuals cease to speak their first language, a critical threshold has been reached, below which the minority language will probably not survive beyond the next generation.

This case of language shift and language attrition is an example of dynamic interactions between and within levels, and of various form–function mappings: new forms (e.g. school or exogamous marriage) lead to other new forms (new language of instruction or languages of child-rearing), and the work function demands a new linguistic form (change of language).

1.3   CONCLUSION

In this chapter we first reviewed a number of definitions of bilingualism, none of which we have found to be satisfactory. One weakness is their unidimensionality; for example, they define the bilingual in terms of competence, ignoring other important dimensions. We discuss the different dimensions in Section 2.1. Another weakness is the failure to take into consideration different levels of analysis (individual, interpersonal and societal). A third and major weakness is that those definitions are not underpinned by a general theory of language behaviour.

In the second part of the chapter we put forward a number of theoretical guiding principles which will underpin our approaches and analyses throughout the book. We view the nature of language behaviour like that of any other complex human behaviours, and indeed view them as being embedded in those behaviours. We consider the following basic principles of language behaviour:

(1)   There is a constant interaction between the societal and the individual dynamics of language.
(2)   Within and between levels there are complex mapping processes between the form of language behaviour and the functions it serves.
(3)   There is a reciprocal interaction between culture and language.
(4)   Self-regulation characterises all higher-order behaviours, and therefore language.
(5)   Valorisation is central to these dynamic interactions.

It is understood that social and psychological realities are simultaneous: any person is at one and the same time an individual, a member of social networks and groups and part of the wider society.

We will examine the issue of languages in contact at the individual and the societal level in the light of these guiding principles which apply equally to the study of bilinguality and of societal bilingualism. In our view form–function mappings occur within and between the languages to different degrees at all levels of analysis. If these guiding principles inform our approach, this does not mean that we do not take into account other theoretical approaches.

In the next chapter we analyse the different dimensions of bilinguality and societal bilingualism. We have already mentioned the multidimensional nature of bilingualism, which calls upon an array of disciplines ranging from neuropsychology to developmental psychology, experimental psychology, cognitive psychology, psycholinguistics, social psychology, sociolinguistics, sociology, the sociology of language, anthropology, ethnography, political and economic sciences, education and, of course, linguistics.

2 Dimensions and measurement of bilinguality and bilingualism

In this chapter first we define the relevant dimensions of bilinguality and bilingualism on the basis of the empirical evidence available in these fields. In the second part we enumerate the main different measures developed in order to try to quantify the relevant concepts.

2.1 DIMENSIONS OF BILINGUALITY AND BILINGUALISM

When qualifiers are used to describe bilingualism or bilinguality, they generally focus on one single dimension of these phenomena which are thereby viewed from a particular angle. If we use some of the classifications put forward by researchers it is because they seem to us to be relevant to the dimension under study; however, we must not lose sight of the fact that bilinguality and bilingualism are multidimensional phenomena which must be investigated as such. In the past, failure to take into account simultaneously other dimensions in addition to linguistic ones has all too often led to incomplete or erroneous interpretations of these phenomena.

2.1.1 Dimensions of bilinguality

In Chapter 1 we made a distinction between bilingualism and bilinguality. We view bilinguality as the psychological state of an individual who has access to more than one linguistic code as a means of social communication. This access is multidimensional as it varies along a number of psychological and sociological dimensions. We have found the following dimensions relevant:

(1)   relative competence;
(2)   cognitive organisation;
(3)   age of acquisition;
(4)   exogeneity;
(5)   social cultural status; and
(6)   cultural identity.

(For a summary of these dimensions see Table 2.1.)

Table 2.1 Summary table of psychological dimensions of bilinguality (Hamers & Blanc, 1989)

Dimension	Type of bilinguality	Comments*
1. according to competence in both languages	(a) balanced bilinguality (b) dominant bilinguality	$L_{A/1}$ competence = $L_{B/2}$ competence $L_{A/1}$ competence > or < $L_{B/2}$ competence
2. according to cognitive organisation	(a) compound bilinguality (b) coordinate bilinguality	$L_{A/1}$ unit equivalent to $L_{B/2}$ unit = one conceptual unit $L_{A/1}$ unit = one conceptual unit 1 $L_{B/2}$ equivalent = one conceptual unit 2

3. according to age of acquisition	(a) childhood bilinguality
	  (i) simultaneous
	  (ii) consecutive
	(b) adolescent bilinguality
	(c) adult bilinguality
		$L_{B/2}$ acquired before age of 10/11
		L_A and L_B = mother tongues
		L_1 = mother tongue; L_2 acquired before 11
		L_2 = acquired between 11 and 17
		L_2 = acquired after 17

4. according to presence of L_2 community in environment	(a) endogenous bilinguality (b) exogenous bilinguality	presence of L_2 community absence of L_2 community
5. according to the relative status of the two languages	(a) additive bilinguality (b) subtractive bilinguality	$L_{A/1}$ and $L_{B/2}$ socially valorised → cognitive advantage L_2 valorised at expense L_1 → cognitive disadvantage
6. according to group membership and cultural identity	(a) bicultural bilinguality (b) L_1 monocultural bilinguality (c) L_2 acculturated bilinguality (d) deculturated bilinguality	double membership and bicultural identity $L_{A/1}$ membership and cultural identity $L_{B/2}$ membership and cultural identity ambiguous membership and anomic identity

* For an explanation of L_A, L_B, L_1, L_2, see p. 372

(1)   The dimension of competence enables us to take into account the relative nature of bilinguality, since it focuses on the relationship between two linguistic competences, one in each language. A distinction has been made between the balanced bilingual who has equivalent competence in both languages and the dominant bilingual for whom competence in one of the languages, more often the mother tongue, is superior to his competence in the other (Lambert, 1955). Balanced bilinguality should not be confused with a very high degree of competence in the two languages; it is rather a question of a state of equilibrium reached by the levels of competence attained in the two languages as compared to monolingual competence. Equivalent competence should not be equated with the ability to use both languages for all functions and domains. Dominance or balance is not equally distributed for all domains and functions of language; each individual has his own dominance configuration.

(2)   Regardless of the state of equilibrium, bilinguality may differ on other dimensions. For example, age and context of acquisition may lead to differences in cognitive functioning. Ervin & Osgood (1954) distinguished between compound and coordinate language systems: in a compound system two sets of linguistic signs come to be associated with the same set of meanings whereas, in a coordinate system, translation equivalents in the two languages correspond to two different sets of representations. This distinction is schematised in Figure 2.1.

This distinction, often misinterpreted in the literature, has to do with a difference of cognitive organisation and not with a difference in the degree of competence, or a difference in the age or context of acquisition. Although there is a high correlation between the type of cognitive organisation, age and context of acquisition, there is no one-to-one correspondence between the form of cognitive representation and the age of acquisition; indeed, an individual who learned both languages as a child in the same context is more likely to have a single cognitive representation for two translation equivalents, whereas one who learned an L_2 in a context different from that of his L_1 will probably have a coordinate organisation, that is, he will have separate representations for two translation equivalents. However, for operational purposes, age and context of acquisition are often used in order to identify the two types of bilinguals. This misinterpretation is often made, even by specialists in bilingual studies who, while noting the relation between age and context of acquisition and type of bilinguality, forget that the distinction refers essentially to differences in semantic organisation in the bilingual (see, for example, Ervin & Osgood, 1954, Fishman, 1964; Gumperz, 1964a; Dodson, 1983). It must be stressed that this distinction is not absolute but that different forms of bilinguality are distributed along a continuum from a compound pole to a coordinate

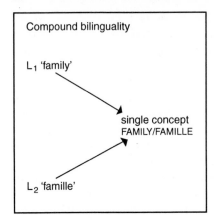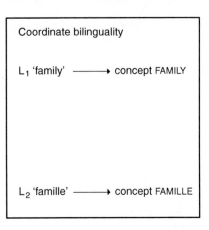

Figure 2.1 Schematic representation of the compound–coordinate
distinction (adapted from Ervin & Osgood, 1954)

pole: a bilingual person can at the same time be more compound for certain
concepts and more coordinate for others. This distinction is further explored in Section 7.1.1.1.

(3)   The age of acquisition plays a part not only in respect of cognitive
representation but also in other aspects of the bilingual's development,
particularly his linguistic, neuropsychological, cognitive and sociocultural
development. Age of acquisition combines with other data from the subject's language biography, such as context of acquisition and use of the two
languages. Indeed, age and context often go together: for instance, early
acquisition of two languages often occurs in the same family context, while
later acquisition of the second language often takes place in a school
context distinct from a family context for the first language.

  A distinction must first be made between childhood bilinguality, adolescent bilinguality and adult bilinguality. In the first of these bilingual
experience takes place at the same time as the general development of the
child; in other words this bilingual experience occurs at the time when the
various developmental components have not yet reached maturity and can
therefore be influenced by this experience. In childhood bilinguality one
must distinguish:

(a)   simultaneous early or infant bilinguality when the child develops two
      mother tongues from the onset of language, which we call L_A and L_B,
      as for example the child of a mixed-lingual family; and
(b)   consecutive childhood bilinguality when he acquires a second lan-
      guage early in childhood but after the basic linguistic acquisition of

his mother tongue has been achieved. In this case and in all other cases of consecutive bilingual acquisition we refer to the mother tongue as L_1 and to the second language as L_2.

While the development of simultaneous bilinguality takes place through informal, unintentional learning, consecutive childhood bilinguality may occur informally, as in the case of the child of an immigrant family, but may also result from intentional learning, as in certain bilingual educational programs. Another important difference between simultaneous and consecutive bilinguality concerns the form–function mapping: in the case of simultaneous bilinguality the child has to map two forms onto one function; we refer to this as compound mapping. In consecutive bilinguality simple mapping (one linguistic form) occurs before the acquisition of the second language for the functions acquired already.

(4)   According to whether the speech communities of both languages are present or not in the child's social environment, we refer to either endogenous or exogenous bilinguality. An endogenous language is one that is used as a mother tongue in a community and may or may not be used for institutional purposes, whereas an exogenous language is one that is used as an official, institutionalised language but has no speech community in the political entity using it officially. Examples of exogenous languages are English or French in West, Central and East African countries; a Benin child from Cotonou, speaking Fon at home and going to a school where French is the exclusive language of instruction develops an exogenous bilinguality in Fon and French.

(5)   In respect of cognitive development, the type of bilinguality is also dependent on the sociocultural environment, in particular the relative status of the two languages in the community. According to whether the two languages are socially valued in his environment, the child will develop different forms of bilinguality. If the two languages are sufficiently valued, the child's cognitive development will derive maximum benefit from the bilingual experience, which will act as an enriching stimulation leading to greater cognitive flexibility compared to his monolingual counterpart; on the other hand, if the sociocultural context is such that the mother tongue is devalued in the child's environment, his cognitive development may be delayed in comparison with a monolingual peer's; in extreme cases, the bilingual child may not be able to make up for this delay. The former type of bilingual experience has been called additive bilinguality; the latter subtractive bilinguality (Lambert, 1974). This distinction relates to the conceptual-linguistic consequences of the sociocultural context of bilingual development.

(6)   Finally, bilinguals can be distinguished in terms of their cultural identity. A bilingual may identify positively with the two cultural groups that speak his languages and be recognised by each group as a member: in this case he is also bicultural. This cultural identity integrating two cultures is probably, at the socio-affective level, the analogue of additive bilinguality at the cognitive level. A balanced biculturalism often goes hand in hand with a balanced bilinguality. However, this is not necessarily the case: in multilingual societies, for example, a multiple cultural membership can coexist with varying degrees of dominant bilingual competence. A high bilingual competence does not always mean a cultural identity with dual cultural membership; a person may become a fluent bilingual while remaining monocultural and identifying culturally with only one of the groups. Bilingual development can also lead a person to renounce the cultural identity of his mother-tongue group and adopt that of the second-language group, in which case he will become an L_2-acculturated bilingual. Sometimes, however, the bilingual may give up his own cultural identity but at the same time fail to identify with the L_2 cultural group, and as a result become anomic and deculturated (Berry, 1980).

Bilinguality has also been described in terms of language use. Weinreich (1953) and Mackey (1962) define bilingualism as the alternate use of two or more languages by the same individual. However, 'use' is not a single dimension but the expression of one or more dimensions of bilinguality. The notion of 'use' means that the bilingual individual has the capacity to call on either language, and this implies that he must have a minimal competence in both languages. Use will tell us whether a bilingual person is more or less dominant in one or the other of his languages for a specific domain or topic. Dodson (1981) proposes the term 'preferred language' to account for choice of language in a particular situation.

2.1.2   Dimensions of societal bilingualism

Sociolinguists have shown how monolingual behaviour varies according to a number of parameters such as, e.g. role relation, relative status of speakers and languages, topic, domain, etc. (see, for example, Ervin-Tripp, 1964a; Fishman, 1965; Labov, 1966; Fishman, 1972). It can be assumed that these variables apply to language-contact situations and that the state of bilinguality interacts with these. The bilingual's language behaviour varies according to whether he interacts with a monolingual or a bilingual interlocutor in a unilingual, bilingual or multilingual environment.

When a person bilingual in L_X, L_Y encounters a monolingual interlocutor in a unilingual community speaking L_X, he will follow the social and linguistic norms of the L_X community. If he encounters a bilingual person like himself (L_X, L_Y) in a similar setting, the two people can follow the unilingual norms of either community or they can create their own set of language norms, as the community defines only the monolingual behaviour norms of L_X.

In a multilingual community, on the other hand, a set of norms exists defining bilingual behaviour. For a bilingual community to exist there must be at least two languages commonly used by some members of the community. Either the community is composed of two groups speaking two different languages as their mother tongue along with a small number of bilinguals speaking both languages, or a small number of both groups speaking a third common language, used as a lingua franca; or, as in the case of an exogenous language, some members of the community speak a second language that has no or few native speakers in the community. Any of these languages may be an official language of the community.

Every bilingual community is situated between the two poles of a continuum, ranging from a set made up of two unilingual groups each containing a small number of bilinguals, to a single group with a more or less large number of members using a second language for specific purposes. At one pole most speakers in each group use only one language for all functions, whereas at the other a varying number of speakers use both languages but for different purposes. One can distinguish the following typical cases:

(1) Territorial bilingualism, in which each group finds itself mostly within its own politically defined territory, with the two (or more) languages having official status in their own territory; the official status of the other national language(s) varies considerably from country to country. Examples of territorial bilingualism can be found in Belgium, Switzerland, Spain, Canada and India, each country applying the principle of territorial bilingualism in its own way.

(2) Another case of bilingual communities can be found in multilingual countries of Africa and Asia where, beside the native languages of indigenous ethnic groups or nations, one or more languages of wider communication exist cutting across these groups and nations native to none or few of them; this can be either a lingua franca, which is like Swahili in Eastern and Central Africa and Tok Pisin in Papua New Guinea, or a superposed language imposed by political decision-making which introduces an exogenous language, normally inherited from a colonial past and used only in certain official domains, as is the case with French or English in several African countries.

(3)   Finally, a bilingual community can be described as diglossic, that is, two languages are spoken by a variable section of the population, but they are used in a complementary way in the community, one language or variety having a higher status than the other and being reserved for certain functions and domains. Examples of diglossic bilingualism are the use of Spanish and Guarani in Paraguay and of French and Creole in Haiti. In these cases both languages have a significant group of native speakers in the community.

Let us stress that monolinguality is more commonly found in economically dominant groups whereas the members of minority or subordinate groups tend to be bilingual or multilingual. Minority does not necessarily imply numerical inferiority, but refers rather to a subordinate status in the community. However, a subordinate group can use its numerical superiority to impose its own language norms through language-planning legislation which aims at ending the subordinate status of that group; in this case the formerly dominant group undergoes a minorisation process.

To the extent that a community's ethnolinguistic duality is officially recognised, the community sets up a number of institutions in order to manage the use of both languages. Inside these institutions members of the different language groups may use one language, which can be a language of the community, a lingua franca, or an exogenous language; alternatively, several languages from the community may be used to a varying extent, as for example when two members of different language groups speak to each other in their respective languages; in this case each understands but does not necessarily speak the other's language, or if they do not understand each other's language they make use of an interpreter.

The various dimensions of bilinguality and bilingualism which we have briefly defined bring out the multidimensional nature of these phenomena. We have called upon notions taken from a variety of disciplines: psychology, psycholinguistics, sociolinguistics, sociology and linguistics. Bilingualism must be approached as a complex phenomenon which simultaneously implies a state of bilinguality of individuals and a state of languages in contact at the collective level. Therefore, this phenomenon should be studied at several levels of analysis: individual, interpersonal, intergroup and societal. Even though the several disciplines involved in the study of bilingualism have developed different methodologies, they all share the problem of operationalising and measuring the concepts they make use of. In the next section we will discuss some of the measures developed by the various disciplines to quantify the dimensions of bilinguality and bilingualism.

2.2 MEASUREMENT OF BILINGUALITY AND BILINGUALISM

In this section we will critically evaluate the measures developed for the assessment of bilinguality and bilingualism. A scientific approach to the study of languages in contact calls for the development of measures relevant to the adopted conceptual framework: conceptualisation and operationalisation of concepts must precede their measurement. To conceptualise is to build a mental representation by organising previous knowledge logically in such a way that some of its features will appear as relevant. To operationalise a concept is to identify those salient features that can be quantified by a specific methodology; normally one measures only the most salient dimensions of a concept. To measure is to compare certain quantities with a standard; an event must be quantified in order to be compared with other events. In order to operationalise a concept its definition will often be reduced to what a test measures. The quantification of a concept, however, should not be confused with the concept itself.

For example, a concept like that of language competence is multidimensional and difficult to operationalise. If one considers that the command of pronunciation, grammar and vocabulary is relevant to linguistic competence, which is one aspect of language competence, one will introduce tests of pronunciation, grammar and vocabulary in the measurement of that competence. These tests, however, measure only some aspects of linguistic competence and do not cover all aspects of language competence.

In the next section we will review some of the measures developed for bilinguality and bilingualism. Without attempting to give an exhaustive list of all measures developed and used in the field, we will try to abstract the basic principles underlying these measures. If a measure has been developed for the specific purpose of assessing languages in contact, we will discuss it in some detail; if it has been developed for another domain, we will only discuss the rationale for its application to the measurement of bilinguality and bilingualism. More specific measures will be introduced in the relevant chapters; for example, the use of electro-encephalic measures in neuropsychology of bilinguality (see Chapter 6). We have also not included in our review qualitative research methods; for these the reader is referred to Davis (1995) and Lazaraton (1995).

2.2.1 The measurement of bilinguality

The measurement of bilinguality must take into consideration the definition of bilinguality, that is, it should assess a psychological state and therefore account for its specificity. If bilinguality is defined as a psychological state of the individual who has access to more than one linguistic code, one might think it sufficient to measure two separate monolingual states to obtain an adequate measure of bilinguality. This is indeed the assumption upon which the majority of measures of bilinguality have been constructed. There are reasons to believe that the bilingual is more than the sum of two monolinguals and that his behaviour displays some unique characteristics. Unfortunately, at present theorising about the bilingual's specific behaviour is still in its infancy and we therefore lack an adequate methodology to capture the specificity of bilingual behaviour.

In the next sections we discuss the following measures of bilinguality:

(1) comparative measures;
(2) measures of bilingual competence;
(3) measures of compound–coordinate bilinguality;
(4) language biographies, self-evaluation and judgements of bilingual production;
(5) measures of bilingual specificity;
(6) measures of cognitive correlates of bilinguality; and
(7) measures of affective correlates of bilinguality.

2.2.1.1   *Comparative measures*

The most frequently used technique for measuring the various dimensions of bilinguality consists in taking measures in each of the bilingual's two languages and comparing them. However, a direct comparison between measures in two languages is extremely difficult even when it is possible. For instance, for us to be able to compare language competence in two languages there must exist measures of language competence in each language and these two sets of measures must be comparable. A measure of language competence implies that we have a clear definition of what a native speaker's competence in that language is. Because there are such wide variations between the competence of native speakers of the same language, it is extremely difficult to identify and thus to operationalise the salient features of a native competence. Moreover, native competence is not necessarily synonymous with a high level of competence; as we have already pointed out, a concept like balanced bilinguality is defined by equilibrium between two native-like competences.

A way round the methodological difficulty of comparing behaviours in two languages consists of making a double comparison: the monolingual competences of a bilingual speaker are compared with monolingual standards in each language. As a consequence of this approach we no longer need the same operational definition of native speaker's competence in the two languages. If, for example, in a series of language tests a bilingual's scores in two languages are in the first percentile, we can conclude that he is highly competent in both languages and that his bilinguality is relatively balanced. Note that the measures used do not need to be similar for each language, since the comparison occurs at the level of a statistical distribution of the competences of native speakers. Such an approach enables us to avoid the problem of directly comparing behaviour in one language with that in another. A problem arises when we want to measure the extent of a bilingual's total vocabulary and compare it with a monolingual's. Pearson, Fernandez & Oller (1993) found that, although bilingual children produce fewer words in each of their languages compared with monolinguals, their production in the two languages together indicates a comparable vocabulary to monolinguals. They used two double-language measures: one of total vocabulary, the other of total conceptual vocabulary, by adding the bilingual's vocabularies in each language and then subtracting the vocabulary shared between the two languages.

This comparative approach is the only valid one when bilinguality is measured on the 'additive–subtractive' dimension. In this case the conceptualisation of the dimension implies that a comparison is made between cognitive measures obtained for bilinguals and monolinguals: the cognitive advantages or disadvantages of additive and subtractive bilinguality are measured in respect of monolingual populations.

2.2.1.2 Measures of bilingual competence

Can language competence be measured and, if so, how?

2.2.1.2.1 Tests of competence in the mother tongue The impossibility of defining native-language competence (Jakobovits, 1970) makes the construction of valid and reliable measures of language competence extremely problematic. This difficulty, however, has not prevented psychometricians from designing such tests. Let us mention, for example, the Peabody Picture Vocabulary Test (Dunn, 1959) measuring receptive vocabulary, Reynell's syntactic complexity test (Reynell, 1969) and the numerous language tests included in traditional test batteries. All these tests measure one aspect of language competence in the mother tongue, but it is far from evident that the particular aspect measured is the most relevant dimension. Is it even justifiable to measure separate skills which supposedly make up language competence? Some tests attempt to capture the unitary nature of competence, for instance, reduced redundancy testing, e.g. the cloze test.[1] Oller (1979: 344) claims that cloze tests are a procedure for testing the learner's internalised system of grammatical knowledge. The main value of the cloze procedure lies in its predictive power of language competence as measured by a battery of other tests.

However, these tests do not measure some aspects of communicative competence, such as knowledge of illocutionary rules and appropriate use of linguistic rules in communication settings (Hymes, 1971; Canale & Swain, 1980). Unfortunately, tests of communicative competence are even less developed than those of linguistic competence, especially in mother-tongue assessment.

Whatever their shortcomings, tests of competence in the mother tongue are useful, as they are the only means of assessing the bilingual's competence and comparing it with that of his monolingual counterpart.

2.2.1.2.2 Tests of competence in a second language   These tests are designed to measure the level of competence in the second language reached by non-native speakers of that language. They are of limited usefulness for the measurement of bilinguality, as we cannot compare them with tests of mother-tongue competence; nonetheless, they are of interest in that they enable us to define levels of dominance in bilinguals, especially at an early stage in the development of bilingual competence. For example, two L_1-dominant bilinguals can be distinguished as to their proficiency in L_2 by means of these tests, which are useful for the identification of stages in the development of a consecutive bilinguality resulting from L_2 teaching program.

In second-language testing there is a large number of tests of linguistic competence (for critical surveys of L_2 tests see Hughes (1989), Alderson & North (1991), Wood (1993) and Bachman & Palmer (1996)).

2.2.1.2.3 Behavioural measures   The difficulty of measuring bilingual competence by means of traditional language tests has led experimental psychologists to design measures which allow a direct comparison between the two languages. These measures are based on the following principle: whenever a task involves a certain degree of verbal competence, a balanced bilingual's performance should be the same whatever the language used in performing the task. A difference in the performance between a task in L_A/L_1 and the same task in L_B/L_2 indicates a dominance in one of the languages. Implicit in this principle is the idea that the relation between L_A/L_1 and the given task is the same as the relation between L_B/L_2 and that task.

(1)   Reaction or latency-time measures. This technique, widely used in experimental psychology, measures verbal fluency in both languages. In these tasks a bilingual subject is asked to verbally either decode or encode

or both; his reaction time to the task in each language is measured. Equal reaction times in the two languages indicate a state of balanced bilinguality. Reaction times have been used as a measure of bilinguality in the following tasks:

(a) Verbal decoding, non-verbal encoding. For example, a subject is asked to react to oral instructions in both languages by pressing one of two keys; if the reaction times to the same instruction in the two languages are equal, subjects are classified as balanced (Lambert, 1955). Another test consists of measuring the reaction time taken for recognising a word presented through a tachistoscope; if the reaction time for the recognition of words in L_A/L_1 is equal to the reaction time to the translation equivalents in L_B/L_2, one will infer that the bilinguality of the subject is balanced. Using this technique, Lambert, Havelka & Gardner (1959) found significant correlations between these measures and traditional linguistic measures of bilinguality.

(b) Non-verbal decoding, verbal encoding. In this technique the subject is asked to respond verbally in one and then in the other language to non-verbal stimuli: for example, a subject is asked to name in each language pictorially presented objects (Ervin, 1964) or colours (Hamers, 1973). A difficulty with this type of measure is that the stimuli might not have the same cultural value in each language; for example, in a colour-naming task the two cultures may have different ways of classifying and naming colours, as in the case of English, Bassa and Shona (H. A. Gleason, 1961).

(c) Verbal decoding, verbal encoding. Here one finds the many tests of reading aloud in both languages. According to Macnamara (1969), speed of reading aloud in both languages is assumed to be a good predictor of bilingual competence. Also in this category are tests of word completion in each language; for example, a bilingual subject is given the beginning of potential words (e.g. the digraph *co-*) and he has to produce as many words as possible in both languages starting with those letters (for example, English: *cob, cock, coin, colt, combination, con, convention, cooperative, copper, cottage, country, court;* French: *combien, combinaison, comme, comment, commerce, conduite, côté, côte, cotelette, courage, couvent, couvert*) (Lambert, 1955).

For all their ingenuity some of these tests come up against a number of problems relating to differences between languages. The main question is one of identity of the task in the two languages: for some pairs of languages it is impossible to find comparable tasks, e.g. completing words starting with the same digraph implies two languages which not only use the same script but also share a vocabulary. Other tasks are not equal in the two languages, either because of the frequency distribution of the translation equivalents or because the decoding processes seem to be different in each language. In this vein, Meara (1984) has demonstrated that while in English the beginning of a word is the most important cue for decoding, in Spanish it is the middle syllable. Non-verbal reaction times to verbal stimuli in different languages seem also to be different regardless of the degree of balance of a subject. For example, it seems that decoding English stimuli is systematically faster than decoding French even for fluent bilinguals dominant in French, as experiments by Treisman (1964) and Hamers (1973) have shown. Decoding tests must therefore be used with caution as a measure of bilingual balance.

(2)   Completion and word-detection tests. The same completion test as described above can be used, but the measure is the number of words produced in one language compared with the number of words produced in the other language. Lambert, Havelka & Gardner (1959) demonstrated that there are significant correlations between results obtained through this technique of measurement and traditional measures of language competence. In another technique developed by the same authors, a bilingual subject is asked to recognise in both languages as many words as possible in a string of nonsense syllables. For example, a French–English bilingual is asked how many French and English words he can recognise in the string *dansonodent*. This test is subject to the same limitations as the previous ones: it can only be used with two languages that have a common graphemic system and have similar graphemic strings. As Baetens Beardsmore (1982) has commented, this type of puzzle may favour the subordinate language since the subject will concentrate on his weaker language at the expense of the stronger; and one might wonder about the validity of this type of technique as a measure of bilingual competence.

(3)   Verbal association tests. Verbal association tests in two languages have been used to measure balance or dominance. A subject is asked to give as many associations as possible to a stimulus word, in the same language as that stimulus, in a given time; this test is repeated for the translation equivalents in the other language. The difference between the total number of words obtained in each language divided by the highest total number of words given in one of the languages gives an index of verbosity (Lambert, 1955). This technique is based on the assumption that the more a learner becomes competent in L_2, the more likely he is to give a high number of associations to L_2 words and the more closely these associations will resemble those of the native speakers of L_2.

(4)   Interlingual verbal flexibility. Other behavioural tests attempt to measure the bilingual's ability to manipulate the two languages simultaneously. Examples are the tests of speed of translation; according to

Lambert, Havelka & Gardner (1959) such a measure is not a good index of the degree of bilingual competence. The same holds for the ability to switch from one language to another without translating (Macnamara, 1969). It is assumed that these tests call upon a different skill from that of bilingual competence. This assumption is supported by clinical data: indeed, in some cases of aphasia a bilingual can lose some aspects of his competence in both languages without losing his ability to translate (Paradis, 1980).

(5)   Use of interlingual ambiguity. Another test developed for measuring the degree of bilingual balance consists in reading aloud a list of cross-language ambiguous words, e.g. *pipe, chance* and *silence* in English and French (Lambert, Havelka & Gardner, 1959). The underlying hypothesis here is that the more balanced a subject is, the less he will decode these words as belonging to one language to the exclusion of the other, and he will obtain equal scores for both languages. This test has been shown to correlate with other measures of bilingual balance. However, its use is limited to languages that have an extensive lexicon in common. Another difficulty comes from the fact that these ambiguous words have very different frequency distributions in each language and it may be that it is the characteristics of the word that condition decoding in one language rather than in the other.

Because of the insufficient operationalisation of concepts like dominance and balance which imply a comparison between two competences, it is premature to want to assess bilinguality on the basis of one type of measure only. We have argued that traditional tests of language competence measure a few aspects of this competence, but give us no answer as to how to compare competences in the two languages with each other. Behavioural measures, on the other hand, have the advantage of being simple and easy to administer, and of permitting direct comparisons; but they rest on the assumption that certain tasks are performed in a similar way in either language. It seems therefore that combining the two kinds of measure should improve the method of quantifying bilingual proficiency. Before discussing further improvements in quantification we will first consider the measurement of the compound–coordinate dimension of bilinguality.

2.2.1.3   *Measures of compound–coordinate bilinguality*

As we saw in Section 2.1.1, the distinction between the compound and coordinate bilingual is one of semantic representation; it implies that for the coordinate bilingual there is a greater semantic independence between his two linguistic codes, while for the compound there is greater semantic interdependence between the two codes. How can the degree of semantic independence and interdependence be measured?

We have seen that this dimension is closely linked to the context of acquisition of the two languages. Therefore, this information can be used to differentiate between compound and coordinate bilinguals who have reached the same level of proficiency in both languages. Some techniques which differentiate between compounds and coordinates and have been used for the purpose are:

- semantic satiation and semantic generalisation (Lambert & Jakobovits, 1960; Jakobovits & Lambert, 1961, 1967; Lambert & Segalowitz, 1969);
- semantic distance (Lambert, Havelka & Crosby, 1958);
- core-concepts technique (Lambert & Rawlings, 1969; Arkwright & Viau, 1974);
- word-association technique (Lambert & Moore, 1966). (For more details of these measures see Section 7.1.1.1.)

2.2.1.4 Language biographies, self-evaluation and judgements of bilingual production

Language biographies provide information on the age and context of acquisition of both languages, their past and present use, their number, the varieties spoken, the degree of literacy, etc. The age, context and use are cues to the type of bilinguality developed by the subject. For example, a person who has acquired two languages in the home from infancy has received his education in both his languages and uses them both regularly at home and at work has most probably developed a balanced and compound bilinguality. On the other hand, a bilingual whose mother tongue is a foreign language in the society where he lives, who has been educated in a language other than his mother tongue, who used his first language only with his family, but has never learned to read or write in it and has ceased to use it altogether, is likely to be a coordinate bilingual, dominant in his L_2. This information, however useful, relates to a declared behaviour as perceived by the subject and not to an actual observable behaviour and should therefore be used in combination with other measures.

Other measures frequently used to evaluate bilingual competence are self-evaluation and evaluation scales. The differential scores between the self-evaluations of proficiency in the two languages are good predictors of the degree of bilingual competence. Evaluation of proficiency in both languages by native speakers of each language can be used as a reliable measure of balanced bilinguality; it is however more difficult to use in order to evaluate the proficiency of a dominant bilingual since it seems less reliable for judging proficiency in a language spoken in a non-native way. Self-evaluation and judgement by native speakers are generally done by assessing a number of language skills on a three-, five- or seven-point scale ranging from 'nil' to 'native-like'.

2.2.1.5   Measures of bilingual specificity

Except for the measures that call upon a simultaneous use of the two languages, such as translation and verbal flexibility, we have so far examined only measures in which the bilingual's behaviour is viewed as the sum of two monolingual behaviours. A bilingual also develops patterns of behaviour that are unique to his state of bilinguality (Grosjean, 1985a). For example, when bilinguals communicate with each other they can make simultaneous use of the resources of each of their languages, for example by borrowing words from one language while using the other (loan words) or by developing mixed or switched codes which are governed by their own specific rules. The study of these specific codes has only just begun. Let us mention Poplack's (1980) attempt to correlate the degree of balance of bilinguals with a high level of competence in rule-governed code-switching. In the same vein, Lavandera (1978) has drawn attention to the inadequacy of monolingual measures to try to evaluate speech production in a bilingual communication situation. The bilingual's total repertoire can be fully exploited by him only in situations in which he can call upon the resources of his two languages and use strategies specific to language contact. The development of tests designed to capture the bilingual's specific competence is an urgent task for researchers. But first a major effort of conceptualisation and operationalisation is required (Grosjean, 1985a).

The specific linguistic behaviour of a bilingual has often been mistaken for interference. Indeed, considered from the angle of monolingual norms, code-mixing and code-switching might seem deviant (Weinreich, 1953). It must be stressed that the notion of interference, if often used, has never been more clearly defined than as the inappropriate use by a speaker of elements or rules of one language while using the other. However, the use of a mixed code is inappropriate only in terms of the monolingual norm. The concept of interference is used extensively in second-language learning methodology and refers to learning processes in which the L_2 learner inappropriately transfers units of his first language to the second. In a traditional language-teaching methodology, interference is perceived as a main source of errors in L_2. At the time of writing there is no operational definition of the concept of interference, still less techniques to measure it. The only attempts are limited to frequency counts of elements often arbitrarily identified as instances of interference.

Even if interference, as defined above, is an expression of the lack of linguistic competence in a dominant bilingual's weaker language, it is by no means proven that it is characteristic of the balanced bilingual. On the contrary, according to Ben-Zeev (1977a), one of the specific mechanisms developed by a balanced bilingual is precisely the use of strategies to avoid interference between one language and the other. Unfortunately, to date we have no reliable measures to capture these specific cognitive and communicative strategies.

2.2.1.6   Measures of cognitive correlates of bilinguality

A considerable amount of empirical evidence suggests that a correlation between the development of bilinguality and cognition exists. The results of these studies are apparently contradictory insofar as they show either a cognitive advantage or a cognitive disadvantage of bilingual development as compared to monolingual development. These research results are discussed in detail in Chapter 4. Because the concepts of cognitive advantage and disadvantage are defined by reference to monolinguals, the only way to demonstrate one or the other is by comparing bilinguals with monolinguals. Depending on which aspect of cognitive development is assumed to be affected by bilingual experience, an experimental design is used to which the results of verbal and non-verbal intelligence tests, verbal creativity, verbal flexibility, divergent thinking, verbal transformations, symbol substitutions, etc. are compared. We refer the reader to the classic study by Peal & Lambert (1962) as an example of an experimental design using a large array of measures in order to assess cognitive differences between bilinguals and monolinguals.

2.2.1.7   Measures of affective correlates of bilinguality

There is always a cognitive and an affective aspect to development. The affective component of bilingual development has to do with the relationships between the bilingual individual and his two languages. Since language is a social phenomenon, all affective reaction towards it is not limited to the language but applies also to the individuals and groups who speak that language.

(1)   One relevant affective aspect of bilingual behaviour concerns value judgements towards languages and their speakers. The most commonly used technique to measure value judgements consists of using Lickert-type evaluation scales, in which subjects are asked to express their degree of agreement or disagreement with a number of statements relating to the languages and their speakers. Such scales have been developed to measure attitudes towards languages and their speakers, motivation to learn or speak a second language, anxiety and confidence in the use of L_2: in other words, all social psychological mechanisms relevant to the affective processes of bilinguality. Among the numerous evaluation scales developed for the measurement of the affective dimensions of bilinguality, we will men-

tion those developed by Gardner & Lambert (1959, 1972), Gardner & Smythe (1975) and Clément (1978).

(2) Another technique adapted to the measurement of the affective dimensions of bilinguality is the semantic differential (Osgood, Suci & Tannenbaum, 1957). As this technique measures the evaluation of a concept it is possible to use it in a differential way and obtain a measure of the relative evaluation of two languages or two groups of speakers. An interesting application of the semantic differential as an affective measure of bilinguality can be found in the matched guise technique (Lambert, Hodgson, Gardner & Fillenbaum, 1960). This technique enables the researcher to measure value judgements towards languages and speakers without having to ask direct questions of the subjects. One objection to the technique is that it ignores all the elements relevant to communication with the exception of voice characteristics.

(3) Of equal importance in the affective domain are the measures of the bilingual's cultural identity. Unlike the bilingual's language competence, which can be viewed as a distinct entity for each of his languages, his cultural identity can be conceptualised only as a single entity which is the outcome of his bilingual/bicultural experience. Even more than in the case of bilingual competence it is not enough to consider two monocultural identities. It is essential to have a technique capable of capturing the specificity of the bilingual's cultural identity. Techniques developed for measuring cultural identity, such as multidimensional scaling, ethnic dolls, role playing, etc., have all been adapted to the measurement of the bilingual's cultural identity (see Chapter 8). Questionnaires have also been used to measure ethnolinguistic group members' perceptions of ethnic identity, like, for example, The Canadian Ethnocultural Questionnaire (Feuerverger, 1991).

2.2.2   Measurement of bilinguality in cultural minorities

The measures of bilinguality previously mentioned are not applicable to all situations of languages in contact; and in particular, there are difficulties when we try to use them in a cultural-minority situation. This is especially critical in the case of the education of cultural-minority children because they follow curricula in the language of the majority, which is usually their weaker language; now psychometric tests of academic proficiency are usually administered in the majority language. As pointed out by, among others, Cummins (1984a), psychometric tests of academic language proficiency are not appropriate for the assessment of minority children because these children have not reached the level of development required for these tests to be valid. Furthermore, results of psychometric tests, e.g. verbal and non-verbal intelligence tests, obtained with minority children who do not have a sufficient linguistic competence in the language of instruction cannot be compared with norms obtained for a different population. (For a fuller treatment of these issues see Chapter 11.)

There is also the problem of the cultural differences between the different groups. For example, if one wants to measure knowledge of vocabulary and the minority child is presented with pictures of familiar objects in the majority culture, as in the Peabody Picture Vocabulary Test (Dunn, 1959), but unfamiliar in the child's culture, lack of response by a minority child has no assessment value. Although attempts have been made to construct culture-free measures applicable to all children, it has proved impossible to eliminate the cultural bias from tests without impairing their validity as measures. (See Samuda, 1975; Samuda, Crawford, Philips & Tinglin, 1980.)

In the case of the child from an immigrant community one solution sometimes put forward is to use norms from the culture of origin; this, however, raises other problems, as the child either is no longer familiar with, or has never been exposed to, that original culture. Sometimes the child's experience of the language and culture of origin may be limited to a small community, even to the immediate family circle. Another solution, which is argued to be culturally fair and which can be used when the minority group is sufficiently large, is to establish group norms; here the problem is that if the minority group is socially disadvantaged, the group norms will then be depressed and results will not be comparable to majority results. It is impossible in these conditions to use these tests diagnostically. (For a discussion of some of these issues see N. Miller, 1984.)

Even if we could design valid psychometric tests, these would still not be capable of measuring the specificity of the minority child's bilingual behaviour, since they would have been developed for monolingual children in each community. The minority child is therefore doubly disadvantaged: on the one hand, the tests used in his case are not adapted to his particular situation, and on the other, no measures capable of assessing the specific character of his bilinguality exist. In the 1980s researchers began to attempt to capture this specificity by resorting to ethnographic/sociolinguistic approaches; it is too early to evaluate the impact of these new approaches on the assessment of bilingual competence. (For more details, see Rivera, 1983; 1984.)

In this section our main objective has been to highlight the problems raised by the use of psychometric tests for the assessment of the competence of children exposed to languages and cultures in contact. In the present state of our knowledge, there are no obvious solutions to these problems. (For a particular discussion of the issues of academic evaluation of minority children in North America see Samuda, 1975; Samuda, Crawford, Phillips & Tinglin, 1980.)

2.2.3   Measurement of societal bilingualism

Few methodologies have been designed specifically for the study of languages in contact at the societal level, and even fewer measures have been developed for the quantification of collective bilingual phenomena. Researchers in this area normally make use of more general methodologies from social science, such as census techniques, polls and surveys as well as applying the methods of sociolinguistics and of the ethnography of communication. Let us note also that most of these methodologies are essentially descriptive in nature and only permit us to make rather crude predictions about collective behaviour in language-contact situations. However, even this descriptive approach is useful to the extent that it enables us to analyse covariations between linguistic and sociological phenomena.

The study of societal bilingualism can be carried out at several levels of analysis, ranging from the macro-sociological to the micro-sociological. These two approaches differ mainly in that at the macro-sociological level the researcher operates with large samples, even whole populations, and as a result, can only ask questions of a very general kind that are easy to analyse, whereas the micro-sociological approach uses in-depth methods of data collection and analysis, thereby reducing the size and representative character of the samples. For this reason the former approach allows mainly questions on reported behaviour, while the study of actual behaviour demands a micro-sociological methodology.

2.2.3.1   Censuses

An instrument frequently used to obtain data on language use is the population census, or rather those questions in such a census that ask for information on the mother tongue(s), the patterns of language use including all language(s) known by the respondents, and the degree of competence in those languages. Because of their magnitude censuses are usually initiated by governments as part of language-planning policies, and as such cover a territory defined by political boundaries. Unfortunately political boundaries are not necessarily coextensive with linguistic and cultural ones. For example, political boundaries in West Africa or in Europe divide linguistic communities which cut across a number of countries; another example is the Canadian census which informs us on the use of French north of the 47th Parallel but tells us nothing about the Franco-Americans of New England.

However, even if censuses were conducted in all countries sharing the same linguistic communities, the results would most probably not be comparable because the basic concepts are not defined in the same way. The concept of mother tongue is a case in point. The Canadian census, for instance, defines the mother tongue as 'the first language learned in childhood and still understood'; in India, on the other hand, it was defined in the 1961 census as the language spoken in childhood by the respondent's mother. The latter definition raises a difficulty in the case of children of mixed-lingual families where the mother's tongue is not the most commonly used language (Pattanayak, 1981). Furthermore, census questions are often vague, ambiguous or worded differently from context to context and from census to census. For example, the question on the mother tongue in the singular does not account for the case of simultaneous infant bilinguals who acquired two mother tongues. The answers from respondents are equally unreliable: they can be ambiguous or mistaken, and respondents may deliberately or unconsciously conceal their linguistic habits or language attitudes. Great care, therefore, should be taken when interpreting or using census data.

For all their flaws and shortcomings census data is nonetheless indispensable: they are the only data of this kind collected on a nationwide scale and at regular intervals, and within limits they enable us to describe patterns of language use in a population. The lack of linguistic census data, as in the case of Belgium where linguistic questions have been prohibited since 1947, hampers research on language behaviour at the societal level.

Censuses also permit us to calculate changes in time and space in the patterns of language use, linguistic diversity, language maintenance and shift, assimilation and acculturation in ethnolinguistic communities. By comparing answers to questions on mother-tongue and language use it is possible to calculate the assimilation rate of a group.

Another measure of societal bilingualism that has been developed on the basis of language-census data is the index of linguistic diversity. To measure the degree of intercommunication between different ethnolinguistic groups in a given community Greenberg (1956) calculated an index (H) of linguistic diversity on a continuum ranging from total lack of intercommunication to complete intercommunication; this index gives the probability that two members of a population taken at random share a common language. Using a refined index, Lieberson (1964) showed that the probability of one Algerian and one European living in the Algeria of 1948 sharing a common language, i.e. able to communicate with each other, was just over two in ten.

An extension of these measures is Kuo's (1980) index of communicativity designed to calculate the potential of a particular language to act as a means of communication between two speakers in a given society. Whereas the former measures linguistic diversity or intercommunication regardless of the languages involved, Kuo's index evaluates the communication power of a given language. Taking Singapore in 1978 as an example, he shows that there are almost two chances in five that two randomly drawn adults would be able to communicate in English with each other. He also suggests that the index can measure the importance of a given language as a medium for intergroup communication.

It must be stressed that indices of linguistic assimilation, diversity and communicativity are mere statistical constructs which tell us little about real intergroup and interpersonal communication needs and practices in a multicultural setting. For a more detailed account of index measures on the basis of census data, see Fasold (1984).

2.2.3.2   Surveys

Surveys differ from censuses in that they are based on a sample of the total population and are specially designed to collect linguistic and language-behaviour data. Although they inform us mostly on reported behaviour, they sometimes include information on actual behaviour. The following are the most commonly used types of survey:

(1) geo-linguistic surveys which describe the geographic distribution of languages and their variations in a given space; one example is The Linguistic Composition of the Nations of the World (Kloss & McConnell, 1974ff, in progress);
(2) linguistic atlases presenting information in a cartographic and analytic form stemming from censuses and geo-linguistic surveys; one example is the geographic atlas of the languages and ethnic groups of India by Breton (1976);
(3) ethnolinguistic studies of multilingual communities like, for example, the Survey of Language Use and Language Teaching in Eastern Africa (Polome, 1982), which covers several countries, the various sociolinguistic surveys in Singapore (E. A. Andersen, 1985), or the Linguistic Minorities Project (The Other Languages of England, 1985), a survey conducted in selected urban areas of England;
(4) inquiries into language behaviour commissioned by governments in multilingual nations, such as the Royal Commission on Bilingualism and Biculturalism in Canada (1967–70) and the inquiry on the status of the French language in Quebec (Gendron, 1972).

Whether they deal with whole populations or large samples, the aforementioned techniques have their limitations in that they do not permit the use of sensitive instruments and refined quantification, such as numerous, precise and detailed questions or the recording of actual language behaviour in a great variety of situations. Other methodological approaches, such as sociolinguistic studies or the ethnography of communication, enable us to use more sophisticated measures and analysis; however, because of the complexity of their use they are limited to small samples.

2.2.3.3   *Sociolinguistic and ethnographic methods*

Sociolinguists study language variation by examining the social distribution of the variants of a number of linguistic variables, as for example Labov's (1966) study of the covariation between phonological variables and social class and stylistic variables. (For a critical review of sociolinguistic methodology see Wardhaugh, 1986.) These techniques, which have been developed for the study of intralingual variation, can be applied to the investigation of situations of language contact. However, to date very few studies have been carried out in multilingual communities; for an application of the methodology to a multilingual context we refer to Labov (1978).

Another sociolinguistic approach is that of Le Page & Tabouret-Keller (1985) in their investigation of language use and attitudes in multilingual communities in Belize and St Lucia. In this field study they collected data on the language behaviour of children and their families by means of questionnaires (reported behaviour) and recorded interviews (reported and actual behaviour). As in the Labovian approach they correlate a number of linguistic variables with sociological ones; but, unlike Labov (1966), they do not use pre-established sociological categories; instead, they examine the covariation of social, cultural, social-psychological, etc. factors with language behaviour.

Finally, the methodology of the ethnography of communication observes small and well-defined multilingual communities in minute detail, calling upon anthropological techniques like participant observation of small groups or social networks and descriptive analyses like, for example, implicational scaling, to describe patterns of language choice. Many ethnographic studies limit themselves to case studies, as for example when language behaviour is observed in one single family. A detailed analysis of the ethnography of communication methodology is given in Saville-Troike (1982).

To sum up, although numerous measures of collective bilingualism exist, most of these still lack sophistication. They are restricted to the description of phenomena and give us only frequencies of occurrence of language variation for a given population. The main reason for this state of affairs is probably the lack of theoretical constructs that are predictive of the different forms taken by societal bilingualism.

2.3   CONCLUSION

In this chapter we first analysed the different dimensions along which bilinguality and bilingualism can vary. We pointed out the multidimensional character of these phenomena by calling successively on a variety of disciplines. Bilingualism is a global phenomenon, which involves simultaneously a psychological state of the individual and a situation of languages in contact at the interpersonal and the collective level. However, a situation of languages in contact can occur at the societal level without implying the bilinguality of individuals, and conversely, individuals can be bilingual without the existence of collective bilingualism.

In Section 2.2 we gave an overview of several relevant measures either developed specifically or adapted from more general social-science methodologies for the study of bilinguality and bilingualism. In our discussion of the measures of bilingual competence we made a distinction between those which reduced this competence to the sum of two monolingual ones and those attempting to evaluate the specificity of bilingual behaviour. We also emphasised the importance of using a variety of measures in order to capture a state of bilinguality. We drew attention to the problems created by the use of psychometric measures in the educational assessment of bilingual children from ethnolinguistic minorities. At the societal level we reviewed a variety of measures which can be used to describe a collective situation of languages in contact.

The main aim of the present chapter has been to draw the reader's attention to the difficulties inherent in the attempt to define and quantify languages in contact at all levels of analysis as well as to the absence of adequate measures and the lack of refinement of existing ones. However, we have to use these measures, as they are the only ones available in the present state of the art. Even if some of the measures are still crude, it is preferable to use them rather than to reject quantification altogether. It is therefore in this critical frame of mind that the following chapters should be read.

3   Ontogenesis of bilinguality

In this chapter we review at some length the present state of the art in the study of the linguistic development in native bilingual speakers (Section 3.1); we further draw attention to linguistic development in consecutive bilinguality (Section 3.2); Section 3.3 describes the specificities of the sign/aural bilingual; in Section 3.4 we discuss how the evidence on bilingual development argues in favour of or against the sensitive-age hypothesis. We finally describe the different cases of attrition in bilinguality (Section 3.5). In the conclusion we discuss how bilingual development can be explained by a more general model of bilingual processing. We do not intend to give detailed linguistic descriptions of the bilingual child's production but rather to give a comprehensive overview of the psycholinguistic factors which can explain bilingual development.

Since the beginning of the twentieth century scholars from a variety of disciplinary backgrounds, such as psychologists, linguists, neurologists and educators, have paid attention to the development of bilinguality; and at the end of the century there has been a research explosion on the subject. During the first half of the century two types of studies were prominent: (1) carefully documented child biographies, such as those by Ronjat (1913) and Leopold (1939–49), and (2) comparative psychometric studies of school tests obtained from bilingual and monolingual children. Whereas the first biographies pointed to a harmonious development of the bilingual child, the early psychometric studies indicated a developmental delay in bilingual children as compared with monolingual peers. This apparent contradiction and the so-called negative consequences of bilinguality are discussed in Chapter 4.

Child biographies are still used today; however, the present methodologies applied to the study of bilingual development are more sophisticated and employ more accurate techniques. For example, rather than simply describe the language development of young bilinguals, scholars attempt to analyse their language in terms of theoretical constructs in language acquisition; bilingual development is described according to psycholinguistic aspects such as the acquisition of interrogative forms and negation or of the mutual-exclusivity constraint rule (children assume that one object has only one label). At the same time, more attention is paid to the control of factors like socio-economic status, parental language, level of proficiency in the language used or degree of bilinguality. An example of a more sophisticated observation of bilingual children is the one given by Saunders (1988) on his three children developing bilingually in English and German. Some recent descriptions of productions by bilingual children and infants can also be found in the CHILDES project (MacWhinney, 1995).

The first description of the linguistic development of a native bilingual child is that of the French psychologist Ronjat (1913), who made detailed records of his son Louis's language behaviour from birth to the age of 4;10 (four years and ten months). The Ronjats, who lived in Paris, were a mixed-lingual family: the father was a native speaker of French, the mother and the nanny native speakers of German. The family adhered to Grammont's Principle (Grammont, 1902) according to which each adult should use exclusively his or her mother tongue with the child. Ronjat's observations can be summarised as follows: a bilingual upbringing has no adverse effect on the child's overall development; the phonology, grammar and lexis of both languages develop in parallel; very early on the child becomes aware of the existence of two distinct linguistic codes and acts as interpreter; he rarely mixes the two languages and mixing tends to disappear as the child grows up; finally, far from delaying the cognitive development of the child, an early bilingual experience fosters a more abstract conception of language. Ronjat concludes that in a mixed-lingual family a child develops normally and in a harmonious way.

The most detailed biography of bilingual development is Leopold's (1939–49), in which the author describes the language acquisition of his two daughters in a German–English mixed-lingual family where Grammont's 'one parent–one language' rule was observed. His conclusions are in agreement with Ronjat's: there are no developmental or linguistic disadvantages; from the start of the acquisition of the syntax, morphology and vocabulary of both languages are separated; mixing is only occasional; soon after the age of three the children discriminate between the languages according to their interlocutor. Leopold also comments on some advantages of early bilinguality, such as a sustained attention to content rather than form and a greater capacity for dissociating the word from its referent. But the author remains imprecise as to his standards of comparison and his conclusions are sometimes difficult to justify on empirical grounds.

Whatever their merits such detailed biographies have their shortcomings (many more have been written since Leopold's; for a review of case studies of simultaneous bilingual acquisition, see McLaughlin, 1984): when the first observations were made there were no scientifically sound theoretical constructs on language development and child language was viewed as an impoverished imitation of adult language. Their contribution to the study of bilingual development is therefore limited to that of well-documented descriptive diaries and contains no information on the developmental psycholinguistic processes relevant to bilinguality. It was not until the 1960s that a renewal of interest in the subject was witnessed, with a number of studies on bilingual development based on general theoretical models of language acquisition.

3.1   BILINGUISTIC DEVELOPMENT

A number of scholars have examined certain specific linguistic dimensions of bilingual acquisition in an attempt to answer some important questions. Examples of these questions are:

- Is it possible to distinguish stages in bilinguistic development?
- If so, how far do they coincide with the developmental stages of monolingual acquisition?
- Is the bilinguistic development delayed compared with the monolingual one?
- How do certain characteristics that are unique to bilingual behaviour like, for instance, code-mixing, loan blends or translation develop?
- How far are the two linguistic systems differentiated (or not) in the early stage of language acquisition?

These approaches, going far beyond the early biographical descriptions, enabled researchers to generate a number of hypotheses and assumptions concerning the development of bilinguality.

3.1.1   Preverbal development

Although the infant does not produce his first words before the end of his first year, a large amount of preverbal linguistic manifestation does occur in the first months of life. How do infants raised in bilingual families process their linguistic input and output compared to their monolingual peers?

3.1.1.1   Early reception

Although the majority of studies of bilinguality in the young child focus on speech production, a few investigators have looked at early perception. Preverbal infants have some acoustic recognition abilities. Discrimination of the maternal language features starts at an early age. Two-to-four-day-old infants have already acquired sensitivity for recognising their mother tongue even when spoken by strangers (see Moon, Panneton-Cooper and Fifer, 1993, studying infants from Spanish-speaking and English-speaking parents; Mehler & Christophe, 1995, studying infants from French-speaking parents). Two-month-old infants from English families discriminate between English and Italian, but not between two foreign languages (Mehler, 1988). Early in life infants are capable of discriminating sounds not present in their linguistic environment (for example, six-month-old infants born in English-Canadian families make phonetic distinctions specific to Hindi), but this ability declines rapidly and disappears before the end of the first year (Werker & Tees, 1984). According to Mehler & Christophe the infant relies on prosodic properties in the first place; at two months of age the infant is capable of recognising basic features of the mother tongue as distinct from another language. By the age of six months infants are capable of segmenting the vowel continuum in accordance with the language they have been exposed to (Kuhl, Williams, Lacerda, Stevens & Lindblom, 1992). Thus, selective attention for speech sounds is either present prenatally or starts in the first days of life and evolves in the first months. But what happens in the case of infants raised in a bilingual environment?

Analysing the perception of phonemes by four-to-eight-month-old infants raised in bilingual (Spanish–English) or monolingual (English) environments, Eilers, Gavin & Oller (1982) found that the former discriminate[1] better than the latter not only between English and Spanish phonemes, but also between the phonemes of English and those of Czech, a language to which they had never been exposed. The authors interpret these results as possible evidence that a richer linguistic input from the environment fosters a better development of the relevant skills, in this case phonemic discrimination. It also appears that prelinguistic infants in bilingual homes are capable of discriminating between the intonation patterns of French and English (Goodz, 1984; 1985). Today, there is a paucity of data on the early speech reception of bilingual children; more research is needed in this area.

3.1.1.2 Early productions

At the production level, infant bilinguals do not differ from monolinguals in the early stages. Evidence for cross-language differentiation at early production levels is two fold. Some research stresses the role of language environment in early production: intonation contour and vowel production of infants resemble those of the language of the environment (de Boysson-Bardies, Halle, Sagart & Durand, 1989); the consonants produced by infants are produced in a way predicted by the language used in the environment (de

Boysson-Bardies & Vihman, 1991). Other studies failed to show differences: no significative differences were obtained between acoustic measures on intonation contours in babbling; adults were not able to identify the infant's linguistic background from babbling (Thevenin, Eilers, Oller & Lavoie, 1985). In a recent longitudinal study Oller, Eilers, Urbano & Cobo-Lewis (1997) found that infants from English–Spanish bilingual and English monolingual backgrounds do not differ in terms of age of onset of canonical babbling (well-formed syllables) or of amount of vocalisation produced. The authors conclude that the phonological precursors of speech do develop in a similar way regardless of the linguistic environment.

So far it seems that an infant exposed to a bilingual environment must develop perceptual skills which will enable him to distinguish between his two languages. Whether this will facilitate the separation of the two languages at the production stage remains a question to be explored. Both bilingual and monolingual infants develop in a similar way: they learn to discriminate the speech features which are relevant to their environment. Contrary to monolinguals, developing bilinguals also have to learn specific processing skills: at the perceptual level they have to discriminate between acoustic patterns in the two languages and they master them in a very short time. There is also some evidence that bilinguals develop specific strategies, different from monolinguals (Goodz, 1985). It would seem that the bilingual child develops two independent phonological systems, which are however not identical to the two monolingual ones. At the production level, they match monolinguals at the phonological level and are indistinguishable from their two monolingual peer groups; they may, however, manifest interference from the other language at the phonetic level (Watson, 1991).

3.1.2   Stages of bilinguistic development

In early literature Ronjat (1913) and Leopold (1939–49) raised the question of a possible delay in linguistic development induced by the exposure to two languages. Both concluded that there was no observable delay and that bilingual and monolingual acquisition followed the same pace. Most authors of bilingual children's biographies agree with these conclusions; however, more detailed observations and direct comparisons with monolinguals tend to indicate that, for some aspects, language acquisition might follow different developmental curves.

3.1.2.1   Lexical development

How does the bilingual child's lexical system develop? There is a general agreement that the bilingual infant produces his first word at the same time as a monolingual infant and that at the holophrastic stage he uses words from his two languages. Volterra and Taeschner (1978), who observed two German–Italian infants, distinguish two stages: first the child has one lexical system which includes words from both languages; later the child discriminates between the two systems and starts using translation equivalents.

Comparing 22 French–English bilingual children, aged between 3;6 and 5;7, with 22 matched monolingual counterparts, Doyle, Champagne & Segalowitz (1977) observed that if the former produced their first word at the same age as the latter, other aspects of language acquisition appeared to follow different developmental curves. They observed that the bilingual children had a smaller vocabulary in their dominant language than their monolingual pairs, but expressed more concepts and showed superior verbal fluency in story-telling.

There have been some claims for a deficit in vocabulary in developing native bilinguals (Doyle, Champagne & Segalowitz, 1977; Rosenblum & Pinker, 1983; Umbel, Pearson, Fernandez & Oller, 1992). However, this is not sustained in other studies; for example, Pearson, Fernandez & Oller (1993), comparing the receptive and productive vocabulary of 25 children raised bilingually with that of matched monolinguals, concluded that: the comprehension ability was comparable in each language; production in each language was smaller for the bilingual children than for the monolingual children, but if the lexical items in the two languages were taken together, production was comparable; translation equivalents in the bilingual child's lexicon are not present for all words and the two lexicons only partially overlap. The discrepancies between the studies can be attributed to the lack of appropriate bilingual norms for measuring vocabulary. When taking into consideration a double-language norm including the total vocabulary and the conceptual vocabulary, bilingual children's lexical productions are comparable to those of monolinguals.

Early lexical development is correlated with the amount of interactive exposure to each language (Huttenlocher, Haight, Bryk, Seltzer & Lyons, 1991). Single-language productions for the simultaneous bilingual child's dominant language are smaller than for monolinguals (Pearson, Fernandez & Oller, 1993). Studying simultaneous bilingual infants (8 months to 2;6 years) who received input in Spanish and English for different amounts of time, Pearson, Fernandez, Lewedeg & Oller (1997) obtained high correlations between the time of interactive exposure and the size of active vocabulary in each language. With as little as 20 per cent of exposure time devoted to one language, some active lexicon still develops; nonetheless a balanced form of bilinguistic development requires 40–60 per cent exposure to each language.

Recent studies compared how the mutual-exclusivity constraint (i.e. children assume that one object has only one label) is applied by monolingual and bilingual young children. Au & Glusman (1990) found that bilingual pre-school children are ready to accept two names for an object provided they come from their two languages. Bilingual children do not differ from monolinguals in their restriction of naming within a language, but are less restrictive between languages (Merriman & Kutlesic, 1993). Comparing the application of the constraint by English monolingual and Greek–English and Urdu–English three- and six-year-old youngsters, Davidson, Jergovic, Imami & Theodos (1997) concluded that bilingual children apply the constraint to a lesser extent than monolinguals and that bilingual three-year-olds are less restrictive than monolingual six-year-olds. Furthermore, bilingual children are more likely to accept a new name for a known object than their monolingual counterparts. These studies are in support of Ronjat's and Leopold's claim that bilingual children have a greater capacity to dissociate the word from the object and a greater flexibility in matching form and function.

3.1.2.2   Grammatical development

Comparing the morphological and syntactic development of a Dutch–English bilingual child with Dutch and English monolinguals for a large number of morphological and syntactic structures (gender, plural, suffixes, word order, etc.) De Houwer (1990) concludes that each language forms a closed system little influenced by the other. This is in contrast with conclusions from other studies which posit a first undifferentiated stage of grammatical development (see Section 3.1.4).

How do grammatical structures evolve in bilinguistic development? Since R. Brown's (1973) pioneering work in developmental psycholinguistics in the late 1960s, in which he identified successive stages[2] in the child's linguistic development, a number of attempts have been made to analyse bilinguistic development in terms of stages. In a longitudinal study of question forms produced by two-to-four-year-old French–English children Swain (1972) found that the formulation of polar questions (i.e. questions requiring a yes or no answer) followed an order of increasing complexity, irrespective of the language used: first intonation and the question tag eh[3] are used; the second to appear are special-purpose question morphemes, first ti[4] and then est-ce-que; in a third stage the constituents are rearranged in the utterance, e.g. inversion of verb and subject pronoun. Analysing the evolution of negation in Spanish–English native bilingual children, Padilla & Lindholm (1976) observed that it followed the same pattern as the one proposed by Klima & Bellugi (1966) for monolingual English children. However, this was not the case for the acquisition of *wh*-questions. Studying the acquisition of English grammatical morphemes by her daughter exposed from birth to Chichewa (a Bantu language) and English, Chimombo (1979) found no significant correlation between the order of their acquisition and the one observed for monolingual English children.

More recent detailed observations of bilinguistic development also analyse it in terms of stages. Apart from comparing bilinguistic development to grammatical development in one language they are concerned with identifying the specificity of bilingual development. One example of such an observation is the DUFDE project (Meisel, 1990) in which detailed longitudinal descriptions of grammatical development of infants (aged from 1 to 3;6 years of age) from mixed-lingual French–German families in Germany are analysed. Based on the assumption that universal grammar (UG) does not require learning the properties of syntactic categories, but that the child must discover from the input in which way lexical items are assigned to the various categories (Meisel, 1990: 16), linguistic descriptions are given for the acquisition of tense and aspect, prepositions, word-order regularities and case morphology, gender, verb agreement, tense, etc. Comparing the bilingual children's productions with those of two monolinguals, Meisel and his associates come to the conclusion that bilinguistic language acquisition does not differ in substantial ways from monolingual acquisition. Although up to now they have not analysed bilingual-specific productions they have found some evidence that bilinguals are able to acquire certain grammatical constructions faster than monolinguals and succeed more easily in decoding underlying grammatical principles. As Meisel notes, these findings might be difficult to explain in the light of the UG, which does assume that linguistic development is independent of cognitive development, considering that bilingual children have to acquire two different systems simultaneously. It is, however, consistent with a more general approach to the cognitive development in bilinguals which assumes that early bilingual experience enhances cognitive processing (see Section 4.2).

Delays in bilinguistic development have been mentioned. For example, Swain (1972) noticed a delay in the development of polar questions: for instance, *est-ce-que* is acquired at 3;2 years by French–English bilinguals compared with 2;6 for French-speaking monolinguals; inversion in the English interrogative is acquired by the age of 3;8 by bilinguals and at 3;2 by English-speaking monolinguals. She interprets this delay as characteristic of the bilinguistic development – since the child concentrates on specific aspects of his dual linguistic system – rather than as an overall delay in his linguistic development.

However, this delay is not confirmed for other grammatical functions: in contrast the DUFDE project shows some evidence for a more precocious development in bilingual children (Meisel, 1990). Apparently conflicting evidence comes also from a study by Padilla & Liebman (1975), who compared the MLU (mean length of utterance) from Spanish–English bilinguals aged between 1;5 and 2;2 with that of Spanish and English monolingual children; they conclude that there is no delay in the formal acquisition of the two languages. From an analysis of the available data on bilinguistic development it appears that certain aspects of linguistic development follow a monolingual pattern closely while others do not. Moreover, bilinguistic development is characterised not only by a different pace of development, but also by linguistic behaviour specific to the bilingual speaker, such as mixing and translation, which are issues addressed in the next section and in Section 9.3.

3.1.3   Bilingual-specific behaviour: linguistic mixing, code-switching and translation

Although these topics are considered at length in Section 9.3, we will discuss them here insofar as they are characteristic of bilingual development. When we refer to mixing in bilinguistic development we include the use of elements from L_B in an utterance in L_A (code-mixing or embedded code-switching) as well as the alternation between L_A and L_B in the same utterance (alternate code-switching). These elements may be lexical, syntactic or semantic. The notion of mixing is close to that of interference (see Section 2.2.1.5), that is, a deviation from the norm in each language due to familiarity with two languages. Language-mixing is produced by all bilinguals but inappropriate language-mixing is more permanent in late bilinguality (I. Taylor, 1990). Mixing is not necessarily a matter of interference but may be the expression of a strategy specific to the bilingual speaker. According to Grosjean (1985a) bilinguals use a bilingual-speech mode with other bilinguals who share their languages and with whom they normally mix languages (code-switching, code-mixing and borrowing). A phenomenon related to mixing is loan-blending, that is borrowing a word from the lexicon of the other language and grammatically adapting it to the language used in the utterance, as for example the verb *mailer* used in a Canadian-French utterance; in this example the French suffix *-er* is added to the English verb *mail* in order to conform with French verb-formation rules.

Many mixings are 'lexical reduplications' or 'spontaneous translations', as when a translation equivalent is supplied as a synonym (for example, *another one, un autre*); spontaneous translations would suggest that the child is aware of the mixing and is deliberately using it as a communication strategy, and when the situation requires, he acts as an interpreter (Swain &

Wesche, 1973). Translation and interpretation are highly specialised skills that usually require formal training. However three-year-old children are perfectly capable of translating when the social context requires it and do so spontaneously (Harris, 1980). Malakoff & Hakuta (1991) found that elementary bilingual Spanish–English school children translate verbal materials that are within their comprehension range in both directions and with relatively few errors.

It would seem that mixing is an integral part of bilinguistic development. It is mentioned in almost all biographies and studies. The majority of mixings are lexical in nature, with nouns as the most frequently substituted words (e.g. *Donne doll à moi?*) (Swain & Wesche, 1973; Lindholm & Padilla, 1978). Redlinger & Park (1980) found that in the mixing of grammatical categories 40 per cent were accounted for by nouns and 6 per cent by verbs. Mixing is not exclusively lexical but may also occur at other levels, as in the example *est-ce que you sleep here?* where a French question morpheme precedes an English sentence. Studying code-mixing in an Estonian–English toddler, Vihman (1985) concluded that function words and not nouns are most frequently mixed in the other language and that mixing patterns from infants are different from those produced by adults. However, Meisel (1990) criticises Vihman's conclusions on the basis of the classification used. Besides the general agreement on the frequency of nouns in mixing, there is a consensus that syntactic categories do not appear at random in mixed elements. According to Meisel (1990; Koppe & Meisel, 1995) grammatical constraints on code-switching apply only to surface structures and can only be applied after the child has acquired functional categories; from the longitudinal analysis of two German–French bilingual toddlers he concludes that after the development of functional categories quantitative and qualitative changes occur in the bilingual productions.

Although probably all bilingual children mix codes, it must be noted that this mixing occurs with a low frequency: according to Swain & Wesche (1973), Lindholm & Padilla (1978) and Redlinger & Park (1980) only 2–4 per cent of utterances of infant bilingual productions are mixings; de Houwer (1990) indicated that 6.5 per cent of utterances are mixed; they are always present in early bilingual speech but their frequency tends to decrease as the child grows older. What role mixing plays in bilinguistic acquisition is still very little known, but the evidence of less frequent language mixing as the child grows older may be a manifestation of his improved capacity to keep his two languages separate. The child uses mixing because he seems to lack the equivalent in the appropriate language: in early mixing words from the weaker language are frequently introduced in the dominant language (Peterson, 1988) and bilingual toddlers mix more in their weaker language (Genesee, Nicoladis & Paradis,

1995). Not all mixing must be attributed to a lack of competence; mixed utterances might express the intended meaning more adequately.

Mixing is not only a matter of mastering lexical and grammatical forms, but also of pragmatics. Some researchers pay attention to the role of context in mixing. Goodz (1989; 1994) observed that language mixing in the child is related to the mixing produced by the parents: at the onset of the child's speech production parents use every possible communication strategy, including mixing; at a later stage however they might revert to a separation between the languages, especially if they notice a lag in the production of one of the child's languages. Lanza (1992) distinguishes between the type of linguistic behaviour produced in a bilingual and in a monolingual context: in a case study of a Norwegian–English two-year-old bilingual she observed that the child's speech was essentially monolingual in a monolingual context, whereas code-switching was frequently used in a bilingual context.

According to Meisel (1994) a distinction must be made between early mixing occurring at 2;0 to 3;0 years and later code-switching around 5;0 to 6;0 years. The latter resembles closely adult code-switching in its pragmatic and sociolinguistic characteristics (see Section 9.3); the former not only lacks the full range of functions observed in adult code-switching, but is also different in form. Lanza (1992) has however questioned this conclusion as the differences might be an artefact due to the nature of the infant's linguistic production; she claims that there are no qualitative differences between adult and infant code-switching.

As already mentioned, translation is also an integral part of bilinguistic development. Besides using translation spontaneously, the bilingual child requests translation equivalents in the other language (for example, a 3;1-year-old French-Flemish bilingual child requesting from a Flemish person the Flemish word for a kit:

wat is een < Flemish > cerf-volant < French >? *Wat is voor jou* < Flemish > un cerf-volant < French >? Comme tu parles < French >, *voor jou* < Flemish >? What is a kit? *What is for you* a kit? Like you speak, *for you*?

> (Hamers, personal observation).

The onset of awareness of two systems is evidenced around the second birthday as is mentioned in a number of biographies. Ronjat mentioned that his son would assign words to his father's or his mother's repertoire before his second birthday; Hoffmann (1991) mentions that around her second birthday her daughter would check with each parent if she got a word and its translation equivalent right. In her biography of an Estonian–English bilingual infant, Vihman (1985) reports that by the age of 2;1 years the child requests translations in either language; furthermore, the child quotes and comments on his own speech act. The author interprets this as proof that language awareness develops at an early age; she argues that language awareness and sensitivity to adult standards motivates language differentiation in the bilingual child.

3.1.4 Differentiation in linguistic systems

One of the key issues in bilingual processing is the ability to keep the two languages functionally separated. At what point in their development do bilingual children use their two codes as separate systems? The evidence on this question seems to be contradictory. On the one hand the one-system hypothesis (Swain, 1972; Volterra & Taeschner, 1978) suggests that the child first develops linguistic rules common to both languages which would then function as two codes of one language; the bilingual child develops differentiation strategies which enable him to distinguish between the two languages. The child develops a common system for rules shared by two languages and separate systems for specific rules; Taeschner (1983) suggests that increased differentiation between linguistic systems follows a number of stages specific to bilinguistic development: in the first stage, the child has one undifferentiated system, both at the lexical and the syntactic level; in stage two the syntax remains undifferentiated but the lexicons are distinct, and in the last stage, both lexicon and syntax are differentiated. Arnberg & Arnberg (1992) observed that bilingual children aged 1;8 to 4;0 who possess a high degree of bilingual awareness (i.e. awareness that there are two separate languages) produce significantly less mixing than their counterparts who have a low level of bilingual awareness.

The existence of an early undifferentiated stage in which the child possesses one lexicon and one grammar has been questioned by several researchers (Padilla & Liebmann, 1975; Goodz, 1989; Genesee, 1989; de Houwer, 1990; Meisel, 1994), who maintain that differentiation between the two systems is established at a much earlier age and that the child is capable of keeping the two phonological systems separate as soon as these develop. The data on preverbal phonetic discrimination (see Section 3.1.1.1) adds support to this view. Studying the acquisition of voicing in an infant from a Spanish–English home in England, Deuchar & Clark (1996) found that the child develops the contrasts earlier in the most frequently heard language; they failed, however, to find evidence for a merged system and suggest that the infant moves from no system to a dual system, without passing through a unified system. According to Padilla & Liebmann a unified but complementary lexicon does not necessarily imply an undifferentiated system: rather it might reflect the developing communicative strategies of the child who makes use of all his resources.

The capacity of bilingual infants to make an appropriate choice of language in accordance with their interlocutor is also in support of an early differentiation: studying parent–child interaction in five infant bilinguals (1;10 to 2;2 years), Genesee, Nicoladis & Paradis (1995) concluded that bilingual children differentiate between their languages before the emergence of two-word utterances. The occurrence of mixing obeying complex grammatical rules argues in favour of two distinct systems (Meisel, 1994); however it can also be argued that code-mixing is a manifestation of an undifferentiated system, a sign that the child lacks awareness of the existence of the two languages. This latter interpretation is however contradicted by evidence of bilingual awareness at an early age: the child, even at the one-word stage, makes the appropriate language choice with strangers and in unfamiliar linguistic surroundings; he is sensitive to his interlocutor's proficiency and is capable of making the necessary adjustment (Genesee, Boivin & Nicoladis, 1996).

The whole issue of whether or not bilinguistic development goes through an undifferentiated stage first cannot be resolved in the present state of our knowledge, although empirical evidence collected so far favours an early onset of distinct systems. It is likely that the reality is more complex and it must be assumed that at some level of processing the two systems are connected at least at the semantic level: whereas the child is perfectly aware of the existence of two systems, used according to the speaker's linguistic characteristics, he is also aware at an early age that two verbal labels can apply to the same object. Studies on the mutually-exclusive constraints demonstrate that, at a very young age, bilingual children are capable of using language cues in a specific way: they allow them to do two function–form mappings combined with a cross-language form–form mapping. This issue of bilingual processing is further discussed in Chapter 7. Only some psycholinguistic aspects have so far been investigated with a very small number of infants and language combinations; from what we know of early language development it might also be expected that large individual differences exist among children developing with two or more languages.

3.1.5   The role of context and interaction in bilinguistic development

A widespread belief among parents and educators is concerned with the separation of languages in terms of the adult models: the assumption is that separate contexts will enhance bilinguistic acquisition, whereas a mixed context will hinder acquisition and induce confusion and interference. This assumption, known as Grammont's Principle (Grammont, 1902), implies that the home environment should introduce a strict 'one language–one person' correspondence. This idea has been adhered to by most bilingual-child biographers but there is no proof of its psycholinguistic reality. Ronjat (1913) adopted it as a proven rule rather than as a hypothesis. The few studies that have investigated its role did not find any support for it. Doyle, Champagne & Segalowitz (1977), studying the impact of language mixing in mixed-lingual families on the bilingual child's vocabulary, failed to find significant differences between children whose parents followed the principle and those whose parents did not. The application of the Grammont Principle has no effect on the cognitive functioning of bilingual children (Bain, 1976). It seems that Grammont's Principle is not as strictly observed as parents pretend: Goodz (1989) found that the observance of the principle was linked to the stage of bilinguistic development reached by the child; when parental attention was focused on the formal features of language the Grammont Principle was more adhered to than when parents attended to content.

Far more important for the development of bilinguality than Grammont's Principle seems to be the role of social networks and the linguistic models they provide the child. The importance of social context for language development in general and for bilinguality in particular is discussed in Chapters 4 and 5. The linguistic context produced by parental interactions determines the bilingual child's productions. Goodz (1989; 1994) observes that certain forms, such as mixing, are related to mixing by parents. Arnberg (1984) has shown that it is not sufficient for a child living in a mixed-lingual family to receive a speech input from one parent only, especially if that parent's language is exogenous, i.e. not spoken as a first language by the speech community. Only if the child has close contacts with the community of his parent's language, by either making prolonged stays in the parent's country of origin or interacting with peers speaking the exogenous language in his environment, or both, will he be able to become a balanced bilingual. We will return to the importance of social networks for bilingual development in Sections 4.3.1 and 5.1.1. Social context can also be a factor in the development of the word–object relationship: according to Rosenblum & Pinker (1983) bilingual children are more likely to attend to sociolinguistic factors associated with the use of words than to grammatical functions.

It must be borne in mind that at a very early age the bilinguistic environment does not necessarily expose the child to similar linguistic experiences. Because in most of the studies on bilinguistic acquisition the parents of the observed children tended to keep to Grammont's Principle, the linguistic environment in which both languages are acquired varies as a function of the social roles of the adults around the child. The amount of time spent interacting with significant others in each language is however important for developing a balanced or dominant competence: an estimate of 20 per cent of the time spent in interaction in one language is considered as necessary for spontaneous production in that language (Pearson, Fernandez, Lewedeg & Oller, 1997).

Goodz (1989) distinguishes five stages in the bilingual child's linguistic development in which parent–child interaction plays a crucial role. In the first two stages (covering the first year), during which the adults provide bilinguistic input, the child becomes capable of discriminating between the two languages. In Stage 3 parents respond to the child by repeating, recasting and expanding the child's utterances, often using both linguistic systems; semantic and pragmatic features are stressed rather than formal ones and this brings about a higher frequency of code-mixing. As the child develops his comprehension and production the parents make greater demands on the child with regard to formal aspects, thus accentuating differences between the languages (Stage 4). As the child becomes proficient in both languages parents once again adopt a more flexible attitude.

Mohanty (1994a) points out that in multilingual environments children are socialised into multilingual modes of communication; in addition to going through the same processes of language socialisation as the monolingual child (see Section 4.1.1), the bilingual child must also acquire some specific behaviours. Mohanty distinguishes a sequence of stages through which the bilingual child is likely to pass in a multilingual environment which can be summarised as follows.

(1) In the stage of emergence of language differentiation the child is aware that communication can take place in a social context in different languages; he knows that some people speak different languages; that some master several languages while others do not; that he himself knows or does not know a given language and that objects have different labels.

(2) In the second stage the child has knowledge of language differentiation, that is he knows that two languages use different forms (for example, a child knows that English is different from Hindi); the child also knows that different speakers use different languages and he will respond in the appropriate language (for example, he will reply in Hindi to a Hindi-speaker and in Oriya to an Oriya-speaker).

(3) In the next stage there is emergence of social awareness of language use; the child speaks in the appropriate language to speakers of different languages and is aware of the appropriate social norms associated with the different languages in different social settings (for example the child is capable of changing language when going from home to school or to the market).

(4) Next, the child develops social understanding of the role of the languages and assigns functional roles to languages. There is an understanding of the hierarchical organisation of languages in the society and awareness of their appropriate contextual use (the child is capable of saying which language to choose in a given social setting and to give an explanation for it; for example, a French–English six-year-old child in Nova Scotia who was asked by an adult in English if she spoke French, replied in English 'yes, but only with the cat, the storekeeper and the man who brings lobsters' and refused to speak French; when asked why she refused, she mentioned it was not appropriate to do so with friends of her parents because they spoke English).

(5) Finally, around the age of seven, the child has developed a rule governed behaviour for multilingual functioning and switches to the appropriate language according to speaker, setting, topic, language hierarchy and social norms. By the end of this stage the child is socially competent to function in a multilingual environment.

In summary then, empirical evidence on bilinguistic development confirms most of the observation described in the biographies: children growing up with two or more native languages are capable of distinguishing their different languages at an early age; they do not lag behind monolingual children, although the developmental curves might be different; they develop a greater awareness of the arbitrariness of language; although they are capable of keeping their two languages separated, they produce a small amount of language mixing. Evidence suggests that native bilinguals develop unique strategies, both at the cognitive and the social level, and that at a very early age a bilingual speech mode is recognisable. However, bilinguistic development must not be viewed in isolation of the socialisation processes; the social and affective bases of prelinguistic and linguistic development are well assessed in the case of monolinguals (J. B. Gleason, 1993) and there is no reason to believe that this is less the case in bilinguistic development, as we shall further see in Chapter 5. But first we turn to another question: are the characteristics of bilinguistic development to be found in children who become fluent in an L_2 at an early age, but after the first language has been developed?

3.2   ONTOGENESIS OF EARLY CONSECUTIVE BILINGUALITY

Languages learned informally before the age of six are generally mastered with native-like proficiency, whereas those learned in adolescence and adulthood will rarely attain a native-like level. According to I. Taylor

(1990), learning an L_2 at a young age means that all the conditions favourable to L_1 acquisition are present, which is not the case for a later learned language. Furthermore, early L_2 acquisition happens often in an informal, natural context, which can be the neighbourhood and the kindergarten or the school, whereas adolescent and adulthood L_2 learning occurs normally, though not always, in a formal L_2 teaching environment.

Evidence from immigrant studies shows an age-of-arrival effect on L_2 proficiency: the younger the age of arrival in the L_2 country, the higher the proficiency in L_2 (Asher & García, 1969; Cummins, 1984b; Flege, 1988). Accent is the most salient feature to mark late L_2 learning: the later an immigrant learns the L_2, the more the foreign accent is evident (Tahta, Wood & Loewenthal, 1981). An age of arrival effect has also been found for comprehension with Italian immigrants who arrived in childhood, adolescence or adulthood (Oyama, 1979). Johnson & Newport (1989) found a linear correlation between age-of-arrival and grammaticality judgements for Korean and Chinese youngsters who had learned English before the age of 10, but no correlation for the immigrants who arrived after puberty. Prepuberty immigrants with a variety of L_1 also scored higher on syntactic skills than highly educated adulthood immigrants, although the latter had received four times more formal instruction in English (Patkowski, 1980).

When we speak of consecutive bilinguality and thus of L_2 acquisition, the first question that comes to mind is, 'to what extent is it similar to L_1 acquisition and/or to bilinguistic acquisition?' In analysing this phenomenon two major aspects should be considered:

(1) L_2 acquisition takes place at a more advanced developmental stage than that attained by children at the onset of language acquisition;
(2) L_2 learners already possess linguistic knowledge in their L_1.

How far, therefore, is this two fold cognitive and linguistic knowledge responsible for different acquisition mechanisms?

3.2.1   Age-related specificities of consecutive bilinguality

The bulk of research on early bilinguality has either been conducted with simultaneous bilinguals or, if not, did not until recently make the distinction between simultaneous and early consecutive bilinguality. Three approaches to the study of childhood bilinguality can be identified: behavioural studies of childhood bilinguals who already master the L_2; studies looking at the developmental aspects of L_2; and studies that relate bilinguality to cognitive development. Because of the specific age at which an early consecutive bilingual learns and masters the L_2, most of the research with early consecutive bilinguals has been concerned with the relation between cognition and bilingual development, which we discuss in Chapter 4.

In the present section we limit our review to the few studies that mention specific behaviours which make early consecutive bilinguals different from late L_2 learners. It must be kept in mind that mastering an L_2 at an early age occurs generally when learning takes place in informal settings or when the child attends school in the L_2 (see Chapter 11), that is context-dependent learning. So far there is no evidence that traditional L_2 teaching to young children in the absence of other contacts with L_2 leads to bilingual proficiency; on the contrary, there is some evidence that children are worse L_2-classroom learners than adults (Snow & Hoefnagel-Hohle, 1978). Once the L_2 is mastered, the behavioural evidence points to similar behaviours in early childhood bilinguals and simultaneous bilinguals, at least insofar as the different features of everyday speech appear to be alike. However, there is some neuropsychological evidence that simultaneous and early consecutive bilinguals use different neurolinguistic strategies (see Section 6.3.2.4).

Adolescents' and adults' mastery of L_2 is seldom native-like, while early consecutive bilinguals are generally considered to have attained the same proficiency levels as simultaneous bilinguals. But are these native-like L_2 speakers processing language in a similar way to the simultaneous bilinguals? There is some evidence that near-native speakers (NNSs) do process the L_2 in a different way from native speakers: comparing native speakers of French with NNSs, Coppieters (1987) observed that NNSs differ not only in accent but develop a grammar different from that of the native speaker. In the same vein Birdsong (1992) found that grammatical structures of native and very fluent non-native speakers were judged differently. However, this data was collected with NNSs who became fluent in L_2 in adolescence or adulthood and does not inform us on early consecutive bilinguality. Reviewing the literature on age of acquisition, Long (1990) concludes that both the rate of acquisition and the ultimate level of attainment in L_2 depends on the age that learning started in different linguistic domains.

One of the supposed characteristics of early childhood bilinguals is that, in many cases, they seem to attain a native-like mastery of the L_2. The term 'true' bilingual is sometimes used to differentiate early native-like bilinguals from near-native bilinguals; sometimes it is used to designate balanced bilinguals and at other times to distinguish childhood bilinguals from proficient L_2 learners. We prefer not to use this term not only because of the lack of agreement on the definition but also on the grounds that it assumes that consecutive bilinguals are incapable of attaining a native-speaker's competence. So far, little empirical evidence is available which entitles us to conclude how close early consecutive bilinguals are to native speakers and simultaneous bilinguals. Nonetheless, it seems reasonable to advance the following principle: the earlier a consecutive bilingual masters the L_2, the more likely his processing will approach that of the simultaneous bilingual. But will it become indistinguishable from native mastery?

The first detailed description of an L_2 acquisition by a young child was given by Kenyeres (1938), who observed her six-year-old daughter whose mother tongue was Hungarian and who was learning French in a school in Geneva. The author concluded that L_2 acquisition, while being achieved in a harmonious fashion, does not follow the same route as L_1 acquisition, and that the majority of errors in L_2 can be attributed to mother-tongue interference. Tits (1948), on the other hand, concluded from his observations of a seven-year-old Spanish-speaking girl acquiring French in Brussels that her L_2 acquisition followed the same stages of development as L_1 acquisition, though at a faster pace. These studies, like the biographies of bilingual children by Ronjat (1913) and Leopold (1939–49), were carried out at a time when no language-acquisition theory was available; for this reason these descriptions, however detailed, tell us very little about the mechanisms involved in L_2 acquisition.

There is some evidence that, in acoustic decoding, early consecutive bilinguals use perceptual strategies different from monolinguals and from simultaneous bilinguals (Watson, 1991). The ability to imitate a foreign accent diminishes by the age of eight (Tahta, Wood & Loewenthal, 1981). Studies comparing early consecutive bilinguals (mainly children who spoke one language at home and attended kindergarten or elementary school in another language) with monolinguals demonstrate that the former process language in a different way: children who become bilingual at an early age have higher levels of awareness in phonological (Rubin & Turner, 1989; Bruck & Genesee, 1995), syntactic (Ben-Zeev, 1977a), and lexical (Diaz, 1985; Hakuta, 1987) processing than do monolinguals. Degree of bilingual competence in early consecutive bilinguals is highly correlated with judgements of referential arbitrariness: studying pre-school bilinguals (4;6 years), from 18 different linguistic backgrounds at the International School of Milan, Edwards & Christophersen (1988) found a highly significant relation between the measure of bilingual competence and two measures of arbitrariness. Unfortunately the authors do not give information about the age of onset of bilinguality. It can only be inferred that they are dealing with early consecutive bilinguals. The study confirms that a certain level of bilingual competence has to be attained in order to be more sensitive to semantic arbitrariness. Age of onset of bilinguality plays a crucial role in early bilinguality insofar as it is responsible for the level of attainment in L_2. According to Ben-Zeev childhood bilinguals develop strategies which will enable them to keep their two languages separate. This issue is further discussed in the section on metalinguistic awareness (Section 4.2.3).

3.2.2   Age-related processing in consecutive bilinguality

In their cross-linguistic study of sentence processing Bates & McWhinney (1989) showed that sentence processing varies across languages. For example, English speakers use word order as a cue for sentence meaning, whereas Italian speakers tend to use animacy as a cue. According to McWhinney (1987), when bilinguals have to deal with two languages for which native speakers use differential strategies, four logical strategies might be used:

(1)   differentiation, in which the listener uses separate strategies for each language, equivalent to the monolinguals;
(2)   forward transfer, a process whereby L_1 strategies for sentence decoding are transferred to L_2;
(3)   backward transfer, a process whereby L_2 strategies are used for sentence processing in L_1; and
(4)   amalgamation, a process whereby a single strategy is used for both languages.

Empirical evidence shows that most bilinguals use forward transfer or amalgamation (for a review, see Liu, Bates & Li, 1992), although Vaid & Pandit (1991) demonstrate that all four strategies can be found in Hindi–English school children: these studies do not however have a strict control over the age of onset of bilinguality.

In a study comparing adult consecutive Chinese–English and English–Chinese bilinguals who had learned the L_2 at different ages, Liu, Bates & Li (1992) found evidence for differential sentence processing as a function of age of exposure to L_2. The early infant bilinguals were native Chinese speakers, born in the USA and exposed to English before the age of four; the early child bilinguals were native Chinese speakers who arrived in the USA between 6–10 years; the adolescent group were native Chinese speakers who arrived between 12–16 years; the two groups of adulthood bilinguals were native Chinese speakers and native English speakers exposed to the L_2 after the age of 20. The bilinguals' processing was also compared with that of two monolingual control groups. During the experiment subjects heard sentences and were asked to determine which object carries out a particular action; for example, in the English sentence *The cow is smelling the pencil*, the word *cow* is the correct answer. Transfer of sentence processing was found in early and late bilinguals: both groups of adulthood bilinguals showed forward transfer in their L_2; childhood bilinguals showed differentiation strategies and behaved like monolinguals in both languages; infant bilinguals showed backward transfer and used English strategies in English and in Chinese; adolescent bilinguals also showed backward transfer.

The authors interpret their data as an indication that the L_1 must be firmly established before exposure to L_2, which is the case for the childhood bilinguals who developed an L_1 fluency before the L_2 was introduced. They attribute the fact that infant bilinguals produce backward transfer to a loss of L_1. It must however be noted that the infant bilinguals were probably dominant in English, as can be inferred from the study, and were schooled in a country that little valorised multilingualism (see Chapter 5). They found little explanation for the backward transfer in the adolescent bilinguals, although they have some evidence that backward transfer is reduced by the use of L_1 in the family. Although this study might shed some light on the way age of onset might interplay with processing, it also confirms that other factors, probably social psychological in nature, must be taken into consideration. In summary, then, this study fails to give the complete picture insofar as it ignores the role played by bilingual competence and by social-psychological features of bilinguality. However, it contributes some important information on language processing in bilinguals, and this is further discussed in Chapter 7.

Some empirical proof that consecutive childhood bilinguals do not process their L_2 in the same way as monolinguals stems from studies by Hyltenstam (1992). He studied Finnish–Swedish and Spanish–Swedish childhood bilinguals for whom the age of onset of the L_2 was either before six or after six but before puberty, and who were indistinguishable from Swedish native speakers for phonology, grammar and lexicon in everyday oral interactions. These groups were compared with matched Swedish monolinguals in a study on spoken and written texts and writing compositions. The material that was produced by their groups was analysed for lexical and grammatical errors. The total number of errors was higher for the bilinguals than for the monolinguals: the late-childhood bilinguals had error frequencies well above those of the monolinguals; the frequency of errors of the early-childhood bilinguals was in between, with some resembling the monolinguals and others the late bilinguals. For the lexical errors no qualitative difference was found between the groups; the most distinctive feature was that bilinguals more frequently gave approximation errors (e.g. *lengthwise* for *in the long run*). The bilinguals, however, produced grammatical errors typical of L_2 learners, such as article deletion or wrong word order. The results support the assumption that ultimate attainment is related to the age of onset. They also confirm that the age of 6–7 is a landmark for distinguishing between native-like and near-native attainment. However, age of onset is not the only factor to explain attainment, especially before the age of 6–7; the large individual differences in that age group point to the relevance of other factors that are cognitive and socio-psychological in nature.

3.2.3   The role of context in childhood L_2 acquisition

Whereas examples abound about later learners who never reach native-like proficiency despite the fact that they live in an L_2 environment, social and conversational context seems to play an important role in childhood native-like L_2 acquisition. As early consecutive L_2 acquisition occurs often in an informal way, social and conversational contexts are bound to play a major role. Wong Fillmore's (1979; 1989; 1991a) research stresses the relevance of social factors in L_2 acquisition in children; according to her the L_2 learner's first task is to establish social relations with his interlocutor. Because he relies on social cognitive strategies to attain this end, he will be able to learn L_2; by interpreting cues from the communication setting, the child begins to guess and understand the other speaker's language and to respond to it. The child will develop the L_2 syntax from this situation of social interaction. The author attributes differences in rate of acquisition mainly to individual differences in social skills. This interpretation is in line with the research on the role of attitudes and motivation in L_2 learning essentially conducted with adolescent and adult learners. According to Wong Fillmore, three types of processes interact in language learning: social, linguistic and cognitive. Social processes include the steps taken by both learner and L_2 speaker to create a social setting in which L_2 communication is possible and desired.

The conversational context of L_2 also plays an important role in L_2 acquisition. Native speakers of L_2, when in interaction with a non-native speaker, simplify the language and make use of foreigner talk (see Section 9.2.2.1). Most speech addressed to non-native speakers by native speakers is however a modified but well-formed version of the L_2: it is structurally more simple, more redundant and repetitive (Larsen-Freeman & Long, 1991). Native-like input also seems to be important, as witnessed by the data on children who went through immersion programs and who never reached native-like L_2 productions (Swain, 1991; Wesche, 1994) (for a further discussion on immersion see Section 11.4).

Keller-Cohen (1979) analysed the conversational aspect of language, and in particular turn-taking. Studying the development of English as L_2 in 4–6-year-old Japanese-, Finnish- and German-speaking children in interaction with native English-speaking adults, she observed that the number of turn-takings under the child's control more than doubled over a period of eight months. The child used two types of strategy for turn-allocation, either questions or attention-directing utterances e.g. *look!* She infers from this that the child must first learn that speaking is turn-taking and turn-allocation for both the child and his interlocutor. She views this aspect as central to L_2 learning. Peck (1978) also insists on the relevance of social interaction in L_2 acquisition, namely on the role of child–child discourse, particularly language involving play. She argues that the child learns the rules of L_2 through discourse produced in social interaction with other children and adults. The role of conversation in acquiring L_2 at an early age is recognised, but the elements of conversation which help the child reach native-like competence are still not identified. In the interactional hypothesis Long (1996) proposes that environmental contributions to acquisition are mediated by selective attention and the learner's developing L_2 processing capacity, and that these resources are brought together during the negotiation for meaning.

Young children are better L_2-learners than older ones in an L_2-context. Age of onset of L_2 learning is an important factor in reaching native-like proficiency in L_2: in the Johnson & Newport (1989) study, it was found that Korean and Chinese speakers who had arrived in the USA between the ages of 3–7 were judged as native-like on production of grammatical structures in English, whereas those who arrived between ages 8–10 were not. That context plays an important role in early L_2 acquisition might reflect the importance of form–function mapping for developing L_2 proficiency in children; children do not override older learners when L_2 is formally taught. But why do older learners who are in similar contexts not reach native-like L_2 competence? This question raises the issue of there being a 'sensitive period' for L_2 learning.

3.3   GESTURAL/ARTICULATED BILINGUALITY

The existence of signed languages allows us another perspective on bilinguality, which combines an aural–oral mode (spoken language) with a visual–gestural mode (sign language). Sign languages, such as American Sign Language (ASL), are fully autonomous languages, which possess all the properties common to all natural languages: formal structuring and organisational principles (Bellugi, Poizner & Klima, 1993). The stages of acquisition of ASL by deaf children parallel the acquisition of spoken languages by hearing children (Newport & Meyer, 1985). Hearing children born to deaf parents often acquire the signed language as the first language or are native bilinguals in signed and articulated language; these children are fully bilingual and often act as interpreters. When referring to a deaf bilingual person it is assumed that we refer to a combination of a gestural, i.e. signed, language and an articulated language, e.g. ASL and English. Just as a hearing person's bilinguality varies on a number of dimensions, so does bilinguality in deaf people who use a gestural and an articulated language: they may vary in their linguistic knowledge of the two languages and in their fluency in each of the languages, according to the age of acquisition of both languages, and in their use of both languages. In recent years the concept of 'deaf culture' has gained recognition and the term is used to refer to the customs and values of the deaf minority in contrast with the hearing majority. A deaf person is often bilingual/bicultural, using sign language within the deaf community and an articulated language with the hearing community (Parasnis, 1996). Furthermore, when deaf people interact with monolinguals, deaf people restrict themselves to one language, whereas in their interactions with other deaf bilinguals they often revert to a bilingual speech mode (Grosjean, 1996).

Only 5–10 per cent of hearing-impaired children are born to deaf parents and have sign language as their native language. The bilingual status of deaf children of hearing parents is more difficult to determine. In the USA about 90–97 per cent of the deaf children born to hearing parents are usually not exposed to sign language in the first years (Mayberry & Fischer, 1989; Meyer & Newport, 1990). Hearing parents generally do not have knowledge of sign language and will often learn it with the child. Furthermore, the degree and the age of hearing loss will determine the degree of input of oral language. Severe prelingual hearing impairment is disruptive of the language-acquisition process and usually leads to severe speech problems, language retardation and dysfunction; however, in milder impairment some input of the articulated language will typically occur. In prelingually deaf infants the articulated language is often introduced, at a later age, through the lip-reading or the written mode, sometimes a sign language is not fully mastered. Prelingually deaf individuals, English is characterised by the production of short, syntactically simple utterances, by an overuse of nouns and articles, and by a restricted use of function words and adverbs (Berent, 1996). It is therefore difficult to ascertain the deaf child's L_1 and his bilingual status.

ASL proficiency declines according to age of onset: native signers develop language at the same rate as children exposed to an oral language and there are marked similarities in the development of sign and of oral language; signers who learned ASL in infancy (between birth and four years) outperform signers who learned ASL in childhood (4–6 years); in turn the latter outperform those who learned ASL after the age of 12 (Newport, 1990). Many deaf learners of English L_2 attain English language knowledge comparable to that of hearing learners but when spoken-language input is severely restricted deaf learners of English develop 'smaller languages'

(Berent, 1996). There is also some evidence that deaf children who developed ASL as a first language develop better English skills than those who did not (Bernstein Ratner, 1997). Provided that linguistic input is not deficient, the mode in which the language is presented does not seem to impinge on the child's linguistic development. Although many parallels can be drawn between hearing and deaf bilingual development, differences also exist. Among these the most important one concerns the context and age of language acquisition: because the vast majority of deaf children are born in normally hearing families which are not familiar with sign language, most deaf children start with severely impoverished communication at home; they more often than not learn sign language outside their home, frequently at an age beyond that of normal language acquisition (Hamers, 1996).

3.4   SENSITIVE-AGE HYPOTHESIS

A controversial area in bilingualism and L_2 acquisition is that of the optimal age of the learner. It is important to distinguish between studies of L_2 learning in a formal classroom situation, and those of informal L_2 acquisition in natural settings. The former indicate that adolescents and adults learn certain aspects of L_2 faster and with greater ease than children (Burstall, 1975; Snow & Hoefnagel-Hohle, 1978); however, studies that address the issue of older learners' advantage normally involve the learning of morphological and syntactic rules, not the final result (Larsen-Freeman & Long, 1991). The relative ease with which a young child masters more than one language, as compared with the effort expended by an adult in learning an L_2, prompted Penfield & Roberts (1959) to assume that this facility might be attributed to the relatively greater cerebral plasticity of the child. Neuropsychological evidence confirms that hemispheric lateralisation for language, although present at birth, will develop during childhood, and that bilingual experience influences this lateralisation and its behavioural correlates (for a discussion see Chapter 6). The relevant questions here are:

(1)   how far will learning an L_2 influence this neuropsychological development in L_2 childhood acquisition?; and
(2)   how far is L_2 acquisition after neuropsychological maturity different from L_2 acquisition during this period?

Lenneberg (1967) hypothesised the existence of a critical period for language acquisition, which terminates with neuropsychological maturity, that is, at around puberty: linguistic development needs to be activated between 3–12 years of age for normal development to occur. This hypothesis implies that all language acquisition, be it L_1 or L_2, beyond the critical period will be qualitatively different from childhood language acquisition. However, this hypothesis is supported by little empirical evidence, most of it stemming from clinical data obtained from feral, hearing-impaired and linguistically isolated children. Because of the overall deprivation suffered in the cases of feral children and of socially isolated abused children this may not be good evidence for a sensitive period. One case is however reported in which language deprivation occurred in the absence of social deprivation: Chelsea, a deaf woman of 31 with no exposure to language, could learn a 2000-word vocabulary with intensive training but failed to develop normal syntactic structures (Curtiss, 1989). Further evidence stems from studies with brain-damaged patients, for whom complete language acquisition rarely happens if the lesion occurs after the age of 5 and substantial recovery rarely occurs after puberty (Stromswold, 1995). If such a critical period exists it is not absolute: there are indications that linguistic competence can be acquired and improved after puberty, although it will not reach normal levels of processing (Curtiss, 1989). For this reason Oyama (1979) prefers to refer to a sensitive rather than a critical period, that is, a developmental period during which there should be a greater receptivity for language.

The existence of a sensitive period for L_2 acquisition has been questioned. As mentioned previously, there is strong evidence which shows that in natural settings early L_2 acquisition is more likely to lead in the long run to native-like competence in all language skills. But can this evidence be used as proof of a sensitive period? Long (1990), relying on the comparison between L_2 acquisition after puberty and L_1 acquisition in language-deprived cases, argues in favour of a sensitive period for L_2. Similarities between L_1 acquisition processes in children and L_2 acquisition in later life have also been used as proof of the sensitive period (Bailey, Madden & Krashen, 1974).

Not all researchers agree however that a sensitive period for L_2 acquisition must be postulated. Summarising some 40 studies on the sensitive period for L_2 acquisition, Ekstrand (1981) concludes that there is no clear evidence for a sensitive period nor for a biologically determined optimal age for L_2 acquisition. According to him the greatest advantage arising from the introduction of an L_2 at an early age rests on the fact that it allows a longer period of learning, starting at a time when the learner has to acquire less linguistic baggage in order to attain native-like competence; this acquisition is, therefore, faster. The young child does not have a greater facility for learning, but a less complex task for which he has more time. Leather & James (1991) view the phonological disadvantage of older learners as resulting from social and individual constraints that make it hard for them to change their way of speaking.

Johnson & Newport (1989) propose two sensitive period hypotheses: the exercise hypothesis holds that early in life human beings have a superior language-learning ability that, if exercised, will remain intact for second language acquisition; the maturational-state hypothesis predicts that, no matter how much exercised, the language learning ability will decline. They argue that empirical evidence supports the maturational hypothesis. However, maturation does not have to be explained by biological factors. McWhinney (1992) argues that the increased automatisation of the L_1 system can make the addition of new auditory, articulatory and semantic contrasts more difficult: the more automatised a system becomes, the less it is available for restructuring, hence the greater the difficulty of acquiring L_2 later in life.

The question as to why children are capable of developing more native-like L_2 proficiency than later learners is still unanswered. The biologically sensitive period explanation does not appear as a necessary one. Social, cognitive and experiential factors might also make the learning task easier for children; restructuring highly atomised behaviour has always proved a difficult task and there is no reason to think it should be different for language. However, neurological maturation as a factor among others, responsible for the lesser L_2 attainment later in life, must not be completely disregarded. It is probably a mixture of these different factors which explains the ease with which a child acquires an L_2 as compared to an adult.

3.5   LANGUAGE ATTRITION AND BILINGUALITY

Language attrition is a generic term used to cover all non-temporary regression in language processing, covering a continuum from mild access problems, i.e. word finding, to complete loss of language. A distinction is made between environmental attrition (due to a reduced use of a language), old-age attrition (due to ageing processes) and pathological attrition (due to disease or trauma) (Hyltenstam & Viberg, 1993). L_2 attrition is a common phenomenon in the cases when an L_2, partially mastered, is no longer learned or used (for a review, see Weltens, 1987); as most documented cases of L_2 attrition refer to late L_2 learners and not to bilinguals, they will not be discussed here. L_1 attrition generally occurs as the result of a restricted use of the L_1, both in adults and children. L_1 attrition in children is common in ethnolinguistic minority children who tend to shift to the official language used in school; the issue of L_1 replacement by L_2 in school-aged children is analysed in the section on subtractive bilingualism in Section 4.2.5.2.

3.5.1   Environmental L_1 attrition in bilinguals

In the present section we are more specifically interested in environmental attrition in bilingual individuals; by environmental attrition we do not mean a total loss of L_1 (which occurs only for very young immigrant children or in post-morbid situations) but a partial loss of certain aspects of a fully developed L_1 stemming from the acquisition and use of an L_2 (Seliger, 1996). Intergenerational attrition is discussed in Section 10.3.4. Although attrition and code-mixing might appear to be similar they must not be confused: code-mixing in L_1 is triggered by the social context, whereas in the case of attrition deterioration occurs even in an L_1 monolingual context. Code-mixing might however be a precursor of attrition. When a person lives long enough in an L_2 environment his productions in L_1 may, though not necessarily, show signs of L_2 interference and of L_1 attrition, especially when the speakers are isolated from other L_1 speakers. L_1 attrition is not only characterised by code-mixing, but also by dynamic processes in L_1: for example, in lexical attrition specific words will be replaced by more basic words; when the basic words are no longer accessible, borrowing words from the L_2 will occur (Viberg, 1993). For a description of the linguistic features of L_1 attrition see Seliger (1996); a further discussion of attrition is also found in Section 10.3.4.

In a study on the L_1 productions of long-term Dutch migrants in France, de Bot, Gommans and Rossing (1991) failed to observe signs of attrition. In contrast, Major (1993) found that English-speaking immigrants who lived in Brazil for at least 12 years had lost their native accent in English. According to Clyne (1977) who studied Dutch adult immigrants residing in Australia for at least 15 years, besides the frequent use of code-switching, the L_1 productions are characterised by code-mixing: lexical, semantic and syntactic transference (e.g. *watch-en* for *kijken*) and phonological integration. Although L_1 attrition is a long-term dynamic process, little change was found when the subjects were retested 16 years later (de Bot & Clyne, 1994): lexical skills did not change over time and the only significant syntactical change was on adverbial order shifted to the English order. A study with German migrants (Waas, 1993) showed that similar attrition occurs after less than 10 years' migration. The authors conclude that L_1 attrition develops during the first decade and remains relatively stable afterwards. However, when they analysed production of the subjects who were weak in their L_1 in the first study, they observed that a mixed code was used either when English or when Dutch was required. They point out that this may be due to an ageing process in bilinguals, resulting in a less controlled code-switching mechanism.

According to Seliger (1996) L_1 attrition depends on the degree of acculturation, the level of literacy in L_1, and the functions served by L_1, as well as on L_1 group characteristics. Seliger distinguishes three stages in L_1 attrition:

- in the first stage the bilingual maintains autonomy for each language, and in the case of code-mixing constraints indigenous to each language are maintained;
- in stage 2, because of the inaccessibility of L_1 data, L_2 becomes the source of evidence affecting L_1 grammar; and
- in stage 3 similar rules in L_1 and L_2 are fused in the direction of that which is less marked.

Attrition in L_1 is not random forgetting but is the result of developing the most parsimonious grammar that can serve both languages: the L_2 rule is assimilated into L_1 and replaces the L_1's more complex rule. The two separate systems which are characteristic of the bilingual speaker fuse into one undifferentiated system.

3.5.2   Age-related and pathological attrition

Whereas L_1 attrition related to ageing is fairly well documented (see Obler, 1997), little is yet known about ageing bilinguals: Obler, Albert & Lozowick (1986) compared language attrition in English-dominant healthy elderly bilinguals (average age 74) and compared them with matched monolinguals. All bilinguals had learned English before the age of six and although some still used their L_1, English was the most used language. The results showed that the bilinguals did not suffer more attrition in their English L_2 than their monolingual Anglophone peers did. In childhood bilinguals age-related L_2-attrition seems not to be different from L_1 attrition in monolinguals. Furthermore no evidence is available that ageing bilinguals lose their specific abilities.

In pathological attrition we make a distinction between post-traumatic aphasia and disease-related attrition. Bilingual aphasia is discussed at length in Chapter 6 on neurolinguistic processing. Among the diseases which cause language attrition, Alzheimer's dementia provokes the most dramatic evolutive changes in language behaviour (Obler, 1997). Only recently have researchers shown interest in bilingual Alzheimer patients; all studies confirm that the language attrition observed in monolingual patients is observed in the bilingual patient's two languages. Hyltenstam & Stroud (1989) found that a German–Swedish bilingual Alzheimer's patient who had acquired Swedish in adulthood showed a preference for the use of L_1, whereas a Swedish–Finnish childhood bilingual patient exhibited no language differences. At similar levels of regression large variations in the behaviour of the Alzheimer patient for language choice and separation can be observed: some will use their L_1 regardless of the interlocutor, whereas others may switch to a language the interlocutor does not know. The ability to make the socially appropriate choice seems to be lost at an early stage, at a time when the two languages remain grammatically adequate (Hyltenstam & Stroud, 1993).

Language attrition in bilinguality is a relatively new topic of interest for researchers. It seems that in normal bilinguals who learned their L_2 in adulthood, L_1 attrition occurs mainly when the L_1 is no longer used in the environment and is replaced by an L_2. This attrition seems to occur during the first decade of isolation and stabilises afterwards. Attrition seems more important when the L_1 proficiency was weak. There are slight indications that severe L_1 attrition might lead to a fused system between L_1 and L_2, but to what extent this is attributable to L_1 isolation or to the ageing process is still unknown. To what extent the merging of two systems may be considered as a manifestation of inadequate mapping or of wrong cue identification remains unanswered. If the L_2 was learned in early childhood and remains a frequently used language, the type of attrition observed is not different from that in native speakers. Although at present very little evidence is available on dementia in bilinguals, it seems that bilingual Alzheimer's patients suffer language attrition in their two languages in a similar way to monolinguals; in addition, the capacity to make appropriate language choices seems to be lost at an early stage.

3.6   CONCLUSION

In this chapter we have presented various facets of bilingual development by looking at its linguistic manifestations, its age of onset and its ontogenesis throughout life. We have discussed the onset of simultaneous bilinguality and several questions were raised about bilinguistic development; for example: Are there stages in bilinguistic development? Is there a lag in this development compared with that of the monolingual child? Are the two linguistic systems differentiated and what is the role of linguistic mixing? How relevant are the linguistic and social contexts in bilinguistic development? We further reviewed some aspects of consecutive bilinguality and the relation between age of L_2 mastering and the attainment of bilingual competence; we also considered the special case of the sign/articulated language bilingual. The descriptive data on the various cases of early bilinguality was further discussed in the framework of a sensitive period for L_2 acquisition, which is still an unresolved problem. Finally we gave a short overview of different types of attrition in bilinguality.

As is the case for monolingual development, bilingual development is deeply rooted in interactions with others. Bilingual lexical development is a function of the amount of time spent in interaction. Bilingual children also seem to show a great sensitivity to sociolinguistic cues in their environment. An early mapping occurs between the choice of language and the function of communication with a specific person, as bilingual children are capable of making the correct choice at an early age.

In our outline of the developmental aspects of language we suggested that there are perceptual/motor prerequisites of language development. From the data discussed in Section 3.1.1, it appears that a bilingual environment plays a role in shaping some of the perceptual prerequisites of language: there are some indications that the prelinguistic infant raised in a bilingual environment discriminates foreign-language phonemes better than his counterpart in a monolingual family. At the same time there is no evidence that a bilingual environment impinges on prelinguistic productions.

MacWhinney (1987) demonstrated that the competition model can be applied to bilingual behaviour. Although he did not demonstrate this for bilinguistic development, early bilinguistic development can also be explained in terms of mapping and cue validity in the same way as monolingual development. The differences in developmental curves of monolingual and bilingual children can also be explained in this way. The small amount of language-mixing produced in bilinguistic development might be an indication that the child is capable of picking up the correct cues as to which language to use in the first stages of bilinguistic development. His capability to act as a translator testifies to his ability to produce a specific and complex combination of form–function and form–form mapping at an early age. It also indicates his sensitivity to the context and to interpersonal interactions.

Relatively few children have the opportunity to develop a simultaneous bilinguality; most bilinguals have acquired an L_2 after their L_1, more often than not through educational programs introduced at various age levels, and these will not necessarily lead to a balanced bilinguality. In this case their linguistic output will be different from that of native speakers, as shown by the empirical studies. To what extent early consecutive bilinguality differs from simultaneous bilinguality remains to be assessed. These differences will only be understood if the two-way relation between linguistic development and cognitive growth is taken into account.

The empirical evidence reviewed is often contradictory, and few theoretical constructs are sufficiently developed to account for these contradictions. Models of bilinguistic development are very often incomplete, and at this stage, are more descriptive than explanatory. A number of methodological questions can also be raised about the empirical evidence itself:

- erroneous generalisations from limited or biased data base, e.g. one or few children;
- vague definition of degree of bilinguality and lack of control of bilingual experience;
- lack of control of co-varying factors;
- lack of validity of measures;
- confusion of independent and dependent variables, which raises the issue of the direction of causality.

In spite of some methodological shortcomings, which should and can be overcome as the most recent research demonstrates, an empirical approach is the only way to unravel the complexities of bilingual development. Only a large body of sound, comparable experimental data will enable scholars to perfect the necessary theoretical constructs, thus giving us a better insight into the ontogenesis of bilinguality. More general theories of language development, like the competition model, are a promising path to a better understanding of bilinguistic development.

However, in our view, these types of models fail to take into account the complex interactions occurring between cognitive growth, linguistic development and social psychological mechanisms. As we already mentioned in Chapter 1, an ontogenetic model of bilinguality should not consider bilinguistic development in isolation from its social and cognitive correlates. In the next chapter we will review the state of the art on the links between bilinguality and cognitive development and discuss how a general model of language processing can explain them.

4 Cognitive development and the sociocultural context of bilinguality

The relation between bilinguality and cognitive development must be viewed in the wider framework of the relationship between language and thought in contemporary theories of behaviour. Furthermore, important empirical studies in the latter part of the twentieth century point to the relevance of the sociocultural context for the cognitive development of bilingual children. In the present chapter we discuss first the state of the art on the relationship between bilinguality and cognitive development; moreover, we insist on the role played by the sociocultural context in this development. If we adopt the theoretical stand that language development and cognitive growth are intimately connected, then we must determine how relevant bilingual development is for intellectual growth and account for the empirical evidence concerning the cognitive development of the bilingual child. In other words, if, besides the fact that they master two languages, bilinguals are different from monolinguals, how and to what extent are they different? And how does it affect their cognitive development? Although in the present chapter we review the empirical evidence on the cognitive consequences of becoming bilingual, we start by discussing some general theoretical views on language development which can lead to a better understanding of this relationship. The relationship between bilinguality and cognitive processes is further discussed in Chapter 5.

4.1   BILINGUALITY AND COGNITION

Whether one considers that language plays an important role in the development of thought or whether both are seen as developing independently of each other will influence the extent to which bilinguality is considered as a relevant factor for the development of cognitive processes. For Vygotsky (1962) language plays an essential role in cognitive development, at least from the time the child has attained a certain level of language competence. Language, first developed as a means of social communication, is later internalised and becomes a crucial tool in the shaping of cognitive processes relevant for the elaboration of the abstract symbolic system which will enable the child to organise thought. In the same vein, Bruner (1975a; 1975b) proposes that the child develops conceptual-linguistic abilities; language comes to play an increasingly powerful role as an implement for knowing; and language permits productive, combinatorial operations in the absence of what is represented.

But there are some important prerequisites before language can develop and be used as a cognitive tool. According to Bruner (1990), in order to internalise symbolic meaning, which is itself deeply rooted in culture, the infant must enter into meaning; therefore he must develop a prelinguistic readiness for meaning. In order to develop this the child must have a set of predispositions to construe the social world in a particular way. Readiness for meaning and language have three characteristics:

(1) interactions with others must occur so that the child will be able to learn *what* to say, *how, where, to whom* and under *what circumstances*; shared routines[1] will facilitate early language-learning;
(2) certain communicative functions and intentions, such as indicating, labelling and requesting, must be developed before the child produces the formal linguistic structures to express them; and
(3) the development of linguistic forms is context-sensitive in the sense that they are easier to learn if there is some prelinguistic grasp of the meaning.

Thus, the social context and in particular the interactions with the primary caretakers is viewed as vital for language development. Interactional routines structure the situation through which socialisation occurs. Routines provide both the linguistic input and the appropriate ways of communicating (Peters & Boggs, 1986). Of particular interest are those aspects of socialisation which relate to language; this is known as language socialisation.

4.1.1   Language socialisation

The definition of language socialisation includes both socialisation through language and socialisation to use language (Ochs, 1986). The goals of language socialisation are:

• orienting towards social status and role-appropriate language use;
• teaching culturally appropriate communication through instruction, practice and exposure; transmitting values and affect;
• setting functional priorities in social communication; and
• developing stylistic preferences and fostering meta-communicative awareness (Mohanty, 1996).

In order to attain these goals the child must rely on the cognitive process of form–function mapping. Furthermore, in order to use language in communication, the child must develop a theory of mind, i.e. a cognitive capacity to recognise, evaluate and exploit the beliefs and desires of others (Bruner, 1990: 68). In order to develop conceptual-linguistic abilities the child must further internalise language as a tool of cognitive functioning, that is, for classifying, reorganising and analysing representations.

In agreement with Vygotsky's and Bruner's approach, we consider that language development and cognitive growth are intermingled and that the ontogenesis of language is deeply rooted in the child's cultural and social environment. In all cultures language is a tool for socialisation and interactions: however, strategies or interactional routines vary greatly from one culture to another (Peters & Boggs, 1986). It is through participation in these routines, that is, through language socialisation, that the child learns the cognitive and affective aspects of language use. There are important cross-cultural differences in the way that language socialisation occurs: in all cultures verbal interactions involving the child and the primary caretakers play an important role in language acquisition; however, language socialisation practices are governed by cultural parameters, which will prioritise some verbal routines and the linguistic forms to express them. For example, in contrast to Western adult–infant interactions, caretakers interacting with four-month-old infants in a Kung! community tend to ignore object manipulation while they focus on social relations (Bakeman, Adamson, Konner & Barr, 1990). Similarly, Rabain-Jamin (1994) observed that Senegal Wolof-speaking mothers living in Paris are less responsive to the child's object-related verbal initiatives but more responsive to social verbal initiatives than their French counterparts, who pay more verbal attention to object manipulation.

4.1.2   Bilinguality and cognitive development

But what happens when two different languages and two different cultures are present around the child? Mohanty (1994b) suggests that in multilingual environments children are socialised into multilingual modes of communication. He proposes a sequence of stages, from language differentiation to the development of code-switching rules, through which a child developing language in a bilingual environment is likely to pass (see Section 3.1.5). From the point of view of a child's development passing through these stages makes the experience of bilingual development unique compared to the monolingual experience. But how does this bilinguistic development influence the child's cognitive development?

In Vygotsky's view, being able to express the same thought in different languages will enable 'the child to see his language as one particular system among many, to view its phenomena under more general categories, and this leads to awareness of his linguistic operations' (Vygotsky, 1962: 110). This early awareness further generalises to other areas of concept learning and thinking. For Vygotsky the evolution of cognitive growth and experiencing with one or more than one language has different consequences for the development of cognitive abilities. He further insists on the role of metalinguistic[2] skills, namely on the control and self-regulation of cognitive processes induced by the use of more than one language.

Viewing bilinguality in a framework of metalinguistic awareness, Segalowitz (1977) suggests that the internalisation of two languages rather than one will result in a more complex, better-equipped 'mental calculus' enabling the child to alternate between two systems of rules in the manipulation of symbols. In the same vein, Lambert (1987) suggests that the bilingual child develops some sort of a tri-dimensional view of language, a stereoscopic perception to which the monolingual child does not have access. This deeper level of processing would lead to a greater cognitive flexibility and a more developed metalinguistic awareness. We speak of metalinguistic awareness when referring to the processes, and of creativity or flexibility when referring to the results of these processes in language behaviour.

In the 1990s several scholars analysed the development of bilinguality in relation to the development of linguistic awareness. For example, some authors argue that bilingual children may have greater cognitive control of information processing than do monolingual children, and that this provides them with the necessary foundation for metalinguistic ability (Bialystok & Ryan, 1985a; Bialystok, 1991). Because experiencing with two languages enhances the awareness of the analysis and control components of language processing, different processing systems develop in order from the ones that operate with one language to serve two linguistic systems. However, before we discuss the role of metalinguistic competence in bilinguality further and propose a theoretical model of bilinguality (see Chapter 5) we review here the existing empirical evidence on the relationship between bilinguality and cognitive development.

4.2   COGNITIVE CONSEQUENCES OF BILINGUALITY

Empirical research on the cognitive consequences of bilingual development can be divided into two periods. The studies, mainly psychometric ones, conducted before the 1960s in which negative consequences are more frequently reported than positive ones; and the period from the 1960s onwards in which studies demonstrating positive effects by far outnumber research which mentions negative effects. An important turning point came in 1962 with the publication of a study by Peal & Lambert: the authors had taken great care in defining concepts they used and in controlling several psychometric aspects of the study.

Although, to date, it is more than 30 years since solid empirical evidence has been available on the positive relationship between bilinguality and general intellectual functioning, and some very persuasive arguments have been put forward in favour of definite cognitive advantages for bilingual children, the stereotype of negative consequences still survives with a number of professional people, such as doctors and teachers who are often the ones to counsel parents in decision-making. For example, it is not uncommon in Europe, Canada or the USA to find anecdotal evidence of teachers who counsel immigrant parents to abandon their mother tongue in favour of the school language, that is the language of the host country. If the parents do not have an excellent command of the host language, this can lead to negative consequences as the child is no longer exposed to an adequate linguistic model in the home. As we shall see later, a strong support of the mother tongue in the home and in the community typically benefits the child's academic results.

4.2.1   Early studies on the cognitive consequences of bilingual development

Early studies on the relationship between bilinguality and cognitive development, sometimes undertaken in order to demonstrate the negative consequences of bilingual development, supported the idea that bilingual children suffered from academic retardation, had a lower IQ and were socially maladjusted as compared with monolingual children. Bilinguality was viewed as the cause of an inferior intelligence. Suffice it to mention the studies by Pintner & Keller (1922), who reported a 'linguistic handicap' in bilingual children, and Saer (1923), who spoke of 'mental confusion' to describe the bilingual's cognitive functioning. For a critical review of these early studies we refer the reader to Darcy (1953) and Peal & Lambert (1962). The evidence from biographies, such as the ones by Ronjat (1913) and Leopold (1939–49) – published in the same period and reporting no negative effect for the development but rather a number of advantages described in terms of verbal flexibility and a greater awareness of the arbitrary character of language – was largely ignored by psychometricians.

Early models of bilingual development postulated that bilingualism inevitably led to a diminished functioning in the two languages. One such tentative explanation of the early research results is that of Macnamara (1966), who attributes the lag in verbal intelligence on the part of bilinguals to a 'balance effect'. According to him, proficiency in L_1 diminishes as proficiency in L_2 increases, so that the sum of the two linguistic proficiencies cannot be superior to the monolingual's proficiency. It does not account for the fact that many bilingual children achieve a high level of competence in both languages and can, as we shall see later in this chapter, surpass their monolingual counterparts in each language; neither does it account for the early research results stemming from the biographies written in the first half of the twentieth century.

A number of methodological criticisms may be levelled at these early psychometric studies:

- the bilingual subjects were often not comparable with monolingual controls in terms of socio-economic background or proficiency in the language of testing;
- bilinguals were often selected on the basis of coming from an immigrant home, having a foreign last name or speaking a foreign language at home;
- the very notion of bilinguality was not adequately defined and tests were often administered in the subjects' weaker language.

Failure to control for the level of the skills in the language of testing, the socio-economic differences and the test bias accounts probably for most of the negative findings in the earlier studies (Lambert, 1977). These variables have been better controlled in more recent studies which make use of more elaborate experimental designs.

4.2.2 The relationship between bilinguality and intelligence: the milestone of the Peal & Lambert study

It was not until the late 1950s that the first of a series of rigorous experimental studies were carried out. Peal & Lambert (1962) compared English–French bilingual ten-year-old elementary-school pupils in Montreal with their monolingual counterparts in each language in order to pinpoint the intellectual components of the bilingual deficit. In contrast with earlier research, great care was taken in their methodological design. Besides matching the groups for age, sex and socio-economic level, the authors also controlled for language proficiency: they calculated a 'balance score' on the basis of tests of vocabulary and association as well as on the basis of a self-evaluation scale in the two languages. Bilingual subjects had to achieve high scores in both languages in order to qualify, whereas monolinguals had to have very low scores on one of the languages.

The bilingual group scored significantly higher than the monolingual controls for most of the measures. Bilinguals scored higher than the monolinguals on tests of verbal and non-verbal intelligence. The bilinguals also showed patterns of a more diversified structure of intelligence. Peal & Lambert suggested that the higher scores of the bilinguals on intelligence measures could be attributed to greater mental flexibility and a greater facility in concept formation. They attributed this to the bilinguals' ability to manipulate two symbolic systems and thus analyse underlying semantic features in greater detail. These results were confirmed in a follow-up study (Anisfeld, 1964).

Since the Peal & Lambert study, a large number of experiments have confirmed and refined their findings. Some comments have been addressed to the fact that they limited their research to balanced bilinguals. This problem, for instance, has been discussed by McNab (1979). She argues that there is no evidence that becoming bilingual leads to cognitive advancement because, by selecting balanced bilingual subjects, one might introduce a bias in favour of more intelligent children; furthermore, non-balanced bilingual children might score lower on cognitive functioning measures to begin with. This criticism has been countered by improvements in statistical methodology which allow for testing of alternative causal models. Hakuta & Diaz (1985), in their study of Spanish-dominant bilingual children, found that more balanced bilingual children scored higher on non-verbal intelligence tests; a stepwise multiple-regression analysis enabled them to demonstrate that the model which claims that degree of bilingualism affects non-verbal intelligence fits the data better than the model claiming the reverse directionality. In the same vein, Scott (1973) found a causal link between bilinguality and divergent thinking in children in the process of becoming bilingual.

The Peal & Lambert study has had an enormous impact on the study of the field. As mentioned above several dozens of studies have confirmed their findings and also refined the notion of cognitive flexibility. In each of the three decades following 1962 the number of empirical studies on the cognitive consequences of bilingualism have almost doubled (Reynolds, 1991). More recently researchers have taken care to verify the degree of bilingual competence and have taken into account the variables which can potentially influence the outcome. Furthermore, the theoretical issues of the relationship between cognitive development and multilingual experience have also been addressed; this is described in the following sections.

4.2.3   The nature of the bilingual's cognitive advantages[3]

Ronjat (1913) and Leopold (1939–49) had already drawn attention to the bilingual child's cognitive and verbal flexibility without being precise about its nature. Since the Peal & Lambert (1962) study, numerous empirical studies in various countries in the western World, Asia and Africa with diverse language and culture combinations and using different cognitive measures have detailed the various aspects of the cognitive advantages of the bilingual child. Since the 1960s most researchers have paid growing attention to methodological issues and research design: special attention has been paid to the level of bilingual competence, some studies referring only to balanced bilinguals, others making a distinction between high and low bilinguals. Studies in the 1960s and 1970s tend to focus on outcomes (cognitive flexibility) whereas more recent experiments try rather to analyse processes (metalinguistic awareness). The vast majority of studies are cross-sectional, although some studies are longitudinal (e.g. Hakuta & Diaz, 1985). Altogether the growing body of research suggests that bilingual children reach a deeper level of information processing which leads to a greater metalinguistic awareness and a greater degree of verbal creativity.

To sum up, the following advantages of bilingualism have been mentioned in studies conducted after the Peal & Lambert study:

- a greater ability in reconstructing perceptual situations (Balkan, 1970);
- superior results on verbal and non-verbal intelligence, verbal originality and verbal divergence tests (Cummins & Gulutsan, 1974);
- a greater sensitivity to semantic relations between words (Ianco-Worrall, 1972; Cummins, 1978); higher scores on Piagetian concept-formation tasks (Liedtke & Nelson, 1968);
- better performance in rule-discovery tasks (Bain, 1975); a better performance with traditional psychometric school tests (WISC-R Block Design) (Gorrell, Bregman, McAllistair & Lipscombe, 1982);
- a greater degree of divergent thinking (Scott, 1973; Da Silveira, 1989): Ben-Zeev (1972; 1977a) observed that English–Hebrew bilinguals had a greater facility in solving non-verbal perceptual tasks and in performing grouping tasks.

Bilinguals are also better at verbal-transformation and symbol-substitution tasks (Ekstrand, 1981); are better at correction of ungrammatical sentences (Diaz, 1985) and at analogical reasoning tasks (Diaz & Klinger, 1991). (For further details, see Diaz & Klinger, 1991; Hamers, 1991; 1996.)

Some research also indicates that the cognitive advantages of bilinguality might extend to non-verbal tasks, e.g. bilingual children show greater originality in creative thinking (Torrance, Gowan, Wu & Aliotti, 1970); Powers & Lopez (1985) observed that four-year-old bilinguals outperform monolinguals not only in following complex instructions but also in perceptual-motor coordination. Bilinguals score higher in analogical reasoning (Diaz, 1985), visual-spatial tasks (Hakuta & Diaz, 1985) and classification tasks (Diaz & Padilla, 1985). Bilinguals also outperform monolinguals in some aspects of matrix-transposition tasks (Ben Zeev, 1977a).

While there are indications that creativity differences between bilinguals and monolinguals might be universal and might therefore be attributable essentially to the child's bilingual experience, some aspects of creativity seem to be influenced by cultural particularities. koh (1980) – comparing the development of bilingual children in Nigeria (bilingual in Yoruba and English) and Wales (Welsh–English) with matched monolinguals in both countries – found that the bilinguals, aged from 9–11, generally scored higher on measures of divergent thinking and verbal creativity; however, on non-verbal creativity tests the Welsh bilinguals scored significantly higher than the Nigerian bilinguals, who did not differ from the monolinguals. Cultural variations in the type of cognitive tasks on which bilinguals show an advantage have also been noted in a study comparing Spanish–English and Vietnamese–English bilinguals (Gorrell, Bregman, McAllister & Lipscombe, 1982).

The conclusions that bilingual children may be potentially more creative than monolinguals are further supported by a number of experiments in India. One such set of studies, conducted by Mohanty and his associates, with bilingual and monolingual children from the same tribal cultural background[4] is of particular interest because bilingual and monolingual groups are comparable on a large number of socio-cultural variables: Kond bilingual children in the State of Orissa, speaking Kui (a Dravidian tribal language) and Oriya (an Indo-European language which is also the state's official language), scored significantly higher than matched Kond monolingual children in Oriya on measures of metalinguistic ability, Raven's Progressive Matrices and Piagetian conservation tasks (Mohanty & Babu, 1983; Pattnaik & Mohanty, 1984; Mohanty & Das, 1987; Mohanty, 1994a). Furthermore, the bilinguals were also better at detecting syntactic ambiguity. In fact, bilingually schooled children outperformed monolingually schooled children on all intelligence and information-processing tasks, but the unschooled bilinguals did not significantly outperform their monolingual counterparts on all measures. Mohanty (1994a) interprets these results as a manifestation of a higher metalinguistic ability and cognitive flexibility developed by the bilinguals; thus, bilingual experience may result in the development of a greater ability to reflect on language, especially when combined with cognitive activities such as the ones developed in schooling.

In the 1980s and 1990s a large number of studies focused on metalinguistic tasks and evidenced further the relationship between bilinguality, cognitive development and metalinguistic awareness (Bialystok, 1990; 1992; Perregaux, 1994). For example, Kessler & Quinn (1982; 1987) reported that bilingual children performed better on problem-solving tasks than their monolingual counterparts; they interpret these results as evidence of greater metalinguistic competence and better-developed creative processes. Bilingual children are better at detection of language mixing (Diaz, 1985). Bilingual children aged from 5–7 outperform monolinguals on metalinguistic tasks which require attention to grammatical features, but not on tasks requiring attention to meaning (Bialystok, 1988). The author suggests that bilingual and monolingual children might call to a different extent on strategies of analysis and control in language processing (this issue is further discussed in Section 5.1.4). Bialystok (1988) also demonstrated that balanced and near-balanced bilingual children systematically outperform partially bilingual children, who, in turn, outperform the monolingual children in solving metalinguistic problems. Diaz & Padilla (1985) found a positive relationship between degree of bilinguality and the use of self-regulatory utterances. Comparing literacy development in monolingual and bilingual children Perregaux (1994) found that bilinguals were better at deletion of phonemic units of non-words, a metalinguistic skill of literacy acquisition.

Although metalinguistic awareness seems to be linked to the level of bilingual competence attained (Bialystok, 1988), there is evidence that it develops at an early stage of bilinguality. Rubin & Turner (1989) observed that 6;6-year-old Anglophone children who had been in a French immersion program for six months obtained superior results on a phonemic segmentation task than did monolingual peers. Yelland, Pollard & Mercuri (1993) demonstrated that, after six months of instruction, 6–7-year-old marginal bilinguals, i.e. Anglophone children who received one hour of Italian instruction a week, showed a higher word awareness than monolingual children who received no L_2 training. Similarly, Galambos & Hakuta (1988) and Galambos & Goldin-Meadow (1990) mention a higher awareness for syntactic structures in children in the process of becoming bilingual through instructional programs. Arnberg & Arnberg (1992) observed that bilingual children aged 1;8 to 4;0 who displayed awareness of the two languages mixed the two languages to a lesser extent than children who did not. The authors interpret these results as evidence that awareness helps the child in organising the two languages and in eliminating a possible confusion between them.

Reviewing the empirical evidence on metalinguistic awareness in bilinguals, Mohanty & Perregaux (1997) conclude that bilingual children probably develop special reflective skills which generalise to other metacognitive processes. Developing these skills enables the child to exercise a greater control over his cognitive functions and use them in more effective ways; he will therefore improve his performance in a variety of academic tasks. The authors assume that, because of their superior metalinguistic skills and greater linguistic sensitivity, bilinguals are better learners.

Several authors have demonstrated that even when bilinguals and monolinguals are equated for cognitive functioning, the former may possess better verbal abilities. A number of studies that have already been mentioned (e.g. Ben-Zeev, 1972; 1977a; Okoh, 1980; Mohanty, 1994a) report bilinguals as being superior in a variety of verbal tasks:

- analytic processing of verbal input;
- verbal creativity;
- awareness of the arbitrariness of language and of the relation between words, referent and meaning; and
- perception of linguistic ambiguity.

Evidence from studies of bilingual education by immersion also points in the same direction: bilingual pupils achieve better results than their monolingual counterparts in tests of complex syntactic structure and in mother-tongue composition (Swain & Lapkin, 1982).

According to Diaz & Klinger (1991) the findings of empirical research conducted since the Peal & Lambert study can be summarised as follows:

- bilingual children show consistent advantages in verbal and non-verbal cognitive tasks;
- bilingual children show advanced metalinguistic abilities, especially in their control of language processing;
- cognitive and metalinguistic advantages can be observed in bilingual situations that involve a systematic use of both languages, such as simultaneous acquisition and bilingual education;
- the cognitive effects of bilinguality appear early in the process of bilingualisation and do not require high levels of bilingual proficiency or a balanced competence.

Bilingual children make more use of language for verbal mediation (Diaz & Padilla, 1985); this leads the child to make a greater use of language as a regulatory tool for cognition.

4.2.4   Negative consequences of bilingual experience

Although since the 1960s the studies reporting positive effects of bilingual development by far outnumber the studies reporting cognitive disadvantages associated with bilinguality, there are still a number of studies reporting negative effects which have to be explained. Some simply mention the negative effects, some mention negative effects along with positive effects, and a few mention an intellectual handicap.

Tsushima & Hogan (1975) found lower scores on tests of verbal ability among 10–11-year-old Japanese–English bilinguals than among monolinguals matched for non-verbal intelligence. Negative effects of bilingual development have also been reported together with positive results for the same children, according to the type of task they are asked to perform. Ben-Zeev (1977b) found that, while Spanish–English bilingual children showed some delay in terms of vocabulary and grammatical structure when compared with monolingual English-speaking peers, at the same time they were better at verbal transformations, analysis of structural complexity, classification and non-verbal tasks requiring perceptual analysis. Lemmon & Goggin (1989) observed that Spanish–English bilingual college students in the USA – carefully selected as proficient in both languages though not balanced – who were given an array of cognitive tasks scored lower than English monolinguals on three cognitive tasks (WAIS-R, the Cattell Culture Fair test and the Guilford fluency/flexibility test). However, when they made a distinction between a group of low bilinguals (who, although proficient enough in English to be considered bilingual, scored low on the Gates–McGinitie Reading Test in their mother tongue) and a group of high bilinguals (who scored high on the Reading test), they observed that the high bilinguals outperformed the low bilinguals on 7 of the 10 cognitive measures. When they paired the high bilingual group with an equally proficient (on the reading test) monolingual group they found no differences on the cognitive tasks.

In a UNESCO investigation in Sweden Skutnabb-Kangas & Toukomaa (1976) found that Finnish migrant children of average non-verbal IQ attending Swedish comprehensive schools were considerably below Finnish and Swedish norms in their literacy skills in L_1 and L_2. They further observed that those children who migrated at age 10 achieved a level in both languages fairly comparable to those norms, whereas children who migrated at an earlier age did not. They also found that the extent to which the mother tongue was developed prior to migration was related to achievement in both languages; from these findings they postulated that competence in the mother tongue had to be sufficiently established before the child could successfully acquire a second language. Similar results are mentioned by Pfaff (1981) in her study on children of Gastarbeiters ('guest workers') in Germany.

Almost all studies mentioning negative effects have been conducted in Western cultures with children of minority groups schooled in the majority language. It must be noted that the more recent studies mentioning negative effects cannot be faulted on the grounds of methodological weakness; for this reason we must find an explanation which takes into account the negative as well as the positive consequences of early bilingual experience.

4.2.5   Explaining positive and negative effects

Most of the studies reporting the positive consequences of bilingual experience also report that bilinguals seem to develop a higher awareness of the arbitrary nature of the linguistic sign. Genesee (1981b) suggested that this increased capacity of the bilingual for dissociating a signifier from its signified could be a manifestation of a more general cognitive ability to analyse the underlying conceptual characteristics in information processing. The empirical evidence on the cognitive development of bilinguals is far from giving a complete picture of those cognitive aspects that might benefit from a bilingual experience. It is reasonable to assume that not all thought processes are enhanced by bilingual experience and that those cognitive tasks which rely more on language will benefit most from that experience.

Ben-Zeev (1977a) has put forward the following hypothesis concerning the cognitive advantages accruing from an early bilingual experience: it would seem that the bilingual child develops a strategy for analysing the linguistic input which enables him to overcome the potential interference arising from a bilingual environment. She distinguishes four mechanisms for resolving interference at the structural level of language:

(1)   a greater capacity for language analysis;
(2)   sensitivity to feedback cues from surface linguistic structure and/or verbal and situational context;
(3)   maximisation of structural differences between languages; and
(4)   neutralisation of structure within a language.

These four mechanisms, developed in the first place to respond to a bilingual environment, are generalised to other information-processing tasks and thus benefit the overall cognitive growth of the child.

Reynolds (1991) suggests that the necessity for the bilingual child to control two language systems improves the efficiency of the metacomponential system of intelligence and his preformance in a variety of meta-cognitive and metalinguistic tasks. His approach is based on Sternberg's (1988) triarchic model of intellectual functioning.[5] The metacomponential system of intelligence controls intellectual functioning by constructing plans, and monitoring and evaluating information processing; it is responsible for a variety of processes such as understanding, selecting strategies, deciding how to perform them and keeping track of what has been done and what remains to be done in problem solving. It is the more efficient use of this metacomponential dimension of intelligence that would give the bilingual advantages in cognitive functioning.

Negative consequences of bilingual experience have been described in terms of a cognitive deficit. The notion of 'semilingualism' has been used to describe the child who fails to reach monolingual proficiency in literacy skills in any language and might be unable to develop his linguistic potential (Skutnabb-Kangas & Toukomaa, 1976). 'Semilingualism' is defined as a linguistic handicap which prevents the individual from acquiring the linguistic skills appropriate to his linguistic potential in any of his languages. It does not imply failure to communicate in ordinary everyday situations since children labelled as 'semilingual' are judged to be quite fluent; but it is suggested that this fluency is only superficial and that it masks a deficit in the knowledge of the structure of both languages.

The use of the notion of 'semilingualism' as an explanatory device has been criticised on the following grounds: the notion is ill-defined; 'linguistic potential' is unexplained; and the deficit is measured only by comparison with standardised norms obtained through traditional psychometric tests and academic results (Brent-Palmer, 1979). From these criticisms, no conclusion can be drawn as to the existence of a linguistic/cognitive deficit; rather, there is enough counter evidence to suggest that sociocultural factors are responsible for poor normative linguistic achievement and scholastic results (Troike, 1984). Many immigrant groups who also come from a different cultural background, but who do not face lower than average socio-economic conditions, perform linguistically and cognitively at least as well as monolinguals. As Troike (1984) points out, if a linguistic handicap resulting from bilingual experience were responsible for poor results in linguistic tests and academic tasks, then the Hispanic Americans – who are socio-economically more deprived than the White Americans from Anglo-Celtic backgrounds but less so than the Black Americans – should perform worse on language tests than both these monolingual groups; this is however not the case: Hispanics Americans perform worse than White Americans but better than Black Americans. It becomes difficult, then, to implicate language proficiency alone as an explanatory factor for poor performance (for further discussion, see Section 11.4.2).

4.2.5.1   *Developmental interdependence and threshold hypotheses*

Cummins (1976; 1979; 1981; 1984a; 1984b; 1991) attempted to explain the contradictory positive and negative results in the following way: One has to assume, first, a 'developmental interdependence' hypothesis and, second, a 'minimal threshold of linguistic competence' hypothesis. The first hypothesis suggests that competence in a second language is a function of competence in the mother tongue, at least at the beginning of exposure to the second language. The threshold hypothesis implies that a first-language competence threshold has to be crossed in order to avoid cognitive deficit

Language competence	Type of bilinguality	State of equilibrium	Cognitive outcome
+ ↑	Additive: high level of competence in both languages	Tends towards equilibrium	Positive effects
Upper threshold of language competence			
	Neutral: high level of competence in at least one of the two languages	Balanced or dominant	No effects
Lower threshold of language competence			
− ↓	'Semilingualism': low level of competence in both languages	Balanced or dominant	Negative effects

Figure 4.1   Cognitive effects of different types of bilinguality (adapted from Cummins, 1979: 230)

linked to childhood bilinguality, and that a second-language competence threshold must be passed if bilinguality is to positively influence cognitive functioning. This is schematised in Figure 4.1.

According to Cummins, the twofold threshold hypothesis explains the apparently contradictory results from the different studies. The first threshold must be reached in order to avoid an intellectual handicap as a consequence of childhood bilingual experience; if this lower threshold is not attained, a below-normal level of competence in both languages might result. Above the first threshold and below the second a handicap will be avoided. But it is only when the second threshold is passed that bilingual experience can have a positive effect on cognitive processing and that competence in both languages tends towards balance. Empirical evidence in support of this construct is found in a number of studies. For example, Duncan & de Avila (1979) found that Hispanic-minority school children in the USA who had developed high levels of proficiency in L_1 and L_2 performed significantly better than monolinguals and other non-proficient bilinguals from the same cultural sample on cognitive tasks. Similarly Hakuta & Diaz (1984) found that fluent bilinguals performed better on cognitive tasks than their non-fluent counterparts. The levels of language competence cannot be determined in absolute terms, rather they 'vary according to the children's stage of cognitive development and the academic demands of different stages of schooling' (Cummins, 1979: 230). The level of language competence seems to act as an intervening variable and play a crucial role in determining the effect of bilingual experience on future cognitive development.

Cummins' other hypothesis, that of developmental interdependence, postulates that the level of competence in L_2 is partly a function of the competence developed in L_1 at the start of exposure to L_2. When certain language functions are sufficiently developed in L_1 it is likely that massive exposure to L_2 will lead to a good competence in L_2 without detriment to competence in L_1. A high level of competence in L_1 is thus related to a high level of competence in L_2. In support of this hypothesis Cummins (1984a) reports, for example, on a Carpinteria Spanish-language pre-school program in California: Spanish-speaking pre-school children who scored much lower on a school readiness test compared with English-speaking peers were exposed to a variety of language-enriching experiences in their mother tongue; at elementary-school entry these children outperformed Spanish-speaking controls in both English and Spanish and compared favourably with English controls on readiness skills (see Section 11.4.2.1).

The interdependence hypothesis has received support from a number of studies. Hakuta & Diaz (1985) found a correlation between English and Spanish academic skills of Hispanic students; this correlation increased over time as the pupils attained a higher degree of bilinguality. Lemmon & Goggin (1989) found that when bilinguals scored high on a reading test in their mother tongue they would also score high on the cognitive tasks in both languages. There is ample evidence that children transfer cognitive functioning acquired in L_1 to the new L_2 at school and, conversely, transfer newly acquired cognitive skills in L_2 to their L_1 (Cummins, 1984a; Harley, Hart & Lapkin, 1986). These observations also extend to immigrant children who have developed academic skills in their L_1 before entering school in the host-country language (Skutnabb-Kangas & Toukomaa, 1976).

The interdependence hypothesis has received support from studies conducted with non-European children living in the West as well as with those living in their own country. The interdependence hypothesis was supported by studies with Vietnamese and Japanese students in North America (Cummins, Swain, Nakajima, Handscombe, Green & Tran, 1984; Cummins & Nakajima, 1987). In Benin, West Africa, Da Silveira (1989) found consistent cross-language correlations for decontextualised tasks: Fon-speaking children, schooled in French, who scored high on cognitive-linguistic tasks in French (Peabody, cloze test, narration, results in the national exam and school results in maths) scored equally high on these tasks in Fon, although they had never performed similar tasks in Fon prior to the study; a regression analysis indicated that the results in maths were a consequence of both the competence in French and the competence in Fon.

These results were interpreted as proof of a linguistic interdependence at the cognitive level (Da Silveira, 1989; Hamers, 1989; Da Silveira & Hamers, 1990).

Decontextualised language skills are highly correlated across languages. Davidson, Kline & Snow (1986), studying indicators of decontextualised language (definitions and definite noun phrases) in French–English bilingual children, found that the correlations between a metalinguistic task in both languages, i.e. the ability to give definitions in French and in English (a skill with a high metalinguistic component), were higher than the correlations between decontextualised and contextualised skills in one language.

Although Cummins did not develop the idea that the interdependence is bi-directional, there is empirical support in favour of this from a study of Swedish children learning English as a second language in Sweden (Holmstrand, 1979): it was found that elementary-school children who already had a high competence in their mother tongue and who started to learn a foreign language at an early age would improve their competence in their mother tongue more than peers who did not have exposure to a foreign language. This evidence suggests that the interdependence hypothesis works in both directions and that language training in one language might be helpful for attaining a higher level of competence in the other language.

According to Cummins (1984a), instruction that develops first-language literacy skills is not only developing these skills but is also developing a deeper conceptual and linguistic competence that is strongly related to the development of general literacy and academic skills. In other words, there is a common cognitive proficiency that underlies behaviour in both languages. The interdependence or common underlying proficiency principle implies, therefore, that experience with either language can promote development of cognitive-linguistic skills, given proper motivation and exposure to both languages.

But what does Cummins mean by 'language proficiency'? The term is conceptualised in such a way that the developmental interrelationships between academic performance and language proficiency in both L_1 and L_2 can be explained (Cummins, 1984b). Note that this model is proposed only in relation to the development of academic skills in bilingual education and is not necessarily appropriate to other skills and other contexts of bilingual development. The author suggests that cognitive academic proficiency can be conceptualised along two independent continua: the first relates to the degree of contextual support available for expressing and receiving meaning (from context-embedded to context-reduced); the second refers to the degree of cognitive involvement in the verbal activity (from cognitively undemanding to cognitively demanding). Thus, a verbal task may be cognitively demanding or not and, at the same time, be more or less context-embedded. Many of the linguistic demands of the school rely on context-reduced and cognitively demanding language behaviour. Most of the studies reporting negative consequences of early bilingual experience are concerned with measures of context-reduced and cognitively demanding behaviour of children who may not have developed the necessary underlying proficiency.

In other words, when bilingual development does not result in cognitive advantages it is always in cases where the children did not possess the skills prerequisite for literacy. It might well be that here we are dealing with a literacy or a metalinguistic problem, not a threshold of linguistic competence: metalinguistic awareness is different from ordinary linguistic communication in the sense that it calls on different cognitive skills, and bilingual children differ from monolingual children on literacy and metalinguistic tasks (Bialystok & Ryan, 1985a; Mohanty, 1994a).

Cummins' model is relevant insofar as it attempts to explain apparently contradictory evidence; it is also useful in providing a model for bilingual education (see Section 11.4.2); however, it lacks explanatory adequacy. On the one hand, it remains silent on the issue of simultaneous bilinguistic development and its cognitive correlates. On the other hand, it fails to explain why some children attain the upper threshold while others never reach the lower one. It may also be an oversimplification to define the threshold levels purely on the basis of language criteria (McLaughlin, 1984). Furthermore, Cummins is vague about his definition of a cognitively demanding task. Finally, cognitive development is also influenced by sociocultural factors apart from language (Hamers & Blanc, 1983).

4.2.5.2 The additivity–subtractivity theory: focus on the sociocultural context

Lambert (1974; 1977) suggests that the roots of bilinguality are to be found in several aspects of the social psychological mechanisms involved in language behaviour, particularly in the perception of the relative social status of both languages by the individual. He was the first to draw attention to the fact that different types of bilinguality may result depending on the sociocultural context in which bilingual experience occurs. He distinguishes between an additive and a subtractive form of bilinguality. In its additive form bilingual development is such that both languages and both cultures will bring complementary positive elements to the child's overall development; this situation is found when both the community and the family attribute positive values to the two languages; the learning of an L_2 will in no case threaten to replace L_1.

Subtractive bilinguality, on the other hand, develops when the two languages are competing rather than complementary; this form will evolve when an ethnolinguistic minority rejects its own cultural values in favour of those of an economically and culturally more prestigious group. In this case, the more prestigious L_2 will tend to replace L_1 in the child's repertoire. This happens, for example, when a minority child is schooled through an L_2 socially more prestigious than his own mother tongue. The degree of bilinguality will 'reflect some stage in the subtraction of the ethnic language and the associated culture, and their replacement with another' (Lambert, 1977: 19). This subtraction will manifest itself at several levels and will influence intellectual development and personality; language competence which first developed via the mother tongue will be affected.

Lambert's views explain why a cognitive advantage linked to bilingual experience is found primarily either among bilingual children from mixed-lingual families or among children from a dominant social group who receive their schooling through the medium of a relatively less prestigious L_2, while the subtractive form is met among children from ethnolinguistic minorities schooled through a dominant, more prestigious L_2. In the additive case, the two languages receive important positive values from the community and consequently from the child himself, whereas in the subtractive condition L_1 is little valorised compared with L_2. Lambert's model relies on the sociocultural environment playing a role in the development of bilinguality. It accords with a more general view of child development: for Bruner (1966) the cultural environment plays a major role in the child's growth once the symbolic stage is reached; culture then serves as a catalyst for cognitive growth. It is therefore crucial to focus on the cultural environment in which bilingual development occurs and to understand its role in the development of bilinguality.

4.3   SOCIAL NETWORKS, LANGUAGE VALORISATION AND LITERACY: THE SOCIOCULTURAL INTERDEPENDENCE HYPOTHESIS

By pointing out the relevance of the sociocultural environment, Lambert stresses the role played by social psychological mechanisms in the development of bilinguality, particularly those involved in the internalisation of societal values. Lambert also introduces the notion of an interdependence hypothesis, but at the level of the internalisation of sociocultural values and language statuses: it is the relative status between the two languages and its internalisation that will determine the nature of bilinguality.

There is ample empirical evidence to support the sociocultural interdependence hypothesis. For example, Long & Padilla (1970) and Bhatnagar (1980) demonstrate that pupils obtained better academic results when their low-status L_1 was valorised and fully used in the home than when L_1 was neglected in the home in favour of L_2. Similarly, Dubé & Herbert (1975) found that school results and language proficiency in both languages improved when the mother tongue was valorised and used in the school system. There is also ample evidence stemming from research on immersion programs (see Section 11.4.1.2) that when a child is a member of a dominant ethnolinguistic group, for whom L_1 is valorised in the community, schooling through the medium of L_2 may be a way to develop high bilinguistic skills, possibly with positive cognitive effects.

However, Lambert's approach is based essentially on correlational evidence; his theoretical construct lacks explanatory adequacy in respect of developmental processes and the development of the socio-psychological mechanisms involved in shaping cognitive growth. The equation 'bilinguality = cognitive advantage' or 'bilinguality = cognitive deficit' may be too simple. Both equations are possible: under the right conditions, bilingual experience may have positive effects on cognitive processes; under adverse sociocultural conditions, bilingual experience may hinder cognitive growth. We still know very little about the social psychological mechanisms that intervene between the socio-cultural environment and intellectual functioning. Lambert's model draws attention to the existence of a relationship but it does not explain how this relationship develops.

4.3.1   Bilinguality and social networks

Language is present in its different aspects in the child's environment and is used to a varying extent and for different functions by speakers with and around the child in his social network. By social network we understand the sum of all the interpersonal relations one individual establishes with others over time. The relevance of a network, centred on the individual, lies in the fact that, on the one hand, it provides the child with a functional and formal linguistic model (or models) and with shared schemata acquired through routines, and, on the other hand, it transmits to the child the system of societal values, attitudes and perceptions relating to the languages and their users (Blanc & Hamers, 1987).

All social network studies, whether they relate to language or not, have shown that close-knit, territorially based social networks act as norm-enforcement mechanisms by exerting pressure on their members to adopt the network norms, values and behaviour, including those pertaining to language (Milroy, 1980). Close-knit network structures are associated with the maintenance of non-standard linguistic norms, whereas loosened structures tend to be associated with changing norms and a shift towards a legitimised standard language. Social networks are important inasmuch as they generate a social status and attribute a place in the social hierarchy (Breitborde, 1983).

In the early years the child is normally surrounded by a close-knit personal network which is often territorially based and consists of clusters of relations where ties of kinship and friendship predominate: first, the older generation of parents and relatives and the contemporary generation of siblings and peers; then, as he grows older, his personal network widens to include neighbours, school peers and teachers. The kinds of norms and values and the language model to which the child is exposed and which he will internalise depend on

(1) whether there is one or more functional and formal model(s) of language around the child;
(2) whether his network is homogeneous or heterogeneous, that is, all its members have a similar language behaviour or some members have a different language behaviour from others; and
(3) whether or not there are competing values and norms.

The relevance of the immediate surroundings for the development of binguality is of the utmost importance. The interaction with the significant others will, through the establishment of routines, shape the form–function mapping necessary for the development of language. In the case of bilingual surroundings we must consider two aspects:

(1) the functions for which language in general and the respective languages in particular are used; and
(2) the degree of relative valorisation attributed to each of the languages.

If a language function is present and used with the child, it is at least valorised by those who use it. However this valorisation varies from one surrounding to another: highly valorised functions may be seldom or never used in families as, for example, the literacy function in an illiterate family; on the other hand, a little-valorised language may be used in the family because of a lack of competence in a more valorised language as, for example, the use of a minority language in an immigrant family. However, more often than not, valorisation and use are closely related (Hamers, 1994).

Family networks are of primary importance in bilingual development. The language used by the parents in interactions will determine the linguistic forms used by the child; for example Goodz (1994) observed that children use language mixing more when parents do than when they do not. Although not always mentioned explicitly, the care taken by parents to valorise both languages in the case of simultaneous bilinguality is obvious. In these cases of planned bilinguality, usually found in middle-class families, parents are careful to maintain both languages, often through the application of Grammont's Principle (Grammont, 1902) and to use them for a variety of functions as evidenced by the descriptions of bilinguistic development discussed in Section 3.1. The same attitudes can be found in some immigrant families who maintain their home language for all functions in the family environment while the child acquires a second language outside the home. In planned bilinguality, parents generally adopt a variety of strategies to maintain the weaker language, such as stays in the country where that language is spoken or attending peer-group sessions. The attainment of balanced bilinguality, however, calls for interaction with peer groups and contacts with the broader language community (Arnberg, 1984). The school network is also crucial in the development of bilinguality: almost by definition the school valorises the literacy-oriented activities which are performed in the language of schooling.

The role of social networks in bilingual development is obvious. Most cases of bilingual biographies discussed in Section 3.1 mention the child's early awareness of social rules and capacity to choose the language as a function of the interlocutor. Mohanty (1994a) insists on the social aspects of multilingual development, and Rosenblum & Pinker (1983) mention that bilingual children attend more to the sociolinguistic factors associated with words than to their grammatical functions.

However, most cases of bilingual development are not carefully planned by parents but are more often the consequence of societal factors such as membership of a minority group, immigration or living in a multilingual setting. In these cases the valorisation of the different languages around the child are of the utmost importance. As we have already mentioned, negative consequences of bilingual experience are so far only evidenced in the schooling of minority children in Western countries. A lack of literacy-oriented activities around the bilingual child does not necessarily lead to a subtractive form of bilinguality. On the contrary, comparing unschooled bilingual with matched unschooled monolingual Kond children on a number of cognitive and metalinguistic tasks, Mohanty & Das (1987) came to the conclusion that the bilinguals outperformed the monolinguals. The authors attribute these results to the social valorisation of bilinguality in India and in the children's social networks.

Valorisation of L_1 and of literacy in the child's social network are both crucial for the development of literacy skills. Landry & Allard (1985) have demonstrated that, in a French-speaking minority setting in New Brunswick, the more the parents valorised the mother tongue, the better the children achieved at school. The authors conclude that negative perceptions of his mother tongue by the minority child can be avoided if L_1 is valorised in the child's social network. If, in addition, the school valorises the child's mother tongue, this reinforces the child's positive perception of his language. The importance of the valorisation process in the family is also demonstrated in a study by Tizard, Schofield & Hewison (1982): non-English-speaking school children in London who had difficulties in English reading skills benefited more from a program which valorised literacy-oriented activities in the home than their counterparts who received English reading remedial classes only.

That social-network characteristics play an important role in multilingual development is also demonstrated in a study by Hamers (1994): both Greek and Arabic first-generation Canadian children develop as highly fluent trilinguals, balanced in at least two of the three languages or as balanced bilinguals in the heritage language and one of the official languages of Canada, provided that the three or the two languages are used for literacy-oriented activities and provided they are valorised in the child's network. Valorisation and language use in the social network determine whether a child becomes balanced in three or in two languages, or dominant in the school language. In a Western country like Canada, valorisation of literacy-oriented activities in the mother tongue seems of the utmost importance. This is however not the case in other cultures: Da Silveira (1994) for example found that Fon-speaking children in Benin who are fluent in both languages and successful in cognitive activities valorise both languages for the role attributed to them by society: they valorise French in its cognitive function and Fon in its communicative function and as a symbol of ethnicity.

4.3.2   Bilinguality and literacy

Because of the importance of literacy for social integration, we have to ask the question why ethnolinguistic minorities do not attain the literacy norms. The educational aspects of the problem are dealt with in Chapter 11. In the present section we limit our discussion to the psychological processes involved in literacy and their possible link with bilinguality.

Literacy plays an important role in bilingual development; as already mentioned the cognitive outcome of bilingual development relies to a large extent on the valorisation of language for literacy-oriented activities, at least in Western cultures. The valorisation of literacy skills per se may have a positive effect on the child's representation of language: Clay (1976), for example, observes that in New Zealand English-medium schools Samoan children are more successful in learning to read than Maori children; the author attributes these results to the greater valorisation of literacy in the

Samoan community. Furthermore, both literacy and bilingual experience foster the development of metalinguistic awareness which plays a crucial role in enhancing cognitive development. Literacy must therefore be considered an important component in the cognitive development of bilingual children.

Literacy deals with the skills of reading and writing, but it refers to much more than the simple skill of encoding and decoding written language. It also has a social and a psychological dimension. In a psychological perspective literacy must be viewed as a cognitive skill which develops as a consequence of mastering the written language, a capacity to employ language as a tool for thinking and communicating (Calfee & Nelson-Barber, 1991); it is used in problem solving, hypothesis construction, and the building of representations. As a new skill it has an impact on cognitive growth in the sense that it empowers the mind and has an effect on language processing and cognitive functioning (Olson, 1988; Chang & Wells, 1990). Literacy, like other higher mental functions, is conditioned by its social context (Hiebert & Raphael, 1996).

Literacy modifies the way language processing is performed at all levels. There are major structural differences between the spoken and the written language: written language relies more heavily on idea units than spoken language (Chafe, 1985); it is decontextualised and depends more on lexicalisation than on the use of paralinguistic and non-verbal signals (Tannen, 1985); it calls upon a visual-spatial mode of speech which is represented as such in memory; it relies heavily on speech analysis; for example: one important skill to develop in reading is the capacity to analyse speech into phonemic segments and illiterate people are poor in this type of task (Bertelson, Morais, Alegria & Content, 1985). Literate people are better in the deletion of phonemic non-word units (Rieben & Perfetti, 1991). Phonological manipulation in the pre-school years is a good predictor of reading achievement (Bryant & Bradley, 1985a). Preschool literacy-related activities predict scholastic success (Wells, 1985a). Children who are skilled in handling the semantic and syntactic structures of language are better able to cope with reading (Torrance & Olson, 1985). Metalinguistic awareness at both the formal and the symbolic level is a precondition of literacy (Bialystok, 1991).

The very skills that develop with the onset of literacy are the ones that develop as a consequence of bilingual experience; for example: a greater linguistic awareness, more analysed language processing, and better developed metalinguistic skills. As is evident from the research reports cited above, bilingual children who start acquiring literacy seem to be advantaged compared to their monolingual counterparts.

For children who have early experience in literacy prerequisites, the bilingual experience is likely to promote their cognitive control to the point where they are able to solve metalinguistic problems (Bialystok & Ryan, 1985b). Empirical evidence indicates that bilingual children are more advanced than monolinguals in an array of metalinguistic tasks. For children who develop simultaneous infant bilinguality, the very situation of being confronted with two interchangeable languages, i.e. two labels for one concept, at a time when they are developing a functional representation of language as a cognitive tool may push them towards developing their analysed knowledge about language. For the child, developing an early representation that language is a cognitive organiser and that his two languages are interchangeable may facilitate the general development of analysed knowledge in all areas. This representation is facilitated further if the child's environment valorises both languages equally. For children who begin to acquire a representation of language as a cognitive tool through their L_1 and are then introduced at an early age to an L_2, this may have similar effects: the introduction of a new language to which they can apply their analytical ability will also prompt them to develop their metalinguistic skills further, thereby enhancing their ability to analyse knowledge.

4.3.3   The sociocultural and cognitive interdependence hypothesis

There is no doubt that sociocultural factors are responsible for the poor linguistic and scholastic results of many ethnolinguistic minorities. However, this need not be the case. Witness the many immigrant groups who also come from different cultural backgrounds but who do not face below average socio-economic conditions; individuals in these groups perform linguistically and cognitively at least as well as monolinguals (Troike, 1984). Schooling can be an important factor in the development of literacy. If we consider the two dimensions relevant to the development of additive bilinguality, that is the development of language in its cognitive use and the valorisation of language and language functions, several possibilities can occur, distributed on a continuum from additivity to subtractivity. At one end of the continuum there is the case of the child who lives in a bilingual social environment at home, in which both languages are valorised around him for both cognitive and communicative functions. At the other extreme there is the case of the child who lives in a unilingual home where the L_1 is little valorised and not used for cognitive functions; furthermore the child is schooled exclusively in a highly valorised language, which is an L_2 for him, but in which he has at best a limited communicative competence; in addition he has to acquire literacy through this language.

In Hamers & Blanc (1989) we suggested that the distinction between additive and subtractive bilinguality must be considered on a continuum

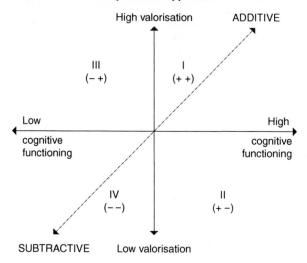

Figure 4.2　The sociocultural and cognitive dimensions of the additive–subtractive continuum (from Hamers & Blanc, 1989)

which is a resultant of two dimensions. The first dimension deals with the cognitive function of language, more specifically with the ability to analyse language and control linguistic cues. The second dimension refers to the degree of valorisation that the child attributes to language. This valorisation results from the child's internalisation of social values attributed to the languages in the community and the surrounding networks. At the additive end of the continuum, the cognitive function of language is well developed and both languages are highly valorised. Because the child valorises both languages to the same extent, he will perceive them as interchangeable. This perception will in turn enhance the overall cognitive functioning. At the other end of the continuum a child who is required to develop the cognitive literacy-oriented language skills in his first devalued language and who is required to develop these skills in a socially more valorised language of which he has little or no knowledge is likely to develop a subtractive form of bilinguality (Hamers & Blanc, 1982; Hamers, 1997). The sociocultural and cognitive dimensions of the additive–subtractive continuum are schematised in Figure 4.2.

The identification of all the conditions that are favourable to an additive form of bilinguality is still a long way off and raises a number of questions. To what extent is the child's perception of these social factors more important than the factors themselves? To what extent can an additive form of bilinguality develop in a subtractive context? In other words, how determining is the sociocultural context for the outcome of bilinguality and how far can the individual develop strategies and social psychological mechanisms that can modify the influence of the social context? The causal link between social psychological roots of bilinguality and their cognitive outcome is still little known. Not all the environmental factors which enable the child to reach the competence necessary for developing additive bilinguality have been identified. In other words, in order to have a better understanding of the development of bilinguality we must view it in relation to language valorisation in the social networks and in relation to the development of literacy.

Why is it that in a subtractive situation the bilingual child is less successful at cognitive tasks than his monolingual peer who also lacks these cognitive skills? First, because of the low value attached by society to his L_1 it is more difficult for this child to see the two languages as interchangeable and therefore to use them for socially valorised activities. Second, schooling reinforces this perception by introducing him to cognitive tasks exclusively in the majority language; he might then perceive the L_2 as the only language suitable for cognitive functioning. Third, whereas in language development it seems necessary for the child to develop a function before he can acquire the linguistic form to express it, the child is here required to learn new forms of language for a language function he has not yet developed.

4.4   CONCLUSION

We first analysed the relationship between bilinguality and cognition in terms of the positive and negative consequences of early bilingual experience for the cognitive development of the child. We looked at the relationship of bilinguality to intelligence and at the nature of the bilingual's cognitive advantages and disadvantages. Second, we examined two explanations, one in terms of the developmental interdependence and dual threshold hypotheses and the other in terms of the additivity–subtractivity model. We showed the importance of social networks, valorisation and the growth of literacy for the development of additive bilinguality and put forward a sociocultural and cognitive interdependence hypothesis to account for the empirical data. We suggested that bilinguality should be conceptualised on an additivity–subtractivity continuum which is the resultant force of two independent factors, that is, valorisation and cognitive functioning.

This approach is congruent with the proposed theoretical guiding principles outlined in Chapter 1. The two dimensions of valorisation and cognitive functioning can be analysed in terms of form–function mapping. In the case of additive bilinguality a relatively high number of form–function mappings occur with many of these having two forms mapped onto one function. For example, when a new function for language – like the use of language as a heuristic in problem solving – is acquired, it is as easy to map two rather than one linguistic form onto it. In this case the bilingual child might develop a more complex set of form–function mappings than his monolingual counterpart, which accounts for the cognitive advantages. On the other hand, in subtractive bilinguality the function that is to be mapped on is missing in the first place; as form–function mapping has not happened, it becomes difficult to map a new form onto absent or at best underdeveloped functions. For example, if the child does not possess the heuristic function of language for problem solving, it is difficult, if not impossible, for him to map a linguistic form onto a new function which he has yet to acquire. If, in addition, he cannot rely on his devalorised first language, he must at the same time acquire a new function with a new form in a little known language.

A crucial question that remains to be answered is: if early bilingual development enhances cognitive development, why is it that not all bilingual experience leads to cognitive enhancement? Positive cognitive consequences of early bilingual experience are almost invariably associated with positive parental attitudes towards both languages and towards literacy. On the other hand, when negative consequences are reported for bilingual experience, they invariably refer to a sociocultural setting which has the following characteristics:

(1)   the child comes from a socially disadvantaged subordinate group;
(2)   he speaks a mother tongue which is little valorised in the society at large; and
(3)   he is schooled through a prestigious L_2 while the school system tends to ignore or denigrate his mother tongue.

So far we have no clear evidence that these negative consequences imply that the child's cognitive processes are less developed; rather, there is plenty of evidence that these children underachieve at school (see Section 11.5).

Because positive consequences of bilingual experience result from the enhancement of cognitive functioning, and negative consequences stem from the social conditions in which the bilingual experience takes place, a general model of bilinguality should bring together both the cognitive aspects and the social aspects of bilingual development. We attempt this integration in the next chapter.

5　Social and psychological foundations of bilinguality

In the present chapter we propose a theoretical approach to bilingual development which is in line with the general guidelines on language behaviour presented in Section 1.2 and takes into account the many dimensions of bilinguality (Section 2.1). As we view bilingual development as a particular case of language development we must first present a general approach to language development. Generally speaking, language development is dependent upon a number of prerequisites, including socialisation processes, the development of the functions for which language will be used, and the existence of language-behaviour models in the child's environment.

5.1　PROCESSES OF LANGUAGE DEVELOPMENT

As explained in our guidelines in Section 1.2 there is a constant interaction between the dynamics of language behaviour at the societal level and language behaviour at the individual level. The child must internalise the language behaviour present in his environment, that is, the language behaviour used in the interpersonal interactions with the significant others in his social network. The child achieves this as follows:

(1)　Through the process of language socialisation the child internalises the different forms and functions of language.
(2)　There is a constant and complex mapping process between forms and functions.
(3)　Mapping processes are particularly important in the development of language as a tool for social interaction and for cognitive functioning.
(4)　The internalisation of forms and functions enables the child to develop social psychological processes which enable him to develop his own social identity.
(5)　Internalisation also permits the use of language as a cognitive tool; furthermore, it plays a constructive role in the growth of cognitive

processes. Language is stored in the form of both social/cultural and propositional representations[1] which are shared by a community; the growing child organises interactive events into more and more complex schemata.[2] As the child develops his own cognitive processes, language in turn becomes an object of cognitive analysis.

(6) As language is a functional tool, valorisation and motivational processes are central to its use and development.

(7) Language behaviour is a self-regulated behaviour. When two languages are present in the child's environment the same processes operate, but each language will be involved to a different degree.

5.1.1   Language socialisation and internalisation

Socialisation is a complex set of learning processes through which the child learns to become a member of his group and builds his social representations; it is also a process by which the child becomes enculturated into a given culture, that is, socialisation practices are governed by cultural parameters; through socialisation processes the child internalises social values and builds up his social, cultural or ethnolinguistic identity. Through internalisation the child reconstructs the world on a psychological plane. These processes shape the child's construction of his shared representation of language, including the development of meaning, the development of social scripts or schemata, and the motivational processes involved in learning or using a language (Hamers & Blanc, 1982). The child learns how to use the appropriate social responses and the appropriate linguistic forms through verbal interactions.

By language socialisation we mean that the child is socialised in the use of language as well as socialised through language; there is a constant interplay between these two mechanisms. Language socialisation is the mechanism by which language behaviour input from the social environment is transformed into intake for the child. Internalisation is the mechanism by which the intake is appropriated by the child. This appropriated intake is further transformed to be used in social and cognitive processes. Language socialisation occurs through the interpersonal interactions in a social network.

Language is present in its different aspects in the child's environment and will be used to a varying extent and for different functions by speakers with and around the child in his social network, that is, the sum of all the interpersonal relations one individual establishes with others over time. The relevance of a network, centred on the individual, lies in the fact that, on the one hand, it provides the child with functional and formal language behaviour model(s) as well as shared schemata; and, on the other hand, it transmits to the child the system of social values, attitudes and perceptions relating to the language(s) and their users (Blanc & Hamers, 1987).

It is through his immediate social network that the child becomes cognisant of the wider social system of intergroup relations, of the place of his network and community within that system, and of the values attributed to, and the status conferred upon, the languages or language varieties and their functions. It is also through his social-network environment that he is exposed to a model or models of language and language behaviour; he internalises the different kinds of social behaviour which are central to him, learns about the social behaviour of outgroups and builds his own social representations of language; these social representations in turn determine how, and for what functions, he will use his linguistic knowledge.

Interaction with others, and in particular child-rearing practices, determine both language and cognition and hence the way in which language and cognition will interact in the child's development. According to Vygotsky (1978), the process of internalisation of higher psychological processes, including language, consists of a series of transformations: an operation that occurred initially externally in interaction with the outside world will become internalised. Furthermore, these transformations from an interpersonal process to an intrapersonal one are the result of an accumulation of developmental events. The internalisation is linked with changes in the rules governing that operation.

The social representation of language – comprising shared meanings, social schemata and the internalisation of social values – plays an essential role in the development of cultural identity. These social cognitive processes determine, in turn, the motivational processes for learning or using a language in its different functions. Socialisation occurs through the interaction between the child and the members of his social network with whom he has frequent and important interactions. Socialisation is thus seen as the interface between a particular social network, which is part of a larger social structure but which has its own pattern of language use, and the individual's social representations, which shape the child's relation to language and languages.

5.1.2   Form–function mapping (fFm)

Language behaviour develops through a complex mapping process between form and function, form–form and function–function (see Section 1.2.1). Of particular interest in the early development is the form–function mapping (fFm). Although the communicative and the cognitive functions of language are closely interrelated, it is generally accepted that language develops first in its communicative function and that it does not develop in its cognitive function without social interaction. The child must first acquire knowledge of the functional aspects of language; he must then develop the cognitive skills necessary for using language as a functional tool of communication (Bruner, 1975b). In order to develop language as a tool of communication he must learn to master both the non-linguistic and the linguistic communicative skills; for example, as mentioned in Section 3.1, the child must develop a theory of mind, that is, develop the necessary skills to evaluate others.

When the child begins to develop linguistic forms, in a first stage there is a one-to-one correspondence between form and function and the child recreates language, in functional terms, using his own forms and rules. In a second stage the child's utterances begin to be plurifunctional and words from the adult language can be identified in his speech. It is also at this stage that he begins to separate his utterances into two main categories of function: he uses language, on the one hand, to satisfy his communicative needs; on the other hand he makes use of language as a cognitive organiser. This usually coincides with a dramatic increase in vocabulary and with the development of dialogue; the child's utterances evolve from holophrases (one-word utterances) into more complex linguistic structures, which combine words in a rule-governed way. From this functional base the child is now ready to develop the linguistic forms and rules approximating to adult language (Halliday, 1975).

Once language is used as a communicative tool, it evolves into a tool of cognitive functioning: the child can develop what Bruner calls 'analytic competence', that is, the conceptual-linguistic abilities involving 'the prolonged operation of thought processes exclusively on linguistic representations [and] propositional structures' (Bruner, 1975b: 72). This development is further discussed in Section 5.1.4.

5.1.2.1 Mapping form onto social function

Before the child can map the forms and formal rules of language with a social function, he must first begin to acquire the functions served by communication; he must also develop a certain amount of conceptual knowledge about the world. The child develops these functions through cooperative action with the adults around him, that is, through joint attention and joint action. For example, the child first learns that he can act upon others ('instrumental function') and at a later stage that he can use language for this function. He will only develop a specific linguistic structure if it can serve a given function for communicating with others. In turn language becomes a constructive element in the development of functions (Karmiloff-Smith, 1979; 1992).

According to Bruner (1975a; Bruner & Sherwood, 1981) the child, through a highly structured interaction with the adult involving the development of joint attention, action and communication, develops a mastery of the rules of social interaction, that is, of culture and language. For example, at the prelinguistic stage infants make requests to adults by gesturing towards a desired object; at about 11 months they use vocalisation as well as gesture and gaze to express requests (Bruner, Roy & Ratner, 1982), and at 14 months they are capable of adjusting vocalisations to the adults' response to the request (Marcos & Bernicot, 1994). In order for the child to learn how to use language in its multiple functions, he must create for himself a functional representation of language; put in simple terms, the child must learn what he can do with language in order to act upon others' utterances.

It is through schemata that children learn how to get things done with the help of others; that they learn about the complex structure of interpersonal interaction and how to use language in this interaction before they have mastered formal linguistic rules (Bruner & Sherwood, 1981). Because schemata serve as a guide to routine encounters in social interactions, they are highly dependent on shared social representations, conventions, norms and language. A shared schema is also an economical device for communication as it presupposes shared knowledge of goal and action which no longer have to be made explicit in the act of communication.

5.1.2.2   *Mapping form onto cognitive function*

Cognitive and social development begins at birth, that is, at the prelinguistic stage. When the child starts internalising language for the cognitive function, he maps a new form onto an existing function; he further maps the acquired form onto a new function, thus transforming the form–function relation. For example, the child first acquires the form *more* in its social function of requesting. At a later stage he uses the form *more* with a new meaning as in *more and more and more and more* for counting objects; the child develops a new concept of quantity for which the mapping with the linguistic form *more* is no longer adequate. He must perform a new form–function mapping by first identifying the adequate form used by adults in order to express the new concept.

As language becomes internalised as an organiser of knowledge it frees itself from the situational context, i.e. it becomes more and more decontextualised; its formal aspects move away from the rules of language used in everyday communication. In so doing, language evolves into autonomous codes, which create their own rules. However, language must necessarily remain a socially shared tool to permit the transmission of knowledge

(Moscovici, 1984). But as language in its cognitive function becomes more autonomous, the communication of knowledge becomes more complex in the sense that it calls upon a higher number of intermediate steps to build a bridge between language as a cognitive organiser and language as a means of communicating knowledge. In order to communicate ideas, it is necessary to use language in a socially decontextualised form, that is, the speaker has to make all the elements of knowledge fully explicit in the text[3] while making optimal use of shared knowledge and shared representations.

Simultaneously, the child develops concepts that are later used linguistically; for example, he learns the concepts of 'agent' or 'attribute' before he is able to express them in linguistic form. The mastery of language thus acts as a catalyst, which in turn amplifies the development of already existing functions. According to Bruner (1971) and Wells (1981), such an amplifier, because of its potential role in the organisation of the child's experience, is essential for shaping his cognitive capacities. This constant dynamic interaction between linguistic form and cognitive functioning shapes both the cognitive and linguistic development of the child.

5.1.3   Development of social psychological processes

The internalisation of language is not a passive intake. By appropriating language the child transforms this intake in order to develop new processing mechanisms, both at the socio-affective and at the cognitive level.

At the socio-affective level the internalisation of language plays a decisive role in the construction of identity. In the socialisation process the child identifies with another person 'when (he) behaves as if he feels like, acts like, and thinks like (that) other person' (Lambert & Lambert, 1973: 29). As a child tends to behave like the people around him, the linguistic models from which he learns his first language play an important part in the language development process. In this identification process the child not only models himself on the adult behaviour, he also internalises the social values associated with the behaviour prevalent in his community. Internalisation involves a reorganisation of the social values in terms of the child's own social experience. Some of these social values are specifically linked to language; for example, the value attributed by a community to a particular accent makes this accent a social marker and the child acquires these values as an integral part of language behaviour and of his identity (Hamers & Blanc, 1982).

Through the socialisation process the child also develops his social/cultural/ethnic identity.[4] The child identifies with the adults around him. The roles played by these adults are to a large extent determined by the hierarchical structure of society and they receive differential values from society. The child not only perceives these different roles but also the values that society attributes to them. He perceives himself as a member of a cultural group and of the different social subgroups with which he identifies; having internalised the values of the cultural and social groups he attaches personal values to this group membership and its values and builds up his own belief system. To the extent that certain aspects of language behaviour, e.g. literacy, are important values for the group, they also become important personal values for the child. We refer to this process as the valorisation process of language.

5.1.4   Development of cognitive processes

As we saw in Section 5.1.2.1, schemata are important in the development of language as a social tool. But a schema is a cognitive construction. It requires a relatively high level of abstraction as it calls for classification, grouping and the recognition of relations; in other words, a schema is highly dependent on the cognitive organisation of knowledge and hence on language. In turn, representations form 'basic building blocks' for subsequent cognitive development (Nelson & Gruendel, 1981).

5.1.4.1   Representations

Higher-order knowledge is stored in the form of representations involving a semiotic function, which is at one and the same time individual and social. Without this semiotic function thought could not be expressed either for the benefit of others or for self (Piaget & Inhelder, 1966). Unlike other aspects of the semiotic function, which can to a large extent be initiated by the child himself as a means of representing the external world (for example, imitation), language is socially transmitted to the child.

Although all mental representations are to a certain extent social in nature, some representations rely more heavily on the physical characteristics of the world and exist partly without the intervention of a structured society. In Bruner's (1975b) classification of representations into echoic, iconic and symbolic modes, the first two rely more on the child's perception and organisation of his knowledge of the physical world, whereas the latter is heavily dependent on culture and language. In a similar vein, J. R. Andersen's (1983) distinction between temporal, spatial and propositional representations also suggests that different modes of organising knowledge depend to a varying extent on the different physical, social or cultural characteristics of the outside world. The evidence from research on memory processes, for example, suggests that complex information is stored in terms of meaning, and thus relies heavily on language (Paivio & Begg, 1981). The organisation of higher-order knowledge draws on these different modes, but mainly on propositional or symbolic representations which use relational categorisations of experience to store and organise information. Linguistic structures are re-encoded into logical structures, such as classes, relations and propositions. For example, linguistic structures enable someone possessing the representations for *eating at home* and *eating at the restaurant* to classify and organise these different physical, social or cultural characteristics of the outside world.

Once knowledge is represented in a propositional form it is important to distinguish between unanalysed and analysed knowledge (Bialystok & Ryan, 1985b); this is similar to Piaget's (1954) distinction between figurative and operative representations. In both kinds of knowledge the proposition is the same, that is, a propositional representation consists of a predicate–argument structure (Miller & Johnson-Laird, 1976); in other words, meaning is the same in both. In unanalysed knowledge, however, the subject uses information routinely without intentional manipulation and with little awareness of the structures and the rules of the proposition; in contrast, in analysed knowledge the subject has access to the structure, which he can transform in order to reorganise knowledge.

5.1.4.2   Cognitive dimensions

Two theoretical frameworks to cognitive processing have been proposed: the information-processing approach and the analysis–control approach. The information-processing model defines acquisition of skills (such as mathematics, language, information technology) as the establishment of complex procedures (procedural knowledge), integrating elementary pieces of information (declarative knowledge) (Andersen, 1983). The analysis–control framework, on the other hand, offers a functional view of skill components. According to Bialystok & Ryan, two cognitive dimensions associated with structuring and accessing knowledge are necessary for higher cognitive operations. First, the dimension of 'analysed knowledge' through which the subject has access to the structure and manipulation of his representations; and, second, the dimension of 'cognitive control', which is responsible for selecting and coordinating the required information within a given time and space. Both approaches are complementary rather than mutually exclusive and go a long way towards explaining how language is transformed into a cognitive tool by the child.

5.1.4.3   Language as a cognitive tool

The cognitive function of language refers to a general psychological process by which the child appropriates language as an organiser of knowledge, i.e. in classifying, forming hierarchies, inferencing, etc. As soon as linguistic communication develops, both the communicative and the cognitive functions become interrelated; this is because communication is not merely exchanging signals that stand in a one-to-one relationship with specific objects, actions and events. Linguistic communication has a cognitive component: it essentially involves exchanging conceptual information. Language used in social interaction thus provides the child with an enlarged database for constructing his knowledge and helps him recognise certain parameters as relevant to problem solving. The extent to which adults, in their interactions with a child, manipulate language in problem-solving enables him to develop language in this function to a greater or lesser degree.

In order for the child to develop language as a cognitive tool, this function must be valorised first in his social network and then by the child himself. Once language has been used in its cognitive function the emphasis is put on this aspect which can no longer be ignored. If, on the other hand, language has been little used as a cognitive tool, it may be neglected in this function.

The different language tasks vary along two dimensions: simple conversational tasks demand a low degree of analysis of knowledge and of cognitive control, while the ability to solve metalinguistic[5] problems requires high levels of information processing in terms of both the manipulation of knowledge and the control exercised over the selection of appropriate information: 'the decrease in contextualisation from conversational to metalinguistic tasks increases the need for analysed knowledge, while the increase of the requirement to focus on form increases the need for cognitive control' (Bialystok & Ryan, 1985a: 233). This conceptual-linguistic ability is a prerequisite for the development of literacy, of reading and writing and is in turn enhanced by them.

5.1.4.4   *Language as an object of cognitive processing*

Our knowledge of and about language varies according to the degree to which it is analysed (Bialystok & Ryan, 1985b). For the child, developing language and cognition means progressing from little-analysed knowledge and limited cognitive control to more-analysed knowledge on which he gradually exercises greater control in terms of attention, selection and priorities. As far as knowledge of language is concerned, the more it is analysed, the more its form is likely to differ from language used in everyday conversational interaction. When Moscovici (1984) argues that, in the internalisation process, language moves away from the form it has in everyday communication, it should be understood that this happens along the following two dimensions: language undergoes more and more transformations through cognitive manipulation, while at the same time the individual has to establish more control procedures to deal with the task.

However, metalinguistic skills are not only required for reaching a certain level of abstraction; they are also necessary for the communication of abstract thought. The metalinguistic skills required for this type of communication are not necessarily the same as those for analysing linguistic input. A speaker who wants to convey information must consider his interlocutor. He must therefore modify and reorganise his language in such a way that he makes use of knowledge, scripts and meanings shared with his interlocutor. These metalinguistic skills interact with social cognition to produce a language of communication which is different from the language of everyday communication. They find their more elaborate expression in literacy skills, such as reading and writing, in which information processing cannot rely on contextual clues.

5.1.4.5 *The development of literacy*

Children develop language first in familiar social interactions for which they construct schemata; language in the early stage is physically and socially contextualised. By this we mean that children, and adults interacting with them, use linguistic units for which the referent is present. This is evidenced, for example, by the deictic use of utterances, such as the 'verbal pointing' that adults use at a very early stage in children's language development, and the frequency of children's first utterances and adult utterances referring to the objects present in the immediate environment. These utterances take their meaning from the configuration of the various physical and social elements in the situation; this meaning is shared by the child and the other people present. The meaning of a linguistic unit can thus be viewed as the shared social representation of its referent (Blanc & Hamers, 1987).

As the child develops and learns to use language as an active organiser in thought processes, adults use language with him in ways that are more and more decontextualised. It must be stressed that the mere mastery of a language for everyday communication is not sufficient to guarantee that it will be used in a more sophisticated organisation of knowledge. To exploit the potential cognitive power of language, a child has to develop:

an enhanced awareness of the symbolic properties of linguistic representations: the realisation that the meaning and implications of a message depend upon the precise linguistic formulation of that message and upon the internal relations and consistency between its constituent parts, rather than upon any necessary correspondence between the message and the perception or memories of the extralinguistic context(s) to which the message might apply. (Wells, 1981: 252)

Decontextualised language – that is, language in which the transmission of the meaning depends on linguistic rather than situational information – finds its ultimate realisation in written texts. In written language we find the same differences between the processes of encoding (writing) and of decoding (reading) as those found in oral language between production and comprehension. However, the task of creating decontextualised written texts is not only different from, but also cognitively and linguistically even more complex than, that of comprehending them. This is because every element of the message has to be produced by the writer and expressed in the text. Although decontextualised language is not confined to the written mode – since cognitively and linguistically complex messages can be produced orally – it is more characteristic of writing; however, not all written language is independent of the context of situation, nor does it necessarily imply a high degree of complexity of the message (as for example in some forms of letter writing, advertising and popular journalism).

In order for a child to acquire decontextualised language, an adequate model must be present in his environment, that is, decontextualised language must be used around and with the child. This development seems to be promoted through a number of shared language-related activities concerned with problem-solving between adult and child, such as extended conversations about meanings that are made explicit, being read to, looking at and talking about books. Familiarity with decontextualised oral language seems to be of the utmost importance for the learning of written skills (see Wells, 1985a). The mere fact of using decontextualised language with a child is sufficient to valorise the decontextualised forms and the functions they apply to.

In literate societies education through schooling stresses the decontextualised use of language and, more particularly, reading and writing; children who as pre-schoolers learned the purposes and mechanics of decontextualised language are the ones who have the greatest advantage in the attainment of literacy at school (Wells, 1985a; Torrance & Olson, 1985). It is not simply the fact of being able to read and write that facilitates the use of decontextualised and symbolic language, but rather the purpose, i.e. the use of language in cognitive organisation, for which the child has learned these skills (Scribner & Cole, 1981). Furthermore, as Luria (1976) has shown, when a traditional society modifies its economic, social and cultural goals and becomes more cognitively oriented with the introduction of literacy, the scope of the functional representation of language moves from being only-context-bound and cognitively-undemanding to become context-free and cognitively demanding.

However, if in a literacy-oriented society the child has not been prepared to use decontextualised language before schooling, he will experience difficulties in learning how to use language as a cognitive organiser for academic tasks, whether oral or written. In order to compensate for this lack of pre-literate skills it appears that it is necessary to promote interactive adult–child literacy-related activities (Tizard, Schofield & Hewison, 1982).

5.1.5   Valorisation and motivational processes

In order for the child to develop overall language competence he must first valorise language, that is, confer a certain positive value to language as a functional tool. To the extent that the adults around him value the use of language for certain functions, the child will also value the use of language for these functions and thus develop those functional aspects of language. The valorised aspects of language are those that enable the child to build up the social psychological mechanisms relevant to his linguistic and social development; it is those very aspects that determine the *evaluative* dimension of language, that is, the child's own affective relationship to language. He will thus construct a certain notion of the prestige that is conferred on language by society and that is to a large extent internalised by him. This affective dimension of language behaviour plays the role of an important mediator in the process of language development (Hamers & Blanc, 1982).

Because of the social attributes of language, the functions that are the most used and valorised with the child are those which he is the most likely to develop. The positive valorisation of all or some of the formal and functional aspects of language help to elaborate and trigger a motivational process for learning and using those aspects of language. These processes first enable the child to develop a competence in the communicative function of language; by developing this competence he valorises language even more as a communicative tool, thereby being further motivated to learn and use it in that function. Second, and provided he is exposed to an adequate functional model, the child also develops a competence in the cognitive function of language; the same social psychological processes are at work here: the child must be exposed to, valorise, and be motivated to learn and use language in its cognitive function. The socially valorised and successful use of language in this function acts as a feedback on the child's valorisation and motivated processes, thus prompting the child to make further use of language for this function. Thus, the two main functional aspects of language, that is the communicative and the cognitive, develop through a number of mediational mechanisms, provided that there is an adequate environment in which the child can pick up the necessary cues from his own social network.

5.1.6   Self-regulated behaviour

Language development, like all higher order behaviour, is a self-regulated behaviour (see, for example, Bandura, 1977; 1986). It is not a simple response to stimuli, but it has an important evaluative component: the child takes into account his past experience in order to judge the present situation. Judgement is arrived at through comparisons both with models of behaviour and with norms stemming from personal, social and collective comparisons. These comparisons enable the child to attribute a certain value to a given behaviour. These self-regulation mechanisms act upon different mediational processes such as motivation and valorisation.

A most important mechanism in higher-order behaviour is the feedback mechanism operating between the different processes involved in the behaviour, as for example between the actual behaviour and the valorisation. By feedback mechanism we mean that the more a child is successful in producing a behaviour the more he valorises it, hence the more motivated he is to produce the behaviour. For example, the more the child is successful in using language for the cognitive function, the more he values language in this function and the more motivated he is to do so. Every psychological mechanism is amplified by the effect of its own feedback mechanism (Hamers & Blanc, 1982).

5.1.7   A sociocognitive interactional model of language development

A comprehensive model of language development should take into consideration the various aspects of language development that we have just discussed. The roots of language development are to be found in the interpersonal interactions occurring in the child's social environment, and these provide the child with a model of language behaviour. Through internalisation processes the child appropriates the social values, forms, functions and existing form–function mappings of language. These functions and forms are valorised and will contribute to the elaboration of the child's social identity. This valorisation further motivates the child for learning and using more form–function mappings. To the extent that linguistic forms are mapped onto communicative and cognitive structures in the environment, these processes lead to the growth of communicative linguistic, conceptual linguistic and metalinguistic competences. These developing processes are also influenced by previous language experience and previously developed representations. The development of conceptual linguistic competence and its accompanying processing mechanisms leads to the further development of language as a cognitive tool and to the processing of language as an object of analysis.

There is an interrelationship between the different components of language competence; these are:

(1) the communicative linguistic competence in which language is put to an interactive use;
(2) the conceptual linguistic competence which requires the manipulation of language as a cognitive tool, as for example in the decontextualised use of language; and
(3) the metalinguistic competence in which the child pays attention to language forms, speaks, thinks, comments on language and is conscious of his ability to manipulate language.

To the extent that language is used for these different functions around and with the child, he will valorise each of these functions and, thus, develop each of these competences.

The competence attained in communicative-linguistic processing, conceptual-linguistic processing and metalinguistic processing of language further enhance – through feedback mechanisms – the valorisation processes. Evaluation of the entire situation (external and internal input) shapes the language behaviour output. This model is depicted in Figure 5.1.

This model is dynamic in the sense that the child's language behaviour output provokes a new input from the environment. Each new input adds to the child's experience and plays a role in further shaping such mechanisms as his representations, his belief system and his social identity. The valorisation of the language behaviour comes from three sources: the external input, the personal experience and the feedback mechanisms. When language is used successfully for a communicative function it is valorised for this function; the child is more motivated to use it in this function which in turn leads to an even greater valorisation and an increase in communicative competence. The same mechanism operates at the cognitive level: if language is valorised as a cognitive tool or as an object of cognitive analysis it is valorised in this function; this further in turn enhances its use in these functions.

5.2   THE DEVELOPMENT OF BILINGUALITY

The development of bilinguality involves the acquisition of two (or more) linguistic codes perceived as socially distinct by the linguistic community. This acquisition is either simultaneous or consecutive. We do not refer to the development of bilinguality after childhood because this book focuses on the role played by a bilingual experience in the development of the child.

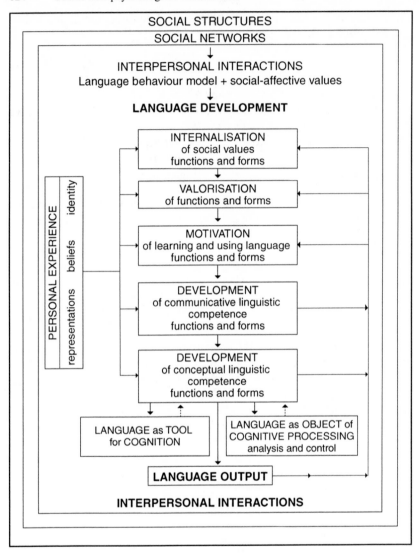

Figure 5.1   Sociocognitive model of language development

To what extent is the child's development affected by exposure to two languages and by the relationship between them?

More specifically, we ask the following questions:

- How does the form–function mapping occur when the linguistic input contains two linguistic systems?

- To what extent is it important that both languages are used for both the communicative and the cognitive function?
- How does the relative valorisation of the two languages affect the child's language development?
- To what extent are the child's social psychological processes affected by this experience?
- To what extent are the different language-behaviour competences affected by the bilingual experience?
- To what extent is the child's cognitive development affected by the bilingual experience?

From the empirical data available on simultaneous bilingual development it appears that children are not only capable of switching from one set of linguistic rules to another – in a socially appropriate manner, at an early stage of language development and long before they have mastered all the rules of adult language – but that they are also aware of the existence of two distinct codes. An infant bilingual spontaneously translates for two adults each of whom speaks one of his languages, thus establishing equivalencies between his two languages (see Section 3.1.3). The ability to use either code for similar interactions is proof that the child is capable of equating the interactional rules of his two languages before he has acquired adult-like language competence and is aware of at least certain dimensions of the social context of language use.

5.2.1   A sociocognitive interactional model of bilinguality

All societies value language as a tool of communication and cognition; however, they tend to valorise some functions more than others; the cognitive function, for example. If different varieties of language are present in a society one variety may be valued to the detriment of others. A similar situation obtains in the case of multilingual societies. One or more languages may be highly valued, while others may be devalorised. At the individual level a similar mechanism operates. To the extent that the adults around the child value the use of language for certain functions, he will also value the use of language for these functions and thus develop these aspects.

   In addition to the processing mechanisms described for monolingual development, five important dimensions determine the type of bilinguality that a child develops:

(1)   the relationship between the two languages, between their statuses, their valorisation and their use for functions, both at the societal and at the individual level;

(2)   the degree to which the form–function mapping overlaps for the two languages;
(3)   the time of onset of bilinguality, i.e. whether it is simultaneous or consecutive;
(4)   the degree of internalisation of the relative values of the languages and of the mappings; and
(5)   the degree to which each language contributes to the development of the communicative, cognitive and metalinguistic competences.

The roots of bilingual development are to be found in the interpersonal interactions occurring in the child's social environment, and these provide the child with a model of language behaviour comprising more than one language. The relative status, valorisation and use of the two languages in the society and around the child determine to what extent the child internalises the two languages as equivalent and interchangeable, or as having different values in terms of social prestige and tools for communicating and thinking.

The degree to which form–function mapping (fFm) overlaps determines to what extent the child has to perform a double mapping or can make a simple mapping. A double mapping can be represented as:

$$\text{(fFm): } (L_A)\text{form–function–}(L_B)\text{form}$$

and a simple mapping can be represented in either of the following ways:

$$\text{(fFm): } (L_A)\text{form–function}$$
$$\text{(fFm): } (L_B)\text{form–function}$$

These representations can be abbreviated, respectively, as: $(f_A f_B Fm)$, $(f_A Fm)$ and $(f_B Fm)$.

Some functions of language, such as agent and action, are universal and are therefore shared by all languages. For these functions the child must internalise the mapping of one function with two forms. If, furthermore, the two languages are used for the same social and cognitive functions, a 'one function–two forms' mapping may also occur. If, however, one language is used for certain functions only and the other for complementary functions, the child has to produce a form–function mapping in the same way as the monolingual child, as is the case in an ideally diglossic situation.

The time of onset of bilinguality – that is, whether it is simultaneous or consecutive – has an effect. In the case of simultaneous bilinguality, language socialisation occurs with two languages present. The child must at the same time learn that two linguistic systems can serve the same social function and that one appropriate social response can be served by two distinct linguistic forms. Development of perceptual skills and discrimina-

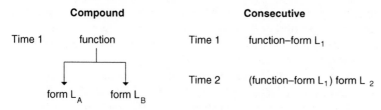

Figure 5.2   Schematised representation of the compound and consecutive form–function mappings

tion of the two linguistic systems in the social environment is an important prerequisite for the bilingual child's development. The child maps two forms onto one function at more or less the same time and in a more or less compound way ($f_A f_B Fm$), whereas in the case of consecutive bilinguality, the child acquires form–function mapping ($f_1 Fm$) first in one language and later maps a new form onto this already existing form–function mapping (f_2–$f_1 Fm$). In the case of simultaneous bilinguality the child is likely to acquire more compound mappings, whereas in the case of consecutive bilinguality it is more likely that a new form mapping will be added to an already existing form–function mapping. This is true as far as the semiotic-linguistic functions are concerned. In each case the task is cognitively different. These (form–function) mappings can be schematised as is shown in Figure 5.2.

The child internalises the social, cognitive and semiotic aspects of language. The kinds of norms, values and language model(s) to which the child is exposed and which he internalises depend on

(1)   whether there is one or more functional and formal model(s) of language around the child;
(2)   whether his network is homogeneous or heterogeneous, that is, whether all its members have a similar language behaviour or some members have a different language behaviour from others; and
(3)   whether or not there are competing values and norms.

The degree of internalisation of the values and of the form–function mapping determines how far the child attributes certain values to certain form–function mappings in one or in both languages, and how far he is thus motivated to use a particular type of form–function mapping in one or both languages.

The degree to which each language is valorised is important for the development of the communicative, cognitive and metalinguistic skills. At the individual level, the positive valorisation of all or some of the values linked to the formal and functional aspects of language helps to elaborate and trigger a motivational process for learning and using those aspects of language. To the extent that these skills are developed, the child elaborates his representation of language which includes the relative use of the two languages for the various functions.

As we suggested in Hamers & Blanc (1982), the use of language as a cognitive organiser is developed by the bilingual child at three different levels: two levels are specific to each language and one abstract level is common to both languages. Language is stored in the form of propositional representations, that is, as relational categorisations; we further argued that propositional representations are related to the general characteristics of language and independent from the specificity of a given language. We therefore propose that the bilingual has propositional representations which are common to both his languages and that he uses this common pool in organising knowledge. Cummins' (1984a) model of 'common underlying proficiency', discussed in Section 4.2.5.1, also suggests that the bilingual develops a literacy-related proficiency common to both languages and that the two languages are interdependent at deeper levels of processing.

When a bilingual child has well-developed propositional representations, his organisation of knowledge is independent of the specific characteristics of his languages and it is likely that he is able to use his two languages interchangeably to communicate this knowledge. On the other hand, if a child has not learned to use language as a cognitive organiser to a significant extent, introducing him to a second language does not promote this function. Thus, the development of propositional representations and the ability to use language as a cognitive organiser must be viewed as psycholinguistic processes that are independent of the specific characteristics of the languages. Bilingual experience may, however, interact with these psycholinguistic processes. What the bilingual child develops are general cognitive mechanisms of information processing; once these mechanisms have been set in motion, the child is able to apply them to all information-processing tasks, even to non-linguistic ones.

5.2.2   Case studies: types of bilinguality

In this section we examine a number of typical cases to illustrate how certain factors determine the outcome of bilinguality.

A   Cases of simultaneous bilinguality

In the case of simultaneous bilinguality the child is not only exposed to two languages, L_A and L_B, during the language development years, but the two languages are used with the child in the socialisation process from birth onwards.

Case 1   The two languages, L_A and L_B, are learned simultaneously and developed equally for the same functions including the literacy functions

A typical case is that of children born into mixed-lingual families where both parents have similar interactions with the child and where language is used for metalinguistic and literacy-related activities (see for example the biographies by Ronjat (1913) and Leopold (1939–49) in Section 3.1). Thus, the child is exposed to a complete model of language behaviour using two languages. The child internalises both languages which are equally valorised for communicative and cognitive functions in his environment. Because there is a compound mapping between two linguistic forms and all functions, the child can equate the two forms as corresponding to one function and therefore as being interchangeable. He may therefore develop a pool or system common to both languages. Thus, the child develops an early metalinguistic awareness (see Section 4.2) which generalises to other areas of concept learning. The use of two languages instead of one for the same functions generally induces the child to develop an increased capacity for abstraction. The child's linguistic environment may be considered more enriched than a monolingual environment. As all functions are developed the child benefits maximally from this enriched environment and he develops not only a balanced but also an additive form of bilinguality (see Section 4.2.5.2).

Case 2   The two languages, L_A and L_B, are learned simultaneously and developed equally for the same functions but no literacy functions are present

This is the case when the child is born into a low-literate bilingual family in which each parent speaks one language, in which both parents have similar interactions with the child, but in which only the communicative functions are valorised in the family, to the exclusion of the cognitive literacy-related functions. The child is exposed to a language-behaviour model in which two linguistic systems are used mainly for communicative functions. The child does not, therefore, valorise the cognitive functions. If at a later stage, for instance at school, the child develops the cognitive functions in one language, he is faced with the same difficulties as the monolingual child who has to learn these functions in the mother tongue at school. Both have to develop a new simple mapping between known forms and new functions. However, because for the bilingual child the two languages are interchangeable, he should have no major difficulties in transferring his cognitive skills from one language to another once these have been acquired through the school language. Any difficulties that he might encounter cannot be attributed to his binguality, but to the absence of cognitive functions in his environment. In this case we have a neutral form of binguality.

Case 3   The two languages, L_A and L_B, are learned simultaneously but one is used for communicative functions only and the other one for all functions

A typical example would be that of a child whose parents speak the same language and a caretaker another language; one language is learned for all functions and the other is learned for a restricted number of functions. Both languages are valorised for the child, but the language that serves the cognitive functions will be relatively more valorised. Through the internalisation process the child valorises both languages to a different extent and is motivated to use them for the functions that are valorised. The tendency is to develop a form of binguality dominant in the more valorised language. Compound mapping occurs between the two linguistic forms and those functions which are valorised in both languages. For the functions valorised in only one language a single mapping occurs. However, as the child masters both languages, it is likely that transfer of the form–function mapping will occur. He will, however, not have the same advantages on the metalinguistic level, as compound mapping occurs for communicative functions and not for cognitive functions. Although the cognitive linguistic dimension of language behaviour might be more developed than in the previous case, the advantages of binguality will be less evident than in Case 1.

In all three cases there is no disadvantage attributable to binguality. The child develops native competence in two mother tongues. The bingual development turns out to be to the child's advantage in cognitive functioning, especially when the two languages are used for all functions (see Chapters 2 and 3 for the empirical evidence). It is understood that if an adequate language-behaviour model is lacking in the child's socialisation process, the child is not able to internalise language behaviour nor develop the necessary form–function mappings required for language development. This happens, for example, when immigrant parents give up their mother tongue in their socialisation practices and replace it by a socially more prestigious but little mastered second language used for a limited number of functions.

B Cases of early consecutive binguality

In the cases of early consecutive binguality one language, L_1, is acquired as the mother tongue and a second language, L_2, is introduced later, after the years of language development but during childhood (before the age of 8–10), either as a language used in the neighbourhood or a language of schooling.

Case 4   The two languages, L_1 and L_2, are learned consecutively, all functions are developed first in L_1 and later in L_2, and both languages are valorised in the child's social networks

In this case the child first develops all functions in his first language: thus, a simple (form–function) mapping occurs and language is valorised for all functions. After being introduced to a second language the child, after a while, develops the second language for all functions. Because he already possesses the necessary (form–function) mappings with his L_1 he easily maps a new form onto an already existing function. As both languages are highly valorised for all functions he internalises these social values for both languages. This is the case of a child who uses a socially highly valorised language at home and who is schooled in a different language which is valorised for the literacy-related cognitive functions and possibly valorised as the language of the peer group (see Section 4.3 and Chapter 11). The child may develop an additive balanced form of bilinguality similar to the child in Case 1; or the child may remain dominant in his first language and develop a near-native command in the second language.

Case 5   The two languages, L_1 and L_2, are learned consecutively, but the child has not developed the literacy-related functions in the devalorised L_1 before he starts to learn L_2 which is the valorised language in society

When L_1 is devalorised in the society, as is the case for many ethnolinguistic minorities, and the child has not developed the literacy-related functions in his L_1, the introduction to a new language at the same time as the introduction of new literacy-related functions presents the child with a supplementary mapping problem because both form and function are new. This is the case of submersion schooling in the majority language. If the conditions do not permit the child to valorise his L_1 sufficiently as compared to his L_2, he is not able to use his L_1 for new literacy-related functions when he starts acquiring them because he can only rely on his limited knowledge of L_2. He will try to use an underdeveloped L_2 to learn new functions. In this case acquiring new language functions, as well as a new language without the support that comes from the valorisation process for the first language, might be too difficult a task for the child. It is therefore primarily a lack of development of the literacy-related functions via L_1 that leads to a lack of development of language as a cognitive tool. In this case the outcome of the bilingual experience is likely to be a

subtractive form of bilinguality. This is not, however, an inevitable outcome: provided that the first language is sufficiently valorised with the child
for literacy-related functions, and the child can develop these in his first
language, he will have less difficulty in mapping new L_2 forms onto these
functions. Not only must the use of L_1 be encouraged but also the development of the literacy-related functions in the L_1 in the family environment.

Case 6   The two languages are learned consecutively, but L_1 is used for a
greater number of functions than L_2

This case is similar to Case 3. It might occur, for example, when a child has
learned his highly valorised L_1 for all functions, including literacy-related
ones, and receives his schooling via an L_2 without having much contact
with people who speak that language. There are neither positive nor
negative consequences from his bilingual experience, but he is likely to
remain dominant in L_1.

C   Cases of language shift

In some cases of bilingual development, a language shift might occur in the
sense that a language present in early development might disappear or
become atrophied.

Case 7   The two languages are learned consecutively or simultaneously,
and the less valorised language L_1 or L_A, disappears or becomes atrophied
after the child has developed the literacy-related functions in the devalorised L_1 or in both languages, before he starts schooling in L_2 which is
the valorised language in society

In this case the child develops all functions but becomes dominant in L_2,
which is likely to become his mother tongue. The degree of bilingual
competence depends on the degree of attrition of the less valorised language. For example, if the first language is no longer spoken, or only used
to a limited extent, the child may even, in an extreme case, become
monolingual. However, because the cognitive aspects of language were
already in place before the language shift occurred, the outcome is a neutral
dominant form of bilinguality.

Case 8   The two languages are learned consecutively or simultaneously,
and the less valorised language L_1 or L_A disappears, or becomes atrophied
before the child has developed the literacy-related functions

In this case the child is in a similar situation to Case 5, that is, he does not only suffer some disadvantage to his cognitive development, but, in addition, he is more likely to become monolingual in the dominant language. This is often the case when immigrant families adopt the more prestigious language of the host country, often before the adults have acquired a sufficient competence in that language.

As already mentioned, the source of language development is to be found in the social environment; if it cannot provide the adequate form–function mappings, the child cannot develop them. Because, in the case of shift in the family language, there might be a lack of an adequate model, we might have a case of subtractive bilinguality in which the second language tends to replace the first language.

5.3   CONCLUSION

We consider this chapter as central to our whole approach to bilinguality and bilingualism. In Section 5.1 we analysed the processes of language development and put forward a sociocognitive interactional model of language development. In Section 5.2 we applied this sociocognitive interactional model to the development of bilinguality. We ended the section by presenting a number of hypothetical case studies to illustrate the main types of bilinguality that may develop.

Language development takes place in the interpersonal interactions which are embedded in social networks and wider social structures. It starts with language socialisation through which the child internalises the social values of his environment and language behaviour used around and with him. Through this internalisation process he valorises either all or only some of the functions of language and is motivated to learn and use language for all or some of the functions. This leads to the development, on the one hand, of communicative linguistic competence, and, on the other, of conceptual linguistic competence. These processes result in language output. One essential feature of this model is the feedback mechanism operating between the different processes involved in the language behaviour. These processes are also influenced by the child's past experience.

Each level of processing (internalisation, valorisation, motivation and competences) is established through a form–function mapping. It should be understood that we view the developing structures in a connectionist approach, that is, as an organised assembly of connections established through experience.

When two languages are present in the child's environment, either a new set of complex compound form–function mapping occurs, $f_A f_B F$, in which two linguistic forms are linked to one function; or, a new form in L_2 is mapped onto an existing f_1F, thus producing f_2f_1F. In the first case, that is of simultaneous bilinguality, both languages are interchangeable for the same functions. In the case of consecutive bilinguality mapping between form and function is first established in one language and a new form is then acquired to fulfil the same function. In this case it is necessary and sufficient that L_1 be used for both the communicative and the cognitive functions to establish a new mapping between the function and the L_2 form.

If, in the case of simultaneous bilinguality, both languages are valorised for all present functions, this is sufficient for the adequate mapping to occur between a function and both the languages; if, however, only some of the functions are present, mapping does not take place, as in the case of a monolingual child. If, in the case of consecutive bilinguality, only some of the functions are present, mapping is established between these functions and the L_1 forms. It is relatively easy to map new L_2 forms on established f_1Fm's. But, if no f_1Fm's exist, mapping a new L_2 form onto a new functions is a more complex task. This has important implications for the education of bilingual children (see Chapter 11).

Bilingual experience, because of its more complex form–function mapping, affects behaviour in general and language behaviour in particular. This more complex mapping occurs not only in language development but also at all levels of behaviour. These other levels are discussed in the following chapters.

6   Neuropsychological foundations of
        bilinguality

Despite the fact that the cerebral organisation of languages in the bilingual person has received a great deal of attention in the latter part of the twentieth century it is still difficult to determine if a bilingual's two languages share the same neural mechanisms. Some early research suggested that brain lateralisation (see Section 6.3) in bilinguals is not different from that occurring in monolinguals and that a bilingual's two languages share the same cerebral substrate (Penfield & Roberts, 1959); on the other hand, early evidence stemming from clinical work with polyglot aphasics has, since the nineteenth century, suggested that a cerebral organisation specific to the bilingual might exist (Minkowski, 1963). Experimental evidence with brain-intact bilinguals since the 1960s tends to support the shared-substrate hypothesis (for a review, see Vaid and Hall, 1991). However, from a more recent study using a refined brain-scanning technique with brain-intact bilinguals, it appears that certain linguistic characteristics are processed in separate anatomical sites for L_1 and L_2 by adulthood bilinguals but not by infancy bilinguals (Kim, Relkin, Lee & Hirsch, 1997; see also Section 6.3.2.4).

In the present chapter we discuss the state of the art of the neuropsychological aspects of bilinguality. Following a brief introduction to the problem of hemispheric preferences for language behaviour and a brief description of the most widely used techniques for assessing hemispheric preferences (Section 6.2) we review the empirical evidence on the neuropsychological development of bilinguals, obtained from brain-damaged and brain-intact bilinguals (Section 6.3). We pay special attention to neuropsychological differences between simultaneous and consecutive bilinguality. We then discuss the neuropsychological state of the bilingual signing person (Section 6.4).

In this chapter we ask six questions:

(1) Is cerebral organisation different in bilinguals and in monolinguals?
(2) Are there separate neural mechanisms for different languages?
(3) Are there age-of-acquisition differences in cerebral processing?

(4) Do differences in learning situations, in competence and in language structure have different effects on cerebral organisation?

(5) Are the same cerebral structures involved in the language of bilinguals using an articulate and a signed language? and

(6) To what extent do different languages rely on different cerebral structures?

6.1   HEMISPHERIC PREFERENCE AND LANGUAGE BEHAVIOUR

Cerebral control of language behaviour is characterised by functional asymmetry,[1] which is a product of neuropsychological maturation. Cerebral lateralisation develops in early childhood: most researchers agree that its first manifestations can be observed around 4–5 years although the claim for a genetically programmed biological basis is well founded (Corballis, 1980; 1991). Generally speaking, the majority of the population has a dominant left hemisphere which exercises a contra-lateral control, i.e. control of the right side of the body (most humans are right-handed); the left hemisphere also controls most of linguistic behaviour. Concordance between hemispheric preference for motricity and for language is however not complete: whereas 96 per cent of right-handers do have a left-hemispheric control for language, 70 per cent of left-handers also have the language control centres in the left hemisphere (Milner, 1975). Right-hand preference is therefore a good indicator of left-hemispheric dominance for language, whereas left-hand preference is not.

Research in the field includes studies on neuro-anatomic structure, and also studies referring to neurophysiological pathways and behavioural strategies. A hemispheric preference does not necessarily equate with a neuro-anatomic structure, and can also refer to an activation or inhibition of a pathway or to a preference in strategies.

The very notion of cerebral dominance[2] or hemispheric preference must not be taken as absolute, but rather as a greater specialisation of one or the other hemisphere for a given task. Bogen (1969), for example, describes the left hemisphere as logical, convergent, analytic, sequential and propositional and the right hemisphere as intuitive, divergent, holistic, parallel and appositional.[3] At the same time, hemispheric specialisation is not exclusive: each hemisphere may be capable of processing information in the other's typical mode (Witelson, 1977). Therefore, both hemispheres will have different degrees of involvement in information processing according to the nature of the linguistic task. However, the two hemispheres must not be viewed as competing but as cooperating; they function in a complementary way in the execution of most higher-order tasks.

Thus, one might expect that for the vast majority of the population the left hemisphere would have a greater involvement in linguistic information processing. The right hemisphere is also involved to a limited extent; according to Schneiderman (1986), right-hemisphere participation in normal language acquisition is that of a limited, specialised role in the perception, retention and basic comprehension of new language stimuli; it also performs a complementary function in that it facilitates processing by the left hemisphere. Right-hemisphere lesions are also known to produce communication deficits and to affect non-explicit speech acts, affective prosody, inference, analogy and non-literate meaning (Paradis, 1990). It must be understood that because of the contra-lateral neurological connections of the human body right-ear advantage and right-visual-field advantage correspond to left-hemispheric preference. For reasons of clarity we refer only to the hemispheric preference (left-hemisphere or right-hemisphere).

6.2 TECHNIQUES FOR MEASURING CEREBRAL PREFERENCE FOR LANGUAGE

In the last three decades researchers in the neuropsychology of language have developed a number of methodologies and techniques in order to assess language hemispheric processing and cerebral localisation. A growing number of studies have been conducted on the cerebral lateralisation of language in brain-damaged and brain-intact bilinguals (for a review of methodological issues, see Obler, Zatorre, Galloway & Vaid, 1982; Vaid & Hall, 1991). Besides traditional psycholinguistic measures of language functioning such as the ones used in test batteries (for a review, see Neils-Strunjas, 1998) and traditional clinical descriptions of the polyglot aphasic's behaviour which span more than one hundred years, specific techniques used with both brain-damaged and brain-intact subjects have been developed in more recent times in order to study cerebral functioning in bilinguals. These techniques include behavioural measures and anatomical/physiological measures.

The most widely used behavioural measures are:

(1) Tachistoscopic techniques in which visual information is presented to either the left hemisphere (LH) or the right hemisphere (RH); better recognition of verbal material presented in the right or the left central visual field is considered a measure of cerebral preference for the contra-lateral side; verbal materials presented to the LH tend to be better and faster recognised than verbal material presented to the RH.

(2) Dichotic listening techniques used to verify the dominance of one or

the other hemisphere for auditory processing: in dichotic listening auditory materials are presented simultaneously to both ears; because in simultaneous auditory stimulation ipsi-lateral neural connections are suppressed in favour of the contra-lateral ones, each stimulus will reach only the contra-lateral hemisphere; a better ear performance is considered as an indication of the contra-lateral hemispheric preference; the right-ear advantage for verbal stimuli is considered as a measure of LH preference.

(3)   Dual-task performance in which a verbal task is performed at the same time as a non-verbal task clearly identified as controlled by one hemisphere, as, for example, right or left finger-tapping while the subject is required to interpret at the same time; a greater disturbance in the task for one side is considered as an indication of hemispheric overload. Hemispheric overload of the LH during a dual task is considered a measure of LH preference for language.

Whereas until the 1970s the use of the anatomical/physiological measures was restricted to brain-damaged patients, new non-invasive measures have been developed since then. These measures allow for the study of cerebral preferences in the brain-intact subjects. Among the physiological and anatomical measures developed to identify LH or RH activity, the most important ones are the following:

(1)   The injection of sodium amytal, a nerve depressant, which anesthetises one hemisphere at a time thereby inducing experimentally temporary aphasia in patients (Rapport, Tan & Whitaker, 1983). This technique, also called the Wada test (Wada & Rasmussen, 1960), is used to determine which hemisphere controls language in brain-surgery patients. If the sodium amytal affects the hemisphere that controls language, speech is disturbed for a few minutes; injection in the other hemisphere will not affect speech.

(2)   The cortical mapping of speech functions, pioneered by Penfield & Roberts (1959), is another physiological measure used only in clinical cases. In this technique, used with brain-surgery patients whose skull is opened under local anaesthesia in order to treat brain diseases, stimulation of precise sites of the dominant hemisphere can be mapped to specific linguistic behaviours such as naming objects, reading aloud, filling in grammatically or semantically correct words or recalling verbal material (Ojemann, 1983). Behavioural impairment during the stimulation of a specified area is considered as an indication of brain localisation of the linguistic behaviour.

(3)   The recording of the electro-physiological stimulation of parts of the brain (evoked potentials), measured through electro-encephalo-

graphic (EEG) techniques. An EEG measures changes in electrical brain waves at rest and during activities; electrical signals are recorded from electrodes fixed on the scalp. EEG techniques are used with both brain-damaged and brain-intact subjects. Electrical signals are recorded from the two hemispheres while subjects are engaged in different verbal activities. An event-related potential (ERP) is an average measure of EEG for a number of events (for example, a series of similar tones as stimuli); the ERP is a more precise measure than the isolated EEG. ERP measures of brain activity are taken during language processing. A higher electrical activity is considered as a measure of hemispheric preference. The LH is more active for analytic and verbal tasks while the RH shows a greater activity during visual-spatial tasks (Moore & Haynes, 1980).

(4) Positron emission tomography (PET), a scanning technique which measures activity-related changes in regional cerebral blood flow (rCBF), is a non-invasive technique used with both brain-damaged and brain-intact subjects. Because the demand for oxygen and glucose is higher during an activity, blood flow increases. This increase is greater in the left hemisphere for verbal tasks and in the right hemisphere for spatial tasks (Gur, Gur, Orbrist, Hungerbuhler, Younkin, Rosen, Skilnick & Reirich, 1982). This scanning method permits a high precision in the anatomic localisation of higher cognitive functions and of the different linguistic functions.

(5) Functional magnetic resonance imaging (fMRI) is another promising non-invasive topographic scanning technique, which allows the researcher to pinpoint with even greater precision than the PET in which parts of the brain the blood flow increases during specific cognitive functioning (for more details, see Damasio, 1995).

(6) The magneto-encephalography technique (MEG), another recent very promising technique, allows the researcher to record minute changes in the magnetic field generated by neuronal aggregates during an experimental task. This completely non-invasive technique allows for the localisation of neurophysiological activity generated in relatively small cerebral regions and the identification of the source of brain activity associated with a variety of linguistic tasks (Papanicolaou, Simos & Basile, 1998).

6.3   NEUROPSYCHOLOGICAL DEVELOPMENT OF BILINGUALS

Is the brain organisation in bilinguals different from the one in monolinguals? Do bilinguals develop different neurological strategies of information processing according to their history and context of acquisition of both languages? Empirical evidence about the neuropsychological organisation of bilinguals stems from clinical data obtained from brain-injured patients who displayed some language-impairment after the injury and from experimental studies conducted with brain-intact bilinguals.

6.3.1   Evidence from polyglot aphasic patients

Numerous studies on polyglot aphasia (for a review, see Paradis, 1989) point to the fact that loss of one language and its subsequent recovery occur in a different way from the loss and subsequent recovery of the other language. Traditionally this evidence suggested a different cerebral organisation for each of a bilingual's languages (Vaid & Lambert, 1979). It would however be dangerous to generalise from clinical evidence to normal behaviour and one must turn to the recent neuropsychological literature on bilingual brain organisation in brain-intact bilinguals to understand the bilingual's cerebral functioning.

We are interested in the case studies on aphasia in bilinguals (referred to in the clinical literature as polyglot aphasia) insofar as they shed some light on bilingual processing. Aphasia is a language disorder, associated in most cases with a localised lesion in the left hemisphere (when associated with the right hemisphere it is referred to as crossed aphasia). Symptoms are numerous and vary according to the type of aphasia; for example, an aphasic may be capable of reading a word but incapable of identifying its referent: he may be incapable of reading a word but able to point to its referent; or he may be incapable of producing the word for a referent but able to recognise the written word. Some aphasics are not capable of naming referents, whereas others who are produce ungrammatical strings of words. It should be noted that in most cases aphasics recover language, especially if the loss is caused by a cranial trauma rather than by a chronic lesion. Recovery patterns also vary widely from one aphasic case to another.

Because aphasia generally occurs in brain-damaged adults and not in children, the view that early brain damage does not impinge on language development (Lenneberg, 1967) prevailed until recently. However, more recent studies indicate that some patterns of linguistic impairment are characteristic of left-hemisphere brain injury, regardless of the age of the injury, albeit in a milder form in cases of infant brain injuries (for a review, see Aram, 1988). Marchman, Miller & Bates (1991) observed that left-brain-injured infants were delayed in preverbal gestural communication and the production of first words when compared to brain-intact infants. Furthermore, their babbling and vocalisations followed different patterns. In the same vein, Thal, Marchman, Stiles, Aram, Trauner, Nass & Bates

(1991) report delays in brain-injured infants but observe that delays tend to disappear and that effects on language behaviour are relatively mild after the age of 4–5. If early brain-damage does delay language development in the early years, permanent impairment, if any, is subtle compared to the effects of a later-occurring brain injury (Styles & Thal, 1993). As no studies to date report effects of early brain damage on bilingual behaviour, we limit the present discussion to data obtained by studying brain-injured adults.

According to Paradis (1993) six basic patterns of recovery are observed in aphasic polyglots:

(1) parallel, when the two (or more) languages progress simultaneously and to the same extent;
(2) differential, when one language is recovered better than the other;
(3) successive, when one language is maximally recovered before the other starts to progress;
(4) selective, when one language is never recovered;
(5) antagonistic recovery, in which one language recovers first, then begins to regress once the second language starts recovering; and
(6) mixed, when the two languages are systematically mixed at the phonological, morphological, syntactic and/or lexical level in a way not present before the brain damage.

The most common patterns of recovery are either the simultaneous recovery of both languages or a selective improvement in one language while the other language or languages remain impaired (Albert & Obler, 1978).

We will not detail the different cases of recovery but rather attempt to answer the following questions:

(1) To what extent is recovery language specific and able to occur in one language to the exclusion of the other?;
(2) To what extent are specific bilingual abilities, such as the ability to translate or code-switch, impaired?; and
(3) does the polyglot aphasic use forms of language mixing which did not occur premorbidly?

Following this, we briefly discuss the relevance of our knowledge on polyglot aphasia for bilingual processing in general.

6.3.1.1 Selective impairment and recovery in polyglot aphasia

Because of the questions we ask above, we have a particular interest in differential or selective impairment/recovery in bilingual aphasics. By differential aphasia or selective impairment/recovery is understood the fact that both languages are not affected in the same way in a polyglot aphasic and/or that recovery does not follow the same pattern. Assumptions about recovery in aphasic polyglots date back to the nineteenth century. Ribot (1882) was the first to assess regularities in recovery; from his clinical observations he stated that the first-learned language is the less impaired and should recover first (Ribot's law). Because this appears true for many, but not all, cases of polyglot aphasia, Pitrès (1895) formulated a second rule: the most familiar or most used language is recovered first (Pitrès' law). However, some cases of polyglot aphasia fit neither of these laws. Therefore, Albert & Obler (1978), reviewing 108 case studies of polyglot aphasia, conclude that Ribot's law does not apply above the level of chance, whereas Pitrès' law is applicable in a number of cases when the patient is under the age of 60. These laws can be modified by a large number of factors determining the nature of the aphasia. Paradis (1977) identified three sources of influence on selective recovery: psychosocial, modality (written language) and hemispheric laterality factors.

Several psychosocial variables have been invoked to explain the patterns of differential impairment and recovery in polyglot aphasics: language-acquisition history, mode of acquisition, linguistic environment during recovery and emotional factors. Some structural variables such as structural similarities between languages and writing systems seem also to play a role. Very few studies mention relative competence as a possible variable influencing selective recovery; it is generally understood that the term 'polyglot aphasic' is used to describe bilinguals who were originally very fluent; unfortunately, what is meant by fluent bilinguals is rarely explained, especially in the earlier case studies; competence in the two languages is generally inferred from information on language acquisition and language use; furthermore, very little data is available on premorbid competence in the two languages. The balanced–dominant issue has not been taken up in the literature on polyglot aphasics and can at the best be inferred from the case descriptions, namely from the language-acquisition history.

Language-acquisition history, which includes age and context of acquisition, appears as the most relevant psychosocial variable for determining the polyglot aphasic's behaviour. According to Lambert & Fillenbaum (1959) language-acquisition history, which is a determining factor in the degree of interdependence of the bilingual's representations, plays an important role in aphasia: they observe that polyglot aphasics, who had presumably developed a compound form of binguality, show more similar symptoms and recovery patterns in both languages than coordinate bilinguals who became aphasic. Although Whitaker (1978) criticises the psychological reality of the compound–coordinate distinction, he admits that it is likely that the earlier a second language is acquired the more likely it is that a neural substrate will be shared by both languages. The clinical literature on polyglot aphasics fails to confirm that coordinate bilinguality in aphasics leads to a greater selective recovery. However, as Vaid (1984; Vaid & Hall, 1991) observes, two-thirds of the clinical observations on aphasic bilinguals are single-case studies and may or may not therefore be representative of the bilingual population at large.

A more recent experimental study (Junque, Vendrell & Vendrell, 1995) does not support Lambert & Fillenbaum's (1959) conclusions on compound and coordinate differences in aphasic bilinguals. In their study 50 fluent Catalan–Spanish bilingual aphasics, whose first language was either Catalan or Spanish and who were classified either as compound or as coordinate bilinguals according to their language history, were compared with brain-intact controls on a word-recognition, a word-finding and a word-translation task. For some of the patients test scores were also obtained after rehabilitation. Although the authors obtained a high percentage of differential recovery (30 per cent) for the aphasic bilinguals, they failed to find more differentiation in coordinate than in compound aphasic bilinguals. The authors suggest that other psychosocial factors stemming from the mode of acquisition, such as a greater metalinguistic knowledge for the second language rather than language organisation per se may be responsible for the selective recovery. It must also be noted that their selection of compound and coordinate bilinguals is not the same as the one used by Lambert & Fillenbaum and that this might explain why they failed to observe differences.

As Chernigovskaya, Balonov & Deglin (1983) point out, the method of appropriating the language is of prime importance. Drawing on a detailed analysis of recovery in Turkmen-Russian aphasics, they maintain that in cases when the last learned language recovers first, this is so because the psychological mechanisms for processing semantic representations and surface structures in the second language are located in the left (injured) hemisphere, while those for processing the semantic representations in the mother tongue are located in the right hemisphere with only the surface structures in the left hemisphere; early childhood bilinguality also follows the latter pattern with semantic representations for both languages in the right hemisphere. This model explains why a second language might be recovered first when it was learned at a later age: once recovery starts, both surface structure and semantic representations in L_2 are available. It also explains why, once L_1 recovery has started, it is recovered faster and more completely. This theoretical framework is tempting inasmuch as it explains a large body of polyglot aphasia data; it lacks, however, strong empirical support that a later learned language has more semantic representation in the left hemisphere.

Earlier studies also mentioned that mode of acquisition affects selective

recovery. For example, Wechsler (1977) mentions a case of polyglot aphasia in which the patient showed severe alexia (the incapacity to read) in his
mother tongue (English), but only a mild form of alexia in French, a
language he had learned in school during adolescence. Several cases of
selective recovery mention the recovery of classical languages (learned
essentially through the written mode) prior to aurally acquired languages
(Whitaker, 1978). From a neuropsychological point of view, it is sound to
postulate that two languages may be affected differentially by brain damage, particularly when they involve visual and auditive modalities to
different degrees (Albert & Obler, 1978). Wechsler (1977) postulated that
later language acquisition would rely more heavily on both hemispheres
and less heavily on the left hemisphere; therefore it would be easier to
recover the later-learned language. A second language learned later in life
might rely more heavily on a greater metalinguistic knowledge and on
more controlled cerebral functions located in the RH (Junque, Vendrell &
Vendrell, 1995). However, no clinical evidence supports the assumption
that becoming bilingual might lead to a transfer of dominance to the right
hemisphere; most aphasic polyglots are left-brain damaged and there are
no more right-brain damaged polyglots than monolingual aphasics.

Emotional factors can also influence selective recovery. Critchley (1974)
mentions the famous case of the French writer Pierre Loti who in a
recovery phase conversed more easily in Turkish – a language to which he
was emotionally attached – than in French, although the latter was his
mother tongue, the language of his literary work and of his environment.
Although emotional factors are often mentioned, very little evidence supports the assumption that emotional relation to the languages is the crucial
factor in recovery.

Recovery patterns are influenced by the linguistic environment during
recovery (Minkowski, 1963); a better recovery of the language used during
the treatment is mentioned in a large number of studies. However,
Voinescu, Vish, Sirian & Maretsis (1977) mention that even if the language
of treatment is favoured in recovery, there is a transfer to the other
languages known by the patient. These findings are also supported by
Junque, Vendrell & Vendrell (1995) who demonstrated that for the 50
aphasics treated in Catalan, only the word-naming task improved more in
Catalan than in Spanish; word-naming was part of the rehabilitation
program. Patients recovered equally well on the Catalan and the Spanish
word-pointing and word-translation tasks, although Spanish was not used
in the rehabilitation program. It must be noted that Spanish and Catalan
are structurally very close. Most studies using structurally more-distant
language combinations (such as Japanese and English) report only partial
transfer of recovery from the language of treatment to the other language in
polyglot aphasics (Watamori & Sasanuma, 1978; Sasanuma & Park, 1995).

It has been postulated that differences in language structure affect selective recovery (Critchley, 1974). There is some support for this assumption: according to Sasanuma & Parks (1995), polyglot aphasics with two structurally related languages such as Japanese and Korean transfer more from the language used during the therapeutic intervention to their other language than do patients with structurally unrelated languages such as Japanese and English. However, before attributing this lack of transfer to structural difference it must be kept in mind that, in the cases of polyglot aphasia where the two languages are structurally different, the two languages were often acquired under different circumstances, making it difficult to attribute differences in recovery to structural differences or to context of acquisition. One study (Stadie, Springer, de Bleser & Burk, 1995) suggests however that for a multilingual aphasic patient with differential recovery, it is easier to recover words in the least recovered language, when they share physical similarities with their translation equivalent in the best recovered language, as in the case of cognates (i.e. similar words such as *bread* in English and *Brot* in German). They explain their data by suggesting that there are some shared structures at least at the phonemic/graphic level. The structural distance hypothesis should thus not be completely disregarded; there are grounds to suggest that positive transfer occurs in post-trauma therapy. Transfer benefits most in the areas where both languages are similar (Sasanuma & Parks, 1995).

The writing system may also play a role. Sasanuma (1985) observed that in Japanese aphasics the syllabic writing system, kana, was recovered differentially from the logographic system, kanji. Whitaker (1978) argues that this might result from different brain locations for phonetically based and visually based languages; it has also been proposed that visual images of words may facilitate recovery (Minkowski, 1963). Because recovery is often reported to occur first for a language of literacy and later for a dialect or a language which is only spoken, it has been suggested that a language one reads and writes has a better chance of being recovered than a language which one only speaks (Grosjean, 1982). It might also be assumed that written language relies on a higher number of controlled processes and a greater metalinguistic awareness which could facilitate recovery.

Selective impairment and recovery appear as the most specific features in bilingual aphasics; however, they account for only 23 per cent of the cases of polyglot aphasia (Whitaker, 1978). In reviewing 138 clinical cases of polyglot aphasics, Paradis (1977) found that more than half were similarly impaired for the different languages and recovered them at the same rate. Furthermore, selective impairment has no equivalent in monolingual aphasics, thereby making any comparison impossible. Selective recovery can be linked to a number of psychological and structural factors, but no clear image of differential neuropsychological functioning emerges from this field. As Paradis (1995a) points out selective recovery must not necessarily be explained by a different anatomical representation for different languages but can be equally accounted for in terms of differential inhibition and control of resources.

6.3.1.2   Bilingual-specific behaviours in polyglot aphasics

When polyglot aphasics recover language use, some specific behaviour absent in the monolingual repertoire can occur. This includes code-mixing, code-switching and the ability to translate. How does brain damage affect these specific bilingual abilities? Several case studies report that polyglot aphasics retain the ability to translate both in simultaneous and selective recovery and, conversely, the ability to translate or code-switch may be lost even in cases of mild impairment in each language; some patients show a unidirectional impairment in translation into their mother tongue (L_1), while retaining the ability to translate into their L_2 (Fabbro & Paradis, 1995). Furthermore, a polyglot aphasic might be able to code-switch but totally unable to translate (Albert & Obler, 1978). He may be impaired in speaking one language but capable of producing a fluent translation in his other language; or he may be incapable of speaking in one language but able to translate into that language; or he may not be able to translate into a language he speaks fluently (Paradis, 1980). Thus, code-switching ability and translation ability seem to be independent of speaking ability.

Surprisingly, aphasic bilinguals rarely produce language-mixing qualitatively different from the code-switching used premorbidly: interlanguage interference is reported as a symptom in only 7 per cent of polyglot aphasia cases, and most patients retain their switching ability (Albert & Obler, 1978). Fredman (1975) reported that aphasic mixing occurred more frequently in older patients; similar language structures (between Hebrew and Arabic) do not induce more mixing than different language structures (as between Hebrew and French or Hungarian), but less; whether this relative absence of mixing between similar languages can be attributed to social factors (the study was conducted in Israel) or to the existence of a control mechanism to keep similar languages separated is open to speculation.

According to Perecman (1984), language-mixing occurs at all levels of linguistic description – i.e. phonological, syntactic and lexical – in polyglot aphasia. She proposes that aphasic language-mixing indicates a 'properly linguistic deficit' while spontaneous translation originates at the conceptual level. However, her interpretation is challenged by Grosjean (1985b), who argues that, because spontaneous translation and language-mixing are common behaviours in the bilingual speech mode, it cannot be concluded that they are abnormal unless they have been compared with the patient's premorbid speech. The data on aphasic language-mixing is still scarce and often we do not know how far aphasic mixing is different from normal code-mixing. A beginning has been made in attempting to unravel the problem of code-switching and to describe the bilingual speech mode (Grosjean & Soares, 1986); before it can be decided what is morbid about aphasic mixing we must be able to describe what is normal about normal bilingual speech-mode processing (see Sections 7.2, 9.2 and 9.3).

One bilingual behaviour often reported in polyglot aphasics which seems to deviate from brain-intact bilinguals is the use of spontaneous translations. There is some reason to believe that translation is a task neuropsychologically independent from understanding and speaking two languages. Spontaneous translation instead of a conventional response to a verbal or non-verbal task (e.g. pointing) is frequently reported (Paradis, Goldblum & Abidi, 1982). Patients may spontaneously translate their own speech without apparent reason, or they may translate verbal commands before or instead of executing them. Spontaneous translations occur in written as well as in spoken language (Lebrun, 1995). Is the spontaneous translation of aphasics similar to the spontaneous translations used by bilingual youngsters dealing with communication problems between speakers of different languages (see Section 3.1.3)? Do they translate verbal commands because they cannot execute them? These questions do not appear to have been investigated to date and are open to speculation. If this is the case, then spontaneous translations must not be viewed as a deviating behaviour but rather as an appropriate response to a disorder of pragmatics in communication.

Because aphasic polyglots might alternate between recovery in their two languages, being one day able to use one language fluently in spontaneous speech but not the other, and vice versa, it must be assumed that there is a functional dissociation between the languages, i.e. that one language becomes restrictively inaccessible for a period of time and under certain conditions (Paradis, Goldblum & Abidi, 1982). Because languages are not destroyed in polyglot aphasia, only inhibited (Green, 1986), this allows us to speculate about bilingual processing.

6.3.1.3   Polyglot aphasia and bilingualism

Summarising the studies on polyglot aphasia, Albert & Obler (1978) suggest that the following data might shed some light on bilingual processing:

(1)   Sometimes there is apparent loss of one language and not the other;
(2)   There is parallel recovery in most cases but not all;
(3)   Regression in the first recovered language can be concurrent with

recovery in the second;

(4)   Affective factors influence recovery;

(5)   Pitrès' law is applicable above chance level;

(6)   There is a possible split between the recovery of formal/literacy and informal language;

(7)   There are possible differences between losses following chronic and traumatic lesions;

(8)   There is a possibility of right-hemisphere initiative in recovery and relearning language functions;

(9)   In some cases there is an apparent loss of switching ability;

(10)   There may be an apparent loss or impairment of translation;

(11)   Lost childhood language can sometimes be recovered through hypnosis; and

(12)   There are indications that multilingualism can have anatomical repercussions.

To what extent does this clinical data inform us about language processing in bilingual aphasics? From the data reviewed it appears that language-acquisition history is a determining factor in polyglot aphasia. This, however, includes a large number of factors such as age, mode and context of acquisition that interact with each other. One of the greatest weaknesses encountered with the evidence stemming from bilingual aphasics is the absence of data on premorbid speech. Fluent bilingual aphasics are at best described using information stemming from their post-hoc language history, but no experimental data is available on their language competence or on their bilingual-specific behaviour. Describing bilingual brain functioning from clinical data alone would be like describing the anatomy of grasping from clinical cases of broken hands. Although the evidence described above can shed some light on bilingual cerebral processing, we must first review the evidence on cerebral functioning in brain-intact bilinguals before we can propose a more general model of the bilingual brain.

6.3.2   Evidence from brain-intact bilinguals

The literature on cerebral dominance in bilinguals does not present a clear, unified picture of how bilinguals process language. Whereas most scholars agree that bilingual experience has some influence on brain functioning, they disagree on the nature of the neuropsychological consequences of this experience. Whereas some researchers contend that bilinguals and monolinguals are equally lateralised, others suggest that bilinguals are more bilateral than monolinguals (Albert & Obler, 1978). However, whereas this might be the case for dominant bilinguals, there is also some evidence which shows that balanced infant bilinguals evince a greater lateralisation (Shanon, 1982). It should come as no surprise, therefore, that in this field we have to deal with a large amount of apparently contradictory evidence; this state of uncertainty can be attributed to the high number of factors influencing the functioning and development of neuropsychological processes. However, researchers are still capable of raising a number of relevant questions on the relationship between bilinguality and brain functioning.

The vast majority of experimental studies on the neuropsychological functioning of bilinguals attempt to answer one or more of the following questions:

(1) Is the neuropsychological development of bilinguals different from that of monolinguals?
(2) Do bilinguals process information in their different languages in a similar way or do they develop specific brain mechanisms for each of their languages?
(3) Does the age of acquisition play a significant role in determining cerebral dominance in bilinguals?
(4) Does the level of competence in the second language influence the hemispheric involvement in language processing?
(5) Is the context of acquisition of and exposure to a second language relevant in determining the degree of lateralisation?
(6) What role do structural differences between languages play in determining the use of both hemispheres?
(7) What effect does a difference in script between languages have on brain functioning in bilinguals?

6.3.2.1 Comparing bilinguals and monolinguals

A direct comparison between the neuropsychological functioning of bilinguals and monolinguals has been made in a number of studies. For example, Barton, Goodglass & Skai (1965) found no differences of lateralisation between Hebrew–English bilinguals and English monolinguals responding to a tachistoscopic task of word recognition presented in the right or the left visual field; both groups had an LH advantage. Tzeng, Hung, Cotton & Wang (1979) found that Chinese–English bilinguals and Chinese monolinguals had similar reaction times to a word-recognition task of English and Chinese words. No differences were found between English–Portuguese bilinguals and English monolinguals, who both showed an LH advantage (Soares & Grosjean, 1981). Similarly, Soares (1984) confirmed that there were no differences between bilinguals and monolinguals; their speech production was equally disrupted when a concurrent task interfered in the left hemisphere. All these studies indicate that LH dominance for language, observed in monolinguals, is equally present in bilinguals. Summarising the results obtained in 17 studies using bilingual and monolingual comparisons, Vaid & Hall (1991) conclude that there are no lateralisation differences between monolinguals and bilinguals when the latter are tested in their mother tongue, but that there is support for bilinguals being less lateralised in studies where they were tested in their second language.

However, some studies seem to contradict the previous conclusion. Walters & Zatorre (1978) argue that bilinguals show a greater degree of heterogeneity in their hemispheric organisation than monolinguals. Indeed, a number of studies mention a greater RH involvement in bilinguals (see, for example, F. W. Carroll, 1978a; Vaid & Lambert, 1979; Galloway, 1980; Sussman, Franklin & Simon, 1982). In the same vein, Mägiste (1992) found less LH involvement in Swedish–German bilinguals than in Swedish monolinguals. Studies mentioning a greater RH involvement and those showing no differences between bilinguals and monolinguals differ in terms of population characteristics such as age of onset of bilinguality and L_2 proficiency. This suggests that a number of experiential factors that are likely to influence the cerebral organisation of the bilingual have to be taken into account.

6.3.2.2   Language-specific cerebral organisation of bilinguals

On the basis of their research in neuropsychology, Penfield & Roberts (1959) put forward the hypothesis that one and the same cerebral mechanism is responsible for the processing of the bilingual's two languages. This hypothesis has been verified by Hamers & Lambert (1977), who concluded that the two hemispheres play a similar part in processing, regardless of the language. In their experiment, balanced French–English bilinguals were asked to respond to a tachistoscopically presented language-recognition task; the results showed that the difference in processing of the two hemispheres is the same for the two languages. This finding was confirmed by H. W. Gordon (1980), who found no differences in lateralisation for the two languages for English–Hebrew subjects responding to a dichotic listening task; a strong lateralisation for one language is highly correlated with a strong lateralisation for the other, regardless of the age of acquisition of L_2, the level of competence in L_2 and the uses of the two languages. In a similar vein, Hoosain (1992) found no evidence for a differential lateralisation in Chinese–English bilinguals. Reviewing the existing experimental and clinical evidence, Zatorre (1989) came to the conclusion that the LH controls both the L_1 and the later-learned L_2 to the same degree. Vaid & Hall (1991) reached a similar conclusion in their review of 39 studies analysing the localisation of the bilingual's two languages.

Empirical support for Penfield & Roberts' assumption that a bilingual's two languages share the same neural substratum also comes from a recent studies using PET scanning (Klein, Zatorre, Milner, Meyer & Evans, 1994; 1995). The authors investigated whether processing in the second language involves the same neurological structures as in the first language; subjects of the study were brain-intact fluent bilinguals who learned their second language after the age of five. They found no support for the assumption that a second language learned in childhood is represented differently from the native language. They conclude that, with the exception of the articulatory demands of L_2 that may require additional processing, the same neural substratum serves both languages. However, they also suggest that using L_1 and L_2 may differ in cognitive demands. It seems likely that bilinguals call upon different strategies in processing L_1 and L_2.

6.3.2.3   Age of acquisition of bilinguality and the onset of laterality

It has been proposed that the age of acquisition of bilinguality or of L_2 is a relevant factor in the development of laterality. Generally speaking, cerebral dominance is more precocious when the child experiences enriching early stimulation (Bever, 1970; Geffner & Hochbert, 1971). Multilingual experience in early childhood seems to speed up the onset of cerebral dominance. One study using a dichotic listening technique with 6–8-year-old Hebrew–French–English trilinguals showed that these children developed laterality earlier than English monolingual counterparts matched for socio-economic background and intelligence (Starck, Genesee, Lambert & Seitz, 1977). But will precocious laterality also determine the relative role of the two hemispheres in verbal information processing? This question has so far received no answer.

6.3.2.4   Age of acquisition and cerebral strategies

Although there is no evidence that cerebral localisation differs as a function of the age of acquisition of bilinguality, a number of empirical studies point to the fact that early and late bilinguals might call upon different cerebral strategies while performing verbal tasks. In which way will bilingual experience influence the relative use of each hemisphere for verbal information processing? The empirical evidence is equivocal with some studies suggesting greater RH involvement in late bilinguals than in early bilinguals and others suggesting equal LH involvement in both early and late bilinguals.

On tasks involving phonetic and syntactic judgements no differences are found between early and late bilinguals; both show an LH superiority (Vaid, 1987). Although generally speaking one might expect a greater reliance on the LH among early than among late bilinguals, not all experiments conducted with early bilinguals point to a greater LH involvement. Group differences are found for synonym judgement tasks (Vaid, 1984) and for shadowing tasks (Vaid, Green, Schweda Nicholson & White, 1989), with early bilinguals showing less asymmetry or greater RH involvement than late bilinguals. In one of her experiments, F. W. Carroll (1978a) found greater RH involvement in the processing of English by early Navajo–English bilinguals than by English monolinguals. However, her Navajo subjects, who were dominant in Navajo, did not show the same pattern in processing Navajo. Therefore, competence in the two languages also plays a role in determining the type of cerebral strategy bilinguals use. Similar results were obtained by Wuillemin, Richardson & Lynch (1994) who found an increased RH involvement in language processing of the L_2 (English and Tok Pisin) with a later age of acquisition.

However, a different set of studies mention more LH involvement in early bilinguals. In one experiment (Genesee, Hamers, Lambert, Mononen, Seitz & Starck, 1978), evoked potentials were measured during a language-recognition task for three groups of balanced French–English bilinguals different in respect of age of acquisition (infant, childhood and adolescent bilinguality), but not in terms of their competence in both languages nor in their language use. The results show that the three groups used different cerebral strategies and thus called on different neuropsychological mechanisms for a similar task: infant and childhood bilinguals relied more on LH processing than did adolescent bilinguals, who relied more heavily on RH. The authors interpreted these results as an indication that early bilinguals rely more on semantic strategies in verbal processing than late bilinguals.

This interpretation is confirmed by another experiment (Vaid & Lambert, 1979) in which early and late bilinguals had to process semantically congruent and incongruent stimuli (F. W. Carroll, 1978b). Using dichotic measures with English–Spanish bilinguals with different language histories, they concluded that the age of bilingual experience is a crucial factor in determining the role played by the left hemisphere in language processing. Shanon (1982) also demonstrated that balanced bilinguals who had developed early childhood bilinguality displayed a greater LH preference than fluent but not balanced bilinguals who had learned L_2 at a later age. In their study with childhood bilinguals who were fluent in L_2 at the age of 7;3, Klein, Zatorre, Milner, Meyer & Evans (1994), although they found no evidence that cortical activity was different for L_1 or L_2, noticed a subcortical activity (in the left putamen) in the production of words in the L_2 which was absent in the production of L_1 and which is also absent in monolinguals. It is however premature to conclude that this is evidence for a neurophysiological distinction between simultaneous and consecutive bilingualism, but it is an indication that even for highly competent childhood bilinguals the L_2 is not processed in the same way as the mother tongue, at least at the articulatory level.

Kim, Relkin, Lee & Hirsch (1997) compared the brain activity of right-handed simultaneous infancy-bilingual adults with that of right-handed bilinguals who started to learn L_2 at the age of 11 and achieved fluency at the age of 19 (after a stay in the L_2 country). The subjects were bilingual in a variety of language combinations. While the subjects were functioning in the two languages they used the FMRI scanning technique. The authors observed no difference in location of activity in Wernicke's area (a cerebral region in which the semantic processing occurs) between the two groups. However, late bilinguals had two distinct spatial sites, one for each language, in Broca's area (a location responsible for grammatical processing). The authors attribute the difference between their study and the study by Klein *et al.* (1994) either to the fact that the FMRI technique permits a higher degree of precision than the PET technique, or to the fact that the consecutive childhood bilinguals used in the Klein *et al.* study would behave in a similar way to the simultaneous bilinguals. They conclude that age of acquisition may be a significant factor in determining the functional organisation in Broca's area, but not in Wernicke's area. If representations of languages in Broca's area are developed and fixed early in life, the acquisition of an L_2 at a later age will necessitate the use of the adjacent cortical area.

6.3.2.5   Bilingual competence and hemispheric preference

A differential involvement of the two hemispheres according to the level of competence attained in L_2 has been mentioned in the scientific literature (for a review see Vaid, 1983). This observation, and the fact that L_1 and L_2 acquisitions occur in a different context, prompted Galloway & Krashen (1980) to postulate the stage hypothesis: they suggest that there is an intermediate stage at the beginning of the acquisition of L_2 during which the right hemisphere might have greater involvement in language processing; as a consequence of an increased competence in L_2, cortical activity during language processing might be shifted to the left hemisphere. In support of this hypothesis, Silverberg, Bentin, Gaziel, Obler & Albert (1979) found a greater RH involvement in the acquisition of reading in L_2 for Hebrew-speaking children who had learned English for only two years than for comparable children who had received 4–6 years of English instruction. Obler (1981) suggests that non-fluent second-language learners call upon a common strategy in which they rely heavily on key words and 'guess' the meaning from the linguistic and the non-linguistic context; intonation patterns, which are processed by the right hemisphere, are part of this context. Furthermore, learners in the beginning stages of L_2 acquisition may be more exposed to drills and to formulaic language, the processing of which involve the RH.

The stage hypothesis has, however, received only limited support from other studies. Schneiderman & Wesche (1980), using a dichotic-listening technique with Anglophones learning French in a formal setting, found that although lateralisation was more pronounced for English than for French, there was no increase in lateralisation for the second language concomitant with an increased competence in that language. Galloway (1980) demonstrated that Spanish-speaking Mexicans who learned English in an informal context had the same LH dominance for Spanish and English; Rupp (1980) reported a greater LH involvement for L_2 in Vietnamese children learning English; and so did Rogers, Ten Houten, Kaplan & Gardiner (1977) with Hopi children learning English.

However, a majority of studies taking into account the competence attained in L_2 do not support the stage hypothesis. Albanese (1985) found no difference in lateralisation between L_1 and L_2 among French–English bilinguals, regardless of their levels of proficiency and the nature of the task. In the same vein, Wuillemin, Richardson & Lynch (1994) failed to find a relation between hemispheric involvement and proficiency in L_2. Analysing 22 comparisons Vaid & Hall (1991) found only five in favour of the stage hypothesis, while eight produced results in the opposite direction. As Albanese points out, the stage hypothesis predicts a large RH involvement at the beginning stage of learning L_2 and a decrease in RH involvement with increasing proficiency; however, this is unsupported by empirical evidence. So far, the stage hypothesis has received support only for learning to read in L_2 (Vaid, 1983).

According to Ojemann & Whitaker (1978), as a language becomes more automatised it will be subserved by a less extensive area of the cortex than a language in which one is less competent. Although the authors produce some experimental evidence in support of this idea, it has so far received no clear-cut answer.

6.3.2.6   *Hemispheric preference and language-acquisition context*

The context in which L_2 is acquired may also influence the hemispheric involvement in bilinguals. According to Vaid (1983) there will be greater RH involvement in L_2 as compared with L_1 if L_2 is learned informally; and conversely, there will be greater LH involvement in L_2 than in L_1 if L_2 is

learned formally. Although a number of experiments support this statement (Albert & Obler, 1978; F. W. Carroll, 1980; H. W. Gordon, 1980) it
may be oversimplified in the sense that the type of formal learning also
influences the hemispheric involvement. It is indeed possible that certain
L_2 teaching methods may call for a greater LH involvement than others
(Krashen, Seliger & Hartnett, 1974). Hartnett (1975), for example, demonstrated a greater LH processing in L_2 learned through a deductive method,
but a greater RH involvement when an inductive method was used. Thus,
even in formal learning, hemispheric involvement may be influenced by the
particular teaching methodology. Formal learning of an L_2 might however
rely more on controlled processing and metalinguistic knowledge and
therefore call more on the RH.

Furthermore, the language-acquisition context cannot be isolated from
age of acquisition, which appears as a major factor in determining cerebral
processing in bilinguals, as we have seen in Section 6.3.2.4.

6.3.2.7   Language differences and hemispheric involvement

The assumption that structural differences between languages may involve
both hemispheres to different degrees has also been advanced. One study
(Rogers, Ten Houten, Kaplan & Gardiner 1977) suggests that Hopi–English bilinguals make greater use of the right hemisphere in processing
elements of Hopi than in processing English. They explain this by the fact
that Hopi is an appositional[4] language that depends more on RH strategies.
While this conclusion is also supported by some studies with Native
American bilinguals (Hynd & Scott, 1980 and Scott, Hynd, Hunt & Weed,
1979 with Navajo–English bilinguals; Vocate, 1984 with Crow–English
bilinguals), it is invalidated by other studies (F. W. Carroll, 1978a and
Hynd, Teeter & Stewart, 1980 with Navajo–English bilinguals).

However, are these differences between hemispheric functioning really
attributable to structural differences between languages, since in all these
cases the language-learning experiences are dissimilar? For example, it is
evident from the experiments by Rogers, Ten Houten, Kaplan & Gardiner
(1977) and by Scott, Hynd, Hunt & Weed (1979) that the experience with
the two languages is very different indeed. It is impossible to attribute
differences in laterality development to structural differences between languages unless one can control the conditions under which both languages
are learned.

6.3.2.8   Script differences and hemispheric preferences

In bilingual speakers whose languages differ in their degree of
sound–symbol correspondence between the spoken and the written lan-

guage, it may be hypothesised that different patterns of hemispheric functioning will occur. Generally speaking, it may be assumed that the more phonetic the script, the greater the LH involvement (Vaid, 1983). Sugishita, Iwata, Toyokura, Yoshioka & Yamada (1978) reported in Japanese commissurectomy patients a RH impairment for reading Japanese in kana (a syllabic script), while the ability to read in kanji (an logographic script), which is supposedly controlled by the left hemisphere, remained intact. Hemispheric differences between processing of kana and kanji scripts have also been observed in normal Japanese subjects in studies using evoked potential measures (Hink, Kaga & Suzuki, 1980) and in tachistoscopic studies (Endo, Shimizu & Hori, 1978; Endo, Shimizu & Nakamura, 1981). These demonstrated a LH superiority for the kana script and a RH superiority for the kanji script. These findings were also confirmed in a study by Hatta (1981); RH involvement has also been reported for Chinese script (Vaid, 1983; Hasuike, Tzeng & Hung, 1986). One study (Cheng & Yang, 1989) confirmed RH processing for single Chinese characters, but LH processing for two-character words. RH superiority in Japanese and Chinese subjects applies only in the case of written material, as LH superiority is reported in dichotic studies with Japanese and Chinese monolinguals (Bryson, Mononen & Yu, 1980). It seems, therefore, that an LH advantage is found when the linguistic material to be processed is sequential.

Differences in modes of writing must affect semantic organisation – as, for example, the difference between a phonetic and an ideographic script – in order for these differences to impinge on brain functioning. More surface differences, like the opposite directionality of two phonetic scripts, do not seem to lead to different processing strategies. This is confirmed by a number of studies with written Yiddish and English (Mishkin & Forgays, 1952; Orbach, 1953), with written Hebrew and English (Barton, Goodglass & Skai, 1965; Gaziel, Obler & Albert, 1978; Shanon, 1982), and with Urdu and Hindi (Vaid, 1983), which all reported a similar LH laterality for both languages. Although a small scanning effect on cerebral processing may exist, it is overridden by other factors.

6.4   HEMISPHERIC PREFERENCES AND THE SIGNING BILINGUAL

Although the literature on bilingual sign aphasia and on cerebral organisation in signing bilinguals is scarce, it offers some valuable insight into the organisation of the brain in bilinguals. On reviewing the published cases of sign aphasics who are bilingual in a gestural and a spoken language, it appears that impairment and recovery follow similar patterns as in bilinguals with two or more spoken languages (Lebrun & Leleux, 1986). When referring to a signing bilingual we include both deaf and hearing people who are fluent in at least one gestural language, such as finger-spelling or ASL, and in one articulated language. Most studies have, however, been conducted with a combination of English and ASL.

Signers with LH damage show language impairments that closely resemble those of hearing aphasics: agrammatism,[5] severe comprehension loss, errors in the formational elements of signs, and errors of spatialised syntax. In contrast signers with a RH lesion produce a fluent, grammatical and unimpaired sign language, even though signing is spatial in nature and spatial skills are controlled by the RH. At the same time they show severe deficits in processing non-verbal spatial relationships (Bellugi, Poizner & Klima, 1993). These observations are confirmed by evidence from brain-intact deaf and hearing signing bilinguals. Left hemisphere specialisation for both languages was demonstrated with a shadowing task of spoken and gestural language (Corina, Vaid & Bellugi, 1992) and in a tachistoscopic sign-recognition task (Grossi, Semenza, Corazza & Volterra, 1996).

In one case, a hearing bilingual signer (ASL–English) treated for epilepsy and identified as LH dominant for the spoken language received an LH injection of sodium amytal. The Wada test caused marked aphasia in both English and ASL. After right temporal-lobe surgery, the patient showed no impairment in English or in ASL (Damasio, Bellugi, Damasio, Poizner & Van Gilder, 1986). When brain-intact native deaf signers are exposed to digitised sequences of ASL signs presented in the left and right central visual field, they show a LH preference for processing ASL signs. This preference is absent in hearing non-signers (Neville, 1988). Bellugi, Poizner & Klima (1993) interpret these results as a proof that the LH specialisation rests on the linguistic function it subserves. The authors conclude that hearing and speech are not crucial for the development of hemispheric specialisation for language. Although visual-spatial relations are normally processed in the RH, once they become a mode to express linguistic functions they appear to be controlled by the LH. Furthermore, the authors found evidence that selective impairment occurs and that sign language is broken down along linguistic lines. These results are in support of the proposal that there is a single anatomical structure for language processing.

6.5   CONCLUSION

At the beginning of this chapter we asked six questions concerning the bilingual's cerebral organisation. How does the behavioural and neuropsychological evidence obtained from brain-damaged and brain-intact subjects contribute to proposing an answer to these questions?

(1)   Is cerebral organisation different in bilinguals from cerebral organisation in monolinguals? In the light of studies to date, the answer seems to be 'no'. From the review by Vaid & Hall (1991) and from subsequent studies, there is no clear-cut evidence that shows basic differences between bilinguals and monolinguals. Neither can the data from the polyglot aphasics studies shed some light on this problem. The vast majority of bilingual aphasics recover their languages in a way similar to that of monolinguals. Furthermore, selective recovery (that occurs in 23 per cent of the patients) is no proof of bilingual–monolingual differences, as there is no comparable mode of recovery in monolinguals. It is specific to bilingual aphasics and might bring some answers to the next question we asked.

(2)   Are there separate neural mechanisms for different languages? As far as localisation is concerned the answer seems to be 'no'. Selective recovery in bilingual aphasics is no proof of differential hemispheric localisation although it might be an indication that cerebral functioning is different for the two languages. Whereas earlier experimental studies are contradictory – with some researchers concluding that there are no differences and others that there are either more LH or more RH preferences – more recent evidence suggests that localisation in the LH serves the bilingual's different languages. Better control of methodological issues in the more recent studies might explain this shift in results. The more recent studies suggest that, although there might be no differences in hemispheric preferences, different neuro-anatomical structures located in the LH might subserve L_1 and L_2. One study (Klein et al. 1994) indicates that there might be some subcortical neural structures specific to an L_2, but this is so far limited to the articulatory level; it is however the first real neuro-anatomical indication that an L_2 does not completely overlap with the L_1. The study by Kim, Relkin, Lee & Hirsch (1997) provides further proof that learning an L_2 at a later age might lead to the development of new neuro-anatomic functions. These specific structures can be explained in terms of the creation of new connections which map new forms onto old functions.

(3)   Are there age-of-acquisition differences in cerebral processing? Here again, in the light of studies to date the answer seems to be 'no'. Bilingual experience seems to enhance the onset of laterality but so do other early enrichment experiences. Furthermore, early onset is no proof of differential organisation. Clinical and experimental evidence on the age of acquisition is contradictory. Some researchers do not support the assumption that a different cerebral structure would develop when bilingual experience occurs at different ages. Most of the evidence mentions greater RH processing. Most studies on the processing of bilinguals deal with consecutive, dominant bilinguals; the few studies referring to early, balanced bilinguals mention greater LH processing (Genesee, Tucker & Lambert, 1978) and a more

pronounced laterality (Shanon, 1982). Some recent neurophysiological evidence suggests that early and late bilinguals process grammar in a neurophysiologically different way. Similar brain structures can be activated by different neural circuits which depend on early experience (Hebb, 1949). From experiments with brain-intact bilinguals it can be argued that hemispheric processing does not only depend on the task, that neurological pathways and the strategies of processing are not necessarily the same for the different types of bilinguals, and that, additionally, they do not appear to be controlled in the same way. However, differences in age of acquisition are often indistinguishable from differences in learning situations.

(4) Do differences in learning situations, in competence and in language structure have different effects on cerebral organisation? Here again, the summarised evidence is in favour of a unique neuro-anatomic structure in the bilingual. Differences in learning situations might promote a differential use of the two hemispheres in language processing. An L_2 is often learned in a classroom situation that will often call for metalinguistic analysis, a process known to be under RH control. There is a small indication that a lesser-known language should be covered by a larger cortical area than a completely automatised language (Rapport, Tan & Whitaker, 1983), but then this is true for all behaviour: when a given behaviour is less automatised it tends to be under control of a larger cortical area. According to Paradis (1995b), when processing language in their weaker language, bilinguals may rely to a greater extent on pragmatics, known to be under RH control. However, here again the evidence is controversial as the stage hypothesis does not receive extensive experimental support. Differences in language structures and scripts might enhance differential processing but the data is not conclusive as to the existence of a separate structure.

(5) Are the same cerebral structures involved in the language of bilinguals using an articulate and a signed language? The small amount of data that exists on signing bilinguals is in support of a shared structure for the signed and the articulated language. Comparisons of processing of sequential visual-spatial units relevant in sign language by signers and non-signers indicate a shift of locus of processing to the LH. This is another argument in favour of a unique cerebral structure for language in the dominant hemisphere.

If the whole body of literature on lateralisation in bilinguals does not entitle us to draw a unified picture of their brain functioning, it nonetheless appears that age of bilinguality and childhood experience in learning different languages are relevant factors in language processing. It is important to make a distinction between evidence on neuro-anatomical localisation – which points to no differential cerebral localisation in bilinguals and monolinguals, or for the bilingual's different languages (with the exception that the cortical area subserving the L_2 at the beginning might be more extended and that subcortical structures might be involved in L_2 production, even in fluent bilinguals) – and the neuropsychological evidence – which indicates differential processing. How do we account for the contradictory results? Herbert (1982) proposed the following explanation for the higher degree of bilateralisation of bilinguals mentioned in a number of studies (see Albert & Obler (1978) for a review): according to Corballis & Morgan (1978; see also Corballis, 1991) the right hemisphere would be more involved in delayed acquisition; because of the delay in maturation between both hemispheres, the left one being slightly ahead and predisposed for language acquisition, early language acquisition should rely essentially on the left hemisphere; in the case of late language acquisition, the difference in maturation between both hemispheres would be lessened and a greater RH involvement would be possible.

It might be argued that bilinguals do not so much use different cerebral structures, but rather the same structures to a different extent, and that they use different strategies for language processing. Green (1986) proposed a general model of bilingual processing which accommodates the performance of brain-intact as well as brain-damaged bilinguals. Assuming that aphasic impairment reflects a problem in controlling intact language systems, he argues that the regulatory mechanisms, specifically the inhibitory resources, are responsible for the different types of impairment: each outcome is a direct consequence of the failure of a specific control system. This framework is interesting insofar as, without having to postulate specific mechanisms, it accounts for pathological as well as for normal behaviour; furthermore, it is congruent with more general models of speech production and skilled action. A number of assumptions in the model, however, have still to be verified. Green's model is further discussed in Section 7.2.2.

Cognitive strategies that are used in the analysis of verbal material and determine the role of each hemisphere are dependent on early language experiences. Even if no clear picture of bilingual brain functioning emerges, the knowledge that early language experience will shape information-processing strategies in later life has important implications for language-teaching methodologists, for parents who want to raise their children in more than one language and for educators who have to introduce children to literacy in a language other than the mother tongue.

(6)   To what extent do different languages rely on different cerebral structures? To summarise, the studies analysing the brain functioning in both brain-damaged and brain-intact bilinguals give little evidence for hemispheric preferences different from the ones found in monolinguals. The idea

prevailing in the 1970s that bilinguals would rely more on the RH is not sustained by the more recent research. Evidence obtained by more sophisticated techniques supports the idea that bilinguals process language in the same way as monolinguals, although they might develop some specific neuro-anatomic structures as a function of the age of L_2 acquisition. Experimental evidence stemming from brain-damaged and brain-intact bilinguals as well as from bilingual signers does not support the assumption that completely separate neuro-anatomic structures serve the bilingual's two languages.

There is a fair amount of evidence to sustain the idea that there might be neurophysiological and neuropsychological specificities in language processing unique to bilinguals: the bilingual would have one structure common to both languages as well as two independent language-specific subsets of neural connections (Paradis, 1995b). However, one has to assume that he also possesses different connections for bilingual-specific processing; this is so far sustained for translation. We lack, however, evidence on cerebral processing of other behaviour specific to the bilingual speech mode, such as code-switching and code-mixing. All three speech modes are used by recovering bilingual aphasics, but to what extent is it used in a different way from how it was used in premorbid speech? The overlap between the bilingual's functional subsets and their activation or inhibition appears to be a function of a variety of factors such as age, context and mode of acquisition of both languages, and to a small extent structural characteristics of the languages involved.

In Chapter 5 we argued that language is stored at the conceptual level, in the form of propositional representations related to the general character- istics of language and independent from the specificity of a given language. Theories of information processing must explain how verbal information is transformed into propositional representations, how one has access to them, how information is stored at the different levels of processing and what the links are between propositional and verbal processes; they must also account for the bilingual's specific behaviour, particularly for the psychological mechanisms which enable him to function alternately in one or the other language while having an extended control on the possible interference. It must equally explain behaviour unique to the bilingual, such as code-switching, code-mixing (discussed in Section 9.3) or the bilingual's capacity to translate. Thus a model of the bilingual's processing must explain at what level of representation the two languages are inter- connected and must be informative about the existing relationship between the bilingual's two codes for every mechanism relevant to language pro- cessing.

In the present chapter we discuss how the bilingual organises, stores and has access to his two languages and propose theoretical frameworks for language representation and processing, which we consider as two separate but interrelated psycholinguistic mechanisms (Section 7.1). We propose a general model of bilingual processing congruent with our approach to language processing (Section 7.2). Finally we discuss briefly the bilingual's non-verbal behaviour and personality (Section 7.3).

7.1   LANGUAGE STORING AND PROCESSING IN BILINGUALS

Psycholinguistic research on bilinguals deals essentially with the relation- ship between the bilingual's two linguistic codes and several psychological mechanisms involved in language organisation and processing. Through- out the present section we analyse the necessity of postulating either the existence of two independent psychological mechanisms – one for each language (independence hypothesis) – or the existence of a single mechanism, common to both linguistic codes (interdependence hypothesis) at different levels of information processing or the existence of a compound mechanism which sometimes calls on separate processors and at other times on common mechanisms. Whether or not separate or common mechanisms are used depends on the type of task required and the depth of processing. Most research on language processing in bilinguals deals with the issue of organisation, storage and memory of lexical units; a smaller body of research addresses the issue of access.

We review the degree of interdependence between the bilingual's two languages for:

(1)   language representation in bilinguals, that is cognitive organisation and memory at different levels of processing; and
(2)   different mechanisms of information processing, that is access to both languages in verbal perception, decoding, encoding and production.

We describe briefly some of the most commonly used experimental techniques and discuss empirical data in terms of the independence–interdependence hypothesis. We close this chapter with a short section on the bilingual's non-verbal behaviour.

7.1.1   Language representation in bilinguals

In this section we attempt to answer the issues raised above, first, by discussing how early bilingual experience might impinge on cognitive representations and, second, by discussing different models of bilingual information processing.

7.1.1.1   *Coordinate vs. compound bilinguals*

The first description of the bilingual's cognitive organisation was given by Weinreich (1953) who made a distinction between compound, coordinate and subordinate bilingualism. When developing the distinction between compound and coordinate bilinguality as a psychological concept, Ervin & Osgood (1954) suggested that for compound bilinguals a verbal label and its translation equivalent have one conceptual representation common to both languages, whereas for coordinate bilinguals there are two distinct representations, one for each language. The compound–coordinate dimension has already been discussed in Sections 2.1.1 and 2.2.1.3, where we insisted on the necessity of viewing this difference as two poles of a continuum on which bilinguals vary. This distinction is relevant to the present discussion insofar as it implies that bilinguals do not all organise verbal material in the same way; coordinate bilinguals are expected to have a more independent organisation than compound bilinguals, as is supported by a number of empirical studies. Because there is an overlap (which is, however, not a complete overlap) between the compound–coordinate dimension and the age of acquisition, compound bilinguals are more often simultaneous bilinguals, whereas coordinate bilinguals tend to be consecutive bilinguals. Furthermore, because coordinate bilinguals are more often than not consecutive, their bilinguality is often not balanced and they may be more proficient in their L_1 than in their L_2.

Lambert, Havelka & Crosby (1958) assumed that, when compared with their compound counterparts, coordinate bilinguals

(1)   make more semantic distinctions between a word and its translation equivalent;
(2)   have two relatively independent association networks for translation equivalents; and
(3)   have greater difficulty with translation.

Hypotheses (1) and (2) were confirmed, as they demonstrated that:

(1)   the semantic difference between translation equivalents, when measured with semantic-evaluation scales, is larger for coordinate bilinguals; and
(2)   repetition of translation equivalents is of more help to the compound bilingual in a recall task, thereby pointing to a greater semantic interdependence.

However, there was no difference in speed of translation; these results suggest that when required both types of bilinguals can switch equally fast from one language to the other (Lambert, 1969).

Semantic satiation and semantic generalisation are two techniques used in the study of bilingual organisation. Semantic satiation controls the effect of continuous repetition of a word on its meaning. For example, a subject is exposed to the continuous repetition of the word *house*; the intensity of the connotative meaning, measured through the semantic differential technique,[1] is greatly diminished through its continuous repetition (Lambert & Jakobovits, 1960). In the bilingual form, one verifies if the semantic satiation obtained for a word in one language is extended to its translation equivalent. Semantic generalisation controls if a conditioning to a word in one language (e.g. a key press to *glove* in English) is extended to its translation equivalent in another language (e.g. *gant* in French). Jakobovits & Lambert (1961; 1967) demonstrated that the degree of semantic satiation for translation equivalents is higher in compound than in coordinate bilinguals; they interpret this data as an indication that compound bilinguals have a common semantic store for both linguistic codes, whereas coordinates would have more independent stores.

A large number of experiments call upon association techniques in order to assess the relationship between the two linguistic codes in compound and coordinate bilinguals. Generally speaking these experiments demonstrate that compound bilinguals have a higher degree of interdependence in the organisation of their two codes than coordinates. For example, compound bilinguals are more adept than coordinates at recognising a core concept (Lambert & Rawlings, 1969); in this experiment subjects were exposed to a bilingual word list in which there were associates from a key word in both languages (e.g. from the French–English list including words such as *chaise, food, desks, bois, manger*, etc. they had to identify the word *table*). The results indicated that it was easier for the compound bilinguals to identify the common concept, whereas coordinate bilinguals were more likely to recognise a frequent associate in one language only (e.g. the word *furniture*, a frequent associate of the English *table*).

However, this compound–coordinate distinction is not always evident. For example, in one study (Dillon, McCormack, Petrusic, Cook & Lafleur, 1973), where the compound–coordinate distinction would predict a lesser degree of interlingual interference in coordinates, no such differences were found. If subjects are constrained to follow an associative schema in a core-concept task this difference also disappears (Arkwright & Viau, 1974). Compound bilinguals may possess dissimilar semantic networks for a word in one language and its translation equivalent (Lambert & Moore, 1966); for the same subject the degree of semantic overlap in two languages is not the same for concrete and abstract words (e.g. Kolers, 1963; Clark, 1978; Hammoud, 1983). Generally speaking, a bilingual subject has a more compound organisation for concrete words and a more coordinate one for abstract words. If such a difference between compound and coordinate bilinguals has some psychological reality, as indeed appears from a number of studies, it must be kept in mind that these differences vary not only according to the subjects but also according to the task and to the linguistic material involved.

From a study on association networks in compound and coordinate bilinguals, Gekoski (1980) concluded that there is only a weak difference between both types of bilingual. However, it should be noted that in this study subjects identified as compound bilinguals had begun learning their second language at the age of 15. In this case, can we speak of a real compound bilinguality? Or, as the author himself observed, are we not dealing rather with differences in degree on a compound–coordinate continuum? As we observed in Section 2.1.1, real compound bilinguality can exist only when the language-acquisition histories are very similar for both languages, which cannot be the case when one of the two languages is learned after childhood. This might account for Gekoski's results, and in this sense his data might be viewed as supporting the distinction.

One methodological difficulty encountered with the experiments on the compound–coordinate issue is the way they define the two types of bilinguals. At best this is done through age of onset and language-acquisition history. But are infant bilinguals the only compound bilinguals? To what extent is a bilingual who learned a second language after childhood compound? Studies which analyse the compound–coordinate dimension often lack an adequate control of the distinction; what is meant by a compound and a coordinate bilingual varies greatly from one experiment to another.

Another body of experimental data also supports the idea that language-acquisition history might play a crucial role in the way bilingual language processing occurs. Bilinguals who learned their two languages in childhood display different association networks from equally fluent bilinguals who learned their second language later in life. Comparing the association networks of Swedish–Lettish childhood and adolescent/adult bilinguals, Rüke-Dravina (1971) observed that while all bilinguals gave associations in both their languages to a stimulus word, those who were dominant in their mother tongue, and had learned their L_2 as young adults, gave only associations which were either translations of the stimulus word or translations of associations already given in their L_1 when they switched languages in the association chain; in other words, when they switched languages they did not introduce a new concept at the same time. On the other hand, in addition to this type of association, childhood bilinguals also gave associations which were new concepts in the other language. Thus, compound bilinguals do not dissociate a semantic task from code-switching, whereas coordinate bilinguals proceed in two steps.

While it is reasonable to assume that all late bilinguals have a coordinate organisation of their two languages, not all childhood bilinguals are compound. Opoku (1983) argues that in developing countries, children who are schooled through an official exogenous language which they use for very different purposes from their mother tongue start developing a compound form of bilinguality which gradually evolves and becomes more coordinate. Comparing the Yoruba and English association networks given by Nigerian Yoruba-speaking children schooled in English, from different age-groups and with different levels of competence in English, he observed that older and more competent children gave more English associations which they could not translate into Yoruba; even though they were equally competent in Yoruba and more competent in English, they had greater difficulty in translating words they had produced. Opoku concluded that the representational system of the bilingual is not stable over time, but evolves, particularly when experiences with the two languages are different.

In conclusion, then, whereas there is some evidence in support of the compound–coordinate distinction, it must be viewed as distributed along a continuum, varying from one bilingual person to another, influenced by language-acquisition experience and by certain word characteristics. At present, this distinction is still questioned and its existence is not recognised by all scholars of bilingual language processing. From the above discussion it is clear that bilingual organisation follows a relatively more interdependent pattern in compound than in coordinate bilinguals. We can conclude that the degree of interdependence is at least partially a function of the bilingual's language-acquisition history and language experience. As we saw in the previous chapters, early bilingual experience can impinge on cognitive functioning and on neuropsychological processing; it also determines a cognitive and semantic organisation in which the two languages are more or less interdependent.

The compound–coordinate distinction was the first statement about two different modes of representation in bilinguals. The apparently contradictory results obtained in studies analysing this distinction have prompted scholars to raise a more general question about bilingual memory: to what degree are the bilingual's two languages stored as separate entities which are language-tagged or to what extend does the bilingual have a common store for both his languages that becomes functionally separated only at the speech-production end? The debate on bilingual memory is slightly different from the one on the compound–coordinate issue: the latter suggests that, according to language experience, the conceptual level of representation is separate or common, whereas the former addresses the problem at the lexical level, assuming commonality at the conceptual level.

7.1.1.2   The bilingual's memory

The most analysed problem of bilingual memory is the degree to which a bilingual's representation of lexical information is common to both his languages. An early view of the problem opposed the independence and the interdependence hypotheses as two mutually exclusive explanations. The independence, or separate-memories, hypothesis stated that there are two independent language-specific memory stores that are in contact with each other via a translation mechanism. The other, the interdependence or common-store hypothesis, viewed bilingual memory as a single system in which information is stored as a complex set of attributes or tags which enables the bilingual to store non-semantic information, such as modality, frequency, spatial and temporal aspects, inclusion in a list and specific language. Language is therefore one of these tags through which the common store taps into two lexical systems via a switching mechanism.

Both types of model postulate the existence of a mechanism which allows the bilingual to switch from one linguistic system to the other; they differ from each other as to where they locate this mechanism during on-line processing. In the common-store model this switch is situated before semantic memory, whereas in the separate-store model it occurs at a much deeper level, and two separate lexical or semantic memory devices are postulated. These two models are schematised in Figure 7.1. Neither the common-store model nor the separate-store model proved satisfactory for explaining the empirical evidence on bilingual memory. More recently a number of hierarchical models have been proposed which assume that at one level a separate store occurs whereas at another level of processing there is a common store. Whereas most scholars nowadays agree that at a surface level there are two separate store systems and at the conceptual level a common store, there are still different approaches as to the degree to which bilinguals develop separate or fully integrated semantic stores for their two languages.

7.1.1.3   Early models of separate and common stores

The first models of bilingual memory posed the problem of separate memories in terms of these being mutually exclusive. If the independence hypothesis proved correct, a balanced bilingual should react as a monolingual in both his languages, independently from what he learned in his other language; if, on the other hand, the interdependence hypothesis reflected the storage processes, then this had to be evidenced in a variety of memory tasks. Generally speaking, the common-store model was supported by evidence indicating that intralingual behaviour did not differ from interlingual behaviour, whereas evidence for the separate-store model stemmed from studies in which bilinguals either responded differently in their two languages or failed to transfer from one language to the other. Most of the evidence that sustained either approach came from experiments with association tasks in the two languages, language-recognition tasks, free recall and recognition of monolingual and bilingual input, and reaction times to bilingual stimuli.

Early studies to test the issue of bilingual memory used a word-association technique. Bilinguals gave different word associations to translation equivalents in their two languages. (For example, a Spanish–English bilingual gives the associations *wood, furniture, chair* to the English word *table*, but associations such as *comer* and *consumir* to its Spanish translation

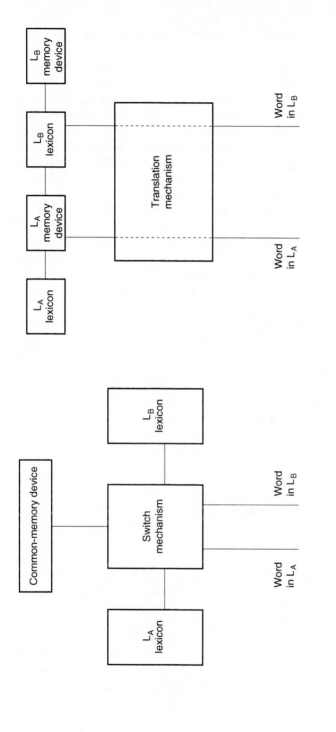

Figure 7.1   The two models of the bilingual's memory

equivalent *mesa*.) Kolers (1963; 1968) interpreted this data as proof of a separate store and argued that if a bilingual person had a common store then the response given in one language should be the translation equivalent of the response in the other language. However, Lambert & Moore (1966) and Dalrymple-Alford & Aamiry (1970) proposed an alternative explanation. They attributed these differences to the fact that translation equivalents do not have identical referential and connotative meanings in both languages, and not to the existence of separate semantic memories. In their view translation equivalents were processed as synonyms in the same language. This latter interpretation has been questioned, as translation equivalents are processed neither as repetitions of the same word in one language (Kintsch, 1970) nor as synonyms; e.g. they are better than synonyms or semantically related words in facilitating recall (McLeod, 1976; Chen & Ng, 1989). This latter finding was also confirmed in a study by Paivio, Clark & Lambert (1988) who found that recall of paired words was higher for translations than for synonyms. Translation equivalents share the same semantic representation, whereas synonyms have distinct representations, which share the same referent.

Another type of evidence proposed in favour of the separate-store model was the fact that bilinguals recall the language of a verbal stimulus above chance level (Kolers, 1965; Lambert, Ignatov & Krauthamer, 1968; Saegert, Hamayan & Ahmar, 1975). According to a number of scholars (Goggin & Wickins, 1971; Rose, Rose, King & Perez, 1975; Paivio & Begg, 1981), this cannot, however, be used as proof for a separate-store model: an alternative explanation is equally valid. Verbal input can be stored in a common semantic or lexical memory with a language tag attached to it. Evidence in favour of this interpretation comes from an experiment by Rose & Carroll (1974): when English–Spanish bilinguals were instructed to recall the language of a stimulus in addition to the word itself, they did this without errors. Light, Berger & Bardales (1975) demonstrated that several non-semantic attributes of a word can be stored if required by the task. However, phonology seems to act as a very powerful tag: Brown, Sharma & Kirsner (1984) observed that it was easy to remember the language of a written stimulus when there were important phonological differences between the two languages, as between English and Urdu, but difficult to remember the language when two stimuli differed in script only, as with Hindi and Urdu. They interpret their data as proof that modalities converge into a common lexical representation and that script is a 'weak' language attribute whereas phonology would be a 'strong' attribute.

Support for the separate-store model stems also from experiments on free recall. Tulving & Colotla (1970), because they observed that trilinguals recall unilingual word lists better than bilingual or trilingual ones (French,

English and Spanish), argue that memory is fairly well organised in one language, but deteriorates when language boundaries have to be crossed in order to form higher-order organisational units; thus, a bilingual would have difficulties in structuring coherent categories across his languages. Although she obtained opposite results on recall of bilingual prose (which is better recalled than monolingual prose), Hummel (1986) also argues for separate stores: a difference in performance results from separate underlying representations. However, this interpretation is not supported by other researchers: as no differences between learning of monolingual and bilingual lists are found, free-recall results in bilinguals are generally interpreted in support of the common-store hypothesis (Nott & Lambert, 1968). Furthermore, recalling a word list in one language (e.g. Spanish) is greatly facilitated if, prior to the recall, a list of translation equivalents (e.g. in English) has been learned (Young & Saegert, 1966; Lopez & Young, 1974).

Kolers & Gonzales (1980) found that word repetition and presentation of a translation equivalent have the same effect on improving recall, whereas this is not the case for a synonym in the same language. They attribute these results to the bilingual's ability to use translation equivalents in an interchangeable way, rather than to a common semantic memory. They argue that postulating two separate stores is more economical than postulating one common semantic store and one for the language tag; however, they do not explain why it is more economical to postulate two semantic stores rather than a common semantic store and a linguistic-tag store. Their argumentation is therefore not very convincing and their results can be equally well interpreted in terms of the common store.

Young & Navar (1968) analysed retroactive inhibition[2] in lists of paired associations in the bilingual's two languages: a bilingual learns first a list of paired associates in one of his languages, e.g. the pair *gato–comer* in Spanish; he is then given a list of paired associates for which the first word of the pair is a translation equivalent but not the second word, in his second language, e.g. in the English list the word *cat* is associated with *house*. When asked to recall the pairs of the first list he will have great difficulty and will often give the translation equivalent of the second pair, e.g. *gato–casa*, instead of the correct response. The authors interpret these results as proof that bilinguals have a common store. These findings have been confirmed in a number of studies: by Kintsch & Kintsch (1969), using free recall of monolingual and bilingual lists with German–English bilinguals; by Lopez, Hicks & Young (1974), using paired-associates lists which differed either on the words only, the language only or on both, with Spanish–English bilinguals; by Liepmann & Saegert (1974), who tested Arabic–English bilinguals for their recall of the novelty of a word in monolingual and bilingual lists; and by Saegert, Kazarian & Young (1973), who used the part–whole transfer paradigm[3] in a bilingual Arabic–English version.

Differences have been found between the processing time in monolingual and bilingual conditions. Kirsner, Brown, Abrul, Chadha & Sharma (1980) observed that Hindi–English bilinguals have longer reaction times in taking lexical decisions[4] (about the novelty of the word) in intralingual than in interlingual conditions; they interpret these results as an indication that bilinguals have separate lexical stores. This interpretation is challenged by Mägiste (1982; 1986), who observed that English–German and Swedish–German bilinguals take more time than monolinguals in mono-lingual verbal processing; according to her this is an indication that bilin-guals have to choose between a larger number of alternatives, thus that they have a common semantic system to which words in different lan-guages are linked by tags, and that in verbal processing they scan through the whole store.

The degree of balance attained by a bilingual also seems to play a certain role in memory. Several studies with dominant bilinguals point to the fact that a higher proficiency in one language influences bilingual memory. Whether this is due to different representations for both languages or to an influence on the retrieval process is not yet clear. Tulving & Colotla (1970) found that the dominant language was more impaired than the weaker language in the recall of items from bilingual and trilingual lists; they attribute these results to the difficulty of forming higher-level units and interpret them as an indication of independence between the different lexical stores. When comparing the effect of a language switch vs. a switch in semantic categories on recall (a semantic switch has a positive effect on recall) in balanced and dominant Spanish–English bilinguals, Goggin & Wickins (1971) observed that the balanced bilinguals evidenced more recovery under language change than the dominant bilinguals; they con-cluded that the balanced bilingual has a greater degree of independence. McCormack (1977), however, argued that an explanation in terms of a language tag is equally consistent: according to Dillon, McCormack, Pet-rusic, Cook & Lafleur (1973) recovery could be attributable to a phonemic switch. This interpretation was confirmed by O'Neil & Huot (1984), who found that balanced bilinguals expressed a similar shift in responding to meaningless trigrams in French and English. Recovery effect observed as a consequence of language shift does not necessarily imply a separate seman-tic system but might simply reflect separate phonological representations.

Berkovits, Abarbanel & Sitman (1984) found that in a sentence-recogni-tion task of mixed-language passages, English-dominant and Hebrew-dominant bilinguals scored higher on the recognition task when the input was in their non-dominant language; furthermore, while they found that dominant bilinguals, proficient in their weaker language, scored higher on a recognition task in the weaker language than those less proficient in their weaker language, no evidence was found that either group of dominant bilinguals would use translation procedure. They interpret these results as an indication that dominant bilinguals do not store information via a translation process, but that they retain material in their weaker language better because processing in a weaker language calls for more controlled analysis and less automaticity.

In summary, then, although there appear to be some contradictions between the different results in early research on bilingual memory, the sum of empirical evidence seems to favour the single-store model. As McCormack (1977) observed, the common-memory model is most attractive both in terms of parsimony and in terms of explanatory power. The one-store model is also consistent with cognitive theories that assume one single conceptual format for all knowledge (Paivio & Begg, 1981). However, it is not entirely satisfactory in the sense that it cannot account for all the empirical evidence. Durgunoglu & Roediger (1987) observed that tasks which are more concept-driven, that is which require focusing on the concepts the stimuli represent (e.g. free recall), generally support the shared-store model, whereas tasks which are data-driven, which require attention for the physical characteristics of the stimuli (e.g. lexical decision), are more in support of the separate-stores hypothesis. In their experiment, Spanish–English bilinguals studied several lists of Spanish and English words; in a subsequent test, one group was tested for free recall, another for fragment completion[5] and a third one for recognition. The results obtained with the fragment-completion task (a data-driven task) supported the independent-store approach while those obtained with the free-recall task (a concept-driven task) showed evidence for a shared-store approach. The authors suggest that the separate–shared storage issue takes into account the demands of the task which can call on different types of memory.

This apparent contradiction between empirical evidence has led a number of scholars to propose models which assume that both type of memories are available to the bilingual. But before we turn to these more recent models, we first review some of the evidence on the independence or interdependence of access mechanisms and information processing.

7.1.2 Separate or common processors for the two languages

Penfield & Roberts (1959) proposed an explanation of the bilingual's capacity to keep the two languages separated: when one linguistic system is in operation this would automatically shut the other one out. This single-switch hypothesis implies the existence of two psycholinguistic systems, one for each language, and a certain degree of independence between two sets of language-specific information processors. The existence of language-specific processors vs. a common mechanism was the major debate in psycholinguistic research on bilingual processing in the 1970s. However more recent models propose alternative explanations, that is mixed models in which coexisting common and separate processors are linked together in a hierarchical structure (Paivio & Begg, 1981; Green, 1986; McWhinney, 1987; Hamers & Blanc, 1989; Kroll & Sholl, 1992).

7.1.2.1 Switching mechanisms in bilinguals

In order to test the independence–interdependence issue a number of techniques used in experimental psychology have been adapted: they rely either on the use of interfering distracters presented in the other language during processing in one language, or on processing in mixed-language tasks.

7.1.2.1.1 Lexical processing and the input switch The Stroop technique[6] was adapted to assess if the same amount of interference would occur when two languages interplayed in the encoding–decoding processes (Preston & Lambert, 1969). In the bilingual version the subject is required to respond to the colour of the ink in one of his languages while a different colour word is presented in his other language. For example, the correct response to the English word *red*, written in green ink, is the French word *vert*. Preston & Lambert observed that the interference in the bilingual condition was only slightly smaller than in the monolingual condition and that the most common error was to give the translation of the stimulus word (e.g. *rouge* for the incongruent stimulus word *red* written in green ink). They interpreted these results as evidence against the existence of a switch mechanism at the input level.

However, if no input switch is postulated, the small but consistent difference between the monolingual and the bilingual conditions must be explained. This difference was reported in several studies using different adaptations of the bilingual Stroop task, with various groups of balanced bilinguals and language combinations (Dalrymple-Alford & Budayr, 1966; Dalrymple-Alford, 1968 and Dalrymple-Alford & Aamiry, 1970 for English–Arabic and English–French; Dyer, 1971 for English–Spanish; Hamers & Lambert, 1972, 1974 for French–English and Dutch–French in an auditory form; Biederman & Tsao, 1979 for Chinese–English; Kiyak, 1982 for Turkish–English; Chen & Ho, 1986 for Chinese–English; Tzelgov, Henik & Leiser, 1990 for Hebrew–Arabic).

One possible explanation is to attribute this difference to the physical difference between the stimulus word and its translation equivalent: Preston & Lambert (1969) demonstrated that interlingual and intralingual interference were almost equal when a stimulus word was physically similar to its translation equivalent (e.g. *red* and *rot*) but that intralingual interference was greater than interlingual interference when the two words were different (e.g. *black* and *schwarz*). These findings are confirmed by studies using language combinations with different scripts: by Biederman & Tsao (1979) in a Chinese version of the Stroop task using different ideographic scripts; by Tzelgov, Henik & Leiser (1990) with Hebrew and Arabic; by Fang, Tzeng & Alva (1981), who found interlingual interference to be higher when the two languages shared the same script (Spanish–English) than when they had different scripts (Chinese–English and Japanese–English).

Furthermore, the degree of interlingual interference depends also on the bilingual's proficiency in both languages. For balanced bilinguals the degree of cross-lingual interference approaches that of intralingual interference; for dominant bilinguals the dominant language caused more interlingual interference than the weaker language (Preston & Lambert, 1969; Mägiste, 1985; Tzelgov, Henik & Leiser, 1990). This may be congruent with other results which found relatively more interlingual interference from the dominant language than from the weaker language. Ehri & Ryan (1980), for example, observed that in a picture-word interference task Spanish–English bilinguals would display greater interlingual interference from Spanish than from English. Analysing responses to a Chinese–English Stroop test with Chinese–English dominant bilinguals, Chen & Ho (1986) found more intralingual than interlingual interference when Chinese was the response language; the more proficient the subjects were in English-L_2 the more interference was produced in the English monolingual condition. Mägiste (1986) also found more interference from the dominant language in bilingual dichotic-listening[7] tasks.

However, can we conclude on the basis of experiments carried out with single words that no input switch exists? Rather than rejecting the switch hypothesis, Macnamara (1967b) proposed a two-switch model: one switch for the verbal input controlled by the environment and an independent output switch under the subject's control. This mechanism would allow the bilingual to encode in one language while decoding in the other. Thus the two languages would be simultaneously activated but independent from each other.

In support of this approach Macnamara and his colleagues (Macnamara, 1967b; Macnamara, Krauthamer & Bolgar, 1968; Macnamara & Kushnir, 1971) cited results from studies using mixed-language reading. They found that, in reading a mixed-lingual text, bilingual subjects would take time to switch from one language to another; they estimated both the input and the output switch to be around 0.2 seconds. The two-switch model has been criticised by several authors. Dalrymple-Alford (1985) argues that no clear conclusion can be drawn from the fact that it takes time to switch languages in a mixed-lingual text. The estimate that the input switch is close to 0.2 seconds cannot be sustained, as there is a wide variation within and between experiments in the time observed. Further-more, the time taken for switching can be accounted for in a different way: alternating languages within sentences in an artificial way must generate unfamiliar syntactically anomalous patterns and this could probably ac-count for slower responding times. I. Taylor (1971) demonstrated that when the subject controls the point of switching no time is taken up by changing languages. Sridhar & Sridhar (1980) argued that code-mixing is a highly structured process of communication whose general properties are violated in those experimental studies. In a similar vein, Chan, Chau & Hoosain (1983) observed that, in reading mixed-lingual texts in two lan-guages as different as Chinese and English, no time was taken for switching when the switch occurred at natural boundaries (as defined by bilinguals who code-switch in a natural setting). They conclude that natural code-switching does not take time for bilinguals familiar with code alternation and that there is no need to postulate the existence of an input switch. Varying language and relatedness in word lists, Dalrymple-Alford (1985) also concluded that the increased time attributed to switching is a result of the novelty of the required task in the experiment.

Grosjean (1985a) and Grosjean & Soares (1986) attempted to identify some of the features in which bilingual speech modes might differ from monolingual ones. They observed that recognition of code-switched words depends on (1) general factors such as word properties (e.g. frequency of the word), preceding context and listener's pragmatic and cognitive knowl-edge; and (2) specific code-switching factors which are either psychosocial (speaker's habits and attitudes, listener's perception and situation) or lin-guistic (e.g. density of code-switching in text or phonotactic characteristics) in nature. (For a further discussion of code-switching, see Section 9.3.)

If, as Macnamara (1967b) suggested, an input switch really operates at a pre-attentive level, it does not account for the interlingual interference observable in the Stroop tasks. Further proof against the existence of an input switch comes from experiments comparing conditions between lan-guages with conditions within a particular language in tasks calling on priming[8] techniques. In the bilingual version of the priming technique the prime is given in one of the bilingual's languages while the stimulus word is given in the other language. Using a cross-language flanker (primer) tech-nique, Guttentag, Haith, Goodman & Hauch (1984) found that a different-language distracter has a similar effect to a same-language distracter. Several studies using cross-language priming confirm these results: for example, semantic facilitation resulting from a cross-language prime is comparable to that stemming from a 'within-language' prime for Spanish–English bilinguals (Schwanenflügel & Rey, 1986). Although Kirsner, Smith, Lockhart, King & Jain (1984) failed to demonstrate cross-language priming effects, the greater facilitation effect of cross-language primes has been demonstrated with French–English bilinguals (Grainger & Beauvillain, 1989), Chinese–English bilinguals (Chen & Ng, 1989) and English–Hebrew bilinguals (Tzelgov & Eben-Ezra, 1992).

Goodman, Haith, Guttentag & Rao (1985) also argue against a voluntary input switch: they observed that the meaning of a distracter affects picture-naming in balanced bilingual children and in beginning-second-language learners as soon as they can read the distracter. Furthermore, several bilingual decoding tasks do not take more time than monolingual ones: responses to two-word signals are unaffected by language mixing (Dalrymple-Alford & Aamiry, 1967); reading mixed-language lists does not take more time than reading unilingual lists (Dalrymple-Alford, 1985); categorisations of words in one language are made equally fast in categories labelled in the same language as in a different language (Caramazza & Brones, 1980), and mixing languages does not affect the judgement of comparisons (Desrochers & Petrusic, 1983).

Certain word characteristics seem however to affect lexical processing in bilinguals in different ways. A number of studies compared the cross-language priming effect of cognate[9] words with that of non-cognate words. If effect of the prime can be attributed to semantic features alone then the priming by cognate and non-cognate words should have a similar effect; if, on the other hand, phonological and graphic similarities between the prime and its equivalent play a role in lexical processing, effect of the prime should be greater for cognate words than for non-cognate words. This was demonstrated with Dutch–English bilinguals (de Groot & Nas, 1991) and with Spanish–English bilinguals (Sánchez-Casas, Davis & García-Alba 1992). Cristoffanini, Kirsner & Milech (1986) observed that memory of the language of presentation was good for words that have non-cognate translation equivalents (e.g. recognising that the word *dog* was presented in English in a Spanish–English list) and poor for words that have cognates as translation equivalents (e.g. the words *rico* and *rich*). The authors interpret this as evidence for an attribute-tagging model of processing in which morphology rather than language determines how representations are tagged. De Groot & Nas (1991) suggest that cognates have links at both the conceptual level and the lexical level, whereas non-cognates have links at the conceptual level only. Structural characteristics of words play a role in lexical decision tasks: Grainger & Dijkstra (1992) demonstrated that lexical decisions about words that are made up of letter strings which are part of both languages (as the English word *time* vs. French *temps* for a French–English bilingual) take more time in bilingual lists than words that have letter strings unique to one language (like the English word *white* in contrast to the French word *blanc*).

Different word types also produce different response patterns in bilinguals. Concrete words share more semantic representations than abstract words (Kolers, 1963). Saegert, Kazarian & Young (1973) analysed translation errors in recall of bilingual lists of paired associates in which Spanish and English translation equivalents had been paired with different words in the same list (e.g. *gato–casa* and *cat–food*); half of the pairs were concrete nouns and half abstract. They assumed that concrete items would be more likely than abstract terms to be stored in a non-verbal form and that this would result in more translation errors with the concrete pairs; this appeared to be the case. They concluded that concrete words are processed as images whereas abstract words are analysed through verbal representations; because the verbal channels are independent this provokes fewer translation errors. According to I. Taylor (1976) concrete words and their translation equivalents produce more primary associates that are translations from each other. Jin (1990) obtained more interlingual semantic priming effects for concrete than for abstract words with English–Korean bilinguals; he interprets this in terms of the dual-coding model (see Section 7.2.3): in addition to being represented in two verbal systems, concrete words are also represented in the imagery system, a representation shared by two translation equivalents. De Groot (1992) also found that Dutch–English bilinguals are faster and more accurate in translating concrete words than abstract words, a finding she attributes to the fact that concrete words share more representations than abstract words.

The input-switch hypothesis is also invalidated by experiments in which a continuous text is used. In bilingual dichotic-listening tasks a subject is unable to attend to a message in one language received in one ear while ignoring a message in the other language, received in the other ear (Treisman, 1964; Mägiste, 1986). If a switch mechanism were operating at a pre-attentive level no interference from the distracting message would occur. Neither would cross-language primers interfere with the given task.

7.1.2.1.2 The output switch   Rather than postulating a switch mechanism, Treisman (1969) suggested that all characteristics of verbal input are analysed regardless of the language used. Treisman's approach has received empirical support from a number of studies. Looking at the errors produced in several Stroop-like interference tasks, Hamers & Lambert (1972;

1974) and Hamers (1973) concluded that the incorrect responses almost always corresponded to the stimulus word which was either read, repeated (in an auditory version) or translated; however, the language in which the response was expected was almost always correctly chosen. From these studies it was concluded that:

(1) an output switch operating somewhere in the on-line output processing had to be responsible for the correct choice of the language in which to encode the response;
(2) there was no evidence for a similar switch operating in the input processing; and
(3) the major source of interference stemmed from semantic similarity between the stimulus word and a possible but incorrect response.

Further proof that bilinguals control their language of output but cannot avoid decoding in both languages comes from experiments using cross-language semantically ambiguous words (Hamers & Lambert, 1974). When bilinguals are presented with written words that can be part of both their languages but have different meanings in each language (e.g. the words *chat*, *ail* and *pain* in French and English) they react to them as to homographs in one language: frequency and grammatical class are more powerful factors than language for identifying the meaning of the word. That is, when a bilingual was, for example, presented with the English words *chat* and *ail* in an English word list, he would give the translation equivalents of the most common associations to the words *chat* and *ail* in French (e.g. *dog* to the word *chat* in the English list). His language of response was however, almost always correct. Professional translators trilingual in French–English–German would also often mistakenly translate these words in the list; for example, the word *chat* in the English list would often be translated into *Katze*, that is, the German word for its French meaning. Hamers & Lambert interpret these results as proof that no switch mechanism is triggered off at the input level and that bilinguals decode all verbal material for meaning.

However, minimal contextual priming, even non-verbal priming such as a background colour corresponding to one language, helps to improve the correct language choice; syntactic primers (for example, the word *chat* preceded by the French article *le*) have a powerful effect in the sense that they disambiguate the processing and allow the subject to make the correct choice of language (Hamers, 1973). When a bilingual is presented with verbal material, his first task is to identify correctly the language in which this material, is presented (Hamers & Lambert, 1977).

In summary, then, the experiments described in this section show that there is a certain degree of independence between decoding and encoding mechanisms, but fail to prove the existence of a switch mechanism in decoding at the semantic level. We cannot, however, exclude the possibility that a switch mechanism may occur at levels of processing which are closer to surface structures. One study (Caramazza, Yeni-Komshian & Zurif, 1974) tested the two-switch model at the phonological level: the authors concluded that, at the phonological level, a switch mechanism had to be postulated for the input as well as for the output process. However, we lack further empirical evidence on that point and we have no answer as to where along the on-line processing of language a switch, if it exists, will be activated. Altenberg & Cairns (1983) showed that, in a lexical-decision task, both sets of phonotactic constraints are simultaneously active during processing by a bilingual, even though the task calls for one language only; they concluded that in language processing, all language-specific processing mechanisms are activated.

7.1.2.2   Syntactic processing in bilinguals

Whereas the vast majority of research on the bilingual's language processing has been conducted at the level of processing of words, there have been a few experiments that address the issue of syntactic processing. Mack (1986) argues that language interdependence is not limited to the semantic level but already exists at the syntactic level: she found that, in a laboratory setting in which they were required to do rapid on-line processing, French–English bilinguals recognised grammatically incorrect English sentences that followed French word order as correct more often than did monolinguals. She concludes that there is no decoding switch mechanism operating but that bilinguals cannot avoid the interaction of their linguistic knowledge when decoding in one language, and thus that keeping the languages functionally separated must occur at a later stage in the on-line processing. She further suggests that a model for verbal decoding in the bilingual must include a mechanism of functional linguistic interdependence. Because the bilingual cannot suppress the automatic activation of one language in rapid on-line processing, he is more likely to use his two languages in active restructuring in either of his languages.

Most research on bilingual memory has been criticised because it addresses the processing of isolated words. Hummel (1986; 1993) argued that the nature of bilingual memory representation cannot be demonstrated from responses to lexical items isolated from their grammatical context. Analysing memory for prose she concluded in her early work that the evidence obtained supports the separate-memory hypothesis. Ransdell & Fischler (1989) arrive, however, at a different conclusion and find on the contrary that memory for prose supports the interdependence hypothesis.

The data on memory for prose appears as inconclusive as the data on single-word processing. More recently Hummel (1993) argues that contextualised units draw more on semantic memory[10] than isolated words do; in processing language smaller linguistic units such as words and sentences are integrated and interpreted with regard to larger units such as discourse; she suggests that in bilingual processing the subject draws on all his resources concerning his knowledge of the world.

This view is supported by several studies based on the form–function mapping model which demonstrate that bilinguals do not process sentences in one language in a way totally independent from their processing mechanisms in the other language. On the contrary, frequently used L_1 word cues, such as, for example, word order or animacy, are applied in sentence processing in L_2, even if L_2 native speakers do not normally rely on these cues (see MacWhinney and Bates, 1989). Examining interpretation strategies of German–English and Italian–English bilinguals in decoding English sentences, Bates & MacWhinney (1981) observed that bilinguals tend to adapt L_1 strategies to English. In the same vein, Kilborn & Ito (1989) demonstrated that Japanese–English and English–Japanese bilinguals who attained a high level of proficiency in Japanese still use English word cues, such as word order in processing Japanese sentences, a decoding strategy not applied by native speakers of Japanese. Analysing strategies in English and Hindi sentence decoding by Hindi–English school children, Vaid & Pandit (1991) found either transfer from L_1 (Hindi), a mixture of Hindi and English strategies used in both languages (amalgamation) or a clear-cut differentiation, subjects behaving like Hindi monolinguals in Hindi and English monolinguals in English.

Liu, Bates & Li (1992) found similar results with Chinese–English late bilinguals who transfer L_1 strategies (word order in English or animacy in Chinese) to their L_2 (forward transfer). The patterns are different for childhood bilinguals: childhood bilinguals who arrived in the US between the ages 6-10 performed as monolinguals in both languages whereas American-born childhood bilinguals transfer L_2 strategies to their L_1 (backward transfer). This latter result might be proof of language attrition in childhood bilinguality (see Section 3.5). The authors conclude that sentence processing varies in bilinguals according to the age of acquisition and the history of their language use. These results can be interpreted as proof that sentence processing in one language is not controlled independently of sentence processing in the other language. However, the bilinguals that had the highest level of balance in the experiment by Liu, Bates & Li are capable of processing in both languages in the same way as do monolinguals in each of their languages. It also points to the fact that language processing is not independent of developmental and societal factors.

If one of the bilingual's two languages cannot be switched off during the decoding of verbal information, we may then wonder which type of mechanism enables the bilingual to function in one language without interference from the other in a natural setting. Hamers & Lambert (1974) demonstrated that context, especially linguistic context (for example, the presence of an article before a word), is a powerful factor in disambiguating cross-language ambiguous words. They interpret this as further proof that all perceptual input, verbal or not, is analysed. A bilingual processes all verbal information he receives and no input switch can account for his capacity to keep his two languages apart; this capacity seems to operate only at the output level and a bilingual must, therefore, have developed some decision mechanism concerning the language of encoding. Indeed, in the Stroop-like tasks there were hardly any errors in the choice of the language of response, even when the task was to name the language of the stimulus in the other language (e.g. respond with the English word *French* to the French stimulus word *anglais* in a list where stimuli in both languages were mixed and the subject was constantly required to switch his response language, Hamers, 1973). It should be noted that this output-switch mechanism is not always in operation and that a bilingual is also capable of using both his languages in verbal production as, for example, in intrasentential code-switching (see Section 9.3). Further proof of the relevance of language context is demonstrated in experiments using lexical-decision tasks: orthographic similarities of prime words affect word recognition in bilinguals, whereas language-specific letter strings have no effect (Grainger & Dijkstra, 1992).

Mägiste (1982; 1985) observed that Spanish–English, English–German and Swedish–German bilinguals took more time than monolinguals to process verbal material in either language and that this was more pronounced with infrequent words than with common words; Soares & Grosjean (1984) also assume that bilinguals search both their lexicons in monolingual processing. Mägiste interprets her data as an indication that bilinguals have a central semantic system and have to take a greater number of decisions, that is, bilingual information processing requires more controlled processing and less automaticity than monolingual processing. Landry (1978) also suggested that bilingual information processing calls for a deeper semantic analysis than verbal processing in one language. Experimental data on both bilingual memory and bilingual access is not conclusive in terms of an either/or explanation for separate or shared processors and indicates rather that there are sometimes shared mechanisms and at other times separate mechanisms which vary along a number of dimensions. This has prompted scholars to propose alternative explanations for the separate and common processor models.

7.2   MODELS OF BILINGUAL INFORMATION
PROCESSING

7.2.1   The monitor model

Obler & Albert (1978) and Albert & Obler (1978) proposed an alternative
to the input-switch model. It seems that a bilingual processes verbal input
through a continuously operating monitor system that controls the input
through an analysis-by-synthesis device, that is, by constantly testing
inputs against their potential correctness. In a first stage, all incoming
stimuli are processed at the phonetic level and assigned to potential phonemes which are in turn assigned to potential words; these are then
interpreted syntactically; decisions on meaning would also take the linguistic and non-linguistic contexts into consideration. The monitor assigns
priorities in interpretation and is prepared to redirect decisions. Such a
model takes into account the fact that all verbal input is processed, that a
subject can constrain output to a single language, but allows borrowings
and language switching when appropriate. Even when the monitor is
primed to decode in one language it can still process the other language.

   The approach presented by Albert & Obler has the merit of proposing a
model that accounts for the empirical evidence on the linguistic-access
mechanisms in the bilingual, both for input and for output processing.
However, from the above discussion it appears that the problem of interdependence between the two languages occurs at a deeper level of processing
than the access mechanisms. At the same time we have to assume that there
is a certain degree of independence between the input and the output
processes and that somewhere in the on-line processing the subject is in
control of the output language. This is apparent from the preceding studies
and also from the existence of simultaneous interpreters.

7.2.2   Green's model of speech control

Any model of language processing must explain how physically different
but functionally equivalent stimuli are interpreted, recognised and remem-
bered as such. This is true for intramodality variations (such as differences
in voice characteristics, accents and dialects), for differences between modalities (as in speech and written language), and for differences between
languages. Where in the on-line processing of language does this equation
occur? Morton (1979a; 1980), for example, suggests that a superordinate
cognitive structure, the logogen,[11] underlies different modalities which
would have access to them via separate lexical stores. Is this also true for
representations in two languages? How does bilingual experience influence

the bilingual's organisation of knowledge, storage and retrieval system? While there is general agreement that the bilingual must have a representation common to both his languages, the controversial question to be addressed is: at what level of processing does this common representation occur?

Green (1986) suggested that in order to account for the data on bilingual processing we must distinguish between three stages of a language system:

(1)   a selective stage, which plays a role in controlling speech output;
(2)   an active stage, in which language plays a role in ongoing processing; and
(3)   a dormant stage, in which language resides in long-term memory but with no role in ongoing processes.

Green assumes that bilingual speech processing is the outcome of an interplay between resource, activation and control. He proposes an inhibitory control model which accounts for selection of one language of output and inhibition of the other; when speaking L_A, devices for recognising L_A must be activated and those for producing L_A must be selected; selection includes activation of L_A and suppression of L_B. In code-switching there is no suppression of L_B, but regulation occurs in such a way that the syntactic rules of both languages are observed in translation (from L_A to L_B) and internal suppression inhibits output in L_A. This approach is interesting insofar as it explains bilingual behaviour in monolingual and bilingual speech modes, and abnormal bilingual behaviour as in polyglot aphasia. This model attempts to explain how a monitor system can regulate bilingual behaviour.

7.2.3   The dual-coding model

In order to resolve the controversy between the common-store and the separate-store model, Paivio & Begg (1981) proposed an alternative model (see also Paivio, 1986; Sadoski, Paivio & Goetz, 1991). Several studies on paired association show that recall is better if there is an interaction between the word to be recalled and another word or an instruction that evokes imagery (Paivio & Begg, 1981). Words are stored in two different ways: verbal representations ('logogens') and non-verbal ones or imagery ('imagens'). The two systems of representation are different from each other by the nature and the organisation of their units, the way they process information and the function they perform in perception, language processing and cognition. Linguistic information is essentially stored as verbal representations, and non-linguistic information as imagery. The bilingual has verbal representations, which correspond to words in each language; the two verbal systems are organised in separate but interconnected associative structures resulting from the experience with the two languages. In addition, each subset also has connections with the imagery system (for example, the image 'cat' will evoke the word *cat* and vice versa). When a word is decoded, representations in each of the subsystems are activated and leave memory traces. Thus storage of a word is a direct function of the two codes: if the two codes are used in memorising a word, its storage is facilitated.

Pavio & Desrochers (1980) suggest that the bilingual has two verbal representations, one for each language, in addition to a representation in the imagery system. These three systems are independent and autonomous from each other but are interconnected at the referential level. Thus, the verbal representation in L_A is in relation with the verbal representation in L_B and a verbal unit (i.e. a logogen) in L_A can activate a verbal unit in L_B. But a logogen in L_A can also activate an imagen in the imagery system, which can in turn activate a logogen in L_B. Translation equivalents do not necessarily activate the same imagen, but there is a degree of overlap between the imagery evoked by both logogens, and this is a function of the bilingual's experience with the two languages. This accounts for the compound–coordinate distinction discussed earlier. Winograd, Cohen & Baressi (1976) postulated the existence of cultural imagery, which implies that bilinguals would have slightly different images associated with translation equivalents. There is no one-to-one correspondence in the imagery system but rather a certain degree of overlap.

The verbal and representational systems function independently from each other, but there is one memory in imagery, which is in constant interaction with the two verbal systems. According to Paivio & Begg (1981) this model explains a larger number of findings on bilingual memory than would either the common-store or the separate-store models. In order to test the dual-coding model, Paivio & Lambert (1981) asked French–English bilinguals to respond to a list composed of either pictures, or French or English words, by either writing the name of the object in the picture in English, rewriting the English word or translating the French word into English; bilinguals were also asked either to copy an English word, to translate it into French, or to draw a picture of the object signified. A recall test for the English words was then given. The results demonstrate that recall improved from the unilingual (copying), to the bilingual (translating) and the dual-coding (naming a picture or drawing the referent of a word) conditions. The authors interpret these results as supporting the dual-coding model and as an indication that the verbal storages are relatively independent of each other.

That translation of concepts leads to better recall than simple repetition was also found by Glanzer & Duarte (1971). Whereas same-language semantic repetitions (through the use of synonyms) lead to better recall scores than simple repetitions, translations lead to an even better recall than synonyms (Paivio, Clark & Lambert, 1988). For Lambert & Paivio this would be due to the fact that, in translation, two verbal stores are put into play instead of one. The dual-coding approach is also supported by experiments on bilingual processing of concrete and abstract words: processing of concrete words is facilitated because they share a common representation at the imagery level in addition to two verbal representations (Saegert, Kazarian & Young, 1973; Jin, 1990). Further support for the dual-coding model comes from an experiment by Arnedt & Gentile (1986), who observed that picture naming is a more powerful means of encoding than verbal means; in addition they found that the translation mode is influenced by language-acquisition history.

However, it must be noted that the dual-coding model concerns the access to representation rather than the organisation of memory. A single semantic store could be reached through two verbal channels; the activation of more than one channel would facilitate recall and recognition. The higher scores obtained in the translation condition may be an indication of the existence of a unique semantic organisation linked to more than one verbal channel. This interpretation is in agreement with Champagnol's (1978; 1979) work: he observed that a change of language between the stimulus and the response word in a recognition task, as, for example, recognising the English word *horse* when the French word *cheval* had been presented, lowers the recognition level of an item. However, when the stimulus word was tagged as to the language of response that would be required (e.g. the French word *cheval* presented simultaneously with the letter *e* indicating that an English translation equivalent had to be recognised), then recognition would reach the same level as in the unilingual condition. Thus, the simple activation of one channel is enough to render information accessible.

The dual-coding model provides a common store for only part of the verbal information that is to be processed, as, for instance, for concrete words which can rely on the imagery processing. However, it keeps the two verbal processors as separate entities, although linked together through associative channels. In contrast, hierarchical models propose at least a two-level approach in which all verbal material is processed at a common conceptual level.

7.2.4   Hierarchical models

The contradictory evidence on the existence of shared or separated mechanisms in bilingual processing prompted some scholars to propose multiple-level models in which at some levels a single store would serve both languages while at other levels two separate stores operate. Collins & Loftus (1975) proposed a two-level model of knowledge representation: concepts are represented at the semantic level, whereas their names are represented at the lexical level.

7.2.4.1   The conceptual-lexical hierarchical models

At the present time the question whether one has to assume the existence of shared processors rather than of separated processors is no longer asked. The question is rather reformulated in the following way: at what level of processing do the systems become separate and at what level do they share common features? Hierarchical models propose that bilingual memory includes at least two levels of storage: in its simplest form it assumes that words are stored at a lexical level whereas semantic features are stored at a conceptual level. Thus, for a bilingual, surface features of a word and its translation equivalent are stored in two separate lexical systems while its semantic features are stored in a shared semantic network (i.e. not in a modal way).

In the experiment by Paivio & Lambert (1981) double verbal coding (translation condition) does not provoke as much recall as dual coding (language and picture); thus, one might assume that there is a store common to both languages different from the one accessible through imagery. Champagnol (1973) postulated the existence of superordinate semantic categories common to both languages in addition to language-specific semantic categories. In the same vein Potter, So, von Eckhardt & Feldman (1984) suggest that in information processing the two languages are linked through a conceptual system; they asked several groups of Chinese–English and English–French dominant bilinguals, varying in their proficiency in the weaker language, to name pictures, read and translate words in both their languages. The findings indicate that dominant bilinguals take longer to translate a word from their dominant language into their weaker language than to name the referent of a picture in their weaker language. This outcome is interpreted as favouring a concept-mediation hypothesis rather than a word-association hypothesis suggested by the dual-coding model. The authors agree with Paivio & Desrochers (1980) that, if there is a single representation, it is shared by the image; they reject, however, the idea that translation equivalents in the two systems might be directly associated and share a linguistic representation which is not conceptual, as this would call for a faster response in L_2 to a word in the dominant language than to a picture.

This independence of the verbal channels is, however, questioned by

Mägiste (1986): she observed not only that Swedish–English and German–English bilinguals are slower than monolinguals in decoding words in their two languages, but also that this difference is relatively more pronounced with infrequent than with frequent words (Mägiste, 1982); she attributes the difference between access times for rare and common words to the degree of automaticity of the task and argues that the difference in time processing between bilinguals and monolinguals may be equally well explained by a separate-store model which calls for access time, or by a common-store model where scanning time would be longer; the interaction between both has to be explained by a common-store model because once the store is accessed it should not take the bilingual relatively more time to process rare words. From their findings that bilinguals take more time than monolinguals to process non-words, Soares & Grosjean (1984) also conclude that bilinguals scan their whole lexicon in verbal processing, but that in decoding bilingual texts they scan the base-language lexicon first.

O'Neil & Dion (1983) found results similar to those of Saegert, Kazarian & Young (1973) with a recognition task for concrete and abstract sentences in the two languages; they suggest that the encoding of concrete verbal items shares more attributes common to both languages than that of abstract items and that, therefore, different-language encoding of abstract verbal information might lead to a greater variability in representation than concrete verbal encoding. Bilingual processing would be a double encoding of similar experiences and can be affected by different attributions and connotations peculiar to the context of encoding and to the particular languages. Bilingual memory organisation, then, varies according to:

(1) the nature of the task, e.g. recognition relies more on perceptual, and recall more on semantic, characteristics (Champagnol, 1978; Durgunoglu & Roediger, 1987);

(2) the context of encoding (Champagnol, 1973; O'Neil & Dion, 1983; Grainger & Dijkstra, 1992);

(3) the non-verbal and verbal characteristics of the stimulus (Saegert, Kazarian & Young, 1973; de Groot & Nas, 1991);

(4) the presence of the two languages in the task (Mägiste, 1986; Hummel, 1986); and

(5) the linguistic nature of the task, i.e. memory for lexical items vs. memory for sentences and prose (Hummel, 1993).

The degree to which storage is language-specific also varies with language-acquisition history and competence in both languages (Tulving & Colotla, 1970; Champagnol, 1973).

As suggested by Paivio & Desrochers (1980), there are several access channels to representations, namely imagery and two verbal channels.

However, Hamers & Blanc (1983; 1989) have proposed that the two verbal channels join in a common semantic store and that there is a referential link between imagery and the totality of the verbal representation structure. For each verbal channel there is a language-specific memory device which stores stimulus-specific features, such as phonology and perceptual aspects and possibly some limited lexical aspects: these are organised in language-specific logogens (in L_A and L_B). The logogens, linked via the referent, are further organised into higher-order semantic structures. This whole structure is related to the imagen through a referential link. We agree with Paivio & Desrochers that, in order to explain the functioning of bilingual memory, imagery is an important component of verbal memory; we disagree with them, however, that semantic memory is language-specific and suggest that postulating a common semantic memory fed by the two separate verbal channels, each one with a surface memory device, is a better explanation for the existing evidence. This model is depicted in Figure 7.2.

This approach is consistent with trends in psycholinguistics and information processing in the late 1990s and has received empirical support. Several researchers (Snodgrass, 1984; Potter, So, von Eckhardt & Feldman, 1984; Durgunoglu & Roediger, 1987) suggest that, according to the level of representation, words are stored in separate and in common stores. In other words, at the lexical level words in each language are stored separately, while at the conceptual level they share a common semantic representation.

7.2.4.2   Asymmetrical storage models

Studies by Kroll & Curley (1988) and Chen & Leung (1989) suggest that this type of model holds only for balanced bilinguals who attained a certain level of fluency in their L_2. The model is symmetrical only for simultaneous balanced bilinguals. Kroll & Sholl (1992) proposed that for all other bilinguals there is an asymmetrical storage model. Consecutive bilinguals fluent in L_2, but dominant in their L_1, retain asymmetrical connections due to residual lexical-level associations. In early stages of consecutive bilingualism L_2 vocabulary access would rely on lexical associations with the L_1; as competence increases the associations become more conceptual in nature. However, even fluent dominant bilinguals retain stronger lexical links from L_2 to L_1 than from L_1 to L_2. Using category attribution of target words presented in French and in English to fluent and less fluent bilinguals, Dufour & Kroll (1995) demonstrated that even novice bilinguals, that is, those who have just started acquiring an L_2, do not use a single translation strategy and have a limited access to conceptual information in their second language.

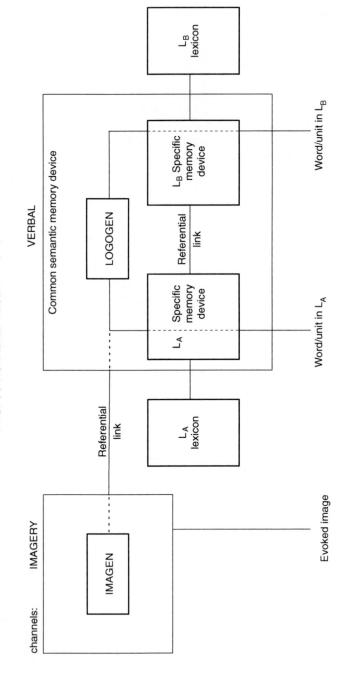

Figure 7.2 Double-coding model adapted to bilingual memory

Representation for a more fluent bilingual

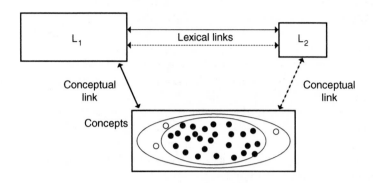

Representation for a less fluent bilingual

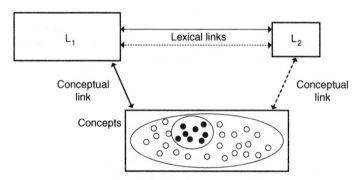

Figure 7.3   Asymmetrical storage models (adapted from Dufour & Kroll, 1995)

This type of model is depicted in Figure 7.3. According to Dufour & Kroll (1995) support for this model stems from experiments with translations. Latency times are faster for L_1 to L_2 translations than for L_2 to L_1 translations (Kroll & Curley, 1988; Kroll & Stewart, 1994; Sánchez-Casas, Davis & García-Alba, 1992). Translations from L_1 to L_2 require access to concepts whereas translations from L_2 to L_1 can rely more on the lexical links between the words in the two languages. Translation asymmetry is greater for less fluent bilinguals than for more fluent bilinguals (Kroll, 1993). Kroll & Stewart (1994) found semantic category interference when fluent bilinguals translate from L_1 to L_2 but not from L_2 to L_1. For dominant bilinguals semantic priming shows a similar effect: L_1 primes L_2 to a greater extent than L_2 primes L_1 suggesting a stronger effect produced by L_1 representations (Tzelgov & Eben-Ezra, 1992; Keatly, Spinks, & De Gelder, 1994). Favreau & Segalowitz (1983) found that L_2 priming was restricted to highly fluent bilinguals. According to Dufour & Kroll this evidence is consistent with the fact that more fluent bilinguals can effectively access lexical and conceptual connections, whereas less fluent bilinguals rely more on the associations from L_2 to L_1. Priming effect from L_2 varies not only with proficiency, but also with the type of lexical relation: cross-language primers belonging to some categories of relations such as synonyms, antonyms and collocations have an effect at an earlier stage of L_2 learning than other categories. Priming effects of L_2 can therefore be interpreted as evidence that a certain autonomy in L_2 is attained (Frenck-Mestre & Price, 1997).

Further evidence for asymmetry in bilingual information processing also stems from a number of earlier studies which used the Stroop test: stimuli in the bilingual's dominant language cause more interlingual semantic interference than stimuli in the weaker language (Preston & Lambert, 1969; Ehri & Ryan, 1980; Mägiste, 1985; Tzelgov, Henik & Leiser, 1990). Research on strategies in sentence processing by bilinguals (Liu, Bates & Li, 1992) is also in line with this interpretation: interfering strategies from the dominant language on the weaker language are stronger than the reverse.

To sum up, then, the hierarchical models are a promising alternative to the unresolved issue of the common-store or the separate-store models. Viewing models as asymmetrical allows bilingual proficiency to be taken into consideration. As we have mentioned before (Hamers & Blanc, 1983), besides a surface level on which two separate representations store specific characteristics, including tagging and perceptual aspects, there is a deeper level, that of semantic storage, which draws on both languages. This higher-order non-language-specific semantic organisation, together with the imaging process, is then further organised into concepts and propositional representations.

Although hierarchical models are different from the competition model we discussed earlier, they are not contradictory in the sense that levels of information can also be explained in terms of form–function mapping, cues and cue validity. McWhinney (1987) applied the competition model to bilingual behaviour. Rather than explaining the experimental data in terms of levels of processing, the competition model offers an explanation in terms of mapping strength and network activation. In the case of bilingual processing a shared representational system comprises mappings between forms and functions. The data on bilingual information processing discussed above (bilingual recall, priming, Stroop test, translation) can be explained in terms of form–function mapping; in addition, an interactive approach like the competition model gives a better explanation for backward transfer. The model also accounts for the asymmetry in processing by dominant bilinguals.

7.3   NON-VERBAL BEHAVIOUR OF THE BILINGUAL

Language processing is not an isolated phenomenon but is integrated in a complex pattern of human behaviour. The use of a language includes not only phonological, syntactic and semantic rules but also a repertoire of non-verbal behaviour. If we take an extreme view of the Whorfian hypothesis (Whorf, 1956), that language moulds thought, then we have to assume that when a bilingual changes languages, he has to rely on a different set of representations. Birdwhistell (1970) suggested that the interaction between culture and language is such that each cultural group possesses a unique non-verbal behavioural repertoire inseparable from language. If this is the case, then the bilingual's non-verbal behaviour must vary according to the language he uses. Bilingual experience will influence not only the paralinguistic behaviour and the gestural behaviour accompanying language but also the totality of the bilingual's behavioural repertoire, including personality traits.

Research in these domains is, however, extremely scarce: there are just a few indications that bilinguals may react in different ways from monolinguals, but the amplitude of these differences is still unknown. More importantly, the whole field lacks theoretical underpinning. In this section we briefly review some empirical data from which it is at present difficult to generalise. However, this data may be an important addition to our knowledge on bilingual behaviour and would therefore indicate directions for further development.

7.3.1   Paralinguistic and gestural behaviour

Wiens, Manuagh & Matarazzo (1976) have studied paralinguistic discourse features in English–German and English–French bilinguals. They took the following paralinguistic measures:

(1)   mean length of individual expressions;
(2)   simple reaction times to verbal input; and
(3)   the frequency of interruptions during conversations in each of the bilingual's two languages.

These three measures remained relatively stable across languages but varied according to content, independently of the language used. These findings suggest that bilinguals do not process their two languages separately but that there is a high degree of overlap in linguistic organisation. For a number of features, one memory structure selected by the content would serve both languages. This is further proof of the relevance of semantic representations in information processing.

Lacroix & Rioux (1978) videorecorded paralinguistic and gestural behaviour of Francophone and Anglophone monolinguals and of French–English bilinguals who spoke in either of their languages. They then asked Francophone and Anglophone judges to identify the language that was spoken from the visual clues only. Whereas it was easy for the judges to recognise the language spoken by monolinguals of both groups, they had great difficulty in guessing the language spoken by bilinguals. The authors concluded that the language spoken did not affect gestural behaviour but that bilinguals develop a unique repertoire that they share across languages. It must however be observed that in this experiment the bilinguals were not balanced and that, although they were highly proficient in their L_2, they could still be identified as Anglophones and Francophones. This calls into question Lacroix & Rioux's findings.

To what extent does a simultaneous infant bilingual develop two distinct sets of non-verbal behaviour and to what extent is he able to switch from one to the other when he switches languages? Although we lack empirical data to answer this question, anecdotal evidence, including our own experience, supports the notion that a balanced bilingual possesses two repertoires of non-verbal behaviour and switches between them when he switches languages. Indeed, a perfectly balanced bilingual can in all aspects behave as a native speaker of both his languages and will be perceived as such by monolingual speakers of each of his languages. We thus postulate an output switch for non-verbal behaviour, similar to the output switch for language discussed in Section 7.1.2.1.

7.3.2   Bilingual behaviour and stress

Non-verbal behaviour affects linguistic behaviour. Stress, for example, affects the bilingual's behaviour. Dornic (1978) reported that environmental noise and mental fatigue affect the bilingual's output, especially in his weaker language. General language-processing mechanisms are affected by stress: semantic generalisation, for example, is influenced by it in the sense that under stress conditions an individual will revert from semantic to phonemic generalisation (Luria, 1981). Javier & Alpert (1986) analysed how stress conditions affect the two languages of the balanced but coordinate bilingual. Measuring the shift from semantic to phonemic generalisation under stress conditions, they concluded that the bilingual's behaviour in both his languages is equally affected by stress conditions, and that therefore both languages are involved in linguistic representations.

7.3.3   The bilingual's personality

Does bilingual experience affect personality? One commonly heard stereotype about bilinguals is that they have 'split minds' (Adler, 1977). This stereotype is supported by anecdotal reports of introspection in which bilinguals affirm that they do not feel the same person when they speak in their different languages (Grosjean, 1982). However, very little experimental evidence on the bilingual's personality is available. Only the studies by Ervin-Tripp are worth mentioning. She observed that bilinguals give different responses to personality measures presented in either of their languages: asking French–English bilinguals to respond to the TAT[12] in both their languages she found that responses which are normally stable when repeated in the same language vary with the language of response (Ervin, 1964). Japanese–English bilinguals were found to give more emotional responses in Japanese than in English when responding to sentence completion (a current personality measure) in both languages (Ervin, 1964) and to picture interpretation (Ervin, 1973). She argues that this may be attributable to a difference in social roles and emotional attitudes linked with the use of each language and does not necessarily reflect personality aspects.

Bilinguals use their two languages in a different way to express affect. Rozensky & Gomez (1983) observed that bilinguals express more affect in their mother tongue during psychotherapeutic sessions; similarly Price & Cuellar (1981) observed that psychiatric bilingual patients express their psychopathology to a greater extent in their mother tongue. However, in one experimental study it was found that both English–Spanish and Spanish–English consecutive bilinguals express more affect in Spanish, and that levels of anxiety and depression varied according to the language in which they were measured (Guttfreund, 1990): the author concludes that characteristics of the language might also play a role in the expression of affect. According to Bond & Lai (1986), a second language is often acquired in an emotionally more neutral setting than a first language and may therefore not be used to the same extent to express emotion.

Thus, the use of one of his languages can make certain of the bilingual's personality traits more salient. What makes the bilingual unique is not some sort of personality split, but rather the fact that he has integrated behaviour patterns from two cultures into his personality and can apply them successfully to appropriate settings. We discuss this issue further in Section 8.3.6.

At the present time very little can be concluded from the bilingual's non-verbal behaviour or personality. The main and very broad conclusion is that bilingual experience impinges on all aspects of human behaviour and is not limited to language processing alone. Language processing is one of the most salient characteristics of human behaviour; if it is impaired, an individual's behaviour is drastically changed. Research on the interaction between language impairment, bilingual experience and behaviour is scarce in some areas, such as in dyslexia, schizophrenia and mutism, and more intensive in others, such as in stuttering and aphasia (see Section 6.3.1 on aphasia).

7.4   CONCLUSION

In this chapter we have reviewed the research and theoretical proposals on language processing in bilinguals. As we have mentioned throughout this chapter, the bilingual's language processing is influenced by the history, context and mode of acquisition of his languages. In the first section we addressed the issue of language representation in bilinguals: is there a psychological reality to the compound–coordinate distinction? We further discussed the controversy between the common-store and the separate-store models of bilingual memory. We discussed the extent to which the two languages are activated in on-line processing and questioned the validity of the switch hypothesis. We then described and discussed some of the recent models of bilingual language representation, including the hierarchical models, and in the case of dominant bilinguality, the asymmetrical hierarchical models. We ended this chapter by discussing briefly the relevance of non-verbal behaviour in bilingual processing.

From the above discussion it emerges clearly that we are just beginning to understand how the bilingual processes languages and how he keeps his two languages separate. Whereas there is general agreement that he is able to keep his two languages functionally separate, the authors disagree as to how and at what level of processing this separation occurs. While being congruent with a general model of language processing, a model of bilingual processing must also account for both the functional separation in output and the activation of all language knowledge during processing. The controversy between the proponents of common-store and separate-store memory is still unresolved; it seems that in the late 1990s all empirical evidence can be interpreted in favour of hierarchical models that assume a common processor at the semantic level and separate processors at surface levels. Hierarchical models are interesting alternatives to the unresolved question of separate vs. common storage. Furthermore, the asymmetrical hierarchical models account for processing in the dominant bilinguals.

One important methodological question arises in experimental studies on bilingual processing: because the age and mode of acquisition seem to play such a crucial role in processing by bilinguals, it is most important that studies on bilingual processing be better documented in terms of language-acquisition history and not treat bilinguals as a homogeneous group. Finally, any model of bilingual processing should account for the different levels of processing by bilinguals in both the monolingual and the bilingual speech mode, while being consistent with a general model of language processing.

8 Social psychological aspects of bilinguality: culture and identity

In the preceding chapters we have discussed the bilingual individual's language development and behaviour. We have insisted all along that the roots of this behaviour are to be found in social interactions which occur in social networks; both are embedded in broader social structures, such as groups, classes, etc. In the present chapter we analyse, from a social psychological perspective, the relationships between the individual and the sociocultural group or groups around him when two or more languages are in contact.

More specifically we focus on the following: the relationship between language and culture (Section 8.1); the development of ethnolinguistic identity (Section 8.2); bilinguality and ethnolinguistic identity (Section 8.3); bilinguality, perceptions and attitudes (Section 8.4) and the social psychological aspects of L_2 acquisition (Section 8.5).

The bilingual's development and behaviour cannot be considered independently from society, its structure and its cultural dimension. It must be borne in mind that the development of language, and hence of bilinguality, is part and parcel of the socialisation process through which a child becomes a member of a given social group (see Section 4.1.1). The psychological mechanisms which result from this process should therefore be analysed within the framework of society and of the cultures in which they develop.

8.1   LANGUAGE AND CULTURE

All definitions of culture agree that language is an important part of culture. There is a consensus that culture is a complex entity which comprises a set of symbolic systems, including knowledge, norms, values, beliefs, language, art and customs, as well as habits and skills learned by individuals as members of a given society. This definition, which was first put forward by Tylor (1873), has been elaborated on by many scholars. Linton (1945), for example, insists that culture is a configuration of learned behaviour and the symbolic meanings attached to it; moreover, the components of culture are transmitted by members of a society to other members and shared among them. Segall, Berry, Dasen & Poortinga (1990) suggest that culture comprises the man-made part of the environment, which includes objects and social institutions regulated by laws, norms and rules. According to Rohner (1984) culture is an organised system of meanings which members of that culture attribute to people and objects that make up the culture. The sharing of symbolic meanings and behaviour is only approximate in the sense that they are equivalent rather than identical for any two individuals and are unevenly distributed in the society. This definition, although pointing to a very important aspect of culture, that is, the shared meaning, fails to include physical objects; however, artefacts also generate meaning and influence behaviour (Jahoda, 1984). For example, an object such as a car influences behaviour: people have increased mobility, can live further away from their work place and can travel. Furthermore, the car becomes a status symbol and may be chosen not for its qualities as a vehicle but because of the symbolic value attached to a particular model.

Bruner (1973; 1990), focusing on the dynamic, developmental aspects of human behaviour, defines culture as being, among other things, a system of techniques for giving shape and power to human capacities; the values, tools and ways of knowing of a culture equip members of a society with amplification systems. A culture is seen as a deviser, a repository and a transmitter of these amplification systems; their significance for the individual's cognitive, affective and social development is that they provide devices for the internal organisation and shaping of experience. These 'amplifiers' are crucial elements in the building up of an individual's social representations, that is representations of external reality shared with other members of the society.

Language is a component of culture along with other entities like, for example, values, beliefs and norms; language is a product of culture, transmitted from one generation to the next in the socialisation process; it also moulds culture, that is to say, our cultural representations are shaped by language. However, unlike other components of culture, language interacts with it in specific ways: for language is a transmitter of culture; furthermore, it is the main tool for the internalisation of culture by the individual. Although culture and language do not exist independently of each other they are, however, not homologous.

An important debate concerning the relationship between language and culture derives from Whorf's (1956) work. Whorf advanced the hypothesis that the structure and nature of the language used by a cultural group shapes the way in which its members think, attribute meaning and behave. However, this approach has been rejected, at least in its strong form.

Whereas it can be recognised that language sometimes shapes values and ideas, the reverse is equally evidenced. Rather than a one-way causal relationship between language and culture we consider there to be a continuous interaction in which language can at times shape ideas and at other times result from the existing cultural values and behaviour.

When more than one culture and/or more than one language are in contact in the same society, culture and language are not isomorphically distributed. To the extent that language is a component of culture, members of a society who do not share the same language do not share all meanings and behaviour of that society; however, there can exist a large degree of overlap between the cultural behaviour of members who do not speak the same language, as is for example the case in numerous societies of Africa and Asia, e.g. Nigeria and India. On the other hand, societies can be culturally very diverse and at the same time speak varieties of the same language, as, for example, English-speaking communities such as are found in Britain, the USA, Australia, the West Indies, Zimbabwe or India, or Francophone communities, such as those in France, Belgium, Switzerland, French Canada or former French colonies in Africa.

8.2   CULTURAL/ETHNIC/ETHNOLINGUISTIC IDENTITY

In the present discussion we use the concept of identity to refer to psychological processes involved in the construction of the self[1] with regard to group membership. Group membership is one aspect of the concept of self and comes into existence through the development of social identity. According to Tajfel (1974; 1981), social identity results from the individual's knowledge of his membership of one or several social groups; it also includes all the values and affective meanings attached to this membership. social group is defined by Tajfel as a psychological concept in the sense that it refers to a cognitive entity in the individual's mind. By a process of 'social categorisation' the individual is able to construct his social environment according to certain criteria. He can recognise that others have common characteristics among themselves and between them and himself; he can then identify with the social groups with whom he shares these characteristics and distinguish himself from those who do not (social identity). Through a mechanism of 'social comparison', he can identify with all or only some of the group's characteristics, but it is necessary that the group recognises him as a member. Similarly, at the collective level a group must perceive itself and be perceived by other groups as a distinctive entity. Thus, an individual may perceive himself as similar to or different from others and act in such a way as to make his own group favourably and psychologically distinct from other groups with which he may compare it (psychological distinctiveness). In complex, multicultural societies distinctiveness between social groups also includes linguistic, cultural and ethnic characteristics.

Similarly Le Page (1968) and Le Page & Tabouret-Keller (1985) state that the individual behaves according to the behavioural patterns of groups he finds it desirable to identify with, to the extent that:

(i) he can identify the groups; (ii) he has adequate access to the groups and the ability to analyse their behavioural patterns; (iii) his motivation to join the groups is sufficiently powerful and is either reinforced or reversed by feedback from the groups; and (iv) he has the ability to modify his behaviour. (Le Page: 182)

Whereas social identity exists within the same society and helps the individual to define himself in relation to the roles and the social groups in that society, one can only become aware of one's cultural identity to the extent that one becomes cognisant of the existence of other cultures inside or outside one's own society. The integration of the complex configuration that is culture into the individual's personality constitutes his cultural identity. Cultural identity is part of, but not the same as, social identity. Cultural identity may comprise a diversity of features such as ancestry, territoriality, institutions, values, norms and language, all of which make one cultural group distinct from another. Ethnic identity is a concept closely related to cultural identity but, in addition, it also refers to physiognomic features or common ancestry. Again it is meaningful only in situations in which two or more ethnic groups are in contact. Ethnic identity refers to that part of an individual's self-concept that concerns how he relates to his own native ethnic group and to other ethnic groups (Phinney, 1990). Giles and Johnson (1981) insist on the self-categorisation aspect of group membership and define an ethnic group as comprising 'those individuals who identify themselves as belonging to the same ethnic category'. In the same vein, Giles and Johnson (1981) define an ethnic unit as 'those individuals who say they belong to ethnic group A rather than B, are willing to be treated as A rather than B, allow their behaviour to be interpreted and judged as A's and not B's, and have shared systems of symbols and meanings, as well as norms and rules for conduct, normatively associated with community A' (p. 106).

Whereas authors differ greatly in their definitions of cultural and ethnic identity, these definitions generally comprise self-perception, a sense of shared values and feelings of belonging. If in a given society certain groups can be identified in terms of ethnic, cultural or linguistic characteristics, these will become salient features, perceived as such by the individual and used by him for ethnic, cultural or linguistic categorisation. An important distinction must be made between ethnicity and ethnic identity. Ethnicity is a sociological concept which refers to objective common indicators of differences, such as race, religion, language and national origin, used in the classification of individuals. Ethnicity is further discussed in Section 10.2.4. Ethnic identity, on the other hand, refers to the subjective experiences of an individual in defining his own affiliation to the group that shares common national, cultural and physical attributes (Kim, 1991a). Social psychologists define ethnic identity as a subjective feeling of belonging to a particular ethnic group (see, for instance, Leets, Giles & Clément, 1996).

When language plays an important role in defining cultural or ethnic identity we refer to identity as ethnolinguistic. Ethnolinguistic identity can thus be viewed as a subjective feeling of belonging to a particular ethnolinguistic group for which the language spoken by the group is an important characteristic. When language is such an important component of culture it is also a salient feature of the individual's social, cultural or ethnic identity, while at the same time being a sociocultural marker of group membership in settings where cultures come into contact, as is the case in multicultural settings. The development of bilinguality, therefore has to be studied in relation to a more general approach to social perception and intergroup behaviour.

8.2.1   The salience of cultural characteristics

The salience of cultural characteristics depends on a number of factors. A group characteristic may become all the more salient if it is not possessed by other groups; for example, if a society consists only of White members, this ethnic trait is totally irrelevant for identifying social groups within the society. If, however, there are individuals of different skin colours, this feature may be used to characterise subgroups; if, furthermore, this feature is correlated with a social characteristic, such as socio-economic status, it may be perceived as a social characteristic and reacted to as such, as is the case in a racist society. From his analysis of the ethnic values of several groups, Driedger (1975) concluded that although ethnic identity is determined by a multiplicity of factors such as language, religion and education, the relative importance of these factors varies from group to group. For example, in the pluralistic Canadian society in Manitoba Jewish people stress endogamy and relations of friendship, whereas Franco-Manitobans insist on language and parish education, and Scandinavians do not attach much importance to any of these characteristics. The last group therefore identify themselves less ethnically or culturally than the first.

In the same vein, Smolicz (1979) puts forward the idea that certain cultural values are particularly salient in construing their cultural identity by members of one particular group, while these same values are less relevant for the elaboration of cultural identity in another group. His model of core values suggests that each culture possesses a number of basic characteristics which are essential for the transmission and the maintenance of that culture; these core values identify a given culture. For example, in the Italian community in Australia, family, religion and language (dialect) appear to be three relevant core values, whereas for the Jewish community they are religion, cultural patrimony and historicity. If in a culturally plural society governed by consensus rather than coercion a variety of power relations exists between the dominant group and subordinate groups, a set of values shared across cultures may evolve. These shared values are what Smolicz (1984) calls overarching core values; an individual can thus possess some values specific to his cultural community while at the same time adhering to wider societal values like, for instance, human rights (see Section 10.2.4).

When language is the core value of a cultural group, it may be an important factor in determining the members' cultural identity. In extreme cases it might even appear as the sole cultural core value, as is evidenced by the Flemings in Belgium or the Quebecois in Canada, who have built their national identity almost exclusively on the defence of their linguistic rights (see Section 10.2.2). The extent to which core values affect the bilingual's cultural identity depends both on the pattern of core values resulting from a specific cultural contact and on the specific social and familial circumstances which shape the type of bilingual experience.

The salience of language in defining identity is, however, not a static phenomenon. It depends on the context in which identity is expressed. Language often becomes an important feature of cultural and ethnic identity in intercultural and interethnic encounters in which often a group status is expressed. Because of the increasing importance of interethnic contacts in today's world, including the continuous growth of immigrant communities in a large number of countries, social scientists are becoming more interested in analysing cultural and ethnic differences and intercultural communication (see, for example, Segall, Dasen, Berry & Poortinga, 1990; Gudykunst & Ting-Toomey, 1990; Kim, 1991b). Although so far scholars interested in intercultural communication diverge in their approaches, there is general agreement that intercultural competence in communication includes a variety of factors among which is the ability to communicate effectively. This ability is primarily mediated through language and comprises linguistic behaviour such as language choice and speech accommodation (for further discussion see Section 9.1). More often than not a certain degree of bilingual competence is required in intercultural communication.

Bilingual competence is not, however, the only feature of intercultural communication in which language plays a role. In addition, the heritage language often acquires a symbolic value in immigrant communities, even in the absence of competence in it. For example, first-generation French adolescents, who are bilinguals dominant in French, and whose parents came from a variety of cultural backgrounds as immigrants to France, refer to the heritage language as 'my language', even if they rarely use it and do not master it to the same extent as they master French (Dabène & Billiez, 1987). This feeling of possessing the language in a symbolic way does occur at an early age, as illustrated in the following example: a six-year-old first-generation Canadian whose parents emigrated from Benin referred to Fon as 'my language' although he did not speak it at all and could hardly understand it. When asked why he referred to Fon as his language, he responded that it was because no child in the neighbourhood spoke it but that his parents, his grandmother and his parents' (African) friends always used it; at the same time he refused the ethnic label African but named himself as a Quebecois which he defined as a French-speaking person.

According to Giles & Coupland (1991) there are at least four reasons for the salience of language in interethnic interactions: it is an attribute of group membership, a cue for ethnic categorisation, an emotional dimension of identity and a means of ingroup cohesion. Linguistic boundaries are perceived as hard or soft. Some ethnic groups attenuate their linguistic variety while others accentuate their linguistic features. The extent to which a particular group will accentuate its linguistic features, thereby insisting on the development of an ethnolinguistic identity, depends on the complex interplay between a number of sociological, sociolinguistic, psychological and psycholinguistic factors in interethnic interactions. Once language has become a salient feature of group identity it plays an important role in the development of the individual ethnolinguistic identity which comprises ethnic, cultural and linguistic features.

8.2.2   Enculturation, acculturation and deculturation

In order to understand the mechanisms by which a child becomes a member of a cultural or ethnolinguistic group, we must first take a closer look at what is meant by the internalisation of a culture. According to Taft (1977), in order to become a member of society a child is 'enculturated to the particular ways and general style of life that constitutes its culture, and as a consequence becomes culturally competent' (p. 130). The child must acquire the means by which his behaviour may become meaningful to the other members of his society and by which he attaches meaning to the other members' behaviour; in other words, the child must learn how 'to mean' and how to communicate (see Chapters 4 and 5).

Enculturation is part of the socialisation process and begins with primary socialisation. If a child is socialised in a bicultural environment, enculturation involves the two cultures. However, if a child lives in a monocultural home surrounded by another culture in the community, enculturation starts in his first culture, in which most of the primary socialisation takes place, and he has to cope with enculturation in a second culture, including the language of that culture; in this case we speak of acculturation. This will also happen to a child or an adult who emigrates to a country with a different culture.

When a child has already been through the enculturation process and comes into contact with a second culture, he has to acculturate in order to adjust to the new culture. Acculturation occurs when an individual experiences changes of behaviour as a result of being in contact with other cultures (Graves, 1967). By acculturation we mean that in communicating with members of a new culture, the child must adjust his behaviour from the old culture to the new one. Acculturation includes 'a combination of acquisition of competence in performing culturally relevant behaviour and the adoption of culturally defined roles and attitudes with respect to that behaviour' (Taft, 1977: 146).

At the societal level acculturation occurs when two independent cultural groups come into contact over an extended period of time, resulting in changes in either or both cultural groups (Berry, Trimble & Olmeda, 1986). In culturally plural societies, that is those in which two or more cultural groups coexist, acculturation is a constant process: groups and individuals influence each other, thereby inducing some degree of change in their way of life and their behaviour (Berry, Kim, Power, Young & Bujaki, 1989). The societal aspects of acculturation are further discussed in Section 10.2.2.

The more advanced the process of enculturation is, the more complex the process of cultural adjustment. In a harmonious acculturation process a person acquires the cultural rules and language skills of the new culture and integrates them appropriately with his primary culture. In other words, his identity becomes bicultural. In this process he also acquires the language of the new culture in addition to his mother tongue, which may be more or less maintained according to circumstances. The adult who has to adapt to a new culture must integrate new cultural elements, including language, in an already well-established identity. According to the requirements of his occupational status he must acquire more or less developed second-language skills (adulthood bilinguality). The older the individual the more difficult his cultural adaptation is (Taft, 1977).

When an individual adapts to a new culture at the expense of his primary culture we speak of a process of deculturation. Deculturation is associated with psychological distress. Extreme deculturation leads to assimilation, which may be accompanied by first-language loss. If no assimilation into the host culture occurs, deculturation leads to anomie, a complex psychological state implying feelings of alienation and isolation vis-à-vis the society one lives in. Acculturation models disagree, however, on the extent to which acculturation processes lead necessarily to a form of deculturation.

Linear models view acculturation as a continuum on which acquiring a new culture and language means a loss to the original culture and language. For example, Moghaddam (1988) suggests the existence of bipolar strategies distributed along a continuum ranging from cultural maintenance to assimilation; these bipolar strategies are applied to the various dimensions of ethnic identity, including language. Clément (1980; 1984) and Giles & Byrne (1982) argue that a strong identification with one's own group leads to a fear of assimilation and thus separation, whereas a weak identification leads to assimilation. For minority groups the acquisition of a new culture and a new language may undermine the original identity.

On the other hand, non-linear models propose alternative explanations: diverse dimensions of acculturation are not viewed on a continuum ranging from isolation to assimilation, but alternative solutions are possible. For example, Berry (1980) proposes four possible modes of acculturation: assimilation, separation, deculturation and integration. Under separation a further distinction is made between segregation, when the dominant group imposes its solution, e.g. the apartheid policy, and separation proper, when the subordinate group decides to isolate itself. Similarly, in deculturation it is possible to distinguish between ethnocide and marginality. In deculturation there is a loss of the original culture without replacement, whereas in integration a second culture is added to the first one without a loss. An individual may adapt to the dominant group while at the same time retaining a number of features of his own identity (Taylor and Moghaddam, 1987). Drawing on Taylor and Moghaddam's approach, van Oudenhoven (1998) suggests that a strong ethnic self-concept is related to integration, while a weak one is related to assimilation, and that ethnic identity is evaluated more positively in integration than in assimilation; at the same time majority members feel more sympathy for assimilating than for integrating immigrants and express more prejudices against those who are integrating. Acculturation processes are further discussed in Section 10.2.2.

The type of bilinguality that evolves in a particular individual is not independent of acculturation and deculturation processes. Learning a new language and becoming fluent in it, while at the same time maintaining or forgetting one's mother tongue, are an integral part of cultural adaptation. The processes of enculturation, acculturation and deculturation play an important role in determining bilingual skills and the bilingual's cultural identity.

8.2.3   The development of cultural and ethnolinguistic identity

How does a child develop the concept of cultural and ethnolinguistic group membership? Before we address this question it is necessary to point out that cultural and ethnolinguistic perceptions are closely linked to the stereotypes and prejudices that one group forms towards another. Speech is a powerful factor of identification. Social, cultural and ethnic categorisations and value judgements based upon language can be expressed about individuals and generalised to whole groups. All of the levels of language (phonology, syntax, semantics, pragmatics) affect the interlocutor's beliefs about, and his evaluation of, the speaker (Bradac, 1990). Many studies have shown that individuals and groups may be positively or negatively evaluated according to the language or language variety they speak. It is usually the 'standard' or 'legitimate' variety, the 'imposed norm' or the majority language, which are valorised, the other languages or varieties being stigmatised (see Section 8.4 for further discussion).

Ethnolinguistic identity is activated and regulated through the dynamics of language and communication (Gudykunst & Ting-Toomey, 1990). In the social comparison process a member of a group generally tends to favour his own salient group characteristics over those of other groups on perceptual, attitudinal and behavioural dimensions (Turner, 1981; Turner, Hogg, Oakes, Reicher, & Wetherell, 1987). An individual adopts positive linguistic distinctiveness strategies with members of outgroups when he identifies with an ingroup which considers its language important, makes insecure comparisons with other ethnic groups, perceives his group's ethnolinguistic vitality (see Section 10.2.3) as high, perceives closed boundaries between his group and other groups, does not identify strongly with other social categories, perceives little category-membership overlap with the interactant and perceives his status as higher in his ethnic group than in other social category memberships (Giles & Johnson, 1981; 1987). Furthermore, he tends to use his own group characteristics as a standard by which to judge and compare other groups (ethnocentrism).

How do these social psychological mechanisms develop? All children have to construe their identity during socialisation. Identity is a process which starts both in the individual and in the group of which the child is a member. Identification is only the beginning process of identity: the child must first identify himself as a member of his own group, that is as similar to other members of the group and different from non-members. The child must internalise identification. Ethnic identity is a broader concept and comprises not only the sense of belonging to an ethnic group, but also the thinking, perception, feelings and behaviour due to ethnic group membership (Rotheram & Phinney, 1987).

The processes of the development of ethnic identity have been studied with ethnic-minority children who are prone to psychological distress. Fewer studies have been conducted on the ethnic identity of majority children.In addition to physical differences, ethnic-minority children are also often different in their cultural practices and linguistic behaviour. The degree of bilinguality attained by children of ethnic minorities varies highly from one group to another and from one child to another. Some ethnic groups use a variety or dialect of the majority language. In other ethnic groups a different language is spoken: some children may know only a few words of the heritage language, mainly for food, household objects and kinship, while others acquire oral proficiency at home. Some children acquire literacy in the heritage language through bilingual education programs or, as may be the case in more educated immigrant communities, may acquire heritage-language literacy skills at home. As language is the most important medium of socialisation, differences in language background are likely to influence the identification processes and the internalisation of values and behaviours.

Several studies (for example, Spencer & Horowitz, 1973; Aboud, 1977; Spencer, 1982; Annis & Corenblum, 1987; Spencer & Markstrom-Adams, 1990) demonstrate that while minority children at a young age are aware of racial and ethnic differences and are capable of identifying correctly their own racial group (Native American, African American, Hispanic American and White American), they also express a preference for the dominant majority group and develop a pro-majority bias in their ethnic attitudes and preferences as well as ingroup negative stereotypes. This discrepancy between identification and other features of ethnic identity is not uncommon in ethnic-minority children; these children often, though not always, experience dissonance between awareness and acceptance (for a more general discussion of identity formation in ethnic minority children, see Spencer & Markstrom-Adams, 1990). According to Rumbaut (1994) a dissonant social context heightens ethnic awareness and boundaries while a consonant context attenuates them.

Most models of development of ethnic identity propose an increasing awareness of a child's ethnic membership as he grows older. Awareness and acceptance vary along a number of lines: age, gender, socio-economic status (Phinney, 1990); intercultural and interethnic encounters (Cross, 1978); child-rearing practices and parental attitudes (Spencer & Markstrom-Adams, 1990; Hamers, 1994). For example, Aboud & Skerry (1984) proposed a three-stage model of development of ethnic attitudes. In a first stage, the child learns to identify and evaluate himself by comparison with other individuals who are different from himself. Then, he perceives himself as a group member and perceives others only as members of other groups; at this stage he accentuates within-group similarities and between-group differences; finally, he becomes capable of focusing on himself and others as individuals as well as group members. In the same vein, Phinney (1990) proposes a three-stage model evolving from an unexamined ethnic identity through a stage of identity search to an achieved and committed identity.

Although little is known about the processes which bring cultural identity into being, some studies suggest that they start at an early age and that by the age of six children have developed some type of cultural identity. According to Lambert & Klineberg (1967) children of diverse ages and ethnic origins prefer to use categories such as being male or female, human, children or pupils to describe themselves; they prefer these over categories such as nationality, religion or race. The latter categories differ according to the child's ethnic origin. It would seem that six-year-olds already possess a concept of ethnic identification which opposes the self to others, that is, to foreigners. It should be further observed that the child's concept of 'foreigner' differs from the adult's.

8.3   BILINGUALITY AND ETHNOLINGUISTIC IDENTITY

8.3.1   The development of ethnic perceptions

If children are capable of developing cultural perceptions at an early age, do children who have an early bicultural experience develop specific cultural perceptions? A frequently used technique for studying ethnic identification consists in asking preschoolers and young elementary school children their preferences for ethnic dolls or pictures that represent members of their own group or a different group. Genesee, Tucker & Lambert (1978) asked Anglo-Canadian children living in Quebec, from different age groups and with different school experiences (English-medium, early immersion in French, and submersion in French; see Section 11.4.1.2), to express friendship preferences for the Franco- and Anglo-Canadian dolls; they also asked the children to imagine they were Franco-Canadians and in this case to identify which doll was most similar to them. Whereas all children from all groups preferred an Anglo-Canadian doll as their best friend and chose a Franco-Canadian doll as the best friend of a Franco-Canadian, children with some bilingual experience showed greater reciprocity in their choices. The younger children from the submersion group perceived all ethnic dolls as more similar to them than did the other children, who identified more clearly with the Anglo-Canadian dolls; however, this difference disappeared with age, the English identity of all the children being well established by the age of 10. The authors conclude that, at least for children from a dominant group, the cultural orientation of the home and surrounding community prevails over the language of schooling in shaping the child's cultural identity. In other words, primary socialisation appears to play a more important role in the process of cultural identification than secondary socialisation.

In a different sociocultural environment, a Francophone minority group in Ontario, Schneiderman (1976) observed that 5-to-12-year-old Franco-Ontarian children bilingual in French and English expressed a preference for the use of English while identifying with Franco-Canadian puppets. She concluded that preference for the majority language does not necessarily mean rejection of one's own cultural identity and that there is no one-to-one correspondence between linguistic assimilation and acculturation.

As already mentioned, mastering the ethnic-group language is not a necessary requisite for ethnolinguistic membership awareness. For example, Edwards & Chisholm (1987) observed that adult Canadians who no longer spoke their heritage language still expressed their membership of the ethnolinguistic group. However, although the role of language per se is still little known, it seems that bilingual competence does play a role in shaping ethnolinguistic identity. The decisions taken by minority and immigrant parents to maintain the heritage language and to raise their children bilingually have important implications for the children's development of identity.

The ethnolinguistic identity of bilingual children depends to a large extent on the primary socialisation processes. Hamers (1994), analysing language use, language competence, ethnic identity and language attitudes in the social networks of first generation lower-middle-class Canadian children from Greek and Arabic ancestry and living in Quebec, observed that heritage-language maintenance in the home correlates positively with a bilingual or trilingual competence and a multicultural identification. However, this bicultural identification is largest when parental language attitudes towards both the official languages (French and English) and the heritage language are positive and when the latter is used for literacy-oriented activities in the home. Greek and Arabic children who use their heritage language for literacy at home are more likely to be balanced trilinguals or bilinguals and to perceive themselves as trilingual or bilingual Canadians and Quebecois. The author interprets this in terms of an ethnolinguistic interdependence hypothesis at the social psychological level of language valorisation and its effects on multilingual development.

When one considers the evolution of ethnolinguistic identity in majority children or in middle-class immigrant children, it is likely that bilingual experience enhances a positive identity and positive attitudes. The results are thus different from the ones obtained with ethnic-minority children (Lambert, 1987). Analysing narratives given by monolingual (in English) and bilingual American children of Armenian descent, Imbens-Bailey (1996) observed that bilingual American-born children used more collective pronouns than did their monolingual counterparts; the author interprets the greater use of the plural 'we' as an expression of a greater sense of ethnic belonging as opposed to the use of 'I'. While both monolinguals and bilinguals showed a strong affinity with their families, bilinguals also expressed a strong affinity with a much more varied group of Armenians. Bilingual children expressed more positive evaluations of their cultural environment than the monolinguals did.

The relationships between bilinguality, language choice and cultural identity in the bilingual are very complex and depend on multiple factors. From the rare experimental evidence to date it appears that early bilingual experience influences the development of ethnolinguistic identity. Bilingual preference does not necessarily coincide with features of cultural identification. The development of cultural identity results from psychological as well as sociological factors. The relationship between bilinguality and ethnolinguistic identity is reciprocal: bilinguality influences the development of ethnolinguistic identity, which in turn influences the development of bilinguality. Differences in ethnolinguistic identity are tolerated to a greater or lesser extent by different communities. Ethnolinguistic identity, like language development, is a consequence of the socialisation process the child undergoes. It is a dynamic mechanism developed by the child and it can be modified by social and psychological events throughout the individual's life. It is important to keep in mind that a bilingual child does not develop two cultural identities but integrates both his cultures into one unique identity.

8.3.2   Self-esteem and plural ethnic identity

Because the development of bilinguality often cooccurs with socialisation in a minority group situation, as is the case for an immigrant child, some developmental consequences of this situation have often been attributed to bilinguality. The best-known example is probably the attribution of personality disorders, such as emotional disorders, to an early bilingual experience (Diebold, 1968). However, the clinical cases cited by Diebold invariably concern bilingual children from socially disadvantaged backgrounds, a fact which is recognised by the author when he concludes that these cases are 'engendered by antagonistic acculturative pressures directed on a bicultural community by a sociologically dominant monolingual society within which the bicultural community is stigmatised as socially inferior and to which its bilingualism is itself an assimilative response' (p. 239).

Not only is there a dearth of convincing empirical evidence on a causal link between bilinguality and personality disorders, but such conclusions rest on controversial presuppositions, namely, that there are fundamental psychological differences between cultural groups, that these differences are mutually exclusive and that they are necessarily reflected in the personality of the individual.

An emotional disorder often attributed to bilinguality is anomie, or disorientation and an absence of norms and values (McClosky & Schaar, 1965). Anomie has often been associated with feelings of anxiety, a lack of cognitive and affective flexibility and a loss of identity. This state can be caused as much by sociological factors as by psychological ones. However, no proof has been given of a causal link between bilinguality and psychological distress and insecurity. On the contrary, several studies conducted with Black Americans, Native Americans and Hispanic Americans indicate that for minority students many sociocultural and social psychological factors other than language combine together and are causes of psychological distress. For example, Markstrom & Mullis (1986) report that Native American female adolescents express more distress in self-perception than do their male counterparts or Anglo-Americans of both sexes. Studying acculturation in two communities of the Native American Florida Seminole Tribe, Lefley (1976) concluded that the less acculturated community had a higher self-esteem than the more acculturated Seminoles. According to Spencer & Markstrom-Adams (1990) several factors, other than linguistic ones, interfere with identity formation: among these are the value conflicts between cultures, the lack of adult role models, the absence of culture-focused specific guidance and the preponderance of negative stereotypes about minorities.

From his study of second-generation Italians in the USA, Child (1943) concluded that Italian adolescent males were faced with a dilemma: should they identify with the culture of their Italian community or should they assimilate into the American mainstream? Child found three typical modes of adjusting to this conflict: some rebelled against their Italian background and assimilated to the dominant culture; others rejected American ways, associating themselves with Italian culture; a third group displayed an apathetic withdrawal (anomie symptoms) and refused to think of themselves in ethnic terms, either by avoiding situations where the issue of cultural background might come up, or by denying that there were any differences between Italians and Americans. It seems that for Child the bilingual's identity can only be either monocultural or anomic. The possibility of a dual allegiance is never envisaged by him. This may be because in the US before the Second World War the values of the 'melting pot' prevailed and there was no room for cultural pluralism.

In their study of adolescents from the Franco-American minorities in Louisiana and New England, Gardner & Lambert (1972) observed similar phenomena. But, unlike Child, they also noticed a fourth subgroup that identified positively with both cultures, the American and the Franco-American. Moreover, this group had acquired a balanced bilinguality and a native-like competence in both their languages, whereas the other groups were either dominant in French, dominant in English or performed poorly in both languages. A high interest in one or the other culture – as manifested by the groups dominant in French or dominant in English – was no guarantee of high proficiency in their dominant language, even though this proficiency was relatively higher than proficiency in their non-dominant language. Studying a group of Franco-American high-school students in Louisiana, Lambert, Just & Segalowitz (1970) found correlations between relative proficiency in the two languages and their cultural allegiance: those subjects who were more attached to American than to Franco-Louisianan values, and showed little interest in the French language, were more competent in English than in French and were relatively more motivated to improve their English; conversely, children who identified with the Francophones had a relatively higher competence in French than in English. Those who had a conflict of cultural identity achieved poorly in both languages; those who identified strongly with both cultures also achieved above average in both languages.

Anomie and low self-esteem are not, therefore, a necessary outcome of bicultural experience but result from the pattern of sociocultural conditions in which socialisation takes place. If the child's two-fold cultural heritage is not valorised, he may either align his identity on one culture at the expense of the other or he may refuse to align himself on either culture, in which case he is likely to develop anomie. If, however, the child's environment encourages the valorisation of both cultures, then the child will be in a position to integrate elements of the two cultures into a harmonious bicultural identity. By harmonious we do not mean that such complex processes are free from tensions, contradictions and conflicts, but that the individual finds personal solutions without having to deny one of his cultures.

8.3.3   Context and the salience of ethnic identity

Several variables both at the macro-level (gender, status, demographic features and institutional support; see also Section 10.2.3 on ethnolinguistic vitality) and at the micro-level (situational variables such as intimacy, formality, the physical setting or the topic) have been known to influence interethnic encounters. Comparing evaluation of White Australian and Aborigine Australian accents, Gallois & Callan (1985) observed that the importance of micro-level situational factors varies with the social distance. They conclude that ethnicity and race judgements are made first. However, how salient are the individual's cultural traits in an interethnic encounter? Clément and Noels (1992) view ethnolinguistic identity as flexible and dynamic: feelings and perceptions of ethnic group membership varies as a function of the social situation in which the interaction takes place. Ethnolinguistic identity is determined in terms of the self but the salience of the ethnic characteristics varies as a function of situational characteristics. For example, the ethnic traits of a first-generation Greek Canadian are more or less salient according to the fact that he is interacting with a fellow Greek Canadian, an Anglo-Canadian, a Franco-Canadian, a mainland Greek, a Haitian immigrant or a Norwegian. Individuals tend to negotiate their ethnolinguistic identity in a given situation in such a way that it provides the most benefits for their self-esteem (Noels, Pon & Clément, 1996).

8.3.4   Bilinguality as a cultural trait

In multicultural communities bilinguality can be perceived as a cultural trait which distinguishes bilinguals from monolinguals. A well-integrated cultural identity enriched by a bicultural situation is, at the affective level, the counterpart of Lambert's (1974) concept of 'additive' bilinguality at the cognitive level. In this case we can speak of additive identity. The development of additive bilinguality is dependent on social factors that lead to the valorisation of both languages and cultures. Similarly, the harmonious integration of two cultures into one's identity calls for a social setting that allows dual cultural or ethnic membership, as in the ideology of multiculturalism. For a child to develop a cultural identity which includes this dual membership, the society in which he lives must not present these two cultures as conflicting nor as mutually exclusive, as was the case with apartheid for example. The individual outcome of an early multilingual experience is not only dependent on the individual but also on the ideology of the society in which the person lives. In other words, to develop a harmonious bilingual bicultural identity the society must integrate multiculturalism as one of its values.

But what exactly is meant by maintaining cultural identity in a multicultural society? Studies on identity maintenance and the ideology of multiculturalism are still scarce. A number of surveys conducted with immigrant groups in North America demonstrated that all groups studied desire to maintain their culture and identity to varying degrees: this type of survey has been conducted with Greeks (Lambert, Mermigis & Taylor, 1986), South Asians (Moghaddam & Taylor, 1987) and Iranians (Moghaddam, Taylor & Lalonde, 1987) in Canada; and with Albanians, Arabs, Poles, Puerto Ricans, Mexican-Americans (Lambert & Taylor, 1990) and Cubans, Nicaraguans and Haitians (Taylor & Lambert (1996) in the USA. According to Taylor & Lambert (1996) a majority of newly arrived immigrants as well as established ethnic groups in the USA and mainstream Black and White Americans agree that it is appropriate to maintain heritage culture and language at home and in social contexts where the ethnic group is the majority (ethnic neighbourhoods, ethnic businesses, churches, ethnic schools) but that at the same time US culture and the English language should predominate in the society. However, the extent to which each group considers it important to maintain the heritage language varies: mainstream respondents consider it far more important to prioritise mainstream culture and language than ethnic cultures and language; on the other hand, although they agree that English language should be used in the public domain, both recently arrived immigrant and established ethnic groups consider maintenance of the heritage language either equally important or more important than adoption of the English language. These surveys do not, however, indicate what is or should be done to assure maintenance of the heritage language. If language maintenance has to be assured, this means the development of bilingual bicultural individuals.

So far, some empirical studies have addressed the issue of the bilingual's cultural identity, for both the majority and the minority bilingual. Aellen & Lambert (1969), using semantic-differential techniques and social-distance scales in order to measure ethnic identification, observed that Canadian adolescents of mixed-lingual French–English families identified harmoniously with both cultures; they displayed less extreme attitudes on authoritarianism and ethnocentrism scales than their monolingual peers. That majority children with bilingual experience are capable of identifying positively with both cultures was also demonstrated by Lambert & Tucker (1972) in their longitudinal study of Anglo-Canadian children attending immersion programs in Montreal.

Employing a multidimensional scaling (MDS[2]) technique Cziko, Lambert & Gutter (1979) found that Anglo-Canadian children schooled in an immersion program attached less importance to language as a cultural marker than did their Anglophone peers in unilingual English-medium schools, that is, they defined themselves less in terms of antagonistic ethnolinguistic traits.

That bilinguality can be perceived as a cultural trait appears also from a study by Taylor, Bassili & Aboud (1973), who found that monolinguals from the two mainstream cultures in Canada perceived themselves as closer to monolinguals of both cultures than to bilinguals of both cultures. Cultural distance was measured by means of MDS. In other words, a discrepancy between culture and language appears as a cultural distance for a monolingual who lacks experience in a second language and culture. Similar results were obtained by Hamers & Deshaies (1982), who also used MDS; they concluded that monolingual Anglophone and Franco-phone elementary and secondary-school students in Quebec perceived language as an important cultural trait for themselves on which they differed not only from children of the other group but also from bilinguals of both groups. In the Quebec context, therefore, language is perceived as the most important cultural trait, and bilinguality as a cultural trait distinct from language. This cultural perception is already present in 10-year-old children.

Guimond & Palmer (1993) suggest that becoming bilingual leads to developing a new ethnolinguistic identity: bilinguals do not need to distin-guish between an ingroup monolingual in L_A and an outgroup monolin-gual in L_B. The authors found some support for Lambert's (1977) assertion that bilinguality leads to increasing tolerance: students who fail to attain a high level of proficiency in an L_2 display more ingroup favouritism and evaluate outgroup members less favourably than those who attain a high level of bilingual proficiency.

How far can these differences between monolinguals and bilinguals be attributed to the child's own experience with language and how far to differences in parental cultural perceptions transmitted to the child? Using MDS, Frasure-Smith, Lambert & Taylor (1975) demonstrated that monolin-gual Anglophone and Francophone parents in the province of Quebec who chose to send their children to unilingual schools of their own culture identified more closely with the monocultural dimension of their group than did monolingual parents of both groups who opted for a school of the other language group for their children; these parents perceived themselves closer to bilingual Canadians of both groups than did the first group of parents. Thus it seems not only that the child's early experience with languages and cultures is relevant for shaping his cultural identity, but that parental cultural allegiance can play a role not only through the trans-mission of their own cultural attitudes but also insofar as they are able to decide to what extent their children will be exposed to other languages and cultures in formal education.

A link between bilinguality and cultural perception has also been dem-onstrated for children of immigrant families in Quebec: first-generation Canadians from Arabic and Greek ancestry who attain a balanced trilinguality in the two official and the heritage languages perceive multilingualism as an important cultural feature that they possess (Hamers, 1994). The role of the parents and the home environment has also been assessed for immigrant minority children. Hamers (1994) found that positive parental attitudes towards the heritage language are linked to a valorisation of the heritage language by the child. However, this link is also related to language use. Valorisation of and competence in the heritage language are highest when parents highly valorise the heritage language and when it is used in the home for literacy-oriented activities. Oral use of the language in everyday activities does not seem to be enough to foster language maintenance and balanced bilinguality in the next generation, but the use of the heritage language as a tool for literacy seems important, at least in a Western host culture.

Feuerverger (1991) came to similar conclusions in her study of students from diverse ethnic background (Italian, Portuguese, Chinese, Korean, Japanese, Hebrew, Ukrainian and Yiddish) who participated in heritage language classes at the university of Toronto. The students insisted on the need for the whole family to be involved in the literacy process and in the role of positive ethnic identification to ensure heritage-language competence. It must, however, be noted that the sample used in this study is biased as it consists of college students who decided to take up heritage-language courses. This might explain their strong sense of commitment towards the ethnic identity.

8.3.5   Bilingual proficiency, identity and acculturation

Several studies mention a link between ethnolinguistic identity and language proficiency: Lambert, Just & Segalowitz (1970) found correlations between Franco-Louisianans' cultural allegiance and their relative proficiency in English and French; bilingual children in Canada view less the French–English difference as a culturally distinct trait (Hamers & Deshaies, 1982); first-generation Canadian children of Greek and Arabic ancestry in Quebec who attain high levels of bilinguality and trilinguality view themselves more as bicultural (as expressed through a hyphenated identity, e.g. Greek-Canadian) than do those children who tend to be monolingual in English or French (Hamers, 1994). Genesee & Bourhis (1988) observed that, in the Quebec setting, Francophone bilingual adolescents are more tolerant of English use than their monolingual counterparts. Bilingualism may influence intergroup attitudes through reduction of assumed psychological differences, facilitation of positive intergroup contacts and enhancement of self-esteem (Guimond & Palmer, 1993).

That language proficiency is closely linked to the formation of ethnic identity has also been shown with adolescent populations. In a large study of more than 5000 youths from several immigrant and refugee ethnic groups in California and Florida (Mexicans, Cubans, Nicaraguans, Colombians, Haitians, Jamaicans, West Indians, Filipinos, Vietnamese, Laotians, Cambodians and other Asians) Rumbaut (1994) found that adolescents who prefer English and are more fluent in English than in the heritage language are more likely to define themselves as American and less likely in terms of their ethnic origin; conversely, those more fluent in their heritage language identify themselves more in terms of their national origin. The fluent bilinguals – that is those who attain a high level of proficiency in English but also maintain a high level of fluency in their heritage language – are more likely to identify themselves as hyphenated Americans (e.g. 'Mexican-Americans'). Rumbaut associates this with an additive form of ethnic identity which includes plural identification.

Thus, so far it seems evident that there is a link between bilingual proficiency and cultural identity. Bilingual children are more likely to have a bicultural identity and positive ethnic perceptions. So far, no causal link can be clearly identified in this relation. Does bilingual experience shape identity or, on the other hand, does identity influence bilingual proficiency? In the case of childhood bilinguality, the child develops both bilinguality and cultural identity in a more or less simultaneous way. From the little empirical evidence obtained so far, it seems reasonable to assume that in childhood it is the bilingual experience which influences and shapes the child's identity, insofar as the languages are core values for the child's identity, rather than the reverse. In the case of adolescent or adulthood bilinguality, a person with an already well-established identity and an ethnic perception of the other group acquires a new language. It is then reasonable to assume that it is the identity and the ethnic perceptions which are likely to influence the bilingual proficiency. But, at the present time, there is a lack of empirical evidence to support any assumption about the causal link between identity and language proficiency.

However, the causal relationship between the two processes is probably not unidirectional. If characteristics of ethnic identity influence L_2 proficiency, the reverse is equally true. In a longitudinal study of Anglophone officer-cadets who received mandatory training in French, Guimond & Palmer (1993) found that failure to achieve a high level of L_2 proficiency negatively affects students' attitudes towards Francophones and increases their ingroup favouritism over time. One possible explanation is that students blame the outgroup for their failure. Rather than implying a unidirectional link between identity, intergroup behaviour and bilingual proficiency, a model has to comprise not only causal directions between features of ethnic identity and bilingual proficiency, but also feedback mechanisms in which language proficiency influences features of identity and intergroup behaviour.

Modes of acculturation and second-language learning are also interrelated (Young & Gardner, 1990), although authors disagree as to the role of L_2 variables such as proficiency, choice and self-confidence in the acculturation process. If acculturation is viewed as a linear process, L_2 variables will be interpreted as a sign of assimilation to the majority culture. On the other hand, if acculturation is viewed as a non-linear process, high scores in L_2 variables will not necessarily be viewed as a sign of linguistic assimilation. Although additive forms of bilinguality are generally found in majority-group members, Gardner (1985) suggests that additive and subtractive bilinguality as acculturation modes are not necessarily linked to majority and minority status, but rather with the individual reaction to L_2 learning. For Chinese minority students in Toronto, self-confidence with English L_2 is related to linguistic assimilation but negatively related to cultural assimilation (Pak, Dion & Dion, 1985). L_2 proficiency in English is linked to both linguistic assimilation and cultural integration (Gardner, Przedzielewsky & Lysynchuk, 1990). However, Noels, Pon & Clément (1996) give a different interpretation to the relationship between L_2 proficiency and acculturation. Studying Chinese students in Ottawa, they found L_2 linguistic self-confidence to be related to contact with English culture and to a lesser involvement with Chinese culture, language and life style; and conversely, greater self-confidence in Chinese was related to a greater contact with Chinese culture and community. They concluded that two modes of acculturation, assimilation and separation were predominant in the Chinese community.

Studying language choice and acculturation in first-generation Canadians of Portuguese lineage in Montreal, Lanca, Alksnis, Roese & Gardner (1994) concluded that language choice and language proficiency are major indices of ethnic identity in modes of acculturation: English and French proficiency is negatively related to rejection and deculturation, two acculturation modes in which individuals refuse to integrate with the majority. High levels of proficiency in English or French were, however, not combined with low levels of proficiency in Portuguese. According to the authors, high L_2 proficiency and a strong acculturation to the North American life style combined with high maintenance of a high proficiency in L_1 is an indicator of an integrative mode of acculturation and reflects the possibility that an additive form of bilinguality can develop in minority groups.

Empirical research on the bilingual's cultural identity and its relation to language proficiency is still scarce. Most of it has been conducted in North America, more specifically in the eastern part of Canada, thus making generalisations difficult. Despite these limitations one may conclude that a bilingual develops a cultural identity different from a monolingual's. Bilinguality and ethnic identity are interrelated; the development of bilinguality influences the development of cultural identity, which in turn is influenced by bilinguality. As we have already mentioned in Sections 4.3 and 5.1.5, language valorisation is central to the child's development. But language valorisation is a process which depends on the social environment. Therefore, this interrelation has to be viewed in the broader context of group relations. How does this developmental interrelationship influence the degree of competence the bilingual attains in his two languages?

Based on the theory of intergroup behaviour it can be assumed that a minority group member approximates to a native-like competence in L_2 in the following cases:

(1) if he identifies weakly with his own cultural group or does not consider his cultural identity to be dependent on language;
(2) if he perceives there are no alternatives to the inferior social status of his cultural group;
(3) if he perceives the vitality of his own group as low compared with that of the dominant group whose language he is acquiring;
(4) if he perceives that social-group mobility is easy, i.e. he can easily 'pass' from one social group to another; and
(5) if he identifies more strongly with social categories other than language and culture, e.g. profession.

Giles & Byrne (1982) claim that ethnic-minority members are most likely to acquire a native-like competence in L_2 provided that their ingroup identification is weak and/or L_1 is not a salient dimension of ethnic-group membership. If, on the other hand, ingroup identification is strong and L_1 is a core value, a person in a bilingual context will be more likely to develop a non-native competence in L_2. This model has the merit of stressing the role of intergroup relations in L_2 proficiency development, but it is limited to the development of L_2 proficiency among members of minority groups. It presumes the existence of a causal link between intergroup behaviour and L_2 proficiency and presupposes that attainment in L_2 is at the cost of L_1 proficiency. Furthermore, it gives no explanation for the development of balanced bilinguality.

8.3.6   The bilingual's cultural identity

If it is true that characteristics of cultural identity influence the degree of proficiency attained in L_2 in a bilingual setting, what then are the specific cultural-identity characteristics of the balanced bicultural bilingual? We suggest that:

(1) he should identify positively with both his cultural/ethnic communities;
(2) his two languages should be highly valorised;
(3) he should perceive the relative status of both his cultural groups as dynamic;
(4) he should perceive a minimum vitality for each of his reference groups; and
(5) he should not perceive any insurmountable contradiction in his membership of the two groups.

Positive identification with one group must be matched by positive identification with the other group. Once again the issue of the interdependence between cultures and between languages is raised.

In Sections 4.3 and 5.1.5 we observed in respect of the development of bilinguality that it is necessary that the two languages be highly valorised if bilinguality is to evolve positively. This valorisation must also extend to the two ethnolinguistic communities in a bilingual setting. In other words, additive balanced bilinguality develops if and only if the characteristics of the bilingual's cultural identity which are relevant for the development of the two languages are present without being conflicting for the individual and if society does not discourage dual membership. At the sociocultural level of analysis, the interdependence hypothesis suggests that a lack of identification with the L_1 culture might be correlated with a lack of identification with the L_2 culture (Clément, 1984); in other words, in order to identify with the cultural group by speaking the other language as L_1 (a condition necessary to attain native-like skills in L_2) a person must first identify with his L_1 group in a strong enough way.

Evidence supporting this sociocultural interdependence hypothesis is still scarce. Berry, Kalin & Taylor (1977) reported a positive correlation between attitudes of Canadians towards their own cultural group and attitudes towards other cultural groups in general: the more one perceives one's own group in a favourable light, the more attitudes towards other groups tend to be favourable. In a similar vein, Clément, Gardner & Smythe (1977a) observed that Francophone Canadian adolescents who expressed positive attitudes towards French Canadians tended also to display positive attitudes towards Anglophones.

Although in the late 1990s we have little empirical evidence for this hypothesis, it appears nonetheless as a plausible assumption because it fits with a more general approach to bilingual development. At the level of cognitive development, Cummins (1979) suggested that an adequate knowledge of L_1 facilitates acquisition of an L_2 and that a deficit in the development of L_2 might be attributed to adverse social conditions for L_1 development. Lambert's (1974; 1977) theoretical approach suggests that the cognitive outcome of bilingual experience is a function of the relative valorisation of the two languages. In their social psychological model of bilingual development Hamers & Blanc (1982; 1987) also suggest that underlying social psychological mechanisms, such as those relating to motivation and identity, are common to both languages and determine certain characteristics of the bilingual child's cultural identity as well as his competence in the two languages.

8.4   BILINGUALITY, PERCEPTIONS AND ATTITUDES

How is a bilingual and bicultural individual perceived by others and how does he in turn perceive monolinguals and bilinguals?

8.4.1   Language, perceptions and attitudes

Because of the wealth of research in the area of language attitudes we are not able to give an extensive review of the literature in this chapter; however, we present a few studies that are relevant to bilingualism (for a review of the field, see for example Giles & Powesland, 1975; Ryan & Giles, 1982; Giles, Hewstone & Ball, 1983). It is important to stress that, linguistically speaking, there is nothing intrinsic to a language or variety that makes it 'superior' or 'inferior' and that it is merely a matter of social evaluation conferred upon a language or variety by social groups; in this section we are dealing with social stereotypes associated with ways of speaking. These value judgements express the stereotypes, attitudes and prejudices that members of a speech community have towards the speakers of another community and their language. These stereotyped judgements have important implications for intergroup relations, the life of individuals and the education of children.

According to Fiske & Neuberg (1990) perceptions and impressions of others are formed through a variety of processes distributed on a continuum ranging from primarily category-based to primarily individuating processes. The more the person's attributes fit the identified category, the more likely the perception is category-based. In this sense language is perceived as a group attribute and thus activates stereotypes and value judgements attributed to the speakers of this language.

In order to measure the stereotypes attributed to languages, varieties, accents, dialects or styles, direct or indirect techniques have been employed. Among the former the most widely used is the attitude questionnaire; however, it fails to reveal unconsciously held or socially undesirable attitudes. To obviate these drawbacks, indirect techniques have been introduced, the most sophisticated being the 'matched guise', developed by W. E. Lambert and his team (Lambert, Hodgson, Gardner & Fillenbaum, 1960; Lambert, 1972). This technique involves judges listening to tape-recordings of a number of bilingual speakers; they are asked to evaluate each speaker on a number of scales describing personality traits such as 'intelligent–stupid', 'interesting–uninteresting', 'good–bad'; the judges are however unaware that they hear the same speaker twice, in two different languages. As the matched recordings do not differ on voice characteristics but only in respect of the language used, differences in personality judgements can be safely attributed to value judgements on the languages. Since it was first used, the technique has been refined and widely applied in numerous studies on language attitudes.

The first study using a matched-guise technique in the context of languages in contact was that of Lambert, Hodgson, Gardner & Fillenbaum (1960). They asked French-Canadian and Anglo-Canadian students in Montreal to judge voices of balanced French–English bilingual speakers on a number of personality traits. It was found that both the English and the French bilinguals judged the English guises more favourably than the French guises; furthermore, the Anglo-Canadian judges rated the French voices higher than did the Franco-Canadians. The authors interpreted these results as evidence of the existence of a negative stereotype about the French minority shared by both communities. This negative stereotype towards one's own cultural-membership group was not found among 10-year-old French-Canadian children in a subsequent study by Anisfeld & Lambert (1964): at the age of 10 both Franco-Canadian and Anglo-Canadian children rated their own group more favourably. However, Franco-Canadian girls had developed the negative stereotype by the age of 12 (Lambert, Franckel & Tucker, 1966). Moreover, in the Anisfeld & Lambert experiment the bilingual 10-year-old judges showed less cultural stereotyping than their monolingual peers and judged French and English guises as more similar.

The effect on cultural stereotypes of learning an L_2 has also been assessed in a different cultural setting, both with children and adults. In a matched-guise study conducted in Wales, Bourhis, Giles & Tajfel (1973) observed that bilingual Welsh–English and monolingual English-speaking Welsh people who attended a course in the Welsh language judged English spoken with a Welsh accent more favourably than did monolingual Anglophone Welsh people who were not learning Welsh. Furthermore, the first two groups also rated their own competence in English more favourably than the monolinguals who did not learn Welsh rated their own English competence. Thus it would seem that being or becoming bilingual in English and Welsh would enhance their self-perception of both their Welsh-accented English and their competence in English. A state of bilinguality seems to attenuate the stereotypes that people have developed about L_2 speakers.

It is important to distinguish between a foreign accent on the one hand and a regional, social or ethnic accent on the other hand. Most studies on evaluation of accented speech indicate that any accent different from the accepted norm is less positively evaluated than the norm itself (see, for example, Giles, 1970; Giles & Powesland, 1975; Giles, Hewstone & Ball, 1983; Cargile, 1997). These findings have been confirmed for a variety of accents in different countries, both with adults and children:

- Jewish accent in Britain (Anisfeld, Bogo & Lambert, 1962);
- Black vs. White accent in the USA (Tucker & Lambert, 1969);
- Mexican-American accent in the USA (Ryan & Carranza, 1975);
- Jamaican accent and Creole in Britain (V. K. Edwards, 1978a);
- German accent and Standard American accent in the USA (Ryan & Bulick, 1982);
- Hispanic-American and Standard American accent in the USA (Giles, Williams, Mackie & Rosselli, 1995);
- Chinese accent vs. English accent in Hong Kong (Gibbons, 1982);
- Italian-accented, Vietnamese-accented and Standard English in Australia (Nesdale & Rooney, 1996).

To summarise the findings, standard-accented speakers are usually rated relatively highly on intelligence and social status compared to non-standard-accented speakers but not on solidarity and attractiveness-related traits (Ryan, Hewstone & Giles, 1984). Speakers of non-Standard American English are perceived as less dynamic than Standard American English speakers by Anglo-American judges (Giles, Williams, Mackie & Rosselli, 1995). However, in a few studies it appears that accented speech is sometimes evaluated in a more favourable way than the standard variety. Bourhis, Giles & Tajfel (1973) found this to be the case for English spoken with a Welsh accent, which was perceived more favourably than RP (received pronunciation) English by Welsh–English bilinguals and Welsh people who were learning Welsh. These favourable ratings, obtained from bilingual adults, were not found in bilingual Welsh–English children living in a predominantly Welsh-speaking environment, who rated the standard variety of English higher than the Welsh-accented one (Price, Fluck & Giles, 1983). Ryan, Carranza & Moffie (1975) had Mexican-American students rate Mexican-American speakers, representing a wide range of accentedness. The results indicated that Mexican-born students rated the speakers more favourably as their accentedness increased, whereas American-born judges rated the least-accented speakers more favourably. Speakers of non-Standard English are sometimes evaluated high on the status and intelligence traits: this is the case for Malaysian (Gill, 1994) and Japanese accents (Cargile & Giles, 1996) and Chinese accents (Cargile, 1997). These apparently contradictory results might be attributed to the raters' self-image, as these results are found only when the evaluated accent is a marker of the judges' ethnic group membership.

Context of evaluation also influences language evaluation. Situational factors influence evaluation of accented speech: personality evaluations given in response to speech vary according to whether the situation is formal or not, stresses status or solidarity, is person centred or group centred (Gallois & Callan, 1985). Cargile (1997) observed that the English accent of a native Chinese–Mandarin speaker did not affect evaluations of attractiveness, status or dynamism by Anglo-Americans in a job-interview situation, but that this evaluation was affected in the context of a college classroom when they rated a professor. The intensity of the accent also plays a role: a mild ethnic accent is better evaluated on status traits whereas a strong accent is better evaluated on solidarity traits (Nesdale & Rooney, 1996).

According to Turner (1981; 1982), comparing oneself favourably with outgroups could be a means of maintaining self-esteem. In this sense, perceiving as positive the 'psycholinguistic distinctiveness' of a group, i.e. using linguistic markers in order to be identified as a member of a group, indicates a high appreciation of that group. Evaluative responses to perceived speech characteristics are the results of an interaction between these perceptions, the social value attributed to one's own speech and social knowledge about ethnic groups and ethnic relations. (For an attempt at a theoretical framework on the role of speech-style evaluation, see Street & Hopper, 1982.)

8.4.2 The evaluation of non-native speech and ethnic clues

Although very few empirical studies have addressed the problem of foreign accents, i.e. speech accented in such a way that it is evident that the speaker is not a member of the ethnolinguistic group, it might be assumed that the pattern of intervening social psychological mechanisms is even more complicated than with regional or social accents. Segalowitz & Gadbonton (1977) studied evaluations of speech of non-balanced, but relatively fluent bilinguals by Francophone judges in Quebec. A non-balanced fluent bilingual, while having reached a high level of competence in his second language, produces speech marked by a series of non-native features, e.g.

accent. Judges would perceive certain markers as the expression of the speaker's ethnic allegiances: for example, a Francophone Quebecois who speaks English with a French accent is judged as having more nationalistic feelings than a Francophone Quebecois who speaks English without a French accent. The perception is independent of the speaker's real feelings: the authors found no correlation between the degree of nationalism expressed by the speakers and their competence in English. Furthermore, the judges' perceptions were not influenced by attitudes towards nationalism or by competence in English; however, their preferences were influenced by their attitudes in the sense that those who had nationalistic feelings preferred a marked accent, whereas those who expressed fewer nationalistic feelings preferred native-like English.

Comparing the evaluative reactions given to RP English, social dialects (e.g. Cockney), regional (e.g. Irish, Yorkshire, Indian) and foreign (e.g. French, Italian) accents in Britain, Giles (1970) observed that RP English was rated more favourably than any accented speech; the ratings given to regional and foreign accents would however vary according to their specificity. For example, English spoken with an Indian accent was not evaluated more favourably than Cockney, whereas English spoken with a French foreign accent was rated in a very favourable way, as superior to any English regional accent and much superior to an Italian or German foreign accent.

A balanced bilingual can be recognised as a native speaker in either one of his languages. However, this is not always the case in everyday ethnic interactions: certain non-linguistic, cultural or ethnic clues can influence the perception of the listener, who categorises the speaker as a member of an ethnolinguistic group. Characteristics of a 'visible minority' influence the listener's perception. The influence of non-linguistic clues is all the greater as these group characteristics are more evident, such as, for example, sex or skin colour.

Using an adapted matched guise, Williams, Whitehead & Miller (1971) presented video-taped recordings of children speaking different varieties of accented English (Mexican-American, Black-American or Anglo-American) to trainee teachers. The films were dubbed with the voices either in a congruent way (e.g. the Black-American child speaking Black English) or an incongruent way (e.g. the same child speaking Anglo-American English). The results indicated that non-linguistic ethnic clues influence the perception of linguistic clues, in the sense that when, for example, a Black American is shown speaking with an Anglo-American accent, this accent is perceived as closer to Black English than when the same accent is produced by an Anglo-American. Hopper (1977) investigated the effect of the interaction between race, accent and professional qualifications on employment interviewers' perception of candidates in the USA; although he found that race and accent were good predictors of employability, he nonetheless observed that when a positively perceived accent (i.e. Standard English) was combined with negatively perceived race characteristics (i.e. Black), e.g. a Black speaker with a Standard accent, the overall perception was highly favourable. Kalin (1982) interprets these results as an indication that language style is a powerful factor in social categorisation. Thus, not only is accent perceived as a marker of social and cultural distinctiveness but also this perception will be influenced by non-linguistic markers of ethnicity. These findings have important implications for the way the bilingual is perceived.

The socio-structural context and situation in which interactions take place influence language evaluation during interethnic encounters (Côté & Clément, 1994). Genesee and Bourhis (1982; 1988) asked judges to evaluate Francophone and Anglophone speakers engaged in code-switching during a situated conversation; the speakers acted either as salesperson or as customer in a large department store in Montreal. The study demonstrates the importance of the situational norm (the salesperson is expected to converge to the customer) but also the effect of a socio-structural variable (French is the only official language of work in Quebec) on code-switching evaluation. Using a modified matched-guise technique, Côté & Clément (1994) examined evaluations and language choice of Anglophone speakers by Francophone students at the University of Ottawa, in both a very intimate and a task-specific situation. Contrary to their expectations the authors did not find a situation effect on the subject's language choice: the Francophones converged to English more often than they maintained their own language, regardless of the situation. However, when the Anglophone speakers used French rather than English they were evaluated more favourably on solidarity and status traits.

Content and message also interact with the accent. Attitude changes of Anglophone respondents concerning the English Only Movement (EOM)[3] were different when the message was delivered by a Standard White-American-accented voice or by a Hispanic-accented voice. When a message against the EOM was delivered in White-American-accented English it reduced support for the issue, but when the message was for the EOM no attitude changes were observed. On the other hand, when the anti-EOM message was delivered in Hispanic accented English no attitude changes were observable, whereas pro-EOM delivered by a Hispanic-accented speaker would induce attitude changes in favour of the EOM. Speakers had no effect on the listener's attitudes when they delivered a message believed to be congruent with their ethnic group membership (Giles, Williams, Mackie & Rosselli, 1995). In other words when the speaker violates the expectations due to his group membership, it has a positive effect in changing the listener's attitudes.

In conclusion, then, evaluation studies of non-native-accented and non-standard-accented speech demonstrate the complexity of language evaluation. Non-native speech evokes ethnolinguistic stereotypes and value judgement, but not in a way independent of other factors, such as context and topic. We are still a long way from understanding the role played by non-native and non-standard speech in intercultural communication. Very few bilinguals speak both languages with a standard native accent; this is the case for many children of mixed marriages where both parents speak their own standard language, and for some majority children schooled through bilingual programs (see Section 11.4.1). Most bilinguals speak one of their languages, if not both, with an accent that is recognised as non-standard. This is because they are members of a minority group that has developed its own accent in the native language and often in the second language, or because through formal schooling or informal contacts they have become proficient, though not native-like, in L_2.

8.5   SOCIAL PSYCHOLOGICAL ASPECTS OF L_2 ACQUISITION

Whereas some individuals become balanced bilinguals either through a mixed-lingual family experience or through informal exposure to two or more languages (as is the case in many African and Asian countries or the case of many immigrant communities), others reach some degree of bilinguality through formal schooling (either through bilingual education or through more traditional L_2 training). In this section we briefly review the most important psychological factors which determine achievement in L_2 acquisition and use of the L_2 in interethnic communication.

The relative importance of psychological factors for L_2 learners has been stressed in a number of correlational studies. For example, Naiman, Fröhlich, Stern & Todesco (1978) attempted to identify the characteristics of 'the good language learner' by correlating a large number of individual factors with achievement in L_2. From this study it appears that individual variables likely to influence L_2 learning are cognitive and socio-affective in nature; they are factors such as intelligence, language aptitude, anxiety, attitudes and motivations, and certain personality factors including cognitive style. In the following sections we briefly analyse the role of some of these factors.

8.5.1   Cognitive variables in L_2 learning

The first individual variables relevant to L_2 acquisition are aptitude variables, that is, variables involved in the cognitive organisation necessary for the internalisation of L_2. They include general cognitive processes, such as generalisation, imitation, analogy, memory, etc. These cognitive mechanisms are relatively well documented and their identification has led to the elaboration of L_2 aptitude tests (see for example, Carroll & Sapon, 1959; Pimsleur, 1966). Language aptitude has been defined as a set of skills similar to intelligence but more specifically related to L_2 competence. J. B. Carroll (1965; 1973) identified four major components of L_2 aptitude: (1) phonemic encoding, (2) grammatical sensitivity, (3) inductive language-learning ability and (4) memory.

Where does L_2 aptitude come from? It has been proposed that aptitude tests draw on skills used in decontextualised language (Skehan, 1986). From research on literacy it seems that skills used in decontextualised language, which are predictive of academic success (Wells, 1985a), are developed in early childhood from the verbal interaction between a child and the adults around him (see Chapter 5). In the follow-up study of 53 adolescents who at the ages of 15–60 months had participated in a research project on L_1 development (Bristol Study, see Wells, 1985b), Skehan demonstrated that foreign-language aptitude and achievement correlated with certain patterns of relations between variables relevant to L_1 development. Examples of these patterns are that:

- L_2 aptitude measures correlate significantly with syntactic L_1 measures (e.g. mean length of utterance, MLU) taken in early childhood;
- L_1 comprehension and vocabulary measures are powerful predictors of L_2 aptitude;
- family background indices, such as parental education, quantity of adult reading to the child, and literacy-oriented behaviour at home seem to play an important role in the development of aptitude;
- a different pattern of childhood L_1 indices correlates with L_2 proficiency tests.

The author concludes that L_2 aptitude is a hybrid combining a language-processing ability with a capacity to handle decontextualised language. Thus, L_2 aptitude can be traced to general language experience at an early age and its social roots (see Chapters 4 and 5 for a discussion in relation to early bilinguality).

8.5.2   Affective variables in L_2 learning

The most-studied affective dimension of L_2 acquisition[4] is probably the attitudinal–motivational variables, which include correlated social psychological factors such as attitudes, anxiety, self-esteem and ethnocentrism. These variables are more specifically of importance in settings where language learning is embedded in the interethnic contacts existing in the community. In an interethnic context the primary reason for language learning is often communication (MacIntyre & Charos, 1996). Therefore interethnic communication processes are closely related to L_2 learning.

The focus on this dimension is justified by the fact that it is the second most important set of variables for predicting achievement in L_2 after aptitude (J. B. Carroll, 1962). Gardner (1980) observed that attitudinal–motivational measures correlate (median correlation = .37) almost as highly with proficiency as do aptitudinal indices (median correlation = .41). The advantage of attitudinal variables is that, unlike aptitude, they can easily be manipulated and modified in order to achieve better results in L_2. A first detailed analysis of these variables was conducted by Gardner & Lambert (1959), who suggested that the learner's motivation to learn an L_2 is influenced by his attitudes towards the target group and by his orientation towards the learning task itself. Motivation is defined as the effort that the learner is prepared to make in order to attain competence in L_2, and his desire to achieve this goal. It is essentially a product of the environment and can for this reason be easily influenced by the latter. The influence of the environment on L_2 achievement is mediated through a complex psychological mechanism which we refer to as 'the motivational process'. Only a better understanding of mediational processes, such as motivation and valorisation, will allow an accurate identification of environmental variables, whose manipulation can lead to greater linguistic, paralinguistic and communicative competence in L_2.

8.5.2.1   Gardner's socio-educative model

The first mediational model proposed by Gardner & Lambert (1972) is a linear one: attitudes influence motivation which in turn influences competence in L_2. The authors identified two orientations towards the learning task: at one extreme, an integrative orientation reflects the learner's desire to resemble members of the L_2 target group; at the other, an instrumental orientation refers to a set of practical reasons for learning L_2. The first studies on orientations indicated the integrative motive as the more important in the motivational process. Besides the empirical evidence gathered by Gardner & Lambert in support of their model it was also demonstrated that for Anglophones learning French in a classroom situation in Western Ontario, integrative orientation was correlated with learners' determination to persist with L_2 learning tasks (Gardner & Smythe, 1975; Clément, Smythe & Gardner, 1978) and with level of activity in the L_2 class (Gliksman & Gardner, 1976).

If integrative orientation appears to be the main determinant of motivation for Anglo-Canadians learning French, this is not necessarily the case for other L_2 learners in other communities. Several studies stress the role of instrumental orientation: it was demonstrated that for Franco-phones learning English in Montreal, instrumental and pragmatic reasons would orientate the learners rather than integrative ones (Gagnon, 1970; Maréchal, Bourdon & Lapierre, 1973). Lukmani (1972) found similar orientations in Marathi high-school learners of English in Bombay. How-ever, these results are not found for all communities: Clément, Gardner & Smythe (1977b) found integrative and instrumental orientation to be equally important for Francophone L_2 learners of English in Quebec; Gardner & Lambert (1972) found similar orientations for Franco-Ameri-can learners of English in New England.

The existence of a positive link between motivational orientations and achievement in L_2 has not been confirmed experimentally by Oller and his associates (Oller, Hudson & Liu, 1977; Oller, Baca & Vigil, 1977; Chihara & Oller, 1978). Oller & Perkins (1978) conclude that the link between motivational orientations and L_2 proficiency is weak if it exists at all. This criticism has been refuted by Gardner (1980) on the basis of methodologi-cal weaknesses on the part of Oller and his associates. Clément & Kruidenier (1983) attribute the disparity between Oller's research and most other studies on motivational orientation to two main sources:

(1) the ambiguity of definitions and concepts such as integrative and instrumental orientation in some of the studies; and
(2) the influence of the language environment on the individual's orienta-tions.

As far as ambiguities are concerned, the definitions of integrative and instrumental orientations used by Oller are different from those used by Gardner and colleagues to the extent that the same item used to measure integrative orientation in one set of studies is used to measure instrumental orientation in the other. As far as the cultural and linguistic environment is concerned Gardner & Lambert (1972) remark that in 'settings where there is an urgency about mastering a second language – as there is in the Philippines and in North America for members of linguistic minority groups – the instrumental approach to language study is extremely effec-tive' (p. 114). From the great number of studies supporting the existence of a relationship between orientations and L_2 proficiency it appears that this relationship varies according to the context of acquisition which must be taken into account by a theoretical model of L_2 acquisition (Clément & Hamers, 1979; Gardner, 1980; Clément & Kruidenier, 1983).

Since the first study by Gardner & Lambert (1959), it is evident that motivational orientations are closely linked to attitudes. Later research stresses, in addition, the relevance of other affective factors. Gardner (1979) demonstrated that in bilingual environments – such as Ottawa, Montreal and Moncton – anxiety is the most important affective factor to predict anglophone learners' proficiency in French, whereas in unilingual environments – such as London, Ontario – motivation is the best predictor of L_2 proficiency. These results confirm the idea developed by Clément & Kruidenier (1983) that the social context of learning at least partly determines the affective dimension of L_2 learning and that anxiety, attitudes and motivation form a complex pattern of interaction which influences the motivation mechanism.

Gardner (1985; 1988) proposed a socio-educational model of L_2 acquisition which accounts for most of the empirical research evidence on motivational processes in L_2. The author also makes use of causal modelling (Jöreskog & Sorbom, 1978) in order to assess the validity of his construct and to test the hypothesised causal link. The model (depicted in Figure 8.1) is composed of four classes of variables: social milieu, individual differences, language-acquisition context and outcomes. The L_2 acquisition process results from a particular causal interplay of these four types of variables. One important feature of the model is that L_2 acquisition occurs in a particular context; it further proposes that attitudes and belief of the community concerning language learning, expectations about the nature of L_2 skill development and individual differences all influence L_2 acquisition. For example, the model predicts that if it is expected that most individuals will learn an L_2, two relevant attitudes – namely, integrativeness and attitudes towards the learning situation – are produced by the sociocultural context.

Further research has shown that in addition to attitudes and motivation, anxiety for L_2 communication correlates with L_2 learning achievement (MacIntyre & Gardner, 1991; 1994). Speaking an L_2 can be a main source of anxiety. Gardner & MacIntyre (1993) suggest that the relation between anxiety and motivation is bi-directional: high levels of anxiety are likely to inhibit motivation and high levels of motivation are likely to diminish anxiety. According to MacIntyre (1994) anxiety influences the perception of competence which is underestimated when anxiety is high. Gardner & MacIntyre (1993) refined Gardner's model and include in the individual differences intelligence, aptitude, strategies, attitudes, motivation and anxiety.

More recently Tremblay & Gardner (1995) expanded the model by making a distinction between motivational behaviour and motivational antecedents. Motivational behaviour refers to the characteristics of an individual that can be observed, such as effort, persistence and attention. Motivational antecedents are the variables that cannot be perceived, but that influence behaviour, as, for example, goal-setting, expectancy, valence

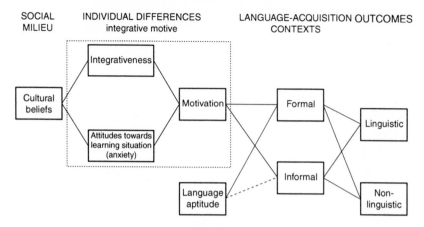

Figure 8.1   Social psychological model of L$_2$ acquisition (adapted from Gardner, 1985)

(the subjective value attributed to the outcome) and self-efficacy (a concept close to self-confidence). In their study in a French school in northern Ontario they demonstrated that achievement in French was equally influenced by French language dominance and by the motivational process. They found that the link between attitudes and motivational behaviour was mediated through a number of intervening variables, of which goal-setting, valence and self-efficacy are the most important.

8.5.2.2   The socio-contextual model

Clément (1980; 1984; 1986) proposes a different model which insists on the importance of the social context and in which he makes a distinction between two motivational processes. Clément & Kruidenier (1983) identified three aspects of learning contexts which are relevant to orientation: learners' ethnic-group membership, the presence of other ethnolinguistic groups in the community and L$_2$ status. Group membership influences orientations, inasmuch as integration with a majority group might equal assimilation, whereas integration with a minority group might be a way of maintaining dominance. For these reasons it might be expected that in Canada, for example, the orientation of Francophones learning English, and of Anglophones learning French, would not be the same. The ethnic composition of the community also plays a role: the learners' orientation is different according to whether they live in a unicultural L$_1$ environment or in a multicultural setting where the relative status of L$_1$ and the target language is more visible. Finally, the sociopolitical status of the target language is relevant: in a multilingual country, learning the official language as an L_2 is not done for the same reasons as learning a foreign language.

Studying the orientation of Francophone high-school learners of English in communities varying in their degree of cultural homogeneity (in the Francophone city of Quebec, in the Anglophone town of London, Ontario, and in the bilingual community of Ottawa), learning either an official language (French or English) or a foreign language (Spanish), Clément & Kruidenier (1985) identified nine different types of orientation, of which four were common to all groups studied. Generally speaking, an L_2 is learned for pragmatic reasons, those included in instrumental orientation, such as better job prospects, but also in order to travel, to create new friendships or to acquire additional knowledge. Other orientations – such as the desire to meet other groups, the recognition of the relevance of a minority, an influence-seeking orientation, an interest in the sociocultural dimensions of the target group, and specific academic interest – were present in certain groups, though not in all. Whereas instrumental orientation was common to all groups, this was not the case for integrative orientation, which was present only in the Francophones and Anglophones who were learning a foreign language (i.e. Spanish) in a multicultural environment. Integrative orientation, in its purest form, was present only in the Anglophone group. The authors conclude that the desire to learn an L_2 in order to identify with members of the target group is found only among individuals who do not feel that their language and culture are threatened and who have experienced close contacts with other ethnolinguistic groups. They further observed that only certain orientations seem to be universal, i.e. when L_2 learning occurs in a context of ethnic group relations. For these reasons, it is important to determine which orientations relevant to L_2 can be considered as universal, and which are context-specific.

Taking into account the context of language learning Clément (1980) proposed a model based on the assumption that there is a close relationship between socio-affective mechanisms in L_1 and L_2. This model is depicted in Figure 8.2. Clément distinguishes between a primary and a secondary motivational process. The primary motivational process, including integrativeness, i.e. the affective predisposition towards the target group, is checked by fear of assimilation, i.e. the fear that learning L_2 may lead to a loss of first culture and language. If the result of these two contrary forces is negative, then motivation to learn L_2 will be low and the learner will not seek contact with the members of the target group. The existence of the primary motivational process has been demonstrated in a number of studies (Gardner & Smythe, 1975; Taylor, Meynard & Rhéault, 1977;

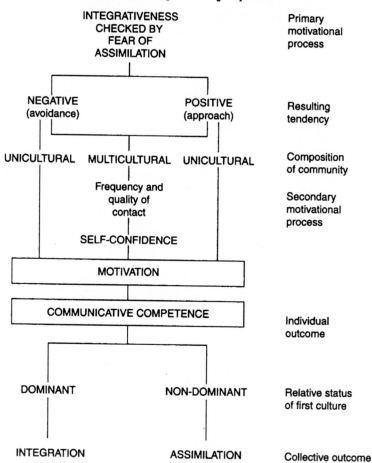

Figure 8.2   Schematic representation of individual motivational
processes (from Clément, 1980)

Clément, 1978) in which negative correlations were found between fear of
assimilation and self-evaluation in L_2, and between fear of assimilation and
integrative orientation.

However, in a multicultural setting a secondary motivational process
might operate. Gardner (1979) found that in bilingual settings in Canada
anxiety to use an L_2 is the best predictor for attitudes and motivation. The
resulting force between the desire to integrate and the fear of assimilation
interact with self-confidence to communicate in L_2. This self-confidence is a
result of specific interethnic contacts. The frequency of these contacts,

however, is not sufficient to increase self-confidence, but their quality is overriding (Amir, 1969). Frequent and agreeable contacts tend to improve self-confidence to use L_2. According to Clément (1980; 1986) the motivation to acquire communicative competence in L_2 is a function of self-confidence and/or a tendency resulting from the primary motivational process, depending on the context. The extent to which these variables are important varies according to the relative status of L_1 and L_2.

This model has been tested with 1180 Francophone students of different age groups learning English in Quebec (Clément & Kruidenier, 1985). The authors made use of a causal-modelling technique in order to verify the causal relationships between the different theoretical constructs utilised. Generally speaking, the results indicated that:

(1)   integrativeness was inversely related to fear of assimilation;
(2)   integrativeness and fear of assimilation have an opposite effect on the secondary motivational process;
(3)   the existence of the secondary motivational process and the causal sequence of contact and self-confidence was supported;
(4)   the secondary motivational process mediated the effect of the primary motivational process; and
(5)   self-confidence is defined by language-use anxiety and self-evaluation in L_2 proficiency.

Thus, the results support the key psychological processes postulated by Clément and their contextual dependency.

Although the affective dimensions underlying the bilingual's cultural identity have essentially been studied in the context of L_2 acquisition, they are also applicable to the development of bilinguality. According to Clément's (1984) general model of L_2 acquisition, several socio-affective mechanisms interact with each other and determine the level of competence in L_2 that a person reaches in a bicultural setting. A first affective mechanism enables the individual to develop certain affective relations with members of both cultural groups and languages; this mechanism determines the 'desire for integration'; a second antagonistic force, 'fear of assimilation', interacts with the first one. If the resultant force is negative the primary process reflects fear of assimilation, and motivation to learn L_2 is relatively low. When the resultant force is positive the primary process reflects integrativeness and a high level of motivation. To these primary processes a secondary motivational process is added, which reflects self-confidence resulting from interaction with the members of the L_2 community. Thus, in a multicultural context, 'an individual's motivation is determined by both the primary and secondary motivational processes operating in sequence' (Clément, 1980: 151). It may be assumed that a similar process operates for the bilingual's cultural identity, i.e. his identity is the result of a desire to integrate with the new culture and a fear of assimilation to the new culture. One important feature of Clément's model is the focus on the context in which L$_2$ learning occurs. By insisting on the role played by self-confidence in L$_2$ learning, Clément puts the whole issue of L$_2$ learning within the scope of interethnic relations.

8.5.3 Cognitive style and personality variables

It has been suggested that learning strategies of L$_2$ learners are influenced by cognitive styles (Richards, 1972; Selinker, 1972). Learning strategies refer to those processes that facilitate the task of learning, such as making memorisation easier, making the task more meaningful, maintaining motivation, encouraging participation and reflecting personal characteristics, as for example, risk-taking (Oxford, 1991). Cognitive style is a choice of, or preference for, particular cognitive strategies; it seems to be a combination of cognitive and affective factors. Its affective dimension stems from the fact that a given cognitive style always covaries with personality factors; for example, cognitive styles in L$_2$ acquisition vary on an impulsivity–reflexivity scale (H. D. Brown, 1973). Impulsivity is a tendency to respond quickly to a problem while taking the risk of giving the wrong response, while reflexivity is the response style which corresponds to a slow but precise response. Examining the relationship between cognitive style and achievement in L$_2$ reading, Doron (1973) demonstrated that reflexive L$_2$ learners were slower at reading in L$_2$ but produced fewer errors than impulsive learners.

Another relevant cognitive-style dimension is that of field dependency–independency: the independent learner is capable of extracting abstract structures from given information whereas a dependent learner is more influenced by the immediate context. Naiman, Fröhlich, Stern & Todesco (1978) showed that an independent style is positively correlated with oral comprehension and imitation in L$_2$; however, this difference has little effect on reading comprehension (Bialystok & Fröhlich, 1977). As these results were not replicated at different age levels the authors concluded that cognitive style is age-related. From a study of university beginners in Spanish as L$_2$, Hansen & Stansfield (1981) concluded that cognitive style plays only a minor role in overall L$_2$ acquisition. It has also been suggested that cognitive style may interact with other factors, as for example the source culture of the learner. Wong Fillmore (1980) showed that L$_2$ learners from Mexican and from Chinese backgrounds called upon different cognitive styles. Politzer (1983) and Politzer & McGoarty (1985) reported that individual differences in strategy use are correlated with differences in proficiency and motivation.

Introversion–extroversion is probably the personality trait most studied in relation to L_2 achievement, but results are inconsistent. According to Skehan (1989) introversion rather than extroversion is the most desirable trait for academic achievement, but either pole of the continuum may favour certain learning situations according to context and method. For example, methods based on competence of communication are likely to favour extrovert learners. Generally speaking, the correlation between extroversion and L_2 achievement is either non-significant or slightly positive, depending on the measures used.

Measuring 18 personality traits Lalonde & Gardner (1984) obtained very low correlations with language achievement, aptitude or perceived competence. However, when they combined the personality traits under two categories labelled 'analytic orientation' and 'seriousness', and applied a causal model for predicting achievement, they obtained significant correlations: analytic orientation predicted integrativeness and seriousness predicted success in the learning situation. Lalonde & Gardner concluded that personality traits have an indirect effect on L_2 achievement mediated through attitudes and motivation.

An interesting development concerning the relation between personality and L_2 learning has been proposed by MacIntyre (1994) who put forward the concept of 'willingness to communicate'. The concept proposed by McCroskey (1992) is defined as a stable predisposition to communicate when free to choose to do so. Willingness to communicate depends on a variety of variables such as anxiety, introversion, alienation, social pressure and lack of communicative competence. MacIntyre & Charos (1996) analysed the following in Anglophone adults taking a French introductory course in evening classes in Ottawa: the relationship between L_2 competence, frequency of communication in French, willingness to communicate in French, integrativeness, motivation, attitudes to language anxiety, the social context (measured by self-reported assessment of encounters with French-speaking people in different settings), and five broad personality traits. The five personality measures were: extroversion–introversion, agreeableness–disagreeableness, conscientiousness–negligence, emotional stability–neuroticism and intellect–unsophistication. In addition to confirming Gardner's model the results suggest that communicating in an L_2 in a bilingual environment is related to the willingness to do so, to the motivation to learn, to the opportunity of contact and to the perception of competence. Major personality traits play an indirect role via their influence on attitudes, anxiety motivation, perceived competence and willingness to communicate. Personality traits and social contexts both contribute to the frequency of communication. Thus, communication in the L_2 is a complex process which depends as much upon language competence, attitudes and personality variables as upon the social context in which it takes place.

8.6   CONCLUSION

In the present chapter we have discussed the relationship between language and culture and its effect on the bilingual's development of identity and behaviour. We first focused on culture, ethnolinguistic identity and its development in a language-contact situation. Cultural identity is an important aspect of personality. The bilingual develops a unique identity, different from that of the monolingual, but which can nonetheless be harmoniously adjusted if society allows it; contrary to received opinion that bilinguality leads to a maladjusted personality, it should be stressed that anomie and psychological distress are not necessary outcomes of bilinguality but develop only when the individual has no possibility of resolving conflicts arising from his dual membership. While the bilingual's ethnolinguistic identity is shaped by his bilingual experience, his bilinguality is in turn influenced by his cultural identity and its social psychological and affective correlates. A balanced bilinguality develops only to the extent that the characteristics of cultural and ethnolinguistic identity relevant to the acquisition of the two languages are salient for the child's identity without conflicting. It is important to stress that a bilingual does not develop two parallel identities but integrates his two cultures into a unique identity in which aspects of both his cultures are closely interrelated (cultural interdependence hypothesis); this integration is the result of an interplay between enculturation, acculturation and deculturation processes. Ethnolinguistic identity is a dynamic process and the salience of certain of its characteristics depends on the context of an interethnic encounter.

Bilingual experience influences ethnic attitudes. Bilinguals focus less on language stereotypes than do monolinguals. Acquiring competence in an L_2 can modify ethnolinguistic attitudes and enhance positive perceptions of the other group. How the bilingual is perceived by members of his own and other communities is a function of the existing relations between the different communities. The level of language competence of a bilingual is also relevant in ethnic interactions. A perfectly balanced bilingual can be perceived as a member of either one of his ethnolinguistic groups provided that no non-linguistic ethnic clues interfere. A dominant bilingual, even if he is highly fluent in his L_2, is however perceived as a member of his own ethnolinguistic group, since the 'foreign' language markers he uses in his speech are identified not only with ethnic-group membership but also with ethnic allegiances. Bilingual proficiency is also related to the social psychological mechanisms implied in ethnolinguistic encounters and there is a constant interplay between proficiency and ethnolinguistic identity. In summary, bilinguality is an important social psychological dimension that influences interethnic relations, is shaped by social factors and, in turn, conditions the development of social psychological mechanisms relevant to the integration of the individual in society.

In Section 8.5 we briefly discussed some social psychological dimensions relevant to L_2 learning. In an interethnic setting the motivational processes are of primary importance and influenced by the interethnic communication situation. It is a combination of aptitude, motivational and personality factors which determines the willingness to communicate in an L_2 in a given social context. As Clément & Bourhis (1996) point out, whereas, since the pioneering work of Gardner & Lambert there has been a wealth of social psychological models of L_2 acquisition and use, there is at the same time a lack of integration between the different approaches. Recent research stresses the role of the social context of L_2 communication. However, scholars still have to integrate the vast domain of social psychological mechanisms in intercultural communication with those of personal characteristics and of L_2 acquisition and bilinguality.

In the next chapter we turn to the social psychological dimensions of intercultural communication.

9   Social psychological aspects of bilinguality: intercultural communication

Whereas in Chapter 8 we focused on the effects of a bilingual experience on social psychological mechanisms relevant to language behaviour, in the present chapter we discuss the result of the interplay of these mechanisms with language behaviour in situations of interpersonal interaction. In order to understand interpersonal communication in an intercultural context one has to understand how meaning is negotiated when the interlocutors are members of different ethnolinguistic groups; how language interacts with processes of social-cognition mediation; and thus how language may become a salient dimension of this interaction (Gudykunst, 1986). In intercultural communication people interact with one another both as individuals and as members of different social groups; social encounters are thus determined by interpersonal as well as by intergroup factors (Tajfel & Turner, 1979), and can be analysed along these two dimensions (Stephenson, 1981).

When two members from different cultural and ethnolinguistic groups communicate with one another, social categorisation occurs in such a way that people have a tendency to exaggerate differences on critical dimensions *between* categories and minimise differences *within* a social category (Tajfel, 1981). Social, cultural or ethnolinguistic groups are perceived as more distinct from each other if they differ on a large number of distinctive features, such as language, race characteristics, religion and social status (as, for example, in an encounter between an Anglo-Celt and an Indian from South India) than if they differ on one or two characteristics only (as would be the case in an encounter between a Briton and an Anglo-Celtic Australian). Furthermore, social categorisation produces ingroup bias which is based on ethnocentrism, that is, on the perception of one's own ethnic group as being superior to an outgroup.

When language is a salient aspect of group identity and an important distinctive feature in a communication between two people, i.e. in a communication dyad, then either person will adopt strategies for positive linguistic distinctiveness if:

(1) he identifies strongly with his own ethnolinguistic group;
(2) he makes insecure intercultural comparisons with regard to his group status;
(3) he perceives the other's ingroup as having high ethnolinguistic vitality (see Section 10.2.3) and closed and hard boundaries;
(4) he does not identify strongly with other social categories, e.g. professions, perceives little overlap between himself and the other person in terms of social group membership, and considers his social identity derived from other categories to be rather inadequate; and
(5) he perceives intragroup status in his cultural group to be relatively higher than intragroup status in other social category groups (Giles & Johnson, 1981).

In intercultural communication these factors interact to determine the choice of language behaviour and the type of speech accommodation an individual will make. Furthermore, his evaluation of the other's language behaviour is a function of his language attitudes, which are determined by two independent dimensions, one being 'person vs. group-centred', the other 'solidarity vs. status-stressing' (Giles & Ryan, 1982).

9.1   SPEECH/COMMUNICATION ACCOMMODATION

One of the most relevant characteristics of interpersonal communication is the adaptation of two speakers to each other's speech. Such adaptation can be observed in all types of verbal interaction, whether monolingual or bilingual, and at all linguistic levels (e.g. phonological, lexical, etc.). Among the many different types of accommodation, those that come most readily to mind are motherese and fatherese, that is, parental speech adjustment to children who are immature speakers (Snow & Ferguson, 1977), and 'foreigner talk', i.e. the simplification of one's language when addressing a non-fluent foreign speaker (Clyne, 1981; see Section 9.2.2.1). It seems that in the course of a conversation between two individuals the most common behaviour for the speakers is to converge towards each other in the speech they use; this has been shown for such features as speech rate, pauses, accent and so on.

9.1.1   Foundations of speech-accommodation theory

In order to explain this tendency to adapt, Giles & Powesland (1975) proposed a model of speech accommodation which focuses on the underlying social cognitive processes mediating between the individual's perception of the communication situation and his communicative behaviour. Briefly stated, speech-accommodation theory which is also sometimes called communication-accommodation theory (Coupland & Giles, 1988), is based on the following social psychological processes:

(1) similarity attraction,
(2) social exchange,
(3) causal attribution and
(4) intergroup distinctiveness.

Through mechanisms of similarity attraction, the more similar an individual's attitudes and beliefs are to others, the more he is attracted to them. By attenuating linguistic differences between himself and his interlocutor the speaker increases social attraction, since he is perceived as more similar by the listener; this process is called 'convergent accommodation'. Accommodation is also the outcome of another social psychological mechanism, that of 'social exchange' through which, prior to acting, one attempts to assess the rewards and costs of alternative courses of action. A speaker accommodates provided he perceives that the cost of accommodation, e.g. a threat to his ethnic identity, is less than the reward gained from an increased social attraction. According to Thakerar, Giles & Cheshire (1982), speakers are motivated to adapt their speech style in order to gain the listener's social approval, increase the efficacy of the communication and maintain a positive social, cultural or ethnic identity. In an interaction the listener interprets the speaker's behaviour in terms of the motives and intentions that he attributes to this behaviour. This process of causal attribution explains how convergent accommodation is perceived as an intention to reduce social distance; speech convergence is perceived more favourably if it is attributed to the speaker's desire to bridge a social gap than if it is attributed to external pressures on the speaker's behaviour, such as the lack of communicative competence of the interlocutor or sociolinguistic norms which impose a specific code. Finally, intergroup distinctiveness also influences speech accommodation (Giles & Smith, 1979). Tajfel (1974) suggested that when two members of different groups interact they compare themselves on relevant dimensions and this leads them to identify those dimensions which make them distinct from each other.

If language is a salient dimension of the speaker's identity, he can use distinctive linguistic markers of his own group to assert his cultural identity and to distinguish himself from his interlocutor. Divergent accommodation, that is, when a person's speech becomes more distinct from his interlocutor's, is a communication strategy which enables the speaker to distinguish himself psychologically from his interlocutor as a member of a distinct ethnolinguistic group. This 'psycholinguistic distinctiveness' (Giles, Bourhis & Taylor, 1977) enables an individual to express ethnolinguistic group allegiances in intercultural interpersonal communication.

Descriptively, convergence and divergence can be labelled 'upwards' or 'downwards', depending on the sociolinguistic status of the interlocutor. One should note, however, that these terms are value laden and based on hierarchical class and speech bias.

9.1.2   Empirical support for speech-accommodation theory

The validity of the speech-accommodation model has been verified in a number of empirical studies in multilingual contexts. How is speech convergence expressed? Studying speech accommodation between Anglo-Canadian and Franco-Canadian bilinguals, Giles, Taylor & Bourhis (1973) demonstrated that Anglo-Canadians perceived Franco-Canadian bilingual speakers in a more favourable light when they also perceived accommodation to be high; in turn, they tended to accommodate more if they attributed a high accommodation intention to the speaker. Simard, Taylor & Giles (1976) observed that lack of accommodation by a speaker is perceived in a different way if it is perceived as resulting from:

(1)   a lack of speaker's competence in the listener's language;
(2)   external pressures on the speech style of the interaction; or
(3)   a lack of effort on the part of the speaker to attenuate dissimilarities and diminish social distance.

The listener reacts more favourably to a lack of accommodation if he perceives it as resulting from a lack of communicative competence rather than from a lack of effort on the part of the speaker.

Because dimensions of status and solidarity are among the most salient characteristics of social interactions they influence speech accommodation in a dyad (Brown & Gilman, 1960). Sociolinguistic stereotypes, that is, stereotypes about how members of certain social groups are 'supposed to speak' and how one 'should' address members of given social groups, are powerful mediating social cognitive processes for speech accommodation (Hewstone & Giles, 1986). In a socially unequal interaction dyad, accommodation generally implies that the speaker with the lower social status accommodates relatively more to his interlocutor rather than the reverse, although in most interactions some form of mutual accommodation can be observed. This is equally true for individual (Thakerar, Giles & Cheshire, 1982) and for ethnolinguistic group status (Taylor, Simard & Papineau, 1978). In an intercultural encounter, cultural-group status interplays with social-group status to determine the power relations and hence the type of speech accommodation.

Deshaies & Hamers (1982) analysed speech accommodation in a role play between bilingual workers, foremen and managers from different ethnolinguistic backgrounds (Francophone, Anglophone and other) in Montreal firms. They observed that, whereas the main goal was to maintain good working relations in the first place (and thus all employees would accommodate linguistically), there was relatively more upwards than downwards convergence in all interactions, the type of linguistic accommodation being tempered, however, by the speaker's linguistic competence. In a different context Valdes-Fallis (1977) found that bilingual Mexican-American women tend to accommodate to male speech by imitating the latter's code alternation (see Section 9.3) when addressing Mexican-American men, whereas they use little code alternation when speaking among themselves. Thus, bilingual speech accommodation is influenced as much by social as by linguistic factors.

Children's speech-accommodation strategies are also influenced by the relative status of the speakers' ethnolinguistic groups. Aboud (1976) observed that when explaining the rules of a game, six-year-old Spanish–English bilingual Chicanos converged more frequently to Anglophone than to Hispanophone interlocutors. However, a fuller knowledge of sociolinguistic norms relating to language use is usually acquired slowly throughout childhood and adolescence, at least in the West (Genesee, 1984). Non-verbal characteristics of the intercultural encounter can also influence speech accommodation: Beebe (1981) found that Chinese–Thai bilingual children used Chinese phonological variants in their Thai speech when interviewed by a speaker of Standard Thai who looked ethnically Chinese.

Many experiments on speech accommodation examine only short interactions; however, in real life interpersonal interactions often extend over a period of time. As verbal interaction is a dynamic phenomenon, little is known about changes in speech accommodation during the course of the interaction. Analysing intercultural speech accommodation, Belair Lockheed (1987) demonstrated that in half-hour-long conversations between Francophone and Anglophone college students in Ottawa, members of a dyad change the way they adjust in the sense that, after a while, interpersonal aspects of the communication overrule intergroup considerations and that content rather than language would become the most important issue.

Linguistic convergence is not always a one-way strategy but is effected by both members of a communication dyad, if not by each of them to the same extent. In experiments with same-sex and mixed-sex dyads, Mulac, Wiemann, Yoerks & Gibson (1983) observed that mixed-dyad participants both converged and met mid-way, whereas in same-sex dyads one member was mainly responsible for convergence. Mutual convergence was also found in a multicultural setting in commercial transactions in Taiwan; in the market place customers converged downwards to salespersons and the latter converged upwards in return, while in banks it was the customer who converged upwards to the clerk who converged downwards to him. Sometimes upwards and downwards convergence may miscarry, as in the cases studied by Platt & Weber (1984) in Singapore and Australia, where aborigines or immigrants tried to match upwardly the speech of native English speakers, and native English speakers mismanaged their downwards convergent attempts towards what they believed the other group sounded like.

Linguistic divergence occurs when a speaker is in an intercultural situation in which he has to affirm his cultural identity. In an experiment carried out in Wales, it was found that when an Anglophone speaker expressed a verbal threat against Welsh cultural identity, an Anglophone Welsh interlocutor learning Welsh would reply in English, but in a style diverging strongly from the speaker's own and characterised by a high number of Welsh markers (Bourhis & Giles, 1977). The expression of psycholinguistic distinctiveness under cultural threat has also been observed in a study of intercultural contacts in Belgium by Bourhis, Giles, Leyens & Tajfel (1979): they found that Flemish-speaking Belgians diverged linguistically from their French-speaking interlocutors when they felt their ethnolinguistic group membership threatened; furthermore, this divergence could go as far as a change of language. According to Sandilands & Fleury (1979), a divergent strategy used by an outgroup speaker is often perceived as impolite, hostile, or insulting. Thakerar, Giles & Cheshire (1982) suggest that there is a hierarchy of strategies to express psycholinguistic distinctiveness: some of these strategies would act more as symbols of social dissociation than others. Maintenance of a speech style or switching to an ingroup code in front of an outgroup interlocutor would be among the most powerful ways of expressing psycholinguistic distinctiveness.

Ethnolinguistic identity is affirmed all the more strongly if the cross-cultural characteristic of an interaction is stressful. In studies with Chinese students bilingual in Cantonese and English from the Chinese university of Hong Kong, Yang & Bond (1980) observed that these students affirmed their Chinese identity more strongly when responding to a questionnaire presented in English than when responding to the same questionnaire presented in Chinese. Similarly, in a second study Bond & Yang (1982) found that students expressed their Chinese identity less strongly in interaction with a Chinese interviewer than with an English interviewer; moreover, they responded to culturally threatening questions by expressing their cultural allegiance but accommodated to Western culture when the questions were neutral. The authors interpret these results as proof that interlocutors feel the need to affirm their cultural identity less in a situation which is culturally congruent with their own cultural background than in a cross-cultural situation.

Over-convergence occurs when the speaker's degree of convergence is perceived by the listener as inappropriate for a given situation, as when for example handicapped, sick or elderly people are talked down to by medical personnel (see Caporael, Lukaszewski & Culbertson (1983), who call this 'secondary baby talk'). Presenting different messages in which an Anglo-Canadian speaker converged towards a British-English listener on three linguistic dimensions (pronunciation, speech rate and message content), Giles & Smith (1979) found that, whereas convergence on each of the dimensions separately was perceived positively, simultaneous convergence on all three dimensions was perceived as negative and patronising. The authors suggest that in a situation of interethnic contact there is a level of optimal convergence beyond which it is perceived as irritating. In their investigation of market-place interaction, Platt & Weber (1984) suggested that over-convergence might be attributed to a wrong stereotypical perception about the other's speech style. Over-convergence, then, can occur because accommodation is a scripted behaviour, the speaker applying a convergence script to what he thinks is his interlocutor's speech style. This is also the case in 'foreigner talk' (see Section 9.2.2.1) when the speaker simplifies his mother tongue in the belief that his interlocutor, perceived as relatively incompetent in that language, will understand better.

Complementing the large number of speech-accommodation studies conducted in the arguably artificial, though well-controlled, laboratory settings, there are a number of field studies of actual language encounters in natural settings which are designed to bolster the external validity of findings (e.g. Bourhis, 1984a; 1984b; Moïse & Bourhis, 1994). Employing a variation of the matched-guise technique, Lawson-Sako & Sachdev (1996) investigated the linguistic reactions of Tunisians of Arab origin randomly approached in the street by ethnically Arab, European and African researchers who asked them for assistance either in fluent Tunisian Arabic or in French. Although respondents were highly accommodating regardless of the language of the request, interesting differences due to the ethnicity of the researcher were also observed. In the initial speaker turns, regardless of the language of the request, the highest levels of convergence were obtained with the European researcher, while the highest levels of divergence were obtained with the African researcher. The highest levels in the use of both Tunisian Arabic and French in the same utterance (i.e. code-switching) were obtained with the Arab researcher (i.e. ingroup member). Responses to a follow-on question posed by the researchers led to increased levels of code-switched responses though the overall difference in linguistic behaviour as a function of ethnicity was maintained, albeit to a lesser degree. Evidently, Tunisian respondents in this study exercised a real choice about which language to use and appeared not to be constrained by questions of linguistic competence. Identification with the African researcher was not popular with many of the respondents as divergence was maintained at relatively high levels, regardless of the language of the researcher and the speaker turn. Lawson-Sako and Sachdev suggest that the high use of code-switching amongst Arabs may indicate its value as an ingroup communication strategy and also 'its ability *simultaneously* to connote both status (via French) and solidarity (via Tunisian Arabic)' (Lawson-Sako & Sachdev, 1996: 75). Indeed, code-switching appeared to play an increasing role as conversations progressed. Overall, these findings reinforce the social psychological underpinnings of speech-accommodation theory in that language choices appear to be strongly influenced by motivational and attitudinal considerations.

9.1.3   Psychological reality of speech accommodation

Linguistic accommodation must not be confused with psychological accommodation, which can be expressed in a variety of ways including linguistic convergence and linguistic divergence (Deshaies, 1981; Deshaies & Hamers, 1982; Thakerar, Giles & Cheshire, 1982). From their study of intercultural interactions in various multilingual work settings in firms in Montreal, Deshaies & Hamers (1982) concluded that, in hierarchical interactions, psychological convergence is a speaker's main concern and that content convergence generally overrides linguistic convergence. Studying the reactions of bilingual Cantonese–English Chinese, dominant in Cantonese but highly fluent in English, to American interviewers who used either English or Cantonese, a language in which they were not very fluent, Pierson & Bond (1982) obtained the following results: social psychologically the interviewees converged upwards towards their higher-status interviewer, but linguistically they adjusted their Cantonese speech style to their interlocutor's lower level of linguistic competence in Cantonese and did not switch to the use of English. The authors interpret these results as showing that, in the power relations existing in the interview situation, the interviewee would perceive that the language to be used was the interviewer's decision. Thakerar, Giles & Cheshire (1982) have suggested that objective linguistic and subjective psychological accommodation are in fact two independent dimensions; for example, linguistic convergence can be the manifestation of a psychological divergence, and vice versa; in addition, the relationship between objective linguistic accommodation and subjective psychological accommodation does not have the same meaning in socially upwards as in socially downwards convergence.

Accommodation behaviour does not necessarily imply a high level of awareness. From an experiment on accommodation to speech rate and response latency, Street (1982) concluded that while subjects were highly conscious of using divergent behaviours, they were unaware of their convergent speech accommodation. In an experimental intercultural interaction between Francophones and Anglophones in Montreal, Taylor & Royer (1980) demonstrated that subjects appeared to be aware not only of their accommodation behaviour but also of the motives for such behaviour; awareness was especially high for ethnically divergent behaviour. The lower level of awareness observed for convergent behaviour might be attributed to the fact that we are dealing with a highly automatised scripted behaviour, the subject applying action schemata to his behaviour (Berger, 1986).

Evaluative speech-accommodation processes interact, however, with the speaker's perception of the listener's linguistic competence (Deshaies & Hamers, 1982) and with the presence of constraining sociolinguistic norms. Ball, Giles, Byrne & Berechree (1984) have observed that speech convergence is evaluated negatively when the convergent act violates the situational norms and that divergence is viewed positively when it adheres to the prevailing situational norms.

9.1.4 Towards a model of speech accommodation

Giles and his colleagues have summarised the theory of speech accommodation in the form of propositions (see, for example, Thakerar, Giles & Cheshire, 1982; Street & Giles, 1982):

(1) Speakers attempt to converge linguistically towards the speech patterns believed to be characteristic of their interlocutors when:
   (a) they desire their social approval and the perceived costs of so acting are lower than the rewards anticipated; and/or
   (b) they desire a high level of communication efficiency; and
   (c) social norms and/or linguistic competence are not perceived to dictate alternative speech strategies.

(2) The degree of linguistic convergence is a function of:
   (a) the extent of the speakers' repertoires; and
   (b) factors (e.g. individual differences and situation) that may increase the need for social approval and/or communication efficiency.

(3)   Speech convergence is positively evaluated by listeners when the resultant behaviour is:
      (a)   perceived as such psychologically;
      (b)   perceived to be at an optimal sociolinguistic distance from them; and
      (c)   credited with positive intent.

(4)   Speakers attempt to maintain their speech patterns or even diverge linguistically away from characteristics they believe their interlocutors possess when they:
      (a)   define the encounter in intergroup terms and desire a positive ingroup identity;
      (b)   wish to dissociate personally from another in an interpersonal encounter; or
      (c)   wish to bring another's speech behaviour to a personally accept-able level.

(5)   The degree of divergence is a function of:
      (a)   the extent of speakers' repertoires; and
      (b)   individual differences and situational actors increasing the sali-ence of the cognitive or affective functions in proposition (4).

(6)   Speech maintenance and divergence is negatively evaluated by lis-teners when the acts are perceived as psychologically divergent, but favourably reacted to by observers of the encounter who define the interaction in intergroup terms and who share a common positively valued group membership with the speaker.

Giles, Mulac, Bradac & Johnson (1986) have reformulated speech-accom-modation theory and refined some of the propositions. They reformulated Tajfel & Turner's (1979) interpersonal–intergroup dialectic by focusing on the concept of 'presentation of self' (Goffman, 1959). According to the model of self-presentation, in a social interaction an individual wishes to create a positive impression along the dimensions desired by others who are socially influential. The latest formulation of the speech-accommoda-tion model stresses the relevance not only of self- and group-presentation but also of relational identities arising from the 'couple comparisons' present in an interpersonal interaction.

    Furthermore, linguistic convergence and divergence may be motivated by the desire to extend one's social influence through individual self-presentation. Convergence strategies are positively evaluated by the lis-tener provided that:

- they match the listener's communication style;
- they match the listener's ethnolinguistic stereotype;
- they are produced as being optimal in terms of linguistic traits;
- the speaker's style conforms to a valued norm;
- the speaker's effort is perceived as high, his language choice as appropriate and his intention as positive.

Divergence is negatively rated by listeners when they perceive:

- a mismatch between the speaker's communication style and their own;
- a mismatch with their linguistic group stereotype;
- the speaker's divergence to be excessively distant and frequent;
- the speaker's style to depart from a valued norm;
- the speaker's effort to diverge as being great and the speaker as intentionally selfish and malevolent (Giles, Mulac, Bradac & Johnson, 1986).

Speech-accommodation theory has the merit of proposing a valid theoretical framework which can explain how and why people modify their language behaviour in different interactional situations. It has been found to be helpful in linking speech style and its modifications to social psychological processes, like cultural identity, attitudes and social perceptions, and to intercultural relations. It stresses the role of language and language variation in these relations, both at the interpersonal and at the intergroup level. It enables us to make predictions with regard to both the monolingual's and the bilingual's behaviour in interethnic contacts. However, because of the complexity of the theory, it may prove difficult to verify it as a whole. It is useful as a series of conceptual constructs, but conclusive empirical assessment might prove too difficult to carry out (Bourhis, personal communication).

9.2   COMMUNICATION STRATEGIES IN INTERCULTURAL INTERACTION

Insofar as intercultural interpersonal communication is concerned, we are interested in interactions between bilingual speakers and between a bilingual and a monolingual speaker, as well as between monolinguals from different ethnolinguistic backgrounds. The distinction between monolinguals and bilinguals is not as clear-cut as might be suggested by this dichotomy: often individuals vary on a continuum from total monolinguality to balanced bilinguality, and multilingual communities also vary on a similar continuum (see Section 10.3.1). However, for the sake of clarity we consider that in a situation of languages in contact, the following interactions may occur (note that for ease of demonstration we ignore the social context of the interactions, in particular the power relations between the interlocutors):

(1) Speakers (x and y) have at least some linguistic competence in common:
   a. both x and y are bilingual in L_A and L_B;
   b. x is bilingual in L_A and L_B; y is monolingual in either L_A or L_B;
   c. x is bilingual in L_A and L_B, but with only a receptive competence in L_B, and y is bilingual in L_A and L_B, but with only a receptive competence in L_A;
   d. both x and y are bilingual but have only one language, L_C, in common; i.e. x is bilingual in L_A and L_C and y in L_B and L_C.

In all four cases x and y can communicate without mediators/interpreters.

(2) Speakers x and y do not share a common linguistic competence:
   a. x speaks L_A and y speaks L_B. In order to communicate they make use of either non-verbal communication strategies, such as gestures, mimicry, etc., or verbal communication strategies like 'foreigner talk', 'broken language', 'pidgin', etc. Note that if each of them decides to speak his own language only, he is engaging in what has been called 'dual-lingualism' (Lincoln, 1979), thus refusing to accommodate.
   b. x and y call on the services of a third speaker, z, who is bilingual in L_A and L_B and acts as interpreter. In this case communication is possible but only through 'relay'. This is typically the case when a professional interpreter is used.
   c. x and y have no linguistic competence in common and call on two interpreters, z and w, who share language L_C, z being bilingual in L_A and L_C and w in L_B and L_C; this is the case of 'double relay', commonly found in multilingual countries.

Before examining bilingual communication strategies in intercultural interactions we must stress that there is a great deal of confusion over the meaning of such terms as 'code selection', 'code-switching', 'code-mixing' and 'bilingual borrowing'. Different authors use these terms in different ways. Let us state at the outset that these are not clear-cut or mutually exclusive categories; they rather stand on a continuum. We define each of the terms as they are introduced.

9.2.1   Code choice/selection

From the model of speech accommodation presented in Section 9.1, it follows that the strategies used to maximise the efficiency of communication in interpersonal interethnic interactions are governed by the following principles:

(1) Linguistic competence principle. The code selected in the interaction
     is that in which the sum of the individual communicative competences
     of the interlocutors is maximum. Code selection or choice is defined
     here as the speaker's decision, in a given communicative interactional
     situation, to use one code rather than another; by code we mean a
     separate language, a language variety, a creole or certain types of
     mixed or switched language. The application of the competence prin-
     ciple may be counteracted by (2), (3) and (4).
(2) Ethnolinguistic affirmation principle. If the gain of choosing a code
     well within the competence of the speaker is perceived by him to be
     less than the cost (e.g. threat) to his ethnic identity, the competence
     principle may not be applied and a code-divergence strategy may even
     be chosen.
(3) Interlocutor-perceived intention. Other things being equal, if the
     speaker perceives hostile intentions on the part of the interlocutor,
     whether at the interpersonal or at the intergroup level, he may refuse
     to converge towards the interlocutor by choosing a code other than
     the most effective one.
(4) Personal, situational and social factors. Examples of these are the
     roles of the interactants, the topic of the communication, the social
     norms or the status of the languages. These factors may also influence
     the application of the competence principle.

It should be stressed that a bilingual's communication strategies vary
within an interactional situation and therefore a code that is optimal at one
point may cease to be so later as a result of changes in the situation, the
topic, role relations, etc. One should add that speakers are not necessarily
conscious of using these strategies.

In any interethnic interpersonal encounter the first speaker selects a code
on the basis of the four principles enunciated above. In response to the
speaker's initial choice his interlocutor in turn will have to choose a code; he
may choose the same code, or the same code with modifications, or he may
change codes, or use both codes. How are the speaker's and the interlocutor's
code choices to be explained? Examining the selection of lingue franche in
the context of multilingual polyglossic Singapore (see Section 10.3.1), Platt
(1980) asks the question: Why do speakers choose a particular lingua franca
for a particular situation? He found that in addition to the appropriateness
of the code and the verbal repertoire of speaker and addressee, other factors
were relevant, like the ethnicity, education, sex, age and socio-economic
background of both speaker and addressee. If the speaker knows the various
characteristics of his addressee, a selection is relatively easy; in many cases,
however (e.g. in transactions with strangers) no prior information is available to the speaker and he has to rely, first, on his direct perception of the

physical and social appearance of his interlocutor and, second, on his appreciation of the domain and situation of interaction.

In the interlocutors' perception of a bilingual interactional situation, Genesee & Bourhis (1982) analysed the role played by social norms, sociocultural status of the languages, ingroup favouritism and interpersonal speech accommodation in determining code choice. English and French Canadians gave evaluative reactions to code selection by Anglophone and Francophone Canadian actors who were heard interacting in a simulated salesperson–customer situation. Four different patterns of code choice, consisting of three or four speaker turns each, were played in each study and subjects' reactions elicited after each turn. The authors found that:

(1)   in the initial stages of a cross-cultural encounter constrained by clearly defined situational norms, interpretations of the interlocutors' language behaviour are significantly influenced by situational norms;
(2)   in bilingual contexts characterised by intergroup conflict (the setting was Montreal in the late 1970s), closely adhering to situational norms ('the customer is always right') is a safe way of behaving in tense interactions with outgroup members;
(3)   language choices at this point in the encounter which clash with situational norms can signal that one or both interlocutors want to redefine the status relationship associated with the roles in question.

For example, a French Canadian salesman's use of French with an English Canadian customer may signify his desire to upgrade his status by not giving in to the traditional dominance of English. It is noteworthy that the bilingual English–French subjects who had followed French immersion programs were more sensitive to sociolinguistic rules than monolingual Francophone or monolingual Anglophone judges.

Scotton (1980) first proposed a sociological framework for interpreting and predicting code choice based on a theory of markedness. For Scotton code choices, although always in situation, are not a function of the situation per se but of negotiations of rights and obligations (RO sets; see Section 9.3.2) between participants. As such, choices are both 'given' and 'new': they are given in the sense that speakers have social representations of the norms of interaction by which they have an expectation of how their choices will be interpreted and how they may interpret the choices of others; they are new because speakers make their own choices to the extent that they construe the speech event. A great deal depends on how conventionalised the exchange is. If the role relationship between participants is well defined, there is usually agreement as to the unmarked code choice for both interlocutors. If speakers choose this unmarked code, they are identifying with the status associated with their given role relationship; if, however, the speakers choose the marked code, they are clearly rejecting that role and making a statement about both the immediate situation and the dominant society. If the situation is weakly defined, however, the unmarked choice is more difficult to identify and a series of exploratory choices will be made to try and identify the type of role relationship and the speakers' identity. In this case, characteristics of personality may be better predictors of language choice than group identities or situational factors. Scotton's approach is complementary to the social psychological theory of speech accommodation (see Genesee & Bourhis, 1982). For an application of the markedness model to code-switching, see Section 9.3.1.

It would seem that perception of physical and social indices as clues for selecting the right code in intercultural interactions begins very early in the bilingual child. In Section 3.1.3 we saw that at the one-word stage infants select the appropriate language with strangers, even in unfamiliar linguistic surroundings (Genesee, Boivin & Nicoladis, 1996). Of course, the most important variable is the significant interactant (McClure, 1981) but soon other clues are used. Fantini (1978) observed that young Spanish–English bilingual children use certain physical clues like hair and skin colour to make decisions about their unknown interlocutors' language. Soon the child is able to detect fluency (or absence of it) in his interlocutors. Bilingual children develop typical strategies for dealing with bilingual situations, learning how to adapt their language to the situation, the roles and the interlocutors, to the extent of playing the role of interpreters between monolingual speakers of different languages (Swain, 1972).

9.2.2   Speech modification strategies

Once the code has been selected the speaker must accommodate to his addressee by selecting from a range of modification strategies. The repertoire at his disposal is of course a function of his bilingual communicative competence (First Principle). If the speaker is monolingual or, though bilingual, does not share a common language with his interlocutor, he can adapt only by modifying his L_1 (we exclude other types of adaptation which call upon non-verbal strategies). Between the choice of one language or the other, for the bilingual speaker there is a whole range of intermediary strategies which include the modification of either code and the relative use of both. Thus, the bilingual speaker possesses a far wider repertoire of adaptive devices and modification devices than the monolingual speaker

(Grosjean, 1985a). Giles, Taylor & Bourhis (1973) have identified some 14 different speech-accommodation strategies. These vary from maximum accommodation, which consists in the exclusive use of the interlocutor's language, to minimal accommodation, where the speaker apologises in his L_1 for not speaking his interlocutor's language.

9.2.2.1 Foreigner talk

One accommodation strategy is 'foreigner talk', which has been studied in connection with the development of pidgins (Ferguson & DeBose, 1977; Mühlhäusler, 1986). In foreigner talk the speaker simplifies his L_1 to make himself understood by an interlocutor who has little knowledge of the other's language (Clyne, 1981). Empirical evidence on foreigner talk is hard to come by, but more recently it has appeared in the form of elicitation experiments, observation and archival research. Typical features of foreigner talk include variable omission of verb inflections (e.g. use of infinitive), deletion of the copula and the article, reduction of personal pronoun to one form (e.g. *me*, *him*), utilisation of lexical words as in telegraphic style, short juxtaposed sentences, slowing down of delivery, voice amplification, the use of expressive devices and so on; some of these are also typical of pidgins and reflect natural intuitions on language simplification (Ferguson & DeBose, 1977; Hinnenkamp, 1982). It is interesting to note with Clyne (1981) that in Australia some immigrant children make use of foreigner talk with their parents and grandparents, sometimes instead of the ethnic language, sometimes in alternation with it, and modelled on their parents' non-fluent English. It is even used by both children and parents with whomever has difficulty with English, whatever their ethnic origin.

9.2.2.2 Broken language

Another adaptive strategy is 'broken language', in which the speaker tries to speak the interlocutor's L_1 although he has little proficiency in it (Ferguson & DeBose, 1977; Kendall, 1980). It is a kind of 'interlanguage'. This strategy uses such devices as simplification, reduction, overgeneralisation, transfer and formulaic language ('prefabricated routines'). It is not an uncommon practice among speakers from different ethnolinguistic backgrounds for one to use foreigner talk in his L_1 while the other tries to speak it in broken language (Clyne, 1981).

9.2.2.3 Communication strategies in L_2 learning/use

The strategies used by second/foreign language learners to deal with communication problems have been analysed by applied linguists, especially in connection with the study of interlanguage. These strategies result from a lack of proficiency in L_2. They are of two main types: avoidance strategies, when speakers give up their original plans; and achievement or compensatory strategies aimed at solving L_2 communication problems. Although these strategies can be used to tackle problems at all linguistic levels, most studies have concentrated on lexical problems, because these play a central role in communication and are easier to identify. Many typologies have been proposed. For example, Faerch & Kasper (1983) distinguish between classes of strategies on the basis of the learner's resources: his L_1; his interlanguage; L_1 and L_2 combined; discourse phenomena; and non-linguistic means. Further subdivisions involve interlanguage strategies of generalisation, paraphrase, neologisms, and restructuring, all based on surface forms. A problem with the use of these typologies is that they proliferate because they are not founded on theories of language use or development and therefore fail to explain the underlying cognitive processes.

To remedy this drawback of using such typologies, some researchers have proposed psychologically-based classifications. For example, a group in Nijmegen, studying compensatory strategies, distinguish between two basic types depending on whether the speaker uses conceptual or linguistic knowledge (Poulisse, 1998). Conceptual strategies are further subdivided into analytic and holistic strategies. Analytic strategies are cases in which the speaker refers obliquely to the intended concept by giving some of its defining properties, e.g. colour, size, uses; and holistic strategies are cases in which the speaker refers to the intended concept by using the word for a related concept (metonymy, e.g. *hammer* for *tool*). Linguistic strategies are based on either morphological innovation (*to ironise* for *to iron*) or transfer from L_1. The Nijmegen approach is similar to that of Bialystok (1990) who distinguishes between analysis-based and control-based strategies. Analysis-based strategies examine and manipulate the intended concept, which must be represented as analysed knowledge (compare the Nijmegen group's conceptual strategies); control-based strategies, on the other hand, examine and manipulate the means of expression. Since Bialystok considers analysis of linguistic knowledge and control of linguistic processing to be the two most important cognitive mechanisms of language processing, she rightly claims that her classification is capable of explaining the functioning of these strategies as cases of language processing (see Section 5.1.4). For a recent critical review of these issues and an inventory of L_2 communication strategies, see Dornyei & Scott, 1997.

9.3   'CODE-SWITCHING', 'CODE-MIXING', 'BILINGUAL BORROWING'

Until the 1970s, only the last of these three phenomena had been studied extensively. The main reason for this lack of interest was the presumed deviant nature of code-switching and code-mixing judged against the prevalent paradigm of monolingualism and of the ideal speaker–hearer in a homogeneous speech community, who knows his language perfectly (Chomsky, 1965). 'Code-switching' and 'code-mixing' were considered as signs of incompetence (in one or both languages; see Section 4.2). Even such informed linguists as Haugen (1950: 211) and Weinreich (1953: 60) saw them as abnormal oversights on the part of bilingual speakers. Since the 1970s, however, these phenomena have received considerable empirical and theoretical attention, as witness the creation of a European Science Foundation Network on Code-switching and Language Contact (Milroy & Muysken, 1995) and the fact that the *International Journal of Bilingualism* devotes many of its articles to these problems.

Since the 1970s, with Blom & Gumperz's (1972) paper 'Social meaning in linguistic structures: code-switching in Norway', it has been widely accepted that these phenomena occur with high frequency whenever two or more speakers who are bilingual in the same languages communicate with one another. These two scholars distinguished between situational code-switching, where there is a change of topic or situation, and conversational code-switching where there is no such change. A comparison of the functions of, and linguistic constraints on, code-switching in different bilingual communities and involving a variety of pairs of typologically related as well as unrelated languages has led researchers, working from several disciplinary viewpoints, to try to determine whether this phenomenon is rule-governed or random and, if rule-governed, whether it obeys universal constraints (etic), is language-specific (emic), or follows discourse principles. However, although large amounts of relatively homogeneous data have been collected so far, we do not to date possess sufficiently diversified data to be able to reach firm conclusions on these questions; the evidence is biased towards certain types of contact situations and languages. Additionally, we are faced with conflicting definitions and explanations.

In a most general and uncontroversial way, code-switching may be defined as 'the juxtaposition within the same speech exchange of passages of speech belonging to two different grammatical systems or sub-systems' (Gumperz, 1982: 59). Two main questions arise:

(1)   Under what social and pragmatic conditions does code-switching operate?
(2)   What are the grammatical rules governing code-switching?

We shall take the second question first, since the sociolinguistic study implied in the first question cannot proceed without a proper linguistic description.

9.3.1 The grammar of code-switching

Some scholars (e.g. Poplack, 1990) distinguish between code-switching and bilingual borrowing. The latter is the adaptation of lexical material to the morphological, syntactic and, usually (but not always), phonological patterns of the recipient language. They further distinguish between established 'loan-words' which show full linguistic integration (i.e. are part of 'langue', and used equally by monolinguals who cannot code-switch) and 'nonce-words' (part of 'parole'). Clyne (1967) calls borrowing 'integrated transfers', nonce-words 'unintegrated transfers', and code-switches 'multiple transfers'. These distinctions are not, however, accepted by all researchers, who consider that code-switching and nonce borrowing are either undifferentiated by the bilingual speaker or operationally indistinguishable (Myers-Scotton, 1992). Following Myers-Scotton, Gardner-Chloros (1995: 74) argues that 'every loan starts off life as a code-switch' (see also Romaine, 1995: 124). We believe that borrowing and code-switching are phenomena at either end of a continuum: an established loan-word is a historically transmitted word that has been integrated with the recipient language, while code-switching is a more or less spontaneous, bounded switch from sentences of one language to sentences of another, affecting all levels of linguistic structure simultaneously. Borrowings may look like code-switches in that they retain a foreign status (especially in phonology), while code-switches often resemble borrowings in brevity and in being fitted into the syntax of another language (Romaine, 1994).

Before we go into the difficult problem of the grammar of code-switching, it is necessary to distinguish between three types of code-switching (Poplack, 1980):

(1) extra-sentential code-switching, or the insertion of a tag, e.g. 'you know', 'I mean', from one language into an utterance which is entirely in another language;
(2) intersentential code-switching, or switch at clause/sentence boundary, one clause being in one language, the other clause in the other, e.g. 'Sometimes I'll start a sentence in English *y termino en español*' ('Sometimes I'll start a sentence in English and finish it in Spanish') (Spanish–English bilingual recorded by Poplack (1980) in the Puerto Rican community of New York City).

(3)   intrasentential code-switching, where switches of different types occur within the clause boundary, including within the word boundary (i.e. loan blend, e.g. *check-er* (English verb *check* + French infinitive morpheme *-er*). The following is an example of intrasentential code-switching: *kio ke* six, seven hours *te* school *de vic* spend *karde ne*, they are speaking English all the time ('Because they spend six or seven hours a day at school they are speaking English all the time') (Punjabi–English bilingual in Britain recorded by Romaine, 1995).

As the concept of clause or sentence is difficult to define in an oral corpus, in which incomplete clauses/sentences tend to predominate, some researchers prefer to speak of 'act' as a functional unit (Dabène & Moore, 1995). This difficulty notwithstanding, it is clear that only intrasentential code-switching poses serious problems for linguistic description. It is to the grammar of intrasentential code-switching that we now turn.

9.3.1.1   Insertional vs. alternational code-switching

There are two main approaches to intrasentential code-switching (Muysken, 1995): code-switching is viewed either as (1) insertional or (2) alternational. In the former approach one language is the dominant or base language into the structure of which a constituent from the other language is inserted (or embedded; this is what Hamers & Blanc (1989) called 'code-mixing'); under this view code-switching is a form of borrowing, the difference between them being the size and type of element inserted (e.g. a single lexical element in borowing, a whole phrase or clause in code-switching). Code alternation is clearly exemplified in intersentential code-switching, while a single borrowed element is a clear case of insertion. However, in other cases it is not easy to decide whether we have alternation or insertion. What criteria are used to allocate code-switching to one or the other category?

- Criteria for determining the base language. Many criteria have been proposed, each of which has its own problems. A pragmatic approach is to say that the base language is that of the interaction or the unmarked code. A statistical answer would be the language with the higher frequency of words. A psycholinguistic solution is to choose the language in which the speaker is more proficient. In a structurally oriented model, it may be the main verb that determines the base. In the lexically based Matrix Language Frame model (Myers-Scotton, 1993a; 1993b; see Section 9.3.1.2.3) the matrix (or base) language determines the order of the elements in mixed constituents and provides the 'system' (or grammatical) morphemes in such constituents.

- Criteria for defining alternation.Alternational code-switching involves properties of both languages. Alternation is likely when there are long stretches of elements from the second language, or when several elements are switched, which together do not form a single constituent. If , however, the switched elements are all single, well-defined constituents (e.g. a prepositional phrase), insertion is more likely. When the switched element is at the edge of an utterance, alternation is more likely; but if the switched string is preceded and followed by elements from the second language, insertion is more likely.

What is the nature of the predictions made above? Some models make absolute claims (DiSciullo, Muysken & Singh, 1986); others, like Poplack (1980), working within a variationist model, propose constraints which are valid for the majority of switches; exceptions are relegated to nonce borrowings. Since we are dealing with performance data, as opposed to competence, probabilistic models are better than absolute ones.

9.3.1.2 *Linguistic factors constraining code-switching*

What are the grammatical constraints on intrasentential switching? Does the switch from one language to the other follow or violate the grammatical rules of either language? A number of models have been proposed.

9.3.1.2.1 The free morpheme and equivalence model Poplack (1980) and Sankoff & Poplack (1981) were the first to postulate linguistic constraints operating on intrasentential code-switching. They defined two such constraints:

(1)   The free morpheme constraint predicts that a switch may not occur between a bound morpheme and a lexical form unless the latter has been phonologically integrated into the language of the bound morpheme (i.e. borrowing); for example, the Spanish–English code-switch *flipeando* is a well-formed Spanish form, whereas *run-eando* is not, because the phonology of *run* is unambiguously English and that of *eando* Spanish.

(2)   The equivalence constraint predicts that the order of sentence constituents immediately adjacent to and on both sides of the switch must be grammatical with respect to both languages simultaneously. The equivalence constraint is illustrated in Figure 9.1, where the dotted lines indicate permissible switch points, and the arrows the surface relationships of the two languages. Switches may occur at, but not between, the dotted lines.

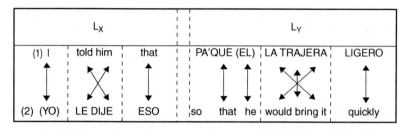

Figure 9.1   Equivalence constraint rule in bilingual code-switching (from Sankoff & Poplack, 1981)

The assumption behind the concept of equivalence is that it facilitates code-switching. There can be equivalence of categories (lexical elements, morphosyntactic features, etc.) and of relations between categories (e.g. word order). However, the very notion of equivalence is problematic: not only is there no exact match between categories in different languages, but, from a psycholinguistic point of view, a speech community may recognise categories from different languages as equivalent, whereas another community may not (Muysken, 1995). Moreover, the equivalence constraint assumes that the two switched languages share the same categories and makes no prediction about categorial mismatches. If switches occur at sites where there is no structural equivalence between the two languages (when, for example, the two languages require a different word order), they sometimes involve omission or repetition of constituents. However, in the following example (Clyne, 1987), the insertion of a subject pronoun follows English word order but violates the Dutch word order constraint: *en dan je realise dat this dat farmleven* . . . (and then you realise that this, that life on the farm . . .), instead of *en dan besef je dat* . . . (inversion of subject in Dutch). The more typologically different the languages are, the more difficult it is to maintain the categorial equivalence constraint. For example, Berk-Seligson (1986) found that in Hebrew–Spanish code-switching many ungrammatical cases occurred as a result of switches from Spanish to Hebrew; the most frequent was the omission of the article (the indefinite article does not exist as a grammatical category in Hebrew). Violations of the equivalence constraint also arise from a mismatch of categories between Yoruba and English. Amuda (1986) found that Yoruba *wa* was often used as a copula with English predicate adjectives, e.g. *ò wa very nice* (it's very nice), instead of *ò dara pupo* (Yoruba never uses *wa* in this way), thus violating Yoruba grammar. In this case it is the addition rather than the omission of categorial marking which is responsible for the violation.

Linguistic performance constrained in this way must be based on simultaneous access to the grammatical rules of both languages. This raises the question of the existence and nature of a bilingual code-switching grammar. Sankoff & Poplack (1981) argue that intrasentential code-switching involves the juxtaposition of constituents from two codes which are too closely connected to be generated by rules from two distinct grammars; an additional argument is that switching often takes place without any pauses or hesitations. The authors postulate the existence of two monolingual grammars and one code-switching grammar. This grammar is made up of the combined lexicons of the two languages as well as the grammatical categories of the two monolingual grammars, limited by the free morpheme and the equivalence constraints.

The hypothesis of a grammar specific to code-switching has been challenged by a number of linguists and psycholinguists. Woolford (1983), for example, proposes an overlap for the two monolingual grammars at the level of phrase-structure rules. When constructing a phrase-structure tree the speaker draws from the phrase-structure rules of either language; when the rules are the same in both languages, then the categories (NP, VP, etc.) may be filled freely from either lexicon. However, when the categories are created by a rule that exists in only one language, they must be filled from the lexicon of that language. The two lexicons remain separate, as do the word-formation components, thus accounting for the free-morpheme constraint. Other criticisms of Sankoff & Poplack's code-switching grammar are based on different language dyads from those used by Sankoff & Poplack or Woolford. For example, Bentahila & Davies (1983) and Berk-Seligson (1986) analysed conversations (the former Arabic–French and the latter Spanish–Hebrew) and found that their subjects switched freely and did not seem to judge switches that broke the equivalence constraint as deviant; the free-morpheme constraint, however, seemed to hold. They concluded from their data that, although code-switching is clearly rule-governed, the equivalence rule is not universal. Moreover, they find it is difficult to accept that intrasentential code-switching is proof of balanced bilinguality (see Section 9.3.2).

One of the problems with this debate is the comparability of the findings. Are the cases reported by the different researchers similar? Are the Spanish–Hebrew speakers and situations of Berk-Seligson and the Arabic–French speakers and situations of Bentahila & Davies really comparable with the (apparently) stable norm-governed bilingual Puerto Rican community described by Poplack (1980)? Until code-switching situations are more clearly defined and a greater variety of contexts have been studied, the universality of the two-constraint rules and the validity of a bilingual code-switching grammar cannot be demonstrated.

9.3.1.2.2 The syntactic-government constraint model   DiSciullo, Muysken & Singh (1986) have put forward a model for code-switching universally constrained by the principle of government. They claim that switching is only possible between elements not related by government binding theory (Chomsky, 1981): if two elements are lexically dependent on one another, there cannot be a switch between them. The government constraint has been tested by Nortier (1990) on data from Moroccan Arabic–Dutch code-switching and been found to be too strong. Counter-examples abound: for example, verbal and prepositional object noun phrases are often in a different language from their governing verb or preposition; switches occur between indirect and direct object, etc. The one advantage of the syntactic-government constraint model is that it predicts that the looser the syntagmatic relation is in the sentence, the easier it is to switch (Muysken, 1995).

9.3.1.2.3 The Matrix Language Frame model   A third approach to intra-sentential code-switching is that of the Matrix Language Frame model of Myers-Scotton (1993a). It rests on the claim that, in every act of bilingual switching, one language is dominant; this is called the Matrix Language or ML. The non-dominant language is the Embedded Language or EL. The ML is the language contributing relatively more morphemes at a discourse level as well as being the code in which the speaker is more proficient. Myers-Scotton further distinguishes three types of constituents:

- ML+EL constituents, made up of elements from both languages;
- ML islands, which draw grammatically and lexically on the ML alone; and
- EL islands, composed of grammatical and lexical elements from the EL only.

The model claims that two interrelated hierarchies direct the structuring of code-switched sentences:

(1)   the borrowing language (ML) vs. the lender (EL) hierarchy, in which the matrix language plays the dominant role; and
(2)   the System vs. Content Morpheme hierarchy (system morphemes are function words and inflectional affixes; content morphemes are noun and verb stems).

The ML determines the morphosyntax of ML+EL *constituents*. (Note that 'the designation of the ML may change across time, and even within a conversation'; p. 69.) From this, two principles follow:

(1)   The Morpheme Order Principle. The surface morpheme order is that of the ML in ML+EL constituents; and

(2)   The System Morpheme Principle. All relevant system morphemes
      must come only from the ML in ML+EL constituents.

These two principles replace the Free Morpheme and Equivalence Constraints of Poplack's model. In the following Alsatian–French example of a
switched sentence Alsatian is the ML, French the EL. Note that the French
past participle *recalé* precedes the auxiliary *wurd* in accordance with Alsatian syntax, but violates French syntax: '*Noch schlimmer, wenne de* client
recalé *wurd am* permis *weje de* panne d'essence' ('Even worse, when the
learner is failed in the (driving) test because the petrol tank is empty')
(Alsatian–French bilingual in Alsace recorded by Gardner-Chloros, 1991.)
      The Matrix Language Frame model rests on the assumption that code-
switched sentences have one base language which determines the order of
the elements in mixed constituents and provides the system morphemes in
such constituents. But, as we saw earlier, defining the base language is
problematic. We return to this question when examining Myers-Scotton's
socio-psycholinguistic model of code-switching (see Section 9.3.2).
      So far, the models we have discussed concentrate on keeping the two
languages separate, discrete and grammatical. But there are many cases of
convergence phenomena which these models cannot accommodate. A
clear example is the case of the compound verb formation in Punjabi–English code-switched speech of bilingual students in Birmingham,
England, described by Romaine (1995: Chapter 4.5). Punjabi verbal oper-
ators, like, e.g. *kerna* (meaning 'do', 'make'), are commonly combined with a
major category (e.g. verb) taken from English to make new verbal compounds which function as a single integrated syntactic unit. For example,
'*ple* kerna', where the first element comes from English '*play*' and the
second from Punjabi. The new mixed compound, which means 'to play' –
and can be replaced by a single, synonymous verb in Punjabi – does not
exist in either language. Similar formations have been attested in (Cypriot)
Greek–English code-switched/mixed utterances by members of the Greek
Cypriot community in London, England (Gardner-Chloros, 1992). Here
major categories from English are combined with the Greek verb *kano*
(*kamno* in Cypriot Greek), which also means 'do', 'make'; it is only used in
Standard Greek to make a new verbal compound when the second element
of the compound is the direct object (i.e. a noun) of *kano* (e.g. *kano*
gimnastiki, 'I do gymnastics'). As with Romaine's Punjabi–English
examples, these mixed compounds exist neither in English nor in Greek:
e.g. *kamno use*, 'to use' (Gardner-Chloros, 1992: 127). In both the
Punjabi–English and the Greek–English cases we are therefore dealing not
with a code-switch between two separate languages, but with a new mixed
verbal formation. The mixed-compound verb is the result of contact

between two systems and should be analysed in terms of its own structure and not as belonging to one or the other language (Romaine, 1995).

9.3.1.3   Conclusions

In conclusion, we cannot but concur with Gardner-Chloros (1995) when she writes:

A lot of effort has been expended within the field of code-switching on setting up a new orthodoxy to replace the old orthodoxy of monolingual norms. This consists in defining code-switching as a special form of skilled bilingual behaviour, to be distinguished from the aberrant manifestations of bilingualism which involve one language influencing another. This new type of ideal speaker-listener, whose existence depends on such discrete alternation, is as much of a rare bird as Chomsky's monolingual original. Code-switching should instead be considered as a much broader, blanket term for a range of interlingual phenomena within which strict alternation between two discrete systems is the exception rather than the rule. (p. 68)

9.3.2   The social meaning of code-switching

Many situational variables seem to affect the type and frequency of code-switching: the topic of conversation, the participants, the setting, the affective aspect of the message and so on. It also seems that 'because of its reliance on unverbalised shared understanding, code-switching is typical of the communicative conventions of closed network situations' (Gumperz, 1982: 71–2). Is code-switching a learned behaviour, and, if so, how is it learned and when? The alternate use of two languages in the same utterance begins early in childhood, but it is different from adult code alternation in a number of ways (Meisel, 1994; see Section 3.1.3). McClure (1981) reports that Mexican-American children use it in different ways depending on their age. Younger bilinguals produce more examples of code-mixing than code-switching; children over the age of nine switch languages for at least a phrase or a sentence as often as they code-mix. In time, code-switching is used as a communicative strategy and a marker of ethnic-group membership and identity.

Studying intergenerational variation in the use of English and Spanish in the Puerto Rican community of New York, Poplack (1983) observed that both English and Spanish are used increasingly in conjunction with each other, without any functional separation, i.e. without diglossia (see Section 10.3.2). Strangely enough, there seems to be no trend towards a convergence of English and Spanish; English loan-words are regularly integrated into Spanish and code-switching is a distinctive communicative resource for the community of skilled bilinguals. But the younger generation diverges markedly from the older one in its use of code-switching. As in the cases studied by McClure (1981) cited above, children switch or mix mostly single nouns, which suggests a lack of lexical availability; learning to code-switch intrasententially is a maturational social process similar to the development of stylistic and repertoire usage, and children learn it later since it requires full development of syntactic rules for both languages. It is interesting to note that bilingual community norms are transmitted down the generations regardless of whether children are taught bilingually or in English only. It looks as though code-switching in this situation has become an institutionalised code, which is the expression of a particular ethnic identity but, as far as its use in the speech community is concerned, it is an unmarked choice (see Scotton, 1986; Myers-Scotton, 1993a; 1993b).

The sociolinguistic context in which code-switching takes place is paramount in determining the type of code and the speakers' relations to it. In the case documented by Poplack (1980) we appear to have a stable, closely knit speech community with focused norms. Its speakers, renewed by fresh immigration, have between them a variable repertoire ranging from Spanish-dominant to balanced Spanish–English bilinguality. Interestingly, Poplack also found that bilinguals dominant in Spanish make greater use of intersentential alternation, while balanced bilinguals use significantly more intrasentential switches. She suggests that this last type of switching might be a good test of balanced bilinguality. Code-switching in this context is not a stage in a language shift from Spanish to English, as is often the case in the acculturation process (for example, with children who are recent immigrants in a foreign country). However, further research is needed before one can confidently come to the conclusion that here we have a more or less stable, non-convergent mixed code.

A further distinction may be made between code-switching which results from the bilingual's communicative competence and code-switching resulting from a speaker's relative lack of competence in L_2. We call the former bilingual code-switching and the latter restricted code-switching. An example of the former is the use of two languages by children of mixed-lingual families; the latter is typical of certain immigrant populations who have acquired a limited functional competence in L_2 but have to resort to their L_1 to compensate for their lack of knowledge of L_2. There is the opposite case of immigrants who have lost some of their competence in L_1 and have to call upon resources of their newly acquired L_2 to communicate, thus resorting to code-switching. Note that it can be a code of transitional competence or interlanguage along the language-shift continuum (see Section 10.3.3). However, this type of code-switching is different from bilingual code-switching as it does not follow the same linguistic rules (Gumperz, 1982).

Myers-Scotton's social psychological markedness model is an extension to code-switching of her theory of markedness for code selection (see Section 9.2.1). In all speech communities types of interaction are conventional and carry fixed 'schemata' about norms and roles for the appropriate socio-psycholinguistic behaviour of speakers. These schemata are the *unmarked* 'rights-and-obligation sets' (RO sets) for specific communicative interactions. In each interaction the speakers infer the unmarked RO set from contextual cues, such as setting, perceived interlocutor's identity, degree of formality, etc. Knowledge of the unmarked RO set for each type of interaction is a normative device that unites the speech community. Since in a multilingual community certain language variants are used more in certain interactional types than in others, each comes to be associated with the unmarked RO set of the relevant interaction type. In this way the members of a speech community arrive at a shared knowledge of the social psychological values of each code as a result of their common communicative experience.

In code-switching the knowledge of the unmarked RO set for an interaction type and the knowledge of the indexical value of each language variety are exploited by the multilingual speaker to fulfil specific communication intentions:

(1)   In any given interaction the speaker may intend to comply with the unmarked RO set, in which case he uses the relevant code. When the context changes, but the speaker still wishes to conform to the expected set, he changes codes. This is 'sequential unmarked code-switching'.

(2)   If the speaker intends to impose a different RO set, he switches from the unmarked RO set to a code characteristic of the RO set he wishes to see prevail. This is 'code-switching as a marked choice'.

(3)   In addition, there is 'unmarked code-switching' as the unmarked choice, when bilingual speakers use code-switching to affirm their multiple group membership.

(4)   If the speaker is not sure what the unmarked choice is for the interaction, or if the speakers do not agree on what is the unmarked choice, we have 'exploratory code-switching'.

This social psychological model, reminiscent of the speech-accommodation model presented in Section 9.1.1, can be criticised on a number of grounds. First, 'marked code-switching', that is, when code-switching is not a common communication pattern, has been omitted. Second, the four types are not all defined by the same criteria. Some arguments, like the definition of the unmarked language, are circular. Above all, this model is a microsocial model which ignores the wider social context of intergroup power relations (Meeuwis & Blommaert, 1994). We will not consider Myers-Scotton's interpretation of her own model in terms of a universal, innate capacity framework: the markedness model stands without it.

We end this section on intersentential code-switching with Sebba's

(1998) 'congruence' approach. His model has a twofold advantage over the other models analysed above. First, it integrates the study of code-switching syntax into a wider framework which takes into account pragmatic, discoursal and ethnographic aspects. It includes the degree of the speaker's bilingual competence as well as the norms of the bilingual speech community. Second, Sebba assumes the equivalence, or congruence, of certain categories across the languages involved, but this categorial congruence is not determined by universal grammar. It is 'constructed' by bilingual speakers in given sociolinguistic situations. Switching takes place between categories which speakers identify as congruent. Which categories are constructed in this way depends not only on the syntactic properties which are part of the grammar of each language, but also on the consensus of speakers to treat suitable categories as equivalent. Speakers may use one of four possible strategies, or any combination of these:

(1) blocking strategies, where switching is not permitted;
(2) harmonisation strategies, where the category is treated as identical in both languages. Examples from Moroccan-Arabic–French code-switching are 'cette *xubza*' and '*had* le pain', both meaning 'this bread', where Arabic and French genders are construed as congruent.
(3) neutralisation strategies, which allows switching by creating a 'slot' for a congruent category in otherwise incompatible languages. In the following example an English lexical item ('to train') is inserted into a Hindustani–Sranan construction: '*train* kare' ('to train'), in which 'kare' serves as the auxiliary verb (cf. the examples taken from Romaine (1995) and Gardner-Chloros (1992) in Section 9.3.1.2.3).
(4) compromise strategies, where switching which results in forms not grammatical in either or both languages are allowed, e.g. Moroccan-Arabic–Dutch 'dik *gesprick*' ('this conversation'), where the Dutch noun lacks the obligatory definite article. (Note that this appears to be the converse of the harmonisation strategy used in the Moroccan-Arabic–French switch which does not violate the grammar of either language.)

Although these four types of strategy may be combined, some are more typical of certain types of bilingual speech communities. For example, harmonisation is more common in old-established communities in which switching is the norm, whereas blocking or neutralisation strategies prevail in communities in which strong sociolinguistic norms militate against switching. We return to the concept of congruence in the discussion of convergence in Section 10.4.

9.3.3   Code-mixing

There is a continuum between code-switching and code-mixing. Code-mixing, like code-switching, is a language-contact communication strategy, but the speaker of a language, L_X, transfers elements or rules of another language, L_Y, to L_X at all linguistic levels of L_X, otherwise they would be considered as loans (in other words, code-mixing, like unintegrated transfers or nonce-words, is a phenomenon of 'parole', not 'langue'). In code-mixing there is necessarily a base language and it should be possible to distinguish in an utterance monolingual chunks in the base language which alternate with chunks calling upon the rules of both languages. For example, in Chiac (a mixed French–English vernacular of New Brunswick) 'je vais back venir' is a French sentence comprising a French phrasal verb 'je vais venir' and an English morpheme 'back', which is prepositioned to the verb according to a French rule unacceptable in English. It is of course possible to observe these two phenomena within a single utterance, in which case code-mixing can be embedded in code-switching, but not the reverse. Note that the distinction between the two is not absolute and there are utterances which can be classified in either category. Note also that code-mixing can trigger off code-switching (Clyne, 1967; Kachru, 1982).

Code-mixing, as we have already explained, is a process characterised by the transfer of elements from a language L_Y to the base language L_X; in the mixed utterance which results we can distinguish monolingual chunks of L_X alternating with chunks of L_Y which refer to the rules of two codes. Unlike borrowing, which is generally limited to lexical units which may be better assimilated or less well assimilated, code-mixing transfers elements of all linguistic levels and units ranging from a lexical item to a sentence, so that it is not always easy to distinguish code-mixing from code-switching. Like code-switching, code-mixing is a strategy of the bilingual speaker (whereas borrowing is not), in the sense that it is a fact of langue, and monolinguals can make use of it. Code-mixing can of course express a lack of competence in the base language, such as, for example, lexical items, and in this case code-mixing can compensate for this deficiency. However, as for code-switching, code-mixing can be a bilingual's specific code which enables him to express attitudes, intentions, roles, and to identify with a particular group.

An interesting case in point is that given by Kachru (1978), who has studied code-mixing in the multilingual and multicultural context of India. He defines three main varieties. The base language can be any one of the languages of India; three languages may be mixed with that language: English, Sanskrit or Persian. The following are three examples of a mixed compound verb in Punjabi (Romaine, 1995: 131):

- Englishised 'pity kerna'
- Sanskritised 'daya karma'
- Persianised 'rahan kerna'

In these examples the basic meaning of the compound verb is determined by the first element 'to pity' and modified by the verbal operator *kerna* 'to do' (see the reference to mixed compound verbs in Section 9.3.1.2.3).

In the first case, called Englishisation, the English language (which is one of the two official languages of India and has great prestige) is mixed with a large number of regional languages in a wide variety of contexts. The resulting mixed code is a marker of high social status and membership of an educated elite; it expresses power and prestige and is characteristic of the Indian middle class. For example, the speech repertoire (see Section 10.3.1) of an educated Indian woman includes a strongly Englishised Hindi, which she speaks with members of her family, and a non-Englishised Hindi, which she reserves for servants. The same woman also uses English and alternates English and Hindi. This Englishised code is used in political, administrative, scientific and technological discourse. It is noteworthy that a bilingual speaker uses a strongly Englishised code in order to hide his social, regional, religious or ethnic identity (neutralisation). One may also wonder if attempts at Englishisation are made by lower-middle-class Indians who have upward social aspirations, and if so, whether hypercorrect forms can be expected.

A second mixed variety results from the mixing of Sanskrit or High Hindi with an Indian language (Sanskritisation). It can be a marker of caste or religious identity. It is used in philosophical, literary or religious (Hindu) discourse. In some contexts Sanskritised speech is a sign of pedantry or political conservatism.

Persianisation is the third kind of code-mixing and is associated with Muslim culture. The language of the law courts borrows its vocabulary from Persian, and in some parts of India Persianised code-mixing is a marker of Muslim religious identity and of professional status.

9.4   CONCLUSION

The interplay between social psychological mechanisms and linguistic behaviour in intercultural interactions has been discussed in this chapter. Accentuating the speech markers of ethnic identity can become an important strategy in intergroup relations, as it enables individuals to affirm their group membership. This psychological differentiation is an important component of speech accommodation in interpersonal intercultural relations. First we analysed some theoretical foundations of speech-accommodation theory and the empirical evidence in its support. We then discussed the psychological reality of convergent and divergent linguistic accommodation through which the speaker expresses his intention to be more similar to, or differentiate himself from, his interlocutor as an individual and as a member of an ethnolinguistic community. We ended this first section by reviewing the current state of the art in speech-accommodation theory.

The second half of this chapter addressed the question of communication strategies in intercultural interaction. We presented research on the principle governing code selection, speech modification and code switching/code-mixing/bilingual borrowing. These last three strategies are not clear cut but overlapping phenomena. Intrasentential code-switching is the most striking communication strategy characteristic of bilingual communication. It is not possible in the present state of our knowledge to determine whether this type of code-switching is random, or governed by universal grammatical (lexical, syntactic) constraints, or is language specific. Rather, there are different kinds of code-switching which seem to vary according to the social context, the identities and roles of the participants and the typological relations between the switched languages. At one end of this continuum we have a type of code-switching which is diffuse, indicating changes in the relationship between the languages (convergence or shift); at the other end we seem to have a more or less stable code with little convergence between the two codes.

Bilingual code-switching can become an autonomous code which develops in closed social settings and identifies an ethnolinguistic group (this type of rule-governed code raises important questions for linguistic description and theory). Code-switching is the outcome of interlinguistic communication strategies. It takes its meaning from intercultural communication. Thus, the bilingual optimises his communication efficiency in terms of the most adequate form–function mapping, by calling upon the whole range of his repertoire. Communication strategies specific to languages in contact arise from the need to continuously accommodate to the intercultural encounters. The outcome can be any type of accommodation ranging from minor modification in one language to mixed-lingual strategies which can evolve into autonomous codes.

Although we have been concerned with the bilingual individual in interaction with others, we have analysed his behaviour primarily as a member of an ethnolinguistic group in an interpersonal communication setting. It is to language behaviour between ethnolinguistic groups and their interrelations that we turn in the next chapter.

10   Societal bilingualism, intergroup relations and sociolinguistic variations

So far, we have been concerned mainly with the bilingual individual, from a number of different points of view and scientific disciplines: bilingual development (Chapters 3 to 5), neuropsychology (Chapter 6), information processing (Chapter 7), cultural and ethnolinguistic identity (Chapter 8), and intercultural communication (Chapter 9). At the points in the two preceding chapters when intergroup relations were mentioned, it was as an interpersonal process in which individuals interact with each other as members of different ethnolinguistic groups. In the present chapter we examine the role of language in intergroup relations at the societal level, when different languages and cultures are in contact.

This chapter differs from the earlier chapters in a number of respects. Having addressed the problems of the bilingual speaker as an individual and in his interpersonal relations, we now consider relations between ethnolinguistic groups. Thus we move from a micro- to a macro-level of analysis and to disciplines which are concerned with socio-structural factors, like, among others, sociology, sociolinguistics and the sociology of language. Because these disciplines deal with a multiplicity of factors and multidimensional phenomena, it is difficult to control all these factors. As a result, theories are thin on the ground and what pass for models are often mere typologies and taxonomies which are more descriptive than predictive; their methodologies include the measures of societal bilingualism reviewed in Section 2.2.3. But social and cultural phenomena have also a psychological reality, and the intergroup and interpersonal levels are the only two poles of the social-interaction dimension. This chapter therefore also considers intergroup relations from the point of view of the individual as member of a group and calls upon disciplines like the social psychology of language and the ethnography of speaking. Our problem is how to integrate these different levels of analysis into a unified interdisciplinary framework. In view of the vast domain encompassed here we limit our analysis to a few fundamental questions and cases and consider only soundly based theories and well-documented evidence.

10.1   ORIGINS OF SOCIETAL BILINGUALISM

According to Blanc (1994) societal bilingualism develops from a variety of language contacts both within and between countries and communities. It is found in border areas between states, either because of constant interchange through visits, trade, work or wars; or because a geographical dialect continuum has been interrupted by political frontiers. One example is the West Romance dialect continuum in Europe, which cuts across the national borders of Portugal, Spain, France, Belgium, Luxembourg, Switzerland and Italy. Although the standard varieties of Portuguese, Spanish, Catalan, French and Italian are more or less mutually unintelligible, the rural dialects of these languages are linked by a chain of mutual intelligibility, such that speakers on either side of the political borders have few problems understanding each other. Moreover, many of these people are bilingual, since they speak the official national language as well as the local dialect. For example, many Galicians in north-west Spain speak Gallego (which is close to Portuguese) and Castilian; most Catalans speak Catalan and Castilian; in the Valle d'Aosta many Italians speak Italian and French, while a majority also speak a Franco-Provençal dialect which has recently received some official status.

Political events may divide people speaking the same language or bring together people speaking different languages. The first situation obtains in many African and Asian countries previously under colonial rule, where the colonial powers drew arbitrary frontiers regardless of ethnolinguistic realities. Conversely, alloglots may be brought together, whether voluntarily or by force. In the former case we have free federations, like Switzerland or the European Union. In the latter case we have more or less enforced federations of nations, like the former Soviet Union or former Yugoslavia. Annexations and invasions, migrations and deportations also bring people and groups from different linguistic and cultural backgrounds together. Examples of these are the many shifts of frontiers in Central and Eastern Europe in the nineteenth and twentieth centuries, with the resulting language contacts and conflicts.

Economic factors can also bring speakers of different languages into contact, whether more or less voluntarily (e.g. the European Union), from necessity (e.g. immigrants to North America or Europe) or by force (e.g. the slave trade).

Religion can be a reason for different linguistic groups who share the same faith to live together, whether temporarily (e.g. pilgrimages) or permanently (e.g. the Indian subcontinent). Conversely, different religious communities may split up a country along linguistic lines; for instance, in 1947, at the time of partition, the Indian subcontinent split up along religious lines, thereby dividing a common lingua franca (Hindustani) into two distinct official languages: Hindi, used by the Hindu community, and Urdu, used by the Muslim community.

Lastly, a society may decide to make a second language available or even compulsory in order to gain access to wider markets or information. An example of this is the increasing use of English as an official or semi-official language in many countries of the world, and its role as an international language.

Whatever the reasons for societal bilingualism, it involves languages in intergroup relations.

10.2 THE ROLE OF LANGUAGE IN INTERGROUP RELATIONS

10.2.1 Language and group boundaries

To the extent that language is a salient dimension of ethnicity and ethnic identity (see Section 8.2.1), it plays an important role in intergroup relations when languages and cultures are in contact, not only as a symbol but also as an instrument for upholding or promoting the groups' ethnic identities. The role of language therefore varies according to its importance as a symbol of group identity and as a function of the power relations holding between the different ethnolinguistic groups. A number of social scientists have investigated the role of language in ethnic-group relations from a variety of theoretical and methodological standpoints.

(1)   First, it is important to stress that an ethnic group is not an objective, rigidly defined, homogeneous category. It can cut across other social categories, such as class, race, caste, religious group or political group. Its boundaries are not closed but more or less permeable, since groups do not develop in isolation from one another and individuals can have multiple group membership, as is the case for the bicultural individual. Boundaries are not fixed but change, since the cultures within them change; conversely, group boundaries may be maintained across generations in spite of social and cultural changes. One cannot assume a one-to-one correspondence between ethnic group and cultural characteristics: some dimensions, e.g. language, may be regarded as significant symbols while others are not. A group may respond differently on different dimensions, and subgroups within a group may react in various, sometimes conflicting, ways.

If there is one point on which most social scientists seem to agree, it is on the subjective definition of ethnic groups (for a sociological critique, see G. Williams, 1992). Only those dimensions which members themselves perceive as significant are defining characteristics of the group (Barth, 1970).

Weber (1968) writes: 'We shall call ethnic groups those human groups that entertain a subjective belief in their common descent. Ethnic membership [is] a presumed identity' (p. 389). Similarly, for Tajfel (1978), who does not deny the importance of objective factors, a social or ethnic group is defined as one which perceives itself and is perceived by other groups as a distinctive entity (see Section 8.2). Thus, the criteria for group membership are defined both externally by objective standards and internally by members themselves. External criteria may be imposed from outside by a dominant group which thereby defines the subordinate group; but individual members may then refuse to identify with that group.

(2)   Second, according to Tajfel's (1978) dynamic theory of intergroup relations, a group aims to differentiate itself from other groups in order to achieve or maintain superiority on some relevant dimension of comparison. Positive group identity therefore occurs not in isolation but through mutual comparisons and differentiations between groups. Social relationships between groups are seldom static, and since any changes in power relations have consequences for the outcome of intergroup comparisons, social identity, which is maintained by such comparisons, also changes; in turn, variations in social identity may alter existing intergroup relations. These changes in identity are explained in Tajfel's theory by 'insecurity', which arises whenever an alternative to the status quo is perceived as possible; because of instability in the positions of the groups, power and status may be perceived as having been acquired illegitimately. Examples to be considered are Quebec in Canada, Flanders in Belgium, and Basque in Spain and France. The consequences of an insecure group identity are a renewed search for positive distinctiveness, either through direct competition on the relevant dimensions of comparison or by redefining or altering the elements of the comparative situation ('social creativity'). Success in imposing a new positive distinctiveness depends partly on some recognition by the other groups; if that recognition is not forthcoming, renewed and more vigorous attempts at differentiation can be expected.

(3)   Third, language itself is dynamic and refers to a very complex objective and subjective reality. Linguistic descriptions, even when they take into account intralanguage and interlanguage variations, do not necessarily correspond to the speakers' own perceptions of what constitutes their language(s), precisely because language is a marker of group ethnolinguistic identity; thus, what is defined by linguists as one and the same language or as a linguistic continuum may in fact be perceived as different languages by different speakers of that language. For example, Hindustani is perceived as Hindi, Urdu or Punjabi according to the cultural, religious or political allegiances of its speakers (Brass, 1974). Languages, like groups, have more or less permeable boundaries. This might help to explain why

the definition of 'speech community' has proved so intractable (Hudson, 1980). A speech community is not necessarily coextensive with a language community. As Romaine states: 'A speech community is a group of people who do not necessarily share the same language, but share a set of norms and rules for the use of language. [Thus,] the boundaries between speech communities are essentially social rather than linguistic' (Romaine, 1994).

A language may be the defining characteristic of an ethnic group, in which case it is necessary to understand and speak it in order to belong to the group; but it is not always a condition of group membership. Trudgill & Tzavaras (1977) have shown that it is not essential for the Albanian Arvanites in Greece to speak Arvanitika in order to be considered 'good' Arvanites. Membership in a community may be established in terms of interactional rather than linguistic norms. In some bilingual Gaelic–English communities in Sutherland, Scotland, speakers who had only a receptive knowledge of Gaelic but shared in interactions with fluent speakers (in other terms, they had pragmatic and communicative competence) nonetheless qualified as group members (Dorian, 1981). An individual or a group can abandon their language for another without necessarily losing their original sense of identity. Ethnicity is sometimes related more to the symbol of a language than to its actual use by members of a group (de Vos & Romanucci-Ross, 1975; Gans, 1979). The nineteenth-century notion of one group (nation/state) corresponding to one language does not match reality either, since some groups (or nations) speak more than one language, and the same language can be spoken by more than one group (or nation). As with the notion of ethnic-group identity, language ethnolinguistic identity is very much a function of the interlocutors' perceptions.

10.2.2   Language as symbol and instrument of group identity

Before we examine in detail the role of language in interethnic-group relations it is useful to define the possible forms that ethnic relations may take in multicultural and multilingual societies. Berry (1980) distinguishes four possible modes of acculturation by individuals or groups: assimilation, integration, segregation or separation, and deculturation. These categories are not discrete but continuous. He further discriminates between cultural acculturation, in which the behaviour of one group becomes more similar to that of another, and structural acculturation, in which one group participates in the economic and social systems of the larger society without losing its cultural distinctiveness. Assimilation for the subordinate group means the surrender of its cultural identity and its absorption into the larger society. Assimilation is complete when the members of the group see themselves as belonging to another group and when that other group accepts them as full members. In the case of integration a group becomes an integral part of the society while retaining its cultural distinctiveness to varying degrees. In the case of segregation the dominant group imposes its solution (e.g. South Africa in the period of apartheid in the second half of the twentieth century); in the case of separation it is the subordinate group that decides to assert its distinctiveness and leave the society. In deculturation, a group loses its cultural identity without gaining another; this happens when the subordinate group is marginalised. Berry's model is, however, rather static and rests on an ideology of liberal pluralism more applicable to individuals than to groups (M. H. Gordon, 1981) and to Western than to Third World societies. Its merit lies in providing us with a useful taxonomy. But it can and should be integrated into a social theory of ethnic-group relations, such as Schermerhorn's (1970), for whom the degree of integration of ethnic groups in the society depends primarily on their power relations.

The relationship between language and ethnic-group identity is not static but varies as a function of the type of power relations obtaining between the groups and the level of economic and social development reached by the groups. From a social historical perspective Ross (1979) has proposed a model of group identity development in four stages; these are successively the communal, minority, ethnic and national group identity modes. Note that a group can remain at a particular stage, that the four stages overlap, and that it is possible for a group to miss a stage and accelerate its development. Building on this taxonomy, Taylor & Giles (1979) have put forward a tentative social psychological theoretical framework for research in intergroup relations, which also posits four similar stages but ignores the communal.

In the communal mode typical of isolated traditional societies, group identity is not an issue: group identity and self-identity are taken for granted, since comparison with other groups is non-existent. The language, which is often not given a name or is named after the group, is the repository of the culture. Communal groups often coexist on the same territory, keep their speech repertoires distinct and do not learn each other's language, with the exception of bilingual intermediaries. Successful territorial bilingualism may be the modern equivalent of the communal mode; in this case, Switzerland would be an example of ethnolinguistic coexistence (McRae, 1983). It is when traditional communal groups come into contact with industrialised societies that problems arise: few resist this impact and most are at worst destroyed, and at best assimilated into the new society. Language shift and language attrition are significant aspects of this assimilation. Ross's view of communal groups is limited and fails to take into account communal groups in such cultures as are found in South

Asia, for example, where intercommunal contacts and conflicts are much greater.

A communal group may not wish, or be allowed, to assimilate; it then becomes a minority group. The existence of a 'minority' implies that of a 'majority' which dominates the society through its ability to impose unequal terms on minority groups rather than through its numerical strength. A minority group is, therefore, characterised by its powerlessness to define the nature of its relation to the majority, and thus define its own identity. Its status is defined by the majority and this is mirrored in the minority's negative self-image. This may extend to the language itself, which comes to reflect the subordinate position of the group. The survival or loss of the minority language is dependent upon the interests of the dominant group or the minority's will and ability to mobilise against assimilation. Sometimes the dominant group decides to maintain minority languages in order to divide and rule. It may do this through segregation or apartheid, as was the case in South Africa, or as in the case of a high-status group of Brahmins in Karnataka, India, who never used their caste dialect with non-Brahmins (Ullrich, 1971). Alternatively, the dominant group may try to achieve the same result by keeping minority groups apart and preserving linguistic differences to prevent interethnic communication, as was the case of Arabic and Berber speakers in North Africa under French rule, or Negro slaves from different ethnolinguistic backgrounds on the plantations (see Section 10.3.5). In modern (post)industrialised societies there is often an 'ethnolinguistic division of labour', where cultural and linguistic boundaries are also class boundaries and upward mobility is denied to minority members (E. C. Hughes, 1970; Hechter, 1975).

More frequently, the majority imposes its own language upon the minority as the only legitimate one and pursues a policy of assimilation. In this case the minority language is devalorised, stigmatised and sometimes even eradicated; in order to survive as individuals, minority-group members have to learn the legitimate language. But not all necessarily develop native competence in L_2, nor even acculturate, let alone assimilate; nor do they always lose their L_1; these members run the risk of marginalisation. However great their desire to assimilate, some minority groups are unable to do so because of some external characteristic, like race, which makes them 'visible'. This may lead to a kind of reactive ethnicity, when the visible minority, or at least some of its members, become aware of the impossibility of complete assimilation.

Minorisation, or the imposition of minority status on subordinate groups by the dominant group, produces negative group identity, and some members strive to achieve a more positive identity by 'passing' into the majority. Passing includes, of course, speaking the legitimate language, and the individuals that do will acculturate linguistically, i.e. they converge upwardly in their speech patterns towards the dominant group, even if for a time some remain bilingual. However, many members are often not able or not allowed to pass because of certain individual characteristics or impermeable group boundaries or both. Some come to realise that status enhancement lies in the redefinition of the minority status of the whole group by raising the group consciousness of its members, persuading them that their status is illegitimate and that only concerted collective action can improve their position. This redefinition is achieved by the transformation of the minority into an ethnic group. Ross (1979) defines an ethnic group as 'a politically mobilised collectivity whose members share a perceived distinctive self-identity' (p. 9). If language is one of the salient features of the ethnic group, it is around the language issue that the group will mobilise; language may of course interact with other factors.

The dominant group usually resists such demands for the recognition of collective rights, including language rights, and if it makes concessions, as in the case of the liberal pluralist ideology, it will only concede individual rights; equality is understood in terms of equal opportunity for individuals only, regardless of ethnic or other characteristics, never in terms of equality of outcome for groups considered collectively (M. M. Gordon, 1981). If a compromise is not reached between ethnic groups and the majority, the conflict can escalate, with calls for autonomy, separation or national self-determination if a homeland exists within the boundaries of the society, or for emigration if it exists outside it. A nationalist solution is reached when an ethnic group acquires a state of its own. With nationhood, however, the issue of a national language and its relation to other dialects and languages, where they exist, arises immediately. Contemporary history abounds in examples of nationalist movements based essentially, though not exclusively, on language demands. For illustrations see C. H. Williams (1984) on ethnolinguistic separatist movements in the West, and Brass (1974) and Das Gupta (1975) on the relationship between ethnicity, language demands and national developments in India.

When it is a salient dimension of group identity, language can play many roles in ethnic mobilisation. First, an ethnic group can revive an ancestral language, as happened when Hebrew, which replaced Yiddish (perceived by Zionists as a symbol of negative self-identity), became once again the expression of, and vehicle for, a revived Jewish state (on the relationship between Hebrew and Yiddish, see Fishman 1985). The ancestral language may be a myth which the group creates for itself as a symbol: in the 1960s many Black Americans took up the study of Swahili in an attempt to promote their new ethnic identity, regardless of the fact that their West African ancestors had never spoken that language. As a symbol of ethnic identity a language need not be used for communication, as the case of Irish testifies (Fishman, 1985). Ethnic mobilisation can unite a group around the defence of its culture from a perceived language threat, especially if the language has a territorial base. Two contemporary examples are Francophone Quebec and the Flemish-speaking half of Belgium. In Quebec the defence of the French language has been directly linked to the demands by the French-speaking population for economic and political power within their province; while polarising the struggle on cultural and linguistic issues, the people of Quebec gained control of the economic and social 'capitals', until then predominantly in the hands of the English-speaking community. The francisation of the province also enabled the Quebecois to lessen their sense of insecurity and partly remove the stigma of inferiority which had attached to them and their language for two centuries, and to build a positive ethnic identity (Bourhis, 1984a). In Belgium the Flemish-speaking population reversed the power relationship which had favoured the dominant French-speaking group, not only by taking over the control of their economy but also by imposing Flemish unilingualism on their French-speaking middle-class elites (Witte & Baetens Beardsmore, 1987). In both cases a territorial form of bilingualism ensures two unilingualisms, with bilingual areas and intermediaries.

A third mode of ethnolinguistic mobilisation is, paradoxically, the use of the dominant language by ethnic groups to voice their demands and rally support; for instance, nationalist elites in India effectively used English in their struggle for independence, while Native Americans in the USA have found English a powerful lingua franca for expressing their ethnic identity.

Finally, when the status of a hitherto stigmatised language is revalorised, the language is usually standardised, modernised and even 'purified' as a symbol of the newly found or reborn ethnic identity, in an effort to mark it off from lower-status varieties. This happened in Quebec in the 1960s with the setting up of a number of boards, like the Conseil de la Langue Française, with the aim of monitoring and implementing the use and 'quality' of a Standard French language (Bourhis, 1984a). Another example is the 1979 campaign for the promotion of Mandarin in Singapore, which was based on the claim that dialects are incapable of expressing educated thoughts and refined feelings (Kuo, 1984).

Conversely, ethnolinguistic groups can redefine a vernacular by valorising it as the symbol of their distinctiveness, despite wider social stigmatisation. Black Americans in the USA (Labov, 1972) and adolescent British Blacks of Afro-Caribbean descent in Britain (Hewitt, 1986) have emphasised their salient ethnic characteristics, like colour ('Black is beautiful') and language (Black English Vernacular, creole, patois). Black British youngsters speak, in addition to a local urban variety of English, a dialect closely related to one of the Caribbean creoles, such as British Jamaican Creole, and code-switch between these varieties (V. K. Edwards, 1986). Prestige Black speech forms of West Indian adolescents are even appropriated and used by some of their White working-class adolescent peers, both unconsciously and consciously, in interracial communication interactions and friendship networks, as the expression of their desire to identify with Black youth culture (Hewitt, 1986). Thus, class and race interact and their boundaries are bridged, albeit temporarily.

For all its dynamic qualities Ross's (1979) model of the interaction between intergroup relations, ethnic-group identity, and language has three main limitations. First, its macro-categories are too general for precise operationalisation to be possible; second, it tends to underestimate individuals' subjective perceptions of the objective societal reality; third, it is 'Western-centric' and predicated on a 'dominant majority – dominated minorities' paradigm. But not all societies are neatly divided into hierarchical social classes with an economically, socially, politically and culturally powerful majority group and a number of ethnolinguistic minority groups which are under pressure to assimilate. Many developing countries in the Third World have multicultural and multilingual communities with different social structures, where communal groups have evolved in a different way. In the next sections we look at these different situations and consider alternative theoretical constructs and methodologies which attempt to account for the role of language in intergroup relations. The first of these is the social psychological model of ethnolinguistic vitality, which tries to bridge the gap between the macro- and micro-levels, that is, between socio-structural factors and individual perceptions of these. It is to this concept that we now turn.

10.2.3   Ethnolinguistic vitality

In order to link social psychological processes underlying inter-ethnolinguistic group behaviour to their proper sociocultural settings and identify the socio-structural factors which promote or impede the maintenance of an ethnic minority language, Giles, Bourhis & Taylor (1977) developed the concept of ethnolinguistic vitality (ELV), which has since been extended and applied in a variety of contexts. They define the vitality of an ethnolinguistic group as 'that which makes a group behave as a distinctive and active collective entity in intergroup situations' (p. 308). ELV can be evaluated by three classes of objective factors, namely, status, demography and institutional support. Briefly stated, the status factors include those variables which reflect a group's economic and political power, its social status, its social-historical standing and the status of the ethnic language(s), relative to the various outgroups. Demographic factors refer to the total population of the group, and its concentration and distribution over a territory; the number of mixed marriages, birth rate and patterns of immigration and emigration are relevant variables here. Institutional support factors refer to the degree of support the group and its language enjoy in the various informal and formal institutions of the society, such as, for example, in the home, the mass media and education.

Giles, Bourhis & Taylor (1977) hypothesised that each of these factors would affect the vitality of an ethnolinguistic group in a positive or negative way. They further proposed that ethnolinguistic communities could be meaningfully grouped according to the above three factors on the basis of the available historical, sociological, demographic and other data. Using such a framework, ethnolinguistic groups could be classified as possessing high, medium or low vitality, which would help define and compare ethnolinguistic groups across cultures. It is argued that the higher the vitality, the more likely a group and its language are to survive as a distinctive entity. So far, our discussion has focused on 'objective' assessments of ELV. But do ethnolinguistic group members perceive their situation along the same lines as the objective analysis? Their subjective assessment may be just as important in determining interethnic group behaviour; members may underestimate or exaggerate the ELV of the ingroup or of the outgroup, and so on. A combination of objective and subjective measures would provide a better understanding of relations between groups in terms of their ethnolinguistic vitality.

The concept of subjectively perceived ethnolinguistic vitality claims to take into account individual members' cognitive representations of the social conditions in which they live and mediates between their intergroup behaviour. This concept provides a theoretical and empirical starting point for bridging the conceptual gap between sociological and social psychological approaches to inter-ethnolinguistic group relations. In order to try to measure perceived ethnolinguistic vitality, a 'Subjective Vitality Questionnaire' (SVQ) was designed by Bourhis, Giles & Rosenthal (1981). On this questionnaire members rate their own group relative to one or more outgroups on the three main vitality dimensions. The relationships between objective and subjective vitality, as well as the validity of the questionnaire, have been investigated in a number of empirical studies.

The findings of a variety of studies across the world have confirmed that perceptions of majorities and minorities match objective ELV estimates on many of the subjective vitality dimensions. For example, some concordance has been reported for majority Anglo-Canadians and minority Italian-Canadian teenagers in Hamilton (Bourhis & Sachdev, 1984), majority Anglo-Australians and minority Greek-Australians in Melbourne

(Giles, Rosenthal & Young, 1985), Welsh bilinguals in Wales (Giles & Johnson, 1987), and Vietnamese in Australia (Willemyns, Pittam & Gallois, 1993). A large-scale study of Francophone minorities across Canada gives the best demonstration of the close match between subjective and objective assessments of vitality (Landry & Allard, 1994).

Surveys of heritage language shift among a wide variety of Nordic peoples – the Sami in Finland, Sweden, Norway and the Kola peninsula (Aikio, 1990), the Inupiat, Yupiks and Aleut in the USA (Bergsland, 1990; Kaplan, 1990), and the Inuit of the Canadian Arctic (Dorais, 1985) – show that those minority languages are gradually giving way to English or French under the impact of strong assimilation policies, the media and education, especially among the younger generation. From the perspective of ethnolinguistic vitality, the colonisation of circumpolar aborigines has left the heritage languages with little in terms of demography, status and institutional support. This low vitality is not always perceived by the communities, as witness the Inuit of Arctic Quebec. Using a non-standard methodology, Taylor, Wright, Ruggiero & Aitchison (1993) asked Inuit caregivers a series of questions about their own fluency in, and present use of, Inuttitut, English and French; furthermore, the caregivers had to estimate their children's present language fluency and usage and to predict their children's future language fluency. The researchers found that there was a considerable optimism about the present and future use of the heritage language and that English and French, far from being a threat, were seen as opportunities for adding new linguistic skills to their repertoire. The authors attributed this positive outlook to a relatively high ethnolinguistic vitality, in particular a degree of control over political, economic and educational institutions. Inuttitut is still the predominant community language. However, as Taylor, Wright, Ruggiero & Aitchison (1993) point out, a concerted effort at strengthening the vitality of the language is needed, in particular by ensuring literacy in Inuttitut. The very optimism of the group might contribute to the demise of the heritage language, since a people confident about the future of its language is unlikely to take action to protect its own ethnolinguistic vitality.

However, discrepancies between subjective and objective vitality assessments have been reported in many studies. Harwood, Giles & Bourhis (1994) have classified these discrepancies into the following categories:

- perceptual distortions in favour of ingroup vitality;
- perceptual distortions in favour of the outgroup (this bias is prevalent among subordinate, low-status minorities); and
- non-consensual vitality perceptions (when group members disagree as to the degree and direction of difference between ingroups and outgroups).

For example, Pierson, Giles & Young (1987) reported that during the period of intense negotiations in the 1990s between the UK and China over the future of Hong Kong, Chinese and Westerners held diametrically opposed perceptions of their relative group vitality. Harwood, Giles & Bourhis identified three main sets of factors affecting ELV perceptions: sociological, social network, and social psychological factors. The first concerns the degree of stability of ELV: the greater the stability the greater the match between objective and subjective assessments. Conversely, in cases of instability, there is less intergroup consensus. The authors fail to consider the possibility that social perceptions might also be based on a conflict of interests over scarce resources (realistic conflict theory) and on competition for positive social identity. The second factor is the concept of individual networks of language contacts. This concept was proposed by Landry & Allard (1994) as a bridge mediating between the sociological and social psychological levels, where the individual lives the totality of his ethnolinguistic experience. The more an individual uses the ingroup language within his networks, the more likely he will perceive the ingroup as having high vitality. Third, motivational processes in striving for positive ethnolinguistic identity account for perceptual distortions in favour of ingroup vitality.

Sachdev & Bourhis (1993) have proposed other motivational and social cognitive factors to account for objective–subjective vitality discrepancies. Subjects have to make judgements when the information available to them on ingroup and outgroup vitality is uncertain or statistically complex, and they resort to a variety of judgement heuristics, of which the availability heuristic is one. It consists of giving a higher frequency or likelihood to objects or events which are more easily accessible from memory or are easier to imagine. In the Bourhis & Sachdev (1984) study of Anglo-Canadian and Italian-Canadian students, both groups were found to share much common information about the wider environment dominated by Anglo-Canadians; however, Italian-Canadians were more familiar with the Italian cultural context than were the Anglo-Canadians. Majorities are often ignorant of and/or prejudiced against minorities, whereas minorities cannot afford to be ignorant of majorities. This is particularly true of first-generation immigrants who, from being members of a majority in their country of origin, become a minority in the new country and experience a drop in status, which leads to perceptual distortions.

Another challenge to motivational explanations of perceptual distortions comes from Allard and Landry who, in addition to the mediating role of social networks, proposed including ELV perceptions in a 'belief system'. The SVQ taps only 'general beliefs' (about 'what is'), and these points contribute only minimally to predictions of language behaviour. Using cognitive orientation theory (Kreitler & Kreitler, 1976), Allard & Landry (1986) found that the predictive power of svq was enhanced when 'normative beliefs' ('what should be'), 'self-beliefs' (what the subject thinks) and 'goal beliefs' (his aims and wishes) about ELV were included in a Beliefs about ELV Questionnaire (BEVQ). They further proposed that self-beliefs and goal beliefs be assigned to 'ego-centric' vitality, and general and normative beliefs to 'exo-centric' vitality. Their findings showed that among French Canadians across Canada, ego-centric beliefs were more predictive of ethnolinguistic behaviour than exo-centric beliefs about Francophone vitality.

More recently Landry & Allard (1994) have extended their model, defining the factors responsible for language use and bilingual development in intergroup contexts on three levels: psychological, social psychological and sociological. The degree to which members of an ethnolinguistic group use their language in a variety of contexts (their 'language behaviour') is indicative of the probability that their language will survive in their community. At the psychological level, this use is dependent, on the one hand, on the language competence of the members and their desire to use their language; on the other, on the opportunities to use their language in a variety of contexts. A group member's choice about which language to use in a given context depends on his language aptitude and competence as well as on his vitality beliefs and ethnolinguistic identity ('cognitive-affective disposition'). At the social psychological level the model postulates that it is in his personal network of language contacts that the individual acquires his language competences, ethnolinguistic beliefs, and ethnic identity (primary and secondary socialisation). At the sociological level, the member's language experiences in his network depend on the respective ethnolinguistic vitality of the linguistic groups with which he is in contact, this vitality being reflected in the demographic, political, economic and cultural (including linguistic) 'capitals' (a concept adapted, rather arbitrarily, from Bourdieu).

Landry, Allard & Henry (1996) applied this model to a study of the vitality of the French community in south-western Louisiana. Four groups of students were formed on the basis of the strength of the Francophone network within the students' immediate family. Although results on social and media contacts with French, as well as the scores on oral French competence, use of French, French identity and beliefs in the vitality of French covary as a function of the proportion of Francophones in the family, the average scores for even the group with the strongest proportion of Francophones in the family are moderate to low. This is attributed by the authors to the small amount of contact with French. They conclude that the present generation of youths of Cajun and French descent will not be able to transmit the French language to their children. An interesting aspect of this study is the authors' extension of the concepts of 'additive' and 'subtractive' bilingualism (Lambert, 1974) from the individual to the group: in this case, for minority group members, learning the majority group's language leads to subtractive bilingualism, that is, valuing, learning and developing competences in the second language at the expense of the first. When most members of the minority group make exclusive use of the majority language, it can be said that language loss has occurred (see Sections 10.3.3 and 10.3.4).

Responding to researchers' findings and reformulations of the initial model of ethnolinguistic vitality and subjective group vitality, Harwood, Giles & Bourhis (1994) proposed a new model designed to articulate situational elements at a number of levels (sociological, social network and social psychological) reminiscent of Landry & Allard's (1994) model which impacts upon the individual's assessment of ingroup and outgroup vitality. Vitality assessment itself is divided into three important components: the degree of cross-group consensus, the salience of vitality concerns, and the degree of accentuation/attenuation of between-group differences. They argue that manifestation of this process of assessment appears in communicative behaviours and intergroup cognitions in terms of social attitudes, attributions, and relational strategies in intra- and intergroup encounters. They further propose adding a discourse dimension to the use of the questionnaire, that is, adding a more qualitative ethnographic type of approach, in which subjects discuss their experiences and perceptions of ingroup and outgroup vitality. Their discourse is analysed in terms of volume (that is, the number of times the participants refer to the vitality of their ethnolinguistic group is indicative of a salient vitality) and tone of vitality (it is argued that groups vary in the affective tone of their discourse about vitality; conversely, the tone varies as a function of how they see other groups and conceive of intergroup competition); the discourse is also analysed in terms of the attitudinal and relational outcomes of vitality assessment. Finally, the authors put forward a number of research propositions which provide useful hypotheses for future research. To date it is too early to assess the validity of this new taxonomic model, which has an essentially social psychological framework.

The construct of ethnolinguistic vitality can be criticised on theoretical grounds from other perspectives. The first objection concerns the status of the socio-structural variables; these form a purely descriptive taxonomy which lacks theoretical justification; that is, they are not based on a social theory. For this reason, the factors and their variables have little predictive value: indeed, any one of them can have diametrically opposed consequences. For example, in his study of factors influencing the maintenance or loss of ethnic-minority languages in the USA, Kloss (1966) showed how the same factor can either enhance or depress the ethnolinguistic vitality of a group. Take, for example, the demographic factor: while there may be safety in numbers and large groups have a greater chance of survival than small ones, this is not always the case; a minority group comprising a relatively large population, unless it is territorially circumscribed, is exposed to multiple contacts with the dominant group and experiences internal divisions and a dilution of its strength. For example, the German-speaking communities in North America were by far the largest and most powerful immigrant groups in the nineteenth century, yet they have gradually been assimilated. Conversely, numerical weakness can lead to greater group solidarity and cohesion; perceptions of inferiority do not necessarily lead to the demise of an ethnic group and its language but can be a spur to the revitalisation of its self-identity, as can the dominant group's policy of enforced assimilation (Glazer, 1966). In all this, group self-awareness and ethnic mobilisation are essential to the survival of a group and its language.

Another critique is directed against the actual or perceived macro–micro (objective–subjective) dichotomy of the ethnolinguistic vitality construct. Husband & Saifullah Khan (1982) maintain that this dichotomy disappears if one analyses intergroup interaction processes at different levels of social organisation, such as primary groups, social networks, interest groups and social classes. They argue that the relationship between, for example, (Pakistani) Punjabi English speakers and English monolingual speakers in Britain can only be understood if one looks at the respective historical, economic and political processes which have led to the present imbalance of power and perceived cultural differences between the two populations. Perceived from within, many Pakistani Punjabis would rate their language rather low relative to the wider context of Britain and Pakistan; however, for its members this language (or variety, since most speak the Mirpuri dialect) is valued as a fundamental part of regional culture and a symbol of group membership and loyalty. The authors criticise the very concept of 'ethnolinguistic group' which, like that of language, refers to too high a level of abstraction; they propose instead that of 'speech community', defined in terms of shared norms and values, and language interactions. Language, as a salient symbol of ethnic identity, is a multidimensional concept varying in space and time. The younger generation of Pakistani Punjabis belongs at the same time both to the Pakistani Punjabi Mirpuri community and to the Anglophone community.

Their view is supported by, among others, a study of linguistic and cultural affiliations amongst first-generation Asian (Gujarati) adolescents in Britain by Mercer, Mercer & Mears (1977). These researchers treat the relationship between ethnic identity and language loyalty as problematic, since the main identifying trait of this group is not language but the physical appearance of the group's members – more specifically their skin colour – and since a common expression of their self-identity in encounters with Whites is their Indian-ness (an ethnic, not an ethnolinguistic label, as Indians speak a variety of Indian languages). Attitudes to language seem to be associated with the individual's conception of the most desirable future for himself and his group within British society. Those who opt for British identity seem to favour assimilation; those who choose Indian identity favour a pluralistic cultural development in which their ethnic identity is maintained. Thus, the wide range of attitudes to the Gujarati language and to traditional Indian culture should warn us against assuming that members of ethnolinguistic minority groups share, by virtue of their common background, a similar set of attitudes to their ethnic language and a similar conception of their place in the new society. Ethnicity is essentially a form of interaction between cultural groups within common social contexts, and different social contexts will generate different ethnic identities. The construct of ethnolinguistic vitality fails to some extent to account for the dynamics of ethnic groups in multilingual communities.

10.2.4   Language and ethnicity in multicultural settings

We have seen that language may be a salient characteristic of a group's ethnic identity. Smolicz (1979) has developed the concept of core values to refer to those values that are regarded by the group as forming the most fundamental components of its culture (see Section 8.2.1); they act as identifying characteristics which are symbolic of the group and its membership. It is through them that groups can be identified as distinctive cultural entities. Rejection of core values carries with it the threat of exclusion from the group. Now cultural groups differ in the extent to which they emphasise certain core values, e.g. language, and there are variations between and within groups over time and in space in the way groups define core values (Smolicz, 1981). For example, there are in many countries of the world people with a strongly developed sense of Jewish identity who speak neither Hebrew nor Yiddish; on the other hand, in Israel today there is no doubt that Hebrew is one of the chief core values of the country and the culture.

There are groups which stress language as the main carrier of their culture and the expression of their identity, and have used it as the main defence mechanism against assimilation. An index of the strength of language as a core value for an immigrant group, for example, can be inferred from the host country's population census data (where such data includes language questions); moreover, cross-national comparisons can be made to see if members of the same groups immigrating to different countries have consistent ethnolinguistic behaviour patterns over generations. A comparison between Australia and Canada, for instance, suggests that in both countries immigrant Chinese, Italians and Greeks exhibit the smallest language shift and the Dutch and Germans the largest, while Poles and Serbo-Croats occupy an intermediate position (Clyne, 1982; Blanc, 1986). In different contexts the 'same' original group may develop differently in terms of core values. Patterson (1975) provides the example of the Chinese who migrated at the same time from the same province of China to the Caribbean. Both groups succeeded economically but developed ethnolinguistically in opposite ways. Those who settled in British Guyana gave up their language and culture and became creolised. The other group, settled in Jamaica, affirmed their ethnolinguistic identity; later, though, they diverged, one subgroup reinforcing their ethnolinguistic distinctiveness through endogamic marriages, while the other subgroup assimilated through creolisation.

In pluralist countries like Australia, Canada and the USA groups or members of those groups that do not assimilate, integrate both their culture and language, but a strong linguistic core value does not prevent them from developing a 'hyphenated' Australian, Canadian or American identity. This is because the different ethnic groups, while representing different cultures, share with minority and majority alike a set of what Smolicz (1984) calls 'overarching core values', such as acceptance of, for example, liberal capitalism and democracy, and the English language as an indispensable medium for national cross-cultural communication and economic and social success. However, this 'hyphenated' identity (see Section 8.3.5) is not as simple as Smolicz suggests. It implies multiple group membership on the part of the minority group and constantly changing self-definition and language use. In his study of two generations of Greek-Australians in Adelaide, Papademetre (1994) shows how time, context and interlocutor impact on the identity and language behaviour of members of the community. Depending on whether the Greek-Australians' identity is self-defined or other-defined, the 'hyphenated' Greek-Australian has to negotiate his identity depending on whether he is interacting with a fellow Greek-Australian, an Anglo-Australian, a member of another minority group, or a Greek in or from Greece (see also Section 8.2.1 on context and salience of ethnic identity). Accordingly, Greek-Australians are defined by others as 'Greeks' or 'new Australians', 'kseni' ('foreigners') or 'afstrali' ('Australians'; the term used by native Greeks), whether they define themselves as 'Greeks' or not. The naming of Greek-diaspora bilinguals by natives in Greece takes on further semantic dimensions; for example: 'ksenoi' (foreigners, strangers, aliens, guests, visitors); 'Afstrali',

'Amerikani', 'metanastes' (migrants, immigrants), etc. (Papademetre: 517). However, diaspora Greeks define themselves as 'new', or 'more', or 'very' Australian, American, Canadian, etc. within their own Greek ethnolinguistic community, depending on the language in which they discuss the issues (Greek or English) and their relative competence in these languages.

But groups and individuals may be forced to adopt the core values of the majority and surrender their own; the loss of core values reduces the culture to mere residues, which represent only superficial manifestations of that culture. When ethnic cultures have been degraded to residues through the loss of their valued language, we have what Smolicz (1984) calls the phenomenon of 'residual multiculturalism'.

So far we have been concerned mainly with situations in which languages and cultures are frequently defined as the distinctive characteristics of separate ethnic groups in competition, conflict or open confrontation with each other. But in many parts of the Third World, especially in those countries which have recently freed themselves from colonial rule, the ethnolinguistic situation can be very different. One such situation has been called 'emergent multilingualism' by Parkin (1977); it usually involves an indigenous, pre-colonial lingua franca and an exogenous, colonial lingua franca which are both used alongside different regional and local vernaculars in ethnically mixed speech communities of recent creation. Unlike the ethnic vernaculars, however, the two lingue franche are not unambiguously regarded as the property of any one ethnic group, nor even of a distinct class or status group (examples are English and Swahili in Eastern Africa, and French and Wolof in Western Africa). The multilingual situation is emergent in the sense that these ethnically and socioculturally unattached lingue franche have the potential of becoming identified with a particular ethnic or sociocultural group (e.g. English, of an elite or of an ethnic group that has become dominant, and Swahili, of an urban proletariat in Kenya). So, though still emergent, the use of one or the other of these lingue franche already carries with it social symbols of identity and connotations as high or low speech varieties.

In the Kenyan case described by Parkin (1977), adolescents from the same ethnolinguistic backgrounds vehemently claim to be either 'Swahili speakers' or 'English speakers', but this distinction does not reflect their actual use of either language: rather, it reflects their perceptions of a socio-economic and educational cleavage between disadvantaged adolescents, expressed as Swahili-speaking, and privileged youths, expressed as English-speaking. This putative difference between Swahili and English usage cuts across the boundaries of everyday vernacular usage, which, for each ethnic group, continues to have great practical and symbolic significance. Parkin compares and contrasts this emergent multilingualism with a more stabilised form of bilingualism where there is an unambiguous association between educational norms, standard speech style, and dominant ethnic group or class. In this kind of situation ethnic–class polarisation is usually reflected in a polarisation between speech styles or languages. Research to test Parkin's model of emergent multilingualism in other Third World multicultural settings has not, to date, been carried out.

To conclude this section, it has become clear in the course of the discussion that – partly because of the variety and complexity of inter-ethnolinguistic group relations in the world, and partly because of the difficulty of bridging the gap between a macro-level (or objective socio-structural level) and the perception of these by individuals at a micro-level (or subjective social psychological level) – there is as yet no adequate theory for the study of language, ethnicity and intergroup relations. We have, however, raised some of the fundamental issues and problems, and have, we hope, suggested in our analysis some fruitful lines of inquiry.

10.3   SOCIOLINGUISTIC VARIATIONS IN LANGUAGE-CONTACT SITUATIONS

In a situation of language contact the status of each language varies, on the one hand, as a function of the nature of intergroup relations – in particular power relations and the values and norms attached to these – and, on the other hand, as a function of the perceptions that speakers form of these relations, their values and norms. It follows that language attitudes and uses vary in social, geographical and historical space as a function of these relations and perceptions. When relations change, status relationships, and therefore perceptions, attitudes and uses, change. It is worth stressing that it is not so much the languages that vary as their speakers, who select from a variety of possible models which are socially marked; as Le Page & Tabouret-Keller point out, change only takes place when the social values of the models change and the behaviour of the speech community also changes (Le Page & Tabouret-Keller, 1985).

10.3.1   Speech repertoires in multilingual communities

In a multilingual speech community a whole range of languages, or repertoire, is available to speakers, who use some of them in their linguistic interactions to perform particular social roles. The term 'repertoire' is also used to refer to the range of dialects, registers and styles typical of a unilingual community of speakers where the choice of one variety over another can have the same social significance as code selection in a multilingual community (Gumperz, 1968). Repertoire applies at two different levels to both the community and the individual. A speaker does not usually control the whole range of the codes that constitute a community's repertoire continuum but only a number of these. An important question to raise is whether the idea of a continuum exists in the minds of the speakers, or whether it is a mere artefact of the sociolinguist. Willemyns (1987) shows convincingly that, while being aware of which code to use when, speakers do not actually experience a continuum but consider their own utterances to be, for example, either dialect or standard language, never something in between. This leaves no room for an intermediate variant.

An illustration of a complex multilingual speech repertoire at both the community and the individual level is given by Platt (1977), who describes Chinese communities in Singapore and Malaysia educated in the English language. The verbal repertoires of both communities consist of various Chinese languages (of which one is regionally dominant), formal and colloquial varieties of English and standard and 'bazaar' varieties of Malay. For a typical English-educated Chinese in Malaysia, a common speech repertoire might include: his mother tongue (one of the Chinese languages), some formal Malaysian English, some colloquial Malaysian English, some Bahasa Malaysia, and Bazaar Malay (a low-prestige lingua franca). Each language or variety is arranged in a 'linear polyglossic distribution' (see Section 10.3.2). An example of how a multilingual speaker might use the different codes in his repertoire is given by Pandit (1979), who describes an Indian businessman living in a suburb of Bombay. His mother tongue and home language is Kathiawari, a dialect of Gujarati (his daily newspaper is printed in the standard Gujarati variety); in the market he uses a familiar variety of Marathi, the state language; at the railway station, where he catches his train for Bombay, he speaks the pan-Indian lingua franca, Hindustani; the language of work is Kachchi, the code of the spice trade; in the evening he watches a film in Hindi or in English or listens to a cricket match commentary on the radio in English. Kachru (1982) has put forward a typology of speech repertoires to which the reader is referred. What role or roles does each of these different languages and varieties perform in the community and the individual?

Juillard (1995) has carried out a sociolinguistic study of a multilingual urban area (Ziguinchor) in Senegal (lingua franca: Wolof; official language: French). She used a variety of elicitation techniques including:

- speakers' evaluation of the relative status of the languages in contact;
- language diaries recording language uses in the speakers' social networks (in answer to the question, 'who speaks what language, to whom, where and when, and for what function?'); and
- direct observation of language interactions in local markets.

Ziguinchor (population: 75,000) is situated in the province of Casamance (population: 750,000) at the crossroads of three countries (Senegal, Gambia and Guinea-Bissau), and numerous ethnic and linguistic groups: eight African, three ex-colonial languages and one 'creole'. She found that her respondents classified languages in three ways: languages of identity, of cross-communication and of culture. In the wider educational domain there are sex differences: boys use French and girls use Wolof. Repertoires varied from a trilingual farmer who used three languages – Mandinka and Diola (the majority language) with men and Wolof with his mother and sister – to a high-school boy who declared using 20 languages and used eight daily. In the market place Peul (Kpelle) is the language of transaction, while Wolof is the language of bargaining power, and French is used to conclude a bargain.

10.3.2   Bilingualism and diglossia

The various codes in a multilingual speech community, as in a bilingual individual, are neither used nor valued in similar ways. If they were, all but one would become redundant. They usually fulfil complementary functions in the twofold sense that they are used differentially according to interlocutor, domain, topic, role and function, and that the choice of one rather than the other involves an 'act of identity' (Le Page & Tabouret-Keller, 1985) on the part of the speaker. When different varieties or languages co-occur throughout a speech community, each with a distinct range of social functions in complementary distribution, we have a situation of diglossia.

The concept of diglossia was originally developed by Ferguson (1959) to describe two functional varieties within a single language, one of which – called the High (H) variety – is reserved for formal functions and is formally learned, the other – the Low (L) variety – is used in informal situations (e.g. Greek Katharevusa and Dhimotiki; Classical and Colloquial Arabic; Standard German and Swiss German; Standard French and Haitian French). H is the language of status, L the speech of solidarity. The notion of diglossia was extended by Gumperz (1971) to multilingual situations, and by Fishman (1967) who distinguished between diglossia and bilingualism, the former referring to the social functional distribution, the latter to an individual's ability to use more than one code (bilinguality in our sense). Whatever the applications of the concept, the defining criterion is that of functional distribution, whether the language forms are separate languages, subsystems of the same language or stylistic varieties. (For a full discussion of the issues, see Fasold, 1984; for a critique of the concept of diglossia, see G. Williams, 1992 and Hudson, 1994.)

There are various types of multilingual diglossia. Examples of these are:

- simple binary contexts; for example: Guarani (L) and Spanish (H) in Paraguay (Rubin, 1968);
- double-overlapping diglossia; for example: African vernaculars (L), Kiswahili (H and L) and English (H) in Tanzania (Abdulaziz Mkilifi, 1978); however, from the perspective of social conflict, Mechaka (1993) shows that, since English is available only to an elite, Kiswahili is the superposed language accorded both higher status and higher prestige; the vernaculars are perceived as the minority languages with low status and low prestige;
- double-nested diglossia, with L and H having both a Low and High; for example: Khalapur in Northern India (Gumperz, 1964b);
- linear polyglossia in Singapore and Malaysia, as quoted above (Platt, 1977).

A full discussion of these types of diglossia is given in Fasold (1984). An equally complex situation is that of Brussels (de Vriendt & Willemyns, 1987), where six groups of speakers are distinguished: monolinguals in Dutch or French, and bilinguals in the two languages but with varying degrees of dominance, each with a High and a Low variety; if one adds to these the increasing number of foreign immigrants, some of whom are bilingual or trilingual, the language configuration of the city is complex indeed. Instead of the High–Low dichotomy of diglossia with bilingualism, a triglossic situation is proposed, with an L (dialect), an H (regional standard) and a 'supreme language' or super-superposed variety which has a higher status than H (T'Sou, 1980); in the multilingual situation of Brussels, the supreme languages are the Standard French of France and the Standard Dutch of the Netherlands, over and above the regional High languages, which are Standard Belgian French and Standard Belgian Dutch (Baetens Beardsmore, 1982). The 'supreme language' concept is not unlike Platt's (1977) notion of 'Dummy High', which refers to a speech variety of which some members of the community have a certain knowledge, and which is given prestige by the speakers, but which is not in fact much used.

Perhaps one of the most complex polyglossic situations is that of Northern India (Khubchandani, 1979). At the local level dialects vary considerably from village to village to the extent of becoming mutually incomprehensible; when a villager visits the bazaar of a neighbouring town he must speak a less localised variety in order to be understood. This is how local trade languages developed and became regional dialects and the mother tongues of town dwellers. Above regional dialects are the state languages recognised as official by the Indian Constitution. Each state language in turn comprises a colloquial and a literary standard form, the

latter being mastered only by literate people, who also speak the vernacular. Over and above these are the two 'supreme languages', Hindi and
English, both official national languages; Hindi is also a regional language
covering several states and diversified into a number of dialects, of which
Khari Boli, the New Delhi standard, is the basis for the official language. In
Northern India the Hindi–Punjabi linguistic-geographic area, comprising
46 per cent of the total Indian population, is a vast polyglossic continuum
where languages and dialects complement, merge or compete with each
other according to functions, domains and group affiliations.

Stable diglossia (called 'broad' by Fasold, 1984) evolves and changes. It
is said to 'leak' when one variety takes over the functions formerly reserved
for the other and this is a sign of the incipient breakdown of the diglossic
relationship, reflecting changes in the power relations between the groups.
The outcome is either a new variety which is a mixture of the former High
and Low varieties (especially when the two languages are structurally
similar) or the replacement of one language by another (especially if they
are structurally dissimilar). An example of the latter is the receding of the
Low German variety spoken in the deprived German-speaking area of
Belgium before the relatively High French variety (Verdoodt, 1972). The
shift from German to French is preceded by widespread bilingualism in
which either language may be used almost indiscriminately. Along the way
to complete shift, the language of the subordinate group comes under the
influence of the dominant language and undergoes important changes. In
turn, the dominant language can be affected by the subordinate language.

10.3.3 Language shift

In stable diglossia a multilingual community maintains its different languages by reserving each of them for certain domains, roles and functions
with little encroachment of one language upon the domains, roles and
functions of another. This maintenance is dependent upon relatively stable
relations between the groups of the community. When these relations
change, however, and one group begins to assimilate to another, language
maintenance starts to break down. Members of that group begin to use the
language of another group for domains, roles and functions hitherto reserved for the first language. Its own language is affected by the dominant
group's language. When the group finally gives up its mother tongue, the
process of language shift is complete. A similar phenomenon occurs when
an indigenous monolingual minority group is absorbed into the dominant
majority, or when an exogenous ethnic group moves to a new society where
the dominant language is different from its own and is assimilated. When
the group's language ceases to be spoken by its members we have a case of

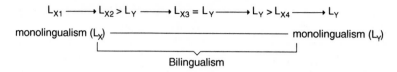

Figure 10.1   Unidimensional model of language shift

'language death', even though the language may continue to be spoken somewhere else. The ethnic identity of the group may survive if its language is not one of its core values.

The various forms of intergroup relations and dependency analysed above mean that when the subordinate groups' internal cohesion is affected, the dominant language spreads and gradually invades the domains, functions and forms of the subordinate language, or rather speakers of the latter gradually adopt the forms of the dominant language in more and more roles, functions and domains. When the family domain is invaded and parents cease to transmit their language to their children, and the latter are no longer motivated to learn it, language shift is almost complete. As groups are not homogeneous, this spread and shift takes place to varying degrees, in different ways and at different rates of development. Taking the group as a whole, with its different generations and social categories, we can represent the process on a continuum ranging from monolingualism in the subordinate language, at one end, to monolingualism in the dominant language at the other. In between we have different levels of bilinguality and bilingualism, from dominant in L_X to dominant in L_Y, with a stage of relative balance between the languages half way along. This period of bilingualism is accompanied by various forms of specific language behaviour, such as code-mixing, code-switching, borrowing, convergence and a reduction in the forms and uses of, and skills in, L_X. This multidimensional process may be schematised on the unidimensional model in Figure 10.1.

The shift also takes place in synchrony; that is, at a given point in time, the first generation is still monolingual in L_X, while the last is already monolingual in L_Y. It is important to note that, as we move along the continuum, L_X does not remain the same but its domains of use, that is, its functions and forms, change in contact with those of L_Y: L_{X1}, L_{X2}, L_{X3} etc. Using a cross-sectional approach to study language shift among Mexican-American high-school students and their parents, Hakuta and D'Andrea (1992) have shown that, if one defines language shift as loss in proficiency in L_1, then it occurs most sharply across generations, especially between those adolescents whose parents were born in Mexico and those whose parents were born in the USA; if shift is defined as a change in choice of code (from L_1 to L_2), then the process begins immediately and proceeds in a progressive manner both across and within generations.

The shift to total assimilation may be halted by a prolonged period of bilingualism, depending on the degree of mobilisation of the group (Paulston, 1992). According to Reitz (1974), who studied the rate of language shift amongst three generations of immigrants to Canada, the most important factors impeding the progress of shift are, in descending order of importance, maintenance of close ties with the ethnic group, identification with the ingroup, endogamy and religious affiliation. In other words, keeping close links with the ethnic social network is the most important factor of language maintenance in Canada. For Fishman (1964) three main classes of factors, or combinations of the three classes, account for language shift:

(1) changes in the way of life of a group that weaken the strength of its social networks;
(2) changes in the power relationships between the groups;
(3) stigmatised attitudes towards the minority group values and language, shared by minority and majority alike.

From a macro-sociological perspective Tabouret-Keller (1968; 1972) has attempted to explain language-shift pattern phenomena from bilingualism to monolingualism in Western and Third World countries by reference to socio-economic, demographic and geographical infrastructures. Using methods of correlational statistics she defined the factors that determined shift in Western European and West African countries, in both rural and urban contexts, and compared nineteenth-century Europe with contemporary Africa. Mutatis mutandis, she found that shift or maintenance can be attributed to the same fundamental economic, technological and social factors, and in particular to urbanisation and schooling. Comparing the evolution of dialects and minority languages within France itself she found a correlation between industrialisation/urbanisation and language shift: social mobility, migration into cities, development of communications and media are factors that accelerate assimilation to the standard. Alsace, where the German dialect survives (Tabouret-Keller & Luckel, 1981), seems to be an exception to the rule because of the following factors: economic (modern intensive farming), historical (recent integration of the province) and social geographical (vicinity of Germany with movements of population across the border). No such favourable factors were found in southern France, where the dialects and languages have been losing ground before the invasion of Standard French.

Socio-structural approaches, however useful for defining macro-factors of change, fail to account for the influence of intervening variables such as the importance of social networks, individual perceptions of the relative ethnolinguistic vitality of groups in contact, and the communication interactions of participants. These may be better apprehended with social psychological or speech-ethnographic methods. Applying Landry & Allard's (1994) ethnolinguistic vitality model (see Section 10.2.3) to the study of language shift in French Louisiana among Francophones, Landry, Allard & Henry (1996) attribute the ongoing language shift from French to English to a very weak network of French-language contacts. Even for the younger generation with the strongest French family network, contacts are closer with the older than with the younger generation; and as their network extends beyond the immediate neighbourhood, the proportion and frequency of contacts with Francophones both diminish. A weak network of French-language contacts is correlated with very poor competences in French, a weak cognitive-affective disposition towards the mother tongue and a low ethnolinguistic vitality conferred on the French language, for now and for the future. The social/cultural identity of those members with strong French networks is defined not in terms of language but on the basis of their Cajun culture. The authors conclude that it is unlikely that French will be passed on to the next generation.

Using techniques of participant observation to study language choice and shift in a Hungarian-German speech community on the border between Austria and Hungary, formerly in Hungary but part of Austria since the end of the First World War (Oberwart in German; Felsoor in Hungarian), Gal (1979) found that, from an original unilingual Hungarian situation, Oberwart had shifted to a German-dominant bilingual community. The local Hungarian dialect is associated with rural values, while German is associated with urban ones. Most peasant children are still growing up bilingual and their religion is identified with the Hungarian language; exogamous marriages, urban employment and schooling benefit German, which has the higher status. At the same time the Hungarian dialect is being devalued by comparison with the standard spoken in Hungary, which is, however, not acceptable because of its different ethnic affiliation. Code-switching occurs in asymmetrical communication interactions, varying as a function of differences in age, ethnic identity, social status and role between interlocutors. Gal predicts that the whole community will be more or less assimilated to an Austrian German culture within a few generations. This study has been criticised for failing to take into account the power struggle inherent in language shift and for accepting too readily the inevitability of language shift. For an analysis of this example of language shift in terms of form–function mapping, see Section 1.2.4.2.

Another case of language-shift and obsolescence is that documented by Dorian (1981) in the Gaelic-speaking fishing community of East Sutherland in the Highlands of Scotland. The shift here is from unilingual Gaelic to unilingual Scottish English (which has higher status). Of greater interest is the lag between this community and the other communities in the area: when the former was unilingual Gaelic-speaking the latter were already Gaelic–English bilingual; when it became bilingual, the other communities had assimilated to English. In this way the shift itself can be a marker of ethnolinguistic distinctiveness. The continuum ranges from fully fluent speakers (subdivided into old and young) to imperfect 'semi-speakers' dominant in English but still making some use of Gaelic though with an aberrant phonology and grammar; another significant subgroup in the community are the 'passive bilinguals' who do not speak Gaelic but understand it sufficiently to be accepted as members of the community: acceptance of group values and knowledge of social norms are as important as active mastery of the language and are sufficient conditions of group membership.

In all the preceding cases language shift has been the result of subordinate groups which are under pressures of various kinds to assimilate and which cease over time to use and transmit their language to the next generation. There are, however, cases of language shift that are not caused by such pressures. Certainly neither the macro-sociological approach to language shift that emphasised the role of industrialisation, urbanisation, migration and political domination, nor a social-network approach would have been of any use in the case of language shift from the local vernacular (Taiap) to the official national creole (Tok Pisin) in the small village of Gapun, an isolated jungle community of Papua New Guinea studied by Kulick (1992). Kulick wanted to find out why adults used both languages in their repertoire while children under 10 no longer actively used the local vernacular but were acquiring instead the second language, Tok Pisin; this was happening despite the fact that their parents valorised the former as the language of their ethnic identity, wanted their children to learn and use it, and wondered why they failed to learn it. He found that, when conversing among themselves, the adults code-switched continually between Taiap and Tok Pisin; they also code-switched when talking to their children, but switching more often to Tok Pisin, even translating from Taiap into it, because they believed that the vernacular was too difficult and Tok Pisin easier for them. But this was not the only reason why adult speech to children was biased towards Tok Pisin. The two languages had become associated with traditional beliefs about the self: Taiap with *hed* (meaning the individualistic, selfish, antisocial aspect of the self) and Tok Pisin with *save* (meaning 'knowledge'), synonymous with men, cooperation and accommodation, modernity and Christianity. Thus, socialisation through accommodation resulted in adults, quite unwittingly, biasing language spoken to children towards Tok Pisin because they wanted them to suppress their *hed* (linked to Taiap) and develop their *save* (best expressed through Tok Pisin).

10.3.4   Language attrition

We have seen that languages become obsolete when speakers no longer communicate with their children in a particular variety, and that children are no longer motivated to acquire an active competence in that language. While 'language shift' denotes the loss of language functions, forms and skills between generations, 'attrition' refers to the loss of language functions, forms and skills in individuals over time. In the 'Cascade' model of attrition and shift among immigrant/minority groups (Gonzo & Saltarelli, 1983) languages are lost by a combination of intragenerational attrition and intergenerational shift: the best input the next generation can have is the already impoverished version of the language used by the previous generation.

At the linguistic level language attrition begins with strong interference from the dominant language on the subordinate one and convergence of the latter towards the former. Mougeon & Béniak (1990) have defined convergence as the gradual elimination of non-congruent forms in contact languages and interference as the introduction of foreign forms/rules into a language where they already exist. An example of convergence is the case of French spoken by the Ontario Francophone minority studied by Béniak, Mougeon & Valois (1984). For example, the prepositional phrase '*chez* + (pro)noun' is being replaced by '*à* + DET + *maison*' (where context permits) as a result of influence from English ('at/to + home/house'). (It may be argued that *à/au* is used in popular French instead of *chez*, e.g. *je vais au coiffeur*, internal simplification working towards the elimination of the less 'transparent' form and this usage may simply be reinforced by the influence of English.) The authors, however, show that the more the French language is in close contact with English at the local level and the more bilingual speakers there are, the more likely it is that the variant *à la maison* will be used.

Attrition may be characterised by a move away from the standard variety. According to Landry & Allard (1994) the lower the vitality of the Francophones in New Brunswick, the less standard and the more restricted their French outside the home and the school. Paradoxically, attrition can lead to the use of a more standardised variety of language. In their study of language shift and attrition in Ontario, Mougeon & Béniak (1994) showed that between 1978 and 1994 the use of French diminished in all interpersonal communication situations, even between siblings, whilst favourable attitudes towards French remained unchanged in the same period; the school is now the last bastion of French language maintenance. However, this has meant that the French of the new generation has become more, not less, standardised. Of course, loss of skills may be asymmetrical, productive skills going before receptive ones, as we saw in the case of attrition in Sutherland.

In their study of Dutch in Australia, de Bot & Clyne (1994) have identified the following linguistic features characteristic of attrition (in terms of both convergence and interference):

- lexical transfer, in both form and meaning;
- phonological integration of lexical transfers;
- compromise forms between English and Dutch;
- semantic and syntactic transfer, transfer of function words and code-switching.

It may be argued that French and English, and even more so Dutch and English, are typologically close. What happens in the case of typologically distinct languages? Romaine (1995) has shown that they too can undergo convergence and interference.

The minority group may mobilise around the defence of its language and resist attrition, especially if its language is a core value. Even if it is not, and the group does not become mobilised, attrition does not always occur, or occurs only incompletely. In a 16-year-long longitudinal study of language attrition among Dutch immigrants in Australia (the group with one of the greatest language shifts), de Bot & Clyne (1994), testing a large sample in 1987, found little sign of language attrition among the informants who had been tested and were still fluent in 1971. These findings are in line with those of de Bot, Gommans & Rossing (1991) who studied Dutch migrants in France. However, Waas (1993), looking at the language performance of German migrants who had been in Australia for less than 10 years, found clear signs of attrition. De Bot & Clyne suggest that language attrition occurs early on and that efforts at maintenance should therefore be concentrated in the first decade after migration, because later on the residual knowledge is likely to remain at the same level.

The subject of language loss affects the state of bilingualism in the world – that is, the fate of ethnolinguistic groups – and research is needed to determine the circumstances under which particular languages come under threat or disappear. Do languages suddenly cease to have speakers and, if so, under what circumstances? If the process is gradual, what linguistic changes occur during the last stages of the 'life' of a language? What are the identifying features of a dying language? Under what conditions should collective corrective measures be taken? What are these measures? (For a discussion of these issues, see Pan & Gleason, 1986 and Fishman, 1991.)

If a language can actually die, there is, however, another situation of languages in contact in which a new language is born out of the contact. This happens in the case of pidginisation.

10.3.5 Pidginisation, creolisation and decreolisation

The processes of pidginisation, creolisation and decreolisation overlap. Only the first and the last arise out of language-contact phenomena, whereas creoles are the outcome of a language shift. In this section we therefore focus on pidginisation and decreolisation and on the relationships between the groups that are involved in these processes. Linguistic descriptions of pidgins and post-creole continua, which have been studied extensively elsewhere (e.g. Todd, 1984; Mühlhäusler, 1986; Romaine, 1988; Lefebvre, 1998), will receive only scanty treatment here.

10.3.5.1 Pidginisation

There is a consensus among linguists and sociolinguists on how pidgins develop. It is assumed that they develop at first through the need for restricted communication between groups which do not share a common language. The starting point is therefore a situation of plurilingualism without bilinguality. Typically, a pidgin evolves out of several low-status mutually unintelligible 'substrate' languages spoken as mother tongues by a majority of the people (e.g. the West African languages of the slaves) in contact with a 'superstrate' language spoken by a relatively small but economically and socially dominant group (e.g. English or French). This situation creates the need for a lingua franca to allow communication between the speakers of the substrate and superstrate languages and among the substrate language speakers themselves. Pidgins are L_2 which result from an incomplete learning of the superstrate owing to a quantitatively and qualitatively restricted input, which may vary from situation to situation. In contrast to slow and regular linguistic change, pidgins develop very rapidly and diverge considerably from their source languages. They are mixed, borrowing from both substrates and superstrate, but in systematic ways: the forms of the lexical items are derived from the superstrate, the syntactic and semantic properties of these lexical items follow the pattern of the substrate languages.

By what processes does a pidgin, despite its almost total lexification from a superstrate, have a syntactic and semantic structure close to the substrate language(s)? Three main processes are involved in the formation of pidgins: relexification, reanalysis and dialect levelling (Lefebvre, 1988):

(1) Relexification is the process of vocabulary substitution in which the
     only information borrowed from the superstrate in the lexical entry is
     the phonological representation. The semantic and syntactic proper-
     ties of these lexical entries are those of the corresponding lexical
     entries in the substrate(s). In the following example, taken from
     Solomon Pidgin (and adapted from Keesing, 1988: 214), the phono-
     logical representations of the pidgin's lexical entries are derived from
     English, but their syntactic and semantic properties correspond to
     those of the substrate language Kwaio, including not only major
     categories (Noun, Verb, Adjective, etc.) but also minor categories
     (functional words, morphemes, Tense, etc.).

(Kwaio:)	Gila	ta-ta	leka
	RO(them)	FUT-3PL	go
(Solomon Pidgin:)	Olketa	bae-i	go
	PRO(them)	FUT-3PL	go
(English:)	all together...	by and by – he	go
(Translation)	They	will	go

When speakers of a pidgin (or early creole; see Section 10.3.5.2) start
targeting the relexified lexicons rather than the superstrate lan-
guage(s), two other processes are used: reanalysis and dialect levelling.

(2) Reanalysis, put simply, is the grammaticalisation of a lexical item
     created by relexification, as when a content word assumes the proper-
     ties of a function word or morpheme, e.g. a verb becomes a tense
     marker (see a similar phenomenon at work in code-switching/code-
     mixing, Section 9.3.1.2).
(3) Dialect levelling refers to the reduction of variation between dialects
     of the same pidgin or creole when their speakers see themselves as part
     of the same speech community and the dialects are brought closer
     together (note that this phenomenon is also known as koine or
     koineisation; Siegel, 1985).

Pidgins have sometimes evolved from trade languages, that is, they
are codes used only for limited exchange. An example of a pidgin that
developed in this way is Neo-Melanesian Pidgin or Tok Pisin, an English-based pidgin used in Papua New Guinea, which evolved in the early
twentieth century as a lingua franca between English administrators and
the indigenous population. The indigenous population speaks a large
number of mutually unintelligible languages. So effective did this pidgin
become that it all but eliminated the local vernaculars and was adopted
as the standard language of the country (Todd, 1984). Another origin of
pidgin is when people from different language backgrounds are thrown
together and have to communicate with one another and with members

of a dominant group in order to survive. This is the situation in which Africans taken as slaves to the plantations of the New World – and separated from each other to prevent intragroup communication and possible rebellion – found themselves. The only way they could communicate with each other and with their masters was through a pidgin which they developed and which remained their only means of intergroup communication. Yet, at the same time, the pidgin was also a means for the dominant group to maintain distance and non-solidarity with their slaves.

10.3.5.2 Creolisation

The classic definition of a creole – that is, a pidgin that has become the mother tongue of a community (a process known as 'nativisation') – was given a language-universal interpretation by Bickerton (1981), who argued that children who learned it as a mother tongue brought their innate linguistic faculties to create, in one generation, a systematic and expanded grammar out of the rudimentary, non-standard pidgin of their parents. Most recent fieldwork studies of pidginisation and creolisation, however, have shown that the most important factor of change is not nativisation per se, but the radical changes in the sociolinguistic environment which have necessitated a function expansion of the code. The crucial point is whether adults or children begin to use the pidgin as the main language of communication to meet an increasingly wide range of social functions. According to Jourdan & Keesing (1997), who have investigated the creolisation process in the Solomon Islands over 15 years, it is adults, for whom the pidgin is a second language, that play a major role in the functional expansion of the pidgin when they first experience urbanisation. 'The adults, the first urbanising generation, and their children, the first nativising generation, play complementary roles as agents of linguistic change' (p. 412). The authors define creole genesis in the following way:

(1) It is a lengthy process which is not speeded up by nativisation.
(2) Different varieties of a pidgin/creole may coexist.
(3) Adults and children play a complementary role in the creolisation process.
(4) Creolisation must be studied in the context of the sociolinguistic complexity of the speech communities where pidgins/creoles develop. (Taken from Jourdan & Keesing, 1997: 417.)

As well as a major expansion of form–function mapping, there is a significant shift in the patterns of language use in the community. When a creole develops it is often at the expense of other languages spoken in the same area, in particular vernaculars. But because a creole has a lower status than the standard superstrate language from which it derives and with which it usually coexists, creole speakers find themselves under pressure to change their speech in the direction of the standard. This process is known as decreolisation.

10.3.5.3 Decreolisation

If creoles are allowed to develop in isolation from the superstrate languages, then they become distinct languages. But the majority of creoles have coexisted with their base languages and this coexistence has brought about a post-creole continuum, often described as decreolisation. This is the process by which the creole is modified at all linguistic levels in the direction of the standard variety of the superstrate. This modification varies as a function of the speakers' attempts to identify with the speakers of the high-status base language. According to Bickerton (1975), the post-creole continuum links a series of 'lects' or varieties, each arising from a minimal restructuring of the preceding one, ranging from the most archaic and socially low lect (called the basilect) to the least creolised and closest to the regional standard (called the acrolect). But since speakers are differentially affected by decreolisation and, according to Bickerton, can even understand and speak different lects, it is not the language that is changing but speakers who use different varieties in different situations (see Le Page & Tabouret-Keller, 1985).

We may have given the impression that the threefold process of pidginisation, creolisation and decreolisation is unidirectional and inevitable. This is not so. We are dealing here with dynamic and changing systems of communication which develop from languages in contact; but creolisation does not follow from pidginisation if the speech community has no need for it; and decreolisation will not occur if the creole remains outside the influence of the base language. Some creoles have disappeared, like Negerhollands in the Virgin Islands; others have developed independently from the superstrate, like the creoles of Surinam, St Lucia or Curaçao; in a diglossic situation, like that of Haiti, the creole not only survives but invades domains and functions hitherto reserved for the High language (in this case, French). There is some evidence that the Creole English of slaves who were released from slavery and returned to West Africa was repidginised by the peoples among whom the ex-slaves settled, and became the Pidgin English of countries like Cameroon (Todd, 1984). We saw earlier how West Indian adolescents in Britain actually recreolise their speech as a symbol of their redefined identity.

Thus, speakers of mutually unintelligible languages in unequal and asymmetrical intergroup relations, like slaves in relation to their slavers, develop a new language for limited communication purposes. When this limited language extends its domains of use and its range of communicative and other functions, it becomes more complex and expands linguistically, begins to stabilise and, if it is learned as a mother tongue, evolves into a creole. Decreolisation occurs in a multilingual situation in contact with the base language and changes in its direction because of social and economic pressures to use the standard. Pidgins and creoles are therefore real languages, suited to the uses for which they are developed. Furthermore, their study enables us to witness and try to understand how languages evolve; their variety and speed of transformation give us insights into language and language behaviour.

In the penultimate section of this chapter we bring together some language-contact phenomena and analyse the implications of these for language behaviour and linguistic theory.

10.4   IMPLICATIONS OF LANGUAGE-CONTACT PHENOMENA FOR LINGUISTIC THEORY

The study of languages in contact has confirmed us in the view that variation and change in language and language behaviour at the group as well as the individual and interpersonal levels are not the exception but the norm. This is because language, in addition to being a tool for communication and a cognitive organiser, is also a symbol and an instrument of individual and group identity and norms, and of intergroup power relations. As these relations, identities and norms change, so do language and language behaviour. But variation and change are not uniform; individuals and groups behave differently and change at different rates on different dimensions. As a result, language contact has differential and at times opposite consequences for language and language behaviour.

When individuals and groups come into contact, their languages inevitably also come into contact. These may either converge or diverge, or converge and diverge at one and the same time. This is because the degree of variation in intralingual and interlingual uses depends on the relative strength of two tendencies in society: the tendency to reduce intergroup and interpersonal differences (convergence) and the tendency to accentuate these differences (divergence). The former, convergence – which Le Page (1978) calls 'focusing' – is found where speakers are in close and constant contact and where there is a consensus on the norms of language behaviour. It is characteristic of small communities with dense and multiplex social networks, or else societies where a standard written language is imposed as the legitimate norm or a linguistic 'commonwealth' (e.g. International French on 'le monde de la Francophonie' or Koranic Arabic on the Islamic world). The latter tendency, divergence – which Le Page (1978) calls 'diffusion' – prevails in situations where there are no imposed or self-imposed norms, where social network links are loose and simplex, leading to wide variations in usage. Language creativity is then at its highest, as in pidgins. In one case we have relative stability, in the other variability. Sometimes both tendencies are at work. A look at a number of cases will make our point clear. We will look in turn at (1) hybrid languages; (2) mixed languages; and (3) code-switching.

(1)   Hybrid languages. The 3000 inhabitants of Kupwar, a small border village in South India, between them speak four languages: Marathi, Urdu (both Indo-European), Kannada and Telugu (both Dravidian). The community is divided into clearly distinct groups or castes, each identified by its language. As the villagers need to communicate they (especially the men) learn each other's languages. These languages have coexisted for centuries and they have converged, at least as far as the syntax is concerned. They have become much more similar than they are elsewhere (the convergence is essentially towards Marathi, the state language). However, they are still totally distinct in their vocabularies, which serve as a powerful symbol of each group's ethnic identity and distinctiveness (Gumperz and Wilson, 1971). This case contradicts universal rules of borrowing, according to which lexical items are the easiest to borrow and syntax the most resistant.

To explain the Kupwar case Hudson (1980) put forward a tentative hypothesis to explain the relations of the different linguistics levels to intergroup relations. Syntax is the marker of social cohesion; in contrast, vocabulary is a marker of caste and religion; pronunciation reflects the permanent groups with which a speaker identifies. 'This results in a tendency for individuals to suppress alternatives, but in contrast to the tendency with syntax, different groups suppress different alternatives in order to distinguish themselves from each other, and some individuals keep some alternatives alive in order to be able to identify their origins even more precisely, by using them in a particular and distinctive proportion relative to other alternatives' (p. 48). This explanation is completely in line with Le Page (1968) on the one hand, and with Tajfel's (1978) theory of social psychological distinctiveness on the other.

(2)   Mixed languages. These are ingroup languages, usually with their grammatical structure from one language and the lexicon from another. Examples of just a few of the many mixed languages are:

• Romani which is a mixture of Persian, Armenian, Greek, Norwegian, English, Basque, Spanish and Serbian;
• Maltese which is Arabic with borrowings from Italian and English;

- Media Lingua which is a mixture of Spanish and Quechua (see Bakker & Mous, 1994).

An intriguing language is Michif, a mixed language spoken by mixed blood buffalo hunters in Western Canada and North Dakota (Papen, 1987; Bakker, 1994). The internal structure (phonology, morphology, syntax and lexis) of the nominal phrase is essentially French (Western Canada variety), while that of the verb phrase is essentially Cree (an Algonquian, polysynthetic language, typologically very different from French). In the following, an extreme example of Michif (Bakker, 1994):

NI	PAKWAT	EN	SI	le*can*	er-YAN	dans le temps	pesant
I	hate	it	COMP	the can	INF-1SG	in the weather	heavy

('I don't like to can in heavy weather.')

a lexical borrowing from English (the verb 'to can') is preceded by the French definite article 'le' and followed by the French infinitive morpheme 'er'. Because of the polysynthetic structure of Cree, it would be impossible for the Michif to have a Cree grammatical system with a French lexicon. Is Michif a case of code-switching? The answer must be no because in stable code-switching (see Section 9.3.2) locutors are competent in both languages, and most speakers of Michif speak neither French nor Cree (it may, of course, have started as code-switching). Is it pidgin? No, because Michif is the mother tongue of its speakers and its grammar is fully developed. Then is it a creole? Insofar as a creole is the development of a pidgin, then Michif is not a creole. Moreover, Michif is an in-group language and creoles are developed for communication across languages. Michif is also different from other mixed languages, like Media Lingua, in that the lexicon of the latter is 90 per cent Spanish, while its syntax is 100 per cent Quechua. Michif – and other mixed languages like it – poses a real puzzle for and challenge to linguistic theory: What is its syntax? What do categorial rules look like, since French and Cree are typologically so different? How should the lexis be organised? Does Michif have one or two phonologies? These are some of the questions which linguists have to answer.

(3)   If we now take the examples of code-switching and code-mixing discussed in Section 9.3, we find very different types of situation. On the one hand, we have those cases where code-switching appears to be random, which may signal that processes of shift are at work in a language or in the relationship between two languages. The situation is a diffuse one, interactants not seemingly engaging in acts of identity, and presumably this type of code-switching is not transmitted, because circumstances are changing all the time. Or, in the case of mixed compound verbs in Punjabi–English

or (Cypriot) Greek–English code-switching we have convergent structures. On the other hand, we seem to have a rule-governed type of code-switching, with constraint/facilitation rules that do not suggest any convergence of the two codes, but which is used as a code for communicating between members of a speech community and symbolising group membership. However, not all members have the same communicative competence of the type which is acquired through a process of syntactic maturation. We have here a focused behaviour converging on a code-switched norm, though it would appear that it is already diversifying through the differential competence of its speakers.

Thus, variation and change are the essence of language because the latter is at once the expression, symbol and instrument of a group's ethnic identity and of its dynamic relations to other groups in a society. As group boundaries are not static (but change), so identity changes; language also changes with it, and so do speakers' relations to language. Languages are not homogeneous entities. The same language – depending on whether its speakers are converging on a stable norm or diverging and causing the language to diffuse – changes little or fragments into different varieties. However, different levels of language change differentially to express varying group identities. From the semantics of one language, the lexis of another and the universal rules of language acquisition, a pidgin evolves to allow its speakers to communicate and express definite relationships between two groups who could not otherwise communicate. A switched code can both borrow and assimilate nouns from one language and be used in alternation with it intrasententially, and yet the two languages do not appear to converge. Language varies along multidimensional continua. Its speakers identify with some of the varieties, and their verbal repertoire is an expression of these identities. But where does all this leave language? Where is the ideal speaker-hearer in a homogeneous speech community? Where is the variable rule which deals with community grammars and alternative ways of saying the same thing? How can one identify, describe and compare every lect on a creole continuum? One tends to forget that when one says 'language' one means its user(s). Only a social and psychological linguistics of the future may be able to tackle these questions. All we can hope to achieve now is to ask some of the right questions.

10.5   LANGUAGE PLANNING

Confronted with many different languages within its boundaries, how does a country solve its communication problems, given the complexities of ethnolinguistic group relations, some of which have been described in the preceding pages? There are a number of alternative solutions. First, a state can impose one official, national language – usually the dominant, legitimised language – upon the population as a whole by devalorising, ignoring or eliminating the other languages. This solution has often been adopted, leading to the extinction of minority and regional languages. France is a case in point. In the pursuit of national unity, the French State, using a variety of methods, succeeded, from the 1539 Ordonnance de Villers-Cotterêts onwards, in imposing the Parisian dialect of the ruling elites upon the whole French population and most of its overseas colonies (Calvet, 1974; Bourhis, 1982).

Today, however, a given state may use the subtler instrument of language planning, which is a particular form of economic and social planning. Indeed, language can be considered as a human resource, and society – or a group claiming to speak on its behalf – takes upon itself the task of organising language communication in interethnic group language relations. Language planning should therefore be studied in the context of the economic, social and cultural conditions in which it is applied. Too many works on the subject fail to examine the assumptions upon which language planners base their practices, namely the legitimising philosophy of the dominant group or groups in society (G. Williams, 1992). Language planning can be a tool for domination and control by the majority; but it can also be used as a potentially revolutionary force by minorities. Fishman (1994) has severely criticised the often unstated assumptions behind language-planning policies. He points out that they are often conducted by elites governed by their own self-interest, that they reproduce social and cultural inequalities, that they inhibit or counteract multiculturalism, and that they are Western-centred and lead to a form of neocolonialism. Two main aspects of language planning can be distinguished: an internal aspect and an external aspect.

Internal planning has also been called language engineering (Wurm, 1977) or language-corpus planning (Kloss, 1969). It constitutes a systematic interference with the internal dynamic processes to which languages are subject. Such interference can be restrictive or creative. Restrictive interference includes standardisation through artificial neutralisation of geographical and social variations, or the 'purification' of the language from foreign influences. Among types of creative interference are the introduction of a writing system for an unwritten language, the standardisation of its alphabet or orthography, or the expansion and modernisation of the lexicon through terminology and neology, etc. The reasons for this interference are implicit in the cases listed above; however, the reasons are not only internal to the language, they are matters of policy decision and implementation, as language reform in China demonstrates (de Francis, 1984).

Confronted with the problems posed by the many mutually unintelligible dialects/languages, Chinese language planners decided to standardise the spoken language (Putonghua, or common speech). They took Northern speech as the basic regional dialect, Beijing pronunciation as the phonetic standard, and modern vernacular as the grammatical norm. The vocabulary was based on modern popular literature, characters were simplified and a new phonetic alphabet, Pinyin, was created (but its use to date remains limited). The reasons put forward for the reform are various and include:

- demographic (70 per cent of Chinese speak the Northern dialect);
- geographic (the chosen dialect is spoken from Manchuria to Yunnan);
- communicative;
- linguistic (the dialects are mutually unintelligible);
- political (the country's diversity is an obstacle to political unity and economic development);
- educational (the rural masses were illiterate); and
- ideological (consider the Marxist-Leninist position on the national-language question).

China is caught in a dilemma: if it maintains the traditional system of characters as the exclusive means of writing, most Chinese will be condemned to illiteracy and the country's modernisation program will be impeded; if it makes Pinyin a proper phonetic alphabet to meet the needs of modern society, it risks a breakdown in communication through the written word.

External language planning (Wurm, 1977), or language-status planning (Kloss, 1969), is concerned with artificially interfering with existing status relations between languages in contact. As we saw in the preceding section, status is a function of the relative economic, demographic, social and political power of the linguistic groups that speak those languages, and of their subjective perceptions of the power relations in the wider society. Two main approaches confront each other: nationalism and nationism (Fishman, 1968). In the case of nationalism, language acts as a powerful symbol of ethnic identification for groups which, resisting fusion into the larger nationality, develop a national consciousness of their own. In the case of nationism, on the other hand, a language is selected for reasons of national efficiency. The requirements of nationalism and nationism can, of course, be in conflict where language is concerned. However, the two notions are not dichotomous; rather they stand on a continuum. Chinese language reform is typical of nationism. The cases of Quebec and Flanders, cited earlier, exemplify a nationalist solution. But most cases fall somewhere between the two, especially in multinational states, where the solution adopted may be variable. Some examples of solutions are:

- one or more indigenous languages are used for all circumstances;
- one or more regional languages are given national status together with an international language;
- an international language is used exclusively as an official language.

All three solutions have their advantages and drawbacks (Le Page, 1964). A comparative study of Singapore and Malaysia is relevant in this respect.

Both Singapore and Malaysia are multicultural, multiethnic, multi-religious and multilingual societies. It is noteworthy that while these countries have evolved along similar historical lines and are composed of the same ethnic communities (though in different proportions), they have chosen radically different approaches to language planning. Malaysia seems to have chosen the solution of nationism (or 'depluralisation'): divided along political, linguistic, ethnic, religious and economic lines, it has followed a path of cultural assimilation with the adoption of Malay (Bahasa Malaysia) as the sole official language of the country. In Singapore, by contrast, the traditional values of each major ethnic group have been fostered, promoting multiculturalism and pluralism: a policy of cultural integration has been pursued, with the four main languages (English, Malay, Mandarin and Tamil) having been declared official. But this policy is not strictly speaking one of nationalism. While encouraging the ethnic languages (the 'symbolic mother tongues') as a cultural foundation for the retention of traditional values and the teaching of literacy at primary school level, it has also emphasised the utilitarian nature of English as the basis for a supra-ethnic Singaporean identity. (See Ward & Hewstone (1985) who have also made cross-cultural comparisons of the two situations in terms of ethnic identity and intergroup relations.)

One of the most intractable but urgent problems of language planning worldwide is ensuring at least functional literacy, that is, a level of literacy that enables people to function in a given society. This is not so much a technical as a social issue, since illiteracy is an obstacle to informed citizen participation in decision-making at all levels of society as well as to national development. Illiteracy is a problem not only for the Third World but also for developed countries which have recently seen a sharp rise in illiteracy rates. This rise is due to the marginalisation of immigrant communities and the rise of unemployment, to falls in public educational standards simultaneously with higher literacy expectations in the labour market, while new electronic media give wider access to information with limited amounts of literacy. Unfortunately, both status and corpus planning are not adequate instruments for tackling the wider social issues of literacy. The limited success of large-scale, state measures would suggest applying small-scale, local solutions with multiple literacy programs at all levels (see Tabouret-Keller, Le Page, Gardner-Chloros & Varro, 1997). Literacy in pidgin vernaculars in multiethnic, multilingual societies raises even greater problems: it is the future of these pidgins as spoken codes different from the base languages (English, French) which is in question. They have come to resemble the standard languages so closely that the problem of writing will soon no longer exist: 'The autonomy of the . . . pidgins will be more and more compromised as they come into contact with their source languages, even that of the basilectal variety, making any literacy in these pidgins for ever impossible' (Charpentier, 1997: 245). We return to the issue of vernacular literacy in Chapter 11.

It is beyond the scope of this chapter to propose a typology of language-planning solutions throughout the world. For recent studies on language planning see, from a political angle, Dua (1996) and, from an economic angle, Grin (1996).

We end this section by examining the presumed link between multilingualism and national underdevelopment. Does the fact that a country is culturally and linguistically diverse and heterogeneous cause that country to be economically disadvantaged? Are nation-states more likely to be stable than multinational states? Given the importance of language for ethnicity and nationalism, is a sense of nation more difficult to develop for a multilingual state than for a unilingual one? Choosing (1) gross domestic product (GDP) per capita as a measure of economic development and (2) the size of the largest native speech community relative to the total population as a measure of linguistic diversity, Pool (1969) calculated these two values and the correlations between them for 133 countries. He concluded that a country can have any degree of linguistic uniformity or fragmentation and still be underdeveloped. He also found that a wholly unilingual country can range from being very rich to being very poor. However, a country that is linguistically highly heterogeneous is always underdeveloped or semideveloped, whereas a country that is highly developed always has considerable language uniformity.

Both Pool's evidence and his methodology have been challenged. First, are the measures valid and reliable? The operationalisation of the concepts is problematic and the data on which the correlations are based is at best unreliable. In any case, correlation does not mean causality: in order to demonstrate causality it would be necessary to use longitudinal data to show that reduction in diversity resulted in increased development and vice versa. Lieberson & Hansen (1974) correlated the Greenberg–Lieberson measure of linguistic diversity (see Section 2.2.3.1) with three measures of development (GNP per capita, urbanisation, literacy) between 1930 and 1960 and concluded that:

- there was only a small tendency for low-language-diversity (i.e. unilingual) nations to have a high per capita GNP;
- diversity was not related to either lack of urbanisation or illiteracy; and
- increasing the time difference to 100 years failed to produce any connection between development and diversity.

A crucial factor seems to be the fact that most less-developed nations are former colonies whose language diversity was artificially produced by the imperial powers who carved up countries (e.g. Africa) without any concern for ethnic and linguistic boundaries.

In reviewing language-planning policies we have seen that languages which were adopted as national languages often had what Kuo (1979) calls high communicativity (e.g. China's Putonghua or Malaysia's Bahasa Malaysia; other examples are Tanzania's Swahili and Indonesia's Bahasa Indonesia). Moreover, today some of the most dynamic cities in the world are among the most ethnically and linguistically heterogeneous: Hong Kong, New York, Singapore, Sydney and Toronto, to name a few. However, we must let Weinreich (1953) have the final word: he rightly points out that the higher the linguistic diversity of a country the higher the degree of bilingualism (bilinguality); where there are many people who speak different languages, people learn each other's languages. In other words, bilingualism compensates for diversity.

10.6   CONCLUSION

This chapter has dealt with languages in contact at the level of intergroup relations. In the first part we looked at language as a symbol of a group's identity. We saw that language is not only a reflection of intergroup and intragroup relations, but that it can also be a powerful factor in the definition, creation, maintenance and transformation of these relations. A social instrumental function should be added to the social symbolic function of language. In the second part we examined the construct of ethnolinguistic vitality as one attempt to explain both the role of socio-structural factors in interethnic group relations and the perception of these factors by individuals in the maintenance or loss of the language(s) of a group. We concluded that the relationship between language and ethnicity is not a simple one: not only is it not a necessary relation, but language and ethnicity do not stand in a one-to-one correspondence. For language to be a salient characteristic of group identity, it must be perceived by members of a group as a core value of their culture. We went on to stress the fact that a group is no more homogeneous in its perception of the role and value of its language(s) than it is in its language behaviour. We surveyed a number of multicultural and multilingual situations in which the relations of ethnolinguistic groups to the different languages in contact are highly complex and vary in geographical and social space as well as over time.

In the third part three sociolinguistic phenomena relating to languages in contact at the intergroup level were examined. These are:

(1) diglossia, a relatively stable situation in which two different languages cooccur throughout the speech community, each with a distinct range of social functions;

(2) language shift, a situation in which over a period of time a social group gives up the use of its first language and replaces it by another spoken in the society; and

(3) pidginisation, or the development of a new code resulting from the need of different groups speaking mutually unintelligible languages in order to communicate with one another over a limited range of social functions; we also followed the evolution of pidgins through the processes of creolisation and decreolisation.

In the penultimate section we briefly discussed the implications of language-contact phenomena for linguistic and sociolinguistic theory. In particular, we argued that the study of speech repertoires, code-switching, pidginisation and decreolisation calls into question certain current views on the nature of language and verbal communication. In the final section we looked at the management of language forms and uses at the national level in language planning.

One of the main concerns of this chapter has been to highlight the necessity of (1) bringing together objective group factors, and their subjective perceptions and interpretations by group members and (2) trying to bridge the conceptual gap between macro (social phenomena) and micro (psychological processes). Our analysis has shown that there is a constant interaction between the dynamics of the societal processes and the dynamics of individual processes. For example, ethnolinguistic vitality is at least a three-dimensional concept: it involves socio-structural factors, interpersonal behaviour, individual perceptions and the interactions between these. According to the outcome of these interactions there will be a self-regulated behaviour: members of an ethnolinguistic group may act upon a change in their perceptions of their vitality and consequently decide to change their behaviour. For example, the consciousness raising of the Quebecois – resulting from a higher level of education and a freeing from traditional institutions – brought about a change in attitudes and language behaviour.

Our analysis has also demonstrated the constant and complex mapping processes between form and function at all levels and across all levels. In the case of pidginisation, the development of new forms of language behaviour is brought about by the introduction of a new function in the community; for example, the need to trade between groups who do not speak the same language results in the creation of a pidgin; because the function is simple, the pidgin is simple; when new functions appear, such as cooperation for work among pidgin-speakers, the latter need new forms to serve these new functions. The pidgin, therefore, becomes more complex and eventually evolves into a creole which, because of its social importance, becomes the mother tongue of the next generation. Concomitantly, the vernaculars hitherto spoken by the community begin to lose some of their functions and, therefore, are reduced in form and eventually become extinct. The same form–function mapping can be seen at work in diglossia, language shift, etc. This interpretation of these phenomena is in line with our connectionist interactional principles.

11   Bilingual education

This chapter addresses the question of bilingual education and the application of theories of bilinguality and bilingualism in this domain. We first raise the problem of literacy (Section 11.1); we then review a number of definitions and discuss some typologies of bilingual education (Section 11.2); in Section 11.3 we analyse various factors which condition bilingual education; we go on to describe two types of bilingual education – one developed for children of the dominant group in society (Section 11.4), the other for ethnolinguistic minorities (Section 11.5) – and discuss their outcome in the light of our model of bilingual development. Finally, other forms of bilingual education are examined (Section 11.6).

In Chapters 4 and 5 we argued that simultaneous and early consecutive bilinguality – in which the two languages are highly valorised and used for all functions with the child – both lead to an additive form, whereas consecutive childhood bilinguality – in which the mother tongue is devalorised and language is not used in all its functions – may lead to a subtractive form. We insisted on the importance for the child of developing the appropriate social representations of language, especially when he is introduced to formal schooling and literacy through a highly valorised L_2 (see Chapter 5).

11.1   LITERACY AND LANGUAGE PLANNING IN EDUCATION

Education, defined as an 'organised and sustained communication designed to bring about learning' (UNESCO, 1976), aims at developing the organisation of knowledge and skilled abilities. In modern societies these goals are attained through the development of literacy skills in a school environment. From an educational perspective, literacy can be viewed as a communication skill which involves a written mode of verbal transmission (reading and writing) employed by literate societies for effective functioning in a changing socio-ecological setting (Srivastava, 1984a). The importance attached to the development of literacy is based on a worldwide conviction

318

that literacy is an instrument for changing the individual's perception and organisation of cognition, and that this leads to economic improvement and is a prerequisite for all functional education.

Since McLuhan's (1962) pioneering work *The Gutenberg Galaxy*, the impact of literacy on the world and on all aspects of life has been broadly recognised. It is of tremendous significance to both the industrialised and the developing countries and is achieved chiefly through schooling. The development of literacy is strongly associated with academic and social success (Ogbu, 1988). In technological societies semi-literate people easily encounter problems of social integration: they have great difficulties in filling in forms, going through job interviews or helping their children with their school work. The semi-literate person is confined to social isolation and to a greatly restricted world (Poissant & Hamers, 1996).

There are millions of semi-literate people in the industrialised countries. For example, in Canada – on the basis of the *Southam Literacy Survey* (Southam News, 1987) defining an illiterate person as someone unable to complete many reading and numeracy tasks that adults commonly face in everyday life – it is estimated that 24 per cent of the adult population is semi-literate. Similar figures exist for the USA and for Britain. Furthermore, the semi-literacy rates of ethnolinguistic minorities exceed the national averages (Poissant & Hamers, 1996). The literacy–illiteracy issue should not be viewed as a dichotomy but rather as a continuum. Tabouret-Keller, Le Page, Gardner-Chloros & Varro (1997) who also view literacy–illiteracy on a continuum distinguish between non-literate societies where literacy is replacing oral traditions, and literate societies where levels of illiteracy at the end of the twentieth century are rising for economic and social reasons (e.g. immigration, unemployment, etc.).

A number of authors have stressed the social collective dimension of literacy. For example, social-literacy approaches, based on Bourdieu's sociological theory (1986), view literacy as social practice. This view marks it off both from a psychological, skill-oriented model of literacy as a purely cognitive activity divorced from the socio-political context, and from a narrow pedagogical perspective. In this approach literacy is a 'cultural capital', which must be 'authorised', that is, valorised by society as a whole for the benefit of all. While schooling undoubtedly promotes specific literacy practices, it is a necessary but not sufficient condition of literacy development, for it produces different kinds and levels of literacy reflecting power relations in society. In other words, there is no one single literacy that can be taught with simple equivalent value in cultural capital (Baker, Cook-Gumperz & Luke, 1997). The school-based literacy practices, therefore, are not sufficient to guarantee economic and social gains to all who demonstrate them. To improve the access to academic and cultural capital of, for example, subordinate ethnolinguistic groups, would require, if it is to be effective, intervention from two directions. On the one hand, intervention is required from other valued social institutions and, on the other hand, it is required from what Fairclough (1992) calls 'critical language awareness'. The latter is an analysis and critique of the power relations associated with particular discourses and texts and, of course, with the very language of instruction. As language use is embedded in context-specific social practices and traditions, different cultural contexts demand a plurality of different literacy practices, using, for example, oral communication, computation, problem-solving and decision-making, as well as written communication skills (see Crandall, 1992; McKay, 1993). In all this the issue of the 'language(s)' of instruction is paramount.

The choice of the language medium through which literacy is achieved is an essential issue in a multicultural setting. Two opposite claims are made by planners concerning the achievement of literacy:

(1) literacy is most effectively achieved in the mother tongue;
(2) it is most effectively achieved in a language of wider communication which possesses a written culture and economic power.

The first claim is based on pedagogical concerns, whereas the second claim relies more on economic preoccupations. These two claims result in two different planning choices with regard to the language of education. The first claim, in its extreme form, leads to a curriculum exclusively in the mother tongue; this is the case in many developed countries, because majority groups whose mother tongue is also a language of wider communication with an extended written tradition (e.g. the Anglophones in the USA and the Francophones in France) can follow the entire curriculum from nursery school to university degrees in one language.

The second claim, in its most extreme form, leads to a monolingual curriculum in an official language which is not the child's mother tongue, as, for example, in some of the former French colonies in Africa where the one and only language of instruction is the exogenous language left by the colonisers (e.g. Benin and Togo, where education starts in French from nursery school onwards). Education exclusively through an L_2 often occurs for minority groups all over the world, for one of three reasons:

- language planning is such that it does not recognise the right to be educated in a non-official language (e.g. France, Belgium, Malaysia);
- the community size is too small to justify mother-tongue education (e.g. the case of many minorities in African and Asian countries, where a limited number of the numerically important national languages are used in education, e.g. Mali, India); or

- the cost of writing down a non-written language, creating teaching materials and training teachers in the mother tongue is too high.

Between these two extreme cases we find a variety of solutions which combine mother tongue and second languages to various extents in the curriculum. Most of these programs are based on the 'linguistic mismatch hypothesis', endorsed by UNESCO (1953), according to which a mismatch between home language and school language is the major cause of poor academic achievement of minority children. Srivastava (1984a; 1990), for example, advocates a literacy model for minority children in India, in which literacy is first introduced in the child's mother tongue; once the basic literacy skills are attained, the curriculum transfers to a formal language of education. Many varieties of these vernacular-cum-transfer literacy models are to be found all over the world. For example, in the numerous African countries where part or whole of elementary school is taught through the child's mother tongue and then education is continued through the exogenous official language, English or French. However, this switch is often not planned through a bilingual education program and children are not always prepared for it.

11.2   DEFINITIONS AND TYPOLOGIES OF BILINGUAL EDUCATION

In the literature the term 'bilingual education' is used to describe a variety of educational programs involving two or more languages to varying degrees. In this chapter we limit our definition to describe any system of school education in which, at a given moment in time and for a varying amount of time, simultaneously or consecutively, instruction is planned and given in at least two languages.

This definition insists on the use of the two languages as media of instruction; it does not include curricula in which a second or foreign language is taught as a subject, with no other use in academic activities, although L_2 teaching may be part of a bilingual education program. We also exclude from our definition the cases in which a switch in the medium of instruction occurs at a given moment with no further planning of the two languages in the curriculum, as happens, for instance, in the numerous cases of 'submersion' in which an individual child attends a program taught in the mother tongue of a different ethnolinguistic group and where the curriculum ignores this child's mother tongue: this is usually the case with immigrant children in mainstream education. However, we do refer to some of these cases insofar as they tell us something about bilingual development in education.

Considering our definition, most programs of bilingual education fit into one of three categories:

(1) Instruction is given in both languages simultaneously.
(2) Instruction is given first in L_1 and the pupil is taught until such time as he is able to use L_2 as a means of learning.
(3) The largest proportion of instruction is given through L_2, and L_1 is introduced at a later stage, first as a subject and later as a medium of instruction.

This is a far cry from Mackey's (1970; 1976) typology in which he distinguishes 90 types of bilingual education. He proposes a typology based on language use and distributed in space and time in four domains: home, school, environment and nation. However detailed this typology may be, it lacks a theoretical base and fails to distinguish wider categories of bilingual education. More satisfactory is the taxonomy developed by Fishman & Lovas (1970) from a sociolinguistic perspective. This taxonomy comprises three main categories defined by three sets of variables: intensity, goal and status. Within the first category (intensity) four types of bilingual program are identified:

(1) transitional bilingualism, in which L_1 is only used to facilitate the transition to an unmarked language (an assimilationist perspective);
(2) monoliterate bilingualism, in which the school uses two languages in all its activities, but only one (L_2) to initiate the child into literacy skills;
(3) partial biliterate bilingualism, in which both languages are used orally and for writing, but academic subjects are divided in such a way that L_1 is used for so-called 'cultural subjects', i.e. history, arts and folklore, and L_2 for science, technology and economics (here we are dealing with a case of educational diglossia);
(4) total biliterate bilingualism, in which all abilities are developed in the two languages for all domains.

Within the second category (goal), bilingual education can be divided into the following three dimensions:

(1) compensatory programs, in which the child is first schooled in his mother tongue in order to be better integrated into mainstream education;
(2) enrichment programs, normally designed for majority-group children, which aim at developing an additive form of bilinguality;
(3) group-maintenance programs, in which the language and culture of the minority child are preserved and enhanced.

The argument against these programs is that they lead to socio-political disruption; the programs are often defended on ideological grounds, in the name of linguistic and cultural pluralism.

The third set of variables (status) comprises four dimensions:

(1) language of primary importance vs. language of secondary importance in education;
(2) home language vs. school language;
(3) major world language versus minor language; and
(4) institutionalised language vs. non-institutionalised language in the community.

Some of these combinations are more predictive of success of bilingual education than others (Fishman, 1977a).

Although these typologies attempt to classify bilingual education, they lack theoretical foundations and tend to ignore the determining factors in bilingual education. These factors are social, historical, socio-structural, cultural, ideological and social psychological in nature. Therefore, only an interdisciplinary approach which takes all these factors into account simultaneously will enable us to understand the problems and sort out the confusion existing in the field of bilingual education (Paulston, 1975). In the next section we examine these factors in detail.

11.3   FACTORS CONDITIONING BILINGUAL EDUCATION

As we have argued, bilingual education is not an independent but an intervening variable in the development of literacy. School can facilitate the introduction of new ideas and methods but it cannot be a powerful counter to social and economic forces; in other words, since it reflects society, it cannot really compensate for deficiencies that a society may have (Bernstein, 1970; Paulston, 1992). What, then, are the factors which condition bilingual education?

11.3.1   Social historical and ideological factors

Since the end of the Second World War the problems of bilingual education have increasingly taken on worldwide importance because of a number of political, economic, ideological and educational events. Politically former colonies became independent: most of these countries are multilingual as a consequence of the arbitrary divisions by colonial powers; furthermore, they are countries facing serious problems of development. As economic development demands the use of a language of wider communication, the language of the coloniser is still used and often remains the official language or one of the official languages as, for example, in many African countries or in India (Calvet, 1974). Furthermore, these countries must cope with problems of language planning and choice of the language of education: often there is a lack of teachers and teaching materials for instruction in national languages (Calvet, 1981; Siguan & Mackey, 1987). From a demographic perspective we have often witnessed massive movements of populations for different reasons:

- internal migration due to the exodus towards rapidly industrialising urban centres;
- external migrations as a consequence of revolutions (e.g. Cuba), wars (e.g. Vietnam) and decolonisation (e.g. the end of colonial empires); or
- migration of labour from undeveloped regions towards highly industrialised countries in Europe, Canada and Australia.

In addition, more and more individuals and their families stay abroad for a lengthy period of time. All these population movements have important consequences for languages in contact and bilingual education (Lewis, 1978; 1981).

The period following the Second World War witnessed an ethnic revolution (Fishman, 1977b) in which numerous minorised ethnic groups (whose status was defined by a dominant group) became conscious of their ethnic identity and mobilised around language as a symbol (see Section 10.2.2). This happened simultaneously:

- for indigenous minorities living in underdeveloped regions of Europe, such as the Welsh in Great Britain, the Bretons and Basques in France, the Basques and Catalans in Spain and the Friesians in Holland;
- for the Native Americans of the USA and Canada;
- for more recently established ethnic minorities in countries like the USA, Canada and Australia. In the USA, for example, ethnic minorities which were thought to be assimilated into the American melting pot started claiming their right to their language, their culture and bilingual education for their children (Glazer & Moynihan, 1963); and
- for guestworkers all over Europe (see J. Edwards, 1984; 1985).

The diversity and expansion of bilingual education programs are also determined by other social historical factors:

- the expansion and democratisation of education throughout the world, and more particularly in developing countries;

- economic, social, political and technical development;
- the universalisation of mass media; and
- recent ideological trends which confer positive values on cultural pluralism.

Developing countries have to plan nationwide education, sometimes for numerous ethnolinguistic groups, some of which speak an unwritten language. Developed countries where education was traditionally monolingual have started planning programs which should answer some of the demands of their ethnic minorities.

In which language should a child be schooled? UNESCO (1953), stressing the relevance of the mother tongue for children's development, recognised for every child the right to be educated through his own vernacular. In a number of countries, where for many children the mainstream language of education is different from the mother tongue, legislation has recognised the right to bilingual education. In the USA, for example, the passage of the Bilingual Education Act (Title vii) in 1968 recognised the right of minority children with limited English-speaking abilities to receive education in their early school years through their mother tongue while they become proficient in English (for further details, see Thernstrom, 1980; J. Edwards, 1985). In 1977, an EEC Council Directive asked its members to take appropriate measures to guarantee guest workers' children the opportunity to learn the host language while maintaining the heritage language and culture, in accordance with the legislation of each country. In the United Kingdom, where the legal responsibility for school curricula lay with local education authorities, several mother-tongue teaching programs were developed in areas with high concentrations of ethnic minorities (V. K. Edwards, 1984).

However, the movement in favour of bilingual education in industrialised countries seems to have peaked in the late 1970s. In the 1980s and 1990s funding for bilingual education programs in the United States has been constantly diminishing (Gray, 1982); special bilingual education programs are still being closed down with resources diverted into ESL programs intended to assimilate children into mainstream programs (Kirp, 1983). In the United Kingdom, an 800-page government report (Education For All, 1985, known as the 'Swann Report') completely misinterpreted research data on mother-tongue teaching and bilingual education. It concluded that better ESL programs should be provided, and that mother-tongue education should be the responsibility of ethnolinguistic minorities. These conclusions, both in the United States and the United Kingdom, were reached on exclusively ideological grounds: they completely disregard the existing empirical evidence on bilingual education, and in particular the consequences for minority children of being taught exclusively through the mainstream language.

Among minority groups we must distinguish, on the one hand, those with a particular territorial status (such as the Basques and the Catalans in Spain), and those who constitute a province or state within a larger political structure (such as Quebec in Canada and several states in India), from, on the other hand, those who coexist with the dominant group without territorial status (such as Native Americans or immigrant groups in Western Europe and North America). In the case of minorities with territorial status, either the national language(s) are used as language(s) of instruction in addition to the official language, or else the latter is taught only as a second language. But language planning in education depends to a great extent on the ethnolinguistic vitality of the group. In Catalonia, for example – where Castilian is not only the official language but is spoken by a majority of immigrant workers, while Catalan, the regional language with official territorial status and a literary tradition, is used by the middle classes, intellectuals and peasants – the autonomous government (the Generalitat) has made the 'catalanisation' of its own workings one of its main objectives. By 1985 it was estimated that half the children received their education through both Catalan and Castilian, while the other half studied Catalan at the rate of five hours a week. In the Basque country, by contrast, the Basque language, which is also promoted by the autonomous Basque government, is encountering difficulties because it is spoken only by a minority, is little used as a literary and scientific medium, is unrelated to Spanish and is thus isolated (Siguan & Mackey, 1987).

In India, where every state has the right to choose regional languages as official languages (Constitution, art. 345), a trilingual education system exists which develops throughout the curriculum (Khubchandani, 1978). This trilingualism can be schematised as in Table 11.1. However, this schema is not always followed and many contradictions can be observed. It is not unusual to come across schools where teachers and students communicate in one language, teaching is conducted in another, school materials are in a third language and homework is done in a fourth (Khubchandani, 1978). Furthermore, only a few of the most important ethnolinguistic groups have a territorial status in India and most communities are minorities inside a State. There are no experimental studies or assessment of the bilingual education programs in India. The same situation held in the former USSR, which also had a complicated pattern of bilingual education (see Lewis, 1972; 1981).

For the second type of minorities, those without territorial status, who are even more subordinate in the sense that the gap between them and the dominant group is wider, we have to distinguish between:

Table 11.1   Trilingual education pattern in India (Khubchandani, 1978)

	Levels of education			
	Elementary	Secondary 1	Secondary 2	Higher
Pupil's L_1	language 1	language 2		
Hindi	Hindi	Regional L_2	English	English
Non-Hindi	L_1	Hindi	English	English

- indigenous minorities, e.g. the Native Americans and Inuit in North America, the Aborigines in Australia and the Maoris in New Zealand;
- minorities who arrived after the dominant group, either through forced immigration (e.g. the African slaves) or free immigration, e.g. the Mexican-Americans and Italian-Americans in the United States; and
- more recent immigrations such as the West Indians, Indians, Bangladeshis and Pakistanis in the United Kingdom and the guest workers in several European countries.

We must also distinguish the indigenous ethnolinguistic minorities who are granted no territorial status in multilingual countries. India, for example, must plan education for 450 tribes with no fewer than 294 mother tongues of which some are not written (Srivastava, 1984b). For all these minorities to survive, some or all of their members must become bilingual and acquire some functional knowledge of an official language.

The UNESCO statement (UNESCO, 1953) that every child has a rightful claim to mother-tongue education is not applied to many minority children. The claim itself has been criticised on the grounds that the economic burden is too big for developing countries: there is a plethora of different vernaculars, some without written forms, and a lack of teaching materials and trained teachers (Bull, 1964). Furthermore, it is not proven that it is better to introduce literacy through the mother tongue per se; Le Page (1964) argues that in multilingual Third World countries children are already multilingual before starting school and the term 'mother tongue' does not have the same meaning as in the West: more relevant are the attitudes of the family and the community who desire social promotion.

Most Third World countries, however, advocate literacy initiation in the vernacular. Srivastava (1984b; 1990) proposes that in a country like India:

(1)   literacy should be initiated 'in the language style in which the child has oral competence and then transfer, if necessary, to the language recognised as the medium of instruction in the formal educational system of the region' (Vernacular-cum-Transfer Model) (1984b: 46); and

(2) if the vernacular has no written system, it should 'select the script of the regional language rather than devise a new script' (1984b: 46). However, if attitudes are strongly negative towards the regional language, the Devanagari script recognised by the Constitution as the official form should be chosen; a tribal language with a written tradition should not be forced to discontinue the use of its own script.

Bamgbose (1984) holds similar views for Nigeria. In the first phase of literacy the local language should be used. Therefore core materials must be developed in all the main Nigerian languages; for minorities for whom this is not possible, either literacy should be initiated through an L_2 in which they have some proficiency, or a transitional period during which they acquire the basic skills should be planned.

To sum up, there is a worldwide claim that literacy for minorities should be initiated through the vernacular. However, whether, once the basic skills have been acquired, education is continued in the vernacular depends essentially on the degree of subordination of the minority: a territorially well-established minority generally has the means and the power to ensure mother-tongue education, at least up to a certain level; a small minority with no territorial claims has neither the means nor the power to demand anything but a transition program in its mother tongue.

11.3.2 Intergroup power-relation factors

According to Schermerhorn (1970), when two ethnolinguistic groups with a different cultural and linguistic history establish lasting contacts, one of the groups tends to dominate the other. The nature of these contacts determines interethnic relations. The degree of integration of both groups in the society depends on a number of factors of which the most important is the power relation (see Section 10.2.2). If we apply our model of intergroup relations to bilingual education, a number of questions arise. Of which group is the child a member? What are the power relations between the dominant and the subordinate group? Who decides about bilingual education and for whom? What are the goals of bilingual education: assimilation, pluralism or segregation? What is the collective outcome? Which group is going to gain by the chosen solution? What are the individual outcomes of bilingual education? Will the child develop an additive or a subtractive form of bilinguality through education? A subtractive form is a negative asset not only for the individual but also for the group, and indeed for society as a whole, since having members who have not developed their full cognitive potential leads to lower economic success. What are the consequences for a group if a member loses his mother tongue? No group wants to lose its members through assimilation, neither does it want to see subtractive bilinguality develop. For these reasons, the minority group tends to minimise the risks of assimilation and subtraction in education. Power relations therefore determine the direction of language planning in education.

It should not be assumed, however, that social factors and power relations are significant only outside the classroom. They also operate within it; they often determine much of what is taught and to whom, as well as how it is taught and by whom; and they also determine how all of those involved in the teaching and learning process interact with each other (Fishman, 1977c).

However, social historical, ideological and power-relation factors are not the only factors that influence bilingual education. Social psychological factors also influence bilingual development and must be taken into consideration in bilingual education.

11.3.3   Social psychological factors

On the basis of our model of bilingual development (see Section 5.2) we formulate a number of hypotheses concerning the consequences of bilingual education. The outcome of bilingual education depends upon a number of pre-school factors as well as upon the way the two languages are planned in education. Two factors are of relevance in education:

(1) To what extent is the child proficient in the school language?
(2) To what extent has he developed the cognitive function in one or both of his languages before starting school?

Considering the interplay of educational factors with the following factors: social psychological and cognitive developmental factors, such as onset of, and proficiency in, both languages; functions developed for language; valorisation of one or both languages for all or a limited number of functions; and the social representations which the child developed as a consequence, we make the following hypotheses:

(1) If both languages are acquired simultaneously or if the child is fully proficient in both languages before entering school, he does not have the double learning burden of acquiring new language skills and literacy skills simultaneously; if, in addition, the child has already developed language as a cognitive tool, the acquisition of literacy skills will be facilitated; and, if the child has also developed an analysed representation of language in which both languages are perceived as interchangeable, thus amplifying cognitive functioning, the acquisition of literacy skills will further amplify this functioning and

the child is more likely to develop an additive form of bilinguality. This is the case of the child in an educated mixed-lingual family.

(2) If the child is only proficient in his L_1 when starting school in L_2, he will have to acquire the primary communicative skills in L_2 at the same time as the literacy skills in L_2. If he has already developed an analysed representation of language through his L_1, he can transfer it to the acquisition of literacy skills; the two languages become interchangeable for cognitive operations, thus amplifying cognitive functioning. Because both languages are valorised in their cognitive function, this transfer is relatively easy. The degree to which his analysed representation of language includes both languages as interchangeable tools determines the degree of additivity. This is the case of immersion-school children and of some advantaged submersion children.

(3) If a child – proficient in his L_1 only, or with a limited knowledge of L_2 at the onset of schooling in a relatively more prestigious L_2 – has not developed the cognitive functions of language in his L_1, he also faces the double burden of acquiring the primary communicative skills in L_2 simultaneously with the literacy skills. Because he does not possess the analytic representation of language, the task of acquiring literacy skills is harder (as is the case for some monolingual children schooled in L_1). If, in addition, his L_1 is devalorised and stigmatised, he will not transfer the newly acquired skills to his L_1 but limit them to an L_2 in which he is not proficient. In the worst case, because he does not use his full language potential as does a monolingual child coping with the problem of acquiring literacy, the development of the analysed representation of language might be slowed down. Further devalorisation of L_1 by society and the school, where it is not used for the development of literacy skills, leads to a perception that his two languages are not interchangeable as cognitive tools and that only L_2 can be used in that function. This might ultimately lead to a subtractive form of bilinguality.

In the next section we discuss some of the bilingual education programs developed for dominant-group and subordinate-group children and analyse the possible outcomes of these language-planning models in education.

11.4   BILINGUAL EDUCATION PROGRAMS

In this section we examine types of bilingual education:

(1) programs for the children of dominant and of socially advantaged groups;

(2)   programs for ethnic-minority children;
(3)   bilingual education programs involving dialects and creoles; and
(4)   community bilingual education programs.

11.4.1   Bilingual education for children of the dominant group

In all cultures and at all times elites have provided their children with bilingual education when they consider it necessary, either by employing a private teacher or by sending the child to an elite school, often in the country where the second language is spoken. In the latter part of the twentieth century, certain dominant groups have adopted a more democratic way of ensuring bilingual education, namely through immersion programs.

11.4.1.1 European 'models' of bilingual education

In Europe there are 9 bilingual schools under EC jurisdiction: these are in Karlsruhe, Munich, Luxembourg, Culham, Bergen, Varese, Mol-Geel and two in Brussels (Baetens Beardsmore, 1980; 1993; Baetens Beardsmore & Swain, 1985). These schools differ significantly from so-called 'International Schools', most of which are international only in recruitment and to some extent in curriculum, but rarely so in the languages they offer. European Schools, on the other hand, are genuinely multilingual both in curriculum and in outcome: they combine two, three or even four languages to a varying extent. For example, the European School in Brussels is primarily meant for children of European civil servants from different countries; it is divided into several linguistic groups; children start elementary education in their mother tongue if it is one of the four working languages of the EU (French, English, German and Italian), otherwise they choose one of these linguistic groups. In the second year an L_2 is introduced which is either French, English or German. At a later stage 'European classes' are organised in which the four working languages are used interchangeably.

To date, very little research has been conducted on the results of bilingual education in the multilingual European schools, and their reputation is essentially based on anecdotal evidence and parental attitudes. The one exception is a comparative study between the Brussels School and an immersion program in Toronto (Baetens Beardsmore & Swain, 1985) which we discuss in Section 11.4.1.2.4. It is very difficult to determine conclusively whether the success of these schools is attributable only to their multilingual programs and not to their elitist character.

11.4.1.2 Immersion programs

It is no accident that immersion programs started developing in Quebec. Because the political evolution of Canada's French province, which expressed itself in the 'Révolution Tranquille' and the subsequent separatist movement in the 1960s and 1970s, transformed Quebec into a unilingual French province (Charte de la Langue Française, known as Bill 101, already mentioned in Section 10.2.2), the Anglo-Quebecois minority, which was essentially monolingual in English, had to adjust and become proficient enough in French to use it as a working language. This prompted the Anglophone minority to provide their children with a better proficiency in French than the one they attained through traditional L_2 teaching methods. Different approaches for improving their working knowledge of French have been developed, and amongst these immersion stands out as the most successful venture. Immersion simply means that a group of L_1-speaking children receive all or part of their schooling through an L_2 as medium of instruction. The immersion approach is based on two assumptions:

(1)   that at the age of immersion an L_2 is learned in a similar way to an L_1; and
(2)   that a language is best learned in a stimulating context which enhances the language functions and exposes the child to the natural forms of language.

In the mid-1960s research in experimental and social psychology started indicating that early bilingual experience might enhance cognitive development and lead to an additive form of bilinguality (see Chapter 4). It is in this political and social psychological context that the first immersion program for Anglophone children was initiated by parents in St-Lambert, a middle-class neighbourhood of Montreal, in collaboration with a team of psychologists from McGill University (Lambert & Tucker, 1972).

11.4.1.2.1 Types of immersion   The term 'immersion' refers to a program in which teaching is planned through the means of an L_2; however, since the St-Lambert program was initiated, many forms of immersion have been developed. Because immersion was first developed in Canada we refer here to French immersion for Anglophones; however it must be kept in mind that immersion programs can be applied to all majority groups schooled in a subordinate language.

(1)   Early Total Immersion. This program was first developed for Anglophone children in the St-Lambert pilot school which serves as the

prototype for all early immersion programs. Education through French starts in kindergarten and is given by Francophone or fluently bilingual teachers. During the first two years of elementary school, instruction is given exclusively through the medium of French; children acquire literacy skills in their L_2; English is introduced in the third year (that is, after three years in French if we include kindergarten), taught as a first language for daily periods of 35 minutes. The amount of time taught in French drops gradually and reaches 50 per cent by the end of elementary. In the early stages children tend to communicate among themselves and with the teachers through the medium of English; however, very soon French is used as a means of communication in the classroom. After the introduction of English there is a bilingual stage in which some subjects are taught in French and others in English; finally, during a consolidation stage, the pupil can choose to take certain subjects in French or English. No particular L_2 methodology is followed.

(2)   Early partial immersion. This differs from total immersion in that both languages are used as means of instruction from the onset of schooling. The relative use of both languages varies widely from one program to another.

(3)   Late immersion. These programs have been designed for high-school students and aim at developing French language skills in students who have so far received a traditional L_2 instruction in French; the goal of the program is to enable the students to attain a functional bilinguality by the time they finish high school. For example, during the first year, 85 per cent of the curriculum is taught through French while in the remaining 15 per cent English is taught as a first language; during the following years the student has a choice and can attend 40 per cent of the classes in French (see Genesee, 1979; Swain & Lapkin, 1982).

11.4.1.2.2 Assessment of immersion programs   Numerous immersion programs have been evaluated since the 1970s. Whereas the St-Lambert project (Lambert & Tucker, 1972) is the prototype of immersion assessment, other large-scale evaluations have also been conducted for different immersion programs in several Canadian cities. Among the most important are those by Genesee (1979; 1984) for Greater Montreal, and by Swain & Lapkin (1982) for Carleton in the Ottawa suburbs and for Toronto. In these follow-up studies, assessments of immersion children were compared with those of monolingual English-speaking children in traditional English programs (English Control Groups) and with those of French-speaking children in French schools (French Control Groups). Three general issues are addressed by the assessment studies:

(1) the effect of receiving instruction through French on English-language skills;
(2) the effect of immersion on academic achievement; and
(3) the effectiveness of immersion for the development of L_2 skills (Genesee, 1984).

A variety of assessment tests have been used in these evaluations: standardised tests in English-L_1 and French-L_1 language skills, speaking, listening comprehension and writing tests in both languages and academic achievement tests. The results of assessment of immersion programs have so far been relatively stable across Canada (Swain, 1982) and can be summarised as follows:

(1) Mother-tongue proficiency. Generally speaking there is no lag in comprehension and expression skills; immersion children lag behind the English controls in literacy skills during the first two years, but this difference disappears once English literacy skills are introduced. Children in partial immersion do not score better on literacy tests in English than children in total immersion once literacy skills in English have been introduced. In late immersion, the students do not lag behind the English controls after their one year's instruction in French. Thus, there is no deficit of mother-tongue skills.
(2) Proficiency in L_2. The results in L_2 are far superior to those obtained by English controls who receive traditional L_2 instruction, to the extent that the tests used with the immersion children are too difficult for the children of the control group. When compared with the French controls, the children in the immersion programs score comparably for oral and written comprehension and on vocabulary tests. However, their written and particularly oral expression skills are not native-like, and they rarely initiate a conversation in French. They perceive themselves, and are perceived by Francophones, as having superior French-language skills to English children in a traditional program. Children in partial immersion do not score as highly on French skills as those in total immersion, while they do not score higher on English skills; thus the reduction of the time spent teaching through French reduces the L_2 skills but does not enhance the L_1 skills. The assessment of children in late immersion follows the same pattern: they achieve higher levels than the English controls but do not reach native-like command of French in expression skills.
(3) Academic achievement. Total immersion children score as highly as their counterparts in English schools on tests of mathematics and science, despite the fact that they receive their instruction in French. Children in late immersion are not impeded by the use of their L_2 as a

medium of instruction and score as highly as the controls in traditional English programs. They also score above the average provincial norms on a number of subjects in French; this last result must however be interpreted with caution as there was a socio-economic bias in favour of the immersion students (Genesee, 1984).

(4) Other assessments. Some studies report other measures taken with immersion children. There are some indications that immersion might lead to cognitive enhancement; IQ measures seem to increase more over the years for immersion students than for children in traditional English programs (Barik & Swain, 1978); immersion children in Grades 5 and 6 (age 10 and 11) score higher on creativity tests (Edwards, Doutriaux, McCarrey & Fu, 1976) and on divergent-thinking measures (Scott, 1973). Comparing below-average, average and above-average students in early immersion programs, Genesee (1981a) observed that below-average students scored significantly lower than average and above-average students on literacy tests in French, but that the three groups did not differ from each other on interpersonal communication tests. This was not the case with late-immersion below-average students, who scored lower than above-average students on interpersonal communication skills in French.

To sum up, with regard to the assessment of immersion programs, it seems that:

(1) immersion programs are superior to traditional programs for French as a second language, with students attaining a high level of proficiency, especially for receptive skills in L_2;
(2) students are not handicapped in mother-tongue skills nor in academic achievement;
(3) when differences occur between results in different immersion programs, they favour the early total immersion over partial immersion (Genesee, 1981b) and over late immersion (Morrison, 1981);
(4) there are some indications that early immersion programs might favour the child's overall cognitive development.

Comparison has also been made between the performance of Anglo-Canadian students in immersion programs and that of Anglophone students who have attended French-medium schools starting in kindergarten or Grade 1 (age 6) where all instruction is given exclusively in French up to Grade 4 (age 9) when English-language arts subjects (i.e. for native speakers of English) are introduced for 30 minutes a day (see Lambert, Genesee, Holobow & Chartrand, 1993). The French-medium group have had an extended exposure to French similar to early total immersion students as a medium of instruction; in addition, French is the language of communication in the school setting. It was found that they performed as well as the French controls on French-language competence, mathematics and writing skills. The notable exception was oral production where the French controls scored higher. But the French-medium students scored significantly higher than the early immersion students on the French cloze test and higher on the written French-language tests. However, they were not different from the early-total-immersion students with respect to oral language skills. This, according to Lambert, Genesee, Holobow & Chartrand (1993), suggests that there may be an upper limit to oral French-language proficiency that can be attained in schools that do not provide opportunity for genuine peer interaction in the language (see below). To explore this possibility, the experimenters collected data on another group of Anglophone students who were also attending classes in an all-French school but one where they were a clear minority, and who therefore had more opportunity for interacting with their French-speaking peers. Tests showed that this group scored at the same level as the first French-medium group on the written tests, but consistently higher on the oral tests. In fact, they are as native-like as the French controls in pronunciation. These results provide some support for the authors' hypothesis that greater peer-group face-to-face interaction and intergroup relations are very advantageous.

What is the long-term effectiveness of immersion programs? Comparing the written skills in English and French of first-year university students who had experienced immersion with those of monolingual English and French students and bilingual Anglophones from French-medium schools, Vignola and Wesche (1991) found that there were no significant differences in English writing skills between the post-immersion group, that is the group of students who attended immersion programs in their elementary education, and Anglophones from English-medium schools; in French writing skills, however, although the post-immersion students were comparable to the French controls in content and compositional skills, they scored below them on vocabulary, verb morphology and tenses, noun gender and number, and prepositions; occasionally, post-immersion students tended to translate from English into French.

Another question concerns the use immersion students make of their acquired skills in French after leaving high school. Reviewing surveys of recent graduates of immersion programs in Canada, Harley (1994) found that few of them made use of their French-language skills and that, while most of the subjects interviewed thought it was important to them to keep up their French, they stressed the problem of motivation. This is in keeping with the findings of Gardner, Moorcroft & Metford (1989) on the factors involved in the retention of L_2 skills in the period following intensive training. On the question of language attrition Harley (1994) drew four conclusions of relevance for those who wished to maintain their skills in French:

(1) self-perceptions of language loss were much worse than objective tests revealed;
(2) the higher the students' initial proficiency, the better their long-term proficiency;
(3) frequency of current use was related to language maintenance of speaking skills; and
(4) renewed exposure to the language leads to rapid recovery of skills thought to be lost.

11.4.1.2.3 A critique of immersion Immersion programs have been criticised from different perspectives: experimental, linguistic, pedagogical and social. From an experimental perspective it has often been noted that the immersion groups were not comparable with the controls, because immersion was selected by parents; or that the results might be attributed to a 'Hawthorne effect'.[1] It has been argued that immersion programs favour gifted children; Genesee (1976; 1991) concluded that they are suitable for all children, since below-average children in early immersion develop the same proficiency in communicative skills in French (L_2) as above-average children. Bruck (1982) argues that children with learning difficulties and slow learners benefit from an immersion program to the extent that they do not lag behind other children with learning difficulties, and in addition learn French; this is not the case in regular programs. Trites (1981), on the basis of a follow-up study, suggests that children with learning difficulties should be removed from immersion programs; Genesee (1984; 1991) argues, however, that unless it can be demonstrated that these children would not experience similar difficulties in traditional programs, Trites' argument does not hold. Immersion programs have often been judged to be suitable only for middle-class children. Assessing working-class children in immersion programs, Bruck, Jakimik & Tucker (1975) found that they were not different from their English counterparts in traditional programs for English skills, but superior to them for French skills; unfortunately they did not follow up their study.

A few studies address the question of the communicative and linguistic output of immersion children. Harley & Swain (1977; 1978) compared the use of verb tenses by immersion children with that by monolingual and infant bilingual children. They observed that immersion children use a reduced tense system: they do not use conditionals and modals. The authors concluded that immersion children develop a competence which allows them to interact with their peers and teachers, but lack the necessary social motivation to develop native-like competence. According to Blanc (1980) and Dodson (1981), teaching methods are partly responsible for this lack of expressive abilities: teaching is too directive, pupils too passive, and texts are not exploited at the linguistic level; furthermore it might be a mistake to postulate that an L_2 is learned in a similar way to an L_1. Swain & Lapkin (1991) confirmed these views, advocating the use of communicative language learning/teaching methods. Cziko, Lambert, Sidoti & Tucker (1978) observed that although students schooled through immersion are capable of functioning in French and are motivated to do so, they hardly come into contact with members of the Francophone community. The relevance of social contacts with members of the ethnolinguistic community has been demonstrated by Chun (1979), who compared the oral expression skills of English children in immersion with English children who spent one year in France; the latter were far superior to the former in oral skills.

11.4.1.2.4 Comparison of immersion with other programs

(1) The Culver City Bilingual Program. This early-total-immersion program is a duplication of the St-Lambert project with Anglo-American children schooled through Spanish (Cohen, 1976). In addition to the St-Lambert program, a small group of Spanish speakers were introduced in Grade 1 (age 6) to serve as models and to stimulate communication in Spanish. The assessment results are comparable to the Canadian immersion evaluations: children compared favourably with monolingual English-speaking controls for English skills and for academic achievement and with Spanish-speaking controls for their Spanish skills, although they did not reach native-like competence. Their attitudes towards Hispanics and the Spanish culture were extremely favourable. However, it must be observed that in the American context Spanish has no 'official' status, unlike French in Canada; additionally, if it is spoken by a large number of Americans it is highly devalorised. The children who participated probably had favourable attitudes before they started the program.

(2) The Cincinnati Immersion Program. This program for French and Spanish is of particular interest because it includes children from lower socio-economic groups and ethnic-minority group (Black) backgrounds, in addition to majority group (White) middle-class children. Immersion children showed the same levels of achievement in English and mathematics as their peers in English-medium schools, and this was equally true for

working-class and Black students. At the same time, the working-class and Black students benefited from learning a second language as much as the middle-class and White students, especially in aural/oral skills; this was despite the fact that their exposure to L_2 was less than in Canadian immersion and the use of languages other than English is not valorised in the USA (Holobow, Genesee & Lambert, 1991; compare two-way bilingual education below).

The next two programmes are not for minority group students but one of the languages involved is a minority language.

(3)   The Welsh Bilingual Project. Beaudoin, Cummins, Dunlop, Genesee & Obadia (1981) compared results of Welsh immersion for Anglophones in Wales with the Canadian results. The Schools Council Bilingual Project aimed at making monolingual English-speaking children fluent bilinguals by the age of 11. Half the school day was conducted in Welsh and the other half in English throughout primary school. The project was very successful for the first two years. Teaching Welsh at the next level, however, was less successful, and in some instances skills in Welsh regressed; but there was no evidence that academic subjects had suffered as a result. In the experimental group only the children with high socio-economic status scored significantly better than the control group.

The difference in performance between the younger and the older school children in the project has been attributed by Dodson (1981) essentially to differences in teaching methods, the approach being far more flexible and dynamic in the earlier years. Furthermore, Dodson has put forward an interesting hypothesis to account for some deficiencies in immersion bilingual programs. He starts from two premises. The first is that learning a second language through immersion is not comparable to the acquisition of the first. The second is that, in the immersion bilingual experience, the child does not have a first and a second language but, rather, 'a preferred' and another language, not necessarily always the same. Consequently the bilingual may be more at ease in one for a set of functions or activities, and more at ease in the other for another set of functions or activities. In the course of evaluating the Welsh program, Dodson found that those schools which followed a 'total' immersion program, in the sense of placing the focus on the message and not the medium, were achieving lower results than those which applied phased methodological sequencing from 'medium-oriented' to 'message-oriented' communication in a continuous cycle. He further advocates the use of both languages, the preferred and the other language, within the same lesson, claiming that the languages reinforce each other.

(4)   Gaelic-medium project in Scotland. This project, involving immersion programs used in Gaelic-medium primary education, is under way in

Scotland (MacNeil, 1994). It occurs in state schools with a monolingual English curriculum. Special units are designated for the project, that is, they are separately staffed and allocated separate classrooms in primary schools. In all the participating schools Gaelic is the only medium used for the first two years. In the third year total immersion ends and English language development is introduced; at this point Gaelic can be subject-based, time-based or age-based, or a combination of all these. There is a high level of support by parents. To date, however, no evaluation of Gaelic-medium immersion programmes has been published.

(5)   Comparison between immersion and EC schools. Baetens Beardsmore & Swain (1985) compared achievement in the L_2 obtained in two different models of bilingual education: a French immersion program in Toronto and the European School in Brussels. They observed that, although the students in the European School received only part of their schooling through French and had thus received much less exposure to the language, both groups of students had a relatively high proficiency in French and achieved equally well. They attribute these results to contextual (social) conditions: the children in the European School used French mainly as a lingua franca in the school; were more exposed to French in the community at large and at home with the parents; and had considerable experience of living in countries where their mother tongue was not spoken. For the children in the immersion program, on the other hand, the L_2 often lacks relevance beyond the classroom. This suggests that classroom activities should be combined with social activities in order to attain native-like command of L_2.

To date, there are few examples, let alone studies, of immersion programs outside Canada. Introducing the majority child to a valorised second language used as medium of instruction at the age of five not only does not delay the child's acquisition of linguistic and academic skills, but it gives him a functional competence in the other language far superior to what he might have achieved by traditional methods. It may even enhance his cognitive skills and produce an additive balanced binguality. However, what has proved valid for the advantaged child of majority groups, whose culture and first language are valorised in his community and who has already reached a sufficient level of analysed language by the time he goes to school, does not necessarily apply in the case of the minority child. It is to him that we now turn.

11.4.2   Bilingual education for ethnic-minority children

When discussing bilingual education for minority children, two important contextual aspects of their development must be emphasised:

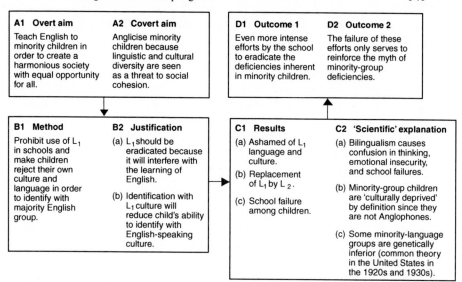

A1 Overt aim	A2 Covert aim
Teach English to minority children in order to create a harmonious society with equal opportunity for all.	Anglicise minority children because linguistic and cultural diversity are seen as a threat to social cohesion.

D1 Outcome 1	D2 Outcome 2
Even more intense efforts by the school to eradicate the deficiencies inherent in minority children.	The failure of these efforts only serves to reinforce the myth of minority-group deficiencies.

B1 Method	B2 Justification
Prohibit use of L_1 in schools and make children reject their own culture and language in order to identify with majority English group.	(a) L_1 should be eradicated because it will interfere with the learning of English. (b) Identification with L_1 culture will reduce child's ability to identify with English-speaking culture.

C1 Results	C2 'Scientific' explanation
(a) Ashamed of L_1 language and culture. (b) Replacement of L_1 by L_2. (c) School failure among children.	(a) Bilingualism causes confusion in thinking, emotional insecurity, and school failures. (b) Minority-group children are 'culturally deprived' by definition since they are not Anglophones. (c) Some minority-language groups are genetically inferior (common theory in the United States in the 1920s and 1930s).

Note: This figure reflects the assumptions of North American school systems in the first half of the twentieth century. However, similar assumptions have been made about minority-language children in the shool systems of many other countries.

Figure 11.1   The myth of the bilingual handicap (adapted from Cummins, 1981)

(1)   they come from a little-valorised mother-tongue background; and
(2)   because they often come from socially deprived communities, their literacy-oriented skills are usually less well developed.

11.4.2.1 The myth of the bilingual handicap

A major problem with education for ethnolinguistic minority children is the so-called 'cognitive handicap' attributed to their binguality; this is what Cummins (1981; 1984a) calls the myth of bilingual handicap. According to this myth the academic failure of minority children is attributed to their state of binguality. Learning the dominant L_2 and using it for education is consequently considered to be the solution to this problem. Cummins's views are schematised in Figure 11.1. In this myth the overt goal of L_2 education is to teach L_2 to the minority child in order to give him equal opportunities, the covert goal being to assimilate him. L_1 may, therefore, be devalorised and children are forbidden to use it in the school, because it could interfere with L_2 acquisition. As a result the child becomes ashamed of his own culture and language, substitutes L_2 for L_1 and obtains poor academic results. These results are, in turn, attributed to the state of bilinguality and to a cognitive deficit and, hence, those responsible for education insist even more on eliminating the 'cause' of the deficit, i.e. the L_1, and reinforce the myth. If this cycle can be broken, then the poor academic achievement of the minority child can be improved. To achieve this, however, one must accept that the school system rather than the child's bilinguality is the main factor responsible for poor achievement. As we argued in Section 4.2.5 it is not the state of bilinguality per se, but socio-structural, sociocultural and social psychological factors which are responsible for poor academic achievement.

The debate on 'semilingualism', although ill-founded, has had a considerable impact on designing education programs for minorities. When 'semilingualism' was introduced as a concept, it was interpreted as an inherent characteristic of the minority child, even though Skutnabb-Kangas (1981) made it clear later that the principal cause was social structural and ideological. Several solutions have been proposed. In order to avoid academic failure, Skutnabb-Kangas & Toukomaa (1976), for example, advocated L_1 shelter-programs in which Finnish immigrant children in Sweden would receive an elementary education exclusively through the medium of Finnish. This solution has been criticised by Ekstrand (1978) on the grounds that it might not only shelter the minority child but also ghettoise him to the extent that he is completely isolated from the wide community; Ekstrand suggests that when a child lives in a bicultural and bilingual environment, this should be reflected in the school, which should also be bicultural and bilingual.

Cummins (1984a; 1994) gives an excellent review of the use made of academic assessment tests to 'demonstrate' the bilingual deficit of minority children. He suggests that language planning in education should opt neither for a 'linguistic mismatch' nor for a 'maximum exposure to L_1' solution. Because there is strong evidence that promoting L_1 literacy skills enhances overall academic achievement, this should always be considered in planning minority education. The school should further employ every means to valorise the child's mother tongue and encourage its use. The factors operating in determining scholastic success for minority children vary from one minority community to another; therefore, no single solution can be proposed but each case should be assessed on its own merits. The following are urgently needed: needs analysis, the definition of specific objectives, the training of community or heritage language teachers and the design of valid and reliable tests for children of ethnolinguistic minorities.

11.4.2.2 Examples of bilingual education programs for minority children

Numerous experiments have been conducted on bilingual education programs for minority children and a certain number of them demonstrate that a subtractive form of bilinguality is not a necessary outcome. We have chosen to describe some of these because they each represent a solution to somewhat different situations.

- The bilingual program for Finnish immigrant children in Sweden (Hanson, 1979). This program uses Finnish as the main language of instruction; Swedish becomes an important means of instruction from Grade 3 (age 3) onwards. At the end of the elementary school children obtain results comparable with Swedish and Finnish control groups. This is an improvement compared with the monolingual and the shelter programs.
- Reading programs for Chiapas children (Modiano, 1973). This program initiates children in Chiapas, South Mexico, who are normally schooled exclusively through Spanish, into reading skills in their mother tongue, which is a highly devalorised language in Mexico. Compared with Chiapas children who learned to read in Spanish only, the experimental group scored higher on written comprehension tests in Spanish after a three-year program. Mutatis mutandis, these results are comparable with those obtained with Navajo children in the United States.
- The Rock Point Experiment with Navajo children (Rosier & Farella, 1976). Before the start of this Navajo–English bilingual education program the Navajo children were two years behind the American norms for reading skills in English at the end of Grade 6 (age 12), despite an extensive teaching program of ESL. The bilingual program used Navajo as the main language of instruction throughout elementary education. The introduction of English was delayed until the reading skills in Navajo were well acquired. At the end of elementary school Navajo children in the program scored slightly higher than the US norms, although they had had less exposure to English than the children in the ESL program.
- The Redwood City Project (Cohen, 1975). In this 'mixed' four-year-long project Mexican-American and Anglo-American children were mixed together in a proportion of two to one. Teachers used both Spanish and English in the same class and translated freely from one language to the other. Results were different for both groups. Anglo-Americans did not acquire much Spanish, as they could use English when they wanted to and were afraid of speaking Spanish. However, the Mexican-Americans learned English; a control group also learned English, receiving exclusively English-language instruction. Both groups scored equally well on mathematics tests and on English-language measures, except in vocabu-

lary. Furthermore their attitudes towards, and their use of, Spanish were positively affected: use of Spanish did not diminish to the same extent as it did in the control group (Hernandez-Chavez, 1978).

- The California experiment (Legaretta, 1979). The author compared three types of bilingual kindergarten programs for Mexican-Americans with two unilingual English programs. The three bilingual education programs were significantly more efficient in developing communicative skills than the English-only programs. The most efficient program shared equal time between Spanish and English.
- The Franco-Manitoban experiment (Hébert, 1976). Franco-Manitoban children in Grades 3, 6 and 9 (ages 8, 12, and 15 respectively) who received bilingual education in French and English made similar progress in English, regardless of the amount of time spent on English. Those who had 20 per cent English and 80 per cent French schooling were as good in English those children who received 80 per cent of their instruction in English and 20 per cent in French (they also had superior results in French skills). In other words mother-tongue skills benefited from a longer exposure time without any loss in L_2 skills.
- The St John's Valley bilingual education program (Dubé & Herbert, 1975). The subtractive situation of Franco-American children was improved when one third of the elementary program was taught in French. After five years these children obtained better scores in academic achievement and English-language skills than control groups in English-only programs; furthermore, they were fluent in French reading and writing skills (Lambert, Giles & Picard, 1975).
- The MOTET Project (Mother Tongue & English Teaching Project) (MOTET, 1981). Two groups of Mirpuri (a Punjabi dialect) mother-tongue children attended a bilingual Mirpuri–English nursery-school program in Bradford, UK. The two languages were each used 50 per cent of the time. The results indicated that one experimental group obtained superior results in English-comprehension skills to the control group, but the reverse was true for the other group; both groups scored higher on English-expression measures and on all Punjabi tests. These results were confirmed in a follow-up study (Fitzpatrick, 1987): the children continued to improve their English and Punjabi skills to a greater extent than Mirpuri children who had not attended a bilingual program. However, significant differences were observed between the children who were dispersed in different schools: if the school did not keep up with the Punjabi language the improvement trends faded out.
- The Carpinteria Spanish-language pre-school program (Carpinteria Unified School District, 1982). The goal of this pre-school Spanish-only program is to bring Spanish-speaking children entering kindergarten to

the level of school readiness attained by the English-speaking children. Children who had attended the program scored higher than Spanish-speaking controls, both on Spanish and on English measures.

11.4.2.3 Features of bilingual education programs for minority children

What can be concluded from this variety of experiments on bilingual education for minority children in Europe and North America? They all deal with potentially highly subtractive contexts; all make use of the mother tongue for formal education, either simultaneously with the dominant language, or before instruction is given in the dominant language. In all cases, academic and linguistic proficiency results in both languages are superior to those obtained by control groups where instruction is in L_2 only. In all cases, the program valorises the mother tongue and culture, motivates the child to learn through his L_1, and develops his linguistic-conceptual capacities to the extent that he will make better progress in an L_2 than his peers schooled exclusively through L_2. These studies provide strong support for the view that, for minority children, the acquisition of literacy skills should be dissociated from the acquisition of L_2 skills, and that formal instruction should valorise the mother tongue. This is exactly what Tizard, Schofield & Hewison (1982) showed with their reading experiments in London (see Sections 4.3.1 and 5.1.4.5).

The large majority of bilingual programs for minority children are transition programs which do not aim at functional bilinguality; this is in contrast to immersion programs. For most programs language planning has been decided by the dominant group, and their ultimate goal is assimilation of the subordinate groups (Wong Fillmore, 1991b). Even if they aim at developing a certain degree of bilinguality, it is likely that in the long run the students will become dominant in L_2 and acculturate. If bilingual education appears to be a necessary condition for children of an ethnolinguistic minority, it is however not a sufficient one. For example, the existence of bilingual education for the Franco-Ontarian minority in Canada is not sufficient to impede assimilation (Mougeon & Canale, 1978). It is the ethnolinguistic vitality of the group (see Section 10.2.3), the use of the mother tongue in the home and in the community, and the allegiance to the cultural group that will ensure cultural survival.

Far from representing a handicap, the use of the mother tongue in the home is an important factor in helping to attain academic achievement. In a longitudinal study Chesarek (1981) demonstrated that, among elementary-school children from a Crow Native American reservation, those who had one Crow-speaking parent and who spoke exclusively English at home scored significantly lower on non-verbal intelligence tests than Crow children who spoke Crow as their first language, or English-speaking Crow children whose parents were both Anglophones. Moreover, after three years of education in Crow, these children scored better than those educated in English only.

In a similar vein, Bhatnagar (1980), studying the adjustment of Italian immigrant children in Montreal, concluded that mother-tongue mainte- nance in the home leads to superior academic achievement, better profi- ciency in their second language, French, and improved social relations. Dolson (1985) obtained similar results with Hispanic children in Califor- nia; those who came from homes where Spanish was spoken scored consist- ently better than Hispanic children from homes that had shifted to English. The relevance of the home in language maintenance has already been discussed in Sections 4.3.1 and 10.2; of all domains it is the family network that most resists the penetration of the dominant language. If the minority language invades the family network the survival chances of the subordi- nate language are extremely slim. (See P. Lieberson, 1970; Fishman, Cooper & Ma, 1971; Gal, 1979, and Mougeon, Brent-Palmer, Bélanger & Cichocki, 1982, among others.)

Using both qualitative and quantitative methods, Feuerverger (1991) studied the perceptions of heritage-language learning and ethnic-identity maintenance by 148 Toronto University students from eight different ethnolinguistic groups. She administered the Canadian Ethnocultural Questionnaire (see Sections 2.2.1.7) and further interviewed two students from each group. She found that three significant factors emerged from the data:

(1) The students saw the need for literacy in the heritage language at home as well as at school.
(2) They favoured family and ethnic-community involvement in the liter- acy process.
(3) They stressed the regenerative effects of identification with the home- land.

They also commented on the fact that the concepts of multilingualism and multiculturalism had not yet been integrated into mainstream education and that, consequently, heritage-language learning/teaching had still not been really accepted in Canada.

In the late 1990s some evidence has emerged that the needs of some minority-group children are not always best served through literacy pro- grams in L_1, but rather through intensive exposure to and instruction in the second language. Elder & Davies (1998), for example, have argued that language distance may be a factor affecting the relationship between L_1 and L_2. While recognising that introducing literacy in L_1 may be an advantage in the case of cognate or typologically close languages, for speakers of typologically distant languages, however, home exposure to L_2 may be a more powerful contributor to literacy development than increased proficiency in L_1 (the so-called 'language distance effect'; see Elder & Davies, 1998). If this were correct, it would throw some doubt on Cummins' claim that there is an underlying proficiency common across all languages and that, once developed, it is transferable from L_1 to L_2, regardless of whether or not the languages are typologically related. However, this linguistic interpretation is questionable: the authors did not prove that linguistic rather than psychological and sociocultural factors were responsible for the difference.

Today there is a general consensus that teaching literacy through the mother tongue is desirable for minority-language speakers, not only for political and cultural reasons, but also for pedagogical reasons, that is, as a means of improving school performance both in L_1 and L_2. Reviewing research carried out in Canada, Danesi (1993) claims that instruction in L_1 is a necessary condition of school success. A similar, though weaker, claim is made by Carson & Kuehn (1994) that literacy development in L_1 facilitates literacy in L_2. We would claim that more than the fact of teaching literacy in L_1, it is the valorisation of L_1 as a cognitive tool by the school which is responsible for the development of literacy.

However, the bilingual education of minority children in the USA has been under attack by, among others, members of the 'English Only Movement' (EOM),[2] whose policy is to make English the official language of the country at national and state levels, and English the only medium of education (Piatt, 1990). They adduce in evidence for their claim Baker & de Kanter's (1981; 1983) reviews of the literature on bilingual education evaluation, which concluded that bilingual education was not effective in meeting educational needs of ethnolinguistic minority students. Analysing Baker & de Kanter's evidence, Willig (1985) argued convincingly that these authors had reviewed the literature uncritically and had not taken into account the methodological flaws of the studies they reported on. Her analysis consistently shows that their evidence goes the other way in support of bilingual education. In evaluation research comparing bilingual education with submersion in English and ESL programs, submersion students scored lowest and bilingual education students highest (Crawford, 1989). Educational research does suggest that policies aimed at promoting English at the expense of minority languages are misguided. Bilingual education, as we have seen, promotes educational achievement, if not additive bilinguality, since most bilingual programs are in effect transitional, designed to enable students to benefit fully from mainstream education. For more details on this issue, see the article prepared for the

American Psychological Association by the panel of experts on English-Only Legislation (Padilla, Lindholm, Chen, Duran, Hakuta, Lambert & Tucker, 1991).

11.4.3   Bilingual education involving dialects and creoles

Similar educational problems arise when the child's mother tongue is a non-standard variety of the language, as for example Black English Vernacular and creoles. There is another myth about the 'linguistic deficit' of Black Americans and West Indians who speak an English-based creole. Bereiter & Englemann (1966), for example, inferred the existence of an intellectual deficit in lower-class Black Americans, on the grounds that they were 'linguistically deficient': they were supposedly incapable of producing complete sentences and answered all questions by yes or no, and their utterances lacked the copula *be* and therefore supposedly could not represent reality. Because of this linguistic deficit compensatory education, in which Black children performed structural exercises in English, was promoted.

Labov (1972), in his studies on Black English, demonstrated the ill-foundedness of Bereiter & Engelmann's theory: first the Black child belongs to a different culture; second, the tests used put him in a totally artificial situation; given a natural communication setting, he expresses himself on all subjects, using the language of his own culture. Inner-city Black children have been described as non-verbal because the school setting does not allow them to express themselves in the ways they are accustomed to. Black English has different rules from Standard English, including the optional use of the copula *be* and the double negation. To attempt to change these rules can only lead to confusion. The Black child does not speak 'improper English', he speaks a different language, stigmatised and devalorised by the school where the standard variety is the only language of instruction.

Three types of solution to bidialectalism have been proposed:

(1)   the creation of compensatory programs, which we have already mentioned and which are based on the notion of a linguistic deficit; these programs aim at changing the linguistic habits of the child and 're-educating' him into speaking the 'proper' language;

(2)   bidialectal programs in which the child learns to use the standard variety at school but is also encouraged by the school to use his vernacular in his own environment (Fasold & Shuy, 1970; Cheshire, 1987);

(3) attempts to reduce the attitudes and prejudices of standard speakers
     of the dominant group, rather than modify the child's behaviour.

In a number of studies on West Indian children in Britain V. K. Edwards
(1978a; 1978b) demonstrated that linguistic factors (differences between
creole and Standard English) and non-linguistic factors (attitudes of peers,
teacher and community members) affect the West Indian child's comprehension of Standard English as well as his motivation to learn it. The low
academic achievement of West Indian children was first attributed to
temporary problems of adjustment, then to a negative self-conception and
racist teaching. There has thus been a shift in the perception of the causes of
low achievement: from blaming it on factors intrinsic to the community
and the child, including his 'improper' language use, we have moved to
attributing it to structural forces in the host society (V. K. Edwards, 1986).

Bidialectal education is facing extremely complex problems which are
socio-economic, sociocultural, social psychological, pedagogical and linguistic in nature. The communities concerned are generally socio-economically and culturally deprived and are often visible minorities (for which
race markers are easily perceived). Bidialectal education has to face attitudes and prejudices developed in the dominant group and often shared by
the subordinate group itself: dialect is often perceived as a stigma to be got
rid of. Several experiments and solutions have been proposed (for example,
Dillard, 1978, for the United States; Le Page, 1981, for the West Indies and
Britain), but too often the problem is ignored and submersion in the
mainstream is the default solution. The results obtained with the bilingual
programs discussed earlier could be used as guidelines for bidialectal
education. Teacher training and re-education should help to change attitudes and expectations of the school. The integration of community
teachers should help the child to valorise his vernacular and to use it in
literacy-oriented activities. Such an approach is now being experimented
with in several programs.

Bilingual education for immigrant children also faces a bidialectal problem. Many immigrants do not speak a standard variety of their home
language. When the L_1 is taught in the host country, should it be the
standard variety, or the dialect which is the child's real mother tongue?
Tosi (1984) stresses the difficulties originating from the dichotomy between
Standard Italian and Sicilian dialect in teaching Standard Italian in bilingual programs for Italian immigrants in Britain. For bidialectal teaching to
become efficient, the dialect must first be valorised. A dominant language
may be threatening, not only for students but also for teachers: Bentolila &
Gani (1981) mention the case of Haiti where the school authorities gave the
impression that Standard French was used in the school; however, in

reality, neither pupils nor teachers were capable of communicating in French. The end result was the use of a mesolect in which French stereotypes and French words took on a symbolic function. Since 1975 Haiti has been experimenting with bidialectal programs and creole is used in the first years of elementary schooling; however, Haitians are now coping with the problem of a written standard for creole. The relative status of both Standard French and creole in Haitian society will determine the future of bidialectal education in Haiti.

11.4.4   Community bilingual education

In an idealised model of bilingual education the different groups of a community decide jointly the languages in which instruction will be given. They not only have pluralist views of education but aim at a 'multicultural synthesis' (Robinson, 1981). Not only the minority children but also the majority children are instructed in both the dominant and the subordinate languages. The choice of the subordinate language varies according to the presence and the size of the minority groups: the school attempts to reflect the linguistic and cultural pattern of the community, hence the name 'community languages' which is sometimes given to this type of bilingual education. Smolicz (1979) and Robinson (1981) have advocated bilingual education in which majority and minority children are both taught together in each other's languages. For example, where the Greek–Australian group is numerous, Anglo-Australian children and Greek–Australian children would be taught the same curriculum in both English and modern Greek (see also Blanc, 1987, for England, and Corson, 1993, for New Zealand). Lambert & Taylor (1990) have suggested a model of community education for American schools: the goals of education and the languages used to attain these goals should be decided by the three main groups: Anglo-Americans, Black Americans and other ethnic minorities. This model implies teaching in at least three codes for all children: Standard English, Black English Vernacular and one heritage language chosen according to the ethnic concentration in the community (e.g. Spanish in California). This ideal has been put into practice in the 'Two-Way Bilingual Education Programs' in the USA (Christian & Mahrer, 1992; Cazabon, Lambert & Hall, 1993; Nicoladis, Taylor, Lambert & Cazabon, 1998). These programs begin in elementary schools and serve an equal number of language-minority and language-majority children, with the goal of bilinguality for both groups. They combine the features of bilingual programs for language-minority students with immersion for majority students. In one program in which Spanish-American, African-American and White American students were taught half the time in English and the other half in Spanish, tests of reading and mathematics in each language were administered. The experimenters (Nicoladis, Taylor, Lambert and Cazabon, 1998) found that although younger African-American students scored significantly lower than the White American group in reading and mathematics in Standard American English, they performed as well as the latter in tests of reading and mathematics in Spanish (L_2). This suggests that the underachievement of African-American children is not genetically determined but the result of social environmental factors; it further suggests that two-way bilingual education can be successful with minority-group children whose home language is different from that of the school.

Interesting though this model may be, it might overlook the power relations existing in the community as well as the ethnolinguistic vitality of each of the groups involved. For example, in his analysis of Franco-Manitoban schools, Hébert (1976) demonstrated that it is sufficient to introduce one English-speaking pupil into a Francophone class in order for all the Francophone students to switch to English. According to Fishman (1980), in a language-contact situation the subordinate language will survive only in a diglossic relation with the dominant language (see Section 10.3.2). Community bilingual education aims at destroying this diglossia by conferring equal status on all languages: will this not make one of the languages redundant (Quinn, 1981)? If that happens then it would be the minority language that becomes redundant. Although community bilingual education might, at first view, appear to be a very promising approach, we wonder whether it can succeed in the long run. The question remains unanswered.

11.5   BILINGUAL EDUCATION AND FORM–FUNCTION MAPPING

According to our social cultural and cognitive interactional model (see Chapter 5) the choice of language as medium of education should be selected as a function of the existing form–function mappings (fFms). In the case of existing fFms education can introduce an L_2 as medium of instruction, whereas in the absence of fFms in the L_1, education should concentrate on establishing these before introducing new L_2 forms. This is in agreement with the social literacy approach (see Section 11.1) and with experiments in literacy development (for example the experiment by Tizard, Schofield & Hewison (1982), mentioned in Sections 4.3.1, 5.1.4.5 and 11.4.2.3).

Mapping L_1 forms onto new functions is also a way of valorising the L_1. By introducing the child who has not acquired literacy skills at home to these new skills via his mother tongue rather than through an L_2, the school valorises the L_1. In this case L_1 and L_2 become interchangeable for literacy functions.

Whether literacy is introduced through the mother tongue or through an L_2, it is essential to integrate formal and functional aspects in teaching it, that is, mapping form onto function (Hamayan, 1994). This is especially true for low-literacy children, that is, children who have had little exposure to literacy-oriented activities even before they start to learn reading and writing, as is often the case for minority children. Hamayan recommends various instructional approaches that provide functional and meaningful literacy activities while teaching the specific forms and structures of written language as part of the teaching environment. These are as follows:

(1) The classroom must be rich with meaningful environmental print.
(2) The construction of meaning must be the basis of all literacy activities.
(3) New literacy skills should be allowed to emerge naturally and in a low-anxiety environment.
(4) These activities must be motivating.
(5) Instruction about linguistic forms and structures should be embedded in meaningful functional language activities.
(6) Literacy instruction should be integrated with instruction of academic content (Hamayan, 1994: 298).

11.6   CONCLUSION

This chapter has dealt with the issues of language planning in bilingual education and their consequences for the child. We first discussed the relationship between the development of literacy and languages of instruction. Bilingual education is determined by social historical, ideological, power-relation and social psychological factors which interact with each other and have to be taken into consideration when deciding on the language or languages of instruction. We looked at bilingual education programs. We began with those designed for majority children, namely in the European schools and in immersion, and discussed the consequences of immersion programs for the child's linguistic skills and academic achievement. Immersion programs appear as an applicable solution for children of dominant and socially advantaged groups. On the other hand, for minority children who have little or no exposure to literacy, it is desirable to introduce literacy in the mother tongue. We further examined the myth of the bilingual handicap of the minority child and showed how it leads to wrong pedagogical decisions. Some examples of bilingual programs for minority children and their results in terms of academic achievement were described. We also reviewed the research on bidialectal and community-language education. We attempted to explain the underlying principles of bilingual education.

For the child to benefit from a bilingual education certain prerequisites have to be met. First, his two languages have to be valorised for both the communicative and cognitive linguistic functions. Second, if the child has already acquired form-L_1–function mapping for literacy functions, mapping between new L_2 forms and functions can occur with relative ease. On the other hand, if these mappings have not been achieved, it is crucial that L_1 forms are first mapped onto these functions before he is introduced to the L_2 forms necessary for these functions.

In the case of immersion programs the children of the dominant/socially advantaged group possess a highly valorised L_1, which in the society is used for a whole range of cognitive and literacy-related activities. Although he is introduced to an L_2 of which he does not yet know the forms, he has reached a state of readiness because he is already familiar with the functions. In the case of a disadvantaged minority child who is little exposed to literacy-oriented activities in his community and who speaks a devalorised minority language, if he is schooled through the more prestigious L_2, he must acquire both the forms in L_2 and the new functions. Because no mapping has occurred previously between these functions and L_1 forms, he has to acquire both elements of the form–function mapping at one at the same time. Furthermore, because of the devalorisation of the L_1 it is not necessary that a form L_1 mapping onto an already existing form-L_2–function mapping occurs. In this sense L_1 does not appear as a necessary form for the function and will be further devalorised.

Whereas there are many indications that the minority child benefits from being introduced to literacy in his mother tongue, for various reasons this is too often ignored. For example, it may be because:

- the covert goal is assimilation of the minority child into the mainstream culture; or
- the means are unattainable or economically too costly (as for example when the language is not written, or when there are no teaching materials or trained teachers available); or
- those who plan education are still ignorant of research results, believe in the myth of the bilingual handicap and are convinced that the earlier the child is introduced to a prestigious L_2 the better he will develop academically.

Bilingual education programs and mother-tongue teaching in the early school years have been shown to benefit minority children and improve their academic achievement. Time spent on teaching the mother tongue does not slow down their proficiency in L_2 and increases their language skills in the mother tongue. Issues of bidialectal education are similar to those of bilingual education.

In contrast with the bilingual education for majority children, bilingual programs designed for minority children do not aim at functional bilinguality; they are rather a way of ensuring a better preparation for further education in a dominant L_2. This is achieved neither by total submersion in the L_2 nor by ghettoisations in a shelter program. Transition programs in which instruction is given entirely or partially in the L_1 enable the minority child to catch up on academic achievement; they do not, however, provide him with the benefits of bilingual education that a majority child can gain from early bilingual experience or immersion programs.

The linguistic mismatch hypothesis which led UNESCO (1953) to declare the right of all children to mother-tongue education is an oversimplification. It is gospel to many educators who do not see the complexity of the problem. That a child can develop an additive form of bilinguality when literacy is taught via an L_2 has been proved by the positive results of immersion programs. The positive consequences of bilingual education can be obtained for all children, provided that the context of development of bilinguality is adequate. By this we mean that education must in the first place ensure that the mapping between linguistic form and cognitive function has been established. There is no simple universal solution to bilingual education, but each program must be planned as a function of the many sociocultural, social structural and social psychological factors relevant to a particular situation (Hamers, 1979).

One of the major differences between bilingual programs for majority and minority children lies in their final goals: functional bilinguality vs. mainstream assimilation. When functional bilinguality is promoted in the minority child – as, for example, when the family valorises the mother tongue sufficiently to maintain it – academic achievement is improved. Community bilingual education aims at promoting functional bilinguality for all children. However, at present we have no empirical evidence that community bilingual education promotes additive bilinguality in minority children. It is not enough to bring majority and minority children together in a community bilingual education program in order to ensure its success. Too many important factors, such as the existing power relations, have been overlooked. Only a better understanding of bilingual development and its relationship to cognitive development and social conditions will help transform community bilingual education from utopia to reality.

Conclusion

In this book we have critically but constructively reviewed the state of the art regarding languages in contact (bilingualism), from individual bilingualism (or bilinguality) to societal bilingualism. We began by examining traditional and current definitions of bilingualism, none of which was found to be adequate. They all show one or more of three main weaknesses. First, they are *unidimensional*: they describe the bilingual in terms of one dimension, such as language competence, ignoring other equally important aspects. Second, they fail to take into account the different *levels of analysis*, from individual to societal. Finally, they are not based on a *general theory of language behaviour*.

To remedy these failings we proposed a multidimensional theoretical model of language behaviour (Figure 1.1), which we also apply to bilingual behaviour and which guides us throughout the book. According to this model *language processing* operates at different levels of organisation which are embedded in one another, from micro- to macro-levels: these are the individual networks, the interpersonal networks, the social networks and the social structures. These levels are not independent of one another but are in dynamic interaction. Within and between these levels there are complex *mappings* of the *forms* of language behaviour onto the *functions* they are supposed to serve. It should be stressed that the social and the psychological dimensions are found at every level simultaneously, in the sense that any speaker is at one and the same time an individual, a member of social networks and groups, and part of the whole society. These different levels of language processing require different types of *analysis* at the individual, interpersonal and societal levels. Finally, these different levels of processing and analysis are best explored by *multidisciplinary and interdisciplinary approaches*: psychological, social psychological and sociological approaches. The linguistic aspect is present throughout, though variously focused.

It is with these guiding principles in mind that in Chapter 2 we analysed the various dimensions and measurements of bilinguality and societal bilingualism. We stressed the specificity and originality of the bilingual's language behaviour which should not be reduced to the sum of two monolingual behaviours.

In Chapters 3 to 5 we examined the evidence on the ontogenesis of bilinguality in the light of our guiding principles. In order to account for the often conflicting results of empirical research we found it necessary at this micro-level to integrate linguistic and cognitive processes with the social cultural context: bilinguistic development is deeply rooted in inter-personal interactions. Children growing up bilingually have specific behaviour with respect to language: they mix and switch codes, translate from one into the other, gradually differentiating between linguistic systems by an appropriate rule-governed behaviour varying according to listener, setting, topic and sociolinguistic norms. From an early stage they are capable of mapping different linguistic forms onto the relevant functions of the languages in their environment. This ability is more evident in simulta-neous bilinguality where two interchangeable forms fulfil the same func-tion. Similarly, in order to explain the contradictory evidence on the relation between bilinguality and cognitive development (Chapter 4), we put forward a hypothesis of sociocultural and cognitive interdependence. In our discussion of several theoretical approaches, we argued that bilin-guality should be conceptualised on an additive–subtractive continuum which is the resulting force of two independent factors: valorisation and cognitive functioning (Figure 4.2). These two factors are then analysed in terms of form–function mapping: in the case of additive bilinguality a high number of form–function mappings occur, with two interchangeable forms mapping onto the same function. When a new, e.g. cognitive, function is acquired, it is relatively easy for the bilingual child to map two linguistic forms onto it. The additive bilingual may thus develop a more complex set of form–function mappings than his monolingual counterpart, which would account for some of the cognitive advantages of the former over the latter. In subtractive bilinguality, on the other hand, form–function map-ping does not take place in the (devalorised) L_1 and it becomes very difficult, if not impossible, for the child to map new L_2 forms onto non-existing functions.

Chapter 5 brings together the various strands in Chapters 3 and 4 into one socio-cognitive interactional connectionist model of language devel-opment (Figure 5.1), which is then applied to the bilingual situation. According to this model language development is rooted in the interper-sonal interactions in the child's social networks which provide him with a model of language behaviour and the socio-affective values attached to it. Through the processes of internalisation, valorisation and motivation, the child appropriates the social values, forms and functions, and the form–function mappings of language; when all or only some of these functions and forms are valorised, the child is motivated to learn and use all, or only some, of these forms and functions. This leads to the development of communicative linguistic competence and conceptual linguistic competence. Each level of processing is established through a form-function mapping. One essential feature of the model is the feedback mechanism operating between the processes involved in language behaviour.

When two or more languages are present in the child's environment either additive or consecutive bilinguality develops. For the former a new set of complex compound form–function mappings is established, in which two interchangeable linguistic forms are mapped onto one function (in simultaneous bilinguality); for adequate mapping to occur between the two languages it is necessary and sufficient that both be valorised for all functions, in which case we have additive bilinguality. In consecutive bilinguality form–function mapping is first established in L_1 and a new form is later acquired in an L_2 to fulfil the same function. In this case, it is necessary and sufficient for the L_1 to be valorised and used for the communicative and cognitive functions in order to establish a new mapping between these functions and the newly acquired L_2 forms. But if no form–function mapping has been established by the time the child learns an L_2, mapping this new L_2 form onto a new function is very difficult, if not impossible, and a subtractive form of bilinguality may ensue. These considerations have far-reaching implications for bilingual education.

In Chapter 6 we reviewed the behavioural and neuropsychological evidence from brain-damaged and brain-intact polyglot bilinguals and found little support for different hemispheric preferences in bilinguals as compared to monolinguals. In Chapter 7 we examined the bilingual's information processing and concluded that hierarchical models were interesting alternatives to the unresolved question of separate vs. common storage models. Although a model of bilingual processing should account for the different levels of processing in both the monolingual and the bilingual speech modes, while being consistent with a general model of language processing, the issue still awaits a solution.

Complex compound form–function mapping also occurs at other levels of language processing. In Chapter 8, which focuses on sociocultural identity of the bilingual, we show that bilingual proficiency is related to the social psychological mechanisms of ethnolinguistic identity. A balanced bilingual is perceived as a member of both his ethnolinguistic groups. A dominant bilingual, on the other hand, even if he is very fluent in his weaker language, is perceived as belonging to his L_1 group, since the foreign language markers he uses are identified with ethnic allegiances. Bilingual proficiency is also related to the social psychological mechanisms implied in ethnolinguistic encounters. Bilinguality is, therefore, an important social psychological dimension which influences interethnic relations, is shaped by social and cultural factors and, in turn, conditions the development of social psychological mechanisms relevant for the integration of the bilingual individual in society. In this chapter we also examined the role of aptitude, motivation and attitude factors as well as the role of social psychological and social factors in second/foreign language learning.

Chapter 9 examined the interplay between social psychological mechanisms and bilingual behaviour and discussed the validity of speech-accommodation theory in explaining how and why speakers modify their speech in situations of interpersonal interaction. Changes of speech style and/or language are linked to social psychological processes, such as cultural/ethnic identity, attitudes and perceptions as well as to interethnic relations at the personal, interpersonal and intergroup levels. In the second part of the chapter we examined the bilingual's intercultural communication strategies in the light of the accommodation model. We suggested that bilingual speakers optimise their communication efficiency in terms of the most adequate form–function mapping by calling upon the whole range of their repertoire. Communication strategies specific to languages in contact arise from the need continually to accommodate to the changes in intercultural encounters, ranging from minor modifications to mixed-lingual strategies which can, in turn, evolve into autonomous codes. We attempted to integrate the study of the grammar of code-switching into a wider multilevel and interdisciplinary framework. This framework takes into account the bilingual competence of the individual and the social norms of the bilingual speech community, and looks at the grammar from pragmatic, discoursal and ethnographic as well as from syntactic viewpoints.

In our study of societal bilingualism in Chapter 10 we stressed the constant interaction between the dynamics of societal processes and individual processes. Ethnolinguistic vitality, for example, is a function of the interaction between sociostructural factors, interpersonal behaviour, individual perceptions, and the interactions between these. The outcome of these interactions is self-regulated behaviour, that is, whether members of an ethnolinguistic group decide to change or not to change their behaviour according to their perceptions of the situation. The analysis of sociolinguistic variations has shown the constant and complex mapping processes between form and function at all levels and across all levels. In the case of pidginisation, for example, the development of new forms of language behaviour is brought about by the introduction of a new social function, for example the need to trade or communicate between groups who do not speak the same language. When new functions appear, new forms are developed to serve these functions and the pidgin becomes more complex; eventually it may evolve into a creole which, because of its social importance, becomes the mother tongue of the next generation. Conversely, the existing vernaculars lose some or all of their functions, are reduced in form and may eventually become extinct. Similar form–function mappings are at work in diglossia, language shift and language planning. This interpretation of these phenomena is in line with the language-processing model set out in Chapter 1.

In the final chapter, Chapter 11, we showed how bilingual education is shaped at all levels by factors which are social historical, ideological, social psychological as well as psychological in nature. As for the best kind of bilingual education for the child, our own social cognitive interactional model of bilingual development provided some answers. According to whether form–function mappings for cognitive-literacy functions are present or absent in the child's L_1, education may or may not introduce an L_2 as the medium of instruction. Immersion programs for the dominant group assume that some mappings are in place in the child's valorised mother tongue, and that he is therefore ready to learn L_2 forms. In the case of a socially disadvantaged group whose L_1 is devalorised, the school should first establish form–function mappings in L_1 before (or at the same time as) introducing L_2 forms. This approach also helps to valorise a usually devalorised L_1. Bilingual education programs based on mother-tongue teaching in the early years have been shown to benefit minority children by improving their academic performance.

Students of languages in contact, whether at the individual, interpersonal or societal level, commonly address the issues from one necessary but insufficient disciplinary perspective, using either a micro- or a macro-level. In order to capture the totality of this complex phenomenon it is essential not only to examine it from different disciplinary viewpoints, but also to integrate these at both the theoretical and methodological level. This approach allows an interdisciplinary model to be designed. In this book we have attempted to apply an interactional connectionist approach to all levels of bilingual processing. In the form–function mapping process, language forms are developed to serve functions. We believe that most language behaviour can be understood through this complex mapping mechanism between form–function, form–form and function–function combinations. Language behaviour is an encultured behaviour and as such follows the rules of higher-order behaviours: it plays an active role in creating representations and is self-regulated. As language is also a valued social object, language behaviour is submitted to the valorisation process. Whether one or more languages are present, these mechanisms come into action. In our analyses of bilinguality and bilingualism we have applied these principles.

However, despite this study of bilinguality and bilingualism, we are only too keenly aware that there is still a long way to go before a truly multidisciplinary and interdisciplinary methodology is developed. At the present time there is a lack of theorising in the field of research in languages in contact. There is almost an overwhelming excess of data gathering on the subject which is not always productive because, as with all observed facts, they are ambiguous unless they can be organised in an interpretative framework. As Clément (1987) rightly comments, 'results are only interpretable in the context of the rationale justifying the choice of the observational paradigm' (p. 4). Examples of uninterpreted data are innumerable in studies on bilingualism, from bilingual child biographies to statistical data on speech communities. These studies become useful only when they can be interpreted in terms of a theoretical model. Typologies, however useful, should not be confused with an explanatory model: putting the data into boxes helps only if the boxes have been assigned a function within a theoretical construct with predictive power. For example, collecting data on who speaks what language to whom and when is of little use unless it is collected in order to test particular hypotheses. Typologies of bilingualism which are a-theoretical can always be invented and reinvented. They tell us nothing about bilinguals except that they are different. They do not, however, tell us why they are different, nor how these differences have come about.

We therefore need to develop further theoretical constructs which can be empirically verified. Such constructs should be interdisciplinary and fit the epistemology of the different disciplines involved. Information technology has eliminated the problem of treating masses of data, but data banks, like typologies, are of use only if the right questions can be asked. One of the problems with interdisciplinary research is that not all the disciplines have reached a similar level of generating hypotheses. In recent years, we have come to know a lot more about information processing in bilinguals than when Weinreich wrote his classic study on languages in contact in 1953. From the conception of the bilingual speaker as someone whose speech shows interferences – and who is at worst cognitively deficient and at best the sum of two monolingual speakers – we have moved to the conception of an integrated person for whom the bilingual experience may enhance cognitive functioning – provided that society recognises this potential. Perhaps it is time that bilinguality and bilingualism be recognised as the norm, and monolinguality and monolingualism as the exception which needs to be explained.

Notes

1 'Polylectality' refers to any speaker's ability to use a repertoire of languages, dialects, language varieties and styles to fulfil a number of social functions.
2 By level of analysis we mean a mode of description and explanation focusing on a particular approach to reality; for example, we can analyse a society in terms of institutions, groups or social networks. These levels are not organised in a hierarchy, but each level refers to a homogeneous approach to reality.
3 A critical mass is a threshold reached when a decisive change occurs, e.g. the temperature reached when water starts to boil.
4 By literacy we understand the type of language processing which develops as a consequence of the decontextualised use of language, which is characteristic of, but not exclusive to, reading and writing. It is a cognitive skill (Venezky, 1991: 49), an amplifier of language as a cognitive tool (Olson, 1998; Chang & Wells, 1990).
5 Theories of connectionism assume that neural connections are created as a result of learning experiences. For example, in Hebb's (1949; 1968) neurophysiological connectionist theory, learning is viewed as a modification of neural transmission routes and a creation of cross-connections between existing routes; as a consequence new and more complex cell-assemblies are formed which are responsible for higher-order behaviour.

2 DIMENSIONS AND MEASUREMENT OF BILINGUALITY AND BILINGUALISM

1 A cloze test is a test of reduced redundancy which consists of a spoken or written text in which single words have been deleted at regular intervals, e.g. every fifth, sixth or seventh word. The ability to fill in the missing words is supposed to be a valid measure of the testee's comprehension of the text and of his expectancy grammar (Oller, 1979). Other tests of reduced redundancy have been proposed in recent years (for a review see, for example, Alderson & North, 1991).

3 ONTOGENESIS OF BILINGUALITY

1 The authors used the Visual Reinforced Infant Speech Discrimination technique (VRISD) in which the infant is first conditioned to turn his head in response to a

change in a continuous auditory stimulation. Once the infant is conditioned this technique can be used to assess other discriminations he is capable of.

2 R. Brown (1973) describes the language of the child in terms of five successive stages. Each stage is mainly defined by a measure of mean length utterance (MLU). Brown's study suggests that child language acquisition is a continuous process of cumulative complexity: before acceding to the next stage the child must master the structures of the previous stage. The author shows that the stages are invariant even if children do not acquire the language at the same pace.

3 This morpheme is characteristic of Canadian English.

4 -ti is a morpheme characteristic of Canadian French.

4 COGNITIVE DEVELOPMENT AND THE SOCIOCULTURAL CONTEXT OF BILINGUALITY

1 An interactional routine is a sequence of exchanges in which a speaker's utterance and its accompanying appropriate non-verbal behaviour calls forth one of a limited set of responses by one or more other participants (Peters & Boggs, 1986).

2 The term 'metalinguistic' refers to an explicit knowledge about the structural components (words, phonology, syntactic structures) of language; 'metalinguistic ability' refers to the capacity to focus on language as an object that can be analysed and reflected upon; 'metalinguistic awareness' refers to the access to this knowledge, i.e. an awareness and a control of linguistic features such as being aware of the arbitrariness of the word–object relation or the capacity to identify and correct syntactic errors. Metalinguistic awareness is considered a major factor in the cognitive growth and the development of literacy; it is a predictor of reading achievement.

3 We refer the reader unfamiliar with psychometric tests to Anastasi (1976).

4 This study is unique insofar as a large number of potentially confounding variables are controlled for: both monolingual and bilingual Konds, also known as Kandhas, are drawn from the same tribal culture and they share common socio-economic conditions, ecology, customs, beliefs, religion and other aspects of culture, except for the language patterns that they use (Mohanty, 1994a).

5 Sternberg's triarchic model of intellectual functioning is composed of three dimensions: a contextual, an experiential and a componential dimension. The contextual dimension describes how intelligence is defined by sociocultural context; the experiential dimension suggests that intelligence is demonstrated in the confrontation of a novel task or in the process of automatisation; the componential dimension describes the structure and processes that underlie intelligent behaviour. The latter dimension has three components: knowledge acquisition which encodes new information and compares it to memorised information; performance which executes plans, and metacomponents which allow one to evaluate, control and monitor information processing.

5 SOCIAL AND PSYCHOLOGICAL FOUNDATIONS OF BILINGUALITY

1 Individuals represent to themselves the outside world and their own actions and experiences. A representation is a stylised model of the world (Charniak &

McDermott, 1985) which comes into existence through the individual's experience. This experience is partly unique to the individual and partly shared with others. Social representations are the sum of the knowledge shared by a community; they are systems of practices, ideas, attitudes and values. Because all higher-order representations have a social component, the individual's organisation of complex human knowledge will depend to a great extent on social interaction and its two salient characteristics: culture and language (see Moscovici, 1984).

2 Through his interaction with others the child first learns to organise his knowledge of interactional events. The representation of events or 'schemata' – also called 'scripts' by Schank & Abelson (1977) and Nelson (1981) and 'formats' by Bruner & Sherwood (1981) – is derived from, and applied to, social contexts. A schema or script is 'an ordered sequence of actions appropriate to a particular spatial-temporal context, organised around a goal' (Nelson, 1981); it is, however, not episodic but serves as a generalised model valid for all instances of a class of events.

3 A text is a sequence of words, either spoken or written, which has a definable communicative function and is characterised by cohesion and coherence.

4 We refer to Tajfel's (1974) model of social identity according to which the child is enabled through socio-psychological mechanisms – such as social comparison, categorisation and distinctiveness – to build up his own social identity and to define himself as a member of the social group, distinct from others on value dimensions.

5 See Chapter 4, Note 2.

6 NEUROPSYCHOLOGICAL FOUNDATIONS OF BILINGUALITY

1 'Functional asymmetry' refers to the fact that, although the two hemispheres of the human brain are anatomically similar, each takes charge of a specific range of behaviour and therefore they differ in the functions each controls. The term 'hemispheric preference' refers to the fact that one hemisphere is preferentially biased to execute a certain task. Although functional asymmetry has some biological basis, there is also evidence that, at birth, there is a certain amount of equipotentiality between both hemispheres: in the case of brain injury to the left hemisphere the right hemisphere can take over linguistic tasks; this shift takes place completely if the injury occurs before the age of 2–4, and to a lesser extent if the patient is older at the time of the injury. For further details see Corballis, 1991.

2 We consider the term 'hemispheric preference' more appropriate than 'cerebral dominance', although the latter has been frequently used.

3 The terms 'propositional' and 'appositional' refer both to typological differences between languages and to differences in modes of thinking related to languages. Thus, for example, Native American languages are polysynthetic and allegedly appositional while English or Chinese are analytic and allegedly propositional.

4 See Note 3.

5 'Agrammatism' is a language disorder that produces speech of a telegrammatic nature, e.g. 'girl speak boy' for 'The girl spoke to the boy'.

7 INFORMATION PROCESSING IN THE BILINGUAL

1 The semantic differential is a technique developed by Osgood, Suci & Tannen-baum (1957) for measuring emotional reactions to words. Subjects are asked to rate each of many words, such as those for a language and its speakers, on twenty bipolar adjective scales, e.g. *happy–sad, hard–soft, slow–fast*. Three domi-nant factors consistently appear across all the cultures and languages, namely *evaluation, potency* and *activity*, which can thus serve as reference points for comparing otherwise culture-bound concepts.

2 In retroactive inhibition (or interference) a new learning inhibits an older established learning; for example, if the association *cat-crazy* has been well established in a previous learning, the subsequent learning of the association *cat-stubborn* will interfere with the previous learning, and the recall of the first paired associate deteriorates.

3 In the part–whole transfer paradigm one learns first a partial list, then a whole list of words which includes the partial list in addition to new words; the subject is required to recognise if a word is part of the whole list or of the partial list.

4 In a lexical decision task the subject has to make a decision whether a string of letters is a word or a non-word (e.g. *cat* and *jik*), or whether a word is part of one language or the other (e.g. *cat* and *chien*); no response requirement is made at the semantic level.

5 In a word-fragment completion task a subject is given a few letters of a word and is asked to complete the word.

6 The Stroop technique was first developed to verify the possible interference between semantic and physical characteristics of a stimulus word. In its original form a subject is presented with a series of colour words, such as *red* and *green*, written in different-coloured inks; the task consists in naming the colour of the ink while ignoring the meaning of the word. For example, the correct response to the word *red* written in green ink is *green*. A subject produces more errors and takes more time to name the colours when the stimulus word is a colour name such as *red*, than when the stimulus-word meaning is unrelated to colours, such as the word *chair*; the most common error is to respond to an incongruent stimulus, i.e. a word denoting a colour different from the ink in which it is written (such as *red* written in blue), by reading the stimulus word instead of naming the colour of the ink. This technique provides an approach for measur-ing the possible interference of a highly automatised verbal decoding process on the required encoding process.

7 In a dichotic-listening technique the subject receives two messages simulta-neously, one in the left ear and the other one in the right. Because in simulta-neous auditory stimulation ipsi-lateral neural connections are suppressed in favour of the contra-lateral ones, each stimulus reaches only the contra-lateral hemisphere. With this technique it is therefore possible to check whether one hemisphere dominates the other in information processing. See also Chapter 6.

8 In the priming technique a stimulus word is presented either together with, or shortly after, another word that is to be ignored. Monolingual studies demon-strate that the subject's response to the stimulus word is influenced by the primer or flanker. For example, when presented with the word *boy* the most likely associate to be given is *girl*; but if the word *boy* is presented just after a

primer like the word *father*, a kinship name like *son* is more likely to be given as a response. A primer which is semantically related to the stimulus word is called a semantic prime and has a facilitating effect on the processing of the stimulus word; for example, processing of the word *teacher* is faster when it is preceded by the word *student* than when it is preceded by the word *cat*. Repetition priming is produced by a repeated presentation of a word (e.g. the stimulus word *cat* has been preceded one or several times by the word *cat*) or, in a bilingual condition, by priming through its translation equivalent (e.g. the English stimulus word *cat* is preceded by the French word *chat*).

9 From a psychological perspective two words are cognates in two related languages when there is a high degree of semantic overlap, a high degree of phonological similarity, and when they are written either in an identical way (the words *table* in French and *table* in English) or in a slightly different graphic form in each language (the words *papier* and *paper*). Non-cognate words which have a high degree of semantic overlap are completely different in their phonological and graphic forms (the French word *chien* and the English word *dog*).

10 The distinction between semantic and episodic memory was introduced by Tulving (1972): semantic memory refers to the storage of representations of the outside world and includes conceptual mechanisms such as categorisation and superordination (e.g. *a cat is an animal*); episodic memory refers to the storage of single events (e.g. *my cat ate my neighbour's goldfish*).

11 Morton (1979b; 1980) uses the word 'logogen' to describe a unit of verbal representation which is not the word but rather the process by which the word becomes accessible in the presence of a given stimulus. For Paivio & Begg (1981) a 'logogen' is a cognitive process which generates a word, while an 'imagen' generates an evoked image.

12 The TAT (Thematic Apperception Test) is a projective technique consisting of one blank card and 19 cards with black and white pictures; the pictures represent people alone or in interaction with others, and the subject is asked to tell a story about each picture and to imagine one for the blank card. It is postulated that the stories reveal certain personality traits.

8 SOCIAL PSYCHOLOGICAL ASPECTS OF BILINGUALITY: CULTURE AND IDENTITY

1 The self-system of identity is a psychological construct which includes concepts like self-development and self-perception; the latter includes mechanisms such as self-recognition, self-awareness, self-esteem and locus of control (Harter, 1983). Identity must be viewed as a psychological construct, capable of synthesis and resynthesis, differentiation and integration, characterised by the attainment of an ever-revised sense of psychological reality supported by a social reality (Spencer & Markstrom-Adams, 1990).

2 The objective of the multidimensional scaling technique is to map a set of objects onto a set of points in multidimensional metric space such that objects which are similar are close together in the space and objects which are dissimilar are distant from each other in the space. This technique enables the social scientist in our particular case to measure perceived social distances between

groups and between self and other groups and to identify the relevant dimensions on which these perceptions vary. For details on MDS, see Kruskal & Wish (1978).

3 The English Only Movement advocates that English is the only language to be officially used in the USA and has to be defended as a national value. Its supporters argue that any bilingual legislation impedes the assimilation and economic achievement of minorities and that services like bilingual education should be abolished.

4 We make a distinction between L$_2$ learning and foreign-language learning. Learning a foreign language is learning a language different from the mother tongue in a setting where no speakers or communities speaking that language are present, as for example learning Swahili in Norway. Learning an L$_2$ is learning a language which is also spoken by speech communities with whom interethnic contacts are present around the learner. This includes a whole array of situations ranging from learning a minority language (e.g. Spanish in California) to learning an official majority language (e.g. learning English in California). The degree of interethnicity present can also vary widely: this is, for example, the case for learning French, one of Canada's official languages, in Quebec, where French is the only official language and the language of the majority; in Ottawa, the national capital where an important Francophone minority lives and where French is present in the federal institutions; or in British Columbia where Francophone communities are almost non-existent and where French has no official status at the provincial level.

11 BILINGUAL EDUCATION

1 'Hawthorne effect' refers to the behaviour-modifying effects of being the subject of social, psychological or educational investigation.

2 See Chapter 8, Note 3.

Glossary

The definitions given in this Glossary correspond to those used in the book and do not necessarily accord with commonly accepted ones. For further information the reader should consult the Subject Index.

acculturation
(acculturated)
The process by which an individual adjusts to a new culture; this usually includes the acquisition of the language(s) of that culture.

acrolect
The speech variety closest to the standard on a creole continuum (see CONTINUUM, DECREOLISATION).

additive
see BILINGUALITY

alloglot
Speaker of languages other than the officially recognised ones in a given society; also called **allophone**.

anomie
A bilingual individual's state of anxiety resulting from an inability to resolve the conflicting demands made by his two cultures.

assimilation
A process by which an individual or group ACCULTURATE to another group by losing their own ethnolinguistic characteristics (see INTEGRATION).
- **fear of assimilation** A process by which an individual refuses to ACCULTURATE for fear of losing his own culture and language.

baby talk
Distinctive linguistic characteristics found in the speech of adults when addressing very young children.

basilect
The oldest and socially lowest speech variety on a creole continuum (see CONTINUUM, DECREOLISATION).

bicultural(ism)
State of an individual or group identifying with more than one culture.
- **bicultural bilingual** Someone who has native competence in his two languages, identifies with both cultural groups and is perceived by each group as belonging.

bidialectal(ism)
- Proficiency in the use of more than one dialect of a language, whether regional or social.
- Principle propounded in sociolinguistics and educational linguistics wherein different speech varieties are accorded equal linguistic validity and used in their appropriate social contexts.

bilingual
- (noun) Individual who has access to two or more distinct linguistic CODES.
- (adjective) Refers to a bilingual individual (or to a community) who uses two or more languages.

bilingual education
Any system of education in which, at a given point in time and for a varying length of time, simultaneously or consecutively, instruction is given in two languages.

bilingualism
The state of an individual (see BILINGUALITY) or a community characterised by the simultaneous presence of two languages (see CONTACT).
- **diglossic bilingualism**   A state of bilingualism in which two languages cooccur, each with a distinct range of social functions.
- **individual** or **personal bilingualism**   see BILINGUALITY
- **territorial bilingualism**   Cooccurrence of two or more languages which have official status within a geographical area; or coexistence of two or more UNILINGUAL areas within a single political structure (e.g. UNILINGUAL regions in a MULTILINGUAL state).

bilinguality
A psychological state of the individual who has access to more than one linguistic code as a means of social communication; this access varies along a number of dimensions.
- **additive bilinguality**   A situation in which a child derives maximum benefit from the bilingual experience for his cognitive development; this is usually the case where the two languages are highly valued in the child's environment.
- **adolescent bilinguality**   State of bilinguality reached after childhood but before adulthood.
- **adult(hood) bilinguality**   State of bilinguality reached after adolescence.
- **balanced bilinguality**   A state of bilinguality in which an equivalent competence is reached in both languages, whatever the level of competence; note that balance is not equally distributed for all domains and functions of language.
- **childhood bilinguality**   State of bilinguality reached before 10–12 years.
- **compound bilinguality**   A state of bilinguality in which two sets of linguistic signs have come to be associated with the same set of meanings; this type of bilinguality is usually linked to a common context of acquisition.
- **consecutive early bilinguality**   Childhood bilinguality in which the second language (L_2) is acquired before 4–5 years but after the acquisition of basic skills in the mother tongue (L_1, then L_2).
- **coordinate bilinguality**   A state of bilinguality in which translation equivalents in two languages each correspond to a distinct set of semantic representations; this type of bilin-

guality is usually linked to different contexts of acquisition.

- **dominant bilinguality** A state of bilinguality in which competence in one language is superior to competence in the other; note that dominance is not equally distributed for all domains and functions of language.
- **infancy bilinguality** State of bilinguality reached during early childhood.
- **simultaneous bilinguality** Infancy bilinguality in which the child develops two mother tongues (L_A, L_B) from the onset of language.
- **subtractive bilinguality** A situation in which the bilingual child's cognitive development is delayed in comparison with his monolingual counterpart; this usually occurs when the mother tongue is devalued in the environment.

borrowing The taking over of linguistic forms (usually lexical items) by one language from another; such borrowings are known as loan words.

broken language A communication strategy by which a speaker attempts to use his interlocutor's mother tongue even though he has a limited competence in it.

code A set of social conventions making use of a system of signs which enable individuals who share these conventions to communicate with one another.

- **linguistic code** A code composed of a system of linguistic rules known by the individuals who use it and stand in a similar relationship to it.

code alternation Generally speaking, a communication strategy used by bilinguals and consisting of the alternate use of two languages in the same utterance or conversation; see CODE-MIXING and CODE-SWITCHING.

code-mixing A communication strategy used by bilinguals in which the speaker of one language L_X transfers elements or rules of a different language (L_Y) to L_X (the base language); unlike BORROWING, however, these elements are not integrated into the linguistic system of L_X.

code-switching A bilingual communication strategy consisting of the alternate use of two languages in the same utterance. There are three types of code-switching: TAG, intersentential and intrasentential code-switching.

competence
- **bilingual competence**: Linguistic competence involving knowledge of the system of rules generating two or more linguistic codes.
- **language** or **communicative competence** This includes linguistic competence and its social and psychological correlates.
- **linguistic competence** An individual's knowledge of the system of rules which generate a linguistic code.

- **native speaker's competence**   The language competence of an individual who knows a language like his mother tongue.

compound (bilinguality)   see BILINGUALITY

contact (languages in)   Cooccurrence of two or more languages either in the individual (BILINGUALITY) or in society (BILINGUALISM).

continuum   Continuous variation between opposite poles, along which variables are situated.

- **linguistic continuum**   Continuous linguistic variation between two or more languages or speech varieties; at each pole of this continuum two distinct linguistic entities are situated which may be mutually unintelligible. A CREOLE is a single continuous chain of varieties connecting the BASILECT at one pole to the ACROLECT at the other.

coordinate (bilinguality)   see BILINGUALITY

creole/ creolisation   A creole is commonly defined as a PIDGIN which has become the first language of a new generation of speakers; this process, called creolisation, is characterised by an expansion of linguistic functions and forms.

critical (optimal/ sensitive) age   Age at which acquisition or learning is achieved in an optimal way; before that age the individual has not reached the necessary maturation stage; after that age he has partially or totally lost the capacity for this acquisition or learning.

- **optimal age for learning a second language**   This is the age period during which the learner acquires native-speaker competence in that language.

decreolisation (post-creole continuum)   The process by which a CREOLE moves towards the dominant (standard) variety at the expense of its most distinctive characteristics.

deculturation   The process by which an individual adapts to a new culture at the expense of his first. Extreme deculturation leads to ASSIMILATION, which may involve loss of the first culture and language.

development (language development)   Refers to the child's language acquisition, including developmental correlates such as the relationship between language and cognitive, affective and social development.

- **bilingual development**   Language development involving the acquisition of two or more languages and including the cognitive, affective and social correlates of this development (see BILINGUALITY).

dialect   A regionally or socially distinctive variety of a language.

diglossia   A situation where two very different varieties of a language or two distinct languages cooccur throughout a SPEECH COMMUNITY, each with a complementary range of social functions.

- **leaky diglossia**   A situation where one variety or language

	spreads into the functions formerly reserved for another.
domain	A group of institutionalised social situations typically constrained by a common set of behavioural rules.
emic/etic	Terms which characterise approaches to the study of culture and language. An **emic** approach is culture and language specific; an **etic** approach sets up universal categories.
enculturation	A part of the socialisation process by which a child acquires the rules of behaviour and the values of his culture.
endogenous (language)	A language that is used as mother tongue within a speech community (see EXOGENOUS).
ethnic identity	see IDENTITY
ethnicity	A sociological concept which refers to objective common indicators of differences, such as race, religion, language, and national origin, used in the classification of individuals.
ethnolinguistic	Refers to a set of cultural, ethnic and linguistic features shared by one social group.
etic	see EMIC
exogenous (language)	A language not used as mother tongue but only as official or institutionalised language in a speech community (see ENDOGENOUS).
feedback	see SELF-REGULATION
first language	see L_1, L_A/L_B, LANGUAGE
foreigner talk	A bilingual communication strategy in which the speaker simplifies his mother tongue to make himself understood by another speaker who has limited competence in it.
form–function mapping (fFm)	A process by which a linguistic form is associated with the function it is meant to serve. Language behaviour is viewed as having two levels: the functional level, where all the meanings and intentions to be expressed are represented; and the formal level, at which all the surface forms used in the language are represented.
handicap (linguistic/ bilingual/ cognitive)	A disadvantage which prevents an individual from achieving expected norms in language or cognitive development.
identity (cultural/ ethnic)	• At the individual level, a psychological mechanism by which a child develops the dimension of his personality pertaining to his membership of a cultural or ethnic group. • At the group level, cultural or ethnic characteristics of the members of a group perceived as a social entity.
immersion (programs)	A type of BILINGUAL EDUCATION in which a group of learners is taught through the medium of a language (L_2) different from their mother tongue (L_1) the latter being used later. • **early immersion** Immersion program in which a second language (L_2) is used exclusively as a medium of instruction in the early years of schooling but together with the mother tongue (L_1) in the later years.

- **late immersion** Immersion program in which a second language (L_2) is introduced as a medium of instruction at a later stage.
- **partial immersion** Immersion program in which both the first (L_1) and the second language (L_2) are used as media of instruction.

independence A psychological state which enables a psychological mechanism or process, or a linguistic code, to function independently of another mechanism, process or linguistic code (see INTERDEPENDENCE).

integration A process by which an individual ACCULTURATES to a new culture without losing his first culture and identity, including language (see ASSIMILATION).

integrative (ness)
- **Integrative orientation** Reasons suggesting that an individual is learning a second language (L_2) in order to form a closer liaison with that other language community.
- **integrative motive** Includes not only the orientation but also the motivation to learn the second language for these reasons.

interdependence Relationship between two linguistic systems or psychological mechanisms which means that one cannot function or develop without reference to the other (see INDEPENDENCE).

interference
- In the field of learning, there is interference when one piece of learning or one associaton inhibits another.
- In second language learning interference refers to learning problems in which the learner unconsciously and inappropriately transfers elements or rules from the first (L_1) to the second (L_2) language.
- May refer to any language behaviour in which a speaker calls upon elements and rules from two or more linguistic codes in the same utterance or communication interaction (see CODE ALTERNATION, CODE-MIXING, CODE-SWITCHING, BORROWING).

interlanguage Refers to successive stages in the processes of acquisition of a second language (L_2) in which the linguistic productions of the learner represent systematic approximations to the target language.

internalisation A psychological process by which a child makes values and behaviour around him his own, thereby transforming it in accordance with his own individual characteristics.

L_1 Denotes the mother tongue or first language.

L_2 Denotes a second language learned after the first.

L_A/L_B Denotes the cooccurrence of two mother tongues learned simultaneously.

L_X, L_Y, L_Z Denotes any natural language.

language
- **auxiliary language** A language which has been adopted by different speech communities for purposes of communica-

tion, it being the native language of none of them (see
LINGUA FRANCA).

- **community** or **heritage language** A minority language
  valued by the community of its speakers who actively encourage its maintenance.
- **first language** or **mother tongue** The linguistic CODE(s) corresponding to the individual's first language (L_1) experience;
  also the linguistic CODE(s) used as mother tongue by most
  members of a speech community.
- **foreign language** Second and subsequently learned lan-
  guage(s) (L_2) which are not widely used by the speech community in which the learner lives.
- **international language** Language of wider communication
  used beyond the national boundaries of a linguistic community for specific purposes.
- **majority** or **dominant language** A language used by a
  socio-economically dominant group in society, or one
  which has received a political or cultural status superior to
  that of other languages in the community.
- **minority** or **subordinate language** A language used by a
  socially subordinate group, or one which has received a
  social or cultural status inferior to that of another (dominant) language in the community.
- **national language** A language which may or may not have
  OFFICIAL status but is used by a large section of the speech
  community.
- **native language** The language or languages which have
  been acquired naturally during childhood (also FIRST
  LANGUAGE, MOTHER TONGUE, L_1).
- **official language** A language which is legally adopted by a
  state as its language of communication for all or some of its
  official transactions; this language may be ENDOGENOUS or
  EXOGENOUS.
- **second language** The language learned by an individual
  after acquiring his first or native language or mother
  tongue; a non-native language which is the mother tongue
  of the speech community (also L_2).
- **source language** The language in which a message is transmitted and which is decoded by the interpreter/translator
  with the aim of recoding it in another language (TARGET
  LANGUAGE), the first language of the second language
  learner.
- **standard language** A language variety which has been accorded a status which is socially and culturally superior to
  other varieties and is used officially.
- **target language** The language into which a message in
  another language is translated or interpreted; the language

	which is the goal of second language acquisition.
language history	The past and present data on the history of acquisition and use of one or more languages.
lect	A collection of linguistic phenomena which has a functional identity within a speech community (see ACROLECT, BASILECT).
lingua franca	An AUXILIARY LANGUAGE (see LANGUAGE) used between groups of people who speak different native languages for the purpose of routine communication.
linguistic code	see CODE
linguistic community	see SPEECH COMMUNITY
linguistic continuum	A continuous linguistic variation between two languages or language varieties; at the opposite poles of this continuum are situated two distinct linguistic entities which may be mutually unintelligible. • **post-creole continuum:** see DECREOLISATION
linguistic handicap	see HANDICAP
literacy	State of an individual or community relating to the decontextualised use of language, especially in the written mode; a use of language which is characteristic of, but not exclusive to, reading and writing. It is a cognitive skill, an amplifier of language as a cognitive tool.
loan blend	A type of BORROWING in which the loan word is modified according to the rules of the borrowing language.
melting pot	A policy of ASSIMILATION which reflected the dominant US ideology towards its ethnic minority groups before the Second World War.
monocultural	Individual identifying with and being identified by only one culture (see also UNICULTURAL).
monolingual	Individual having access to only one linguistic code (see also UNILINGUAL).
mother tongue	see FIRST LANGUAGE under LANGUAGE
multilingual/ multilingualism	see BILINGUAL/BILINGUALISM
native speaker	An individual for whom a particular language is a 'native language' (see FIRST LANGUAGE under LANGUAGE).
network	see SOCIAL NETWORK
optimal age	see CRITICAL AGE
pidgin/ pidginisation	A new language developed by two speech communities attempting to communicate and characterised by reduced grammatical structure and lexis; the process by which this language develops.
planning (language planning)	The official organisation of the relations between languages within a given territory. • **external/statusplanning** Interferencewiththeexistingstatus relations between languages in contact in a given territory.

	• **internal/corpus planning** Interference with the internal dynamic processes of a language.
pluralism	A cultural and linguistic policy by which ethnolinguistic minority groups are integrated into the wider society while being allowed to maintain their linguistic and cultural characteristics to varying degrees.
preferred language	The language chosen by a bilingual speaker in a given situation from among his REPERTOIRE.
received pronunciation (RP)	The name given to the regionally neutral but socially prestigious accent in British English.
repertoire (speech repertoire)	The range of codes, languages or varieties available for use by a speaker, each of which enables him to perform a particular social role; the range of languages or varieties within a speech community.
second language	see L$_2$, LANGUAGE
segregation	Process by which an individual or group is kept linguistically and culturally isolated within a society.
self-regulation	• A characteristic of all higher-order behaviours by which a feedback is given which allows readjustment of behaviour. • At the individual level it calls upon the past experience, the evaluation and the individual's cognitive and emotional functioning allowing for readjustment of the response.
semilingualism	A term used to denote a state in the language development of a bilingual who has reached native-speaker competence in none of his languages (see SUBTRACTIVE BILINGUALITY under BILINGUALITY).
sensitive age	see CRITICAL AGE
separatism	A political process by which an ethnolinguistic group chooses the solution of language nationalism to its linguistic and cultural problems.
shift (language shift)	Process in which a speech community gives up a language completely in favour of another one.
social network	The sum of all the interpersonal relations existing in a community, or that one individual establishes with others over time including their own characteristics.
speech accommodation	The process by which interlocutors modify their speech style (e.g. accent) or switch codes in order to converge towards, or diverge from, each other in communication interactions.
speech community	Any regionally or socially definable human group identified by the use of a shared linguistic system(s) and by participation in shared sociolinguistic norms.
standard	The prestige variety of language used within a speech community; the natural or artificial process by which a dialect becomes a standard language is called standardisation.
submersion	A form of education in which a child is taught in a school where the medium of instruction is a language other than his mother tongue.

subtractive	see BILINGUALITY
switch (mechanism)	Psychological mechanism by which the bilingual is enabled to shut out one of his linguistic systems while using another.
translation equivalent	A linguistic unit in one language corresponding to a linguistic unit in another language at the semantic level.
unicultural	Group identifying with and being identified by only one culture (see also MONOCULTURAL).
unilingual	Group having access to only one linguistic code (see also MONOLINGUAL).
universal grammar (UG)	Grammar that specifies the properties common to all languages.
valorisation	A psychological process by which a child or an adult attributes certain values to a physical or social object.
variety	Any system of linguistic expression whose use is governed by situational variables, such as region, occupation, etc.
vernacular	The indigenous language or dialect of a speech community.
vitality (ethnolinguistic vitality)	That which makes an ethnolinguistic group likely to behave as a distinctive and active collective entity in intergroup relations.

References

Abdulaziz Mkilifi, M. H. (1978) Triglossia and Swahili–English bilingualism in Tanzania. In J. A. Fishman (ed.) *Advances in the Study of Societal Multilingualism*. The Hague: Mouton.

Aboud, F. E. (1976) Social development aspect of language. *Papers in Linguistics*, 9, 15–37.

Aboud, F. E. (1977) Interest in ethnic formation: a cross-cultural developmental study. *Canadian Journal of Behavioral Science*, 9, 134–46.

Aboud, F. E. & Skerry, S. A. (1984) The development of ethnic attitudes: a critical review. *Journal of Cross-Cultural Psychology*, 15, 3–34.

Adler, K. (1977) *Collective and Individual Bilingualism: A Socio-Linguistic Study.* Hamburg: Helmut Buske Verlag.

Aellen, C. & Lambert, W. E. (1969) Ethnic identification and personality adjustments of Canadian adolescents of mixed English–French parentage. *Canadian Journal of Behavioral Science*, 1, 69–86.

Aikio, M. (1990) The Finnish perspective: language and ethnicity. In D. R. F. Collis (ed.) *Arctic Languages: An Awakening.* Paris: UNESCO.

Albanese, J. F. (1985) Language lateralization in English–French bilinguals. *Brain and Language*, 24, 284–96.

Albert, M. & Obler, L. (eds.) (1978) *The Bilingual Brain.* New York: Academic Press.

Alderson, J. C. & North, B. (eds.) (1991) *Language Testing in the 1990s: The Communicative Legacy.* London: Modern English Publications/British Council.

Allard, R. & Landry, R. (1986) Subjective ethnolinguistic vitality viewed as a belief system. *Journal of Multilingual and Multicultural Development*, 7, 1–12.

Altenberg, E. P. & Cairns, H. S. (1983) The effect of phonotactic constraints on lexical processing in bilingual and monolingual subjects. *Journal of Verbal Learning and Verbal Behavior*, 22, 174–88.

Amati, Mehler, J., Argentieri, S. & Canestri, J. (1990) *La Babele Dell'Inconscio: Lingue Madre e Lingue Straniere nella Dimensione Psicoanalitica.* Milano: Raffaello Corina Editoré.

Amir, Y. (1969) Contact hypothesis in ethnic relations. *Psychological Bulletin*, 71, 319–42.

Amuda, A. A. (1986) Yoruba–English Code-Switching in Nigeria: aspects of its Functions and Form. PhD Thesis. University of Reading.

Anastasi, A. (1976) *Psychological Testing.* 4th edn. New York: Macmillan.

Andersen, E. A. (1985) Sociolinguistic surveys in Singapore. *International Journal of the Sociology of Language*, 55, 89–114.

Andersen, J. R. (1983) *The Architecture of Cognition*. Cambridge, MA: Harvard University Press.

Anisfeld, E. (1964) A comparison of the cognitive functioning of monolinguals and bilinguals. Unpublished PhD dissertation. Montreal: McGill University.

Anisfeld, E. & Lambert, W. E. (1964) Evaluation reactions of bilingual and monolingual children to spoken language. *Journal of Abnormal and Social Psychology*, 59, 89–97.

Anisfeld, M., Bogo, N. & Lambert, W. E. (1962) Evaluational reactions to accented English speech. *Journal of Abnormal and Social Psychology*, 65, 223–31.

Annis, R. & Corenblum, B. (1987) Effects of test language and experimenter race on Canadian Indian children's racial and self-identity. *Journal of Social Psychology*, 126, 761–73.

Aram, D. (1988) Language sequelae of unilateral brain lesions in children. In F. Plum (ed.) *Language, Communication and the Brain*. New York: Raven Press.

Arkwright, T. & Viau, A. (1974) Les processus d'association chez les bilingues. *Working Papers on Bilingualism*, 2, 57–67.

Arnberg, L. N. (1984) Mother tongue playgroups for pre-school bilingual children. *Journal of Multilingual and Multicultural Development*, 5, 65–84.

Arnberg, L. N. & Arnberg, P. W. (1992) Language awareness and language separation in the young bilingual child. In R. J. Harris (ed.) *Cognitive Processing in Bilinguals*. Amsterdam: Elsevier.

Arnedt, C. S. & Gentile, J. R. (1986) Test of dual coding theory for bilingual memory. *Canadian Journal of Psychology*, 40, 290–9.

Asher, J. & García, R. (1969) The optimal age to learn a second language. *Modern Language Journal*, 8, 334–41.

Au, T. K. F., & Glusman, M. (1990) The principle of mutual exclusivity in word learning: to honor or not to honor. *Child Development*, 61, 1474–90.

Bachman, L. F. & Palmer, A. S. (1996). *Language testing in practice*. Oxford: Oxford University Press.

Baetens Beardsmore, H. (1980) Bilingual education in International Schools, European Schools and Experimental Schools: a comparative analysis. In Lim Kiat Boey (ed.) *Bilingual Education*. Singapore: Singapore University Press.

Baetens Beardsmore, H. (1982) *Bilingualism: Basic Principles*. Clevedon: Multilingual Matters.

Baetens Beardsmore, H. (ed.) (1993) *European Models of Bilingual Education*. Clevedon & Philadelphia: Multilingual Matters.

Baetens Beardsmore, H. & Swain, M. (1985) Designing bilingual education: aspects of immersion and 'European School' models. *Journal of Multilingual and Multicultural Development*, 6, 1–15.

Bailey, N., Madden, C. & Krashen, S. (1974) Is there a 'natural sequence' in adult second language learning? *Language Learning*, 24, 235–43.

Bain, B. (1975) Toward an integration of Piaget and Vygotsky: bilingual considerations. *Linguistics* 16, 5–20.

Bain, B. (1976) Verbal regulation of cognitive processes: a replication of Luria's procedure with bilingual and unilingual infants. *Child Development*, 47, 543–6.

Bakeman, R., Adamson, L. B., Konner, M. & Barr, R. G. (1990) Kung! infancy: the social context of object exploration. *Child Development*, 61, 794–801.

Baker, C. D., Cook-Gumperz, J. & Luke, A. (eds.) (1997) *Literacy and Power*. London: Taylor and Francis.

Baker, K. & de Kanter, A. A. (1981) *Effectiveness of Bilingual Education: A Review of Literature*. Washington, DC: US Department of Education, Office of Planning, Budget and Evaluation.

Baker, K. & de Kanter, A. A. (1983) *Bilingual Education: A Reappraisal of Federal Policy*. Lexington, MA: Lexington.

Bakker, P. (1994) Michif. In P. Bakker & M. Mous (eds.) *Mixed Languages: Fifteen Case Studies in Language Intertwining* (Studies in Language and Language Use, 13) Amsterdam: Institute for Functional Research into Language and Language Use.

Bakker, P. & Mous, M. (eds.) (1994) *Mixed Languages: Fifteen Case Studies in Language Intertwining* (Studies in Language and Language Use, 13). Amsterdam: Institute for Functional Research into Language and Language Use.

Balkan, L. (1970) *Les Effets du Bilinguisme Français–Anglais sur les Aptitudes Intellectuelles*. Brussels: Aimav.

Ball, P., Giles, H., Byrne, J. L. & Berechree, P. (1984) Situational constraints on the evaluative significance of speech accommodation: some Australian data. *International Journal of the Sociology of Language*, 46, 115–29.

Bamgbose, A. (1984) Minority languages and literacy. In F. Coulmas (ed.) *Linguistic Minorities and Literacy*. Berlin: Mouton.

Bandura, A. (1977) *Social Learning Theory*. Englewood Cliffs, NJ: Prentice-Hall.

Bandura, A. (1986) *Social Foundations of Thought and Action: A Social Cognitive Theory*. Englewood Cliffs, NJ: Prentice-Hall.

Barik, H. C. & Swain, M. (1978) A longitudinal study of bilingual and cognitive development. *International Journal of Psychology*, 11, 251–63.

Barth, F. (1970) *Ethnic Groups and Boundaries: The Social Organization of Culture Difference*. London: Allen and Unwin.

Barton, M. I., Goodglass, H. & Skai, A. (1965) Differential recognition of tachistoscopically presented English and Hebrew words in right and left visual fields. *Perceptual and Motor Skills*, 21, 431–7.

Bates, E. & MacWhinney, B. (1981) Second language acquisition from a functionalist perspective: pragmatic, semantic and perceptual strategies. In H. Winitz (ed.) *Annals of the New York Academy of Sciences Conference on Native and Foreign Language Acquisition*. New York Academy of Sciences.

Bates, E. & MacWhinney, B. (1982) Functionalist approaches to grammar. In E. Wanner & L. Gleitman (eds.) *Language Acquisition: The State of the Art*. Cambridge and New York: Cambridge University Press.

Bates, E. & MacWhinney, B. (1987) Language universals, individual variation, and the competition model. In B. MacWhinney (ed.) *Mechanisms of Language Acquisition*. Hillsdale, NJ: Erlbaum.

Bates, E. & MacWhinney, B. (1989) Functionalism and the competition model. In B. MacWhinney & E. Bates (eds.) *The Cross-Linguistic Study of Sentence Processing*. New York: Academic Press.

Beaudoin, M., Cummins, J., Dunlop, H., Genesee, F. & Obadia, A. (1981) Bilingual education: a comparison of Welsh and Canadian experience. *Canadian Mod-*

ern Language Review: Revue Canadienne des Langues Vivantes, 37, 498–509.

Beebe, L. (1981) Social and situational factors affecting communicative strategies of communicative code-switching. *International Journal of the Sociology of Language*, 46, 139–49.

Belair Lockheed, J. (1987) Le Contact Inter-Ethnique: Antécédents, Processus et Conséquences. Unpublished PhD dissertation. Université d'Ottawa.

Bellugi, U., Poizner, H. & Klima, E. S. (1993) Language, modality and the brain. In A. H. Johnson (ed.) *Brain Development and Cognition: A Reader*. Oxford: Blackwell.

Béniak, E., Mougeon, R. & Valois, D. (1984) Sociolinguistic evidence of a possible case of syntactic convergence in Ontarian French. *Journal of the Atlantic Provinces Linguistic Association*, 6/7, 73–88.

Bentahila, A. & Davies, E. E. (1983) The syntax of Arabic–French code-switching. *Lingua*, 59, 301–30.

Bentolila, A. & Gani, L. (1981) Langues et problèmes d'éducation en Haiti. *Languages*, 61, 117–27.

Ben-Zeev, S. (1972) The Influence of Bilingualism on Cognitive Development and Cognitive Strategy. Unpublished PhD dissertation. University of Chicago.

Ben-Zeev, S. (1977a) Mechanisms by which childhood bilingualism affects understanding of language and cognitive structures. In P. A. Hornby (ed.) *Bilingualism: Psychological, Social and Educational Implications*. New York: Academic Press.

Ben-Zeev, S. (1977b) The effect of bilingualism in children from Spanish–English low economic neighbourhoods on cognitive development and cognitive strategy. *Working Papers on Bilingualism*, 14, 83–122.

Bereiter, C. & Engelmann, S. (1966) *Teaching Disadvantaged Children in the Preschool*. Englewood Cliffs, Prentice Hall.

Berent, G. P. (1996) The acquisition of English syntax by deaf learners. In C. Ritchie & T. K. Bhatia (eds.) *Handbook of Second Language Acquisition*. New York: Academic Press.

Berger, C. R. (1986) Social cognition and intergroup communication. In W. B. Gudykunst (ed.) *Intergroup Communication*. London: Edward Arnold.

Bergsland, K. (1990) The Aleut language in Alaska. In D. R. F. Collis (ed.) *Arctic Languages: An Awakening*. Paris: UNESCO.

Berk-Seligson, S. (1986) Linguistic constraints on intrasentential code-switching: a study of Spanish–Hebrew bilingualism. *Language in Society*, 15, 313–48.

Berkovits, R., Abarbanel, J. & Sitman, D. (1984) The effects of language proficiency on memory for input language. *Applied Psycholinguistics*, 5, 209–21.

Bernstein, B. (1970) Education cannot compensate for society. *New Society*, 387, February 1970.

Bernstein Ratner, N. (1997) Atypical language development. In J. B. Gleason (ed.) *The Development of Language*. 4th edition Boston: Allyn & Bacon. .

Berry, J. W. (1980) Acculturation as varieties of adaptation. In A. Padilla (ed.) *Acculturation: Theory and Models*. Washington: AAAS.

Berry, J. W., Kalin, R. & Taylor, D. M. (1977) *Multiculturalism and Ethnic Attitudes in Canada*. Ottawa: Supply and Services Canada.

Berry, J. W., Kim, U., Power, S., Young, M. & Bujaki, M. (1989) Acculturation attitudes in plural societies. *Applied Psychology: An International Review*, 38(2), 185–206.

Berry, J. W., Trimble, J. & Olmeda, E. (1986) The assessment of acculturation. In W. J. Lonner & J. W. Berry (eds.) *Field Methods in Cross-Cultural Research*. London: Sage.

Bertelson, P., Morais, J., Alegria, J. & Content, A. (1985) Phonetic analysis capacity and learning to read. *Nature*, 313, 73–4.

Bever, T. G. (1970) Are there Psycho-Social Interactions that Maintain a Low IQ Score of the Poor? Unpublished manuscript. University of Columbia.

Bhatnagar, J. (1980) Linguistic behaviour and adjustment of immigrant children in French and English schools in Montreal. *International Journal of Applied Psychology*, 29, 141–58.

Bialystok, E. (1988) Levels of bilingualism and levels of linguistic awareness. *Developmental Psychology*, 24, 560–7.

Bialystok, E. (1990) *Communication Strategies*. Oxford: Blackwell.

Bialystok, E. (1991) Metalinguistic dimensions of bilingual language proficiency. In E. Bialystok (ed.) *Language Processing in Bilingual Children*. Cambridge University Press.

Bialystok, E. (1992) Selective attention in cognitive processing: the bilingual edge. In R. J. Harris (ed.) *Cognitive Processing in Bilinguals*. Amsterdam: Elsevier.

Bialystok, E. & Fröhlich, M. (1977) Aspects of second language learning in classroom setting. *Working Papers on Bilingualism*, 13, 2–26.

Bialystok, E. & Ryan, E. B. (1985a) Toward a definition of metalinguistic skill. *Merill-Palmer Quarterly*, 31, 229–51.

Bialystok, E. & Ryan, E. B. (1985b) A metacognitive framework for the development of first and second language skills. In D. L. Forrest-Pressley, G. E. MacKinnon & T. Gary Waller (eds.) *Metacognition, Cognition, and Human Performance*. New York: Academic Press.

Bickerton, D. (1975) *Dynamics of a Creole System*. Cambridge University Press.

Bickerton, D. (1981) *Roots of Language*. Ann Arbor, MI: Karoma.

Biederman, I. & Tsao, Y. C. (1979) On processing Chinese ideographs and English words: some implications from Stroop-test results. *Cognitive Science*, 2, 125–32.

Birdsong, D. (1992) Ultimate attainment in second language acquisition. *Language*, 68, 706–55.

Birdwhistell, R. L. (1970) *Kinesics and Context*. Philadelphia: University of Pennsylvania Press.

Blanc, M. H. A. (1980) Réflexions sur quelques Classes d'Immersion. Unpublished manuscript. Birkbeck College, University of London.

Blanc, M. H. A. (1986) Canada's non-official languages: assimilation or pluralism? *The London Journal of Canadian Studies*, 3, 46–56.

Blanc, M. H. A. (1987) A project of community bilingual education: some theoretical and applied issues. In M. H. A. Blanc & J. F. Hamers (eds.) *Theoretical and Methodological Issues in the Study of Languages/Dialects in Contact at the Macro- and Micro-logical Levels of Analysis*. Quebec: International Center for Research on Bilingualism, B-160.

Blanc, M. H. A. (1994) Bilingualism, Societal. In R. E. Asher (ed.) *Encyclopedia of*

382   References

Language and Linguistics. Oxford: Pergamon, 354–8.

Blanc, M. H. A. & Hamers, J. F. (1987) Réseaux sociaux et comportements langagiers. In A. Prujiner (ed.) *L'interdisciplinarité en Sciences Sociales pour l'Étude du Contact des Langues.* Quebec: International Center for Research on Bilingualism, B-158.

Blom, J.-P. & Gumperz, J. J. (1972) Social meaning in linguistic structures: code-switching in Norway. In J. J. Gumperz & D. Hymes (eds.) *Directions in Sociolinguistics: The Ethnography of Communication.* New York: Holt, Rinehart and Winston.

Bloomfield, L. (1935) *Language.* London: Allen and Unwin.

Bogen, J. E. (1969) The other side of the brain 2: an appositional mind. *Bulletin of the Los Angeles Neurological Society,* 34, 191–220.

Bond, M. H. & Lai, T. (1986) Embarrassment and code-switching into a second language. *Journal of Social Psychology,* 126, 179–86.

Bond, M. H. & Yang, K. S. (1982) Ethnic affirmation vs. cross-cultural accommodation: the variable impact of questionnaire language. *Journal of Cross-Cultural Psychology,* 13, 165–85.

Bourdieu, P. (1982) *Ce que Parler Veut Dire. L'Économie des Échanges Linguistiques.* Paris: Fayard.

Bourdieu, P. (1986) The forms of capital. In J. G. Richardson (ed.) *Handbook of Theory and Research for the Sociology of Education.* New York: Greenwood Press.

Bourhis, R. Y. (1982) Language policies and language attitudes: le monde de la francophonie. In E. B. Ryan & H. Giles (eds.) *Attitudes towards Language Variation: Social and Applied Contexts.* London: Edward Arnold.

Bourhis, R. Y. (ed.) (1984a) *Conflict and Language Planning in Quebec.* Clevedon: Multilingual Matters.

Bourhis, R. Y. (1984b). Crosscultural communication in Montreal: two field studies since Bill 101. *International Journal of the Sociology of Language,* 46, 33–47.

Bourhis, R. Y. & Giles, H. (1977) The language of intergroup distinctiveness. In H. Giles (ed.) *Language, Ethnicity and Intergroup Relations.* London: Academic Press.

Bourhis, R. Y., Giles, H., Leyens, J. P. & Tajfel, H. (1979) Psychological distinctiveness: language divergence in Belgium. In H. Giles & R. N. Sinclair (eds.) *Language and Social Psychology.* Oxford: Blackwell.

Bourhis, R. Y., Giles, H. & Rosenthal, D. (1981) Notes on the construction of a 'Subjective Vitality Questionnaire' for ethnolinguistic groups. *Journal of Multilingual and Multicultural Development,* 2, 145–54.

Bourhis, R. Y., Giles, H. & Tajfel, H. (1973) Language as a determinant of Welsh identity. *European Journal of Social Psychology,* 3, 447–60.

Bourhis, R. Y. & Sachdev, I. (1984) Vitality perceptions and language attitudes: some Canadian data. *Journal of Language and Social Psychology,* 3, 97–126.

Bradac, J. J. (1990) Language attitudes and impression formation. In H. Giles & W. P. Robinson (eds.) *Handbook of Language and Social Psychology,* 2nd edition. Chichester: John Wiley & Sons.

Brass, P. R. (1974) *Language, Religion and Politics in North India.* Cambridge University Press.

Breitborde, L. B. (1983) Levels of analysis in sociolinguistic explanation: Bilingual code switching, social relations and domain theory. *International Journal of the Sociology of Language*, 39, 5–43.

Brent-Palmer, C. (1979) A sociolinguistics assessment of the notion 'im/migrant semi-lingualism' from a social conflict perspective. *Working Papers on Bilingualism*, 17, 135–80.

Breton, R. J. L. (1976) *Atlas Géographique des Langues et des Ethnies de l'Inde et du Subcontinent*. Quebec: International Center for Research on Bilingualism / Presses de l'Université Laval, A-10.

Brown, H. (1973) Effective variables in second language acquisition. *Language Learning*, 23, 231–44.

Brown, H., Sharma, N. K. & Kirsner, K. (1984) The role of script and phonology in lexical representation. *Quarterly Journal of Experimental Psychology*, 36a, 491–505.

Brown, R. (1973) *A First Language: The Early Stages*. Cambridge, MA: Harvard University Press.

Brown, R. & Gilman, A. (1960) The pronouns of power and solidarity. In T. Sebeok (ed.) *Style in Language*. New York: Wiley.

Bruck, M. (1982) Language-impaired children's performance in an additive bilingual education program. *Applied Psycholinguistics*, 3, 45–60.

Bruck, M., & Genesee, F. (1995) Phonological awareness in young second language learners. *Journal of Child Language*, 22, 307–24.

Bruck, M., Jakimik, J. & Tucker, G. R. (1975) Are French immersion programs suitable for working class children? A follow up investigation. *Word*, 27, 311–41.

Bruner, J. S. (1966) *Towards a Theory of Instruction*. New York: Norton.

Bruner, J. S. (1971) *The Relevance of Education*. New York: Norton.

Bruner, J. S. (1973) *Beyond the Information Given*. London: Allen & Unwin.

Bruner, J. S. (1975a) The ontogenesis of speech acts. *Journal of Child Language*, 2, 1–20.

Bruner, J. S. (1975b) Language as an instrument of thought. In A. Davies (ed.) *Problems of Language and Learning*. London: Heinemann.

Bruner, J. S. (1990) *Acts of Meaning*. Cambridge, MA and London: Harvard University Press.

Bruner, J., Roy, C. & Ratner, N. (1982) The beginnings of request. In K. E. Nelson (ed.) *Children's Language*, Volume 3. Hillsdale, NJ: Erlbaum.

Bruner, J. S. & Sherwood, V. (1981) Thought, language and interaction in infancy. In J. P. Forgas (ed.) *Social Cognition*. London: Academic Press.

Bryant, P. E. & Bradley, L. (1985) *Children's Reading Difficulties*. Oxford: Blackwell.

Bryson, S., Mononen, L. & Yu, L. (1980) Procedural constraints on the measurement of laterality in young children. *Neuropsychologia*, 18, 243–6.

Bull, W. (1964) The use of vernacular languages in fundamental education. In D. Hymes (ed.) *Language in Culture and Society*. New York: Harper & Row.

Burstall, C. (1975) Factors affecting foreign-language learning: a consideration of some recent research findings. *Language Teaching and Linguistics Abstracts*, 8, 1–18.

Calfee, R. C. & Nelson-Barber, S. (1991) Diversity and constancy in human thinking: critical literacy as amplifier of intellect and experience. In E. H. Hiebert
(ed.) *Literacy for a diverse society: Perspectives, Practices and Policies.* New
York: Teachers College Press.

Calvet, J. L. (1974) *Linguistique et Colonialisme: Petit Traité de Glottophagie.* Paris:
Payot.

Calvet, J. L. (1981) *L'alphabétisation ou la scolarisation: le cas du Mali.* In A. Martin
(ed.) *L'État et la Planification Linguistique,* Volume 2. Québec: Éditeur Officiel
du Québec.

Canale, M. & Swain, M. (1980) Theoretical bases of communicative approaches to
second language teaching and testing. *Applied Linguistics,* 1, 2–43.

Caporael, L. R., Lukaszewski, M. P. & Culbertson, G. H. (1983) Secondary baby
talk: judgements by institutionalised elderly and their caregivers. *Journal of
Personality and Social Psychology,* 44, 746–54.

Caramazza, A. & Brones, L. (1980) Semantic classification by bilinguals. *Canadian
Journal of Psychology,* 34, 77–81.

Caramazza, A., Yeni-Komshian, G. & Zurif, E. (1974) Bilingual switching at the
phonological level. *Canadian Journal of Psychology,* 28, 310–18.

Cargile, A. C. (1997) Attitudes toward Chinese-accented speech. *Journal of Language and Social Psychology,* 16, 434–43.

Cargile, A. C. & Giles, H. (1996) Language attitudes toward varieties of English: An
American–Japanese context. Paper presented at the Speech Communication
Association, San Diego, November 1996.

Carpinteria Unified School District (1982) Title VII Evaluation Report 1981–1982.
Carpinteria, CA: Unpublished report.

Carroll, F. W. (1978a) Cerebral Lateralization and Adult Second Language Learning. Unpublished PhD dissertation. Albuquerque: University of New Mexico.

Carroll, F. W. (1978b) Cerebral dominance for language: a dichotic listening study
of Navajo–English bilinguals. In H. H. Key, G. G. McCullough & J. B. Sawyer
(eds.) *The Bilingual in a Pluralistic Society.* Long Beach: California State
University.

Carroll, F. W. (1980) Neurolinguistic processing of a second language: experimental
evidence. In R. Scarcella & S. Krashen (eds.) *Research in Second Language
Acquisition.* Rowley, MA: Newbury House.

Carroll, J. B. (1962) The prediction of success in intensive foreign language training.
In R. Glazer (ed.) *Training, Research and Education.* University of Pittsburgh
Press.

Carroll, J. B. (1965) The contribution of psychological theory and educational
research to the teaching of foreign languages. *Modern Language Journal,* 49,
273–7.

Carroll, J. B. (1973) Implications of aptitude test research and psycholinguistic
theory for foreign language teaching. *International Journal of Psycholinguistics,* 2, 5–14.

Carroll, J. B. & Sapon, S. M. (1959) *Modern Language Aptitude Test. Form A.* New
York: The Psychological Corporation.

Carson, J. E. & Kuehn, P. A. (1994) Evidence of transfer and loss in developing
second-language writers. In A. Cumming (ed.) *Bilingual Performance in Read-*

ing and Writing. Ann Arbor, MI: Research Club in Language Learning, 257–81.

Cazabon, M., Lambert, W. E. & Hall, G. (1993) *Two-way Bilingual Education: A Progress Report on the Amigos Program* (Research Report No 7). Santa Cruz, CA: National Center for Research on Cultural Diversity and Second Language Learning.

Chafe, W. L. (1985) Linguistic differences produced by differences between speaking and writing. In D. R. Olson, N. Torrance & A. Hildyard (eds.) *Literacy, Language and Learning.* Cambridge University Press.

Champagnol, R. (1973) Organisation sémantique et linguistique dans le rappel libre bilingue. *L'Année Psychologique,* 73, 115–34.

Champagnol, R. (1978) Effets des consignes de traitement 'perceptif' et 'sémantique' sur la reconnaissance et le rappel des mots français et anglais. *Psychologie Française,* 23, 115–25.

Champagnol, R. (1979) Reconnaissances interlangues et intermodalités avec indicateurs de transformation. *L'Année Psychologique,* 79, 65–85.

Chan, M. C., Chau, H. L. H. & Hoosain, R. (1983) Input/output switch in bilingual code switching. *Journal of Psycholinguistic Research,* 12, 407–16.

Chang, G. L. & Wells, G. (1990) . Concepts of literacy and their consequences for children's potential as learners. In S. P. Norris & L. M. Phillips (eds.) *Foundation of Literacy Policy in Canada.* Calgary, Alberta: Detselig Enterprises Ltd.

Charniak, E. & McDermott, D. (1985) *Introduction to Artificial Intelligence.* Reading, MA: Addison-Wesley.

Charpentier, J.-M. (1997) Literacy in a pidgin vernacular. In A. Tabouret-Keller, R. B. Le Page, P. Gardner-Chloros, & G. Varro (eds.) *Vernacular Literacy: A Re-Evaluation.* (Oxford Studies in Anthropological Linguistics) Oxford: Clarendon Press.

Chen, H. C. & Ho, C. (1986) Development of Stroop interference in Chinese-English bilinguals. *Journal of Experimental Psychology: Learning, Memory and Cognition,* 12, 397–401.

Chen, H. C. & Leung, Y. S. (1989) Patterns of lexical processing in a nonnative language. *Journal of Experimental Psychology: Learning, Memory and Cognition, 12,* 316–25.

Chen, H. C. & Ng, M. L. (1989) Semantic facilitation and translation priming effects in Chinese–English bilinguals. *Memory & Cognition,* 17, 454–62.

Cheng, C. M. & Yang, M. J (1989) Lateralization in the visual perception of Chinese characters. *Brain and Language,* 36, 669–89.

Chernigovskaya, T. V., Balonov, L. J. & Deglin, V. L. (1983) Bilingualism and brain functional asymmetry. *Brain and Language,* 20, 195–216.

Chesarek, S. (1981) Cognitive Consequences of Home on School Education in a Limited Second Language: a Case Study in the Crow Indian Bilingual Community. Ailie House, VA: Paper presented at the Language Proficiency Assessment Symposium.

Cheshire, J. (1987) A survey of dialect grammar in British English. In M. H. A. Blanc & J. F. Hamers (eds.) *Theoretical and Methodological Issues in the Study of Languages/Dialects in Contact at the Macro- and Micro-Logical Levels of Analysis.* Quebec: International Center for Research on Bilingualism, B-160.

Chihara, T. & Oller, J. W. (1978) Attitudes and attained proficiency in EFL: a sociolinguistic study of adult Japanese speakers. *Language Learning*, 28, 55–68.

Child, I. L. (1943) *Italian or American? The Second Generation in Conflict.* New Haven, CT: Yale University Press.

Chimombo, J. (1979) An analysis of the order of acquisition of English grammatical morphemes in a bilingual child. *Working Papers on Bilingualism*, 18, 201–30.

Chomsky, N. (1965) *Aspects of the Theory of Syntax.* Cambridge, MA: MIT Press.

Chomsky, N. (1981) *Lectures on Government and Binding.* Dordrecht: Foris.

Christian, D. & Mahrer, C. (1992) *Two-Way Bilingual Programs in the United States, 1991–1992.* Washington, DC: National Center for Research in Cultural Diversity and Second Language Learning. Center for Applied Linguistics.

Chun, J. (1979) The importance of the language-learning situation: is immersion the same as the 'sink or swim' method? *Working Papers on Bilingualism*, 18, 131–64.

Clark, M. J. (1978) Synonymity of Concreteness Effects on Free Recall and Free Association: Implications for a Theory of Semantic Memory. Unpublished PhD dissertation. London, Ontario: University of Western Ontario.

Clay, M. M. (1976) Early childhood and cultural diversity in New Zealand. *Reading Teacher*, 29, 333–42.

Clément, R. (1978) *Motivational Characteristics of Francophones Learning English.* Quebec: International Center for Research on Bilingualism Presses de l'Université Laval, B-70.

Clément, R. (1980) Ethnicity, contact and communicative competence in second language. In H. Giles, W. P. Robinson & P. M. Smith (eds.) *Language: Social Psychological Perspectives.* Oxford: Pergamon Press.

Clément, R. (1984) Aspects socio-psychologiques de la communication inter-ethnique et de l'identité culturelle. *Recherches Sociologiques*, 15, 293–312.

Clément, R. (1986) Second language proficicency and acculturation: An investigation of the effects of language status and individual characteristics. *Journal of Language and Social Psychology*, 5, 271–90.

Clément, R. (1987) Meta-theoretical Comments on Language and Social Psychology: an Introduction to Theoretical Issues. Bristol: Paper presented at the Third International Conference on Social Psychology of Language. Bristol, 20–23 July 1987.

Clément, R. & Bourhis, R. (1996) Bilingual and intergroup communication. *International Journal of Psycholinguistics*, 12(2), 171–91.

Clément, R., Gardner, R. C. & Smythe, P. C. (1977a) Motivational variables in second language acquisition: a study of francophones learning English. *Canadian Journal of Behavioral Science*, 9, 123–33.

Clément, R., Gardner, R. C. & Smythe, P. C. (1977b) Inter-ethnic contact: attitudinal consequences. *Canadian Journal of Behavioral Science*, 9, 205–15.

Clément, R. & Hamers, J. F. (1979) Les bases sociopsychologiques du comportement langagier. In G. Bégin & P. Joshi (eds.) *Psychologie Sociale.* Quebec: Presses de l'Université, Laval.

Clément, R. & Kruidenier, B. G. (1983) Orientations in second language acquisition: the effects of ethnicity, milieu and target language on their emergence. *Language Learning*, 33, 273–91.

Clément, R. & Kruidenier, B. G. (1985) Aptitude, attitude and motivation in second language proficiency: a test of Clément's model. *Journal of Language and Social Psychology*, 4, 21–37.

Clément, R. & Noels, K. (1992) Towards a situated approach to ethnolinguistic identity: The effect of status on individuals and groups. *Journal of Language and Social Psychology*, 11, 203–32.

Clément, R., Smythe, P. C. & Gardner, R. C. (1978) Persistence in second language studies: motivational considerations. *Canadian Modern Language Review*, 34, 688–94.

Clyne, M. G. (1967) *Transference and Triggering*. The Hague: Nijhoff.

Clyne, M. G. (1977) Bilingualism in the elderly. *Talanya*, 4, 45–65.

Clyne, M. G. (ed.) (1981) Foreigner Talk. *Special issue of International Journal of the Sociology of Language 28*. The Hague: Mouton.

Clyne, M. (1982) *Multilingual Australia*. Melbourne: River Seine Publications.

Clyne, M. (1987) Constraints on code-switching: How universal are they? *Linguistics*, 25, 739–64.

Cohen, A. D. (1975) *A Sociolinguistic Approach to Bilingual Education: Experiments in the Southwest*. Rowley, MA: Newbury House.

Cohen, A. D. (1976) The acquisition of Spanish grammar through immersion: some findings after four years. *Canadian Modern Language Review*, 32, 572–4.

Collins, A. M. & Loftus, E. (1975) A spreading activation theory of semantic processing. *Psychological Review*, 82, 407–28.

Coppieters, R. (1987) Competence differences between native and near-native speakers. *Language*, 63, 544–73.

Corballis, M. C. (1980) Laterality and myth. *American Psychologist*, 35, 284–95.

Corballis, M. C. (1991) *The Lopsided Ape: Evolution of the Generative Mind*. Oxford: Oxford University Press.

Corballis, M. C. & Morgan, M. (1978) On the biological basis of human laterality. *The Behavioural and Brain Sciences*, 1, 261–9.

Corina, D. P., Vaid, J. & Bellugi, U. (1992) The linguistic basis of left hemisphere specialisation. *Science*, 255, 1258–60.

Corson, D. (1993) *Language, Minority Education and Gender: Linking Social Justice and Power*. Clevedon: Multilingual Matters and Toronto: Ontario Institute for Studies in Education.

Côté, P. & Clément, R. (1994) Language attitudes: an interactive situated approach. *Language and Communication*, 14 (3), 237–51.

Coupland, N. & Giles, H. (1988) Communicative accommodation: recent developments. *Language and Communication*, 8, 175–327.

Crandall, J. (1992) Adult literacy development. *Annual Review of Applied Linguistics 12*, 105–16.

Crawford, J. (1989) *Bilingual Education: History, Politics, Theory and Practice*. Trenton, NJ: Crane.

Cristoffanini, P. K., Kirsner, K., & Milech, D. (1986) Bilingual lexical representation: the status of Spanish–English cognates. *Quarterly Journal of Experimental Psychology*, 38A, 367–93.

Critchley, M. (1974) Aphasia in polyglots and bilinguals. *Brain and Language*, 1, 15–27.

Cross, W. (1978) The Thomas and Cross models of psychological nigrescence: A literature review. *Journal of Black Psychology*, 4, 13–31.

Cummins, J. (1976) The influence of bilingualism on cognitive growth: a synthesis of research findings and explanatory hypotheses. *Working Papers on Bilingualism*, 9, 1–43.

Cummins, J. (1978) Bilingualism and the development of metalinguistic awareness. *Journal of Cross-Cultural Psychology*, 9, 139–49.

Cummins, J. (1979) Linguistic interdependence and the educational development of bilingual children. *Review of Educational Research*, 49, 222–51.

Cummins, J. (1981) The role of primary language development in promoting educational success for language minority students. In *Schooling and Language Minority Students: A Theoretical Framework*. Los Angeles, CA: Department of Evaluation, Dissemination and Assessment Center.

Cummins, J. (1984a) *Bilingualism and Special Education: Issues in Assessment and Pedagogy*. Clevedon: Multilingual Matters, 6.

Cummins, J. (1984b) Wanted: a theoretical framework for relating language proficiency to academic achievement among bilingual students. In C. Rivera (ed.) *Language Proficiency and Academic Achievement*. Clevedon: Multilingual Matters, 10.

Cummins, J. (1991) Interdependence of first and second language proficiency in bilingual children. In E. Bialystok (ed.) *Language Processing in Bilingual Children*. Cambridge University Press

Cummins, J. (1994) Knowledge, power, and identity in teaching English as a second language. In J. C. Richards (ed.) *Educating Second Language Children*. Cambridge University Press.

Cummins, J. & Gulutsan, M. (1974) Some effects of bilingualism on cognitive functioning. In S. T. Carey (ed.) *Bilingualism, Biculturalism and Education*. Edmonton: University of Alberta Press.

Cummins, J. & Nakajima, J. (1987) Age of arrival, length of residence, and interdependence of literacy skills among Japanese immigrant students. In B. Harley, P. Allen, J. Cummins, & M. Swain (eds.) *The Development of Bilingual Proficiency*. Final Report submitted to the Social Science and Humanities Research Council. Toronto: Ontario Institute for Studies in Education.

Cummins, J., Swain, M., Nakajima, J., Handscombe, D., Green, D., & Tran, C. (1984) Linguistic interdependence among Japanese and Vietnamese immigrant students. In C. Rivera (ed.) *Communicative Competence Approaches to Language Proficiency Assessment: Research and Application*. Clevedon: Multilingual Matters.

Curtiss, S. (1989) The independence and task-specificity of language. In A. Bornstein & J. Bruner (eds.) *Interaction in Human Development*. Hillsdale, NJ: Erlbaum.

Cziko, G. A., Lambert, W. E. & Gutter, R. (1979) French immersion programs and students' social attitudes: a multidimensional investigation. *Working Papers on Bilingualism*, 19, 13–28.

Cziko, G. A., Lambert, W. E., Sidoti, N. & Tucker, G. R. (1978) Graduates of early immersion: retrospective views of Grade 11 students and their parents. Unpublished research report. Montreal: McGill University.

Dabène, L. & Billiez, J. (1987) Le parler des jeunes issus de l'immigration. In G. Vermès & J. Boutet (eds.) *France, Pays Multilingue, Tome 2: Pratiques des langues en France*. Paris: L'Harmattan.

Dabène, L. & Moore, D. (1995) Bilingual speech of migrant people. In L. Milroy &

P. Muysken (eds.) *One Speaker, Two Languages: Cross-disciplinary Perspectives on Code-Switching.* Cambridge University Press.

Dalrymple-Alford, E. C. (1968) Interlingual interference in a color-naming task. *Psychonomic Science*, 10, 215–16.

Dalrymple-Alford, E. C. (1985) Language switching during bilingual reading. *British Journal of Psychology*, 76, 111–22.

Dalrymple-Alford, E. C. & Aamiry, A. (1967) Speed of responding to mixed language signals. *Psychonomic Science*, 9, 535–6.

Dalrymple-Alford, E. C. & Aamiry, A. (1970) Word associations of bilinguals. *Psychonomic Science*, 21, 319–20.

Dalrymple-Alford, E. C. & Budayr, B. (1966) Examination of some aspects of the Stroop color-word test. *Perceptual and Motor Skills*, 23, 1211–14.

Damasio, H. (1995) *Human Brain Anatomy in Computerised Images.* New York: Oxford University Press.

Damasio, A., Bellugi, U., Damasio, H., Poizner, H. & Van Gilder, J. (1986) Sign language aphasia during left hemisphere amytal injection. *Nature*, 322, 363–5.

Danesi, M. (1993) Literacy and bilingual education programs in elementary school: assessing the research. *Mosaic*, 1, 6–12.

Darcy, N. T. (1953) A review of the literature on the effects of bilingualism upon the measurement of intelligence. *Journal of Genetic Psychology*, 82, 21–57.

Das Gupta, J. (1975) Ethnicity, language and national development in India. In N. Glazer & D. P. Moynihan (eds.) *Ethnicity: Theory and Experience.* Cambridge, MA: Harvard University Press.

Da Silveira, Y. I. (1989) Rôle de quelques facteurs socio-psychologiques dans le rendement scolaire en contexte diglossique africain. In H. Krief & F. Gbénimé-Sendagbia (eds.) *Espace francophone: État de la langue française en Afrique Centrale.* Université de Bangui.

Da Silveira, Y. I. (1994) Valorisation langagière par le milieu et développement bilingue: importance du contexte de contact des langues. In J. Blomart & B. Krewer (eds.) *Perspectives de l'Interculturel.* Paris: L'Harmattan.

Da Silveira, Y. I. & Hamers, J. F. (1990) Scolarisation et bilingualité en contexte africain: un défi? *Langage et Société*, 52, 23–58.

Davidson, D., Jergovic, D., Imami, Z., & Theodos, V. (1997) Monolingual and bilingual children's use of the mutual exclusivity constraint. *Journal of Child Language*, 24, 3–24.

Davidson, R., Kline, S., & Snow, C. E. (1986) Definitions and definite noun phrases: indicators of children's decontextualized skills. *Journal of Research in Childhood Education*, 1, 37–48.

Davis, K. A. (1995) Qualitative theory and methods in Applied Linguistics Research. *Tesol Quarterly*, 29, 427–53.

de Bot, K. & Clyne, M. (1994) A 16-year longitudinal study of language attrition in Dutch immigrants in Australia. *Journal of Multilingual and Multicultural Development*, 15, 17–28.

de Bot, K., Gommans, P. and Rossing, C. (1991) L1-loss in an L2 environment: Dutch immigrants in France. In H. Seliger & R. Vago (eds.) *First Language Attrition: Structural and Theoretical Perspectives.* Cambridge University Press.

de Boysson-Bardies, B., Halle, P., Sagart, L. & Durand, C. (1989) A cross-linguistic investigation of vowel formants in babbling. *Journal of Child Language*, 16, 1–17.

de Boysson-Bardies, B. & Vihman, M. M. (1991) Adaptation to language: evidence from babbling and first words in four languages. *Language*, 67, 297–319.

de Francis, J. (1984) *The Chinese Language: Facts and Fantasy*. Honolulu: University of Hawaii Press.

de Groot, A. M. B. (1992) Determinants of word translation. *Journal of Experimental Psychology: Learning, Memory and Cognition*, 18, 1001–18.

de Groot, A. M. B. & Nas, G. L. J. (1991) Lexical representation of cognates and noncognates in compound bilinguals. *Journal of Memory and Language*, 30, 90–123.

de Houwer, A. (1990) *The Acquisition of Two Languages from Birth: A Case Study*. Cambridge University Press.

Deshaies, D. (1981) *Le Français Parlé dans la Ville de Québec: Une Étude Sociolinguistique*. Quebec: International Center for Research on Bilingualism, G-1.

Deshaies, D. & Hamers, J. F. (1982) *Étude des Comportements Langagiers dans Deux Entreprises en Début de Processus de Francisation*. Quebec: International Center for Research on Bilingualism, G-3.

Desrochers, A. & Petrusic, W. M. (1983) Comprehension effects in comparative judgements. In J. C. Yuille (ed.) *Imagery, Memory and Cognition*. Hillsdale, NJ: Erlbaum.

Deuchar, M. & Clark, A. (1996) Early bilingual acquisition of the voicing contrast in English and Spanish. *Journal of Phonetics*, 24, 351–65.

de Vos, G. & Romanucci-Ross, L. (1975) *Ethnic Identity*. Palo Alto: Mayfield.

de Vriendt, S. & Willemyns, R. (1987) Sociolinguistic aspects: linguistic research in Brussels. In E. Witte & H. Baetens Beardsmore (eds.) *The Interdisciplinary Study of Urban Bilingualism in Brussels*. Clevedon: Multilingual Matters.

Diaz, R. M. (1985) Bilingual cognitive development: addressing the gaps in current research. *Child Development*, 56, 1376–88.

Diaz, R. M. & Klinger, C. (1991) Towards an explanatory model of the interaction between bilingualism and cognitive development. In E. Bialystok (ed.) *Language Processing in Bilingual Children*. Cambridge University Press.

Diaz, R. M. & Padilla, K. A. (1985) The self-regulatory speech of bilingual preschoolers. Paper presented at the Meeting of the Society for Research in Child Development, Toronto, April 1985.

Diebold, A. R. (1968) The consequences of early bilingualism in cognitive and personality information. In E. Norbeck, D. Price-Williams & W. M. McCord (eds.) *The Study of Personality: An Interdisciplinary Appraisal*. New York: Holt, Rinehart & Winston.

Dillard, J. L. (1978) Bidialectal education: Black English and Standard English in the United States. In B. Spolsky & R. L. Cooper (eds.) *Case Studies in Bilingual Education*. Rowley, MA: Newbury House.

Dillon, R., McCormack, P. D., Petrusic, P., Cook, M. & Lafleur, L. (1973) Release from proactive interference in compound and co-ordinate bilinguals. *Bulletin of the Psychonomic Society*, 2, 293–4.

DiSciullo, A.-M., Muysken, P. & Singh, R. (1986) Government and code-mixing. *Journal of Linguistics*, 22, 1–24.

Dodson, K. (1981) A reappraisal of bilingual development and education. In H. Baetens Beardsmore (ed.) *Elements of Bilingual Theory*. Free University of Brussels.

Dodson, K. (1983) Bilingualism, language teaching and learning. *British Journal of Language Teaching*, 21, 3–8.

Dolson, D. P. (1985) The effects of Spanish home language use on the scholastic performance of Hispanic pupils. *Journal of Multilingual and Multicultural Development*, 6, 135–55.

Dorais, L. J. (1985) La survie et le développement de la langue des Inuit. *Revue de l'Université Laurentienne*, 18, 89–103.

Dorian, N. C. (1981) *Language Death: The Life Cycle of a Scottish Gaelic Dialect*. Philadelphia: University of Pennsylvania Press.

Dornic, S. (1978) The bilingual's performance: language dominance, stress and individual differences. In D. Gerver & H. W. Sinaiko (eds.) *Language, Interpretation and Communication*. New York: Plenum Press.

Dornyei, Z. & Scott, M. L. (1997) Communication strategies in second language: definitions and taxonomies. *Language Learning*, 47, 173–210.

Doron, S. (1973) Reflexivity-Impulsivity and their Influence on Reading for Inference for Adult Students of ESL. Unpublished manuscript. University of Michigan.

Doyle, A., Champagne, M. & Segalowitz, N. (1977) Some issues in the assessment of linguistic consequences of early bilingualism. *Working Papers on Bilingualism*, 14, 21–30.

Driedger, L. (1975) In search of cultural identity factors: a comparison of ethnic students. *Canadian Review of Sociology and Anthropology*, 12, 150–62.

Dua, H. R. (ed.) (1996) Language Planning and Political Theory. *International Journal of the Sociology of Language*, 118.

Dubé, N. C. & Herbert G. (1975) Evaluation of the St John Valley Title VII Bilingual Education Program, 1970–1975. Unpublished report. Madawaska, Maine.

Dufour, R. & Kroll, J. F. (1995) Matching words to concepts in two languages: A test of the concept mediation model of bilingual representation. *Memory and Cognition*, 23, 66–80.

Duncan, S. E. & de Avila, E. A. (1979) Bilingualism and cognition: some recent findings. *NABE Journal*, 4, 15–50.

Dunn, L. M. (1959) *Peabody Picture Vocabulary Test*. Tennessee: American Guidance Service.

Durgunoglu, A. Y. & Roediger, H. L. (1987) Test differences in accessing bilingual memory. *Journal of Memory and Language*, 26, 377–91.

Dyer, F. N. (1971) Color-naming interference in monolinguals and bilingual. *Journal of Verbal Learning and Verbal Behavior*, 10, 297–302.

Education For All (1985) *The Report of the Committee of Inquiry into the Education of Children from Ethnic Minority Groups*. London: Her Majesty's Stationery Office.

Edwards, D. & Christophersen, H. (1988) Bilingualism, literacy and meta-linguistic awareness in preschool children. *British Journal of Developmental Psychology*, 6, 235–44.

Edwards, H. P., Doutriaux, C. W., McCarrey, H. A. & Fu, L. (1976) Evaluation of Second Language Programs: Annual Report 1975–1976. Unpublished manuscript. Ottawa: Roman Catholic Separate School Board.

Edwards, J. (ed.) (1984) *Linguistic Minorities, Policies and Pluralism*. London: Academic Press.

Edwards, J. (1985) *Language, Society and Identity*. Oxford: Blackwell.

Edwards, J. & Chisholm, J. (1987) Language, multiculturalism and identity: a Canadian study. *Journal of Multilingual and Multicultural Development*, 8(5), 391–407.

Edwards, V. K. (1978a) Language attitudes and underperformance in West Indian children. *Educational Review*, 30, 51–8.

Edwards, V. K. (1978b) Dialect interference in West Indian children. *Language and Speech*, 21, 76–86.

Edwards, V. K. (1984) Language policy in multicultural Britain. In J. Edwards (ed.) *Linguistic Minorities, Policies and Pluralism*. London: Academic Press.

Edwards, V. K. (1986) *Language in a Black Community*. Clevedon: Multilingual Matters.

Ehri, L. C. & Ryan, E. B. (1980) Performance of bilinguals in a picture word interference task. *Journal of Psycholinguistic Research*, 9, 285–302.

Eilers, R. E., Gavin, W. J. & Oller, D. K. (1982) Cross-linguistic perception in infancy: early effects of linguistic experience. *Journal of Child Language*, 9, 289–302.

Ekstrand, L. H. (1978) Migrant adaptation: a cross-cultural problem. In R. Freudenstein (ed.) *Teaching the Children of Immigrants*. Brussels: Didier.

Ekstrand, L. H. (1981) Theories and facts about early bilingualism in native and migrant children. *Gräzer Linguistische Studien*, 14, 24–52.

Elder, C. & Davies, A. (1998) Performance on ESL examinations: Is there a language distance effect? *Language and Education*, 11, 1–17.

Endo, M., Shimizu, A. & Hori, T. (1978) Functional asymmetry of visual fields for Japanese words in kana (syllable-based) writing and Japanese shape-recognition in Japanese subjects. *Neuropsychologia*, 16, 291–7.

Endo, M., Shimizu. A. & Nakumara, I. (1981) Laterality differences in the recognition of Japanese and Hangul words by monolinguals and bilinguals. *Cortex*, 17, 1–19.

Ervin, S. M. (1964) Language and TAT content in bilingual. *Journal of Abnormal and Social Psychology*, 68, 500–7.

Ervin, S. M. & Osgood, C. E. (1954) Second language learning and bilingualism. *Journal of Abnormal and Social Psychology, Supplement*, 49, 139–46.

Ervin-Tripp, S. M. (1973) Identification and bilingualism. In A. Dil (ed.) *Language Acquisition and Communicative Choice*. Stanford University Press.

Fabbro, F. & Paradis, M. (1995) Acquired aphasia in a bilingual child. In M. Paradis (ed.) *Aspects of Bilingual Aphasia*. New York: Elsevier.

Faerch, C. & Kasper, G. (eds.) (1983) *Strategies in Interlanguage Communication*. Cambridge, MA: MIT Press.

Fairclough, N. (ed.) (1992) *Critical Language Awareness*. London: Longman.

Fang, S. P., Tzeng, O. J. & Alva, L. (1981) Intralanguage versus interlanguage:

Stroop effects in two types of writing systems. *Memory and Cognition*, 96, 609–17.

Fantini, A. E. (1978) Bilingual behaviour and social cues: case studies of two bilingual children. In M. Paradis (ed.) *Aspects of Bilingualism*. Columbia: Hornbeam Press.

Fasold, R. (1984) *The Sociolinguistics of Society*. Oxford: Blackwell.

Fasold, R. & Shuy, R. W. (eds.) (1970) *Teaching Standard English in the Inner City*. Washington, DC: Center for Applied Linguistics. Urban Language Series.

Favreau, M. & Segalowitz, N. (1983) Automatic and controlled processing in first- and second-language reading in fluent bilinguals. *Memory and Cognition*, 11, 565–74.

Ferguson, C. A. (1959) Diglossia. *Word*, 15, 125–40.

Ferguson, C. A. & DeBose, C. E. (1977) Simplified register, broken language and pidginization. In A. Valdman (ed.) *Pidgin and Creole Linguistics*. Bloomington: Indiana University.

Feuerverger, G. (1991) University students' perceptions of heritage language learning and ethnic identity maintenance. *The Canadian Modern Language Review / Revue Canadienne des Langues Vivantes*, 47, 660–77.

Fishman, J. A. (1964) Language maintenance and language shift as a field of inquiry. *Linguistics*, 9, 32–70.

Fishman, J. A. (1965) Who speaks what language to whom and when? *La Linguistique*, 2, 67–8.

Fishman, J. A. (1967) Bilingualism with and without diglossia; diglossia with and without bilingualism. *Journal of Social Issues*, 32, 29–38.

Fishman, J. A. (1968) Nationality–nationalism and nation–nationism. In J. A. Fishman, C. A. Ferguson & J. Das Gupta (eds.) *Language Problems of Developing Nations*. The Hague: Mouton.

Fishman, J. A. (1972) *The Sociology of Language: An Interdisciplinary Social Sciences Approach to Language in Society*. Rowley, MA: Newbury House.

Fishman, J. A. (1977a) Language and ethnicity. In H. Giles (ed.) *Language, Ethnicity and Intergroup Relations*. London: Academic Press.

Fishman, J. A. (1977b) The sociology of bilingual education. In B. Spolsky & R. L. Cooper (eds.) *Frontiers of Bilingual Education*. Rowley, MA: Newbury House.

Fishman, J. A. (1977c) The social science perspective. In *Bilingual Education: Current Perspectives*. Arlington, VA: Center for Applied Linguistics.

Fishman, J. A. (1980) Bilingualism and biculturalism as individual and societal phenomena. *Journal of Multilingual and Multicultural Development*, 1, 1–13.

Fishman, J. A. (1985) 'Nothing new under the sun': a case study of alternatives in language and ethnocultural identity. In J. A. Fishman, M. H. Gertner, E. G. Lowy & W. G. Milan (eds.) *The Rise and Fall of the Ethnic Revival: Perspectives on Language and Ethnicity*. Berlin: Mouton.

Fishman, J. A. (1991) *Reversing Language Shift: Empirical Foundations*. Clevedon: Multilingual Matters.

Fishman, J. A. (1994) Critiques of language planning: A minority languages perspective. *Journal of Multilingual and Multicultural Development*, 15, 91–9.

Fishman, J. A., Cooper, R. & Ma, R. (1971) *Bilingualism in the Barrio*. Bloomington: Indiana University Press.

Fishman, J. A. & Lovas, J. (1970) Bilingual education in sociolinguistic perspective. *TESOL Quarterly*, 4, 215–22.

Fiske, S. T. & Neuberg, S. L. (1990) A continuum of impression formation, from category-based to individuating processes: Influences from information and motivation on attention and interpretation. In L. Berkowitz (ed.) *Advances in Experimental Social Psychology*, 23, New York: Academic Press.

Fitzpatrick, F. (1987) *The Open Door*. Clevedon: Multilingual Matters.

Flege, J. E. (1988) Factors affecting degree of perceived foreign accent in English sentences. *Journal of Acoustic Society of America*, 84, 70–9.

Frasure-Smith, N., Lambert, W. E. & Taylor, D. M. (1975) Choosing the language of instruction for one's children: a Quebec Study. *Journal of Cross-Cultural Psychology*, 6, 131–55.

Fredman, M. (1975) The effect of therapy given in Hebrew on the home language of the bilingual and polyglot adult aphasic in Israel. *British Journal of Disorders of Communication*, 10–61.

Frenck-Mestre, C. & Price, P. (1997) Second language autonomy. *Journal of Memory and Language*, 37, 481–501.

Gagnon, M. (1970) *Échelle d'Attitude à l'Égard de la Langue Seconde, l'Anglais pour Francophones: Manuel et Normes*. Montreal: Lidec.

Gal, S. (1979) *Language Shift: Social Determinants of Linguistic Change in Bilingual Austria*. New York: Academic Press.

Galambos, S. J. & Goldin-Meadow, S. (1990) The effects of learning two languages on metalinguistic awareness. *Cognition*, 34, 1–56.

Galambos, S. J. & Hakuta, K. (1988) Subject-specific and task-specific characteristics of metalinguistic awareness in bilingual children. *Applied Psycholinguistics*, 9, 141–62.

Gallois, C. & Callan, V. J. (1985) Situational influences on perceptions of accented speech. In J. Forgas (ed.) *Language and Social Situations*. New York: Springer-Verlag, 159–73.

Galloway, L. (1980) The Cerebral Organization of Language in Bilingual and Second Language Learners. Niagara Falls, Ontario: Paper read at the Symposium on Cerebral Lateralisation in Bilingualism, Babble Conference.

Galloway, L. & Krashen, S. (1980) Cerebral organisation in bilingualism and second language. In R. Scarcella & S. Krashen (eds.) *Research in Second Language Acquisition*. Rowley, MA: Newbury House.

Gans, H. (1979) Symbolic ethnicity: the future of ethnic groups and cultures in America. *Ethnic and Racial Studies*, 2, 1–20.

Gardner, R. C. (1979) Social psychological aspects of second language acquisition. In H. Giles & R. St Clair (eds.) *Language and Social Psychology*. Oxford: Blackwell.

Gardner, R. C. (1980) On the validity of affective variables in second language acquisition: conceptual, contextual and statistical considerations. *Language Learning*, 30, 255–70.

Gardner, R. C. (1985) *Social Psychology and Second Language Learning: the Role of Attitudes and Motivation*. London: Edward Arnold.

Gardner, R. C. (1988) The socio-educational model of second language learning: assumptions, findings and issues. *Language learning*, 38, 101–26.

Gardner, R. C. & Lambert, W. E. (1959) Motivational variables in second-language acquisition. *Canadian Journal of Psychology*, 13, 266–72.

Gardner, R. C. & Lambert, W. E. (1972) *Attitudes and Motivation in Second Language Learning*. Rowley, MA: Newbury House.

Gardner, R. C. & MacIntyre, P. D. (1993) On the measurement of affective variables in second language learning. *Language Learning*, 43, 157–94.

Gardner, R. C., Moorcroft, R. & Metford, J. (1989) Second language learning in an immersion programme: Factors influencing acquisition and retention. *Journal of Language and Social Psychology*, 8, 287–305.

Gardner, R. C., Przedzielewsky, E. & Lysynchuk, L. M. (1990) *A Multidimensional Investigation of Acculturation and Language Proficiency*. Research Bulletin 692, London, Ontario: University of Western Ontario.

Gardner, R. C. & Smythe, P. C. (1975) *Second Language Acquisition: A Social Psychological Approach*. London, Ontario: University of Western Ontario, Department of Psychology, Research Report 332.

Gardner-Chloros, P. (1991) *Language Selection and Switching in Strasbourg*. Oxford: Clarendon Press.

Gardner-Chloros, P. (1992) The sociolinguistics of the Greek-Cypriot community in London. *Plurilinguismes: Sociolinguistique du Grec et de la Grèce*. Paris: CERPL.

Gardner-Chloros, P. (1995) Code-switching in community, regional and national repertoires: The myth of the discreteness of linguistic systems. In L. Milroy & P. Muysken (eds.) *One Speaker, Two Languages: Cross-Disciplinary Perspectives on Code-Switching*. Cambridge University Press.

Gaziel, T., Obler, L. & Albert, M. (1978) A tachistoscopic study of Hebrew–English bilinguals. In M. Albert & L. Obler (eds.) *The Bilingual Brain*. New York: Academic Press.

Geffner, D. S. & Hochbert, I. (1971) Ear laterality performance of children from low middle socio-economic levels on a verbal dichotic listening task. *Cortex*, 3, 193–203.

Gekoski, W. L. (1980) Language acquisition context and language organisation in bilinguals. *Journal of Psycholinguistic Research*, 9(5), 429–49.

Gendron, J. D. (1972) *Rapport de la Commission d'Enquête sur la Situation de la Langue Française et sur les Droits Linguistiques au Québec. Livre 1. La Langue de Travail. La Situation de la Langue Française au Québec*. Québec: Éditeur Officiel du Québec.

Genesee, F. (1976) The role of intelligence in second language learning. *Language Learning*, 26, 267–80.

Genesee, F. (1979) *Les Programmes d'Immersion en Français du Bureau des Écoles Protestantes du Grand Montréal*. Québec: Études et Documents du Ministère de l'Éducation du Québec.

Genesee, F. (1981a) Cognitive and social consequences of bilingualism. In R. C. Gardner & R. Kalin (eds.) *A Canadian Social Psychology of Ethnic Relations*. London: Methuen.

Genesee, F. (1981b) Evaluation of the Laurendale Early Partial and Early Total Immersion Program. Unpublished manuscript. Montreal: McGill University.

Genesee, F. (1984) French Immersion Programs. In S. Shapson & V. D'Oyley (eds.)

Bilingual and Multicultural Education: Canadian Perspective. Clevedon: Multi-lingual Matters.

Genesee, F. (1989) Early bilingual development: One language or two? *Journal of Child Language*, 16, 161–79.

Genesee, F. (1991) L'immersion et l'apprenant défavorisé. *Études de Linguistique Appliquée*, 82, 77–93.

Genesee, F., Boivin, I. & Nicoladis, E. (1996) Talking with strangers: A study of bilingual children's communicative competence. *Applied Psycholinguistics*, 17, 427–42.

Genesee, F. & Bourhis, R. Y. (1982) The social psychological significance of code-switching in cross-cultural communication. *Journal of Language and Social Psychology*, 1, 1–27.

Genesee, F. & Bourhis, R. Y. (1988) Evaluative reactions to language choice strategies: the role of sociostructural factors. *Language and Communication*, 8, 229–50.

Genesee, F., Hamers, J. F., Lambert, W. E., Mononen, L., Seitz, M. & Starck, R. (1978) Language processing in bilinguals. *Brain and Language*, 5, 1–12.

Genesee, F., Nicoladis, E. & Paradis, J. (1995) Language differentiation in early bilingual development. *Journal of Child Language*, 22, 611–31.

Genesee, F., Tucker, G. R. & Lambert, W. E. (1978) The development of ethnic identity and ethnic role taking skills in children from different school settings. *International Journal of Psychology*, 13, 39–57.

Gibbons, J. (1982) The issue of language of instruction in the lower forms of Hong Kong secondary schools. *Journal of Multilingual and Multicultural Development*, 3, 117–28.

Giles, H. (1970) Evaluative reactions to accents. *Educational Review*, 22, 211–27.

Giles, H., Bourhis, R. Y. & Taylor, D. M. (1977) Towards a theory of language in ethnic group relations. In H. Giles (ed.) *Language, Ethnicity and Intergroup Relations*. London: Academic Press.

Giles, H. & Byrne, J. L. (1982) An intergroup approach to second language acquisition. *Journal of Multilingual and Multicultural Development*, 3, 17–40.

Giles, H. & Coupland, N. (1991) *Language: Contexts and Consequences.* Bucking-ham: Open University Press.

Giles, H., Hewstone, M. & Ball, P. (1983) Language attitudes in multilingual settings: prologue with priorities. *Journal of Multilingual and Multicultural Development*, 4, 81–100.

Giles, H . & Johnson, P. (1981) The role of language in ethnic group relations. In J. C. Turner & H. Giles (eds.) *Intergroup Behaviour*. Oxford: Blackwell.

Giles, H. & Johnson, P. (1987) Ethnolinguistic identity theory: a social psychological approach to language maintenance. *International Journal of the Sociology of Language*, 68, 69–99.

Giles, H., Mulac, A., Bradac, J. J. & Johnson, P. (1986) Speech accommodation theory: the first decade and beyond. *Communication Yearbooks*, 10, 8–34.

Giles, H. & Powesland, P. F. (1975) *Speech Style and Social Evaluation.* London: Academic Press.

Giles, H., Rosenthal, D. & Young, R. K. (1985) Perceived ethnolinguistic vitality: the Anglo- and Greek-Australian setting. *Journal of Multilingual and Multicultural Development*, 6, 253–69.

Giles, H. & Ryan, E. B. (1982) Prolegomena for developing a social psychological theory of language attitudes. In E. B. Ryan & H. Giles (eds.) *Attitudes towards Language Variation: Social and Applied Contexts.* London: Edward Arnold.

Giles, H. & Smith, P. M. (1979) Accommodation theory: optimal levels of convergence. In H. Giles & R. N. St Clair (eds.) *Language and Social Psychology.* Oxford: Blackwell.

Giles, H., Taylor, D. M. & Bourhis, R. Y. (1973) Towards a theory of interpersonal accommodation through speech: some Canadian data. *Language in Society,* 2, 177–92.

Giles, H., Williams, A., Mackie, D. M. & Rosselli, F. (1995) Reactions to Anglo- and Hispanic-American accented speakers: Affect, identity, persuasion and the English-only controversy. *Language and Communication,* 14, 102–23.

Gill, M. (1994) Accent and stereotypes: their effect on perception of teacher's and learner's comprehension. *Journal of Applied Communication Research,* 22, 348–61.

Glanzer, M. & Duarte, A. (1971) Repetition between and within languages in free recall. *Journal of Verbal Learning and Verbal Behavior,* 10, 625–30.

Glazer, N. (1966) The process and problems of language maintenance: an integrative review. In J. A. Fishman (ed.) *Language Loyalty in the United States.* The Hague: Mouton.

Glazer, N. & Moynihan, D. P. (eds.) (1963) *Beyond the Melting Pot.* Cambridge, MA: MIT/Harvard University Press.

Gleason, H. A. (1961) An Introduction to Descriptive Linguistics. Revised edition. New York: Holt, Rinehart & Winston.

Gleason, J. B. (1993) Neurolinguistics aspects of first language acquisition and loss. In K. Hyltenstam & A. Viberg (eds.) *Progression and Regression in Language.* Cambridge University Press.

Gliksman, L. & Gardner, R. C. (1976) Some Relationships between Students' Attitudes and their Behaviour in the French Classroom. London, Ontario: Language Research Group, Department of Psychology, University of Western Ontario, Research Bulletin, 5.

Goffman, E. (1959) *The Presentation of Self in Everyday Life.* New York: Doubleday.

Goggin, J. & Wickins, D. D. (1971) Proactive interference and language change in short-term memory. *Journal of Verbal Learning and Verbal Behavior,* 10, 453–8.

Gonzo, S. & Saltarelli, M. (1983) Pidginization and linguistic change in immigrant language. In R. Andersen (ed.) *Pidginization and Creolization as Language Acquisition.* Rowley: Newbury House.

Goodman, G. S., Haith, M. M., Guttentag, R. E. & Rao, S. (1985) Automatic processing of word meaning: intralingual and interlingual interference. *Child Development,* 56, 103–18.

Goodz, N. (1984) Variables Influencing Parental Language Mixing. Paper presented at the Ninth Annual Meeting of the Boston University Conference on Child Development, Boston, MA.

Goodz, N. (1985) Parent-to-child speech in bilingual and monolingual families. Toronto: Paper presented at the Society for Research on Child Development.

Goodz, N. (1989) Parental language mixing in bilingual families. *Infant Mental Health Journal*, 10, 25–43.

Goodz, N. (1994) Interactions between parents and children in bilingual families. In F. Genesee (ed.) *Educating Second Language Children: The Whole Child, the Whole Curriculum, the Whole Community*. Cambridge University Press.

Gordon, H. W. (1980) Cerebral organization in bilinguals. *Brain and Language*, 9, 255–68.

Gordon, M. M. (1981) Models of pluralism: the American dilemma. *The Annals of the American Academy of Political and Social Science*, 454, 178–88.

Gorrell, J. J., Bregman, N. J., McAllistair, H. A. & Lipscombe, T. J. (1982) A comparison of spatial role-taking in monolingual and bilingual children. *Journal of Genetic Psychology*, 140, 3–10.

Grainger, J. & Beauvillain, C. (1989) Associative priming in bilinguals: Some limits of the interlingual facilitation effect. *Canadian Journal of Psychology*, 12, 261–73.

Grainger, J. & Dijkstra, T. (1992) On the representation and use of language information in bilinguals. In R. J. Harris (ed.) *Cognitive Processing in Bilinguals*. Amsterdam: Elsevier.

Grammont, M. (1902) *Observations sur le Langage des Enfants*. Paris: Mélanges Meillet

Graves, T. D. (1967) Acculturation in a tri-ethnic community. *Journal of Anthropology*, 23, 337–50.

Gray, T. (1982) Bilingual program? What's that? *Linguistic Reporter*, 24, 1–5.

Green, D. W. (1986) Control, activation, and resource: a framework and a model for the control of speech in bilinguals. *Brain and Language*, 27, 210–23.

Greenberg, J. H. (1956) The measurement of linguistic diversity. *Language*, 32, 109–15.

Grin, F. (ed.) (1996) Economic approaches to language and language planning. *International Journal of the Sociology of Language*, 121.

Grosjean, F. (1982) *Life with Two Languages: An Introduction to Bilingualism*. Cambridge, MA: Harvard University Press.

Grosjean, F. (1985a) The bilingual as a competent but specific speaker–hearer. *The Journal of Multilingual and Multicultural Development*, 6, 467–77.

Grosjean, F. (1985b) Polyglot aphasics and language mixing: a comment on Perecman. *Brain and Language*, 26, 349–55.

Grosjean, F. (1996) Living with two languages and two cultures. In I. Parasnis (ed.) *Cultural and Language Diversity and the Deaf Experience*. New York: Cambridge University Press.

Grosjean, F. & Soares, C. (1986) Processing mixed language: some preliminary findings. In J. Vaid (ed.) *Language Processing in Bilinguals: Psycholinguistic and Neuropsychological Perspectives*. Hillsdale, NJ: Erlbaum.

Grossi, G., Semenza, C., Corazza, S. & Volterra, V. (1996) Hemispheric specialization for sign language. *Neuropsychologia*, 34, 737–40.

Gudykunst, W. B. (1986) Towards a theory of intergroup communication. In W. B. Gudykunst (ed.) *Intergroup Communication*. London: Edward Arnold.

Gudykunst, W. B. & Ting-Toomey, S. (1990) Ethnic identity, language and communication breakdowns. In H. Giles & W. P. Robinson (eds.) *Handbook of*

Language and Social Psychology, 1st edition. Chichester: John Wiley.

Guimond, S. & Palmer, D. L. (1993) Developmental changes in ingroup favouritism among bilingual and unilingual Francophone and Anglophone students. *Journal of Language and Social Psychology*, 12, 318–51.

Gumperz, J. J. (1964a) Linguistic and social interaction in two communities. *American Anthropologist*, 66, 137–53.

Gumperz, J. J. (1964b) Hindi–Punjabi code-switching in Delhi. In H. Hunt (ed.) *Proceedings of the Ninth International Congress of Linguistics*. The Hague: Mouton.

Gumperz, J. J. (1968) The speech community. In D. L. Sills (ed.) *International Encyclopaedia of the Social Sciences*, Volume 9. New York: Macmillan.

Gumperz, J. J. (1971) *Language in Social Groups*. Stanford University Press.

Gumperz, J. J. (1982) Social network and language shift. In J. J. Gumperz (ed.) *Discourse Strategies*. Cambridge University Press.

Gumperz, J. J. & Wilson, R. (1971) Convergence and creolization: a case from the Indo-Aryan/Dravidian Border in India. In D. H. Hymes (ed.) *Pidginization and Creolization of Language*. Cambridge University Press.

Gur, R. C., Gur, R. E., Orbrist, W. D., Hungerbuhler, J. P., Younkin, D., Rosen, A. D., Skilnick, B. E. & Reirich, M. (1982) Sex and handedness differences in cerebral blood flow during rest and cognitive activity. *Science*, 217, 659–61.

Guttentag, R. E., Haith, M. M., Goodman, G. S. & Hauch, J. (1984) Semantic processing of unattended words by bilinguals: a test of the input switch mechanism. *Journal of Verbal Learning and Verbal Behavior*, 23, 178–88.

Guttfreund, D. G. (1990) Effects of language usage on the emotional experience of Spanish–English and English–Spanish bilinguals. *Journal of Consulting and Clinical Psychology*, 58, 604–7.

Hakuta, K. (1987) Degree of bilingualism and cognitive ability in mainland Puerto Rican children. *Child Development*, 58, 1372–88.

Hakuta, K. & D'Andrea, D. (1992) Some properties of bilingual maintenance and loss in Mexican background high-school students. *Applied Linguistics*, 13, 72–99.

Hakuta, K. & Diaz, R. M. (1984) The relationship between degree of bilingualism and cognitive ability: a critical discussion and some longitudinal data. In K.E. Nelson (ed.) *Children's Language*, Volume 5. Hillsdale, NJ: Erlbaum.

Halliday, M. A. K. (1973) *Explorations in the Functions of Language*. London: Arnold.

Halliday, M. A. K. (1975) *Learning How to Mean: Explorations in the Development of Language*. London: Edward Arnold.

Hamayan, E. V. (1994) Language development of low-literacy students. In F. Genesee (ed.) *Educating Second Language Children: The Whole Child, the Whole Curriculum, the Whole Community*. Cambridge University Press.

Hamers, J. F. (1973) Interdependent and Independent States of a Bilingual's Two Languages. Unpublished PhD dissertation. Montreal: McGill University.

Hamers, J. F. (1979) Le rôle du langage et de la culture dans les processus d'apprentissage et dans la planification éducative. *Recherche, Pédagogie et Culture*, 43, 24–31.

Hamers, J. F. (1981) Psychological approaches to the development of bilinguality.

In H. Baetens Beardsmore (ed.) *Elements of Bilingual Theory*. Free University of Brussels.

Hamers, J. F. (1987) The relevance of Social Network Analysis in the psycholinguistic investigation of multilingual behaviour. In M. Blanc & J. F. Hamers (eds.) *Problèmes Théoriques et Méthodologiques dans l'Étude des Langues/Dialectes en Contact aux Niveaux Macrologique et Micrologique*. Quebec: International Center for Research on Bilinguism, B-160.

Hamers, J. F. (1989) La scolarisation et le développement langagier en Afrique francophone: considérations socio-psychologiques. In H. Krief & F. Gbénimé-Sendagbia (eds.) *Espace Francophone: Revue de Langue et Littérature*, Volume 2. Bangui: Département des Lettres Modernes, Université de Bangui.

Hamers, J. F. (1991) L'ontogénèse de la bilingualité. In A. G. Reynolds (ed.) *Bilingualism, Multiculturalism and Second Language Learning: The McGill Conference in Honour of Wallace E. Lambert*. Hillsdale, NJ: Erlbaum.

Hamers, J. F. (1994) L'interaction entre les réseaux sociaux, la valorisation du langage et les croyances dans le développement biculturel. In J. Blomart & B. Krewer (eds.) *Perspectives de l'Interculturel*. Paris: L'Harmattan.

Hamers, J. F. (1996) Cognitive and bilingual development of bilingual children. In I. Parasnis (ed.) *Cultural and Language Diversity and the Deaf Experience*. Cambridge University Press.

Hamers, J. F. (1997) Les situations plurilingues et leurs enjeux. In M. L. Lefèbvre & M. A. Hily (eds.) *Les situations plurilingues et leurs enjeux*. Paris: L'Harmattan.

Hamers, J. F. & Blanc, M. (1982) Towards a social-psychological model of bilingual development. *Journal of Language and Social Psychology*, 1, 29–49.

Hamers, J. F. & Blanc, M. (1983) *Bilingualité et Bilinguisme*. Série Psychologie et Sciences Humaines, 129. Brussels: Mardaga.

Hamers, J. F. & Blanc, M. (1987) Social Psychological Foundations of Bilingual Development. Paper presented at the Third International Conference on the Social Psychology of Language, Bristol, 20–23 July 1987.

Hamers, J. F. & Blanc, M. H. A. (1989) *Bilinguality & Bilingualism*. 1st Edition. Cambridge University Press.

Hamers, J. F. & Deshaies, D. (1982) Les dimensions de l'identité culturelle chez les jeunes Québécois. In J. D. Gendron, A. Prujiner & R. Vigneault (eds.) *Identité Culturelle: Approches Méthodologiques*. Quebec: International Center for Research on Bilingualism, B-113.

Hamers, J. F. & Lambert, W. E. (1972). Bilingual interdependencies in auditory perception. *Journal of Verbal Learning and Verbal Behavior*, 11, 303–10.

Hamers, J. F. & Lambert, W. E. (1974) Bilingual reactions to cross language semantic ambiguity. In S. T. Carey (ed.) *Bilingualism, Biculturalism and Education*. Edmonton: University of Alberta, Printing Department.

Hamers, J. F. & Lambert, W. E. (1977) Visual field and cerebral hemisphere preferences in bilinguals. In S. J. Segalowitz & F. A. Gruber (eds.) *Language Development and Neurological Theory*. New York: Academic Press.

Hammoud, R. (1983) *Utilisation de l'Image Mentale et du Champ d'Association dans l'Enseignement du Vocabulaire d'une Langue Étrangère à des Débutants Adultes*

Francophones en Contexte Canadien. Quebec: International Center for Research on Bilingualism, B-129.

Hansen, J. & Stansfield, C. (1981) The relationship of field dependent–independent cognitive styles to foreign language achievement. *Language Learning*, 31, 349–67.

Hanson, G. (1979) The position of the second generation of Finnish immigrants in Sweden: the importance of education in the home language to the welfare of second generation immigrants. Split, Paper presented at the Symposium on the Position of Second Generation Yugoslav Immigrants in Sweden.

Harley, B. (1994) After immersion: maintaining the momentum. *Journal of Multilingual and Multicultural Development*, 15, 229–44.

Harley, B., Hart, D. & Lapkin, S. (1986) The effects of early bilingual schooling on first language skills. *Applied Psycholinguistics*, 7, 295–322.

Harley, B. & Swain, M. (1977) An analysis of verb form and function in the speech of French immersion pupils. *Working Papers on Bilingualism*, 14, 31–46.

Harley, B. & Swain, M. (1978) An analysis of verb systems used by young learners of French. *Interlanguage Studies Bulletin*, 3, 35–79.

Harris, B. (1980) How a three-year-old translates. In *Patterns of Bilingualism.* RELC Anthology Series, Volume 8. National University of Singapore Press.

Harter, S. (1983) Developmental perspectives on the self-system. In E. M. Hetherinton (ed.) *Handbook of Child Psychology. Volume 4: Socialization, Personality and Social Development.* New York: Wiley.

Hartnett, D. (1975) The Relation of Cognitive Style and Hemispheric Preference to Deductive and Inductive Second Language Learning. Unpublished PhD dissertation. Montreal: McGill University.

Harwood, J., Giles, H. & Bourhis, R.Y. (1994) The genesis of vitality theory: historical patterns and discoursal dimensions. *International Journal of the Sociology of Language*, 108, 167–206.

Hasuike, R., Tzeng, O. & Hung, D. (1986) Script effects and cerebral lateralization: the case of Chinese characters. In J. Vaid (ed.) *Language Processing in Bilinguals: Psycholinguistic and Neuropsychological Perspectives.* Hillsdale, NJ: Erlbaum.

Hatta, T. (1981) Differential processing of Kanji and Kana stimuli in Japanese people: some implications from Stroop-test results. *Neuropsychologia*, 19, 87–93.

Haugen, E. (1950) The analysis of linguistic borrowings. *Language*, 26, 210–31.

Hebb, D. O. (1949) *The Organization of Behavior.* New York: John Wiley.

Hebb, D. O. (1968) Concerning imagery. *Psychological Review*, 15, 466–77.

Hébert, R. (1976) *Rendement Académique et Langue d'Enseignement chez les Élèves Franco-Manitobains.* Saint-Boniface, Manitoba: Centre de Recherches du Collège Universitaire Saint-Boniface.

Hechter, M. (1975) *Internal Colonialism: the Celtic Fringe in British National Development, 1530–1966.* London: Routledge and Kegan Paul.

Herbert, R. K. (1982) Cerebral asymmetry in bilinguals and the deaf: perspectives on a common pattern. *Journal of Multilingual and Multicultural Development*, 3, 47–59.

Hernandez-Chavez, E. (1978) Language maintenance, bilingual education and philosophies of bilingualism in the United States. In J. E. Alatis (ed.) *International Dimensions of Bilingual Education*. Washington, DC: Georgetown University Press.

Hewitt, R. (1986) *White Talk Black Talk: Inter-racial Friendship and Communication amongst Adolescents*. Cambridge University Press.

Hewstone, M. & Giles, H. (1986) Social groups and social stereotypes in intergroup communications: a review and model of intergroup communication breakdown. In W. B. Gudykunst (ed.) *Intergroup Communication*. London: Edward Arnold.

Hiebert, E. H. & Raphael, T. E. (1996) Psychological perspectives on literacy and extensions to educational practice. In D. C. Berliner & R. C. Calfee (eds.) *Handbook of Educational Psychology*. New York: Simon & Shuster / Macmillan.

Hink, R., Kaga, K. & Suzuki, J. (1980) An evoked potential correlate of reading ideographic and phonetic Japanese scripts. *Neuropsychologia*, 18, 455–64.

Hinnenkamp, V. (1982) *Foreigner Talk and Tarzanisch*. Hamburg: Helmut Buske Verlag.

Hoffmann, C. (1991) *An Introduction to Bilingualism*. London: Longman.

Holmstrand, L. E. (1979) The effects on general school achievement of early commencement of English instruction. University of Uppsala Department of Education, *Uppsala Reports on Education*, 4, 1–45.

Holobow, N., E. Genesee, & Lambert, W. E. (1991) The effectiveness of a foreign language immersion program for children from different ethnic and social class backgrounds: Report 2. *Applied Psycholinguistics*, 12, 179–98.

Hoosain, R. (1992) Different cerebral lateralization of Chinese–English bilingual functions. In R. D. Harris (ed.) *Cognitive Processing in Bilinguals*. Amsterdam: North Holland.

Hopper, R. (1977) Language attitudes in the job interview. *Communication Monograph*, 44, 346–51.

Hudson, R. A. (1980) *Sociolinguistics*. Cambridge University Press.

Hudson, R. A. (1994) Diglossia. In R. E. Asher (ed.) *Encyclopedia of Language and Linguistics*. Volume 1. Oxford: Pergamon.

Hughes, A. (1989) *Testing for Language Teachers*. Cambridge University Press.

Hughes, E. C. (1970) The linguistic division of labor in industrial and urban societies. *Georgetown Monograph Series on Language and Linguistics*, 23, 103–19.

Hummel, K. M. (1986) Memory for bilingual prose. In J. Vaid (ed.) *Language Processing in Bilinguals: Psycholinguistic and Neuropsychological Perspectives*. Hillsdale, NJ: Erlbaum.

Hummel, K. M. (1993) Bilingual memory research: From storage to processing issues. *Applied Psycholinguistics*, 14, 267–84.

Husband, C. & Saifullah Khan (1982) The viability of ethnolinguistic vitality. *Journal of Multilingual and Multicultural Development*, 3, 193–205.

Huttenlocher, J., Haight, W., Bryk, A., Seltzer, M., & Lyons, T. (1991) Early vocabulary growth: Relation to language input and gender. *Developmental Psychology*, 27, 236–48.

Hyltenstam, K. (1992) Non-native features of near-native speakers: on the ultimate attainment of childhood L2 learners. In R. J. Harris (ed.) *Cognitive Processing in Bilinguals.* Amsterdam: Elsevier.

Hyltenstam, K. & Stroud, C. (1989) Bilingualism in Alzheimer's dementia. In K. Hyltenstam & L. K. Obler (eds.) *Bilingualism across the Lifespan: Aspects of Acquisition, Maturity and Loss.* Cambridge University Press.

Hyltenstam, K., & Stroud, C. (1993) Second language regression in Alzheimer's dementia. In K. Hyltenstam & A. Viberg (eds.) *Progression and Regression in Language.* Cambridge: Cambridge University Press.

Hyltenstam, K. & Viberg, A. (1993) Linguistic progression and regression: an introduction. In K. Hyltenstam & A. Viberg (eds.), *Progression and Regression in Language.* Cambridge: Cambridge University Press, 3–36.

Hymes, D. (1971) *On Communicative Competence.* Philadelphia: University of Pennsylvania Press.

Hynd, G. & Scott, S. (1980) Propositional and appositional modes of thought and differential speech lateralization in Navajo Indian and Anglo children. *Child Development,* 51, 909–11.

Hynd, G., Teeter, A. & Stewart, A. (1980) Acculturation and the lateralization of speech in the bilingual native American. *International Journal of Neuroscience,* 11, 1–7.

Ianco-Worrall, A. D. (1972) Bilingualism and cognitive development. *Child Development,* 43, 1390–400.

Imbens-Bailey, A. L. (1996) Ancestral language acquisition: implications for aspects of ethnic identity among Armenian American children and adolescents. *Journal of Language and Social Psychology,* 15, 422–43.

Jahoda, G. (1984) Do we need a concept of culture? *Journal of Cross-Cultural Psychology,* 15, 139–52.

Jakobovits, L. A. (1970) *Foreign Language Learning: a Psycho-linguistic Analysis of the Issues.* Rowley, MA: Newbury House.

Jakobovits, L. A. & Lambert, W. E. (1961) Semantic satiation among bilinguals. *Journal of Experimental Psychology,* 62, 576–82.

Jakobovits, L. A. & Lambert, W. E. (1967) A note on the measurement of semantic satiation. *Journal of Verbal Learning and Verbal Behavior,* 6, 954–7.

Javier, R. A. & Alpert, M. (1986) The effect of stress on the linguistic generalization of bilingual individuals. *Journal of Psycholinguistic Research,* 15, 419–35.

Jin, Y. S. (1990) Effects of concreteness on cross-language priming in lexical decisions. *Perceptual and Motor Skills,* 70, 1139–54.

Johnson, J. S. & Newport, E. L. (1989) Critical effects in second language learning: the influence of maturational state on the acquisition of English as a second language. *Cognitive Psychology,* 21, 60–99.

Jöreskog, K. G. & Sorbom, D. (1978) *LISREL: Analysis of Linear Structural Relationships by the Method of Maximum Likelihood.* Chicago: International Educational Services.

Jourdan, C. & Keesing, R. (1997) From Fisin to Pidgin: creolization in process in the Solomon Islands. *Language in Society,* 26, 401–20.

Juillard, C. (1995) *Sociolinguistique Urbaine. La Vie des Langues à Ziguinchor (Sénégal).* Paris: CNRS.

Junque, C., Vendrell, P. & Vendrell, J. (1995) Differential impairments and specific phenomena in 50 Catalan–Spanish bilingual aphasic patients. In M. Paradis (ed.) *Aspects of Bilingual Aphasia*. New York: Elsevier.

Kachru, B. B. (1978) Code-mixing as a communicative strategy. In J. Alatis (ed.) *International Dimensions of Bilingual Education*. Washington, DC: Georgetown University Press.

Kachru, B. B. (1982) The bilingual's linguistic repertoire. In B. Hartford, A. Valdman & C. R. Foster (eds.) *Issues in International Bilingual Education: the Role of the Vernacular*. New York: Plenum Press.

Kalin, R. (1982) The social significance of speech in medical, legal and occupational settings. In E. B. Ryan & H. Giles (eds.) *Attitudes Towards Language Variation*. London: Edward Arnold.

Kaplan, L. D. (1990) The language of the Alaskan Inuit. In D. R. F. Collis (ed.) *Arctic Languages: An Awakening*. Paris: UNESCO.

Karmiloff-Smith, A. (1979) *A Functional Approach to Child Language*. Cambridge: Cambridge University Press.

Karmiloff-Smith, A. (1992) *Beyond Modularity: A Developmental Perspective on Cognitive Science*. Cambridge, MA: MIT Press.

Keatly, C. W., Spinks, J. A. & De Gelder, B. (1994) Asymmetrical cross-language priming effects. *Memory & Cognition*, 22, 70–84.

Keesing, R. M. (1988) *Melanesian Pidgin and the Oceanic Substrate*. Stanford University Press.

Keller-Cohen, D. (1979) Systematicity and variations in the non-native child's acquisition of conversational skills. *Language Learning*, 29, 27–44.

Kendall, M. B. (1980) Radical grammars: interplays of form and function. In H. Giles, W. P. Robinson & P. M. Smith (eds.) *Language: Social Psychological Perspectives*. Oxford: Pergamon.

Kenyeres, A. (1938) Comment une petite Hongroise de sept ans apprend le français. *Archives de Psychologie*, 26, 321–66.

Kessler, C. & Quinn, M. E. (1982) Cognitive development in bilingual environments. In B. Hartford, A. Valdman & C. R. Foster (eds.) *Issues in International Bilingual Education: The Role of the Vernacular*. New York: Plenum Press.

Kessler, C. & Quinn, M. E. (1987) Language minority children's linguistic and cognitive creativity. *Journal of Multilingual and Multicultural Development*, 8, 173–86.

Khubchandani, L. M. (1978) Multilingual education in India. In B. Spolsky & R. L. Cooper (eds.) *Case Studies in Bilingual Education*. Rowley, MA: Newbury House.

Khubchandani, L. M. (1979) A demographic typology for Hindi, Urdu, Panjabi speakers in Northern India. In W. C. McCormack & S. A. Wurm (eds.) *Language and Society*. The Hague: Mouton.

Kilborn, K. & Ito, T. (1989) Sentence processing strategies in adult bilinguals. In B. MacWhinney & E. Bates (eds.) *The Cross Linguistic Study of Sentence Processing*. Cambridge University Press.

Kim, K. H. S., Relkin, N. R., Lee, K. M., & Hirsch, J. (1997) Distinct cortical areas associated with native and second languages. *Nature*, 388, 171–4.

Kim, Y. Y. (1991a) Interethnic communication: The context and the meaning.

Paper presented at the 4th International Conference on Social Psychology and Language. Santa Barbara.

Kim, Y. Y. (1991b) Intercultural communication competence: A systems-theoretic view. In S. Ting-Toomey & F. Korzenny (eds.) *Cross-Cultural Interpersonal Communication*. Newbury Park, CA: Sage, 259–75.

Kintsch, W. (1970) Recognition memory in bilingual subjects. *Journal of Verbal Learning and Verbal Behavior*, 9, 405–9.

Kintsch, W. & Kintsch, E. (1969) Interlingual interference and memory processes. *Journal of Verbal Learning and Verbal Behavior*, 8, 16–19.

Kirp, D. (1983) Elusive equality: race, ethnicity, and education in the American experience. In N. Glazer & K. Young (eds.) *Ethnic Pluralism and Public Policy*. London: Heinemann.

Kirsner, K., Brown, H. L., Abrul, S., Chadha, N. K. & Sharma, N. K. (1980) Bilingualism and lexical representation. *Quarterly Journal of Experimental Psychology*, 32, 585–94.

Kirsner, K., Smith, M. C., Lockhart, R. S., King, M. L. & Jain, M. (1984) The bilingual lexicon: Language specific units in an integrated network. *Journal of Verbal Learning and Verbal Behavior*, 23, 519–39.

Kiyak, H. A. (1982) Interlingual interference in naming color words. *Journal of Cross Cultural Psychology*, 13, 125–35.

Klein, D., Zatorre, R. J., Milner, B., Meyer, E. & Evans, A. C. (1994) Left putamen activation when speaking a second language: evidence from PET. *Cognitive Neuroscience and Neuropsychology*, 5, 1721, 2295–7.

Klein, D., Zatorre, R. J., Milner, B., Meyer E. & Evans, A. C. (1995) The neural substrate of bilingual language processing: evidence from positron emission tomography. In M. Paradis (ed.) *Aspects of Bilingual Aphasia*. New York: Elsevier.

Klima, E. S. & Bellugi, U. (1966) Syntactic regularities in the speech of children. In J. Lyons & R. J. Wales (eds.) *Psycholinguistic Papers: The Proceedings of the 1966 Edinburgh Conference*. Edinburgh University Press.

Kloss, H. (1966) Conceptual background: an analysis of factors influencing language maintenance outcomes. In J. A. Fishman (ed.) *Language Loyalty in the United States*. The Hague: Mouton.

Kloss, H. (1969) *Research Problems in Group Bilingualism*. Quebec: International Center for Research on Bilingualism.

Kloss, H. & McConnell, G. D. (1974ff.) *Composition Linguistique des Nations du Monde*. Quebec: International Center for Research on Bilingualism / Presses de l'Université Laval.

Kolers, P. A. (1963) Interlingual word association. *Journal of Verbal Learning and Verbal Behavior*, 2, 291–300.

Kolers, P. A. (1965) Bilingualism and bicodalism. *Language and Speech*, 8, 122–6.

Kolers, P. A. (1968) Bilingualism and information processing. *Scientific American*, March, 78–86.

Kolers, P. A. (1978) On the representation of experience. In D. Gerver & H. W. Sinaiko (eds.) *Language, Interpretation and Communication*. New York: Plenum Press.

Kolers, P. A. & Gonzales, E. (1980) Memory for words, synonyms and translation.

Journal of Experimental Psychology, Human Learning and Memory, 6, 53–65.

Koppe, R. & Meisel, J. M. (1995) Code-switching in bilingual first language acquisition. In L. Milroy & P. Muysken (eds.) *One speaker, two Languages: Cross-disciplinary perspectives on code-switching.* Cambridge University Press.

Krashen, S., Seliger, H. & Hartnett, D. (1974) Two studies in adult second language learning. *Kritikon Litterarum,* 3, 220–8.

Kreitler, H. & Kreitler, S. (1976) *Cognitive Orientation and Behaviour.* New York: Springer Verlag.

Kroll, J. F. (1993) Accessing conceptual representation for words in a second language. In R. Schreuber & B. Weltens (eds.) *The Bilingual Lexicon.* Philadelphia: John Benjamin.

Kroll, J. F. & Curley, J. (1988) Lexical memory in novice bilinguals: The role of concepts in retrieving second language words. In M. Gruneberg, P. Morris & R. Sykes (eds.) *Practical Aspects of Memory,* Volume 2. London: John Wiley.

Kroll, J. F. & Sholl, A. (1992) Lexical and conceptual memory in fluent and non-fluent bilinguals. In R. J. Harris (ed.) *Cognitive Processing in Bilinguals.* Amsterdam: Elsevier.

Kroll, J. F. & Stewart, E. (1994) Category inference in translation and picture naming: evidence for asymmetric connections between bilingual memory representations. *Journal of Memory & Language,* 33, 149–74.

Kruskal, J. B. & Wish, M. (1978) *Multidimensional Scaling.* Newbury Park, CA & London: Sage.

Kuhl, P., Williams, K., Lacerda, F., Stevens, K. & Lindblom, B. (1992) Linguistic experience alters phonetic perception in infants by 6 months of age. *Science,* 255, 606–8.

Kulick, D. (1992) *Language Shift and Cultural Reproduction: Socialization, Self, and Syncretism in a Papua New Guinea Village.* Studies in the Social and Cultural Foundations of Language 14. Cambridge University Press.

Kuo, E. C. Y. (1979) Measuring communicativity in multilingual societies: the case of Singapore and West Malaysia. *Anthropological Linguistics,* 21, 328–40.

Kuo, E. (1984) Mass media and language planning: Singapore's 'Speak Mandarin' campaign. *Journal of Communication,* 34, 24–35.

Labov, W. (1966) *The Social Stratification of English in New York City.* Washington, DC: Center for Applied Linguistics.

Labov, W. (1972) *Language in the Inner City: Studies in the Blacks' English Vernacular.* Oxford: Blackwell.

Labov, W. (1978) The design of a sociolinguistic project. In D. P. Pattanayak (ed.) *Papers in Indian Sociolinguistic* CIIL Conference and Seminars Series 2. Mysore: Central Institute for Indian Languages.

Lacroix, J. M. & Rioux, Y. (1978) La communication non verbale chez le bilingue. *Canadian Journal of Behavioral Science,* 10, 130–40.

Lalonde, R. N. & Gardner, R. C. (1984) Investigating a causal model of second language acquisition: where does personality fit? *Canadian Journal of Behavioural Science,* 16, 224–37.

Lambert, W. E. (1955) Measurement of the linguistic dominance in bilinguals. *Journal of Abnormal and Social Psychology,* 50, 197–200.

Lambert, W. E. (1969) Psychological studies of interdependencies of the bilingual's two languages. In J. Puhvel (ed.) *Substance and Structure of Language.* Los Angeles: University of California Press.

Lambert, W. E. (1972) *Language, Psychology and Culture: Essays by Wallace E. Lambert,* A. S. Dil (ed.), Stanford University Press.

Lambert, W. E. (1974) Culture and language as factors in learning and education. In F. E. Aboud & R. D. Meade (eds.) *Cultural Factors in Learning and Education.* Bellingham, WA: Western Washington State University.

Lambert, W. E. (1977) Effects of bilingualism on the individual. In P. A. Hornby (ed.) *Bilingualism: Psychological, Social and Educational Implications.* New York: Academic Press.

Lambert, W. E. (1987) The effects of bilingual and bicultural experiences on children's attitudes and social perspectives. In P. Homel, M. Palij & D. Aaronson (eds.) *Childhood Bilingualism: Aspects of Linguistic, Cognitive and Social Development.* Hillsdale, NJ: Erlbaum Associates.

Lambert, W. E. & Fillenbaum, S. (1959) A pilot study of aphasia among bilinguals. *Canadian Journal of Psychology,* 13, 28–34.

Lambert, W. E., Franckel, H. & Tucker, G. R. (1966) Judging personality through speech: a French Canadian example. *Journal of Communication,* 16, 305–21.

Lambert, W. E. Genesee, F. Holobow, N. E. & Chartrand, L. (1993) Bilingual education for Majority English-speaking children. *European Journal of Psychology of Education,* 8, 3–22.

Lambert, W. E., Giles, H. & Picard, O. (1975) Language attitudes in a French American community. *International Journal of the Sociology of Language,* 4, 127–52.

Lambert, W. E., Havelka, J. & Crosby, C. (1958) The influence of language acquisition contexts on bilingualism. *Journal of Abnormal and Social Psychology,* 56, 239–44.

Lambert, W. E., Havelka, J. & Gardner, R. C. (1959) Linguistic manifestations of bilingualism. *American Journal of Psychology,* 72, 77–82.

Lambert, W. E., Hodgson, R. C., Gardner, R. C. & Fillenbaum, S. J. (1960) Evaluation reactions to spoken languages. *Journal of Abnormal and Social Psychology,* 60, 44–51.

Lambert, W. E., Ignatov, M. & Krauthamer, M. (1968) Bilingual organisation in free recall. *Journal of Verbal Learning and Verbal Behavior,* 7, 207–14.

Lambert, W. E. & Jakobovits, L. A. (1960) Verbal satiation and changes in the intensity of meaning. *Journal of Experimental Psychology,* 60, 376–83.

Lambert, W. E., Just, M. & Segalowitz, N. (1970) Some cognitive consequences of following the curricula of Grades One and Two in a foreign language. *Georgetown Monograph Series on Languages and Linguistics,* 23, 229–79.

Lambert, W. E. & Klineberg, O. (1967) *Children's View of Foreign Peoples: A Cross National Study.* New York: Appleton-Century-Croft.

Lambert, W. E., Mermigis, L. & Taylor, D. M. (1986) Greek Canadians' attitudes towards own group and other Canadian ethnic groups: a test of the multiculturalism hypothesis. *Canadian Journal of Behavioral Science,* 18, 35–51.

Lambert, W. E. & Moore, N. (1966) Word-association responses: comparison of American and French monolinguals with Canadian monolinguals and bilinguals. *Journal of Personality and Social Psychology*, 3, 313–20.

Lambert, W. E. & Rawlings, C. (1969) Bilingual processing of mixed-language associative networks. *Journal of Verbal Learning and Verbal Behavior*, 8, 604–9.

Lambert, W. E. & Segalowitz, N. (1969) Semantic generalization in bilinguals. *Journal of Verbal Learning and Verbal Behavior*, 8, 559–66.

Lambert, W. E. & Taylor, D. M. (1990) *Coping with Cultural and Racial Diversity in Urban America*. New York: Praeger.

Lambert, W. E. & Tucker, G. R. (1972) *Bilingual Education of Children: The St Lambert Experiment*. Rowley, MA: Newbury House.

Lambert, W. W. & Lambert, W. E. (1973) *Social Psychology*, 2nd edition. Foundations of Modern Psychology Series. Englewood, NJ: Prentice Hall.

Lanca, M., Alksnis, C., Roese, N. J. & Gardner, R. C. (1994) Effects of language choice on acculturation: a study of Portuguese immigrants in a multicultural setting. *Journal of Language and Social Psychology*, 13, 315–30.

Landry, R. (1978) Le bilinguisme: le facteur répétition. *Revue Canadienne des Langues Modernes/Canadian Modern Language Review*, 34, 548–76.

Landry, R. & Allard, R. (1985) Choix de la langue d'enseignement: une analyse chez des parents francophones en milieu bilingue. *Canadian Modern Language Review*, 4, 480–510.

Landry, R. & Allard, R. (1994) The Acadians of New Brunswick: Demolinguistic realities and the vitality of the French language. *International Journal of the Sociology of Language*, 105, 187–215.

Landry, R., Allard, R. & Henry, J. (1996) French in South Louisiana: Towards language loss. *Journal of Multilingual and Multicultural Development*, 17, 442–68.

Lanza, E. (1992) Can bilingual two-year-olds code-switch? *Journal of Child Language*, 19, 633–58.

Larsen-Freeman, D. & Long, M. H. (1991) *An Introduction to Research on Second Language Acquisition*. London: Longman.

Lavandera, B. R. (1978) The variable component of bilingual performance. In J. Alatis (ed.) *International Dimensions of Bilingual Education*. Washington, DC: Georgetown University Press.

Lawson-Sako, S. & Sachdev, I. (1996) Ethnolinguistic communication in Tunisian streets: convergence and divergence. In Y. Suleiman (ed.) *Language and Identity in the Middle East and North Africa*. Richmond, Surrey: Curzon Press.

Lazaraton, A. (1995) Qualitative research in Applied Linguistics: a progress report. *TESOL Quarterly*, 29, 455–72.

Leather, J. & James, A. (1991) The acquisition of second language speech. *Studies in Second Language Acquisition*, 13, 305–41.

Lebrun, Y. (1995) The study of bilingual aphasia: Pitres' legacy. In M. Paradis (ed.) *Aspects of Bilingual Aphasia*. New York: Elsevier Science, Pergamon.

Lebrun, Y. & Leleux, C. (1986) Central communication disorders in deaf signers. In J. L. Nespoulous, P. Perron, & A. Lecours (eds.) *The biological foundations of gestures*. Hillsdale, Erlbaum.

Leets, L., Giles, H. & Clément, R. (1996) Explicating ethnicity in theory and communication research. *Multilingua*, 15, 115–47.

Lefebvre, C. (1998) *Creole Genesis and the Acquisition of Grammar: The Case of Haitian Creole*. Cambridge University Press.

Lefley, H. P. (1976) Acculturation, child-rearing and self-esteem in two North American tribes. *Ethos*, 4, 385–401.

Legaretta, D. (1979) The effects of program models on language acquisition by Spanish speaking children. *TESOL Quarterly*, 13, 521–34.

Lemmon, C. R. & Goggin, J. P. (1989) The measurement of bilingualism and its relationship to cognitive ability. *Applied Psycholinguistics*, 10, 133–55.

Lenneberg, E. H. (1967) *Biological Foundations of Language*. New York: Wiley.

Leopold, W. F. (1939–1949) *Speech Development of a Bilingual Child*. Evanston, IL: Northwestern University Press, 4 Volumes.

Le Page, R. B. (1964) *The National Language Question*. Oxford University Press.

Le Page, R. B. (1968) Problems of description in multilingual communities. *Transactions of the Philological Society*, 189–212.

Le Page, R. B. (1978) Projection, focussing, diffusion or steps towards a sociolinguistic theory of language, illustrated from the survey of multilingual communities. Stage I: Cayo District, Belize (formerly British Honduras) and Stage II: St Lucia. School of Education, St Augustine's, Trinidad: Society for Caribbean Linguistics Occasional Paper No. 9. Reprinted in *Report Papers in Linguistics*, 9, 1980.

Le Page, R. B. (1981) *Caribbean Connections in the Classroom*. London: Mary Glasgow Language Trust.

Le Page, R. B. & Tabouret-Keller, A. (1985) *Acts of Identity: Creole-based Approaches to Language and Ethnicity*. Cambridge University Press.

Lewis, G. (1972) *Multilingualism in the Soviet Union: Language Policy and its Implementation*. The Hague: Mouton.

Lewis, G. (1978) Types of bilingual communities. In J. E. Alatis (ed.) *International Dimensions of Bilingual Education*. Georgetown University Round Table on Languages and Linguistics. Washington, DC: Georgetown University Press.

Lewis, G. (1981) *Bilingualism and Bilingual Education*. Oxford: Pergamon Press.

Lieberson, P. (1970) *Language and Ethnic Relations in Canada*. New York: Wiley.

Lieberson, S. (1964) An extension of Greenberg's linguistic diversity measure. *Language*, 40, 526–31.

Lieberson, S. & Hansen, L. K. (1974) National development, mother tongue diversity, and the comparative study of nations. *American Sociological Review*, 39, 523–41.

Liedtke, W. W. & Nelson, L. D. (1968) Concept formation and bilingualism. *Alberta Journal of Education Research*, 14, 225–32.

Liepmann, D. & Saegert, J. (1974) Language tagging in bilingual free recall. *Journal of Experimental Psychology*, 103, 1137–41.

Light, L. L., Berger, D. & Bardales, D. E. (1975) Trade-off between memory for verbal items and their visual attributes. *Journal of Experimental Psychology: Human Learning and Memory*, 104, 188–93.

Lincoln, P. C. (1979) Dual-lingualism: Passive bilingualism in action. *Te Reo*, 22, 65–72.

Lindholm, J. J. & Padilla, A. M. (1978) Language mixing in bilingual children. *Journal of Child Language*, 5, 327–35.

Linton, R. (1945) *The Cultural Background of Personality*. New York: Appleton-Century.

Liu, H., Bates, E. & Li, P. (1992) Sentence processing in bilingual speakers of English and Chinese. *Applied Psycholinguistics*, 13, 451–84.

Long, K. K. & Padilla, A. M. (1970) Evidence for Bilingual Antecedents of Academic Success in a Group of Spanish-American College Students. Unpublished research report. Bellingham, WA: Western Washington State College.

Long, M. H. (1990) Maturational constraints on language development. *Studies in Second Language Acquisition*, 12, 251–85.

Long, M. H. (1996) Modality and the linguistic environment in second language acquisition. In C. Ritchie & T. K. Bhatia (eds.) *Handbook of Second Language Acquisition*. New York: Academic Press.

Lopez, M., Hicks, R. E. & Young, R. R. (1974) Retroactive inhibition in a bilingual A-B, A'-B' paradigm. *Journal of Experimental Psychology*, 103, 85–90.

Lopez, M. & Young, R. R. (1974) The linguistic interdependence of bilinguals. *Journal of Experimental Psychology*, 6, 981–3.

Lüdi, G. (1986) Forms and functions of bilingual speech in pluricultural migrant communities in Switzerland. In J. A. Fishman, A. Tabouret-Keller, M. Clyne, B. H. Krishnamurti & M. Abdulaziz (eds.) *The Fergusonian Impact in honor of Charles A. Ferguson on the Occasion of His 65th birthday. Volume 2: Sociolinguistics and the Sociology of Language*. Berlin: Mouton de Gruyter.

Lukmani, Y. (1972) Motivation to learn and language proficiency. *Language Learning*, 22, 261–73.

Luria, A. R. (1976) *Cognitive Development: its Cultural and Social Foundations*. Cambridge, MA: Harvard University Press.

Luria, A. (1981) *Language and Cognition*. Washington, DC: Winston.

MacIntyre, P. D. (1994) Variables underlying willingness to communicate: a causal analysis. *Communication Research Reports*, 11, 135–42.

MacIntyre, P. D. & Charos, C. (1996) Personality, attitudes, and affect as predictors of second language communication. *Journal of Language and Social Psychology*, 15, 3–26.

MacIntyre, P. D. & Gardner, R. C. (1991) Language anxiety: its relation to other anxieties and to processing in native and second languages. *Language Learning*, 41, 513–34.

MacIntyre, P. D. & Gardner, R. C. (1994) The subtle effects of language anxiety on cognitive processing in the second language. *Language Learning*, 44, 283–305.

Mack, M. (1986) A study of semantic and syntactic processing in monolinguals and fluent early bilingual. *Journal of Psycholinguistic Research*, 15, 463–88.

Mackey, W. F. (1962) The description of bilingualism. *Canadian Journal of Linguistics*, 7, 51–85.

Mackey, W. F. (1970) A typology of bilingual education. *Foreign Language Annals*, 3, 596–608.

Mackey, W. F. (1976) *Bilinguisme et Contact des Langues*. Paris: Klincksieck.

Macnamara, J. (1966) *Bilingualism and Primary Education*. Edinburgh University Press.

Macnamara, J. (1967a) The bilingual's linguistic performance. *Journal of Social Issues*, 23, 58–77.

Macnamara, J. (1967b) The linguistic independence of bilinguals. *Journal of Verbal Learning and Verbal Behavior*, 6, 729–36.

Macnamara, J. (1969) Comment mesurer le bilinguisme d'une personne? In L. G. Kelly (ed.) *Description and Measurement of Bilingualism*. Toronto University Press.

Macnamara, J., Krauthamer, M. & Bolgar, M. (1968) Language switching in bilinguals as a function of stimulus and response uncertainty. *Journal of Experimental Psychology*, 78, 208–15.

Macnamara, J. & Kushnir, S. (1971) Linguistic independence of bilinguals: the input switch. *Journal of Verbal Learning and Verbal Behavior*, 10, 480–7.

MacNeil, M. M. (1994) Immersion programmes employed in Gaelic-medium units in Scotland. *Journal of Multilingual and Multicultural Development*, 15, 245–252.

Mägiste, E. (1982) Automaticity and interference in bilinguals. *Psychological Research*, 44, 29–43.

Mägiste, E. (1985) Development of intra and interlingual interference in bilinguals. *Journal of Psycholinguistic Research*, 14, 137–54.

Mägiste, E. (1986) Selected issues in second and third language learning. In J. Vaid (ed.) *Language Processing in Bilinguals: Psycholinguistic and Neuropsychological Perspective*. Hillsdale, NJ: Erlbaum.

Mägiste, E. (1992) Learning to the right: hemispheric involvement in bilinguals. In R. D. Harris (ed.) *Cognitive Processing in Bilinguals*. Amsterdam: North Holland.

Major, R. C. (1993) Sociolinguistic factors in loss and acquisition of phonology. In K. Hyltenstam & A. Viberg (eds.), *Progression and Regression in Language*. Cambridge University Press.

Malakoff, M. & Hakuta, K. (1991) Translation skills and metalinguistic awareness in bilinguals. In E. Bialystok (ed.) *Language Processing in Bilingual Children*. Cambridge University Press.

Marchman, V. A., Miller, R. & Bates, E. (1991) Babble and first words in children with focal brain injury. *Applied Psycholinguistics*, 12, 1–22.

Marcos, H. & Bernicot, J. (1994) Addressee co-operation and request formulation in young children. *Journal of Child Language*, 21, 677–92.

Maréchal, R., Bourdon, P. & Lapierre, J. (1973) *La Motivation des Enseignants et des Étudiants Francophones face à la situation linguistique au Québec*. Québec: Éditeur Officiel du Québec.

Markstrom, C. A. & Mullis, R. L. (1986) Ethnic differences in the imagery audience. *Journal of Adolescent Research*, 1, 289–301.

Mayberry, R. I. & Fischer, S. D. (1989) Looking through phonological shape to lexical meaning: The bottleneck of non-native sign language-processing. *Memory and Cognition*, 17, 740–54.

McClosky, H. & Schaar, J. H. (1965) Psychological dimensions of anomy. *American Sociological Review*, 30, 14–40.

McClure, E. (1981) Formal and functional aspects of the code-switched discourse of bilingual children. In R. Duran (ed.) *Latino Discourse and Communicative*

Behavior. Norwood, NJ: Ablex Publishing Group.

McCormack, P. D. (1977) Bilingual linguistic memory: the independence–interdependence issue revisited. In P. A. Hornby (ed.) *Bilingualism: Psychological, Social and Educational Implications*. New York: Academic Press.

McCroskey, J. C. (1992) Reliability and validity of the willingness to communicate scale. *Communication Quarterly*, 40, 16–25.

McKay, S. L. (1993) Examining L2 composition ideology: A look at literacy education. *Journal of Second Language Writing 2*, 65–81.

McLaughlin, B. (1984) *Second-Language Acquisition in Childhood. Volume 1: Pre-school Children*, 2nd edition. Hillsdale, NJ: Erlbaum.

McLaughlin, B. (1987) *Theories of Second-Language Learning*. London: Edward Arnold.

McLeod, C. M. (1976) Bilingual episodic memory: acquisition and forgetting. *Journal of Verbal Learning and Verbal Behavior*, 15, 347–64.

McLuhan, M. (1962) *The Gutenberg Galaxy: The Making of Typographic Man*. University Press of Toronto.

McNab, G. (1979) Cognition and bilingualism: a reanalysis of studies. *Linguistics*, 17, 231–55.

McRae, K. D. (1983) *Conflict and Compromise in Multilingual Societies: Switzerland*. Waterloo, Ont.: Wilfrid Laurier University Press.

McWhinney, B. (1987) Applying the competition model to bilingualism. *Applied Psycholinguistics*, 8, 315–27.

McWhinney, B. (1992) Transfer and competition in second language learning. In R. J. Harris (ed.) *Cognitive Processing in Bilinguals*. Amsterdam, North Holland: Elsevier.

McWhinney, B. (1995) *The CHILDES Project: Tools for Analyzing Talk*. Hillsdale, NJ: Lawrence Erlbaum Associates.

McWhinney, B. & Bates, E. (eds.) (1989) *The Cross Linguistic Study of Sentence Processing*. Cambridge University Press.

Meara, P. (1984) Word recognition in foreign languages. In A. K. Pugh & J. Ulijn (eds.) *Reading for Special Purposes*. London: Heinemann Educational Books.

Mechaka, R. D. K. (1993) Is Tanzania triglossic? The status and rôle of ethnic community languages. *Journal of Multilingual and Multicultural Development*, 14, 307–20.

Meeuwis, M. & Blommaert, J. (1994) Review article: 'Markedness Model' and the absence of society: remarks on codeswitching. *Multilingua*, 13–14, 387–423.

Mehler, J. & Christophe, A. (1995) Maturation and learning of language in the first year of life. In M. S. Gazzaniga & E. Bizzi (eds.) *The Cognitive Neuroscience*. Cambridge, MA: MIT. Press.

Mehler, J., Jusczyk, P., Lambertz, G., Halsted, N., Bertoncini, J. & Amiel-Tison, C. (1988) A precursor of language acquisition in young infants. *Cognition*, 29, 143–78.

Meisel, J. M. (ed.) (1990) *Two First Languages: Early Grammatical Development in Bilingual Children*. Dordrecht: Floris.

Meisel, J. M. (1994) The acquisition of grammatical constraints. *Studies in Second Language Acquisition*, 16, 413–40.

Mercer, N., Mercer, E. & Mears, R. (1977) Linguistic and cultural affiliation amongst young Asian people in Leicester. In H. Giles & B. Saint-Jacques (eds.) *Language and Ethnic Relations*. Oxford: Pergamon Press.

Merriman, W. E. & Kutlesic, V. (1993) Bilingual and monolingual children's use of two lexical acquisition heuristics. *Applied Psycholinguistics*, 14, 229–49.

Meyer, R. & Newport, E. (1990) Out of the hands of babes: on a possible sign advantage in language acquisition. *Language*, 66, 1–23.

Miller, G. A. & Johnson-Laird, P. N. (1976) *Language and Perception*. Cambridge, MA: Harvard University Press.

Miller, N. (ed.) (1984) *Bilingualism and Language Disability. Assessment and Remediation*. London: Croom Helm.

Milner, B. (1975) Psychological aspects of focal epilepsy and its neuro-surgical management. In D. P. Purpura, J. K. Penry & R. D. Walker (eds.) *Advances in Neurology*. New York: Raven Press.

Milroy, L. (1980) *Language and Social Networks*. Oxford: Blackwell.

Milroy, L. & Muysken, P. (eds.) (1995) *One Speaker, Two Languages. Cross-Disciplinary Perspectives on Code-Switching*. Cambridge University Press.

Minkowski, M. (1963) On aphasia in polyglots. In L. Halpern (ed.) *Problems of Dynamic Neurology*. Jerusalem: Hebrew University.

Mishkin, M. & Forgays, D. (1952) Word recognition as a function of retinal locus. *Journal of Experimental Psychology*, 43, 43–8.

Modiano, N. (1973) *Indian Education in the Chiapas Highlands*. New York: Rinehart, Holt & Winston.

Moghaddam, F. M. (1988) Individualistic and collective integration strategies among immigrants: towards a mobility model of cultural integration. In J. W. Berry & R. C. Annis (eds.) *Ethnic Psychology: Research and Practice with Immigrants, Refugees, Native Peoples, Ethnic Groups and Sojourners*. Lisse, Switzerland: Swets & Zeitlinger.

Moghaddam, F. M. & Taylor, D. M. (1987) The meaning of multiculturalism of visible minority immigrant women. *Canadian Journal of Behavioral Science*, 19, 121–36.

Moghaddam, F. M., Taylor, D. M. & Lalonde, R. N. (1987) Individualistic and collective integration strategies among Iranians in Canada. *International Journal of Psychology*, 22, 301–13.

Mohanty, A. K. (1994a) *Bilingualism in a Multilingual Society: Psychosocial and Pedagogical Implications*. Mysore: Central Institute of Indian Languages.

Mohanty, A. K. (1994b) Language socialization in a multilingual society. Paper presented at the International Conference on Early Childhood Communication, Bhubaneswar, December 1994.

Mohanty, A. (1996) *Language Behaviour and Language Processes*. CAS in Psychology. Bhubaneswar: Utkal University.

Mohanty, A. K. & Babu, N. (1983) Bilingualism and metalinguistic ability among Kond tribals in Orissa, India. *The Journal of Social Psychology*, 121, 15–22.

Mohanty, A. K. & Das, S. P. (1987) Cognitive and metalinguistic ability of unschooled bilingual and unilingual tribal children. *Psychological Studies*, 32, 5–8.

Mohanty, A. K. & Perregaux, C. (1997) Language acquisition and bilingualism. In J. W. Berry, P. R. Dasen & T. S. Saraswathi (eds.) *Handbook of Cross-Cultural Psychology. Volume 2: Basic Processes and Human Development*. 2nd edition. Boston, MA: Allyn & Bacon.

Moïse, L. C. & Bourhis, R. Y. (1994) Langage et ethnicité: communication interculturelle à Montréal, 1977–1991. *Canadian Ethnic Studies*, 26, 86–107.

Moon, C., Panneton-Cooper, R. & Fifer, W. P. (1993) Two-day-olds prefer their native language. *Infant Behavior and Development*, 16, 495–500.

Moore, W. H. & Haynes, W. O. (1980) A study of alpha hemispheric asymmetries for verbal and non-verbal stimuli in males and females. *Brain and Language*, 9, 338–49.

Morrison, F. (1981) Evaluation of the Second Language Learning (French) Programs in School of the Ottawa and Carleton Boards of Education: Eighth Annual Report. Ottawa: Ottawa Board of Education Research Center.

Morton, J. (1979a) Word recognition. In J. Morton & J. Marshall (eds.) *Psycholinguistics 2. Structures and Processes*. Cambridge, MA: MIT Press.

Morton, J. (1979b) Facilitation in word recognition: experiments causing change in the logogen model. In P. A. Kolers, M. E. Wrolstad & M. Bouma (eds.) *Processing of Visible Language*. New York: Plenum Press.

Morton, J. (1980) The logogen model and orthographic structure. In U. Frith (ed.) *Cognitive Process in Spelling*. London: Academic Press.

Moscovici, S. (1984) The phenomenon of social representations. In R. M. Farr & S. Moscovici (eds.) *Social Representations*. Cambridge University Press/Paris: Éditions de la Maison des Sciences de l'Homme.

MOTET (Mother Tongue and English Teaching Project)(1981) Summary of Report 1 and 2. Bradford: University of Bradford.

Mougeon, R. & Béniak, E. (1990) *Linguistic Consequences of Language Contact and Restriction: the Case of French in Ontario, Canada*. Oxford University Press.

Mougeon, R. & Béniak, E. (1994) Bilingualism, language shift, and institutional support for French: The case of the Franco-Ontarians. *International Journal of the Sociology of Language: Special Issue, 105–106. French–English Language Issues in Canada*, 99–126.

Mougeon, R., Brent-Palmer, C., Belanger, M. & Cichocki, W. (1982) *Le Français Parlé en Situation Minoritaire*. Quebec: International Center for Research on Bilingualism B-105.

Mougeon, R. & Canale, M. (1978) Maintenance of French in Ontario: is education in French enough? *Interchange*, 9, 30–9.

Mühlhäusler, P. (1986) *Pidgin and Creole Linguistics*. Oxford: Blackwell.

Mulac, A., Wiemann, J., Yoerks, S. & Gibson, T. W. (1983) Male/female language differences and their effects in like-sex and mixed-sex dyads: a test of interpersonal accommodation and the gender-linked language effect. Paper presented at the Second International Conference on Social Psychology of Language, Bristol, 18–22 July 1983.

Muysken, P. (1995) Codeswitching and grammatical theory. In L. Milroy & P. Muysken (eds.) *One Speaker, Two Languages. Cross-disciplinary Perspectives on Codeswitching*. Cambridge University Press, 177–98.

Myers-Scotton, C. (1992) Comparing codeswitching and borrowing. *Journal of Multilingual and Multicultural Development 13: Special Issue on Codeswitching*, 19–39.

Myers-Scotton, C. (1993a) *Social Motivation for Codeswitching: Evidence from Africa*. Oxford: Clarendon Press.

Myers-Scotton, C. (1993b) *Duelling Languages: Grammatical Structure in Code-Switching*. Oxford: Clarendon Press.

Naiman, N., Fröhlich, M., Stern, H. H. & Todesco, A. (1978) *The Good Language Learner*. Toronto: Ontario Institute for Studies in Education.

Neils-Strunjas, J. (1998) Clinical Assessment Strategies. In B. Stemmer & H. A. Whitaker (ed.) *Handbook Of Neurolinguistics*. San Diego: Academic Press.

Nelson, K. (1981) Social cognition in a script framework. In J. H. Flavell & L. Ross (eds.) *Social Cognitive Development*. Cambridge University Press.

Nelson, K. & Gruendel, J. M. (1981) Generalized event representations: basic building blocks of cognitive development. In M. Lamb & A. L. Brown (eds.) *Advances in Developmental Psychology*, Volume 1. Hillsdale, NJ: Erlbaum.

Nesdale, D. & Rooney, R. (1996) Evaluations and stereotyping of accented speakers by pre-adolescent children. *Journal of Language and Social Psychology*, 15, 133–54.

Neville, H. J. (1988) Cerebral organization for spatial attention. In Stiles-Davis, J., Kritchevsky, M. *et al.* (eds.) *Spatial Cognition: Brain Bases and Development*. Hillsdale, NJ: Lawrence Erlbaum.

Newport, E. L. (1990) Maturational constraints on language learning. *Cognitive Science*, 14, 11–28.

Newport, E. & Meyer, R. (1985) The acquisition of sign language. In D. Slobin (ed.) *The Cross-Linguistic Study of Language Acquisition*, Volume 1. Hillsdale, NJ: Lawrence Erlbaum.

Nicoladis, E., Taylor, D. M., Lambert, W. E. & Cazabon, M. (1998) What Two-Way Bilingual Programs Reveal about the Controversy Surrounding Race and Intelligence. Montreal: McGill University, Unpublished Paper.

Noels, K., Pon, G. & Clément, R. (1996) Language identity and adjustment: The role of linguistic self-confidence in the acculturation process. *Journal of Language and Social Psychology*, 15, 246–64.

Nortier, J. M. (1990) *Dutch–Moroccan Arabic Code-Switching among Young Moroccans in the Netherlands*. Dordrecht: Foris.

Nott, R. & Lambert, W. E. (1968) Free recall of bilinguals. *Journal of Verbal Learning and Verbal Behavior*, 7, 1065–71.

Obler, L. K. (1981) Right hemisphere participation in second language acquisition. In K. C. Diller (ed.) *Individual Differences and Universals in Language Learning Aptitude*. Rowley, MA: Newbury House.

Obler, L. (1997) Development and Loss: Changes in the adult years. In J. B. Gleason (ed.) *The Development of Language*. 4th edition. Boston, MA: Allyn & Bacon.

Obler, L. & Albert, M. (1978) A monitor system for bilingual language processing. In M. Paradis (ed.) *Aspects of Bilingualism*. Columbia: Hornbeam Press.

Obler, L., Albert, M. & Lozowick, S. (1986) The ageing bilingual. In J. Vaid (ed.) *Language Processing in Bilinguals: Psycholinguistic and Neuropsychological Perspectives*. Hillsdale, NJ: Erlbaum Associates.

Obler, L., Zatorre, R., Galloway, L. & Vaid, J. (1982) Cerebral lateralization in bilinguals: methodological issues. *Brain and Language*, 15, 40–54.

Ochs, E. (1986) Introduction. In B. B. Schieffelin & E. Ochs (eds.) *Language and socialization across cultures*. Cambridge University Press.

Ogbu, J. U. (1988) Literacy and schooling in subordinate cultures: The case of Black Americans. In E. R. Kingten, B. M. Kroll & M. Rose (eds.) *Perspectives on*

Literacy. Carbondale: Southern Illinois University Press.

Ojemann, G. A. (1983) Brain organization for language from the perspective of electrical stimulation mapping. *Behavioural and Brain Sciences*, 6, 189–230.

Ojemann, G. A. & Whitaker, H. A. (1978) The bilingual brain. *Archives of Neurology*, 35, 409–12.

Okoh, N. (1980) Bilingualism and divergent thinking among Nigerian and Welsh school children. *The Journal of Social Psychology*, 110, 163–70.

Oller, D. K., Eilers, R. E., Urbano, R., & Cobo-Lewis, A. B. (1997) Development of precursors to speech in infants exposed to two languages. *Journal of Child Language*, 24, 407–25.

Oller, J. W. (1979) *Language Tests at School*. London: Longman.

Oller, J. W., Baca, L. & Vigil, A. (1977) Attitudes and attained proficiency in ESL: a sociolinguistic study of Mexican-Americans in the South-West. *TESOL Quarterly.*, 2, 173–83.

Oller, J. W., Hudson, A. J. & Liu, P. F. (1977) Attitudes and attained proficiency in ESL: a sociolinguistic study of native speakers of Chinese in the United States. *Language Learning*, 27, 1–27.

Oller, J. W. & Perkins, P. (1978) Intelligence and language proficiency as sources of variance in self-reported affective variables. *Language Learning*, 28, 85–97.

Olson, D. R. (1988) From utterance to text: the bias of language in speech and writing. In E. R. Kington, B. M. Kroll & M. Rose (eds.) *Perspectives in Literacy*. Carbondale: Southern Illinois University Press.

O'Neil, W. & Dion, A. (1983) Bilingual recognition of concrete and abstract sentences. *Perceptual and Motor Skills*, 57, 839–45.

O'Neil, W. & Huot, R. (1984) Release from proactive inhibition as a function of pronunciation shift in bilinguals. *Canadian Journal of Psychology*, 38, 54–62.

Opoku, J. Y. (1983) The learning of English as a second language and the development of the emergent bilingual representational systems. *International Journal of Psychology*, 18, 271–83.

Orbach, J. (1953) Retinal locus as a factor in the recognition of visually perceived words. *American Journal of Psychology*, 65, 555–62.

Osgood, C. E., Suci, G. I. & Tannenbaum, P. H. (1957) *The Measurement of Meaning*. Urbana, IL: University of Illinois Press.

Oxford, R. (1991) *Language Learning Strategies: What every Teacher should know*. New York: Newbury House.

Oyama, S. (1979) The concept of the sensitive period in developmental studies. *Merill Palmer Quarterly*, 25, 83–103.

Padilla, A. M. & Liebmann, E. (1975) Language acquisition in the bilingual child. *The Bilingual Review/ La Revista Bilingüe*, 2, 34–55.

Padilla, A. M. & Lindholm, K. J. (1976) Development of interrogative, negative and possessive forms in speech of young Spanish/English bilingual. *The Bilingual Review/ La Revista Bilingüe*, 3, 122–52.

Padilla, A. M., Lindholm, K. J., Chen, A., Duran, R., Hakuta, K., Lambert, W. E. & Tucker, G. R. (1991) The English-Only Movement: Myths, Reality and Implications for Psychology. *American Psychologist*, February 1991, 120–30.

Paivio, A. (1986) *Mental Representations: A Dual-Coding Approach*. New York: Oxford University Press.

Paivio, A. & Begg, I. (1981) *Psychology of Language*. Englewood Cliffs. NJ: Prentice-Hall, Inc.

Paivio, A., Clark, J. M. & Lambert, W. E. (1988) Bilingual dual-coding theory and semantic repetition effects on recall. *Journal of Experimental Psychology: Learning, Memory, and Cognition*, 14, 163–72.

Paivio, A. & Desrochers, A. (1980) A dual-coding approach to bilingual memory. *Canadian Journal of Psychology*, 34, 388–99.

Paivio, A. & Lambert, W. E. (1981) Dual coding and bilingual memory. *Journal of Verbal Learning and Verbal Behavior*, 20, 532–9.

Pak, A., Dion, K. L. & Dion, K. K. (1985) Correlates of self-confidence with English among Chinese students in Toronto. *Canadian Journal of Behavioural Science*, 17, 369–78.

Pan, A. B. & Gleason, J. B. (1986) The study of language loss: models and hypotheses for an emerging discipline. *Applied Psycholinguistics*, 7, 193–206.

Pandit, P. B. (1979) Perspectives on sociolinguistics in India. In W. C. McCormack & S. A. Wurm (eds.) *Language and Society*. The Hague: Mouton.

Papademetre, L. (1994) Self-defined, other-defined cultural identity: Logogenesis and multiple group membership in a Greek-Australian sociolinguistic community. *Journal of Multilingual and Multicultural Development*, 15, 507–25.

Papanicolaou, A. C., Simos, P. G. & Basile, L. F. H. (1998) Applications of magneto-encephalography to neurolinguistic research. In B. Stemmer & H. A. Whitaker, (eds.) *Handbook Of Neurolinguistics*. San Diego: Academic Press.

Papen, R. A. (1987) Le métif: Le nec plus ultra des grammaires en contact. *Revue Québécoise de Linguistique Théorique et Appliquée*, 6, 57–70.

Paradis, M. (1977) Bilingualism and aphasia. In H. Whitaker & H. A. Whitaker (eds.) *Studies in Neurolinguistics*. New York: Academic Press.

Paradis, M. (1980) Contributions of neurolinguistics to the theory of bilingualism. In R. K. Herbert (ed.) *Applications of Linguistic Theory in the Human Sciences*. Chicago: Michigan State University, Department of Linguistics.

Paradis, M. (1986) Foreword. In J. Vaid (ed.) *Language Processing in Bilinguals: Psycholinguistic and Neuropsychological Perspectives*. Hillsdale, NJ: Erlbaum.

Paradis, M. (1989) Bilingual and polyglot aphasia. In F. Boller & J. Grafman (eds.) *Handbook of Neuropsychology*, Volume 2. Amsterdam: Elsevier.

Paradis, M. (1990) Language lateralization in bilinguals: Enough already! *Brain and Language*, 39, 576–86.

Paradis, M. (1993) Multilingualism and aphasia. In G. Blanken, J. Dittmann, H. Grimm, J. C. Marshall & C. W. Wallesch (eds.) *Linguistic Disorders and Pathologies*. Berlin: W. de Gruyter.

Paradis, M. (ed.) (1995a) Introduction: The need for distinction. In M. Paradis (ed.) *Aspects of Bilingual Aphasia*. New York: Elsevier.

Paradis, M. (ed.) (1995b) Epilogue: Bilingual aphasia 100 years later: consensus and controversies. In M. Paradis (ed.) *Aspects of Bilingual Aphasia*. New York: Elsevier.

Paradis, M. (1998) Language and communication in multilinguals. In B. Stemmer & H. A. Whitaker (eds.) *Handbook Of Neurolinguistics*. San Diego: Academic Press.

Paradis, M., Goldblum, M. C. & Abidi, R. (1982) Alternate antagonism with paradoxical translation behaviour in two bilingual aphasic patients. *Brain and Language*, 15, 55–69.

Parasnis, I. (1996) On interpreting the deaf experience within the context of cultural and language diversity. In I. Parasnis (ed.) *Cultural and Language Diversity and the Deaf Experience*. New York: Cambridge University Press.

Parkin, D. (1977) Emergent and stabilized multilingualism: polyethnic peer groups in urban Kenya. In H. Giles (ed.) *Language, Ethnicity and Intergroup Relations*. London: Academic Press.

Patkowski, M. (1980) The sensitive period for the acquisition of syntax in a second language. *Language Learning*, 30, 449–72.

Pattanayak, D. P. (1981) *Multilingualism and Mother Tongue Education*. New Delhi: Oxford University Press.

Patterson, O. (1975) Context and choice in ethnic allegiance: a theoretical framework and Caribbean case study. In N. Glazer & D. P. Moynihan (eds.) *Ethnicity: Theory and Experience*. Cambridge, MA: Harvard University Press.

Pattnaik, K. & Mohanty, A. K. (1984) Relationships between metalinguistic and cognitive development of bilingual and unilingual tribal children. *Psycho-Lingua*, 14, 63–70.

Paulston, C. B. (1975) Ethnic relations and bilingual education: accounting for contradictory data. *Working Papers on Bilingualism*, 6, 368–401.

Paulston, C. B. (1992) *Sociolinguistic Perspective on Bilingual Education*. Clevedon: Multilingual Matters.

Peal, E. & Lambert, W. E. (1962) The relation of bilingualism to intelligence. *Psychological Monographs*, 76, 1–23.

Pearson, B. Z., Fernandez, S. C., Lewedeg, V., & Oller, D. K. (1997) The relation of input factors to lexical learning by bilingual infants. *Applied Psycholinguistics*, 18, 41–58.

Pearson, B. Z., Fernandez, S. C. & Oller, D. K. (1993) Lexical development in bilingual infants and toddlers: Comparisons to monolingual norms. *Language Learning*, 43, 93–120.

Peck, S. (1978) Child–child discourse in second language acquisition. In E. M. Hatch (ed.) *Second Language Acquisition: a Book of Readings*. Rowley, MA: Newbury House.

Penfield, W. P. & Roberts, L. R. (1959) *Speech and Brain Mechanism*. London: Oxford University Press.

Perecman, E. (1984) Spontaneous translation and language mixing in a polyglot aphasic. *Brain and Language*, 23, 43–63.

Perregaux, C. (1994) *Les Enfants à Deux Voix: Des Effets du Bilinguisme sur l'Apprentissage de la lecture*. Berne: Lang.

Peters, A. M. & Boggs, S. T. (1986) Interactional routines as cultural influences upon language acquisition. In B. B. Schieffelin & E. Ochs (eds.) *Language and socialization across cultures*. Cambridge University Press.

Peterson, J. (1988) Word-internal code-switching constraints in a bilingual child's grammar. *Linguistics*, 26, 479–93.

Pfaff, C. (1981) Sociolinguistic problems of immigrants. *Language in Society*, 10, 155–88.

Phinney, J. S. (1990) Ethnic identity in adolescents and adults: review of research.

Psychological Bulletin, 108, 499–514.

Piaget, J. (1954) *The Construction of Reality in the Child*. New York: Ballantine Books.

Piaget, J. (1970) *Genetic Epistemology*. New York: Columbia University Press.

Piaget, J. & Inhelder, B. (1966) *L'Image Mentale chez l'Enfant*. Paris: Presses Universitaires de France.

Piatt, B. (1990) *Only English: Law and Language Policy in the United States*. Albuquerque: University of Mexico Press.

Pierson, H. D. & Bond, M. H. (1982) How do Chinese bilinguals respond to variations of interviewer language and ethnicity? *Journal of Language and Social Psychology*, 1, 123–39.

Pierson, H. D., Giles, H. & Young, L. (1987) Intergroup vitality perceptions during a period of political uncertainty: The case of Hong Kong. *Journal of Multilingual and Multicultural Development*, 8, 451–60.

Pimsleur, P. (1966) *Language Aptitude Battery*. New York: Harcourt, Brace, Jovanovich.

Pinker, S. (1996) *Language Learnability and Language Development*, 2nd edition. Cambridge, MA: Harvard University Press.

Pintner, R. & Keller, R. (1922) Intelligence tests for foreign children. *Journal of Educational Psychology*, 13, 214–22.

Pitrès, A. (1895) Étude sur l'aphasie. *Revue de Médecine*, 15, 873–99.

Platt, J. T. (1977) A model for polyglossia and multilingualism (with special reference to Singapore and Malaysia). *Language in Society*, 6, 361–78.

Platt, J. T. (1980) The lingue franche of Singapore: an investigation into strategies of inter-ethnic communication. In H. Giles, W. P. Robinson & P. M. Smith (eds.) *Language: Social Psychological Perspectives*. Oxford: Pergamon Press.

Platt, J. T. & Weber, H. (1984) Speech convergence miscarried: an investigation into inappropriate accommodation strategies. *International Journal of the Sociology of Language*, 46, 131–46.

Poissant, H. & Hamers, J. F. (1996). Multicultural Development, Literacy and Scholastic Achievement in Ethnolinguistic Minorities. Unpublished paper, Montreal: UQAM.

Politzer, R. L. (1983) An explanatory study of self-reported language learning behaviors and their relation to achievement. *Studies in Second Language Acquisition*, 6, 54–68.

Politzer, R. L. & McGoarty, M. (1985) An explanatory study of learning behaviors and their relationship to gains in linguistic and communicative competence. *TESOL Quarterly*, 19, 103–23.

Polome, E. C. (1982) Sociolinguistically-oriented language surveys: reflections on the survey of language use and language-teaching in Eastern Africa. *Language in Society*, 11, 265–83.

Pool, J. (1969) National development and language diversity. *La Monda Lingo-Problemo*, 1, 140–56.

Poplack, S. (1980). Sometimes I'll start a sentence in English y termino en español: toward a typology of code-switching. *Linguistics*, 18, 581–618.

Poplack, S. (1983) Intergenerational variation in language use and structure in a bilingual context. In C. Rivera (ed.) *An Ethnographic/Sociolinguistic Approach to Language Proficiency Assessment.* Clevedon: Multilingual Matters.

Poplack, S. (1990) Variation theory and language contact: concept, method and data. Papers for the Workshop on Concepts, Methodology and Data. Held in Basel, 12–13 January 1990. Strasbourg: European Science Foundation, 33–66.

Potter, M. C., So, K.-F., von Eckhardt, B. & Feldman, L. B. (1984) Lexical and conceptual representation in beginning and proficient bilinguals. *Journal of Verbal Learning and Verbal Behavior,* 23, 23–8.

Poulisse, N. (1998) Compensatory strategies and the principles of clarity and economy. In G. Kasper & E. Kellerman (eds.) *Advances in Communication Strategy Research.* London: Longman.

Powers, S. & Lopez, R. L. (1985) Perceptual, motor, and verbal skills of monolingual and bilingual Hispanic children: a discriminant analysis. *Perceptual and Motor Skills,* 60, 999–1002.

Preston, M. S. & Lambert, W. E. (1969) Interlingual interference in a bilingual version of the Stroop color-word task. *Journal of Verbal Learning and Verbal Behavior,* 8, 295–301.

Price, C. S. & Cuellar, I. (1981) Effects of language and related variables on the expression of psychopathology in Mexican-American psychiatric patients. *Hispanic Journal of Behavioral Sciences,* 3, 145–60.

Price, S., Fluck, M. & Giles, H. (1983) The effects of language of testing on bilingual pre-adolescents' attitudes towards Welsh and varieties of English. *Journal of Multilingual and Multicultural Development,* 4, 149–61.

Prujiner, A., Deshaies, D., Hamers, J. F., Blanc, M., Clément, R. & Landry, R. (1984) *Variation du Comportement Langagier lorsque Deux Langues sont en Contact.* Quebec: International Center for Research on Bilingualism, G-5.

Quinn, T. J. (1981) Establishing a threshold-level concept for community language teaching in Australia. In M. Garner (ed.) *Community Languages: their Role in Education.* Melbourne/Sydney: River Seine Publications.

Rabain-Jamin, J. (1994) Language socialization of the child in African families living in France. In P. M. Greenfield & R. R. Cocking (eds.) *Cross-cultural roots of minority child development.* Hillsdale, NJ: Erlbaum.

Ransdell, S. E. & Fischler, I. (1989) Effects of concreteness and task context on recall prose among bilingual and monolingual speakers. *Journal of memory and Language,* 28, 278–91.

Rapport, R. L., Tan, C. T. & Whitaker, H. A. (1983) Language function and dysfunction among Chinese and English speaking polyglots: cortical stimulation, wada testing and clinical studies. *Brain and Language,* 18, 342–66.

Redlinger, W. E. & Park, T. Z. (1980) Language mixing in young bilinguals. *Journal of Child Language,* 7, 337–52.

Reitz, J. G. (1974) Language and ethnic community survival. *Canadian Review of Sociology and Anthropology,* 104, Special Issue.

Reynell, J. (1969) *Reynell Development Language Scales Manual.* Littleton, MA: PSG Publishing.

Reynolds, A. G. (1991) The cognitive consequences of bilingualism. In A. G. Reynolds (ed.) *Bilingualism, Multiculturalism and Second Language Learning: The McGill Conference in Honour of Wallace E. Lambert.* Hillsdale, NJ: Erlbaum, 145–82.

Ribot, T. (1882) *Diseases of Memory: An Essay in the Positive Psychology*. London: Paul.

Richards, J. C. (1972) Social factors, interlanguage and language learning. *Language Learning*, 22, 159–88.

Rieben, L. & Perfetti, C. (1991) *Learning to Read*. Hillsdale, NJ: Erlbaum.

Rivera, C. (ed.) (1983) *An Ethnographic/Sociolinguistic Approach to Language Proficiency Assessment*. Clevedon: Multilingual Matters.

Rivera, C. (ed.) (1984) *Language Proficiency and Academic Achievement*. Clevedon: Multilingual Matters.

Robinson, G. L. N. (1981) Bilingual education in Australia and the United States. In M. Garner (ed.) *Community Languages: Their Role in Education*. Melbourne/Sydney: River Seine Publications.

Rogers, L., Ten Houten, W., Kaplan, C. D. & Gardiner, M. (1977) Hemispheric specialisation of language: An EEG study of bilingual Hopi children. *International Journal of Neuroscience*, 8, 1–6.

Rohner, R. (1984) Toward a conception of culture for cross-cultural psychology. *Journal of Cross-Cultural Psychology*, 15, 11–38.

Romaine, S. (1988) *Pidgin and Creole Languages*. London/New York: Longman.

Romaine, S. (1994) 'Borrowing'. In R.E. Asher (ed.) *Encyclopedia of Language and Linguistics*. Oxford: Pergamon.

Romaine, S. (1995) *Bilingualism*, 2nd edition. Oxford: Blackwell.

Ronjat, J. (1913) *Le Développement du Langage Observé chez un Enfant Bilingue*. Paris: Champion.

Rose, R. G. & Carroll, J. (1974) Free recall of mixed language list. *Bulletin of the Psychonomic Society*, 3, 267–8.

Rose, R. G., Rose, P. R., King, N. & Perez, A. (1975) Bilingual memory for related and unrelated sentences. *Journal of Experimental Psychology: Human Learning and Memory*, 1, 599–606.

Rosenblum, T. & Pinker, S. A. (1983) Word magic revisited: monolingual and bilingual children's understanding of the word–object relationship. *Child Development*, 54, 773–80.

Rosier, P. & Farella, M. (1976) Bilingual education at Rock Point: some early results. *TESOL Quarterly*, 10, 379–88.

Ross, J. A. (1979) Language and the mobilisation of ethnic identity. In H. Giles & B. Saint-Jacques (eds.) *Language and Ethnic Relations*. Oxford: Pergamon Press.

Rotheram, M. J. & Phinney, J. S. (1987) Introduction: definitions and perspective in the study of children's ethnic socialization. In J. S. Phinney & M. J. Rotheram (eds.) *Children's Ethnic Socialization*. Newbury Park, CA: Sage.

Royal Commission on Bilingualism and Biculturalism (1967–1970) Ottawa: Queen's Printer, 4 Volumes.

Rozensky, R. H. & Gomez, M. Y. (1983) Language switching in psychotherapy with bilinguals. Two problems, two models, and case examples. *Psychotherapy: Theory, Research and Practice*, 20, 152–60.

Rubin, H., & Turner, A. (1989) Linguistic awareness skills in grade one children in a French immersion setting. *Reading and Writing: An Interdisciplinary Journal*, 1, 73–86.

Rubin, J. (1968) *National Bilingualism in Paraguay*. The Hague: Mouton.

Rüke-Dravina, V. (1971) Word associations in monolingual and multilingual individuals. *Linguistics*, 74, 66–84.

Rumbaut, R. G. (1994) The crucible within: ethnic identity, self-esteem, and segmented assimilation among children of immigrants. *International Migration Review*, 28, 748–94.

Rupp, J. (1980) Cerebral language dominance in Vietnamese-English bilingual children. Unpublished doctoral dissertation. Albuquerque: University of New Mexico.

Ryan, E. B. & Bulik, C. (1982) Evaluation of middle class and lower class speakers of standard American and German-accented English. *Journal of Language and Social Psychology*, 1, 51–61.

Ryan, E. B. & Carranza, M. A. (1975) Evaluative reactions of adolescents towards speakers of standard English and Mexican American accented English. *Journal of Personality and Social Psychology*, 31, 855–63.

Ryan, E. B., Carranza, M. A. & Moffie, R. W. (1975) Mexican American reactions to accented English. In J. W. Berry & W. J. Lonner (eds.) *Applied Cross-Cultural Psychology: Selected Papers from the Second International Conference of the IACCP*. Amsterdam: Swets & Zeitlinger.

Ryan, E. B. & Giles, H. (eds.) (1982) *Attitudes Towards Language Variation: Social and Applied Contexts*. London: Edward Arnold.

Ryan, E. B., Hewstone, M. & Giles, H. (1984) Language and intergroup attitudes. In J. Eiser (ed.) *Attitudinal Judgement*. New York: Springer-Verlag.

Sachdev, I. & Bourhis, R. (1993) Ethnolinguistic vitality: some motivational and cognitive considerations. In M. H. Hogg & D. Abrams (eds.) *Group Motivation: Social Psychological Perspectives*. New York: Harvester Wheatsheaf.

Sadoski, M., Paivio, A. & Goetz, E. T. (1991) A critique of schema theory in reading and a dual coding alternative. *Reading Research Quarterly*, 24, 463–84.

Saegert, J., Hamayan, E. & Ahmar, H. (1975) Memory for language of input in polyglots. *Journal of Experimental Psychology: Human Learning and Memory*, 1, 607–27.

Saegert, J., Kazarian, S. & Young, R. K. (1973) Part/whole transfer with bilinguals. *American Journal of Psychology*, 86, 537–46.

Saer, O. J. (1923) The effects of bilingualism on intelligence. *British Journal of Psychology*, 14, 25–8.

Samuda, R. J. (1975) *Psychological Testing of American Minorities: its Use and Consequences*. New York: Dodd, Mead & Co.

Samuda, R. J., Crawford, D., Phillips, L. & Tinglin, W. (1980) *Testing, Assessment, Counselling and Placement of Ethnic Minority Students: Current Methods in Ontario*. Toronto: Ontario Ministry of Education.

Sánchez-Casas, R., Davis, C. W. & García-Alba, J. E. (1992) Bilingual lexical processing: exploring the cognate/non-cognate distinction. In A. M. B. de Groot & C. Barry (eds.) *The Multilingual Community: Bilingualism. A Special Journal issue of the European Journal of Cognitive Psychology*. Hillsdale, NJ: Erlbaum.

Sandilands, M. L. & Fleury, N. C. (1979) Unilinguals in des milieux bilingues: une analyse of attributions. *Canadian Journal of Behavioral Science*, 11, 164–8.

Sankoff, D. & Poplack, S. (1981) A formal grammar for code-switching. *Papers in Linguistics*, 14, 3–46.

Sasanuma, S. (1985) Surface dyslexia and dysgraphia: How are they manifested in Japanese? In K. E. Patterson, J. C. Marshall & M. Coltheart (eds.) *Surface Dyslexia: Neurological and Cognitive Studies of Phonological Reading*. Hillsdale, NJ: Erlbaum.

Sasanuma, S. & Park, H. S. (1995) Patterns of language deficit in two Korean–Japanese bilingual aphasic patients. In M. Paradis (ed.) *Aspects of Bilingual Aphasia*. New York: Elsevier.

Saville-Troike, M. (1982) *The Ethnography of Communication: An Introduction*. Language in Society, Volume 3. Oxford: Blackwell.

Saunders, G. (1988) *Bilingual Children from Birth to Teens*. Clevedon: Multilingual Matters.

Schank, R. C. & Abelson, R. P. (1977) *Scripts, Plans, Goals, and Understanding*. Hillsdale, NJ: Erlbaum.

Schermerhorn, R. A. (1970) *Comparative Ethnic Relations: a Framework for Theory and Research*. New York: Random House.

Schmandt-Besserat, D. (1992) *Before Writing: Volume I. From Counting to Cuneiform*. Austin, TX: University of Texas Press.

Schneiderman, E. (1976) An examination of the ethnic and linguistic attitudes of bilingual children. *ITL Review of Applied Linguistics*, 33, 59–72.

Schneiderman, E. (1986) Learning to the right: some thoughts on hemisphere involvement in language acquisition. In J. Vaid (ed.) *Language Processing in Bilinguals: Psycholinguistic and Neuropsychological Perspectives*. Hillsdale, NJ: Erlbaum.

Schneiderman, E. & Wesche, M. (1980) Right hemisphere participation in second language acquisition. Los Angeles: Paper presented at the Los Angeles Second Language Research Forum.

Schwanenflügel, P. J. & Rey, M. (1986) Interlingual semantic facilitation: evidence for a common representational system in the bilingual lexicon. *Journal of Memory and Language*, 25, 605–18.

Scott, S. (1973) The relation of divergent thinking to bilingualism: cause or effect? Unpublished research report. Montreal: McGill University.

Scott, S., Hynd, G. W., Hunt, L. & Weed, W. (1979) Cerebral speech lateralization in the Native American Navajo. *Neuropsychologia*, 17, 89–92.

Scotton, C. M. (1980) Explaining linguistic choices as identity negotiations. In H. Giles, W. P. Robinson & P. M. Smith (eds.) *Language: Social Psychological Perspectives*. Oxford: Pergamon Press.

Scotton, C. M. (1986) Diglossia and code switching. In J. A. Fishman, A. Tabouret-Keller, M. Clyne, B. Krishnamurti & M. Abdulaziz (eds.) *The Fergusonian Impact in Honor of Charles A. Ferguson on the Occasion of His 65th Birthday. Volume 2: Sociolinguistics and the Sociology of Language*. Berlin: Mouton de Gruyter.

Scribner, S. & Cole, M. (1981) *The Psychology of Literacy*. Cambridge, MA: Harvard University Press.

Sebba, M. (1998) A congruence approach to the syntax of code-switching. *International Journal of Bilingualism*, 2, 1–19.

Segall, M. H., Berry, J. W., Dasen, P. R. & Poortinga, Y. H. (1990) *Human Behavior in the Global Perspective: An Introduction to Cross-Cultural Psychology*. New York: Pergamon Press.

Segalowitz, N. (1977) Psychological perspectives on bilingual education. In B.

Spolsky & R. Cooper (eds.) *Frontiers of Bilingual Education.* Rowley, MA: Newbury House.

Segalowitz, N. & Gadbonton, E. (1977) Studies of the non-fluent bilingual. In P. A. Hornby (ed.) *Bilingualism: Psychological, Social and Educational Implications.* New York: Academic Press.

Seliger, H. W. (1996) Primary language attrition in the context of bilingualism. In C. Ritchie & T. K. Bhatia (eds.) *Handbook of Second Language Acquisition.* New York: Academic Press.

Selinker, L. (1972) Interlanguage. *International Review of Applied Linguistics*, 10, 209–31.

Shanon, B. (1982) Lateralization in the perception of Hebrew and English words. *Brain and Language*, 17, 107–23.

Siegel, J. (1985) Koines and Koineization. *Language in Society*, 14, 357–78.

Siguan, M. & Mackey, W. F. (1987) *Education and Bilingualism.* London: Kogan Page / UNESCO.

Silverberg, R., Bentin, S., Gaziel, T., Obler, L. K. & Albert, M. L. (1979) Shift of visual field preference for English words in native Hebrew speakers. *Brain and Language*, 8, 184–90.

Simard, L. M., Taylor, D. M. & Giles, H. (1976) Attribution processes and interpersonal accommodation in a bilingual setting. *Language and Speech*, 19, 374–87.

Skehan, P. (1986) Where does language aptitude come from? *British Studies in Applied Linguistics*, 1, 95–113.

Skehan, P. (1989) *Individual Differences in Second Language Learning.* London: Edward Arnold.

Skutnabb-Kangas, T. (1981) *Bilingualism or Not: The Education of Minorities.* Clevedon: Multilingual Matters.

Skutnabb-Kangas, T. & Toukomaa, P. (1976) Teaching migrant children's mother tongue and learning the language of the host country in the context of the socio-cultural situation of the migrant family. Tampere: UNESCO Report, *University of Tampere Research Reports*, 15.

Smolicz, J. J. (1979) *Culture and Education in a Plural Society.* Canberra: Curriculum Development Center.

Smolicz, J. J. (1981) Core values and cultural identity. *Ethnic and Racial Studies*, 4, 75–90.

Smolicz, J. J. (1984) Multiculturalism and an overarching framework of values: some educational responses for ethnically plural societies. *European Journal of Education*, 19, 11–23.

Snodgrass, J. G. (1984) Concepts and their surface representations. *Journal of Verbal Learning and Verbal Behaviour*, 23, 3–22.

Snow, C. E. & Ferguson, C. A. (eds.) (1977) *Talking to Children.* Cambridge University Press.

Snow, C. E. & Hoefnagel-Hohle, M. (1978) The critical period for language acquisition: evidence from second language learning. *Child Development*, 49, 1114–28.

Soares, C. (1984) Left-hemisphere language lateralization in bilinguals: use of the concurrent activities paradigm. *Brain and Language*, 23, 86–96.

Soares, C. & Grosjean, F. (1981) Left hemisphere language lateralization in bilinguals and monolingual. *Perception and Psychophysics*, 29, 599–601.

Soares, C. & Grosjean, F. (1984) Bilingual in a monolingual and bilingual speech mode: the effect on lexical access. *Memory and Cognition*, 12, 380–6.

Southam News (1987) *L'Analphabétisme au Canada: Rapport d'Enquête Préparé par Southam News*. Ottawa: Le Groupe Innova.

Spencer, M. B. (1982) Personal and group identity of black children: An alternative synthesis. *Genetic Psychology Monographs*, 103, 59–84.

Spencer, M. B. & Horowitz, F. D. (1973) Racial attitudes and color concept-attitude modification in Black and Caucasian preschool children. *Developmental Psychology*, 9, 246–54.

Spencer, M. B. & Markstrom-Adams, C. (1990) Identity processes among racial and ethnic minority children in America. *Child development*, 61, 290–310.

Sridhar, S. N. & Sridhar, K. K. (1980) The syntax and psycholinguistics of bilingual code-mixing. *Canadian Journal of Psychology*, 34, 407–16.

Srivastava, R. N. (1984a) Consequences of initiating literacy in the second language. In F. Coulmas (ed.) *Linguistic Minorities and Literacy*. Berlin: Mouton.

Srivastava, R. N. (1984b) Literacy education for minorities: a case study from India. In F. Coulmas (ed.) *Linguistic Minorities and Literacy*. Berlin: Mouton.

Srivastava, R. N. (1990) Multilingualism and school education in India. In D. P. Pattayanak (ed.) *Multilingualism in India*. Clevedon: Multilingual Matters, 37–53.

Stadie, N., Springer, L., de Bleser, R. & Burk, F. (1995) Oral and written naming in multilingual aphasic patient. In M. Paradis (ed.) *Aspects of Bilingual Aphasia*. New York: Elsevier.

Starck, R., Genesee, F., Lambert, W. E. & Seitz, M. (1977) Multiple language experience and the development of cerebral dominance. In S. J. Segalowitz & F. A. Gruber (eds.) *Language Development and Neurological Theory*. New York: Academic Press.

Stephenson, G. M. (1981) Intergroup bargaining and negotiation. In J. C. Turner & H. Giles (eds.) *Intergroup Behaviour*. Oxford: Blackwell.

Sternberg, R. J. (1988) *The Triarchic Mind: A New Theory of Human Intelligence*. New York: Viking.

Street, R. L. (1982) Evaluation of noncontent speech accommodation. *Language and Communication*, 2, 13–31.

Street, R. L. & Giles, H. (1982) Speech accommodation theory: a social cognitive approach to language and speech behaviour. In M. Roloff & C. Berger (eds.) *Social Cognition and Communication*. Newbury Park, CA: Sage.

Street, R. L. & Hopper, R. (1982) A model of speech style evaluation. In E. B. Ryan & H. Giles (eds.) *Attitudes towards Language Variation*. London: Edward Arnold.

Stromswold, K. (1995) The cognitive and neural basis of language acquisition. In M. S. Gazzaniga & E. Bizzi (eds.) *The Cognitive Neuroscience*. Cambridge: MIT Press.

Stroop, J. R. (1935) Studies of interference in serial verbal reactions. *Journal of Experimental Psychology* 118, 643–61.

Styles, J. & Thal, D. (1993) Linguistic and spatial cognitive development following early focal brain injury: patterns of deficit and recovery. In A. H. Johnson (ed.) *Brain Development and Cognition: A Reader*. Oxford: Blackwell.

Sugishita, M., Iwata, M., Toyokura, Y., Yoshioka, M. & Yamada, R. (1978) Reading of ideograms and phonograms in Japanese patients after partial commissurotomy. *Neuropsychologia*, 26, 417–26.

Sussman, H., Franklin, P. & Simon, T. (1982) Bilingual speech: bilateral control? *Brain and Language*, 15, 125–42.

Swain, M. (1972) Bilingualism as a first language. Unpublished PhD dissertation. Irvine: University of California.

Swain, M. (1982) Immersion education: applicability for nonvernacular teaching to vernacular speakers. In B. Hartford, A. Valdman & C. R. Foster (eds.) *Issues in International Bilingual Education: the Role of the Vernacular*. New York: Plenum Press.

Swain, M. (1991) French immersion and its offshoots: getting two for one. In B. F. Freed (ed.) *Foreign Language Acquisition Research and the Classroom*. Lexington, MA: D. C. Heath.

Swain, M. & Lapkin, S. (1982) *Evaluating Bilingual Education: A Canadian Case Study*. Clevedon: Multilingual Matters.

Swain, M. & Lapkin, S. (1991) Programmes d'immersion au Canada et enseignement des langues aux adultes. Existe-t-il un lien? *Études de Linguistique Appliquée*, 82, 24–38.

Swain, M. & Wesche, M. (1973) Linguistic interaction: case study of a bilingual child. *Working Papers on Bilingualism*, 1, 1–34.

Tabouret-Keller, A. (1968) Sociological factors of language maintenance and shift: a methodological approach based on European and African examples. In J. A. Fishman, C. A. Ferguson & J. Das Gupta (eds.) *Language Problems of Developing Nations*. New York: Wiley.

Tabouret-Keller, A. (1972) A contribution to the sociological study of language maintenance and language shift. In J. A. Fishman (ed.) *Advances in the Sociology of Language*, Volume 2. The Hague: Mouton.

Tabouret-Keller, A. & Luckel, F. (1981) Maintien de l'alsacien et adoption du français: éléments de la situation linguistique en milieu rural en Alsace. *Langages*, 61, 39–62.

Tabouret-Keller, A., Le Page, R. B., Gardner-Chloros, P. & Varro, G. (eds.) (1997) *Vernacular Literacy: A Re-Evaluation*. Oxford Studies in Anthropological Linguistics. Oxford: Clarendon Press..

Taeschner, T. (1983) *The Sun is Feminine*. Berlin: Springer Verlag.

Taft, R. (1977) Coping with unfamiliar cultures. In N. Warren (ed.) *Studies in Cross-Cultural Psychology*, Volume 1. London: Academic Press.

Tahta, S., Wood, M., & Loewenthal, K. (1981) Age changes in the ability to replicate foreign pronunciation and intonation. *Language and Speech*, 24, 363–72.

Tajfel, H. (1974) Social identity and intergroup behaviour. *Social Science Information*, 13, 65–93.

Tajfel, H. (ed.) (1978) *Differentiation between Social Groups: Studies in the Social Psychology of Intergroup Relations*. London: Academic Press.

Tajfel, H. (1981) *Human Groups and Social Categories: Studies in Social Psychology*. Cambridge University Press.

Tajfel, H. & Turner, J. C. (1979) An integrative theory of intergroup conflict. In

W. G. Austin & S. Worchel (eds.) *The Social Psychology of Intergroup Relations*. Monterey: Brooks / Cole.

Tannen, D. (1985). Relative focus on involvement in oral and written discourse. In D. R. Olson, N. Torrance & A. Hildyard (eds.) *Literacy, Language and Learning*. Cambridge University Press.

Taylor, D. M., Bassili, J. N. & Aboud, F. E. (1973) Dimensions of ethnic identity: an example from Quebec. *Journal of Social Psychology*, 89, 185–92.

Taylor, D. M. & Giles, H. (1979) At the crossroads of research into language and ethnic relations. In H. Giles & B. Saint-Jacques (eds.) *Language and Ethnic Relations*. Oxford: Pergamon Press.

Taylor, D. M. & Lambert, W. E. (1996) The meaning of multiculturalism in a culturally diverse urban American area. *Journal of Social Psychology*, 36, 727–40.

Taylor, D. M., Meynard, R. & Rheault, E. (1977) Threat to ethnic identity and second-language learning. In H. Giles (ed.) *Language, Ethnicity and Intergroup Relations*. New York: Academic Press.

Taylor, D. M. & Moghaddam, F. M. (1987) *Theories of Intergroup Relations: International Perspectives*. New York: Praeger.

Taylor, D. M. & Royer, L. (1980) Group processes affecting anticipated language choice in intergroup relations. In H. Giles, W. P. Robinson & P. M. Smith (eds.) *Language: Social Psychological Perspectives*. Oxford: Pergamon Press.

Taylor, D. M., Simard, L. M. & Papineau, D. (1978) Perceptions of cultural differences and language use: a field study in a bilingual environment. *Canadian Journal of Behavioral Science*, 10, 181–91.

Taylor, D. M., Wright, S. C., Ruggiero, K. M. & Aitchison, M. C. (1993) Language perceptions among the Inuit of Arctic Quebec: the future of the heritage language. *Journal of Language and Social Psychology*, 12, 195–206.

Taylor, I. (1971) How are words from two languages organized in a bilingual's memory? *Canadian Journal of Psychology*, 25, 228–40.

Taylor, I. (1976) Similarity between French and English words: a factor to be considered in bilingual language behavior? *Journal of Psycholinguistic Research*, 5, 85–95.

Taylor, I. (1990) *Psycholinguistics: Learning and Using Language*. Englewood Cliffs, NJ: Prentice Hall.

Thakerar, J. N., Giles, H. & Cheshire, J. (1982) Psychological and linguistic parameters of speech accommodation theory. In C. Fraser & K. R. Scherer (eds.) *Advances in the Social Psychology of Language*. Cambridge University Press.

Thal, D., Marchman, V. A., Stiles, J., Aram, D., Trauner, D., Nass, R. & Bates, E. (1991) Early lexical development in children with focal brain injury. *Brain and Language*, 40, 491–527.

The Other Languages of England (1985) Linguistic Minorities Project. London: Routledge & Kegan Paul.

Thernstrom, A. (1980) Language: issues and legislation. In S. Thernstrom, A. Orlov & O. Handlin (eds.) *Harvard Encyclopedia of American Ethnic Groups*. Cambridge, MA: Harvard University Press.

Thevenin, D., Eilers, R. E., Oller, D. K. & Lavoie, L. (1985) Where's the drift in babbling drift? A cross-linguistic study. *Applied Psycholinguistics*, 6, 3–15.

Titone, R. (1972) *Le Bilinguisme Précoce*. Brussels: Dessart.

Tits, D. (1948) *Le Mécanisme de l'Acquisition d'une Langue se Substituant à la Langue Maternelle chez une Enfant Espagnole Agée de Six Ans*. Brussels: Veldeman.

Tizard, J., Schofield, W. N. & Hewison, J. (1982) Collaboration between teachers and parents in assisting children's reading. *British Journal of Educational Psychology*, 52, 1–15.

Todd, L. (1984) *Modern Englishes: Pidgins and Creoles*. Oxford: Blackwell.

Torrance, A. P., Gowan, J. C., Wu, J. M. & Aliotti, N. C. (1970) Creative functioning of monolingual and bilingual children in Singapore. *Journal of Educational Psychology*, 61, 72–5.

Torrance, N. & Olson, D. R. (1985) Oral and literate competencies in early school years. In D. R. Olson, N. Torrance & A. Hildyard (eds.) *Literacy, Language and Learning*. Cambridge University Press.

Tosi, A. (1984) *Immigration and Bilingual Education*. Oxford: Pergamon Press.

Treisman, A. M. (1964) Verbal cues, language and meaning in selective attention. *American Journal of Psychology*, 77, 210–19.

Treisman, A. M. (1969) Strategies and models of selective attention. *Psychological Review*, 76, 282–99.

Tremblay, P. F. & Gardner, R. C. (1995) Expanding the motivation construct in language learning. *The Modern Language Journal*, 79, 505–18.

Trites, R. (1981) *Primary French Immersion: Disabilities and Prediction of Success*. Toronto: OISE Press.

Troike, R. C. (1984) SCALP: Social and cultural aspects of language proficiency. In C. Rivera (ed.) *Language Proficiency and Academic Assessment*. Clevedon: Multilingual Matters, 10.

Trudgill, P. & Tzavaras, G. (1977) Why Albanian-Greeks are not Albanians: language shift in Attica and Biotia. In H. Giles (ed.) *Language, Ethnicity and Intergroup Relations*. London: Academic Press.

T'Sou, B. (1980) Critical sociolinguistic realignment in multilingual societies. In E. Afendras (ed.) *Patterns of Bilingualism*. Singapore University Press.

Tsushima, W. T. & Hogan, T. P. (1975) Verbal ability and school achievement of bilingual and monolingual children of different ages. *Journal of Educational Research*, 68, 349–53.

Tucker, G. R. & Lambert, W. E. (1969) White and Negro listeners' reactions to various American–English dialects. *Social Forces*, 47, 463–8.

Tulving, E. (1972) Episodic and semantic memory. In E. Tulving & W. Donaldson (eds.) *Organisation of Memory*. New York: Academic Press.

Tulving, E. & Colotla, V. (1970) Free recall of trilingual lists. *Cognitive Psychology*, 1, 86–98.

Turner, J. C. (1981) The experimental social psychology of intergroup behaviour. In J. C. Turner & H. Giles (eds.) *Intergroup Behaviour*. Oxford: Pergamon Press.

Turner, J. C. (1982) Towards a cognitive redefinition of the social group. In H. Tajfel (ed.) *Social Identity and Intergroup Relations*. Cambridge University Press.

Turner, J. C., Hogg, M. A., Oakes, P. J., Reicher, S. D. & Wetherell, M. S. (1987) *Rediscovering the Social Group: A Self-Categorization Theory*. Oxford: Basil

Blackwell.

Tylor, E. B. (1873) *Primitive Culture: Researches into the Development of Mythology, Philosophy, Religion, Language, Art and Custom.* London: John Murray.

Tzelgov, J. & Eben-Ezra, S. (1992) Components of the between-language semantic priming effect. *European Journal of Cognitive Psychology*, 4, 253–72.

Tzelgov, J., Henik, A. & Leiser, D. (1990) Controlling Stroop interference: Evidence from a bilingual task. *Journal of Experimental Psychology: Learning, Memory and Cognition*, 16, 760–71.

Tzeng, O. J. O., Hung, D. L., Cotton, B. & Wang, W. S. Y. (1979) Visual lateralization effects in reading Chinese nouns, adjectives and verbs. *Nature*, 282, 499–501.

Ullrich, H. E. (1971) Linguistic aspects of antiquity: a dialect study. *Anthropological Linguistics*, 13, 106–13.

Umbel, V. M., Pearson, B. Z., Fernandez, M. C., & Oller, D. K. (1992) Measuring bilingual children's receptive vocabularies. *Child Development*, 63, 1012–20.

UNESCO (1953) *The Use of Vernacular Languages in Education.* Paris: UNESCO.

UNESCO (1976) *International Standard Classification of Education.* Paris: UNESCO, Division of Statistics on Education.

Vaid, J. (1983) Bilingualism and brain lateralization. In S. J. Segalovitz (ed.) *Language Function and Brain Organization.* New York: Academic Press.

Vaid, J. (1984) Visual, phonetic, and semantic processing in early and late bilinguals. In M. Paradis & Y. Lebrun (eds.) *Early Bilingualism and Child Development.* Lisse: Swets & Zeitlinger.

Vaid, J. (1987) Visual field asymmetries for rhyme and syntactic category judgements in monolinguals and fluent early and late bilinguals. *Brain and Language*, 30, 267–77.

Vaid, J., Green, A., Schweda Nicholson, N. & White, N. (1989) Hemispheric specialisation for shadowing versus interpretation: a dual task study of simultaneous interpreters and matched unilingual controls. *Investigaciones Psicológicas*, 7, 43–54.

Vaid, J. & Hall, D. G. (1991) Neuropsychological perspectives on bilingualism: right, left, and center. In A. J. Reynolds (ed.) *Bilingualism, Multiculturalism, and Second Language Learning. The McGill Conference in Honour of Wallace E. Lambert.* Hillsdale, NJ: Erlbaum.

Vaid, J. & Lambert, W. E. (1979) Differential cerebral involvement in the cognitive functioning of bilinguals. *Brain and Language*, 8, 92–110.

Vaid, J. & Pandit, P. B. (1991) Sentence interpretation in normal and aphasic Hindi speakers. *Brain and Language*, 41, 250–74.

Valdes-Fallis, G. (1977) Code switching among bilingual Mexican-American women: towards an understanding of sex-related language alternation. *International Journal of the Sociology of Language*, 7, 65–72.

van Oudenhoven, J. P. (1998) Integration and assimilation of Moroccan immigrants in Israel and the Netherlands. Unpublished manuscript. Groningen: University of Groningen.

Venezky, R. L. (1991) The development of literacy in the industrialized nations of the west. In R. Barr, M. L. Kamil, P. B. Mosenthal and P. D. Pearson (eds.) *Handbook of Reading Research*, Volume 2, New York: Longman.

Verdoodt, A. (1972) The differential impact of immigrant French speakers on indigenous German speakers: a case study in the light of two theories. In J. A. Fishman (ed.) *Advances in the Sociology of Language*, Volume 2. The Hague: Mouton.

Viberg, A. (1993) Cross-linguistic perspectives on lexical organisation and lexical progression. In K. Hyltenstam & A. Viberg (eds.) *Progression and Regression in Language*. Cambridge University Press.

Vignola, M.-J. & Wesche, M. B. (1991) L'écriture en langue maternelle et en langue seconde chez les diplômés d'immersion française. *Études de Linguistique Appliquée*, 82, 94–115.

Vihman, M. (1985) Language differentiation by the bilingual infant. *Journal of Child Language*, 12, 297–324.

Vocate, D. R. (1984) Differential cerebral speech lateralization in Crow Indian and Anglo children. *Neuropsychologia*, 22, 487–94.

Voinescu, I., Vish, E., Sirian, S. & Maretsis, M. (1977) Aphasia in a polyglot. *Brain and Language*, 4, 165–76.

Volterra, V. & Taeschner, T. (1978) The acquisition and the development of language by bilingual children. *Journal of Child Language*, 5, 311–26.

Vygotsky, L. S. (1962) *Thought and Language*. Cambridge, MA: MIT Press.

Vygotsky, L. S. (1978) *Mind in Society: the Development of Higher Psychological Processes*. Cambridge, MA: Harvard University Press.

Waas (1993) Language attrition among German speakers in Australia: a sociolinguistic inquiry. Unpublished doctoral dissertation, Macquarie University, Sydney.

Wada, J. & Rasmussen, T. (1960) Intracarotid injection of sodium amytal for the lateralization of cerebral speech dominance: experimental and clinical observation. *Journal of Neurosurgery*, 17, 266–82.

Walters, J. & Zatorre, R. J. (1978) Laterality differences for word identification in bilinguals. *Brain and Language*, 6, 158–67.

Ward, C. A. & Hewstone, M. (1985) Ethnicity, language and intergroup relations in Malaysia and Singapore: a social psychological analysis. *Journal of Multilingual and Multicultural Development*, 6, 271–96.

Wardhaugh, R. (1986) *An Introduction to Sociolinguistics*. Oxford: Blackwell.

Watamori, T. S. & Sasanuma, S. (1978) The recovery process of two English-Japanese bilingual aphasics. *Brain and Language*, 6, 127–40.

Watson, I. (1991) Phonological processing in two languages. In E. Bialystok (ed.) *Language Processing in Bilinguals*. Cambridge University Press.

Webster, N. (1961) *Webster's Third New International Dictionary of the English Language*. London: Bell & Sons. Weber, M. (1968) *Economy and Society: an Outline of Interpretive Sociology*. New York: Bedminster Press.

Wechsler, A. (1977) Dissociative aphasia. *Archives of Neurology*, 34, 257.

Weinreich, U. (1953) *Languages in Contact*. The Hague: Mouton.

Wells, C. G. (1981) *Learning through Interaction. The Study of Language Development*. Cambridge University Press.

Wells, C. G. (1985a) Preschool literacy-related activities and success in school. In D. R. Olson, N. Torrance & A. Hildyard (eds.) *Literacy, Language, and Learning: The Nature and Consequences of Reading and Writing*. Cambridge

University Press.

Wells, C. G. (1985b) *Language Development in the Pre-school Years.* Cambridge University Press.

Weltens, B. (1987) The attrition of foreign-language skills. *Applied Linguistics,* 8, 22–38.

Werker, J. F. & Tees, R. C. (1984) Cross-language speech development: Evidence for perceptual reorganization during the first year of life. *Infant Behavior and Development,* 7, 49–93.

Wesche, M. B. (1994) Input, interaction and acquisition. In B. Richards & C. Gallaway (eds.) *Input and Interaction in Language Acquisition.* Cambridge University Press.

Whitaker, H. A. (1978) Bilingualism: a neurolinguistic perspective. In W. C. Ritchie (ed.) *Second Language Acquisition Research.* New York: Academic Press.

Whorf, B. (1956) *Language, Thought and Reality.* Cambridge, MA: MIT Press.

Wiens, A. N., Manuagh, T. S. & Matarazzo, J. D. (1976) Speech and silence behaviour of bilinguals conversing in each of two languages. *Linguistics,* 172, 79–93.

Willemyns, M., Pittam, J. & Gallois, C. (1993) Perceived ethnolinguistic vitality of Vietnamese and English in Australia. *Journal of Multilingual and Multicultural Development,* 14, 481–97.

Willemyns, R. (1987) The investigation of 'language continuum and diglossia'. In M. Blanc & J. F. Hamers (eds.) *Theoretical and Methodological Issues in the Study of Languages/Dialects in Contact at the Macro- and Micro-logical Levels of Analysis.* Quebec: International Center for Research on Bilingualism, B-160.

Williams, C. H. (1984) More than tongue can tell: linguistic factors in ethnic separatism. In J. Edwards (ed.) *Linguistic Minorities, Policies and Pluralism.* London: Academic Press.

Williams, F., Whitehead, J. L. & Miller, L. M. (1971) Ethnic stereotyping and judgements of children's speech. *Speech Monographs,* 38, 166–70.

Williams, G. (1992) *Sociolinguistics: A Sociological Critique.* London and New York: Routledge.

Willig, A. C. (1985) A meta-analysis of selected studies on the effectiveness of bilingual education. *Review of Educational Research,* 55, 269–317.

Winograd, E., Cohen, C. & Baressi, J. (1976) Memory for concrete and abstract words in bilingual speakers. *Memory and Cognition,* 4, 323–9.

Witelson, S. F. (1977) Early hemisphere specialisation and interhemispheric plasticity: an empirical and theoretical review. In S. J. Segalowitz and F. A. Gruber (eds.) *Language Development and Neurological Theory.* Cambridge, MA: MIT Press.

Witte, E. & Baetens Beardsmore, H. (eds.) (1987) *The Interdisciplinary Study of Urban Bilingualism in Brussels.* Clevedon: Multilingual Matters.

Wong Fillmore, L. (1979) Individual differences in second language acquisition. In C. J. Fillmore, D. Kempler & W. S.-Y. Wang (eds.) *Individual Differences in Language Ability and Language Behaviour.* New York: Academic Press.

Wong Fillmore, L. (1980) Cultural perspectives on second language learning. *TESOL Reporter,* 14, 22–31.

Wong Fillmore, L. (1989) Language learning in social context. In R. Dietrich & C. Graumann (eds.) *Language Processing in Social Context*. Amsterdam: Elsevier.

Wong Fillmore, L. (1991a) Second-language learning in children: a model of learning in social context. In E. Bialystok (ed.) *Language Processing in Bilingual Children*. Cambridge University Press.

Wong Fillmore, L. (1991b) When learning a second language means losing the first. *Early Childhood Research Quarterly*, 6, 323–346.

Wood, R. (1993). *Assessment and testing: A survey of research*. Cambridge University Press.

Woolford, E. (1983) Bilingual code-switching and syntactic theory. *Linguistic Inquiry*, 14, 520–36.

Wuillemin, D., Richardson, B. & Lynch, J. (1994) Right hemisphere involvement in processing later-learned languages in multilinguals. *Brain & Language*, 46, 620–36.

Wurm, S. A. (1977) Pidgins, creoles, lingue franche and national development. In A. Valdman (ed.) *Pidgin and Creole Linguistics*. Bloomington: Indiana University Press.

Yang, K. S. & Bond, M. H. (1980) Ethnic affirmation by Chinese bilinguals. *Journal of Cross-Cultural Psychology*, 1, 411–25.

Yelland, G. W., Pollard, J. & Mercuri, A. (1993) The metalinguistic benefits of limited contact with a second language. *Applied Psycholinguistics*, 14, 423–44.

Young, M. Y. & Gardner, R. C. (1990) Modes of acculturation and second language proficiency. *Canadian Journal of Behavioral Science*, 22, 59–71.

Young, R. K. & Navar, M. (1968) Retroactive inhibition with bilinguals. *Journal of Experimental Psychology*, 77, 109–15.

Young, R. K. & Saegert, J. (1966) Transfer with bilinguals. *Psychonomic Science*, 6, 161–2.

Zatorre, R. J. (1989) On the representation of multiple languages in the brain: old problems and new directions. *Brain and Language*, 36, 127–47.

Subject index

Author index

CPSIA information can be obtained at www.ICGtesting.com
Printed in the USA
LVOW08s1847180813

348430LV00001B/15/A